UTAH CAMPING

MIKE MATSON

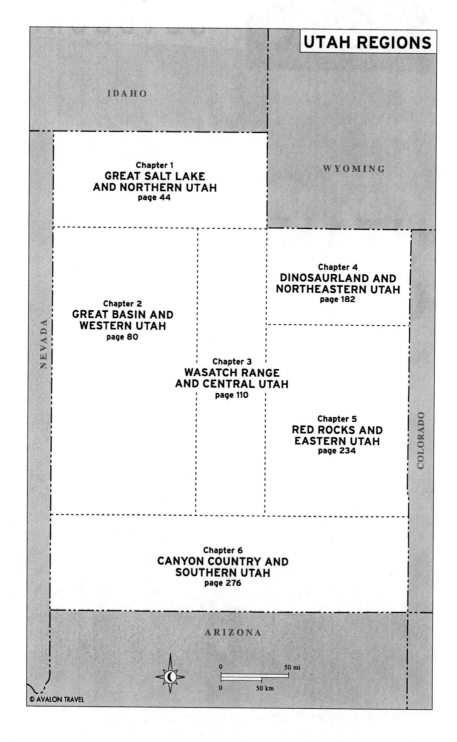

UTAH REGIONS

IDAHO

WYOMING

NEVADA

COLORADO

ARIZONA

Chapter 1
GREAT SALT LAKE
AND NORTHERN UTAH
page 44

Chapter 4
DINOSAURLAND AND
NORTHEASTERN UTAH
page 182

Chapter 2
GREAT BASIN AND
WESTERN UTAH
page 80

Chapter 3
WASATCH RANGE
AND CENTRAL UTAH
page 110

Chapter 5
RED ROCKS AND
EASTERN UTAH
page 234

Chapter 6
CANYON COUNTRY AND
SOUTHERN UTAH
page 276

0   50 mi

0   50 km

© AVALON TRAVEL

Contents

How to Use This Book

ABOUT THE CAMPGROUND PROFILES

The campgrounds are listed in a consistent, easy-to-read format to help you choose the ideal camping spot. If you already know the name of the specific campground you want to visit, or the name of the surrounding geological area or nearby feature (town, national or state park, forest, mountain, lake, river, etc.), look it up in the index and turn to the corresponding page. Here is a sample profile:

Campground name and number →

General location of the campground in relation to the nearest major town or landmark

Map the campground can be found on and page number the map can be found on

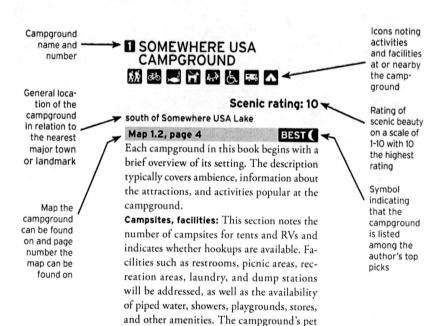

Icons noting activities and facilities at or nearby the campground

Rating of scenic beauty on a scale of 1-10 with 10 the highest rating

Symbol indicating that the campground is listed among the author's top picks

■ SOMEWHERE USA CAMPGROUND

Scenic rating: 10

south of Somewhere USA Lake

Map 1.2, page 4   **BEST (**

Each campground in this book begins with a brief overview of its setting. The description typically covers ambience, information about the attractions, and activities popular at the campground.

Campsites, facilities: This section notes the number of campsites for tents and RVs and indicates whether hookups are available. Facilities such as restrooms, picnic areas, recreation areas, laundry, and dump stations will be addressed, as well as the availability of piped water, showers, playgrounds, stores, and other amenities. The campground's pet policy and wheelchair accessibility is also mentioned here.

Reservations, fees: This section notes whether reservations are accepted, and provides rates for tent sites and RV sites. If there are additional fees for parking or pets, or discounted weekly or seasonal rates, they will also be noted here.

Directions: This section provides mile-by-mile driving directions to the campground from the nearest major town or highway.

Contact: This section provides an address, phone number, and website, if available, for the campground.

ABOUT THE ICONS

The icons in this book are designed to provide at-a-glance information on activities, facilities, and services available on-site or within walking distance of each campground.

- 🥾 Hiking trails
- 🚴 Biking trails
- 🏊 Swimming
- 🎣 Fishing
- 🚤 Boating
- 🛶 Canoeing and/or kayaking
- ❄️ Winter sports

- ♨️ Hot springs
- 🐾 Pets permitted
- 🛝 Playground
- ♿ Wheelchair accessible
- 🚐 RV sites
- ⛺ Tent sites

ABOUT THE SCENIC RATING

Each campground profile employs a scenic rating on a scale of 1 to 10, with 1 being the least scenic and 10 being the most scenic. A scenic rating measures only the overall beauty of the campground and environs; it does not take into account noise level, facilities, maintenance, recreation options, or campground management. The setting of a campground with a lower scenic rating may simply not be as picturesque that of as a higher rated campground, however other factors that can influence a trip, such as noise or recreation access, can still affect or enhance your camping trip. Consider both the scenic rating and the profile description before deciding which campground is perfect for you.

MAP SYMBOLS

▦▦▦	Expressway	(80)	Interstate Freeway	✈	Airfield
⋯⋯⋯	Primary Road	(101)	U.S. Highway	✈	Airport
▦▦▦	Secondary Road	(21)	State Highway	○	City/Town
▫▫▫	Unpaved Road	(66)	County Highway	▲	Mountain
⋯⋯⋯	Ferry		Lake	⬧	Park
▬ ▬ ▸	National Border		Dry Lake	⤬	Pass
▬ ▬ ▬	State Border		Seasonal Lake	◉	State Capital

ABOUT THE MAPS

This book is divided into chapters based on major regions in the state; an overview map of these regions precedes the table of contents. Each chapter begins with a map of the region, which is further broken down into detail maps. Campgrounds are noted on the detail maps by number.

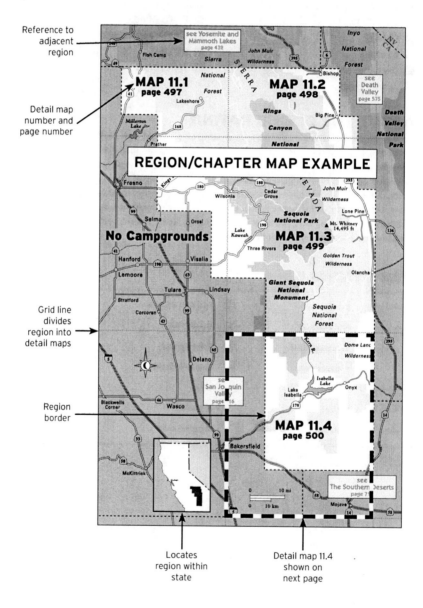

Reference to adjacent region

Detail map number and page number

Grid line divides region into detail maps

Region border

Locates region within state

Detail map 11.4 shown on next page

REGION/CHAPTER MAP EXAMPLE

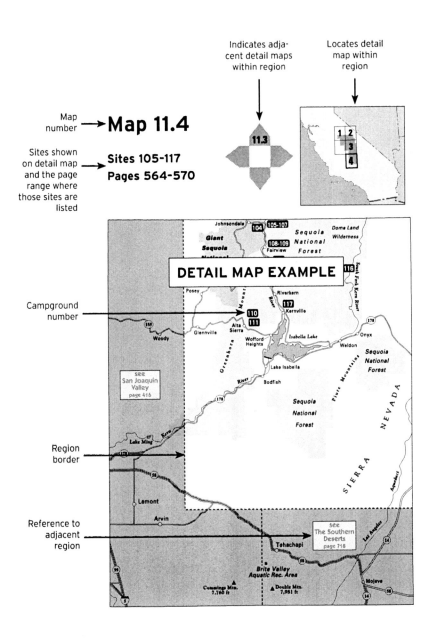

Indicates adjacent detail maps within region

Locates detail map within region

Map number → **Map 11.4**

Sites shown on detail map and the page range where those sites are listed → **Sites 105-117**
Pages 564-570

11.3

1 2
3
4

Johnsondale · 105-107 · Dome Land
104 · Sequoia · Wilderness
Giant · 108-109 · National
Sequoia · Fairview · Forest

DETAIL MAP EXAMPLE

Posey · Riverkern
110 · 117 · Kernville
111

Campground number →

Glennville · Alta · Sierra · Isabella Lake · Onyx
Woody · Wofford · Heights · Weldon · Sequoia National Forest
Lake Isabella

see
San Joaquin
Valley
page 418 · Bodfish

Sequoia National Forest

Lake Ming

Region border →

Lemont

Reference to adjacent region →

Arvin · see The Southern Deserts page 718 · Los Angeles
Tehachapi

Brite Valley Aquatic Rec. Area

Cummings Mtn. 7,760 ft · Double Mtn. 7,981 ft · Mojave

INTRODUCTION

© MIKE MATSON

Author's Note

Utah is a state of extreme natural beauty. In the south, the landscape is dominated by the wonderfully twisted red rock geology of the Colorado Plateau. The Plateau is a world of hard alien landscapes and soft textured layers—a place where history and time can be seen in the land itself, where dinosaur bones lay half unearthed and ancient Anasazi writings are literally carved into the varnished desert rock, the soft rusting sandstone at once telling a story and awaking a sense of wonder. In the north, Utah is basin and range country, defined by boldly majestic mountains and wide, expansive valleys. The Wasatch Mountains reach up to scrape the sky, topping out above 11,500 feet, while the Bonneville Salt Flats stretch so far and flat they appear to become one with the sky, melting away the horizon in a shimmering, featureless white.

Utah has a small, concentrated population and a huge amount of open, public land. The state boasts a whopping five national parks—Zion, Bryce Canyon, Capitol Reef, Arches, and Canyonlands—which preserve some unique and spectacular parts of the Colorado Plateau. Nearly as impressive are seven national monuments: the sprawling Grand Staircase-Escalante, the breathtaking Cedar Breaks, the intriguing Dinosaur, the historic Hovenweep, the remote Rainbow Bridge, the subterranean Timpanogos Cave, and the often overlooked Natural Bridges. These monuments capture some of the best of Utah and remain relatively crowd free, if only because they weren't designated the prestigious title of "national parks." Their monument designation is held dear by those who know them well as a blessing in disguise. Two national recreation areas protect the lifeblood of the whole Southwest Region, the waters of the Green and Colorado Rivers. The Flaming Gorge National Recreation Area surrounds the Green River as it enters Utah in the state's northeast corner, while the Glen Canyon National Recreation Area encompasses the land around Lake Powell, where the waters of the Colorado River leave Utah and flow into northern Arizona.

Finally, there are Utah's state parks. In 42 parks, the state system protects a variety of lands ranging from small reservoirs to geologic wonders to public golf links—some of the very best lands in Utah. Desert parks like Kodachrome Basin, Coral Pink Sand Dunes, Goblin Valley, and Snow Canyon stand out as glowing examples of how smaller, well-run state parks can outshine some of the internationally acclaimed national parks in the area. If you visit, you'll notice these parks have the best-designed, best-maintained, and most user-friendly campgrounds in the state of Utah. It's a testament to the abundance of beauty in Utah that there are so many spectacular sites protected on state lands.

Exploring all this splendor is no small task. Whether you're a native Utahan looking to experience your home state in a new way, or a visitor coming to see the state for the first time, there is no better way to absorb all Utah has to offer than camping. Camping offers an opportunity to get out and experience the natural world firsthand—to feel the desert's heat, and smell the freshness of the mountain air. It's an opportunity to simplify life for a few days, build a campfire, read a book, or just hang out in a beautiful place. Young or old, couples or families, solo or in a group, there's something for everyone to enjoy. For many travelers, camping is just part of the story—a vehicle to access the unique recreation opportunities the region has to offer.

KEEP IT WILD

"Enjoy America's country and leave no trace." That's the motto of the Leave No Trace program, and I strongly support it. Promoting responsible outdoor recreation through education, research, and partnerships is its mission. Look for the Keep It Wild Tips, developed from the policies of Leave No Trace, throughout the Camping Tips portion of this book. This copyrighted information has been reprinted with permission from the Leave No Trace Center for Outdoor Ethics. For more information or materials, please visit www.LNT.org or call 303/442-8222 or 800/332-4100.

For fly-fishers, camping might mean spending the night in the alpine lake–dotted Uinta Mountains, poised for the perfect moment when a trout will rise. To rock climbers, maybe it's about celebrating with a cold beer on the pickup's tailgate after a day spent scaling a perfect desert crack. And to the mountain biker, it could mean nursing a sore saddle after negotiating the ups and downs of the Slickrock Trail outside Moab, the most famous mountain bike destination in the world.

For others, camping itself is the adventure—a first night spent sleeping out under the stars, noticing the fresh scent of a pine forest in the morning air, or rising before dawn to watch sunrise over Bryce Canyon. To parents, camping might simply be enjoying the way their kids unplug from everyday life and notice the natural world around them. Or maybe it's the magic of a campfire and the tall tales it inspires.

Regardless of your camping style, this guide is designed to facilitate your camping experience. All told, there are over 400 campgrounds in Utah, and they're as varied as the landscapes they're in. Some are built for RVs, others cater to tents, and some can only be accessed with a sturdy 4WD vehicle. One thing I've painfully discovered writing this guide is that just because there's a campground on the map doesn't necessarily mean it exists. Things change: Campgrounds are transitioned into picnic areas or removed altogether. If a campground is listed in this book, however, you can bet it'll exist, because we've been there.

I hope this book makes planning and executing your camping trips more efficient. Perhaps it will inspire the confidence to explore new places and discover fresh adventures. In writing this book, my Utah "to do" list has only grown longer: take my parents on the Southwest grand tour of national parks in an RV; mountain bike Kokopelli's Trail 142 miles from Moab to Loma, Colorado, with my wife; raft the Colorado River through Cataract Canyon and Canyonlands National Park with my rowdy band of river rat co-workers—to name a few. What's on your list?

Enjoy—
Mike Matson

Best Campgrounds

When only the best will do . . . Here are my recommendations on the best campgrounds in Utah in the following 10 categories.

◖ Best Escapes from Salt Lake City
Rockport State Park, Wasatch Range and Central Utah, page 119
Smith and Morehouse, Wasatch Range and Central Utah, page 120
Redman, Wasatch Range and Central Utah, page 123
Tanner's Flat, Wasatch Range and Central Utah, page 129
Granite Flat, Wasatch Range and Central Utah, page 133
Washington Lake, Dinosaurland and Northeastern Utah, page 197

◖ Best for Families
Perception Park, Great Salt Lake and Northern Utah, page 71
Lagoon RV Park and Campground, Great Salt Lake and Northern Utah, page 74
Ledgefork, Wasatch Range and Central Utah, page 120
Devils Garden, Red Rocks and Eastern Utah, page 243
Coral Pink Sand Dunes State Park, Canyon Country and Southern Utah, page 313
Kodachrome Basin State Park, Canyon Country and Southern Utah, page 321

◖ Best Free Camping
Cathedral, Wasatch Range and Central Utah, page 171
Buckhorn Wash, Red Rocks and Eastern Utah, page 239
Lava Point, Canyon Country and Southern Utah, page 287
Mosquito Cove, Canyon Country and Southern Utah, page 293
Cedar Mesa, Canyon Country and Southern Utah, page 318

◖ Best for Hiking
Spruces, Wasatch Range and Central Utah, page 122
Spirit Lake, Dinosaurland and Northeastern Utah, page 192
Browne Lake, Dinosaurland and Northeastern Utah, page 214
Squaw Flat, Red Rocks and Eastern Utah, page 269
Snow Canyon State Park, Canyon Country and Southern Utah, page 289
Sunset, Canyon Country and Southern Utah, page 303

◖ Best for Mountain Biking
Redman, Wasatch Range and Central Utah, page 123
Dewey Bridge, Red Rocks and Eastern Utah, page 244
Sand Flats Recreation Area, Red Rocks and Eastern Utah, page 254
Williams Bottom, Red Rocks and Eastern Utah, page 256
Willow Flat, Red Rocks and Eastern Utah, page 267
Te-ah, Canyon Country and Southern Utah, page 309

⟨ Best for Nature Photography
Devils Garden, Red Rocks and Eastern Utah, page 243
Dead Horse Point State Park, Red Rocks and Eastern Utah, page 264
Willow Flat, Red Rocks and Eastern Utah, page 267
North, Canyon Country and Southern Utah, page 303
Kodachrome Basin State Park, Canyon Country and Southern Utah, page 321
White House, Canyon Country and Southern Utah, page 322
Goulding's Monument Valley RV Park, Canyon Country and Southern Utah, page 327

⟨ Best Public RV Campground
Hailstone at Jordanelle State Park, Wasatch Range and Central Utah, page 123
Lucerne Valley, Dinosaurland and Northeastern Utah, page 212
Green River, Dinosaurland and Northeastern Utah, page 229
Red Canyon, Canyon Country and Southern Utah, page 300
North, Canyon Country and Southern Utah, page 303
Watchman, Canyon Country and Southern Utah, page 312

⟨ Best for Rock Art and Ruins
Castle Rock at Fremont Indian State Park, Great Basin and
   Western Utah, page 97
Rainbow Park, Dinosaurland and Northeastern Utah, page 230
San Rafael Bridge, Red Rocks and Eastern Utah, page 240
Jaycee Park, Red Rocks and Eastern Utah, page 255
Hamburger Rock, Red Rocks and Eastern Utah, page 268
Calf Creek, Canyon Country and Southern Utah, page 321
Natural Bridges, Canyon Country and Southern Utah, page 331
Hovenweep, Canyon Country and Southern Utah, page 333
Sand Island, Canyon Country and Southern Utah, page 335

⟨ Best for Wildflowers
Albion Basin, Wasatch Range and Central Utah, page 130
Timpooneke, Wasatch Range and Central Utah, page 135
Ferron Reservoir, Wasatch Range and Central Utah, page 164
Elkhorn, Wasatch Range and Central Utah, page 171
Point Supreme, Canyon Country and Southern Utah, page 305

⟨ Best for Wildlife
**Bridger Bay and White Rock Bay Group Sites at Antelope Island
   State Park,** Great Salt Lake and Northern Utah, page 51
Anderson Meadow, Great Basin and Western Utah, page 102
Bridger Lake, Dinosaurland and Northeastern Utah, page 189
Canyon Rim, Dinosaurland and Northeastern Utah, page 216
Antelope Flat, Dinosaurland and Northeastern Utah, page 217
Portal RV Resort, Red Rocks and Eastern Utah, page 252
Blue Spruce, Canyon Country and Southern Utah, page 317

Camping Tips

GEAR SELECTION AND MAINTENANCE

You'll encounter many different forms of camping in Utah, from the 50-foot land yacht to minimalist backpackers with under 30 pounds on their backs. You may choose to take as little or as much camping equipment as you'd like. Selecting, buying, and accumulating all the gear for your adventures is all part of the fun. If you're reading this guide because you're just getting started, or you're trying to fine-tune your established setup, here are a few tips to help with selecting your gear.

Tents

Tents come in all shapes, styles, and sizes. In general, a good tent should keep you dry and warm and shield you from the elements. It should also be easy to pitch, have enough room for your needs, be well ventilated, and be adaptable enough to work well in a range of environments. Utah weather can be anything from blistering hot to polar cold, from a gentle breeze to a blinding red sandstorm, so choose accordingly.

The character and size of your tent will largely be dictated by your style of camping. Backpackers choose sleek, lightweight tents that are quick to set up and easy to tear down. These dome style tents have just enough space inside for their occupants and a small amount of gear. Their smaller size is sometimes offset by a large rain-fly vestibule that provides additional dry storage for shoes, backpacks, and other equipment. Weight is of paramount concern, and some backpacking tents tip the scales at as little as 3–4 pounds. There is usually a trade-off, however, between weight and comfort. As tents get lighter, the strength and protection they offer is reduced as well. Manufactures address this by labeling tents according to the seasons they are suitable for. Three-season tents will suffice for spring, summer, and fall and are usually incredibly light. Four-season tents are engineered to withstand winter storms, have much stronger pole structures, and are substantially heavier and more expensive.

a lit tent near Kent's Lake, Tushar Mountains

© MIKE MATSON

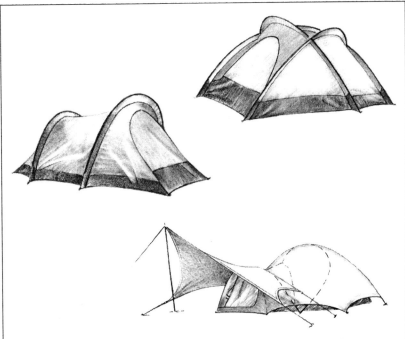

With the world going high-tech, **tents** of today vary greatly in complexity, size, price, and put-up time. And they wouldn't be fit for this new millennium without offering options such as moon roofs, rain flies, and tent wings. Be sure to buy the one that's right for your needs.

Car campers who never plan to carry their tent farther than from the trunk to a tent pad may be better served by a roomier tent. Wall tents and A-frame tents provide lots of space for campers and their gear. Often these tents are spacious enough to sleep the whole family. On the downside, these larger tents are more complex to pitch and not usually freestanding. They are not as strong or wind resistant as smaller dome tents and are intended for summer weather and warmer temperatures. They are usually much less expensive than the high-tech, low-profile backpacking tents. For family camping in developed campgrounds, this is the way to go.

Once you've invested in a good tent, you'll want to take care of it. After all, it's going to be your home away from home. After each trip, be sure to set up your tent and let it dry before you pack it away. Stowing away a tent that is even a bit damp can lead to mildew. Once mildew takes hold, it is almost impossible to remove. Be careful when packing away your tent. For the longest possible tent life, it is recommended to store your tent loosely packed; stuffing it in a pillowcase is a good option. The idea is to avoid rolling your tent in similar pattern each time you put it away, eventually this could lead to wearing along a repeated crease or fold line. Be gentle with the zippers as well. Zippers tend to be the weakest link in tents and are the first thing to break down as tents age. Keep this in mind before you whip the mosquito netting closed or put your body weight on a half-open door. Finally, when breaking down your tent, go easy on the poles and take them apart from the center out, it puts less stress on the delicate shock cords and keeps them taut.

Sleeping Bags

Sleeping bags break down into two basic categories: those stuffed with a synthetic lining and those filled with goose down.

Modern synthetic sleeping bags are filled with high-tech polyester fabric with names like Primaloft, Polarguard HV (High Void), and LiteLoft. You'll notice these names all incorporate loft or void, which refers to the fabric's air-trapping qualities. These fabrics mimic down feathers and create dead air space within the sleeping bag, which in turn traps body heat. Synthetic fill bags have several advantages over down bags. If synthetic bags get wet, they won't collapse, they maintain their loft, and as a result will still retain as much as 65 percent of a camper's body heat. In contrast, down bags are a clumpy, useless disaster when they get wet and take forever to dry. Synthetic bags also don't cause any allergic reactions like goose feathers do for some people. Finally, synthetic bags are significantly cheaper than otherwise-comparable down bags.

Why, then, would anyone want a down sleeping bag? Down bags continue to be popular for several reasons. First and foremost there are no synthetic fabrics that will compare with down for its warmth-to-weight ratio. Down sleeping bags are significantly lighter than synthetic bags. They also pack into small spaces much better than bulky synthetic bags. For backpackers and climbers trying to shave pack weight and space this is a huge advantage. Down bags are also better in frigid conditions. If you're considering doing any winter, early spring, or late fall camping in Utah, you'll definitely want to consider buying the warmest bag you can find, which will certainly be down. In addition, Utah's climate is overwhelmingly dry, and the chances of your sleeping bag getting really wet are relatively slim.

Regardless of whether you choose a down or synthetic insulated sleeping bag, store your bag unstuffed. This keeps the lining fluffy and prolongs the lifespan of the loft (insulating properties of the bag). Either hang the bag in the closet or loosely stuff it in the large cotton stuff sack it comes in. Always store your sleeping bag in a cool dry place where it isn't likely to get damp or mold.

Sleeping Pads

Camping doesn't mean sleeping on the cold hard ground like it once did. Much has changed since John Muir used to cut himself a bed of pine bows for a bed. There's now a good selection of sleeping pad options for campers to choose from that will vastly improve a night spent outdoors. They'll also help keep you warm. Self-inflating air

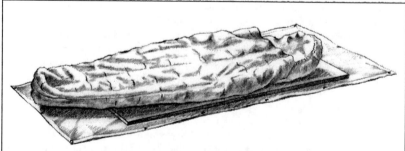

Even with the warmest sleeping bag in the world, if you just lay it down on the ground and try to sleep, you will likely get as cold as a winter cucumber. That is because the cold ground will suck the warmth right out of your body. The solution? A sleeping pad.

mattresses have earned a reputation as the best sleeping pads around. They come in a variety of thicknesses and lengths and some are even cut to fit a human body. Closed cell foam pads are also still popular, especially among backcountry travelers trying to go extremely light. Consider using a combination of a foam pad and a self inflating mattress on cold nights or when camping in the snow, the extra insulation is well worth any added cost and weight. If you choose a self inflating pad, it's a good idea to buy a patch kit because sooner or later, your sleeping pad is bound to spring a leak.

Lighting

Hopefully part of the fun of camping is becoming more in tune with the natural cycle of the earth. Go to bed when it gets dark, wake up at first light. Ah, the simple life! Realistically though, sooner or later, you're going to need a light source to set up camp, cook a meal, or find the bathroom in the dark. There's a huge assortment of camping specific lighting. Depending on your camping style you might want a bright lantern or featherweight LED headlamp. Some lanterns run on white gas while others are battery operated, and more

traditionally are candle lanterns. Headlamps, perfected by spelunkers so they could see the caverns they were exploring, come in all shapes and sizes and are popular because they are not only hands free, but light up wherever you look. Whatever you choose to brighten the night, remember extra batteries, and don't forget to turn everything off once in a while and enjoy the stars!

Food and Cooking Gear

A big part of any successful camping trip is the food. Whether it's roasting hot dogs over the fire, carbo-loading on pasta in the backcountry, or teaching your five-year-old how to make his first s'more, everything tastes better when you're camping. However, while learning to go without is a valuable part of the camping experience, not every meal can be prepared over an open flame. It's important to have at least some basic ware for your camping kitchen.

STOVES

Large, two-burner stoves are ideal for camping in developed campgrounds. These simple, reliable stoves run on white gas or propane fuel. Don't be seduced by stoves boasting they

DUTCH OVEN PINEAPPLE UPSIDE DOWN CAKE

1 yellow cake mix

3 eggs

1 - 20 ounce can of pineapple slices with juice

1/3 cup vegetable oil

1/4 cup butter

1/2 cup brown sugar

8 to 10 maraschino cherries

Preheat a Dutch oven (12" works best) with about 10 coals under the Dutch oven and 20 coals on the lid.

Melt the butter in the preheated Dutch oven. Sprinkle the brown sugar on the butter, then add the pineapple slices, placing a maraschino cherry in each pineapple slice. In a mixing bowl, combine the cake mix, pineapple juice, oil, and eggs. Mix well and spread the batter evenly over the pineapple slices.

Bake for about 35 minutes or until the center is done and the cake is fluffy. Let the oven cool. Carefully remove the cake by running a spatula around the edges and invert the cake onto a plate.

Serves 6 to 8

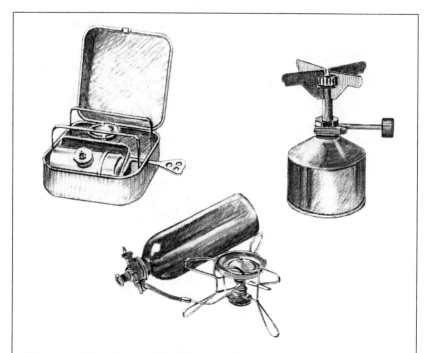

Stoves are available in many styles and burn a variety of fuels. These are three typical examples. Top left: **White gas stoves** are the most popular because they are inexpensive and easy to find; they do require priming and can be explosive. Top right: **Gas canister stoves** burn propane, butane, isobutane, and mixtures of the three. These are the easiest to use but have two disadvantages: 1) Because the fuel is bottled, determining how much fuel is left can be difficult. 2) The fuel is limited to above-freezing conditions. Bottom: **Liquid fuel stoves** burn Coleman fuel, denatured alcohol, kerosene, and even gasoline; these fuels are economical and have a high heat output, but most must be primed.

operate on other fuels like kerosene or unleaded gas; white gas is much cleaner and a superior fuel. Steer clear of alternative fuels except as a last resort. The dirty burn will end up all over your pots and pans and cause far more headaches than finding the right fuel.

Smaller backpacking stoves are also a good option, especially if you'll be preparing simple meals. They're compact, light, and easy to use, and they heat up very quickly. Traditionally, lightweight stoves have run off white gas, while some high-end stoves can run on a variety of fuels in a pinch. These stoves are more versatile, especially if you'll be using them on

international expeditions where your fuel options might be severely limited. If this is the case, take the time to learn how to clean and maintain the stove in the field. Be especially careful not to allow the tiny fuel jet to become clogged by a buildup of carbon from the gas. An hour of practice at home can save major headaches down the road. Again, choose your fuels carefully—not all are created equal. These days, many backpacking stoves run off pressurized butane fuel, which is very efficient and simple to control in temperature, though more expensive than white gas. This is probably the simplest, most user-friendly fuel on the market. Look for stoves with an ignition button to avoid being stuck with a cold, partially hydrated dinner because you forgot the matches.

When storing your stove, remember that white gas is extremely refined and sensitive. White gas that has been opened and stored for a period of time won't burn as cleanly as new gas. When possible, only buy as much gas as you'll need for your next trip.

POTS, PANS, AND UTENSILS

Pots and pans for camping should be versatile, efficient, and easy to clean. Tight fitting lids are a must for quickly boiling water and retaining heat in blustery weather. Nonstick surfaces and good heat distribution are important because camping heat sources are usually too hot and difficult to adjust. Keep in mind there won't always be a sink to tidy up in. Interchangeable pot grippers save weight on backpacking cook sets and allow you to handle the pot without burning yourself. They are a small but essential part of any good cook set. Cook sets are made out of a variety of lightweight metals like stainless steel, aluminum, and titanium. Their price is inversely related to their weight. If you're really trying to shave weight, there are also stove and pot combinations integrated into one, hyper-efficient unit. These units cut fuel use in half and work especially well in windy conditions.

Bet you didn't know Utah has a State Cooking Pot! Well, it does: the Dutch oven. For chefs itching to take their outdoor meals to the next level, a Dutch oven is a fun way to expand the realm of possibilities. These cast iron pots are tough enough to sit directly in hot coals and have a rimmed lid to hold additional coals on top. It's the perfect set-up for baking in the campground. Try dishes you would never attempt outside, like scalloped potatoes and double chocolate cake—they're easy and delicious. Dutch ovens have long been a staple on overnight river-rafting trips because they create so many opportunities for gourmet cooking. In fact, there are

entire cookbooks of recipes specifically designed for Dutch ovens.

Camping utensils can be as simple a single "spork," the do-anything spoon-fork hybrid, to a full kitchen in an RV. It all depends upon your individual style. I always make sure to include a multi-functional utility knife, a plastic bowl, and a mug for coffee or other hot drinks. The mug will also keep your soup warm long enough to finish it in cold weather. Other handy items I like to include in my camping kitchen include a spatula and small cutting board.

SPICE KIT

Nothing can add more to the flavor of camping meals than carrying a simple spice kit. I've created a special spice kit that I keep with my camping gear so I'll always have a little extra flavor for everything I end up cooking in camp. I use a half-dozen tiny screw-top Nalgene containers (old film canisters work just as well), fill them with my favorite spices, and stash it with my cook set. It's easy, light for backpacking, and always ready to go. My kit usually includes garlic salt, pepper, cayenne, Montreal steak seasoning, mushroom powder, and onion powder.

COFFEE

Can't stand the idea of waking up without a cup of coffee? You're not alone. There are lots of options for making a good morning brew even when you're sleeping outdoors. Mini French press coffee makers, drip-style filters, and percolator pots have brought the quality of camping coffee closer to what you might expect from a local latte stand. There are even tiny hand-held bean grinders for those who crave extra fresh flavor.

Water Containers

Utah is a desert. While many of the campgrounds listed in this guide provide drinking water, many do not. Dead Horse State Park trucks its drinking water 32 miles for the campground to use. Do the planet a favor and buy a five-gallon water container and fill it before the trip. It's much cheaper than buying gallon jugs at the grocery store and saves on plastic as well. Having a reserve of water also makes you a more flexible camper, able to choose from more campgrounds or even well-suited undeveloped spots. Another good strategy is to fill old water jugs and bottles at home, freeze them, and then fill your cooler. They'll double as a bag of ice and, when they melt, drinking water as well.

WATER TREATMENT

If you're camping in the backcountry and drawing water from a natural source, it should be treated. With cattle and countless wild animals sharing Utah's wilderness with us, it's mandatory to treat all drinking water. Small, efficient water pumps do a great job of filtering out unwanted parasites, bacteria, and cysts that would otherwise wreak havoc on our digestive systems. Water filters force water through microscopic holes to filter out the unwanted. Unfortunately, many of Utah's rivers, especially in the southern half of the state, have extremely high sediment loads. These suspended solids can quickly clog the tiny holes of the filter and render it useless. To combat this, pump the clearest water possible and wrap a coffee filter or bandanna around the intake to your filter to keep it from getting clogged. For the record, water filters are notorious for breaking down when they are needed the most. So, relying solely on a filter isn't a wise plan. Carry at least one backup treatment method just in case.

A good alternative way to treat water is with iodine tablets. The small tabs take about 30 minutes to treat a quart of water. They weigh almost nothing, are simple to use, and will never clog or break down when needed most. Iodine tablets used to leave treated water tasting rather undesirable, but an effective flavor neutralizer has been developed and is included with the iodine.

The more traditional way to treat water is to boil it. To be totally safe, water should be brought to a rolling boil for at least 5 minutes.

This option is the most foolproof way to treat water; however, it uses lots of fuel, which is relatively heavy and wasteful compared to the other options.

CLOTHING

Clothing choices for camping depend greatly on the activities you'll be doing on your camping trip. Packing for camping can be as simple as going to the closet and grabbing a warm jacket and pajamas, or it might mean being ready for any kind of weather Mother Nature can deliver.

Staying warm and comfortable in inclement weather can be a real challenge. The best way to ensure you'll be cozy when you're active in stormy weather is to dress in layers. Insulating layers that sit close to your body should be made of wool or synthetic material that will keep you warm even when they are damp or wet. As a general rule, the more breathable the fabric is, the better. Modern synthetic fabrics made of petroleum and recycled plastic bottles do a great job of wicking moisture away from your skin and keeping you warm and dry. They also trap odor, as anyone who spends much time in polyester long underwear will tell you. For this and other reasons, there will always be people who prefer natural fabrics. Merino wool is currently in vogue because it insulates well without retaining as much undesirable funk. However, it can carry quite a hefty price tag. When temperatures get really cold, or if you're lounging around camp in chilly weather, you'll want a middle layer of insulation as well. Down or synthetic "puffy" jackets fill this need nicely. Like a fitted mummy sleeping bag, they trap air close to the body and retain an amazing amount of body heat. In the case of a storm, you'll also want a nylon shell jacket as an outer layer, preferably one that's very water repellent but still breathes enough to transfer moisture out, away from your body.

Shoes

Like clothing, your choice of footwear for

RECYCLED CLOTHING

In the modern world we don't always know where our clothing comes from. As competing manufacturers of outdoor clothing constantly strive to invent the latest, lightest, most high-tech equipment, consumers are often left wondering, "What am I wearing?"

You might be surprised to learn that many high-tech fabrics are, at their core, petroleum products. Petroleum-based synthetic fabrics like nylon are used in many types of outdoor clothing because they don't absorb moisture and help people retain body heat even when the fabrics become wet. Fabrics that have become household names, like fleece, Capilene, Polartec, and Gore-Tex, all start out as crude oil.

Fortunately, engineers have developed a process to make many of these same products with post-consumer waste, namely, recycled plastic water bottles. Soda pop and water bottles are refined and purified, then chopped down and spun into fiber strands. These strands can then be knitted and woven into new fabrics. Manufacturers have also started recycling the clothes themselves. Your worn-out long underwear, made out of these same petroleum-based products, can now be recycled in similar fashion. Some companies are even recycling cotton T-shirts in addition to synthetic fabrics. The outdoor clothing manufacture Patagonia has a recycling program called Common Threads Garment Recycling. Clothing can be recycled at their retail stores or mailed to:

Patagonia Service Center
ATTN: Common Threads
Recycling Program
8550 White Fir Street
Reno, NV 89523-8939
800/638-6464
www.patagonia.com

The benefits of recycled clothing are simple. Recycling plastic bottles and used clothing reduces the total amount of waste we produce, in turn decreasing the amount of toxic emissions produced by incinerators and reducing the overall pressure on landfills. In short, it helps preserve the natural environment we enjoy when we go camping.

camping will be dictated by the activities you plan on doing during your camping trip. You may need anything from casual sandals to heavy mountaineering boots, depending upon your trip's agenda. If there's any significant hiking planned, boots or comfortable hiking or running shoes are a good idea. They'll provide support and protect your feet from potential hazards or injury. When you'll be carrying a heavy pack or moving through uneven terrain, boots with ankle support can save a twisted or sprained ankle. Remember, your feet will swell on long hikes, so size your boots and hiking shoes appropriately. When shopping for hiking boots, also consider the socks you'll be wearing.

If you like to wear thick wool socks or two pair at once, add at least a half size to your boots. Desert canyon hiking may require athletic sandals; consider water-specific neoprene shoes if river crossings are necessary. Regardless of the shoes you choose, make sure to break them in before you embark on major hikes.

Socks

The right pair of socks can be as vital to foot comfort as the appropriate shoes. The activity, weather, and shoes you'll be wearing will all play a role in choosing the best socks. For big hikes, wool and wool-synthetic blended fabric socks do a great job of keeping your feet warm and dry.

Both wool and synthetic fabrics do a good job of transferring moisture away from your skin and helping your feet breathe. Thicker wool socks will provide some cushioning and help reduce friction inside your boots, minimizing blisters. A thin synthetic liner sock worn together with a wool sock is a great combination for heavy boots and long hikes. For backpacking trips I always take an extra pair of wool socks to sleep in. On hot days and shorter hikes, thin cotton socks may be more appropriate and will keep your feet cool and comfortable.

Foot care

Regardless of the footwear combination you end up choosing, it's important to pay attention to your feet when outdoors, especially on long trips. Address any hotspots or rubbing as soon as you feel them. Carry a small foot care kit on big hikes; a few ounces of moleskin or athletic tape can save you from painful blisters. Consider taking sandals or light shoes with you on backpacking trips to wear around camp. They will let your feet air out after a long day in heavy boots. Also, keep

UTAH'S ORIGINAL CAMPERS

People have been camping in Utah for thousands of years. In the past, camping wasn't thought of as recreation, but simply a way of life.

Part of what makes the Colorado Plateau such a fun place to explore are the visible signs left by these long ago peoples. Everywhere you go in southern Utah you'll find reference to the Anasazi (Ancient Ones). The name Anasazi is actually a word from the Navajo language, while the Anasazi were the ancestors of the modern-day Pueblo Indians living in Arizona and New Mexico. These people are thought to have inhabited the Four Corners region from around A.D. 1 to A.D. 1300. Anasazi rock art panels, known as petroglyphs (figures carved out of the desert varnished rock) and pictographs (painted on the rock), can be found in many locations in southern Utah on the soft, red desert sandstone. Depending on the site, these art panels may be as simple as a single figure or as complex as hundreds of different characters. One of most elaborate panels can be seen at Newspaper Rock near the southern entrance to Canyonlands National Park. The most widely recognizable figures in these petroglyphs are the Kokopelli. Kokopelli was a fertility deity usually depicted in rock art as a humpback flute player. The Kokopelli was believed to be the god of childbirth and agriculture but was also thought of a mischievous trickster.

Perhaps more impressive than their rock art are the Anasazi people's dwellings and storehouses, known as kivas and granaries. Their stone structures are tucked into the deep, protected canyons of the Colorado Plateau. These intricately constructed and complex buildings have lasted hundreds of years and were built by a culture with highly developed masonry skills. The best displays of these cliff dwellings are protected in the Four Corners region in the Hovenweep National Monument, Chaco Canyon National Historical Park, Mesa Verde National Park, Bandelier National Monument, and the Canyon de Chelly National Monument. Of these parks and monuments, only Hovenweep lies within Utah, but all are clustered within a short distance of each other. Other smaller, isolated structures can be found around the southwest. Finding these structures or other ancient artifacts on your own can be a rewarding experience. If you do come across one of these treasures in the backcountry, please be respectful in your admiration.

your feet as clean as possible. Sand, dirt, and small pebbles inevitably find their way inside your shoes on hikes and can rub your feet raw. Be sure to take your shoes off occasionally and clean them out. Last but not least, don't forget your toenails. Trim them before you leave to avoid any uncomfortable rubbing they might cause.

CLIMATE AND WEATHER

Utah has a climate with four distinct seasons, each with its own charm. Camping is possible year-round but is a vastly different experience depending upon the season.

Winter

Winters are cold and white, with the northern part of the state receiving the bulk of the snowfall. The Wasatch Mountains receive an average of 500 inches of snow a year. These mountains transform into a winter playground for skiers and snowboarders from all over the world, who come to sample some of the best, most accessible powder on the planet. Camping in northern Utah during winter is a chilly prospect, though still a possibility. Yurts, strategically placed to access some of the best backcountry skiing, offer an opportunity for backcountry travelers to winter camp in relative comfort. The original yurts were portable structures used by nomads in Mongolia. Traditionally made of slats covered by wool felt, Mongolian yurts were similar to the tepees used by the Plains Indians of North America. Modern versions have thick plastic walls and a skylight in the center and are outfitted with a woodstove to help combat the inevitable sinking temperatures of a winter night in Utah's mountains. The Big Water Yurt is located in Mill Creek Canyon in the Wasatch Mountains, just a short drive from Salt Lake City. It can be reserved from December through April and offers a great escape from the city.

The southern half of the state stays dry in winter but receives considerable snowfall as well, the white snow highlighting the rusty red beauty of the desert landscape. Bryce Canyon National Park is particularly beautiful in winter, its higher elevation catching more snow to contrast the pink and red hoodoo wonderland. Utah winter weather is unpredictable and can vary greatly from year to year. Camping in the winter might seem crazy in some years and perfectly viable in others. St. George, in the extreme southwest corner of Utah, consistently posts the state's warmest winter temperatures and is a great place to head for mid-winter warmth and camping. Regardless of the daytime temperatures, be prepared for bitterly cold nights. The dry desert air combined with short winter days can make for some of the coldest sleeping conditions you're ever likely to experience. So, if you plan on winter camping anywhere in Utah, be prepared. Also, the wise winter camper will watch the weather forecast closely and always have a backup plan. The tradeoff: solitude and empty campgrounds.

Spring

Spring weather in Utah is borderline schizophrenic, oscillating between warm sunshine, snow showers, and the occasional rainsquall. Spring rain and the melting snowpack bring new life to an otherwise stark landscape. The northern mountains burst into fresh green, and wildflowers bloom in the desert. Taken as an average, temperatures in spring are ideal for outdoor recreation. While the high peaks melt out from their winter blanket, it is prime time to visit southern hot spots. Outdoor lovers of all kinds descend upon the desert recreation mecca of Moab in April and May to soak up the sun and enjoy its unique, freakish geology. It's also a great time to explore less popular desert treasures like Grand Staircase–Escalante National Monument and the mysterious San Rafael Swell. Keep in mind winter and spring storms often take the form of strong wind and sandstorms in Southern Utah. These storms are no fun to be out in, and certainly not enjoyable to camp in, as described by

Edward Abbey in his novel about a season spent in Arches National Park, *Desert Solitaire:* "After the reconnoitering dust devils comes the real, serious wind, the voice of the desert rising to a demented howl and blotting out sky and sun behind yellow clouds of dust, sand, confusion, embattled birds, last year's scrub-oak leaves, pollen, the husks of locust, bark of juniper…" Again, come prepared and be ready to be flexible.

Summer

Summer in Utah is hot, and it's the time to flee for the hills and the lakes. The higher elevations provide relief from the heat and offer excellent camping. Aspen and cottonwood trees mix with alpine spruce and ponderosa pines in a mosaic of green. High mountain lakes provide great fishing for cutthroat and rainbow trout, while hiking and biking trails are snow-free and begging to be enjoyed. The Wasatch and Uinta Mountains offer alpine retreats in the north and the Sevier and Aquarius Plateaus provide respite in the south. The volcanic peaks of the San Juan, Henry, and Abajo Mountains in the southeast corner of the state are cool escapes as well. If you prefer water recreation as means to cool down, Utah has plenty of options for you as well. Lake Powell, a man-made reservoir created by the Glen Canyon Dam on the Colorado River, draws every kind of boater imaginable. It's possible to see people on personal watercraft and in sea kayaks exploring the lake's canyons side by side in a melting pot of recreation style. Northern notable boating options include Bear Lake and Flaming Gorge. Summer is the busiest time to camp; when possible, call ahead and reserve your sites.

THUNDER AND LIGHTNING STORMS

The majority of the summer precipitation in Utah arrives in the form of thunderstorms. Thunderstorms can be both beautiful and dangerous. It is not wise to be exposed on mountain ridges when summer storms develop. A direct lightning strike will almost certainly be fatal—and it doesn't take a direct strike to injure or kill you. Electrical current can travel through the ground after it strikes and still be quite dangerous. Tall, billowing cumulus clouds are associated with thunderstorms. These clouds are created by the rapid heating of air near the ground. Heated air rises quickly through cooler air in cells or vertical columns called thermals. As the air rises and cools, water condenses and huge dark clouds form. The dramatic shifting of air and strong updrafts create electronic imbalances within these clouds. Lightning is the result of these imbalances equalizing in dramatic and violent ways. To avoid being exposed in an electrical storm, plan summer hikes in the morning. Thunderstorms become dangerous in the afternoon, so make certain you're down in safe terrain by noon or 1 P.M. when thunderstorms threaten. In the mountains, open exposed ridges are the worst place to be in a storm, because lighting seeks the path of least resistance. Avoid tall individual trees and objects that might attract a strike. Also avoid standing by a lake or body of water as it can act as a conductor of electricity.

Fall

Autumn is by far the prettiest season in Utah. The mountains turn into a wild display of fall colors. The aspen groves quake golden and the scrub oak turn a fiery burnt red. Evenings and mornings feel crisp and fresh, and afternoon temperatures climb into the mid 70s. Fall is the perfect time to camp almost anywhere in the state, the snow long gone and weather ideal. Nights can start to get chilly, especially at higher elevations, so it's time to pull out the warm down sleeping bag! Fall is also the safest time to explore the labyrinth of slot canyons in Southern Utah, when sudden rainstorms and flash floods are least likely to develop. If you enjoy landscape photography, fall is one of the most rewarding times to plan a trip. Not only are the leaves in full regalia, but the frenzied crowds of spring and summer have moved on to other pursuits.

SAFETY AND FIRST AID

While no one wants to think about getting injured while they're camping, the possibility always exists. Be smart and have a plan for injury before it happens.

Plants

There are the usual poisonous and irritating plants in Utah. You'll find poison oak, poison ivy, and stinging nettles in isolated parts of the state. Poison ivy and poison oak can be found in Utah's mountains, especially in the canyons. They can be recognized by their green almond-shaped leaves, which grow in groups of three, inspiring the cautionary phrase, "Leaves of three, let them be." The leaves turn a dark red in autumn.

Both poison ivy and poison oak produce a resin called urushiol that can cause an allergic reaction when exposed to human skin. The reaction to urushiol usually appears 2–3 days after exposure, in the form of rash and

Avoiding Poison Oak: Remember the old Boy Scout saying: "Leaves of three, let them be."

curved lines of itchy red bumps or blisters on the skin.

Stinging nettles are a herbaceous flowering plant that grow in moist areas during summer months. The nettles' stems and leaves are very hairy, and the tips of these hairs contain a combination of chemicals that produces a stinging sensation when touched. Nettle stings may cause an unpleasant rash or itch for anywhere from a few hours to several days.

Itch creams and lotions can help mitigate any nasty encounters with poison ivy, poison oak, or stinging nettles. In extreme cases, seek the advice of a doctor.

Insects and Reptiles

There are a staggering number of ways to get hurt in the outdoors. If you don't think so, turn on the 5 o'clock news and listen. Nearly every day you'll hear another unbelievable story of someone getting into trouble in the outdoors. Luckily, compared to everyday life the chances of getting injured are extremely low. You're much more likely to get hurt driving your car or crossing the street than going camping. So don't let this cautionary list get in the way of an enjoyable trip.

TICKS

There are a few bugs to watch out for while camping in Utah. Ticks are not a major concern but they are around, especially in spring and early summer in the mountains during snowmelt. Ticks drop out of trees onto people and crawl around for a while before they find a nice warm, dark place to bed down and dig in. It's a good idea to do a quick tick check after any hike just to be safe. Look particularly close in the dank, hairy parts of your body—ticks love armpits and crotches. If you do find a tick lurking, carefully remove it; the longer it's imbedded, the more likely it could pass on Lyme disease. The best and only safe way to remove a tick is with tweezers. Pinch the tick as close to the skin as possible, pull gently but firmly on the tick without breaking off its body. You will need to be patient and pull for a while until the tick slowly backs out. If the tick has been embedded for more than 24 hours or you have reason to believe you've contracted Lyme disease, go to a doctor. The symptoms and signs of Lyme disease include a circular rash around the site of the tick bite, lack of energy, headache, stiff neck, fever and chills, or muscle and joint pain.

MOSQUITOES

Mosquitoes can be a problem in areas near standing water in early summer. Most recently, concern has been on the rise about West Nile Virus. While cases in Utah have been very isolated, they are starting to occur. If you're in an area where West Nile has been reported, be safe. Mosquito repellent does a good job keeping these pests away. The most effect mosquito repellents contain an active ingredient called DEET (N,N-diethyl-m-toluamide). Other effective repellants include Picaridin (KBR 3023), or the oil of lemon eucalyptus (p-menthane 3,8-diol (PMD). Where mosquitoes pose little threat and are simply a pesky nuisance, a less toxic option is a mosquito coil, incense that, like a good fire, keeps mosquitoes at bay. There are also mosquito head nets if you're heading to an area that has particularly nasty mosquitoes or black flies. When camping without a tent, head nets are nice security for bugs in general.

SCORPIONS

Scorpions are an unlikely but potentially painful encounter. Southwestern Utah is home to dozens of species of scorpions. Bark scorpions are the most dangerous, and the only scorpions that have a potentially life-threatening sting. If young children are stung, they should be taken to a medical facility quickly. Adults are unlikely to need medical treatment, but keep careful watch on the sting site to be sure. If you camp in the desert, check your shoes in the morning before you slide them on.

SPIDERS

Black widows and tarantulas are the two poisonous spiders found in Utah. Tarantulas are common in the Topaz Mountain area along the Thomas Range in Millard County. Their bites create redness and irritation, but little more. Black widows can be found almost anywhere in the United States, but again their bites are not life threatening. Elevate the bite site, apply a cold compress, and take aspirin or Tylenol.

BEES

Bees are especially worrisome to campers who are allergic. If you are, take the time to get an epinephrine pen from your doctor and learn how to use it. In the outdoors, and certainly in the backcountry, it can be difference between life and death.

GILA MONSTERS

Your chances of seeing a Gila monster in the wild are extremely rare. If you do, consider yourself lucky! And give it space. Gila monsters might appear slow and lethargic, but they can actually move very quickly. Trying to pick them up is a very bad idea. They have a venomous bite that can overpower prey but is rarely fatal to humans. In the event of a bite, seek immediate medical attention.

RATTLESNAKES

Encountering rattlesnakes is far more likely. The Southwest has the largest variety of rattlesnakes in the world, and many of these live in Utah. They can often be found sunning their cold-blooded bodies on warm, south-facing rocks in the early morning. If disturbed, they shake their rattles to indicate irritation. Again, just give them a wide berth. The warning rattle is a good indicator you're too close. Back slowly away and go on with your day. You'll both be happy you did. Rattlesnake bites rarely kill people but do make for a terrible experience. In the case of a bite, again find immediate medical attention. The best way to counteract the bite is with antivenin, which you'll only find at a medical facility. Remove any rings or jewelry before swelling begins. Keep the bite below your heart and limit movement and physical exertion to an absolute minimum. Don't cut the wound to suck out the venom like you've seen in old Westerns, you'll only risk infection and worsen the wound.

Wildlife

BEARS

Everyone's got a bear story. I saw my first grizzly bears in the wild backpacking in Yellowstone when I was 19. We spotted the mother and two cubs across an open, grassy meadow just before sunset. The experience was scary yet calming at the same time; the bears looked peaceful and at home in their environment. They quietly went their way and we ours, better off for the encounter. Unfortunately, most bear stories are neither as short nor as benign. Too many involve established campgrounds and bears pursuing human food. Camping in bear country carries with it a responsibility. When bears gain access to human food, it hurts the bears and creates a potentially dangerous situation. Human food is far more nutritious than the natural bear diet. When bears start eating human food, they'll go to great lengths to continue. Because relocation efforts are largely unsuccessful, the tragic end to this story is that "problem" bears are generally killed. As the old adage goes, "a fed bear is a dead bear." Make every effort to keep human food out of the bear's diet. In developed campgrounds, use provided bearproof lockers and

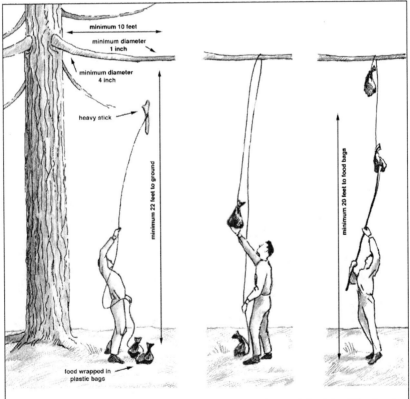

In an area frequented by bears, a good **bear-proof food hang** is a must. Food should be stored in a plastic bag 10 feet from the trunk of the tree and at least 20 feet from the ground.

in the backcountry carry bear canisters or effectively hang your food.

Moose

Northern Utah has a surprisingly large moose population living in relatively close proximity to the Salt Lake Valley. Moose are particularly visible in the Wasatch Mountains on the Park City side of the Range as well as Big Cottonwood Canyon. These goofy, awkward-looking animals are at the same time beautifully serene and extremely dangerous. Male moose during the fall mating season have a reputation as one of the most aggressive animals you're likely to encounter. Keep your distance and enjoy these giants respectfully.

Mountain Lions

Mountain lions, also known as cougars or pumas, live in a wide range of habitat in Utah. They prey on deer, elk, moose, mountain goats, and most commonly deer. Cougars are rarely seen in the wild because they are active mostly at night. As a rule they'll go to great lengths to avoid contact with humans, but encounters do occasionally occur. While it is possible to be attacked by a cougar, the chances of this happening are so negligible it is hardly worth worrying about. In all of North America over the past 100 years only 25 people have been fatally wounded by a cougar attack. It doesn't take a math wiz to figure out there are a lot more dangerous things to think about on your next camping trip. If you're still worried, make sure to keep an eye on the kids—don't let them wander off alone, as they are more likely to be perceived as possible prey than a grown adult.

Coyotes

Coyotes are exceptionally adaptable animals. They're scavengers that eat a varied and flexible diet and inhabit most environments in Utah. Like bears, however, they prefer human food to their natural diet because of its superior nutritional value. Please don't feed coyotes or let them have access to your food. Help keep these wild animals wild and alive!

First Aid

First-Aid Kits

The prudent camper will carry a first-aid kit. Prepackaged first-aid kits come in all shapes

a bull moose in the Wasatch Mountains

© MIKE MATSON

and sizes and provide anything you might need for an injury short of stitches or a plaster cast. A simple first-aid kit is probably all you'll need if you camp exclusively in developed campgrounds. Most campgrounds are not far from emergency services, so the part of the first-aid kit you'll access most will probably be ibuprofen and adhesive bandages. Of course, a larger kit can't hurt, so if it makes you feel better equipped to handle an emergency, put one in the car and it'll be there if you need it.

If you plan on traveling and camping in the backcountry, a small but useful first-aid kit should always be included in your pack. Even more important in the case of a backcountry injury than a first-aid kit, however, is a cool head and resourceful, creative approach. Using what you have with you, rather than pounds of first-aid supplies, will get you through most injuries. For example, the metal stays in your backpack's frame combined with an ace bandage make a perfectly functional splint for a broken arm. A cut-up cotton T-shirt doubles as a bandage or gauze and a cold mountain stream will reduce the swelling in a sprained ankle as well as any icepack. If you plan on spending a lot of time in the backcountry, I recommend taking a Wilderness First Responder (WFR) course. This weeklong first-aid training course will boost your confidence in an emergency and fill your mind with creative solutions for any backcountry trauma you'll encounter.

What to include in a minimalist backcountry kit? There are a few items you shouldn't leave the trailhead without. The most versatile piece of any first-aid kit is a small roll of one-inch cotton medical tape. Other must-haves include ibuprofen or other painkillers and antihistamines in the event of an allergic reaction. If you or someone in your group is prone to strong allergic reactions, an epinephrine pen can save a life. Make sure the trip leader or someone who isn't allergic knows how to use it. If you feel more comfortable with a larger kit, by all means bring it. In my

experience, larger, heavier kits tend to get left behind, while smaller, less cumbersome kits are there when you need them.

HANTAVIRUS PULMONARY SYNDROME
This rare respiratory ailment is contracted by breathing in dust particles from deer mice feces. It progresses quickly, and anyone suffering from symptoms needs to be hospitalized immediately. The first symptoms are generally flu-like and include fever, headache, stomach pain, pain in the joints and lower back, coughing, and sometimes nausea and vomiting. The main symptom is difficulty breathing, as the lungs fill with fluid. Luckily, the chances of actually contracting hantavirus are so minuscule it's hardly worth mentioning.

ALTITUDE SICKNESS
Altitude sickness can and does affect visitors to Utah. The Wasatch Mountains reach almost 11,000 feet and are within a half hour's drive of Salt Lake Airport. Travelers arrive and are quickly whisked up into the mountains without stopping to acclimatize. On rare occasions, especially when people hike, ski, or exercise too hard, too quickly, they will feel the effects of altitude. Acute Mountain Sickness (AMS) is the most common illness associated with going high in a hurry. It can begin as low as 7,000 to 9,000 feet. Symptoms include nausea, dizziness, loss of appetite, headache, and trouble sleeping. The best way to deal with AMS is to simply descend and acclimatize.

DEHYDRATION
Stay hydrated! Utah in the summer is a hot, dry, windy place. Campers need to drink lots of water to stay hydrated. Drinking three to four quarts of water a day is a good starting point, but if you're exercising or exposed to the sun all day, double that isn't too much. How do you know if you're drinking enough? It's simple: If you're well hydrated, your urine will be clear and copious. The more water you drink the happier and more comfortable you'll be.

HEAT EXHAUSTION AND HEAT STROKE

It's easy to get overheated in Utah's wild places. The day starts out cool, the sky blue and beautiful—perfect weather to head out on the Slickrock on a mountain bike. But by 9 A.M. the thermometer is showing 85°F, your hydration pack is empty, and you've still got miles to go to complete your loop. Just a few hours later the mercury is pushing the century mark and you're in trouble, you're tired, you have a pounding headache, and you feel nauseated. These are the symptoms of heat exhaustion. You've sweated out a lot of water and salt, and your body is out of balance. Find a shady spot to rest and drink lots of water. A small, salty snack and a couple hours of rest will help replace what you've lost and you'll start feeling better. If you continue the ride without rest and water you risk progressing toward the far more serious heat stroke. Indicators of heat stoke are hot red skin and bizarre personality changes. In heat stroke, the victim's body is losing its ability to cool itself and producing heat faster than it can release it. The body's core temperature must be cooled down fast. Get out of the heat and seek medical attention.

HYPOTHERMIA

Hypothermia is the most likely way to get into a life-threatening situation in the outdoors. When the body's core temperature falls too far below its normal 98.6°F hypothermia starts to set in. Hypothermia can be the result of exposure to very cold temperatures, but it is more often caused by a combination of wet clothing, wind, and fatigue. The first signs of lowered core temperature are chattering teeth and uncontrollable shivering. This is the time to take action. Change out of wet clothes, prepare hot drinks, eat food, and, if possible, get out of the environment that's causing hypothermia. If the core temperature continues to drop you'll notice impaired motor skills and poor judgment. A hypothermic person's body is pulling into itself in an effort to conserve whatever heat it can for its vital core. This is

the threshold between mild and severe hypothermia. A very clear indicator of severe hypothermia is a partial or full lack of consciousness. At this point, a full-scale effort to re-warm the person is urgently needed. Use hot water bottles as heat packs and bundle the victim in warm, dry, insulating layers, including a waterproof vapor barrier like a tarp or tent fly to insure no heat is escaping. Get the victim professional medical treatment as soon as possible.

The best way to combat hypothermia is to prevent it in the first place. Wear clothing like wool or fleece that continues to insulate even if it gets wet. Dress in layers you can easily remove or add in order to regulate your body temperature. Also, bring lots of water and snacks when you head out on adventures. Your body needs calories and water to stay warm in cold environments, even if you have plenty of warm clothing.

FROSTBITE

Frostbite only happens to mountaineers on exotic peaks like Denali and Mount Everest, right? Not necessarily. I've had mild frostbite on my cheek in less than five minutes after getting off the tram at Snowbird Ski Resort in the Wasatch Mountains. The wind was blowing hard, my face felt numb, and my friend pointed out I had a large white circle under my goggles. We went inside quickly to warm up and luckily all I was left with was a scab the size of a quarter on my face. But if you don't watch for and recognize frostbite quickly, it can lead to far greater consequences. Monitor your friends closely when you're in really cold situations—sometimes you'll know better than they do if they're getting too cold.

SUNBURN

In case you've been living under a rock for the past 30 years and haven't heard, too much exposure to the sun's ultraviolet (UV) rays will cause sunburn. Long-term sun exposure will lead to wrinkled skin, premature aging, and possibly skin cancer. The short-wave, high-energy UV rays actually destroy DNA molecules in the skin, which is why too much exposure can lead to cancer. In fact, one in six Americans is now expected to develop skin cancer in his or her lifetime.

To prevent sunburn, wear protective clothing, wide-brimmed hats, and sunscreen. Consider avoiding the sun altogether between 10 A.M. and 4 P.M. when it is directly overhead and at its strongest. Cloudy overcast days are often when people are unexpectedly burned. The clouds diffuse but don't block the sun's UV rays. Most people know the sun's rays reflect off water and snow, but remember they will reflect off rocks as well, especially in southern Utah.

BLISTERS

Blisters are almost always the result of poor preparation. New shoes or boots that haven't been broken in properly cause blisters by rubbing on heels, toes, and other soft spots on hikers' feet. Blisters are formed by friction. As the blister forms, a small pocket of fluid called plasma builds within the outer layers of skin. The blister forms in effort to prevent further damage to the skin. Before a full-blown blister develops, you'll probably notice a hot spot or rubbing in your boot. This is the time to address the problem. If a hot spot is detected early enough, a blister usually can be avoided. Take off the boot, assess the blister, and take appropriate action. Small hot spots might only need a small piece of cotton medical tape, while full-blown blisters need to be dressed with several pieces of moleskin, tape, and an additional sock to make things more comfortable. Be careful not to cause a new source of friction by adding too many bulky coverings.

Here's how you avoid getting a blister in the first place: The first step is to break in new boots or hiking shoes long before their first hike. Wear them while you walk the dog, around town, or to the office. You might think you look silly, but you'll be happy when you don't get a blister on your first big hiking adventure. If you'll be carrying a heavy load on the hike, break in those boots with a big pack, too. Many people are surprised when they get blisters in the same boots they've worn on other hikes the first time they carry serious weight. Heavy backpacks change the way your feet displace weight, and sometimes new blisters form where you've never had a problem before. Simulate the hike at home and you'll be more comfortable on the trail. Wearing two pairs of socks, one thin liner sock and one thick wool sock, will also help keep your feet happy. The liner will reduce friction and act as an extra layer of skin between your foot and the boot. Finally, don't lace your boots too tight. Many hikers lace their boots as tight as possible and are surprised when they develop blisters. Give your feet a little wiggle room. They need space to breathe, so they don't get too hot, and to swell (most hikers' feet will expand by a half size to a size on long hikes). Remember to lace up a little tighter when if you're heading into a long downhill section of trail; it'll keep your toes from banging too much on the front of your boots.

Navigational Tools

Staying found, especially while you're traveling in the backcountry in Utah, can sometimes be a challenging task. There are many scenarios where even the most spatially aware travelers can become disoriented. Wandering across wide-open desert, hiking through the twisting corners of deeply carved slot canyon, or backcountry skiing through a whiteout blizzard can throw almost anyone for a loop. Luckily, there are modern technologies like Global Positioning Systems (GPS) and the age-old system of maps and compass to help us out.

MAP READING

Accurate map reading is one of the most essential tools for traveling safely in the outdoors. Nothing will build your confidence more than knowing exactly where you are in the backcountry at all times. But staying found does take work, and the only way to get good at

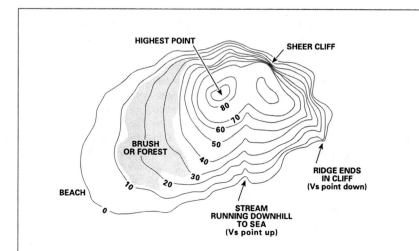

HIGHEST POINT

SHEER CLIFF

80
70
60
50
40
30
20
10
0

BRUSH
OR FOREST

BEACH

RIDGE ENDS
IN CLIFF
(Vs point down)

STREAM
RUNNING DOWNHILL
TO SEA
(Vs point up)

The **topographical map** is easier to read than many believe. Lines close together mean steep gradients; lines farther apart mean gentle gradients; V-shaped sets of lines pointing to higher elevations mean gulleys or stream-beds; V-shaped sets of lines pointing to lower elevations mean ridges.

reading maps is to practice. As we all know from driving in the car, accurate navigation can be a full-time job. Checking the map regularly while you're traveling in the backcountry, whether it's on foot, a horse, a bike, or in a boat, and comparing the landscape to what is drawn on the map, is the best way to keep track of where you are. So keep the map handy and pull it out often. The United States Geologic Survey (USGS) makes the most detailed and useful maps for backcountry travel. The scale of 1:24,000 is very detailed and provides travelers with lots of information about what's around them. National Geographic specializes in maps of the national parks and other popular recreation areas that aren't as detailed as the USGS maps but cover a greater, sometimes more practical area. Both these types of maps represent a three-dimensional world on a flat piece of paper and use contour lines to show elevation changes and a grid system for distance. A compass can make your map reading a lot easier by telling you exactly which way you are facing. Good maps will have a key at the top to orient your compass and help adjust it from Magnetic North to True North. If you don't have a compass, the sun and stars can provide you with an approximation of directions if you pay close attention.

GPS

Handheld GPS units take most of guesswork out of map reading and tell you precisely where you are at all times. It does take some work to get good at reading a GPS as well, so don't assume that buying one will automatically keep you found. In addition, GPS maps do not provide the same level of detail as the USGS topographic maps; in some cases you might need both. To make things easier we've included the GPS coordinates in the description of each campground reviewed in this guide.

CAMPING ETHICS
Kids and the Outdoors
Is there anything more fun for kids than going camping? When I was a kid I remember setting up my grandfather's huge Army green wall tent, with its metal poles and canvas walls, and

camping out in the backyard day after day. Some nights, it seemed like the whole neighborhood would fit in there, our sleeping bags spread out across the floor. We even ran an extension cord out the window so we could watch the summer Olympics on the tiny black-and-white TV. It was the time of our lives, and we didn't even leave the yard!

Camping can be a truly wonderful experience for children. It's a change from everyday life, a time to see new places and have new experiences. It's an opportunity to learn new skills and understand nature in a new way. It's also a chance for the family to spend time together in a stimulating environment. Of course, taking the kids camping isn't always a good time. On one memorable camping trip when I was just three years old, we arrived late at night, and as soon as I exited the car I tripped on a root and split my forehead open on a tree stump. End of trip.

In Utah, some campgrounds are certainly better suited for children than others. Places like Coral Pink Sand Dunes State Park, with

EDWARD ABBEY

If there is one author who defines the red rock country of southern Utah's Colorado Plateau most aptly, it has to be Edward Abbey. While there are many factors contributing to the current popularity of the Four Corners region, southern Utah, and the greater Colorado River environment, Edward Abbey's books *Desert Solitaire* and *The Monkey Wrench Gang* rank at the top of the list. Abbey has been compared to some of the most respected nature writers in Western literature, like Ralph Waldo Emerson and Aldo Leopold, and at the same time called an anarchist and eco-terrorist.

Abbey wrote *Desert Solitaire* while spending two seasons as a Park Service ranger in Arches National Monument during the late 1950s. Arches was a seldom-visited place at that time, and Moab was known as a quiet Uranium mining town rather than the outdoor recreation mecca it is today. *Desert Solitaire* is a love letter of sorts to nature, wilderness, and the desert landscape. Abbey's own words describe his personal passion for the 1950s version of Arches best: "Standing there, gaping at this monstrous and inhuman spectacle of rock and cloud and sky and space, I feel a ridiculous greed and possessive-ness come over me. I want to know it all, possess it all, embrace the entire scene intimately, deeply, totally, as a man desires a beautiful woman. An insane wish? Perhaps not – at least there's nothing else, no one human, to dispute possession with me."

The Monkey Wrench Gang picks up where *Desert Solitaire* leaves off, its focus protecting the landscape rather than admiring it. *The Monkey Wrench Gang* is a novel that's equal parts adventure narrative, anarchist manifesto, and environmental conservation plea. "But the love of wilderness is more than a hunger for what is always beyond reach; it is also an expression of loyalty to the earth, the earth which bore us and sustains us, the only home we shall ever know, the only paradise we ever need – if only we had the eyes to see. Original sin, the true original sin, is the blind destruction for the sake of greed of this natural paradise which lies all around us – if only we were worthy of it."

Edward Abbey's books both inspire and offend. His writing and views are as unpredictable as they are powerful. Perhaps it's the undeniable contradictions and stark contrasts that make him such a perfect spokesman for the desert wilderness of the American Southwest.

its huge, safe, kid-friendly dunes, are a perfect example. Kodachrome Basin is another state park that seems well suited for children. Families of all ages and sizes can enjoy the short hikes and scenic landscape of the place. Other campgrounds offer playgrounds and activities geared toward children. Many of the national park campgrounds have amphitheaters and ranger programs designed specifically for families with young kids. Some of the more developed campgrounds have paved campground loops or bike trails, which are great for kids with bikes to safely explore.

To keep kids from getting bored, bring lots of things to do to supplement the local activities. Bring fishing poles, kayaks, canoes, and boats to lakes; Frisbees and footballs to open campgrounds; and badminton and volleyballs where courts are provided. Binoculars will add to the excitement of seeing wildlife and make the tiny bird in the bushes more interesting. Building a campfire and roasting hot dogs and marshmallows is far more fun than cooking on a camp stove. Encourage the kids to learn while they play. Bring along a star chart to point out constellations at night, or a field guide to learn about wildflowers. As kids get older, invite friends so they can keep exploring with someone their own age, and when ready encourage them to head out on their own. Remind them that camping takes some work, too, and get them involved with camp chores. Jobs like pitching a tent and building a fire will quickly become something they look forward to rather than try to avoid. The more kids go camping, the more they'll enjoy it. They'll build life skills and lasting memories. So go get started, get them out there watch their experience grow.

In setting up camp, always be mindful of potential ecological disturbances. Pitch tents and dispose of human waste at least 200 feet from the water's edge. In grizzly bear territory, increase the distance between your tent and your cooking area, food-hang, and the water's edge threefold. In other words, if you're in grizzly country, do all your cooking 100 yards (not feet) downwind of your sleeping area. If you can establish an escape tree nearby, all the better.

Campground Etiquette

Camping etiquette can be boiled down to one word: respect. Respect the land, other people, the wildlife, and the facilities. Campgrounds have all sorts of signs posted, outlining their particular rules and version of camping ethics. While it's important to follow the posted rules, it's better to understand the philosophy behind them. As campers we are visitors in an otherwise natural area. Hopefully, these natural areas maintain as much of their wild character as possible. It's easy to be shortsighted while camping and have a negative impact on the natural character of a campground. Perhaps you forgot to bring firewood from home and gathered some dead wood and twigs to burn. Or maybe you were being lazy and left out the Fig Newtons during a midday nap, only to wake up to a group of ravens enjoying them for lunch. These seemingly small misdeeds add up quickly, and their cumulative effect is that many of the campgrounds we visit to experience nature aren't very wild at all. A quick look around popular campgrounds will reveal there's almost no dead wood on the ground and even the lower branches on trees have been removed for firewood. Wildlife in and around campgrounds are dependent upon human food and aren't truly wild at all. Poke around bushes and behind trees outside camp spots and you notice carelessly half-buried toilet paper flapping in the wind; the person who left it has long since gone home and forgotten, but the overall effect is the campground feels less like a cherished wilderness and more like the city we came to escape.

With this in mind, please be respectful while you camp. Come prepared with everything you need and take nothing from the land. Give wildlife room to breathe but nothing to eat—it will be healthier in the long run. Be quiet at night and respectful of other campers. If you arrive late or leave early, don't flash high beams into campsites for a better view. Noise is the biggest source of conflict in campgrounds. Be respectful of your neighbors. If you have a larger group and anticipate you'll be loud, find a spot away from other campers. Often times designated group sites are available and are separated from the main campground for this very reason. If you're in a big rig, keep in mind generators can be at least as loud and obnoxious as a rowdy group of campers. Be respectful of those who came for the peace and quiet, and remember: what goes around, comes around.

Wilderness Ethics

Backcountry campers need to be even more aware of their potential impact on the places where they travel and camp. "Take only pictures and leave only footprints" is a simple and sound rule in the backcountry. The Wilderness Act of 1964 defines wilderness as ". . . an area where the earth and its community of life are untrammeled by man, where man himself is a visitor who does not remain." As more and more people travel in the backcountry, it becomes increasingly important to practice low-impact camping and treat these areas with the utmost respect. Utah is home to a wonderfully unique landscape and a staggering amount of wilderness. Within these wilderness areas are extremely fragile ecosystems, rock formations, native art, artifacts, and ancient dwellings; all can be destroyed by careless campers and backcountry travelers. It is our privilege and responsibility to enjoy, preserve, and care for these natural and historic treasures—to love them, but not love them to death.

CAMPING EQUIPMENT CHECKLIST

Sleeping

- ground tarp
- pillow
- rain fly
- sleeping bag
- sleeping pad
- tent

Cooking

- bottle opener/wine key
- coffee
- cooler
- dishes
- dish soap
- food
- fuel
- lighter/matches
- paper towels
- pots and pans with lids
- spatula
- spices
- sponge/dishrag
- stove
- utensils
- utility knife/pocketknife
- water bottle/container
- zip-top resealable bags/plastic containers with lids

Recreation

- bike and helmet
- books
- camera
- day pack
- fishing gear
- Global Positioning System (GPS)
- hiking boots/athletic shoes
- journal
- maps
- pen
- playing cards
- sandals
- tripod

Clothing

- bandanna
- gloves
- hat
- jacket

- long-sleeve shirt
- long underwear
- non-cotton pants
- raincoat

- socks
- swimsuit
- T-shirts
- underwear

Toiletries

- comb
- shampoo
- soap
- toilet paper

- toothbrush
- toothpaste
- towel

Protection

- bug repellent
- first-aid kit

- sunglasses
- sunscreen

Luxuries

- barbecue grill
- camp chair
- camp table

- charcoal briquettes
- Dutch oven

Other

- batteries
- candles
- firewood
- hatchet
- headlamp

- kindling/newspaper for fire building
- lantern
- naturalist guidebook
- star chart

GREAT SALT LAKE AND NORTHERN UTAH

© MIKE MATSON

BEST CAMPGROUNDS

⟨ Families
Perception Park, **page 71**
Lagoon RV Park and Campground, **page 74**

⟨ Wildlife
Bridger Bay and White Rock Bay Group Sites at
   Antelope Island State Park, **page 51**

Utah's northernmost region is a land of transition.

In the wide blunt panhandle extending north of the 41st parallel, two of North America's major geographic regions come together in a fascinating landscape. The Great Basin Desert ends abruptly with the undeniable western front of the Wasatch Mountains. The Great Basin Desert, a huge arid region covering most of Nevada and part of northern Arizona, spreads into the western part of Utah's northern panhandle. Known as the Great Salt Lake Desert in Utah, this basin and range landscape is defined by north-to-south-oriented mountain ranges separated by wide, flat valleys. Collected in the bottom of this system is the Great Salt Lake.

The Great Salt Lake is the largest natural lake west of the Mississippi River and is the remnant of an even larger ancient inland sea named Lake Bonneville. At one time Lake Bonneville covered much of northern Utah and eastern Nevada. Over time, as the region's climate has become increasingly arid, the lake's waters have evaporated and receded to the present-day Salt Lake. The present-day lake has no outlet other than evaporation, leaving its waters at least three times as salty as the ocean. Almost nothing will live in the lake environment, except for tiny brine shrimp, which multiply by the billions. These brine shrimp attract a wide assortment of birds, including seagulls normally found only on or near the ocean. While many people write the Great Salt Lake off as a shallow, putrid-smelling cesspool, the lake actually presents some unique, if not overtly inviting, recreational opportunities.

Antelope Island, a 42-square-mile island near the southeast shore of the lake, is one of Utah's best wildlife-viewing sites. Early settlers brought a small group of American bison to the island in 1893, when fears for the species' survival sparked early conservation measures. Today, the free-roaming herd is maintained at around 600 animals and has acted as an important genetic pool for breeding purposes. Herds of pronghorn antelope and bighorn sheep live on the island as well. Shorebirds come here by the millions during migrations to breed and feed on the abundant, reliant food source of countless brine shrimp. Antelope Island is a perfect day trip getaway from Salt Lake City, or a worthy camping destination.

Willard Bay State Park on the northeast arm of the Great Salt Lake represents another wildlife-viewing opportunity paired with camping. Willard Bay is a freshwater lake created by an extensive dike system separating it from the saltwater. The freshwater environment attracts a wide variety of birds, including fish-eating species not found near the Great Salt Lake like bald eagles, hooded mergansers, common terns, and loons.

The other major defining characteristic of Utah's northern panhandle is the Wasatch Mountain Range. The Wasatch Mountains are one of the westernmost ranges in the greater Rocky Mountains; they mark a distinct border between the Great Basin Desert and Rocky Mountain ecosystems. This transition of natural systems makes northern Utah an incredibly diverse environment. The dramatic elevation change of the Wasatch Front from the valley floor encourages winter storms to consistently drop loads of snow. This valuable source of moisture, coupled with a cooler, alpine climate, leads to completely different plant communities than those found in the basin and range ecosystem to the west. The upper northern Wasatch is covered in a mosaic of aspen and lodgepole pine forests. Down in the deep-cut canyons of the range, hardwood deciduous trees like box elder and Rocky Mountain maples create a lush, green environment that couldn't feel farther from the starkness of the basin and range ecosystem. These canyons are also home to some of the best recreation and most popular campgrounds in northern Utah.

Logan Canyon, cutting through the Bear River Mountains, is one such example. Logan Canyon is carved from black-and-gray limestone that offers challenging rock climbing right off the scenic byway. The canyon is cut by the clear Logan River, which offers trout fishing along its cool shaded banks. In similar fashion, the South Fork of Beaver Creek features popular fishing sites up and down its length. Both these streams are lined with Forest Service campgrounds that capitalize on the relaxing, shaded environment of these beautiful canyons.

The Great Salt Lake, the stark beauty of the surrounding desert, and the contrasting green forests of the Wasatch Mountains all draw campers to Utah's northern panhandle. You'll find a wide variety of campgrounds from which to choose in a landscape that transitions from desert to mountains and from desolate to inviting.

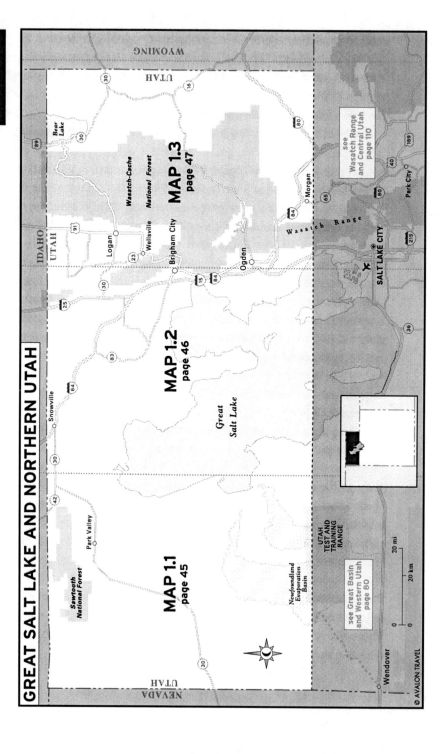

GREAT SALT LAKE AND NORTHERN UTAH

Map 1.1

Campground 1
Page 48

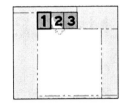

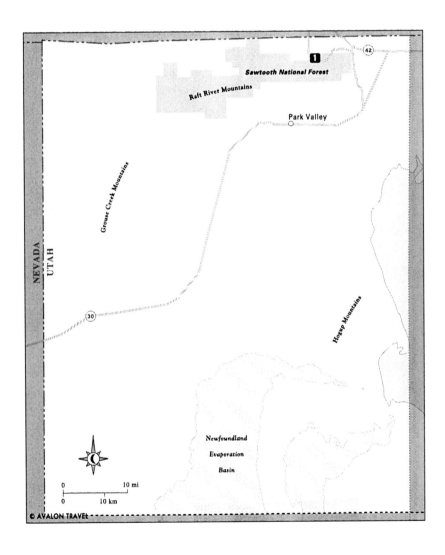

Map 1.2

Campgrounds 2-7
Pages 48-51

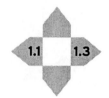

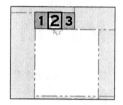

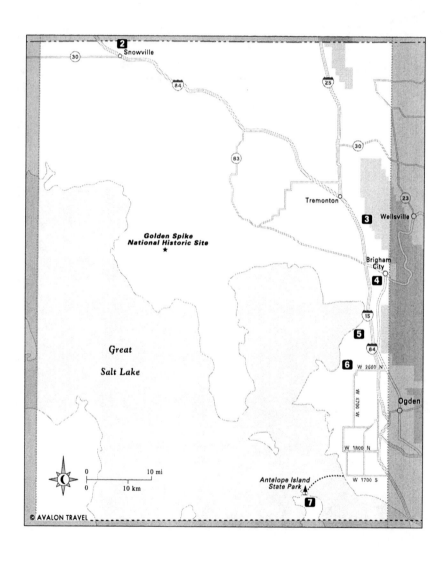

Map 1.3

Campgrounds 8-48

Pages 52-74

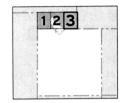

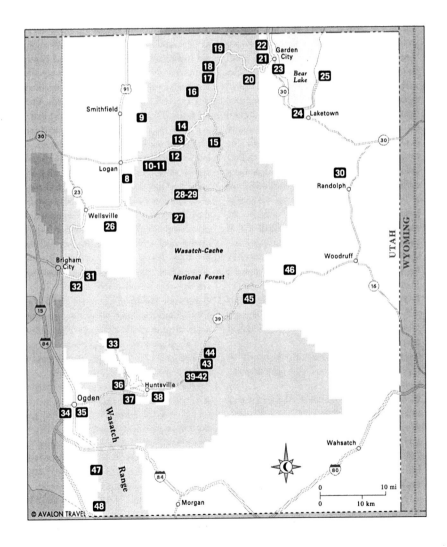

◯ CLEAR CREEK

Scenic rating: 7

west of Snowville in the Sawtooth National Forest

Map 1.1, page 45

Clear Creek is located in the extreme northwest corner of Utah, in the remote Raft River Mountains. This is cow country; several bovine were grazing at the entrance to the campground and around the sites. Clear Creek runs through the campground and offers trout fishing. The campground is unremarkable, with simple sites partially shaded by a mix of aspen and pinyon pine trees. Sagebrush grows around the sites and blankets the hills around the campground. Clear Creek Campground is the trailhead for the Bull Flat Trail. The trail leads through fir and pine trees to Bull Lake in a striking alpine cirque below steep cliffs. It's possible to continue to the summit of Bull Mountain at 9,331 feet. The campground, trail, and Raft River Mountains are well out of the way and see very little use. If you're interested in solitude, the campgrounds should be high on your list. Consider visiting the nearby City of Rocks in southeastern Idaho if you're in the area.

Campsites, facilities: There are 14 sites. Picnic tables, concrete fire rings, and vault toilets are provided. There is no drinking water. Leashed pets permitted.

Reservations, fees: Reservations are not accepted. There is no fee. Open June through September.

Directions: From Snowville, drive east two miles on I-84 and take Exit 5 onto Rte. 30. At the intersection of Rte. 30 and Rte. 42 stay to the right and continue eight miles to Strevell. Turn west (left) and continue 3.2 miles and turn left again and travel 6.1 miles to the campground.

GPS Coordinates: N 41° 57.198' W 113° 19.372'

Contact: Minidoka Ranger District, 208/678-0430.

◯ LOTTIE-DELL RV PARK

Scenic rating: 5

in Snowville

Map 1.2, page 46

Lottie Dell RV Park in Snowville is a throwback to another time. Located at the edge of a vast expanse of open country and wide-open blue sky, the campground feels like an old western outpost teetering on the brink of a long lost frontier. The campground features an impressive collection of old rusting tractors, antique cars, and farming equipment. Nailed to the fence running along the yard is everything from old wooden telemark skis to wood stoves to ironing boards. Views from the RV park are 90 percent sky and 10 percent rolling hills. The campground is completely exposed with no shade or trees at all, but this somehow feels right, considering the surrounding landscape. Gravel parking slips and gravel loop roads lead to grass and clover sites. The sites are close together, but most days there'll be plenty of room between you and the next camper. In the field to the north of the campground are yardage markers for a golf practice range. If you neglected to bring the clubs, there's a healthy selection of antique blade irons and woods in the office to borrow.

Campsites, facilities: There are 51 RV sites, a tent grass area, and five cabin rooms. Amenities include picnic tables, garbage service, pull-through sites, modern restrooms with showers, and a driving range. Laundry and ice are available. Leashed pets permitted.

Reservations, fees: Reservations are accepted at 435/872-8273. RV sites are $25, tent sites are $15, and the cabin rooms are $30. Open April 1 through November 1.

Directions: From I-84 take Exit 7, drive one block north on Stone Road, turn left and continue 0.7 mile west on Main Street. Lottie-Dell will be on the right side of the road.

GPS Coordinates: N 41° 57.973' W 112° 43.417'

Contact: Lottie-Dell RV Park, 435/872-8273.

3 CRYSTAL HOT SPRINGS WATERPARK AND CAMPGROUND

Scenic rating: 5

in the town of Honeyville

Map 1.2, page 46

Crystal Hot Springs Waterpark and Campground is a private developed hot spring in the town of Honeyville below the Wellsville Mountains. The springs at the park are a bit of a geographic oddity, with both a natural hot spring and cold spring within 50 feet of each other. The hot spring water temperature is around 140°F. The water is very salty, with a dissolved slurry of other minerals including calcium, iron, fluoride, magnesium, and potassium. The swimming complex features two swimming pools, several hot tubs for soaking, and a water slide. The campground is located on the south side of the water park. The campground has good views up the Wellsville Mountain Wilderness Area, a long, narrow, north-to-south mountain range above town. The grounds at the campground are grass and shaded by large cottonwood trees. There are occasional picnic tables and fire grills, though hardly enough for everyone if the campground is full. The camp loop and parking spots are gravel and the facility has a large group picnic area.

Campsites, facilities: There are 83 full hookup sites and 37 tent sites. Picnic tables, barbecue grills, fire pits, modern restrooms with showers, a swing set, a group picnic area, a stocked fishing pond, a game room, a basketball court, a sand volleyball court, drinking water, and garbage service are provided. A snack bar, swimming pools, water slides, and hot tubs are available. Leashed pets permitted.

Reservations, fees: Reservations are accepted at 435/279-8104. Full hook-up sites are $25 and non-hook-up/tent sites are $15. Open year-round.

Directions: From I-15 take Exit 372 (Honeyville). Drive east on Rte. 240 for 1.1 miles, turn left onto Rte. 38 and continue 1.8 miles. The Crystal Hot Springs will be on the left side of the road.

GPS Coordinates: N 41° 39.514' W 112° 05.181'

Contact: Crystal Hot Springs Water Park and Campground, 435/279-8104, www.crystal-hotsprings.net/camping/

4 BRIGHAM CITY KOA

Scenic rating: 5

south of Brigham City

Map 1.2, page 46

Brigham City KOA is south of Brigham City along a stretch of Highway 89 lined by fresh-fruit stands. Towering above the highway is the dramatic 9,763 foot Willard Peak. The campground occupies a rural setting bordered by farmland. Entering the RV park, you'll be greeted by an imposing grizzly bear statue and a welcoming A-frame office. The KOA has a relaxed country feel, with mature deciduous trees casting a shadow on almost every site on the grounds. The tent areas have grass lawns and the RV sites feature narrow grass strips. The RV spaces are close together and everyone in the park can see one another, so don't expect lots of privacy. While Highway 89 is audible in the distance, the campground maintains a quiet, peaceful atmosphere.

Campsites, facilities: There are 40 full hookup (30, 50 amps) sites, 22 partial hook-up sites, four deluxe tent sites, 13 tent sites, and eight cabins. Picnic tables, barbecue grills, a swimming pool, Wi-Fi, horseshoes, a recreation room, a playground, drinking water, modern restrooms with showers, garbage service, and a dump station are provided. Firewood, ice, a convenience store, a snack bar, and laundry facilities are available. Leashed pets are permitted, but not in the pool area, in the buildings, or at the playground.

Reservations, fees: Reservations are accepted

at 800/562-0903 or online at https://koa.com/ where/ut/44103/reserve/. Full hook-up sites are $31–39, partial hook-up sites are $29.50, deluxe tent sites (with electricity) are $26, tent sites are $23, and cabins are $44. Open year-round.

Directions: From I-15, take Exit 364 drive east on Hwy. 91 for two miles and turn south (right) onto Hwy. 89. Continue 3.5 miles, turn right onto 3600 S and drive one block. Brigham City KOA will be on the right side of the road.

GPS Coordinates: N 41° 26.688' W 112° 02.438'

Contact: Brigham City KOA, 435/723-5503, www.koa.com/where/ut/44103/

⑤ NORTH CAMPGROUND AT WILLARD BAY STATE PARK

🧗 🏊 🚣 🛶 🏕 ♿ 🚐 ⛺

Scenic rating: 7

north of Ogden on the Great Salt Lake

Map 1.2, page 46

Willard Bay is a large freshwater bay in the northeast arm of the Great Salt Lake where the Bear River empties into the lake. Willard Bay and Bear River Bay together form an extensive wetland ecosystem protected by the likes of the Bear River Migratory Bird Refuge and Willard Bay State Park. The Willard Bay State Park has two campgrounds in addition to boat ramps for lake access. The freshwater lake created by the 14.5-mile-long Arthur V. Watkins Dam is popular for boating, swimming, waterskiing, and fishing. Fish species living in the reservoir include black crappie, walleye, smallmouth bass, bluegill, gizzard shad, and channel catfish. The North Campground at Willard Bay has two loops, Willow Creek and Cottonwood. The paved loops lead to grass campsites shaded by large cottonwood and box elder trees. The sites have views up to the impressive twisted strata of Ben Lomond and Willard Peaks east of the town of Willard. Other sites look west out across Willard Bay and the Great Salt Lake and to a finger of land protruding into the north end of the lake, the Promontory Mountains. Sites 18 and 20 have outstanding 360° views. A small creek runs through the campground and birds can be heard chirping in the trees around the sites. The campground facilities are in excellent shape. The Willow Creek Loop is designed for tent campers, while the Cottonwood Loop features full hook-ups for RVs. There is a nature trail following Willard Creek through the campground.

Campsites, facilities: There are 24 single sites and 15 double sites in the Willow Creek Loop. Site 6 is wheelchair accessible in the Willow Creek Loop. There are 37 single sites and two double sites in the Cottonwood Loop. Sites 5 and 19 are wheelchair accessible in the Cottonwood Loop. One group area is available at Pelican Beach for up to 200 people. Picnic tables, barbeque grills, modern restrooms with showers, drinking water, docks, a boat ramp, WiFi, a day-use group area, garbage service, and a dump station are provided. Leashed pets are permitted, but not on Eagle Beach.

Reservations, fees: Reservations are accepted at 800/322-3770 or online at www.reserveamerica.com. Single-site reservations must be made a minimum of two days in advance and can be arranged up to 16 weeks in advance. Group reservations can be made up to 11 months in advance. There is a nonrefundable reservation fee of $8 for individual sites and $10.25 for group sites. Willow Creek Loop single sites are $16, double sites are $32, and extra vehicles are $8. Cottonwood Loop single sites with full hook-ups are $25, double sites with full hook-ups are $41, extra vehicles are $13, and day use is $10. Pelican Beach Group Area is $225 for up to 75 people plus $3 for each additional person (maximum of 200 people). Cottonwood Loop is open year-round, Willow Creek is open April through October, and Pelican Group Area and Eagle Beach are open March through November.

Directions: From Ogden, drive north on I-15 for 15 miles. Take Exit 357 and turn left onto

State Street. The entrance station to Willard Bay is on State Street.

GPS Coordinates: N 41° 25.155' W 112° 03.202'

Contact: Willard Bay State Park, 435/734-9494, http://stateparks.utah.gov/stateparks/parks/willard-bay/

6 SOUTH CAMPGROUND AT WILLARD BAY STATE PARK

🏊 🚣 🚐 🐾 🚗 ⛺

Scenic rating: 6

north of Ogden on the Great Salt Lake

Map 1.2, page 46

Willard Bay State Park's South Campground offers a low-key, relatively primitive camping experience compared with the park's northern sites. While the facilities are developed and adequate, they pale in comparison to the northern offerings. The broad, paved camp loop features some covered picnic tables, while others are out in the open. The south loop sits below the level of the dam, which limits views of the lake to the west. There are still views of the northern Wasatch Mountains to the east. While the distinct layers of Willard Peak are an impressive sight, the distant views can't compare with the panorama of beauty at the northern end of the park. Large cottonwood trees shade part of the loop. The campground is bordered to the south by tall rows of corn. A short path leads from the campground across a murky canal, over the dike system and onto a rocky ocean-like beach. A plethora of birds use the state park's beach, campground, and wetlands. Warblers stop in during spring and fall migrations; nesting species include black-headed grosbeak, yellow-headed blackbird, gray catbird, and song sparrow. Since the introduction of gizzard shad fish to the reservoir, fish-eating species like bald eagles, common loons, and hooded mergansers feed in the park as well. During the middle of the week, this quiet campground is all but deserted.

Campsites, facilities: There are 25 sites. Picnic tables (some are covered), barbeque grills, fire grills, modern restrooms with showers, drinking water, a boat ramp, and garbage service are provided. Leashed pets permitted.

Reservations, fees: Reservations are not accepted. Sites cost $16, extra vehicles cost $8, and day use is $10. Open April through October.

Directions: From Ogden, drive north on I-15 for eight miles. Take Exit 351 and turn right at 4000 N. Drive 1.3 miles and turn right onto 2000 W. Continue 0.7 mile and turn onto the entrance road for Willard State Park.

GPS Coordinates: N 41° 21.162' W 112° 04.557'

Contact: Willard Bay State Park, 435/734-9494, http://stateparks.utah.gov/stateparks/parks/willard-bay/

7 BRIDGER BAY AND WHITE ROCK BAY GROUP SITES AT ANTELOPE ISLAND STATE PARK

🚶 🚴 🏕 ♿ 🚗 ⛺

Scenic rating: 8

on Antelope Island in the southeast corner of the Great Salt Lake

Map 1.2, page 46   **BEST (**

Bridger Bay is located on the northwest tip of Antelope Island State Park in the Great Salt Lake. The park is home to a stunning collection of wildlife including a very visible herd of around 700 free-roaming buffalo, pronghorn antelope, bighorn sheep, coyotes, and an endless collection of birds. Birders love the island for all the species of waterfowl that stop through during migrations to feast on the brine shrimp living in the salty waters of the lake. Look carefully for a pair of burrowing owls nesting below the road near the Buffalo Bistro. The sandy, sagebrush-dotted campsites look north across the vast shallow lake. Each site features covered, cement-floored picnic table platforms containing deep-bowled fire pits. The sites are well spaced, but all are within view of each other

© MIKE MATSON

an American Bison, also known as a buffalo, grazing in Antelope Island State Park

because of the open nature of the landscape. Between the campground and the lake is a sandy beach that varies greatly in size depending on the level of the ever-fluctuating lake. This park and campground is a great place for families to get out of the city and experience nature. White Rock Bay Group Area is located right at the White Rock Loop Trailhead; horses are allowed in this camping area.

Campsites, facilities: There are 26 sites for tents and RVs up to 90 feet in length at Bridger Bay. Sites 12 and 20–22 are wheelchair accessible. Amenities include picnic tables, fire grills, pull-through sites, garbage service, drinking water, and vault toilets. Flush toilets and showers are available at the day-use area. There are 12 primitive sites at White Rock Bay, which can all be reserved together for up to 70 people. White Rock Bay has picnic tables, fire pits, barbeque grills, and vault toilets. There is no drinking water. Leashed pets permitted.

Reservations, fees: Reservations are required for the group sites and can be arranged by calling 801/733-2941. Reservations are accepted at 800/322-3770 or online at www.reserveamerica.com for the single sites and must be made a minimum of two days in advance and can be arranged up to 16 weeks in advance. There is an $8 nonrefundable reservation fee for individual sites. The fee is $13 per vehicle (includes causeway fee), the group sites are $3 pp ($60 minimum), and the day-use fee is $9. Open year-round.

Directions: Traveling north from Salt Lake City on I-15, take the Syracuse exit (Exit 332), then turn left (west) on West Antelope Drive. Drive seven miles to the park entrance, and then cross out to the island on the 7.5-mile causeway.

GPS Coordinates: N 41° 02.476' W 112° 15.363'

Contact: Antelope Island State Park, 801/773-2941, http://stateparks.utah.gov/stateparks/parks/antelope-island/

8 TRAVELAND RV CACHE VALLEY

Scenic rating: 5

in Logan

Map 1.3, page 47

The Traveland RV Cache Valley is tucked behind a Motel 6 in the town of Logan. Unlike many RV parks behind motels, this Traveland facility is its own separate entity. The campground has nice, well-kept facilities with paved driveways and neatly trimmed grass lawns. There are good views to Minersville Peak and other Logan Mountain summits above town. Cattle graze off to the side of the park in an open range and farmland. The motel functions as a buffer from the road, making the campground quiet and peaceful despite being only a block from a major arterial. Sites are tightly packed into neat rows, and there is very little shade. There are no tent sites available at this RV park.

Campsites, facilities: There are 45 pull-through, full hook-up sites (30, 50 amps) for RVs up to 60 feet in length. Tents are not permitted. Picnic tables, modern restrooms with showers, a playground, a basketball hoop, a volleyball court, cable TV, WiFi, a horseshoe pit, drinking water and garbage service are provided. Laundry and a small store are available. Leashed pets permitted.

Reservations, fees: Reservations are accepted at 435/787-2020. RV sites are $35.86. Open year-round.

Directions: From the intersection of Hwy. 89/91 and Rte. 30, drive 3.3 miles south on Hwy. 89/91 and turn left into the Traveland RV park behind Motel 6.

GPS Coordinates: N 41° 41.691' W 111° 51.676'

Contact: Traveland RV Cache Valley, 435/787-2020, www.travelandrvpark.net/cachevalley.htm

9 SMITHFIELD

Scenic rating: 7

northeast of Smithfield, in Smithfield Canyon

Map 1.3, page 47

Smithfield Campground is a small, secluded campground near the west side of the Mount Naomi Wilderness. Summit Creek, a tributary to the Bear River, runs through the campground as it drains off 9,979-foot Naomi Peak. Fishing for cutthroat trout is possible in Summit Creek. While there are trails to the top of the surrounding summits of Mount Elmer and Naomi Peak, none leaves directly from Smithfield Campground. Two miles up the road is the trailhead for the Smithfield Canyon Trail, popular with horseback riders. Shafts of sunlight penetrate the dense hardwood forest canopy and catch the dust kicked up from dirt spur roads in Smithfield Canyon. The campground is secluded and quiet, with sounds limited to the cascading creek and other campers. The thick trees provide lots of privacy and shade for each site. Drinking water can be pumped from an old-school green well. In addition to the tiny loop of campsites within the developed campground, a few dispersed sites can be found

along the road and across the bridge leading over Summit Creek.

Campsites, facilities: There are seven sites. Picnic tables, fire grills, a picnic area, vault toilets, garbage service, and drinking water are provided. Leashed pets permitted.

Reservations, fees: Reservations are not accepted. Sites are $13, extra vehicles are $6, and day use is $7–13. Open May through September.

Directions: From the intersection of Main and Center in Smithfield, turn east on Center Street and drive 0.2 mile. Turn left onto 200 E and continue one block. Turn right onto 50 N, drive one block, and turn left onto Canyon Road. Follow Canyon Road for 4.5 miles to Smithfield Campground.

GPS Coordinates: N 41° 52.219' W 111° 45.236'

Contact: Logan Ranger District, 435/755-3620, www.fs.fed.us/r4/uwc/recreation/wcnf/camping/logan-camping.shtml#smithfield

10 BRIDGER

Scenic rating: 7

in Logan Canyon in the Wasatch-Cache National Forest

Map 1.3, page 47

Bridger Campground is named after mountain man Jim Bridger, one the earliest Anglo trappers to use Logan Canyon. Bridger and other early trappers used to stockpile underground caches of fur and animal pelts in this region, thereby lending the name Cache Valley to the broad plain below the Wasatch Range. The Bridger Campground is a small wooded loop on the Logan Canyon Scenic Byway. The Logan River flows through the campground and offers fishing for brown and rainbow trout. The campground loop leads to sites shaded by maple and box elder trees. Limestone boulders line the loop and keep vehicles on the road. Bridger is best for tent camping, as the tight loop is not accommodating to RVs and large vehicles.

Campsites, facilities: There are 10 sites. Picnic tables, fire grills, flush toilets, garbage service, and drinking water are provided. Firewood is available. Leashed pets permitted.

Reservations, fees: Reservations are not accepted. Sites are $13, extra vehicles are $6, and day use is $7–13. Open May through September.

Directions: From Logan, drive east 5.8 miles on Hwy. 89 and turn right into the Bridger Campground.

GPS Coordinates: N 41° 44.867' W 111° 44.037'

Contact: Logan Ranger District, 435/755-3620, www.fs.fed.us/r4/uwc/recreation/wcnf/camping/logan-camping.shtml#bridger

11 SPRING HOLLOW

Scenic rating: 8

in Logan Canyon in the Wasatch-Cache National Forest

Map 1.3, page 47

Spring Hollow Campground sits at 5,100 feet in Logan Canyon. The campground is located at the edge of a popular fishing pond, created by the small Third Dam on the Logan River. There is a four-trout limit on fishing. Above the campground is an alluvial bench that looks to an undiscerning eye like a simple gravel hill. A roadside geologic marker explains the bench was formed at the edge of the ancient Lake Bonneville. The prehistoric lake covered much of northern and western Utah and is the ancestor of the Great Salt Lake. The campground is the trailhead for a handful of trails including the Riverside Nature Trail, which follows the Logan River upstream for 1.3 miles to the Guinavah–Malibu Campground. Other trails leaving from the campground are Spring Hollow, Mill Hollow, Crimson, River, and Bridger Lookout Trails. The camp loop is paved with a unique entrance leading right through a small creek. The vegetation in and around the campground is very lush, with dense underbrush, tall

grass, and a variety of broad-leaved deciduous trees like maples, box elders, and cottonwoods. These trees provide shade for all the sites. The campground occupies a relatively small area; as a result, the sites are clustered closely together. A narrow creek rushes through the campground before joining the Logan River. Because of the plentiful water and the campground's proximity to the pond, bugs can be a nuisance.

Campsites, facilities: There are 12 sites and two group areas. Wheelchair-friendly picnic tables, fire grills, stove tables, garbage service, drinking water, and flush toilets are provided. Firewood is available. Leashed pets permitted.

Reservations, fees: Reservations are accepted at 877/444-6777 or online at www.recreation.gov and must be made a minimum of four days in advance. Sites are $15, extra vehicles are $6, the group area is $35, and day use is $8–15. Public parking is free. Open May through September.

Directions: From Logan, drive east 6.5 miles on Hwy. 89 and turn right into Spring Hollow Campground.

GPS Coordinates: N 41° 45.185' W 111° 43.003'

Contact: Logan Ranger District, 435/755-3620, www.fs.fed.us/r4/uwc/recreation/wcnf/camping/logan-camping.shtml#springhollow

12 GUINAVAH-MALIBU

Scenic rating: 7

in Logan Canyon in the Wasatch-Cache National Forest

Map 1.3, page 47

Guinavah–Malibu is a dual looped campground set in the river-bottom environment along the Logan River. The Guinavah loop branches off to the left as you enter the campground and features an amphitheater and the trailhead for the Riverside Nature Trail. The Riverside Trail follows the Logan River 1.3 miles downstream to the Spring Hollow Campground. Along the way 12 interpretive stations explain the vegetation and riparian habitat found along the creek. Malibu Loop bends to the right and features thick deciduous forests with exceptionally shaded sites. Both camp loops are a mix of gravel and old pavement, and the campsite parking spots are small. Many of the sites are right on the Logan River, offering both front-door fishing and soothing natural audio to drown out the nearby road. Some of the sites with openings in the forest canopy sneak peeks up to the limestone cliffs along the upper reaches of Logan Canyon.

Campsites, facilities: There are 40 sites and three group sites. Picnic tables, fire grills, garbage service, drinking water, flush toilets, and amphitheater are provided. Firewood is available. Leashed pets permitted.

Reservations, fees: Reservations are accepted at 877/444-6777 or online at www.recreation. gov and must be made a minimum of four days in advance. Single sites are $15, double sites are $30, extra vehicles are $6, and day use is $8–15. Open May through early October.

Directions: From Logan, drive east eight miles on Hwy. 89 and turn right into the Guinavah–Malibu Campground.

GPS Coordinates: N 41° 45.662' W 111° 41.808'

Contact: Logan Ranger District, 435/755-3620, www.fs.fed.us/r4/uwc/recreation/wcnf/camping/logan-camping.shtml#guinavahmalibu

13 PRESTON VALLEY
🏃 🛶 🏕 🚐 ⛰

Scenic rating: 7

in Logan Canyon in the Wasatch-Cache National Forest

Map 1.3, page 47

Preston Valley Campground is located beside the Logan River in Logan Canyon. Fishing for brown and rainbow trout is excellent in the shallow river. The campground is one of many historical summer home sites in Logan Canyon. The summer home sites were used by Mormon settlers from Logan who came to the canyon to escape the summer heat and

commune with the outdoors. The small campground is shaded by Rocky Mountain maple and box hollow trees, with tall grass growing in and around the sites. Thickets of willows trees grow along the river. Drivers of large vehicles should be aware there is no turn-around on the left side of the loop by sites 1 and 2. Like many of the sites in Logan Canyon, Preston Valley Campground is very close to the road. Expect to hear traffic from all the sites. The Preston Valley is near the Wind Caves Trailhead. The Wind Caves Trail leads 1.9 miles to a triple arch and a limestone cave.

Campsites, facilities: There are eight sites. Picnic tables, fire grills, drinking water, flush toilets, and garbage service are provided. Firewood is available. Leashed pets permitted.

Reservations, fees: Reservations are not accepted. Sites are $13, extra vehicles are $6, and day use is $7–13. Open May through early October.

Directions: From Logan, drive east 10.5 miles on Hwy 89 and turn right into the Preston Valley Campground

GPS Coordinates: N 41° 46.406' W 111° 39.283'

Contact: Logan Ranger District, 435/755-3620, www.fs.fed.us/r4/uwc/recreation/wcnf/camping/logan-camping.shtml#prestonvalley

14 WOODCAMP
🏃 🏕 🚐 ⛰

Scenic rating: 7

in Logan Canyon in the Wasatch-Cache National Forest

Map 1.3, page 47

Woodcamp is beside the Logan River in the heart of Logan Canyon. Logan Canyon is a beautiful canyon carved out of the Bear River Mountains. Steep, imposing limestone cliffs rise above the river. In recent years, rock climbers have developed hundreds of bolted sport routes up these vertical-to-overhanging walls. In fact, some of the hardest routes in the country can be found in Logan Canyon on the China Wall. In addition to the difficult test pieces, the canyon has a wide variety of rock climbing routes of varying difficulty, with something almost every climber can enjoy. Woodcamp is the closest campground to the China Wall and China Cave, where many of the routes are concentrated. The camp is set in a stand of box elder (also known as ash-leaved maple), maple, and cottonwood trees. The dense trees provide plenty of shade for the campground and the Logan River adds to the camp's refreshing appeal. The small loop is gravel with gravel parking. On the downside, Woodcamp is right next to the Logan Canyon Scenic Byway, and road noise filters into the campground. Just upstream from the campground is a hiking and horseback riding trail into the Mount Naomi Wilderness.

Campsites, facilities: There are six sites for tents and RVs up to 20 feet in length. Picnic tables, fire grills, pull-through sites, and vault toilets are provided. There is no drinking water. Leashed pets permitted.

Reservations, fees: Reservations are not accepted. The fee is $13, extra vehicles are $6, and day use is $7–13. Open May through early October.

Directions: From Logan, drive east on Hwy. 89 for 12 miles and turn left into the Woodcamp Campground.

GPS Coordinates: N 41° 47.83' W 111° 38.681'

Contact: Logan Ranger District, 435/755-3620, www.fs.fed.us/r4/uwc/recreation/wcnf/camping/logan-camping.shtml#woodcamp

15 LODGE

Scenic rating: 8

in Logan Canyon in the Wasatch-Cache National Forest

Map 1.3, page 47

Lodge Campground is beneath a dense maple forest in the Right Fork of Logan Canyon, about a mile off the main road. It is the only campground in Logan Canyon that is not right next to the scenic byway. If being away from the road is important to you, consider making the short side trip up the creek to this site. The road is well maintained and the detour is brief, but it feels a lot farther from the passing traffic. Lodge has a gravel access loop leading to shaded forest sites with dirt floors. Site 7 peeks out from beneath an enormous cottonwood tree to the dramatic gray and black cliffs of the upper canyon. Fishing for trout in the creek is possible.

Campsites, facilities: There are ten sites for tents and RVs up to 20 feet in length. Picnic tables, fire grills, drinking water, vault toilets, and garbage service are provided. Firewood is available. Leashed pets permitted.

Reservations, fees: Reservations are not accepted. Sites are $13, extra vehicles are $6, and day use is $7–13. Open May through early October.

Directions: From Logan, drive east on Hwy. 89 for 11 miles, turn right, and continue 1.3 miles. Take a sharp right into the Lodge Campground.

GPS Coordinates: N 41° 46.655' W 111° 37.216'

Contact: Logan Ranger District, 435/755-3620, www.fs.fed.us/r4/uwc/recreation/wcnf/camping/logan-camping.shtml#lodge

16 TONY GROVE LAKE

Scenic rating: 9

in Logan Canyon in the Wasatch-Cache National Forest

Map 1.3, page 47

Tony Grove Lake sits in a lovely alpine valley on the eastern edge of the Mount Naomi Wilderness. The lake is walled in by black-and-gray limestone rock and surrounded by lush green vegetation sprinkled with wildflowers. A low earthen dam holds back the reservoir's water while doubling as a lakeside trail. Tony Grove Campground is perched on a gentle slope above the lake. Alpine spruce and fir trees conceal the campsites, which are well dispersed among the forest. Sites feature pine needle forest floors, and flat tent-pitching possibilities vary considerably from site to site. Several trails leave from the day-use parking lot by the campground, including the 6.8-mile Naomi Peak Nature Trail, the 4.5-mile White Pine Lake Trail, and the Cold Springs Trail. Trout fishing and nonmotorized boating are possible on the lake.

Campsites, facilities: There are 34 single sites and one double site. Sites 16B–18B are wheelchair accessible. Picnic tables, fire grills, flush toilets, vault toilets, and garbage service are provided. There is no drinking water. Firewood is available. Leashed pets permitted.

Reservations, fees: Reservations are accepted at 877/444-6777 or online at www.recreation.gov and must be made a minimum of seven days in advance. Single sites are $15, double sites are $30, extra vehicles are $6, and day use is $8–15. Open May through September, weather permitting.

Directions: At the intersection of Hwy. 89 and Rte. 30 in Garden City, head west on Hwy. 89 for 18 miles, turn right and take the next left onto Forest Road 003. Continue 6.8 miles and turn left into the Tony Grove Lake Campground.

GPS Coordinates: N 41° 53.626' W 111° 38.391'

Contact: Logan Ranger District, 435/755-3620, www.fs.fed.us/r4/uwc/recreation/wcnf/camping/logan-camping.shtml#tonygrovelake

17 LEWIS M. TURNER
🏕️🛶🏠⛰️

Scenic rating: 7

In the Wasatch-Cache National Forest

Map 1.3, page 47

The Lewis M. Turner Campground is located along the Logan Canyon Scenic Byway in the Bear River Mountains. The area is popular for hiking and horseback riding in summer and snowmobiling in winter. This Forest Service campground is set in mature stands of aspen

and surrounded by sagebrush-covered hills. Lodgepole pines mixed with aspen provide patchy shade for sites. Most sites are surrounded by tall grass and brush, with a small patch of bare ground for a tent. The campground has a paved access loop, parking aprons, and path to a central restroom facility. Trout fishing is possible near the campground on the Logan River. Lewis M. Turner is a calm, peaceful alternative to the busy campground at Tony Grove Lake.

Campsites, facilities: There are 10 sites. Picnic tables, fire grills, drinking water, flush toilets, and garbage service are provided. Leashed pets permitted.

Reservations, fees: Reservations are not accepted. Sites are $13, extra vehicles are $6, and day use is $ 7–13. Open May through September, weather permitting.

Directions: At the intersection of Hwy. 89 and Rte. 30 in Garden City, head west on Hwy. 89 for 18 miles, turn right and continue 0.5 mile to the Lewis M. Turner Campground.

GPS Coordinates: N 41° 53.120' N 111° 34.287'

Contact: Logan Ranger District, 435/755-3620, www.fs.fed.us/r4/uwc/recreation/wcnf/camping/logan-camping.shtml#lmturner

18 RED BANKS
🛶🏠🚐⛰️

Scenic rating: 7

In the Wasatch-Cache National Forest

Map 1.3, page 47

Red Banks Campground is in the upper reaches of Logan Canyon near the Beaver Mountain Ski Resort. The campground sits between the scenic byway and the Logan River. It's named after the steeply rising red dirt banks on the opposite side of the river from the campsites. Dense thickets of brush and willows grow along the river where fishing for trout is possible. The river is closed to fishing January 1–July 1, and there is a two-trout limit during the summer months. The campground loop and parking spots are gravel, and the sites are well shaded by aspen and cottonwood trees. Sites 4, 5, 8, 9, 10, and 11 are right on the creek, where you'll hear the river at night rather than the adjacent road. Hiking trails leading into the Mount Naomi Wilderness are available nearby at Tony Grove Lake.

Campsites, facilities: There are 15 sites for tents and RVs up to 20 feet in length. Picnic tables, barbeque grills, fire grills, garbage service, vault toilets, and drinking water are provided. Leashed pets permitted.

Reservations, fees: Reservations are not accepted. Sites are $13, extra vehicles are $6, and day use is $ 7–13. Open May through September, weather permitting.

Directions: At the intersection of Hwy. 89 and Rte. 30 in Garden City, head west on Hwy. 89 for 17.1 miles and turn right into the Red Banks Campground.
GPS Coordinates: N 41° 53.915' W 111° 33.891'

Contact: Logan Ranger District, 435/755-3620, www.fs.fed.us/r4/uwc/recreation/wcnf/camping/logan-camping.shtml#redbanks

19 BEAVER MOUNTAIN RV AND CAMPGROUND

Scenic rating: 8

at the Beaver Mountain Ski Resort

Map 1.3, page 47

Beaver Mountain Ski Resort is a small, family-run ski area on the northern border of Utah. The handiwork of its namesake animals can be plainly seen in a series of dams and ponds built downstream on the Logan River. Beavers brought the first Anglo trappers to the region, mountain men like Jim Bridger, Jedediah Smith, and Peter Skene Ogden, who used the Logan Canyon area to trap and store fur. The Beaver Mountain RV and Campground is a resourceful way for the ski area to use its parking lots during summer months. The campground is one of the most scenic RV parks in the state. Views look down to mountain slopes forested

in aspen and lodgepole pine trees. RV sites run in a row along the side of the parking lot and back up to a 30-foot-wide strip of natural forest. Some sites have excellent tent pads on the narrow ribbon of forest. The campground also features walk-in style tent sites in a separate area near the base of the ski lifts. These sites are well spread out and private and feel very natural despite being near the ski area base.

Campsites, facilities: There 16 full hook-up (20- and 30-amp) sites and seven tent sites. Picnic tables, fire rings, a basketball hoop, modern restrooms with showers, drinking water, garbage service, and a dump station are provided. Firewood and ice are available. Leashed pets permitted.

Reservations, fees: Reservations are accepted at 435/563-5677. Full hook-up sites are $25 Thurs.–Sat. and $20 Sun.–Wed., tent sites are $12 and overnight parking is $10. Open Memorial Day through Labor Day.

Directions: At the intersection of Hwy. 89 and Rte. 30 in Garden City, head west on Hwy. 89 for 12 miles, turn right onto Rte. 243 and continue 1.2 miles to the Beaver Mountain Ski Area.
GPS Coordinates: N 41° 58.145' W 111° 32.399'

Contact: Beaver Mountain RV and Campground, 435/563-5677, info@skithebeav.com

20 SUNRISE

Scenic rating: 8

west of Bear Lake in the Wasatch-Cache National Forest

Map 1.3, page 47

Sunrise Campground is located on the eastern slopes of the Bear River Mountains on a ridge above Bear Lake. The entrance to the campground weaves through a grove of tall, skinny, bone-white aspen trees. In the campground proper, spruce and lodgepole pine trees provide shade, and tall grass grows from the forest floor. The sites are clean and feature nice cushiony pine needle floors. The camp loop and parking spots are paved. Sites are well spread out and allow lots of privacy. Sunrise has a comfortable, alpine feel even in hot weather. Near the campground is the trailhead for the Limber Pine Nature Trail. The 1.3-mile trail leads to a 2,560-year-old Limber Pine tree. Limber Pines can be recognized by their flexible branches and needles that grow in clusters of five. Look for tiny Clark's Nuthatch birds along the path. Also near the campground is the Bear Lake Summit, where there is an informative overlook station. The view down to Bear Lake is worth a stop in itself.

Campsites, facilities: There are 27 sites for tents and RVs up to 35 feet in length. Picnic tables, fire grills, drinking water, pull-through sites, garbage service, and vault toilets are provided. Firewood is available. Leashed pets permitted.

Reservations, fees: Reservations are accepted at 877/444-6777 or online at www.recreation.gov and must be made a minimum of four days in advance. Sites are $15, extra vehicles are $6, and day use costs $8–15. Open May through September.

Directions: At the intersection of Hwy. 89 and Rte. 30 in Garden City, head west on Hwy. 89 for 5.3 miles. Turn left into the campground.

GPS Coordinates: N 41° 55.232 W 111° 27.754

Contact: Logan Ranger District, 435/755-3620, www.fs.fed.us/r4/uwc/recreation/wcnf/camping/logan-camping.shtml#sunrise

21 TRAVELAND RV PARK AT BEAR LAKE

🚲 ⛺ 🏕️ 🚐 ⛺

Scenic rating: 6

in Garden City

Map 1.3, page 47

Traveland RV Park is one of many RV park–style campgrounds in the resort town of Garden City, on the southwest shore of Bear Lake. The campground is sunny and exposed with very few trees. The facilities are new, well

done, and inviting. The loop is paved and leads to a wide variety of sites, with pull-through options for big rigs at one extreme, and a separate grass tenting area at the other. The Traveland is three blocks off the main strip in Garden City, giving it a quiet, relaxed feel, especially compared to the other options in town. At the same time, it's still close to the shops and restaurants of Garden City and all the recreation opportunities on Bear Lake. The campground is near the four-mile paved Bear Lake Scenic Trail that runs through Garden City.

Campsites, facilities: There are 63 pull-through sites with full hook-ups (30, 50 amps) for RVs up to 60 feet in length and 12 tent sites. Picnic tables, fire rings, a playground, WiFi, cable TV, modern restrooms with showers, a basketball court, a sand volleyball court, drinking water, and garbage service are provided. Laundry is available. Leashed pets permitted.

Reservations, fees: Reservations are accepted at 435/946-8444. RV sites are $32 and tent sites are $22. Open year-round.

Directions: At the intersection of Hwy. 89 and Rte. 30 in Garden City, head north on Rte. 30 for two blocks and turn west (left) on 200 N and drive 0.3 mile. Traveland RV Park will be on the left.

GPS Coordinates: N 41° 56.956' W 111° 24.028'

Contact: Traveland RV Park, 435/946-8444, www.travelandrvpark.net/bearlake.htm

22 BEAR LAKE KOA

🚲 🏊 🏕️ 🏍️ ♿ 🚐 ⛺

Scenic rating: 4

in Garden City

Map 1.3, page 47

The Bear Lake KOA is a huge RV park in the resort community of Garden City on the southwest beach shore of Bear Lake. Garden City occupies a prime strip of land between the tantalizing blue waters of Bear Lake and the upland beauty of the Bear River Mountains. Bear Lake KOA is right in the middle of the action. With bike rentals and front-door access to the paved Bear Lake Scenic Trail, there's lots of traffic and fun to be had. An extensive playground and mini-golf course add to the amusement park feel of the place. The campground itself is not particularly scenic, considering the surroundings, but is well kept and offers a shaded, comfortable camping environment. Rows and rows of sites stretch away from the entrance in a semi-circle of camping exuberance. Like most large RV parks, privacy is limited, so expect to get to know your neighbors. A central covered cooking and eating pavilion helps add to the communal spirit. There are cabins for those who'd like more privacy.

Campsites, facilities: There are 53 full hook-up (30, 50 amps) sites, 52 partial hook-up sites (all RV sites are pull-through), one super RV site with full hook-ups and a hot tub, 34 tent sites, 12 deluxe cabins, and 22 cabins. Picnic tables, fire grills, WiFi, modern restrooms with showers, drinking water, tennis courts, horseshoe pits, a dog walk, a jumping pillow, a swimming pool, a wading pool, ping pong, shuffleboard, a cooking area (covered picnic tables), garbage service, and a dump station are provided. Bike rentals, mini-golf, firewood, a convenience store, a gas station, and laundry are available. Leashed pets permitted.

Reservations, fees: Reservations are accepted at 435/946-3454 or online at https://koa.com/where/ut/44101/reserve/. Full hook-up (50 amps) sites are $47–49, full hook-ups (30 amps) are $43–46, partial hook-ups are $39–41, the super site is $85–91, improved tent sites are $39–41, and tent sites are $29–31, depending on the day of the week. Open March 15 through November 15.

Directions: At the intersection of Hwy. 89 and Rte. 30 in Garden City drive north on Hwy. 89 for one mile. The Bear Lake KOA is on the left side of the road.

GPS Coordinates: N 41° 57.333' W 111° 23.873'

Contact: Bear Lake KOA, 435/946-3454, www.koa.com/where/ut/44101/

23 IDEAL BEACH RV PARK

Scenic rating: 7

south of Garden City

Map 1.3, page 47

Ideal Beach is a private beach south of the resort town of Garden City on Bear Lake. Bear Lake is a large, natural, freshwater lake sitting on the Utah–Idaho border. The lake has been dubbed the "Caribbean of the Rockies," and gorgeous, open Ideal Beach certainly reinforces the comparison. The gray-sand beach feels like it's on the ocean, with miles of water stretching out in front of it. You can rent almost any water toy you'd like at Ideal Beach. The RV park is perched on a flat bluff above the beach. The sites ring the perimeter of the yard under the intermittent shade of aspen and fir trees. The sites are close together and offer no privacy whatsoever. Unfortunately, a fence blocks the best views down to the lake. In addition to beach recreation, the four-mile paved Bear Lake Scenic Trail passes by the entrance to Ideal Beach.

Campsites, facilities: There are 20 full hook-up (50 amps) sites and six tent sites. Picnic tables, fire grills, modern restrooms with showers, drinking water, and garbage service are provided. A convenience store and ATV, personal watercraft, boat, canoe, and pedalboat rentals are available. Leashed pets permitted.

Reservations, fees: Reservations are accepted at 435/946-5800. RV sites are $45 and tent sites are $30. Open Memorial Day through Labor Day.

Directions: From Garden City, drive 0.5 mile southeast on Rte. 30 and enter Ideal Beach on the left side of the road.

GPS Coordinates: N 41° 53.983' W 111° 22.159'

Contact: Ideal Beach RV Park, 435/946-5800, www.bearlakefun.com/rvpark.html

24 RENDEZVOUS BEACH AT BEAR LAKE STATE PARK

🏊 ⛵ 🚐 ❄️ 🏕️ ♿ 🚌 ⛰️

Scenic rating: 7

on Bear Lake at the Rendezvous Recreation Area

Map 1.3, page 47

Rendezvous Beach is named after the historic meeting spot of Shoshone Native Americans and fur trappers. Between 1825 and 1840 the natives and fur trappers would meet on the southern shore of Bear Lake to swap goods, tell stories, and socialize for several weeks in late summer. In modern times, Bear Lake has become a destination for summer fun. The lake is popular for waterskiing, sailing, swimming, and even scuba diving. In winter, visitors come to snowmobile and ice fish. Rendezvous Beach is the heart and soul of the Bear Lake State Park facilities, with an expansive marina and four campground loops. The Willow Loop is the first loop encountered after entering the state park. Willow is a group-oriented site, with three covered pavilions and many campsites scattered amongst the willows and other trees. The parking spaces are marked with numbered sites, but the actual tent site boundaries are up to each camper's discretion. Birch is the next loop, moving east along the lake shore. The Birch Area is wide open and feels a lot like an RV park. Views of the lake are mostly blocked by cottonwood trees along the shore. The Cottonwood Area is designed for large groups and is the closest of the Rendezvous Beach loops to the actual beach. Three large group pavilions become surrounded sporadically by pitched tents when the site is busy. The Big Creek Loop is the easternmost of the camping loops. At the entrance to the loop a pioneer-era cabin greets campers; four "mountain man" cabins are available to rent. The cabins are designed to look like cabins used by mountain men like Jim Bridger who used the site for their annual rendezvous. The rest of the loop is fairly open, with young trees planted between sites. A wall of cottonwood trees lines the lake shore and diminishes any views from the campground. Take the time to explore the four large loops, because the facilities and sites vary dramatically.

Campsites, facilities: There are 45 full hook-up (15 amps) sites in the Big Creek Loop, 60 full hook-up (15 amps) sites in the Birch Loop, 30 parking spots spread out over three group sites for up to 80 people in the Willow Loop, and 37 walk-in sites in the Cottonwood Loop. Site 3 in the Big Creek Loop; Sites 7, 9, 19, and 27 in the Birch Loop; and Group Site 3 in the Willow Loop are wheelchair accessible. Picnic tables, fire grills, barbeque grills, modern restrooms with showers, drinking water, pull-through sites, garbage service, and a dump station are provided. Leashed pets are permitted but not allowed on the beaches.

Reservations, fees: Reservations are accepted at 800/322-3770 or online at www.reserveamerica.com for the single sites and group sites. Single-site reservations must be made a minimum of two days in advance and can be arranged up to 16 weeks in advance, and group-site reservations can be arranged up to 11 months in advance. There is a non-refundable reservation fee of $8 for individual sites and $10.25 for group sites. Big Creek and Birch Loop sites are $25, Cottonwood Loop is $16, group sites are $75 for the first 25 people and $3 for each additional person (maximum 80 people), extra vehicles are $8–13, and day use is $8. Cabin reservations are accepted at 435/946-8600. Open year-round.

Directions: From Garden City drive eight miles southeast on Rte. 30 and enter the Rendezvous Beach on the left side of the road. GPS Coordinates: N 41° 50.782' W 111° 20.950'

Contact: Bear Lake State Park, 435/946-3343, http://stateparks.utah.gov/stateparks/parks/bear-lake/

25 SOUTH EDEN AT BEAR LAKE STATE PARK

Scenic rating: 8

on the southeast shore of Bear Lake

Map 1.3, page 47

Bear Lake is a large natural lake straddling the Utah–Idaho border. Its turquoise waters and gray-sand beaches give the lake a tropical feel, earning its nickname, "The Caribbean of the Rockies." The lake is a popular destination for a variety of recreational pursuits, including boating, sailing, waterskiing, swimming, fishing, and snowmobiling. And at 20 miles long and eight miles wide, there's plenty of lake for everyone to enjoy. Sport fish species on the lake include mackinaw, Bonneville Cisco, Bonneville whitefish, and Bear Lake whitefish. South Eden Campground is the less-developed camping facility in Bear Lake State Park. The relatively primitive sites stretch out across two terraces in the gently rising hillside above the southeast shore of the lake. Below the campground is a wide sandy beach. Sagebrush grows between sites while a few small trees add very little to the campground. A mile north of South Eden proper is Cisco Beach, the official overflow campground at Bear Lake. Steep hills rise above Cisco Beach. Cisco Beach is very rocky and slopes steeply up to a long narrow strip of undeveloped sites. Tents can be pitched on the grass and rocks, but some sites are far more comfortable than others. Two sites feature covered picnic areas, while most are out in the open. Views from both Cisco Beach and South Eden are hard to beat stretching out to southern Idaho and the Bear River Mountains across the lake.

Campsites, facilities: There are 20 single sites and two group areas for up to 30 or 50 people depending on the site at South Eden. Cisco Beach is a long strip of undesignated sites. Picnic tables, fire grills, garbage service, vault toilets, and drinking water are provided. Leashed pets permitted.

Reservations, fees: Reservations are accepted at 800/322-3770 or online at www.reserveamerica.com for the single and group sites. Single-site reservations must be made a minimum of two days in advance and can be arranged up to 16 weeks in advance,; group site reservations can be arranged up to 11 months in advance. There is a nonrefundable reservation fee of $8 for individual sites and $10.25 for group sites. Single sites cost $10, group sites cost $75, and day use is $5. Open year-round.

Directions: From Garden City, drive southeast 10 miles on Rte. 30 to the intersection of Main Street and 30th West in Laketown. Turn north (left) on 30th West and continue 8.1 miles to the South Eden Campground on the left side of the road.

GPS Coordinates: N 41° 55.828' W 111° 16.972'

Contact: Bear Lake State Park, 435/946-3343, http://stateparks.utah.gov/stateparks/parks/bear-lake/

26 HYRUM STATE PARK

Scenic rating: 8

west of Hyrum on Hyrum Reservoir in the Cache Valley

Map 1.3, page 47

Hyrum State Park is located on the shores of Hyrum Reservoir. The lake is popular for boating, swimming, and fishing. A paved boat ramp accesses the lake. Sport-fishing species in the lake include rainbow, cutthroat, and brown trout, as well as largemouth bass, yellow perch, and bluegill. The trail along the north shore of the reservoir from the Ranger Station to the beach parking lot offers good birding. During fall, winter, and spring, birders can expect to see and hear yellow-rumped warblers, black-capped chickadees, and song and white-crowned sparrows. A bald eagle pair lives near the lake and can be seen circling on thermals hunting for their next meal. Other wildlife in the park includes small mammals like raccoons, foxes, and muskrats. Lovers of charismatic mega-fauna

© MIKE MATSON

boating on Hyrum Reservoir in Hyrum State Park

pavilion are provided at the group site. Leashed pets are permitted, but not on the beach.

Reservations, fees: Reservations are accepted at 800/322-3770 or online at www.reserveamerica.com. Reservations for the single sites must be made a minimum of two days in advance and can be arranged up to 16 weeks in advance. Group site reservations can be arranged up to 11 months in advance. There is an nonrefundable reservation fee of $8 for individual sites and $10.25 for group sites. Sites are $16, the group area is $150, and day use is $6. Open year-round.

Directions: From the intersection of 800 W and Main Street in Hyrum, drive west on Main Street for 1.7 miles. Turn left onto 400 W and continue 0.4 mile to the entrance of Hyrum State Park.

GPS Coordinates: N 41° 37.619' W 111° 51.995'

Contact: Hyrum State Park, 435/245-6866, http://stateparks.utah.gov/stateparks/parks/hyrum/

will be interested to note that the Cache Valley was home to the last surviving grizzly bear in the state of Utah. A sheepherder named Frank Clark trapped the last grizzly, nicknamed Old Ephraim, near Hyrum State Park in 1923. The campground sits on a bluff above the reservoir, with the perfect vantage point to enjoy all the activity on the lake. Views from camp extend beyond the reservoir to distant hills that glow pink at sunset. The campground's paved loop leads to clean, well-manicured grass sites with long parking slips and trees for shade. The state park is equally comfortable for tent or RV campers and has a relaxed natural atmosphere despite its proximity to the town of Hyrum.

Campsites, facilities: There are 26 sites and a group area for up to 100 people. Site 9 is wheelchair accessible. Picnic tables, barbeque grills, modern restrooms with showers, drinking water, a boat ramp, a fish-cleaning station, garbage service, and aluminum recycling are provided. Horseshoes, a volleyball net, and a

27 PIONEER

Scenic rating: 7

southeast of Logan in the Bear River Mountains in the Wasatch-Cache National Forest

Map 1.3, page 47

Pioneer Campground is on Route 101 on the Blacksmith Fork River in the Bear River Mountains. The campground is popular with ATV riders who use the nearby Great Western Trail. There's fishing for wild brown trout and stocked cutthroat and rainbow trout in the river. The Blacksmith Fork receives little fishing pressure compared to more popular regional streams like the Logan River. The campground has views up to the craggy hills above. Pioneer features a gravel loop and parking spaces between very dense undergrowth. A forest of maple and box elder trees creates a shady, jungle-like atmosphere for campers. The flat river bottom sites have great, level tent pads. Sites 16–18 are on the creek on their own spur, making them ideal for those who prefer privacy. Sites 3–5 also offer seclusion but are not on the creek. Both clusters of sites are on dead-end spurs, making turning around difficult for larger vehicles.

Campsites, facilities: There are 18 sites. Picnic tables, fire grills, drinking water, garbage service, and vault toilets are provided. Leashed pets permitted.

Reservations, fees: Reservations are not accepted. Sites are $13, extra vehicles are $6, and day use is $7–13. Open May through September.

Directions: From Hyrum, drive east on Rte. 101. After eight miles turn right into Pioneer Campground.

GPS Coordinates: N 41° 37.707' W 111° 41.585'

Contact: Logan Ranger District, 435/755-3620, www.fs.fed.us/r4/uwc/recreation/wcnf/camping/logan-camping.shtml#pioneer

28 FRIENDSHIP
⛵ 🏕 🔼

Scenic rating: 7

southeast of Logan in the Bear River Mountains in the Wasatch-Cache National Forest

Map 1.3, page 47

Friendship is a small, remote campground along the Left Hand Fork of the Blacksmith Fork River. The Blacksmith Fork River drains off the western slopes of the Bear River Mountains east of Hyrum. This surprisingly remote area is off-road vehicle heaven. The Great Western ATV Trail can be accessed directly from Friendship Campground. In fact, you'll probably want an ATV to get to the campground in the first place. The forest road is rocky and rough and will take its toll on any vehicle that wasn't designed to absorb a few bumps and bruises. Motorbikes and four-wheelers rule the road, so be prepared for them to come whipping around the next bend. This relatively primitive campground is

covered by a lush forest of hardwoods. The forest floor is dusty and dry despite being next to the creek. The dense forest and remote location of the campground contribute to quiet, private sites. The facilities are simple but adequate. The trout fishing is good in this little-used branch of the Blacksmith Fork River.

Campsites, facilities: There are five sites and one group site for up to 25 people. Picnic tables, fire grills, and a vault toilet are provided. There is no drinking water. Leashed pets permitted.

Reservations, fees: Reservations are accepted only for the group site at 877/444-6777 or online at www.recreation.gov and must be made a minimum of four days in advance. Sites are $7, the group area is $35, extra vehicles are $4, and day use is $7. Open May through September.

Directions: From Hyrum, drive east on Rte. 101 for 7.2 miles. Turn left into the Left Hand Fork Canyon. Continue 3.6 miles up the canyon and enter Friendship Campground on the right side of the road.

GPS Coordinates: N 41° 39.671' W 111° 39.906'

Contact: Logan Ranger District, 435/755-3620, www.fs.fed.us/r4/uwc/recreation/wcnf/camping/logan-camping.shtml#friendship

29 SPRING
🥾 ⛵ 〰 🏕 🔼

Scenic rating: 7

southeast of Logan in the Bear River Mountains of the Wasatch-Cache National Forest

Map 1.3, page 47

Spring Campground is even farther off the beaten path than Friendship Campground. Like Friendship, Spring is on the Left Hand Fork of the Blacksmith Fork River on Forest Road 245. The road is a herky-jerky experience, best traversed with an off-road vehicle. If you can get there, the campground is a quiet little haven in the forest. Broad-leaved maples and box elder trees shade a walk-in-style campground that feels like it's been around forever. Three flat sites stretch out over the forest floor around a house-sized boulder. The campground accesses the Great Western Trail for ATV riders, and nearby is a loop hiking trail leading to Hog Hole, Pig Hole, Boar Hole, and Sow Hole cold springs. Ah, springs named after pigs—tempting, isn't it?

Campsites, facilities: There are three sites. Picnic tables, fire grills, and a pit toilet are provided. There is no drinking water. Leashed pets permitted.

Reservations, fees: Reservations are not accepted. Sites are $7, extra vehicles are $4, and day use is $7. Open May through September.

Directions: From Hyrum, drive east on Rte. 101 for 7.2 miles. Turn left into the Left Hand Fork Canyon. Continue 4.2 miles up canyon and enter Spring Campground on the right side of the road.

GPS Coordinates: N 41° 39.716' W 111° 39.243'

Contact: Logan Ranger District, 435/755-3620, www.fs.fed.us/r4/uwc/recreation/wcnf/camping/logan-camping.shtml#spring

30 LITTLE CREEK

Scenic rating: 7

west of Randolph

Map 1.3, page 47

Little Creek Campground is a small campground located below the wide, short earthen dam of Little Creek Reservoir. The midsize reservoir is drained each summer for irrigation. During late summer the reservoir appeared to be defunct, with very little water actually collected behind the dam. Little Creek trickled out of the bottom of the dam, unmolested and free flowing. The reservoir is stocked with rainbow trout each spring and offers fishing opportunities in spring and early summer, but be aware boats must be carried to the lake. The Wasatch Audubon Society identifies Little Creek Reservoir as a birding destination during migrations. Birders may spot downy woodpeckers, warbling vireos, dusty flycatchers, or western tanagers. The campground is managed jointly by the City of Randolph, Rich County, and the BLM. The site is a small, fenced, grass plot with a covered pavilion. The pavilion has four picnic tables and a large barbeque grill on a cement pad. There's room to pitch about a dozen tents in the grass around the eating area. A gravel parking lot has room for plenty of cars and RVs. Although the campsites are below the level of the dam, the scenery isn't bad, with views of the sagebrush-dotted hills surrounding the reservoir and eastward to Rex Peak in the Crawford Mountains.

Campsites, facilities: This campground can function as one large group unit or a communal setup for several unaffiliated parties. A central pavilion with picnic tables, a barbeque grill, drinking water (available seasonally), and a vault toilet are provided. Leashed pets permitted.

Reservations, fees: Reservations are not accepted. There is no fee. Open May through October, weather permitting.

Directions: From the junction of N. Main Street and W. Canyon Street in Randolph, drive west (left). After 2.1 miles take the right fork and continue 0.3 mile to the campground on the right.

GPS Coordinates: N 41° 40.668' W 111° 13.567'

Contact: Salt Lake Field Office, 801/977-4300, www.blm.gov/ut/st/en/fo/salt_lake/recreation/camping/little_creek.html

31 MOUNT HAVEN RV PARK

Scenic rating: 4

in the town of Mantua

Map 1.3, page 47

Mount Haven RV Park is located in the small town of Mantua on the shores of Mantua Reservoir. Mantua (pronounced MAN-a-way) is an Italian word meaning "beautiful gown." The small settlement was established in the pioneer era as an agricultural operation to grow flax for clothing. While Mount Haven RV Park doesn't have direct access to the reservoir, it is only a short walk away. The campground yard is well shaded by a variety of broad-leaved trees, and lush green grass grows in the sites. Views from Mount Haven are limited to the back side of the dam for Mantua Reservoir. The Mantua Reservoir (also known as Brigham City Reservoir) offers boating, waterskiing, swimming, and fishing. Ice fishing is possible on the lake in winter. Fish species include smallmouth and largemouth bass, rainbow and Bonneville cutthroat trout, bluegill, and yellow perch.

Campsites, facilities: There are 32 sites for tents and RVs up to 33 feet in length. Picnic tables, modern restrooms with showers, drinking water, and garbage service are provided. A convenience store is available. Leashed pets permitted.

Reservations, fees: Reservations are accepted at 435/723-1292. RV and tent sites are $24. Open Memorial Day through mid-October.

Directions: From Brigham City, drive east on Hwy. 89/91 for 4.5 miles and take the first Mantua exit (300 W). Follow 300 W until the junction with Main Street. Turn left on Main Street and continue 0.5 mile; Mount Haven RV Park will be on the right side of the road.

GPS Coordinates: N 41° 29.957' W 111° 56.599'

Contact: Mount Haven RV Park, 435/723-1292.

32 BOX ELDER

Scenic rating: 7

near Mantua in the Wasatch-Cache National Forest

Map 1.3, page 47

Box Elder Campground is located near the little community of Mantua at the margins of the Cache National Forest. In one direction are the steep ridges of Willard and Ben Lomond Peaks, and in the other are the waters of the Mantua Reservoir. ATV riders will love the winding, rutted road leading to Willard Peak. Mantua Reservoir (also known as Brigham City Reservoir) offers boating, waterskiing, and fishing. Ice fishing is possible on the lake in winter. Fish species include smallmouth and largemouth bass, rainbow and Bonneville cutthroat trout, bluegill, and yellow perch. Not surprisingly, Box Elder Campground is shaded by a dense forest of box elder trees and cottonwood trees. A gravel loop leads to sites with good, flat tent spots and gravel parking. The dense forest provides privacy between sites. The aging campground is in a convenient location close to highway, but far enough away to be quiet. Box Elder Creek runs through the campground and offers a different fishing experience than the nearby reservoir.

Campsites, facilities: There are 26 sites for tents and RVs up to 35 feet in length, four group sites for up to 50, 60, or 100 people depending on the site, and a day-use area. Picnic tables, fire grills, drinking water, garbage service, and flush toilets are provided. Firewood is available. Leashed pets permitted.

Reservations, fees: Reservations are accepted at 877/444-6777 or online at www.recreation. gov and must be made a minimum of four days in advance. Single sites are $15, extra vehicles are $6, and day use is $8–15. Open May through October.

Directions: From Brigham City, drive east on Hwy. 89/91 for 4.5 miles and take the first Mantua exit (300 W). Drive 0.2 mile, turn right, and continue 0.2 mile to the campground.

GPS Coordinates: N 41° 29.726' W 111° 57.106'

Contact: Logan Ranger District, 435/755-3620, www.fs.fed.us/r4/uwc/recreation/wcnf/camping/logan-camping.shtml#boxelder

33 NORTH FORK PARK

🚶 🏕 ♿ 🚐 ⛰

Scenic rating: 7

near the town of Eden

Map 1.3, page 47

North Fork Park is a Weber County park below the impressive east face of Ben Lomond Mountain. The park offers a low-key experience in a beautiful valley. The campground has views up to the steep rock faces of the mountains to the west. Groves of Gambel oak trees grow around the sites and long grass mixed with thick underbrush crowds in around the picnic tables. The campground is accessed via a gravel loop and the parking spots are mostly grass and dirt. The parking slips are long and can accommodate large trailers or even RVs. The park isn't very busy, even on weekends. It's a hot, dry spot that doesn't feel very well taken care of. The loop and parking spaces look to be in danger of being reclaimed by the forest and many of the picnic tables are old and peeling. Loop B features horse corrals and the trailhead for the Ben Lomond Trail, which leads to the summit of the 9,712-foot Ben Lomond Peak.

Campsites, facilities: There are 182 individual sites and six group sites for up to 200–300 people. Sites 83 and 84 in Loop B are wheelchair accessible. Picnic tables, fire grills, garbage service, drinking water, flush toilets, horse corrals, volleyball poles, and a horseshoe pit are provided. Leashed pets permitted.

Reservations, fees: Reservations are accepted at 801/399-8491 and are accepted in November for the following season. The fee is $15, horse stalls are $5, the corral group site is $30, and all the other group sites are $65 for up to 30 people. Additional people are $1.25 per night and extra vehicles are $3. Open May 1 through mid October.

Directions: From the intersection of Rte. 162 and Rte. 158, drive northwest on Rte. 162 for three miles. Turn left onto 4100 N and drive 0.2 mile, then turn right onto 3300 E and continue 1.1 miles. Take the left fork onto North Fork Road and drive 1.1 miles, turn left onto 5950 N at the sign for Weber County North Fork Park and the Ben Lomond Trailhead, and drive one mile to the campground.

GPS Coordinates: N 41° 22.269' W 111° 54.158'

Contact: Weber County Parks and Recreation, 801/399-8491, www.co.weber.ut.us/parks/nf-park.php.

34 CENTURY RV PARK

🏊 🏕 ♿ 🚐 ⛰

Scenic rating: 3

in Ogden

Map 1.3, page 47

Century RV Park is a large, popular RV park located in Ogden next to I-15. The RV park presents an interesting dichotomy, with a nice, community feel right next to the largest, busiest freeway in the state of Utah. Huge concrete walls rise above the campground, and cars can be heard buzzing by on six lanes overhead. But regardless of these undeniable reminders of the urban environment, the campground maintains an attractive atmosphere. There are some trees in the park, providing intermittent shade for the RV slips. Open grass lawns add green to the campground, where playing kids spill out onto the access loops. Flower baskets hang from green street signs, adding a neighborhood feel to the place. If you're passing through Utah on I-15 or want to spend a couple of nights in town, this is a good, easy option.

Campsites, facilities: There are 139 full hookup (30, 50 amps) sites, eight partial hook-up sites, 30 sites with electricity only, and 27 tent sites. Amenities include picnic tables, dog walk, playground, swimming pool, hot tub, covered pavilion, WiFi, cable TV, laundry, garbage service, modern restrooms with showers, and drinking water. Leashed pets permitted.

Reservations, fees: Reservations are accepted at 801-731-3800. Full hook-up sites are $27.01; sites with electricity and cable TV sites are $25.01; sites with electricity, water, and cable TV are $25.26; electricity-only sites are $23.66; sites with electricity and water are $24.66; and no hook-ups/tent sites are $20.91. Open year-round.

Directions: From I-15, take Exit 343. Drive west one block on Rte. 104 (2100 S) and turn left into the Century RV Park.

GPS Coordinates: N 41° 13.574' W 112° 00.810'

Contact: Century RV Park, 801/731-3800, http://centuryrvpark.googlepages.com/

☰ FORT BUENAVENTURA PARK
🏊 🐴 🚐 🏕

Scenic rating: 6

in Ogden

Map 1.3, page 47

Fort Buenaventura was the first Anglo settlement in the state of Utah and the Great Basin Region. The fort was established in 1846 near present-day Ogden along the Weber River, built by mountain men and trappers for trading. Fort Buenaventura Park is currently owned and operated by Weber County. The fort at the park isn't original, but it has been reconstructed as accurately as possible, including classic mortise and tenon joints. The park contains Native American tepees, rusting farming equipment from the pioneer era, and a visitors center to explain all the history. The campground is set under a thick canopy of broad-leaved deciduous trees. The facilities are more reminiscent of a nice Forest Service campground than what you might expect from a county park. Limited views up to the Wasatch Mountains above town add to the scenic atmosphere. The sites have good spacing, and the forest offers a natural setting despite being within the city limits.

Campsites, facilities: There are 15 sites, two with electricity hook-ups, and two group areas for up to 150 people. Picnic tables on concrete pads, concrete fire rings, garbage service, a dump station, modern restrooms, drinking water, and a visitors center are provided. Canoe rentals are available. Leashed pets permitted.

Reservations, fees: Reservations are accepted at 801/399-8099 and are accepted in November for the following year. Sites are $15 without hook-ups, $20 with hook-ups (electricity only). Group areas are $65 plus $1.25 per person over 30 people, and extra vehicles are $3. Open May 1 through mid-October.

Directions: From I-15, take Exit 342 for Rte. 53 and turn right onto Pennsylvania Avenue (Rte. 53). Drive 0.8 mile and turn right onto A Avenue. Continue one block and turn left onto the Fort Buenaventura Park entrance road.

GPS Coordinates: N 41° 13.005' W 111° 59.253'

Contact: Fort Buenaventura Park, 801/399-8099, www1.co.weber.ut.us/parks/fortb/

☰ ANDERSON COVE
🏊 🚣 🍴 🐴 ♿ 🚐 🏕

Scenic rating: 7

on the Pineview Reservoir in the Wasatch-Cache National Forest

Map 1.3, page 47

Anderson Cove is a Forest Service campground on the shore of Pineview Reservoir near Huntsville. The reservoir is the most popular reservoir of its size in the state of Utah. Only a half-hour drive from Ogden, Pineview is a good place to retreat from the summer heat by boating, swimming, and fishing the lake's waters. Sport-fishing species include largemouth bass, black crappie, bluegill, bullhead catfish, and tiger muskellunge. Tiger muskellunge are a sterile hybrid cross between a northern pike and a muskellunge. These fish can be over 50 inches long and weigh up to 30 pounds. A paved boat ramp at the Anderson Cove Campground provides easy access to the lake for campers. The campground loop is spread out in a flat grass field with broad-leaved trees offering shade for most of the sites. The loop and parking spots are paved, and the campground is equally comfortable for tents and RVs. The campground offers views of the surrounding green and brown hills but feels more like a city park than what you might expect from the Forest Service. Weekends are particularly busy here, so make reservations.

Campsites, facilities: There are 58 single sites, nine double sites, one quad site, and two group sites for up to 100 people. Over 30 of the sites and the group sites are wheelchair accessible. Picnic tables on concrete pads, fire pits, garbage service, aluminum recycling, sand volleyball courts, horseshoe pits, drinking water, a boat ramp, a dump station, and vault toilets are provided. Firewood and ice are available. Leashed pets permitted.

Reservations, fees: Reservations are accepted at 877/444-6777 or online at www.recreation.gov and must be made a minimum of four days in advance. Single sites are $18, double sites are $36, and the group sites are $32–160. Open May through September.

Directions: From the intersection of Rte. 39 and Rte. 167 southwest of Huntsville drive west on Rte. 39 for 0.7 mile. Anderson Cove Campground will be on the right side of the road. GPS Coordinates: N 41° 15.000' W 111° 47.174'

Contact: Ogden Ranger District, 801/625-5306, www.fs.fed.us/r4/uwc/recreation/wcnf/camping/ogden-camping.shtml#andersoncove

❚37❚ JEFFERSON HUNT

🧗 🏕 🚐 ⛺

Scenic rating: 7

near the Pineview Reservoir in Huntsville in the Wasatch-Cache National Forest

Map 1.3, page 47

The campground is set on the historical Winter family's homestead site known as Winter's Grove. Winter's Grove is located at the southeast tip of Pineview Reservoir near the town of Huntsville. The South Fork of the Ogden River flows by the campground, contributing to the site's river-bottom feel. Mature willow and cottonwood trees shade the sites and make the place feel both secluded and protected. Long seeding grass grows thick around the sites. The small loop is gravel but has room for moderately large RVs and trailers. The Winter's Grove Nature Trail starts just outside the entrance to the campground. The trail travels through a forest of tall trees that house the northern oriole. Woodpeckers and raptors also use the large trees to build cavity nests, and other avian species like warblers, vireos, and kinglets can be seen and heard along the nature trail. Moose, deer, and raccoons also live in the wetland environment at the end of the lake. The trail is open to hikers and horses.

Campsites, facilities: There are 29 sites. Picnic tables, drinking water, fire pits, garbage service, and vault toilets are provided. Leashed pets permitted.

Reservations, fees: Reservations are not accepted. The fee is $14. Open May through September.

Directions: From the intersection of Rte. 39 and Rte. 167 southwest of Huntsville, drive east on Rte. 39 for 0.1 mile. Turn left, drive a short distance, and turn right into Jefferson Hunt Campground. GPS Coordinates: N 41° 14.962' W 111° 46.105'

Contact: Ogden Ranger District, 801/625-5306, www.fs.fed.us/r4/uwc/recreation/wcnf/camping/ogden-camping.shtml#jeffersonhunt

❚38❚ CHRIS' RV PARK

🏕 🚐 ⛺

Scenic rating: 4

in Huntsville

Map 1.3, page 47

Chris' RV Park is a small campground in the backyard of a café and gas station in the town of Huntsville. Pioneer-era wagon wheels decorate the entrance to the facility, and a green dinosaur statue will confirm you've found the right place. The RV park is near the popular Pineview Reservoir, which offers summer fun in the form of swimming, boating, and fishing. Sport-fishing species in the lake include largemouth bass, black crappie, bluegill, bullhead catfish, and tiger muskellunge. There are decent views out of the park to the golden brown hills surrounding town. The layout has small patches of grass in tightly spaced sites between permanent trailers and an old barn. The RV park is neighbored by the Jackson Fork Inn and has a cramped feel to it.

Campsites, facilities: There are 10 sites for tents and RVs. Picnic tables, drinking water, modern restrooms with showers, garbage service, a café, a convenience store with camping supplies, and a gas station are provided. Leashed pets permitted.

Reservations, fees: Reservations are accepted at 801/745-3542. RV sites are $25 and tent sites are $15. Open year-round.

Directions: From the intersection of Rte. 39 and Rte. 167 southwest of Huntsville, drive east on Rte. 39 for 0.1 mile. Chris' RV Park will be on the right side of the road.

GPS Coordinates: N 41° 14.754' W 111° 46.288'

Contact: Chris' RV Park, 801/745-3542.

campground is shaded by a thick canopy of broad-leaved trees like maples, box elders, and cottonwoods. Northern flicker woodpeckers, swallows, bluebirds, small owls, and kestrels nest in the many dead trees near Magpie Campground. Townsend's big-eared bats, little brown bats, and spotted bats take over where the birds left off when darkness falls. Long grass grows around sites, adding to the intensely green atmosphere. The short drive-through loop and parking slips are gravel. When the campground fills to capacity, the camp hosts close the gate.

Campsites, facilities: There are 12 sites. Picnic tables on cement pads, fire pits, drinking water, garbage service, stove stands, and vault toilets are provided. Firewood is available. Leashed pets permitted.

Reservations, fees: Reservations are not accepted. Single sites are $14 and double sites are $28. Open May through October.

Directions: From Huntsville, drive 6.3 miles east on Rte. 39 and enter Magpie Campground on the right side of the road.

GPS Coordinates: N 41° 16.210' W 111° 40.024'

Contact: Ogden Ranger District, 801/625-5306, www.fs.fed.us/r4/uwc/recreation/wcnf/camping/ogden-camping.shtml#magpie

39 MAGPIE

Scenic rating: 7

on the Ogden River Scenic Byway in the Wasatch-Cache National Forest

Map 1.3, page 47

Magpie Campground is the first campground in a series of river-bottom campgrounds in South Fork Canyon along the South Fork of the Ogden River. Fishing for brown, cutthroat, and rainbow trout is popular along the clear, shallow river. Tubing the river is equally popular, which can have a detrimental effect on the fishing. The creek flows next to the campground, offering a pleasant atmosphere and drowning out the busy highway through the trees. The

40 BOTTS

Scenic rating: 7

on the Ogden River Scenic Byway in the Wasatch-Cache National Forest

Map 1.3, page 47

Botts is the second campground in South Fork Canyon along the South Fork of the Ogden River. Fishing for brown, cutthroat, and rainbow trout is popular along the gently cascading river. The creek is especially popular in late summer, when the water is low and the temperatures are hot; beer-toting tubers cruise the river then and scare the trout into hiding. The campground is similar to Magpie in many ways but is generally more open and receives better sun than its neighbor. Its open nature allows for views across the creek to a steep canyon wall. Old gnarled cottonwoods provide shade for sites, and there's plenty of lush vegetation and long seeding grass. On the downside, Botts' open feel amplifies the nearby road and traffic passing by.

Campsites, facilities: There are eight sites. Picnic tables on cement pads, fire pits, drinking water, garbage service, and vault toilets are provided. Firewood is available. Leashed pets permitted.

Reservations, fees: Reservations are not accepted. Single sites are $14. Open May through October.

Directions: From Huntsville, drive 7.1 miles east on Rte. 39 and enter Botts Campground on the right side of the road.
GPS Coordinates: N 41° 16.639' W 111° 39.477'

Contact: Ogden Ranger District, 801/625-5306, www.fs.fed.us/r4/uwc/recreation/wcnf/camping/ogden-camping.shtml#botts

41 SOUTH FORK
🛶 🏕 ♿ 🚐 ⛺

Scenic rating: 7

on the Ogden River Scenic Byway Canyon in the Wasatch-Cache National Forest

Map 1.3, page 47

As you drive northeast of Huntsville on Route 39 in South Fork Canyon, South Fork is the first major campground encountered. While Bott and Magpie offer a preview of what you'll find at South Fork, this campground is much larger, featuring two loops and more developed facilities. Like all the Forest Service sites in the canyon, South Fork hugs the banks of the river. Cottonwood and Rocky Mountain maple trees provide the sites with ample shade, and dense underbrush and grass add green everywhere you look. The sites have nice, flat tent pads on the dirt forest floor. Many of the sites have direct access to the creek on little game trails tunneling through the dense vegetation. South Fork

was reworked in 1996 to provide better facilities and limit the sites' impact on the Ogden River. The campground is packed on weekends, so be safe and make reservations.

Campsites, facilities: There are 33 single sites and 11 double sites. Sites 1–3, 6, 7, 9–11, 14, and 16–19 are wheelchair accessible. Picnic tables on cement pads, fire pits, drinking water, garbage service and vault toilets are provided. Firewood is available. Leashed pets permitted.

Reservations, fees: Reservations are accepted at 877/444-6777 or online at www.recreation.gov and must be made a minimum of four days in advance. Single sites are $14 and double sites are $28. Open May 15 through September 30.

Directions: From Huntsville, drive eight miles east on Rte. 39 and enter South Fork Campground on the right side of the road.
GPS Coordinates: N 41° 16.923' W 111° 39.238'

Contact: Ogden Ranger District, 801/625-5306, www.fs.fed.us/r4/uwc/recreation/wcnf/camping/ogden-camping.shtml#southfork

42 PERCEPTION PARK
🛶 🏕 ♿ 🚐 ⛺

Scenic rating: 7

on the Ogden River Scenic Byway in the Wasatch-Cache National Forest

Map 1.3, page 47   **BEST (**

Perception Park is a first-rate Forest Service facility on the banks of the South Fork of Ogden River. The shallow South Fork is popular for its trout fishing and tubing. The campground was developed specifically for campers with special needs—the whole place is wheelchair accessible. In 1975, the Women's Conservation Council lobbied heavily for a facility where special needs campers could enjoy the outdoors. Perception Park was built in the mid-1980s as a result of its efforts. The campground has paved walkways and benches along the river and wheelchair-accessible water fountains. All campers will appreciate these improvements and the overall quality of the site. Large, water-loving trees like cottonwoods offer shade for many of the campsites; dense grass and other vegetations grows around the campground. Facilities like sand volleyball courts, wood jungle gyms, and horseshoe pits give the place a parklike atmosphere and make it one of the best campgrounds for families with small children.

Campsites, facilities: There are 24 single sites and three group sites. McKay Group Site can accommodate up to 60 people, WCCU Group Site up to 40 people, and GFWC up to 50 people. Picnic tables on cement pads, fire pits, barbeque grills, drinking water, garbage service, a playground, horseshoe pits, volleyball courts (sand and paved), and flush toilets are provided. Firewood is available. Leashed pets permitted.

Reservations, fees: Reservations are accepted at 877/444-6777 or online at www.recreation. gov and must be made a minimum of four days in advance. Single sites are $16, group sites are $150, and day use is $5. Open May 15 through September 30.

Directions: From Huntsville, drive east 8.8 miles on Rte. 39 and enter Perception Park on the right side of the road.

GPS Coordinates: N 41° 16.923' W 111° 39.238'

Contact: Ogden Ranger District, 801/625-5306, www.fs.fed.us/r4/uwc/recreation/wcnf/camping/ogden-camping.shtml#perceptionpark

43 UPPER AND LOWER MEADOWS
🛶 🎠 🚐 ⛺

Scenic rating: 7

on the Ogden River Scenic Byway in the Wasatch-Cache National Forest

Map 1.3, page 47

Meadow Campground is broken into two loops, the Upper Meadows loop on the south bank of the South Fork of the Ogden River, and the Lower Meadows on the stream's north bank. Recreation along the river includes fishing for trout and riding the pint-sized rapids on inflated inner tubes. Both loops are gravel and offer

well-spaced, private campsites. The nearby road is within earshot but doesn't weigh too heavily on the natural character of the Meadows. This campground is popular with tent campers who like the flat tent sites under the trees. Leafy trees provide plenty of shade for sites.

Campsites, facilities: There are nine sites at the Upper Meadows Loop and 19 single sites and two double sites at the Lower Meadows Loop. Both loops can accommodate RVs up to 25 feet in length. Picnic tables on cement pads, fire pits, drinking water, garbage service, and vault toilets are provided. Firewood is available. Leashed pets permitted.

Reservations, fees: Reservations are not accepted. Singles sites are $14, double sites are $28, extra vehicles are $6, and day use is $7. Open May 15 through September 30.

Directions: From Huntsville, drive east nine miles on Rte. 39 and enter Meadows on the right side of the road.

GPS Coordinates: N 41° 17.206' W 111° 38.627'

Contact: Ogden Ranger District, 801/625-5306, Upper Meadows www.fs.fed.us/r4/uwc/recreation/wcnf/camping/ogden-camping.shtml#uppermeadows, Lower Meadows www.fs.fed.us/r4/uwc/recreation/wcnf/camping/ogden-camping.shtml#lowermeadows

44 WILLOWS
🛶 🎠 🚐 ⛺

Scenic rating: 7

on the Ogden River Scenic Byway in the Wasatch-Cache National Forest

Map 1.3, page 47

Willows is the final South Fork Canyon Campground on Route 39. The campground is very similar to the whole cluster of Forest Service campgrounds lining the South Fork of the Ogden River. Copious thick-leaved trees provide shade and cover for tent-friendly campsites on the river-bottom floor. Picnic tables sit on cement pads squeezed by the lush, encroaching undergrowth. Green dominates the visual landscape, and the soothing sounds of the rushing river and chirping birds provide the audio backdrop. Weekends see heavy traffic both on the road next to the campground and in the sites themselves. Fishing for brown, rainbow, and cutthroat trout is possible on the river, though heavy tubing traffic on weekends tends to keep the fish wary. For this reason, spring, fall, and winter offer the best fishing.

Campsites, facilities: There are 12 single sites and three double sites. Picnic tables on cement pads, fire pits, stove stands, drinking water, garbage service, and vault toilets are provided. Firewood is available. Leashed pets permitted.

Reservations, fees: Reservations are not accepted. Sites are $14, double sites are $28, extra vehicles are $7, and day use is $6. Open May 15 through September 30.

Directions: From Huntsville, drive east 9.2 miles on Rte. 39 and enter Willows Campground on the right side of the road.
GPS Coordinates: N 41° 17.514' W 111° 38.063'

Contact: Ogden Ranger District, 801/625-5306, www.fs.fed.us/r4/uwc/recreation/wcnf/camping/ogden-camping.shtml#willows

45 MONTE CRISTO
🏃 🏕 ♿ 🚐 ⛺

Scenic rating: 8

in the Bear River Range of the Wasatch-Cache National Forest

Map 1.3, page 47

Monte Cristo Campground is located across from the Forest Service Guard Station on the crest of the Bear River Mountains. At around 9,000 feet in elevation, the air at Monte Cristo is refreshingly crisp and clean even during the dog days of summer. Five camp loops are woven into mature Engelmann spruce and aspen trees. Loop D borders a gorgeous open grass and wildflower meadow that offers views eastward down to the rolling hills and valleys of southwestern Wyoming. Thick patches of purple fireweed grow along the paved access loop. Pine needles pad the forest floor campsites and offer ideal tenting grounds. The sites are well spread out along the loops and the trees provide shade and privacy for campers. Monte Cristo is popular with ATV riders.

Campsites, facilities: There are 47 single sites for tents and RVs up to 25 feet in length and two group sites for up to 80 or 100 people, depending on the site. Picnic tables, fire grills, pull-through sites, drinking water, garbage service, and vault toilets are provided. Firewood is available. Leashed pets permitted.

Reservations, fees: Reservations are accepted only for the group sites at 877/444-6777 or online at www.recreation.gov and must be made a minimum of four days in advance. Sites are $14, group areas are $125, extra vehicles are $7, and day use is $7. Open July through October, weather permitting.

Directions: From Huntsville, drive east 31 miles on Rte. 39 and enter Monte Cristo Campground on the right side of the road.
GPS Coordinates: N 41° 27.778' W 111° 29.860'

Contact: Ogden Ranger District, 801/625-5306, www.fs.fed.us/r4/uwc/recreation/wcnf/camping/ogden-camping.shtml#montecristo

46 BIRCH CREEK
🚣 🏕 🚐 ⛺

Scenic rating: 5

on the east slopes of the Monte Cristo Range

Map 1.3, page 47

Birch Creek Campground is as simple as campgrounds get. In fact, if it weren't listed by the BLM it wouldn't be included in this guide. The "campground" is a gravel parking lot with a few possible campsites scattered among the sagebrush. For those with campers, trailers, or small RVs, the site may hold some interest as a convenient, free place to stay to access fishing on the Birch Creek Reservoir or hunting in the surrounding mountains. There are actually two Birch Creek Reservoirs: The larger upper lake is called Birch Creek Reservoir #2, and the lower pond is Birch Creek Reservoir #1. The reservoirs are stocked with rainbow and cutthroat trout. Fishing is most likely from the shoreline, because it is difficult to get a boat up to the upper reservoir. The reservoir is also drained down to a 25-foot-deep retaining pond by mid-summer for irrigation. Expect to encounter cows grazing the sagebrush and grasslands around the reservoir.

Campsites, facilities: There is an undeveloped site at the base of an earthen dam and another at the lower end of Birch Creek Reservoir #1 (Lower Reservoir). A fire ring and a vault toilet are provided at the site below the dam. There is no potable water. Leashed pets permitted.

Reservations, fees: Reservations are not accepted. There is no fee. Open May through October, weather permitting.

Directions: From Woodruff, drive eight miles west on Rte. 39 and turn right on a gravel road signed for Birch Creek Reservoir. Follow the road one mile to the reservoir at the end of the road.

GPS Coordinates: N 41° 30.329' W 111° 19.124'

Contact: Salt Lake Field Office, 801/977-4300, www.blm.gov/ut/st/en/fo/salt_lake/recreation/camping/birch_creek.html

47 CHERRY HILL

Scenic rating: 5

in Kaysville

Map 1.3, page 47

Cherry Hill Recreation Park is a water and amusement park located in Kaysville. The Cherry Hill complex has batting cages, miniature golf, and a 30-foot artificial climbing wall. Cherry Hill also features a large, pleasant RV park and campground for those who plan to spend more than a day at the fun-land. The RV park has green grass and plentiful shade provided by mature hardwood trees. While some of the sites are near Main Street

and suffer from the hustle and bustle of the busy entrance, other sites in the back of the campground are as calm and quiet as you'll experience in any RV park. The campground is equally accommodating for tents and RVs, with nice spots to comfortably pitch a tent. The paved loop makes for easy access to the sites and gives the place a first-class feel. On the downside, the RV park is huge and offers a very urban camping experience.

Campsites, facilities: There are 112 full hookup sites (20-, 30-, and 50-amp), 10 sites with electricity only, 58 no hook-up/tent sites, and one group site. Amenities include modern restrooms with showers, WiFi, laundry, drinking water, garbage service, dump station, miniature golf, game room, baseball batting cages, gift shop, convenience store, restaurant, swimming pool, covered picnic pavilions, climbing wall, and water park. Leashed pets permitted.

Reservations, fees: Reservations are accepted at 888/4GO-CAMP (888/446-2267). Full hook-up sites are $34 and tent sites are $28. Open April through early November; limited winter camping is available.

Directions: From I-15 take Exit 324 onto Hwy. 89. Drive two miles north on Hwy. 89 and take Exit 397 onto Rte. 273. Cherry Hill will be on the right side of the road.

GPS Coordinates: N 41° 00.797' W 111° 54.815'

Contact: Cherry Hill, 801/451-5379, www.cherry-hill.com/

48 LAGOON RV PARK AND CAMPGROUND

Scenic rating: 3

in Farmington

Map 1.3, page 47   BEST (

Lagoon RV Park is part of the Lagoon Park, a huge amusement park in Farmington. The park is rich in history, having been around in one form or another since 1886. Lagoon has over 40 rides, shows at its theater, a small zoo, a water park, and a historic pioneer village. The RV and campground is at the south end of the park and borders the zoo. From camp you can see elk, camels, llamas, and more. The camping situation is less than ideal but will suffice as a convenient spot to stay to enjoy the Lagoon Park experience. Big trees provide plenty of shade for the sites. There are decent views of the mountains of Bountiful Peak and the Wasatch Range above town. On the downside, the campground suffers from the constant and significant noise created by the amusement park rides and their screaming passengers. While that's to be expected, the noise is hard to ignore and dominates the campground's atmosphere. The sites are small and crowded with no privacy. While the unique campground is more utilitarian than aesthetic, it offers cheap accommodations at a park built for family entertainment.

Campsites, facilities: There are 90 full hookup (20-, 30-, and 50-amp) sites, 59 partial hook-up sites, 58 electricity only/tent sites, and one group site. Amenities include modern restrooms with showers, drinking water, laundry, a dog walk, drinking water, garbage service, a dump station, and an amusement park. Leashed pets permitted.

Reservations, fees: Reservations are accepted at 801/451-8100 or 800/748-5246 and can be arranged in February for the following season. Full hook-ups are $33.50 (pull-through), full hook-ups (back-in) are $31.50, electricity only/tent sites are $27.50, and partial hook-up sites are $29.50. Open May through mid-October, weather permitting.

Directions: From I-15, take Exit 322 for Rte. 227 and Lagoon Drive. Take the Lagoon ramp and continue on Lagoon Drive 0.8 mile; Lagoon RV Park will be on the left side of the road after the entrance to the main park.

GPS Coordinates: N 40° 58.973' W 111° 53.808'

Contact: Lagoon RV Park and Campground, 801/451-8100 or 800/748-5246, www.lagoon-park.com/camping.php

GREAT BASIN AND WESTERN UTAH

© MIKE MATSON

BEST CAMPGROUNDS

Western Utah is a desert in the truest form of
the word. It is part of the Great Basin Desert, the largest desert in the
Southwest. Extending south from the Great Salt Lake and west from the
Wasatch Mountains, the Great Salt Lake Desert forms the eastern edge
of this parched ecosystem. This desert is a dry, desolate landscape with
featureless basins stretching toward the horizon in unbroken monotony. It
is salt flats so consistently smooth and barren they've become the testing
grounds for the land speed record at Bonneville Flats. It is featureless sand
dunes and mud flats deemed so utterly worthless the military uses them
to test explosives and chemical weapons. The Dugway Proving Grounds
and Deseret Test Center are littered with so many hazards they're closed
to public access.

But not all of Utah's desert is wasteland. Rising from the Great
Salt Lake Desert are a series of beautiful north-to-south mountain ranges. The Basin and Range landscape has been formed by the gradual
stretching of the earth's surface. During the stretching process, the
crust thinned, and mountain ranges rose along north-to-south fault lines.
Examples of this geologic phenomenon can be seen in the western Utah
desert in ranges like the Deep Creek Range, the Stansbury Mountains,
the Sheeprock Mountains, and the Wah Wah Mountains. These peaks
climb in stark relief from the flat valleys below. Like tiny islands in the sky,

desert mountains catch winter snows and act as isolated microclimates for plant communities and desert wildlife.

The largest of these ranges, the Stansbury Mountains are protected by the Deseret Peak Wilderness and offer a lush, wooded canyon and excellent hiking to the summit of Deseret Peak. Another notable mountain retreat in the western Utah region is the Tushar Mountains. A collection of lovely upland reservoirs on the Beaver River offers fly fishing among volcanic rock. Trout-stocked lakes, lush meadows, and cool alpine air make the dry, barren desert feel far away.

There are attractions in the basins of the Great Salt Lake Desert, too. In the Sevier Desert, a huge complex of white sand dunes has collected at Sand Mountain. The Little Sahara Recreation Area is a playground of constantly shifting dunes for motorcycles, ATVs, and dune buggies. There's history in the Great Salt Lake Desert as well. Southwest of the Dugway Proving grounds is the historic Pony Express Trail. Simpson Springs was a reliable watering hole for the mail-packing horsemen on their way across the imposing desert wilderness. A reconstructed cabin and monument marks the spot.

While many dismiss western Utah's desert as a wasteland, open-minded travelers will discover an extreme landscape with surprising beauty. Throw your preconceptions aside and go explore the vast, empty space on the Utah map.

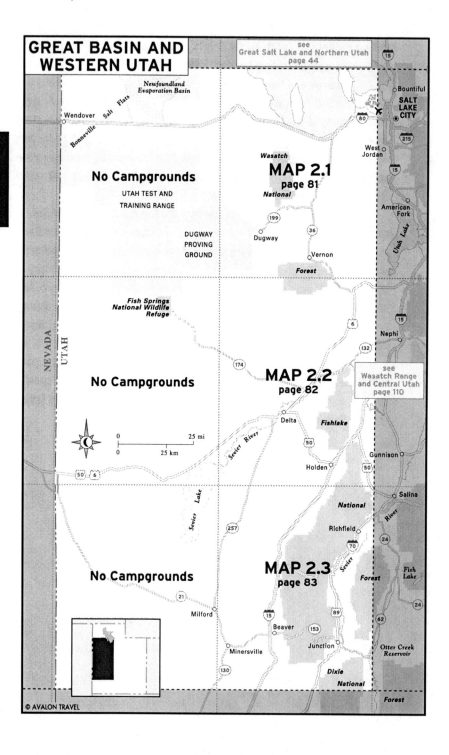

GREAT BASIN AND WESTERN UTAH

see
Great Salt Lake and Northern Utah
page 44

Newfoundland
Evaporation Basin

Bountiful

SALT
LAKE
CITY

Wendover

Salt Flats

Bonneville

West
Jordan

Wasatch

MAP 2.1
page 81

National

American
Fork

Utah Lake

No Campgrounds

UTAH TEST AND
TRAINING RANGE

199

36

DUGWAY
PROVING
GROUND

Dugway

Vernon

Forest

Fish Springs
National Wildlife
Refuge

NEVADA   UTAH

6

Nephi

132

174

MAP 2.2
page 82

see
Wasatch Range
and Central Utah
page 110

No Campgrounds

0   25 mi
0   25 km

Delta

Fishlake

Sevier River

50

Gunnison

50

Holden

Sevier Lake

Salina

National

River

257

Richfield

70

24

50   6

MAP 2.3
page 83

Sevier

Forest

Fish
Lake

24

21

Milford

15

89

62

Beaver

153

Junction

Otter Creek
Reservoir

Minersville

130

Dixie

National

© AVALON TRAVEL

Forest

Map 2.1

Campgrounds 1-8
Pages 84-88

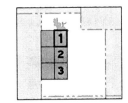

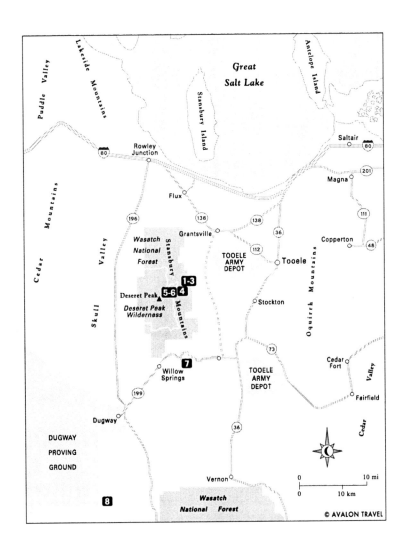

Map 2.2

Campgrounds 9-18
Pages 88-94

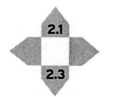

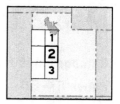

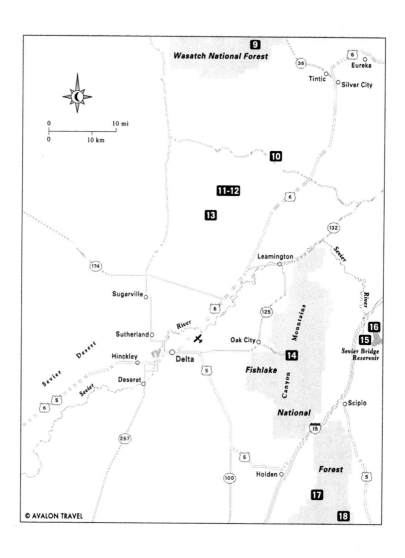

Map 2.3

Campgrounds 19-41
Pages 94-105

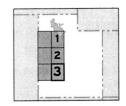

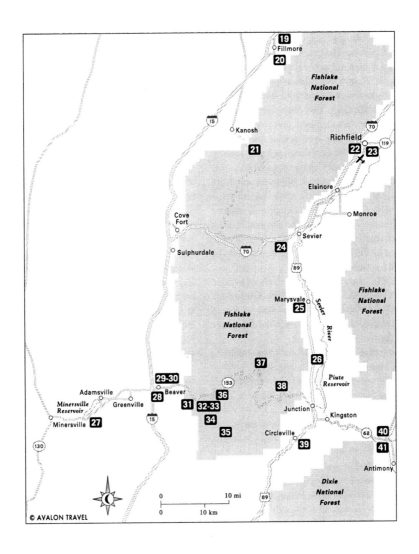

1 COTTONWOOD
🏠 ⛺

Scenic rating: 7

in the Stansbury Mountains in the
Wasatch-Cache National Forest

Map 2.1, page 81

Cottonwood Campground is a tiny Forest Service unit on the east flanks of the Stansbury Mountains. The Stansbury Mountains are one of the most dramatic and appealing ranges in the basin and range country of western Utah. Deseret Peak is the crown jewel of the range, with steep rock walls rising to a summit of over 11,000 feet. Cottonwood is the first campground encountered driving up South Willow Canyon. The canyon is cut deeply into the mountains by a year-round stream that adds life to the otherwise dry environment and character to the areas campgrounds. The Cottonwood Campground is really only two sites along the creek. Big cottonwood and juniper trees define the spot. The sites are close to the road, but not compared to some of the units farther up the canyon. Hiking and horseback-riding trails leading into the Deseret Peak Wilderness are available at the upper terminus of the road.

NOTE: Cottonwood is currently closed because of a fire in the summer of 2008. The fire left upstream slopes unstable, and there is concern a landslide or flash flood could be dangerous in the riverside sites.

Campsites, facilities: There is one single site and one double site. Picnic tables, a communal fire ring, and a vault toilet are provided. There is no drinking water. Leashed pets permitted.

Reservations, fees: Reservations are not accepted. The single site is $10 and the double site is $20. Open late May through early October, weather permitting.

Directions: From Grantsville, drive south on Cooley Street for five miles. Turn right on South Willow Road and continue four miles to the Cottonwood Campground on the left side of the road.

GPS Coordinates: N 40° 30.107' W 112° 33.591'
Contact: Salt Lake City Ranger District, 801/466-6411, www.fs.fed.us/r4/uwc/recreation/wcnf/camping/slrd/stansbury_mtn_cg.shtml#cottonwood-cg

2 INTAKE
🏠 ⛺

Scenic rating: 7

in the Stansbury Mountains in the
Wasatch-Cache National Forest

Map 2.1, page 81

Intake Campground is the second campground encountered heading up South Willow Canyon. The canyon cuts into the Stansbury Mountains below the impressive Deseret Peak Wilderness. Deseret Peak climbs to 11,031 feet in a dramatic fashion. The small campground is shaded by box elder and cottonwood trees and sits in narrow ribbon of forest by South Willow Creek. The South Willow Guard Station is just up the road from Intake Campground. Stop by to see the whitewashed buildings and a noteworthy collection of hummingbird feeders. Hiking to Deseret Peak's summit is possible on the Mill Fork Trail starting up the road at Loop Campground.

NOTE: The Forest Service temporarily closed Intake in 2008 because a fire left upstream slopes unstable, which could cause a landslide or flash flood in the riverside sites.

Campsites, facilities: There are four sites. Picnic tables, fire rings, and a vault toilet are provided. There is no drinking water. Leashed pets permitted.

Reservations, fees: Reservations are not accepted. Sites are $10. Open late May through early October, weather permitting.

Directions: From Grantsville, drive south on Cooley Street for five miles. Turn right on South Willow Road and continue 4.7 miles to Intake Campground on the left side of the road.

GPS Coordinates: N 40° 29.898' W 112° 34.267'

Contact: Salt Lake City Ranger District, 801/466-6411, www.fs.fed.us/ r4/uwc/recreation/wcnf/camping/slrd/ stansbury_mtn_cg.shtml#intake-cg

3 BOY SCOUT

Scenic rating: 7

in the Stansbury Mountains in the
Wasatch-Cache National Forest

Map 2.1, page 81

Boy Scout Campground sits beneath Little Bald Mountain in the Stansbury Mountains. Little Bald Mountain burned in a 558-acre forest fire in late July and early August of 2008. While the fire left the hills above Boy Scout Campground looking a little charred, it didn't have any direct effect on the campground. South Willow Creek acted as a natural fire line and protected the campground. The sites are shaded by box elder trees and offer a quiet setting next to the gently flowing creek. The forest canopy is dense, and the remote nature of the campground makes it feel both private and safe. Boy Scout is near the trailhead for the Medina Flat Trail, which is popular with ATV riders and also leads to the Mining Fork Trail. The Mining Fork Trail can be reached at the end of Mining Fork Road (with a four-wheel-drive vehicle). The trail leads past abandoned mines to South Willow Lake. Hiking and horseback riding are also possible farther up the creek, near Loop Campground.

Campsites, facilities: There are five tent sites (RVs are not recommended). Picnic tables, fire rings, and a vault toilet are provided. There is no drinking water. Leashed pets permitted.

Reservations, fees: Reservations are not accepted. Sites are $10. Open late May through early October, weather permitting.

Directions: From Grantsville, drive south on Cooley Street for five miles. Turn right on South Willow Road and continue 5.2 miles to the Boy Scout Campground on the left side of the road.

GPS Coordinates: N 40° 29.691' W 112° 34.741'

Contact: Salt Lake City Ranger District, 801/466-6411, www.fs.fed.us/ r4/uwc/recreation/wcnf/camping/slrd/ stansbury_mtn_cg.shtml#boy-scout-cg

4 LOWER NARROWS

Scenic rating: 8

in the Stansbury Mountains in the
Wasatch-Cache National Forest

Map 2.1, page 81

As the South Willow Canyon winds up into the Stansbury Mountains, tightly spaced limestone walls create two narrow slots that the road and creek must navigate through. The Lower Narrows Campground is located near the first of these tight slots. As the road climbs into the mountains, the forest becomes more diverse and lush. Spruce and fir trees join box elder and aspens in the forest setting at Lower Narrows. The refreshing South Willow Creek flows between the sites, and the forest floor, littered with pine needles and leaves, provides an ideal place to pitch your tent. You park along the side of the road and walk in to the campground, and a bridge leads across the creek to some of the sites. Old woodstoves give campers an opportunity to cook 19th-century-style and contribute to the quaint character of the campground.

Campsites, facilities: There are five tent sites (RVs are not recommended). Picnic tables, fire rings, wood stoves, garbage service, and a vault toilet are provided. There is no drinking water. Leashed pets permitted.

Reservations, fees: Reservations are not accepted. Sites are $10, and day use is $6. Open late May through early October, weather permitting.

Directions: From Grantsville, drive south on

Cooley Street for five miles. Turn right on South Willow Road and continue 5.9 miles to the Lower Narrows Campground on the left side of the road.
GPS Coordinates: N 40° 29.543' W 112° 35.491'
Contact: Salt Lake City Ranger District, 801/466-6411, www.fs.fed.us/r4/uwc/recreation/wcnf/camping/slrd/stansbury_mtn_cg.shtml#lower-narrows-cg

5 UPPER NARROWS
🏕 ⛺

Scenic rating: 8

in the Stansbury Mountains in Wasatch-Cache National Forest

Map 2.1, page 81

Upper Narrows Campground is near the second limestone tunnel along South Willow Creek. The trickling creek becomes particularly pretty in this part of the canyon, with crystal-clear water flowing through green, moss-covered rocks. The sites at Upper Narrows are shielded by a very lush forest canopy with surprising diversity for this part of the desert. Box elder, cottonwood, spruce, fir, and aspen trees all contribute to the rich forest palette. A sturdy bridge leads from the roadside parking to the private camp sites tucked into the woods. The walk-in sites are spread out in a chain along the creek. The campground is unique in the South Willow Canyon because sites can be reserved in blocks for group use.
Campsites, facilities: There are eight walk-in sites (RVs are not recommended). Picnic tables, fire rings, garbage service, and a vault toilet are provided. There is no drinking water. Leashed pets permitted.
Reservations, fees: Reservations are accepted at 800/444-6777 or online at www.recreation.gov and must be made at minimum of four days in advance. Sites are $10, group sites 1–4 are $35 for up to 30 people and five vehicles, group sites 1–6 are $60 for up to 50

people and eight vehicles. Extra vehicles are $6. Open late May through early October, weather permitting.
Directions: From Grantsville, drive south on Cooley Street for five miles. Turn right on South Willow Road and continue 6.1 miles to the Upper Narrows Campground on the left side of the road.
GPS Coordinates: N 40° 29.510' W 112° 35.687'
Contact: Salt Lake City Ranger District, 801/466-6411, www.fs.fed.us/r4/uwc/recreation/wcnf/camping/slrd/stansbury_mtn_cg.shtml#upper-narrows-cg

6 LOOP
🚶 🏕 ⛺

Scenic rating: 8

in the Stansbury Mountains in Wasatch-Cache National Forest

Map 2.1, page 81

Loop Campground is the last campground in the upper reaches of South Willow Canyon. It's the biggest, most developed campground in the canyon. The trailhead for the Mill Fork Trail leaves from the upper end of the camp loop. Mill Fork Trail leads up 11,031-foot Deseret Peak in the Deseret Peak Wilderness. The peak is the highest point in Tooele County, with commanding summit views of the Bonneville Salt Flats to the west and the Oquirrh Mountain Range to the east. The trail is popular with hikers and horseback riders, and there's a horse corral at the trailhead. The campground has a cool, relaxing atmosphere and offers views of the surrounding Stansbury Mountains. Mornings are particularly nice at the campground, sites are in the shade, temperatures are cool, and the warm morning sun lights up the east face of Deseret Peak. An open and varied forest provides shade for campers. The forest is mostly box elder, Douglas fir, and aspens. Boy Scouts planted many of the fir trees around the sites in 1966 in a mass planting

© MIKE MATSON

Deseret Peak seen through aspen trees from Loop Campground

effort called the Beauty Project. The campground loop and parking aprons are gravel, and the road is not in great shape—bring your high clearance vehicle.

Campsites, facilities: There are eight single sites (1A is a walk-in site) and one double site (RVs are not recommended). Picnic tables, fire pits, a horse corral, garbage service, and vault toilets are provided. There is no drinking water. Leashed pets permitted.

Reservations, fees: Reservations are not accepted. Single sites are $10, double sites are $20, and extra vehicles and day use are $6. Open late May through early October, weather permitting.

Directions: From Grantsville, drive south on Cooley Street for five miles. Turn right on South Willow Road and continue 7.2 miles to the Loop Campground at the end of the road.

GPS Coordinates: N 40° 28.976' W 112° 36.438'

Contact: Salt Lake City Ranger District, 801/466-6411, www.fs.fed.us/ r4/uwc/recreation/wcnf/camping/slrd/ stansbury_mtn_cg.shtml#loop-cg

▼ CLOVER SPRINGS

Scenic rating: 7

In the Onaqui Mountains, southwest of Tooele

Map 2.1, page 81

Clover Springs Campground is located near Johnson's Pass in the modest Onaqui Mountains. The campground sits just east of the mysterious Dugway Proving Grounds, where the U.S. Army tests and maintains chemical and biological weapons. Clover Springs is a BLM campground managed by Tooele County. The campground is in a desert setting with Juniper trees, sagebrush, Mormon tea, and wild grasses. The facility is divided into two loops, one for equestrians and one with standard campsites. The access loop and parking aprons are gravel. A hiking and horseback-riding trail leads out from sites 10 and 11. No motor vehicles are allowed on the trail. A small creek runs by site 6. Along the creek box elder and cottonwood tress provide some shade. This out-of-the-way campground is good place to find peace and solitude.

Campsites, facilities: There are 10 single sites—two are equestrian-only (sites 8 and

9)—and one group site for up to 50 people and 10 vehicles. Picnic tables, fire pits, fire grills, two horse corrals, and vault toilets are provided. Site 5 is wheelchair accessible via a paved trail to the toilet and parking. Site 1 has a covered picnic table. There is no drinking water. Leashed pets permitted.

Reservations, fees: Reservations are required for the group site by calling 801/977-4380. Individual sites are $6 and the group site is $20. Open May through October.

Directions: From Tooele, drive south 16 miles on Rte. 36 and turn west (right) onto Rte. 199. Continue 6.1 miles and turn left into the Clover Springs Campground.

GPS Coordinates: N 40° 20.823' W 112° 33.045'

Contact: Salt Lake BLM Field Office, 801/977-4300, www.blm.gov/ut/st/en/fo/salt_lake/recreation/camping/clover_creek.html

8 SIMPSON SPRINGS

Scenic rating: 8

west of the Sheeprock Mountains on the historic Pony Express Trail

Map 2.1, page 81

Simpson Spring is a rare reliable water source in the barren desert east of the Dugway Proving Grounds. The springs were utilized by the Pony Express riders on their lonely rides across the inhospitable landscape. There is a historic marker and refurbished Pony Express cabin, used as a layover spot for riders on their way from Missouri to California. The riders pushed hard and rode fast, traveling more than 1,800 miles in 10 days. Simpson Springs is also the site of a Civilian Conservation Corps (CCC) camp 1939–1942. The CCC worked on road development and range of projects along the Pony Express Trail. The camp included barracks, a mess hall, officer quarters, a recreation hall, swimming pool, and support bunkers. The builders were disassembled at the start of World War II. In the present-day campground, juniper

trees, sagebrush, and Mormon tea grow around the campsites. The campground is open and exposed, with minimal shade. It gets pretty hot, so bring some shade if you plan on spending any time here. The gravel loop leads to tightly spaced sites that feel too close together in such a vast landscape. Sites look out west toward the Dugway Proving Grounds, the Deep Creek Range, the Dugway Mountains Range, and up north to the Simpson Mountains. A note of caution: Simpson Springs is about as close as the government will allow civilians to the Dugway Proving Grounds. Take care not to wander too far west, and avoid touching any mysterious objects. Undetonated explosives have been found outside the Proving Grounds boundaries.

Campsites, facilities: There are 20 sites. Picnic tables, barbeque grills, rock fire rings, pull-through sites, and vault toilets are provided. There is no potable water. Leashed pets permitted.

Reservations, fees: Reservations are not accepted. The fee is $5. Open year-round.

Directions: From Tooele, drive south 16 miles on Rte. 36 and turn west (right) onto Rte. 199. Travel 21 miles and turn left at the end of Rte. 199 before the restricted entrance to Dugway. After seven miles stay to the right at the Y intersection, and again in three miles take the right fork. Continue 10 miles and turn left into the Simpson Springs Campground.

GPS Coordinates: N 40° 02.134' W 112° 46.970'

Contact: Salt Lake BLM Field Office, 801/977-4300, www.blm.gov/ut/st/en/fo/salt_lake/recreation/camping/simpson_springs.html

9 VERNON RESERVOIR

Scenic rating: 6

southeast of Vernon in the Wasatch-Cache National Forest

Map 2.2, page 82

Vernon Reservoir is a small reservoir east of the Sheeprock Mountains. The reservoir is used to irrigate local farms and is routinely drawn down in late summer. It still offers fishing, though, and is stocked with rainbow trout. The main campground area at Vernon is a glorified parking lot with sites circling the lot. Views look down on the reservoir and across to the rolling juniper- and sagebrush-covered hills. There are three separate areas circling the lake where simple sites are located. On the southwest shore a fence with a narrow gate allows anglers access but keeps the cows at bay. Sites offer covered picnic tables on cement pads, but they are dirty and rather unappealing. The campground has a forgotten feel to it, with a sign advertising for its adoption. Vernon will appeal to campers looking for solitude and a quiet place to fish. Unless it's a busy weekend, you should be able to have the peaceful spot all to yourself.

Campsites, facilities: There are nine single sites and one double site. Covered picnic tables on concrete pads, fire grills, and vault toilets are provided. There is no drinking water. Leashed pets permitted.

Reservations, fees: Reservations are not accepted. There is no fee. Open June through October.

Directions: From Vernon, drive south on Rte. 36 for 0.6 mile, turn right and after five miles and turn left at the intersection. Continue 2.6 miles and turn right into the main Vernon Reservoir campground area.

GPS Coordinates: N 39° 59.553' W 112° 23.161'

Contact: Spanish Fork Ranger District, 801/798-3571, www.fs.fed.us/r4/uinta/recreation/camping/spanish_fork/index.shtml#vernon

🔟 WHITE SANDS
🏃 🏕 ⛰

Scenic rating: 8

In the Little Sahara Recreation Area

Map 2.2, page 82

The Little Sahara Recreation Area is a huge sand dune complex on the eastern edge of the Sevier Desert. Sevier Desert is part of the vast expanse of barren land in the central part of western Utah. The sand is left over from the last ice age, when much of western Utah was covered by a huge inland sea, now referred to as Lake Bonneville. The sand was deposited where the Sevier River used to empty into the lake. Lake Bonneville has since receded dramatically, and southwesterly winds have transported the white sands north to create the Little Sahara Recreation Area. The recreation area encompasses 124 square miles of giant, free-flowing sand dunes around Sand Mountain. Little Sahara offers two distinct experiences for visitors. Sand Mountain has a 700-foot wall of sand, the ultimate proving ground for ATV, dune buggy, and motorcycle riders. Steep slopes, open bowls, convex rollovers, arcing ridges, and gentle dunes of sand create a complex playground to test both man and machine. Riders and non-riders agree this part of the park can get crazy. Every year, there are serious accidents on the dunes. For a peaceful, nonmotorized desert experience, head to the Rockwell Outstanding Natural Area. The Rockwell Area protects 9,000 acres of natural habitat for deer, birds, and reptiles. White Sands Campground is a relatively primitive campground located at the northeast end of the white sand dunes. The campground loops are literally in and around the dunes. Sand is everywhere. The access loops are made of sand, which makes getting into the sites in a passenger car a little sketchy, though not impossible. Except for the picnic tables, the sites are entirely sand, a good or bad thing depending on your perspective. If you aren't interested in camping directly in the sand, check out the other campgrounds in the park. The campground has juniper trees growing around the campsites. These scrubby trees offer a little shade at the edges of day, but not much during the hottest hours.

Campsites, facilities: There are 100 sites in Loops A, B, and C. Picnic tables, garbage service, flush toilets (vault toilets only in the winter), barbeque grills, fire pits, drinking water, and a fenced sand play area are provided. Leashed pets permitted.

Reservations, fees: Reservations are not accepted. The entrance fee is $8 ($10 on holidays) per vehicle and includes use of the campgrounds. Open year-round.

Directions: From Delta, drive north on Hwy. 6 for 34 miles and turn left at the sign for the Little Sahara Recreation Area. Drive 4.4 miles, turn left, continue 2.1 miles (past the entrance station), and turn right. Continue 1.4 miles to the White Sands Campground.

GPS Coordinates: N 39° 44.440' W 112° 18.988'

Contact: Fillmore Field Office, 435/743-3100, www.blm.gov/ut/st/en/fo/fillmore/recreation/special_recreation/little_sahara_recreation.html

11 JERICHO

Scenic rating: 8

in the Little Sahara Recreation Area

Map 2.2, page 82

If you're looking for shade in Little Sahara Recreation Area, Jericho may be the only place to find it. This modest campground loop features covered picnic tables that may help abate the midday heat and blinding white glare reflecting off the dunes. Jericho started out as a picnic area and then was adapted to a campground when the hundreds of other sites in the park proved inadequate. That doesn't make it a bad place to camp. Jericho is in a beautiful setting, below a picturesque sand hill. It's small compared to the other campgrounds in Little Sahara, and it is off by itself, where the throngs of weekend warriors feel at least an arm's length away. There's just one tree in the actual campground, so except for the covered tables, you'll be out in the open. And while there may be fewer other campers around you, there's still very little privacy when the park is busy.

Campsites, facilities: This is a large picnic area, overflow camping area, and a group camping area. Amenities include 40 covered picnic tables, a fenced sand play area, fire pits, barbeque

grills, flush toilets, drinking water, and an amphitheater. Leashed pets permitted.

Reservations, fees: Reservations are not accepted. The entrance fee is $8 ($10 on holidays) per vehicle and includes use of the campgrounds. Open year-round.

Directions: From Delta, drive north on Hwy. 6 for 34 miles and turn left at the sign for the Little Sahara Recreation Area. Drive 4.4 miles, turn left, and continue seven miles (past the entrance station). Turn left and drive 0.5 mile to the Jericho Campground.

GPS Coordinates: N 39° 41.222' W 112° 22.032'

Contact: Fillmore Field Office, 435/743-3100, www.blm.gov/ut/st/en/fo/fillmore/recreation/special_recreation/little_sahara_recreation.html

12 OASIS

Scenic rating: 7

in the Little Sahara Recreation Area

Map 2.2, page 82

Oasis is the most developed of all the campgrounds in the Little Sahara Recreation Area. Compared with the sand loops of White Sands Campground and the undeveloped free-for-all at Sand Mountain, Oasis is more of a traditional campground, like you'd expect to find at a destination park or recreation area. The campground has well-defined sites with tent pads, picnic tables, paved loops and parking, and modern restrooms with running water. These amenities and an RV dump station make it stand out as the most accommodating campground in Little Sahara. The sites are mostly gravel and sand, with juniper trees providing some separation between you and your neighbors. Sites are fairly close together, but that's a necessity considering the popularity of the park.

Campsites, facilities: There are 115 sites. Picnic tables, drinking water, flush toilets, a dump station, garbage service, barbeque

© MIKE MATSON

Sand Mountain in the Little Sahara Recreation Area

grills, and fire pits are provided. Leashed pets permitted.

Reservations, fees: Reservations are not accepted. The entrance fee is $8 ($10 on holidays) per vehicle and includes use of the campgrounds. Open year-round.

Directions: From Delta, drive north on Hwy. 6 for 34 miles and turn left at the sign for the Little Sahara Recreation Area. Drive 4.4 miles, turn left, and continue seven miles (past the entrance station) to the Oasis Campground on the right side of the road.

GPS Coordinates: N 39° 41.347' W 112° 21.279'

Contact: Fillmore Field Office, 435/743-3100, www.blm.gov/ut/st/en/fo/fillmore/recreation/special_recreation/little_sahara_recreation.html

13 SAND MOUNTAIN

Scenic rating: 8

in the Little Sahara Recreation Area

Map 2.2, page 82

If you want to maximize your riding and spectating time on the dunes and don't mind the comings and goings of the Sand Mountain scene, you might as well camp right at the base of the biggest dune of them all, Sand Mountain. The campground at Sand Mountain is simple. Paved parking leads to open sites that are perfect for RV camping and front-door access to riding opportunities. Views from the campsites look right up to the sand playground above. The wide-open format and vendor area make it feel like a rock concert parking lot on busy weekends. The tradeoff for all this convenience is the bare-bones facility.

Campsites, facilities: This is a primitive camping area without designated sites. An open, paved parking/camping area, a vendor area, garbage service, flush toilets (vault toilets in the winter), and drinking water are provided. Leashed pets permitted.

Reservations, fees: Reservations are not accepted. The entrance fee is $8 ($10 on holidays) per vehicle and includes use of the campgrounds. Open year-round.

Directions: From Delta, drive north on Hwy. 6 for 34 miles and turn left at the sign for the Little Sahara Recreation Area. Drive 4.4 miles, turn left, and continue 11.3 miles (past the entrance station) and enter the Sand Mountain Camping Area.

GPS Coordinates: N 39° 38.527' W 112° 23.169'
Contact: Fillmore Field Office, 435/743-3100, www.blm.gov/ut/st/en/fo/fillmore/recreation/special_recreation/little_sahara_recreation.html

14 OAK CREEK

Scenic rating: 8

in Fishlake National Forest

Map 2.2, page 82

Oak Creek is a small, peaceful Forest Service campground in a narrow, scenic canyon. The landscape around the campground is made up of crags and rock hills in the Canyon Mountains. A group-oriented loop has a large amphitheater that is shaded by a grove of gambel oaks and cedars trees. The group loop also features a covered group picnic area of timeless character, with generations of names carved into the brown wood roof. The roof protects two long picnic tables from the elements. Group Unit 1 is next to Oak Creek, where it's easy to spot small trout swimming in the pools. The quiet campground has well-spaced individual sites. These sites are well shaded by all the oak trees and feel cool even with temperatures in the high 80s. The campground also has a central field with volleyball poles. Bring your own net to string up on the poles.

Campsites, facilities: There are six single sites and four group sites for up to 32, 48, 50, or 96 people, depending on the site. Picnic tables, fire pits, barbeque grills, vault toilets, and a volleyball court are provided. There is no drinking water. Leashed pets permitted.

Reservations, fees: Reservations are accepted for the group sites only at 877/444-6777 or online at www.recreation.gov. The fee is $10 per night for individual sites, $30–60 for group sites, and $5 for extra vehicles. Open May through September.

Directions: From Oak City, drive east for 4.2 miles on Forest Road 89.
GPS Coordinates: N 39° 21.002' W 112° 15.984'
Contact: Fillmore Ranger District, 435/743-5721, www.fs.fed.us/r4/fishlake/recreation/camping/oakcreek.htm

15 OASIS AT YUBA STATE PARK

Scenic rating: 7

on Yuba Reservoir

Map 2.2, page 82

Yuba Reservoir is a 22-mile-long reservoir on the Sevier River. The state park has three different campgrounds, each with unique character. The lake is rimmed with white sand swimming beaches and has a seemingly endless surface area to boat on. The wind blows hard in the open valley, making it a great place for windsurfing and sailing. Two boat ramps provide access to the lake. Year-round fishing is possible on the reservoir for rainbow trout, northern pike, walleye, perch, and catfish. Oasis Campground is set in the northwest shore of the lake, offering shorefront camping in a developed campground with all the modern amenities you'd expect at a Utah State Park. The camp loop is paved and leads to sites with everything from green grass lawns to unimproved gravel with native vegetation. Sagebrush grows around the campground, and cottonwood trees shade many of the sites. Lower water levels leave several hundred yards between the campground and the water, but this doesn't seem to be an inconvenience for swimmers enjoying the lake's aquamarine waters.

Campsites, facilities: There are 28 campsites and a group area for up to 75 people. Site 1 is wheelchair accessible. Picnic tables, fire grills, pull-through sites, modern restrooms with showers, drinking water, a dump station, and garbage service are provided. Ice is available. Leashed pets permitted.

Reservations, fees: Reservations are accepted at 800/322-3770 or online at www.reserveamerica.com and must be made a minimum of two days in advance and can be arranged up to 16 weeks in advance. Sites are $14, the group site is $100, extra vehicles are $8, and the day-use fee is $7. Open year-round.
Directions: From Nephi, drive south 25 miles on I-15, take Exit 202, drive south five miles, and turn left into the campground.
GPS Coordinates: N 39° 22.610' W 112° 01.659'
Contact: Yuba State Park, 435/758-2611, http://stateparks.utah.gov/stateparks/parks/yuba/

16 NORTH AND WEST BEACHES AT YUBA STATE PARK

Scenic rating: 7

on Yuba Reservoir

Map 2.2, page 82

The North and West Beaches at Yuba State Park offer a wide-open, unrestricted camping experience right on the shore of the lake. The half moon of white beach that rings the northern tip of the lake fills up with RVs, tents, and campers and their watercraft. The facilities at the beach sites are minimal, but that doesn't affect its popularity. Bring everything you need, from sunshades to lawn chairs. There are fire pits and a smattering of picnic tables, but that's about it. With one look, you'll know if the North and West Beaches are for you. Expect a party, not a nature experience.
Campsites, facilities: This area is for dispersed beach camping, and there are no designated sites. Picnic tables, fire pits, garbage service, and vault toilets are provided. Leashed pets permitted. Leashed pets permitted.
Reservations, fees: Reservations are accepted at 800/322-3770 or online at www.reserveamerica.com; they must be made a minimum of two days in advance and may be arranged up

to 16 weeks in advance. Sites are $10 and the day-use fee is $7. Open year-round.
Directions: From Nephi, drive south 25 miles on I-15 and take Exit 202, then drive south five miles and turn left into the campground.
GPS Coordinates: N 39° 24.475' W 112° 01.665'
Contact: Yuba State Park, 435/758-2611, http://stateparks.utah.gov/stateparks/parks/yuba/

17 MAPLE HOLLOW

Scenic rating: 7

in the Fishlake National Forest

Map 2.2, page 82

Maple Hollow is a quiet, walk-in, tent campground in the Fishlake National Forest. A hiking trail starting at Maple Hollow leads up to Jack's Peak (10,072 feet) and Coffee Peak (10,005 feet) in the Pavant Mountains. Birds chirp quietly in the maple, gambel oak, spruce, and cottonwood trees that shade the campsites. The forest canopy provides protected habitat for hummingbirds, which buzz between wildflowers in the tall grass. It's also home to yellow-and-black swallowtail and orange painted lady butterflies. At almost 7,000 feet, the forest is quiet, shaded, cool, and comfortable. A system of concrete and gravel paths connects sites and leads to water spigots and bathrooms. Sites vary tremendously in quality and style, so take a quick walk around before choosing your site.
Campsites, facilities: There are 12 walk-in sites. Sites 2 and 10 are wheelchair accessible via paved paths. Picnic tables, cement fire rings, vault toilets, and drinking water are provided. Leashed pets permitted.
Reservations, fees: Reservations are not accepted. There is no fee for the sites. There is a $25 fee to rent the entire campground for a group. Open Memorial Day to Labor Day.
Directions: From Holden, drive east six miles on Forest Road 098. The campground is on the left side of the road.

GPS Coordinates: N 39° 03.707' W 112° 10.351'

Contact: Fillmore Ranger District, 435/743-5721, www.fs.fed.us/r4/fishlake/recreation/camping/maplehollow.htm

18 MAPLE GROVE

Scenic rating: 7

in Fishlake National Forest

Map 2.2, page 82

Maple Grove Campground sits at the northern end of the Pavant Mountains east of Coffee Peak. The campground was constructed by the Civilian Conservation Corps in 1938. Like the name suggests, the campground is carved out of grove of broad-leaved maple trees. Gambel oak and juniper trees add to the site's lush green décor, and long, waving grass grows around the campsites. Reddish-brown rock cliffs stand guard over the forest. The parking slips and campground loop are both paved. Views from camp look down over Highway 50 at the distant Valley Mountains. A hiking trail leaving from Site 10 leads up into the Pavant Mountains and eventually to the summit of 10,005-foot Coffee Peak.

Campsites, facilities: There are 22 single sites and three group sites for up to 56, 96, or 100 people, depending on the site. The group sites and many of the individual sites are wheelchair accessible. Picnic tables, barbeque grills, vault toilets, and drinking water are provided. Leashed pets permitted.

Reservations, fees: Reservations are accepted for the group sites only at 877/444-6777 or online at www.recreation.gov. Individual sites are $10, group sites are $50–90, and extra vehicles are $5. Open mid-May through mid-September.

Directions: From Salina, drive northwest on Hwy. 50 for approximately 13 miles, turn left at Mile Marker 146, and continue 3.6 miles to the campground.

GPS Coordinates: N 39° 01.111' W 112° 05.344'

Contact: Fillmore Ranger District, 435/743-5721, www.fs.fed.us/r4/fishlake/recreation/camping/maplegrove.htm

19 WAGON WEST RV PARK

Scenic rating: 5

in Fillmore

Map 2.3, page 83

Wagon West RV Park is right off Main Street in Fillmore. The RV park has views up Pavant (also spelled Pahvant) Mountain Range east of town. It's near the historical Territorial House State Park. On September 8, 1851, Governor Brigham Young designated Fillmore the state's capital and named the town after President Millard Fillmore. The red rock capitol building was constructed 1852–1855. The state park has a nice rose garden, informative interpretive signs, open grass lawns, and other pioneer-era buildings complementing the capitol building. The historical park doesn't offer camping, making Wagon West RV Park the closest place to spend the night. Wagon West features a gravel yard and grass sites, some of which are shaded by large-leaved trees. The campground is popular with ATV enthusiasts who station themselves in centrally located Fillmore to enjoy the surrounding network of trails. The 275-mile-long Paiute ATV Trail can be accessed in Fillmore. Riders often spend three or four days traversing the trail, stopping to camp out, fishing, taking pictures, and watching wildlife.

Campsites, facilities: There are 55 RV sites. There are no tent sites. Amenities include a dump station, a RV washing station, cable TV, drinking water, garbage service, modern restrooms with showers, and a convenience store. Leashed pets permitted.

Reservations, fees: Reservations are accepted at 435/743-6188. RV sites are $26. Open year-round.

Directions: From I-15, take Exit 167 and drive south on Main Street toward downtown Fillmore. Wagon West RV Park will be on the right side of the road.
GPS Coordinates: N 38° 58.857' W 112° 19.358'
Contact: Wagon West RV Park, 435/743-6188.

20 FILLMORE KOA

Scenic rating: 5

near the town of Fillmore

Map 2.3, page 83

The Fillmore KOA is set in a quiet rural lot a half mile off Main Street and far enough from I-15 to be out of earshot of the highway. Views of the Pavant Mountains can be enjoyed from the campground. Like Wagon West RV, the Fillmore KOA is busy with ATV riders traveling on or accessing the epic Paiute ATV Trail. The KOA sites are grass with gravel parking slips. Tall trees add to the campground's rural, relaxed feel. Tight spacing of sites guarantees you'll get to know your neighbors.

Campsites, facilities: There are 49 RV sites, seven tent sites, and five cabins. Picnic tables, drinking water, modern restrooms with showers, a swimming pool (open seasonally), a playground, a volleyball court, a horseshoe pit, WiFi, and garbage service are provided. Firewood is available. Leashed pets permitted.

Reservations, fees: Reservations are accepted at 800/562-1516 or online at https://koa.com/where/ut/44150/reserve/. Full hook-up sites are $26.50–30, partial hook-up sites are $23, tent sites are $21, and cabins are $40–47. Open March through early December.

Directions: From Main Street in Fillmore, turn east onto 200 S (Canyon Road). Continue for three miles until it turns into Forest Road 100 and becomes gravel. The Fillmore KOA will be on the left side.
GPS Coordinates: N 38° 56.927' W 112° 20.128'

Contact: Fillmore KOA, 435/743-4420, www.koa.com/where/ut/44150/

21 ADELAIDE

Scenic rating: 6

on the west side of the Pavant Mountains in Fishlake National Forest

Map 2.3, page 83

Adelaide is a Forest Service campground set on the banks of Corn Creek near the town of Fillmore. Corn Creek has good fishing for brown trout, which don't seem to mind its slightly murky waters. Watch for rattlesnakes down by the water—the creek bottom is notorious for frequent reptile encounters. The flat, gravel loop accesses shaded sites under mature cottonwood trees. The campground is small, quiet, and far enough off the beaten path to only fill up on weekends. A group site features an amphitheater and a group fire ring.

Campsites, facilities: There are eight individual sites and one group site for up to 48 people. Picnic tables, drinking water, fire grills, vault toilets, and an amphitheater are provided. Leashed pets permitted.

Reservations, fees: Reservations are accepted only for the group site at 877/444-6777 or online at www.recreation.gov and must be made a minimum of one day in advance. Individual sites are $8, and the group site is $50. Open mid-May through mid-September.

Directions: From I-15, take Exit 158 and travel south on Rte. 133 to Kanosh. Turn left on 300 S (Corn Creek Road) and drive six miles southeast to the campground. Corn Creek Road turns into Canyon Road (Forest Road 106).
GPS Coordinates: N 38° 75.361' W 112° 36.361'
Contact: Fillmore Ranger District, 435/743-5721, www.fs.fed.us/r4/fishlake/recreation/camping/adelaide.htm

22 RICHFIELD KOA

Scenic rating: 3

in Richfield

Map 2.3, page 83

Richfield KOA is located in a quiet neighborhood in Richfield. Richfield is near the Paiute ATV Trail, Yuba Reservoir, the Sevier Plateau, and the remote Pavant Mountains. It's also relatively close to Fish Lake and the little-visited northern part of Capitol Reef National Park. The KOA is bordered by a school, a road, and the Red Hills Trailer Park. The full-service RV park is clean and well maintained. Lots of large cottonwood trees shade the grounds, and open grass lawns give the campground a city park feel. With a swimming pool and a miniature golf course, it almost feels like an amusement park. Richfield is a good pit stop while exploring south central Utah, and this KOA is by far the best camping option in Richfield.

Campsites, facilities: There are 87 RV sites, five tent areas, and three cabins. Amenities include picnic tables, barbeque grills, modern restrooms with showers, horseshoe pits, a swimming pool, a basketball court, drinking water, a pet walk area, a playground, WiFi, cable TV, and garbage service. Laundry, miniature golf, firewood, and bicycle rentals are available. Leashed pets permitted.

Reservations, fees: Reservations are accepted at 888/562-4703 or online at www.koa.com/where/ut/44109/reserve/. Full hook-up RV sites are $29–31.50, tent sites are $20, and cabins are $37.50. Open March through October.

Directions: From I-70, take Exit 40 and drive two miles south on Main Street/Hwy. 89, then turn west (right) on 600 S and drive 0.4 mile to the Richfield KOA.

GPS Coordinates: N 38° 45.609' W 112° 05.703'

Contact: Richfield KOA, 435/896-6674, www.koa.com/where/ut/44109/

23 RICHFIELD RV PARK

Scenic rating: 1

in Richfield

Map 2.3, page 83

The Richfield RV Park is not an inspiring campground—in fact, quite the opposite. Crammed behind a convenience store on a tiny lot off Main Street in Richfield, the RV park more closely resembles a truck stop than a campground. A single row of sites lines a chain link fence looking out over the adjacent farmland. The amenities are minimal. Small wood fences divide tightly packed sites. Because room is limited, parking spaces for additional vehicles aren't provided. The lot is close enough to Main Street to expect road noise, and the sites are so close together it doesn't really matter. You're more likely to hear your neighbor snoring through the night than trucks lumbering past on the business loop. Many of the sites are occupied by long-term campers.

Campsites, facilities: There are 21 full hook-up (20, 30 amps) and 17 pull-through sites. There are no tent sites. A dump station, garbage service, drinking water, and modern restrooms are provided. Laundry, a convenience store, and RV washing station are available. Leashed pets permitted.

Reservations, fees: Reservations are not accepted. RV sites are $19. Open year-round.

Directions: From I-70, take Exit 40 and drive 2.2 miles south on Main Street/Hwy. 89. The Richfield RV Park will be on the left side of the road.

GPS Coordinates: N 38° 45.468' W 112° 05.034'

Contact: Richfield RV Park, 435/896-5609.

24 CASTLE ROCK AT FREMONT INDIAN STATE PARK

🏃 🏕 ♿ 🚐 ⛰

Scenic rating: 8

southwest of Richfield

Map 2.3, page 83   BEST (

Fremont Indian State Park is located on the northern slopes of the Tushar Mountains. The state park features a museum celebrating a collection of Fremont Indian artifacts and rock paintings in Clear Creek Canyon. The pictographs and thousands of artifacts were stumbled across during the construction of I-70, when the largest known Fremont Indian village was discovered at Five Finger Ridge. Twelve interpretive trails leaving from the park museum lead to the pictograph panels. The Castle Rock Campground at the state park is set in a lovely canyon carved out of unique hoodoo rock towers. The towers are similar to those found in Bryce Canyon National Park but are brown in color and much smaller. The towers have distinct sedimentary layers near the top of the formation, which also distinguishes them from other famous Utah rock forms. The camp loop is tucked into a forest of aspen, cottonwood, juniper, and pinyon pine trees adjacent to the rocks. Joe Lott Creek runs through the campground and adds to the already pleasant atmosphere. The parking spaces are gravel and are adequate for small RVs as well as passenger cars. Sites are well distributed in the forest and offer privacy from other campers.

Campsites, facilities: There are 31 sites. Sites 10 and 28 are wheelchair accessible. Picnic tables, barbeque grills, modern restrooms, vault toilets, drinking water (seasonally), and garbage service are provided. Firewood is available. Leashed pets permitted.

Reservations, fees: Reservations are accepted at 800/322-3770 or online at www.reserveamerica.com for single sites; they must be made a minimum of two days in advance and can be arranged up to 16 weeks in advance. Single sites are $12, double sites are $28, extra vehicles are $6, and day use is $6. Fees include access to the museum. Open year-round.

Directions: From Richfield, drive 23 miles southwest on I-70 and take Exit 17. Drive south across the freeway overpass and continue 1.2 miles to the Castle Rock Campground. GPS Coordinates: N 38° 33.287' W 112° 21.328'

Contact: Fremont Indian State Park, 435/527-4631, http://stateparks.utah.gov/stateparks/parks/fremont/

25 LIZZIE AND CHARLIE'S RV/ATV PARK

🏃 🏕 🚐 ⛰

Scenic rating: 7

in Marysvale

Map 2.3, page 83

Lizzie and Charlie's RV/ATV Park is ATV heaven. As its slogan proclaims, it is "located in the exact center of the ATV Universe." What distinguishes the exact center of the ATV universe from the middle of nowhere? Well, that's debatable, but in this case, Lizzie and Charlie's is near the Paiute ATV Trail system. The Paiute Trail, a network of 900-plus miles of trails in south-central Utah, has been rated in the top 10 in the country by two popular ATV riding magazines. What sets Lizzie and Charlie's apart from other RV parks in the region is its enthusiasm and hospitality for RV riders. The park lets riders ride their ATVs into the campground to their sites. A gravel camp loop leads to tightly spaced sites. The sites are shaded by cottonwood trees, and a separate tenting area offers a grass lawn to pitch shelters on. On Saturday nights, Lizzie and Charlie's offers potluck-style Dutch oven meals.

Campsites, facilities: There are 100 full hookup (30, 50 amps) RV sites, seven tent sites, seven cabins, and one cottage. Picnic tables, WiFi, horseshoes, flush toilets, garbage service, a group pavilion, and drinking water are provided. Laundry, a convenience store, a Saturday night Dutch oven dinner, showers, ATV wash station, a dump station, and ice are available. Leashed pets permitted.

Reservations, fees: Reservations are accepted at 435/326-4213. RV sites with 50-amp hook-ups are $30, sites with 30-amp hook-ups are $25, tent sites are $12, cabins are $45, and the cottage is $149. Open May through October.

Directions: From the junction of I-70 and Hwy. 89 (Exit 23), drive 12.5 miles south on Hwy. 89. Lizzie and Charlie's RV Park will be on the left side of the road.

GPS Coordinates: N 38° 26.586' W 112° 13.406'

Contact: Lizzie and Charlie's RV/ATV Park, 435/326-4213, www.lizzieandcharlies.com/

26 PIUTE STATE PARK

Scenic rating: 7

north of the town of Junction on the Piute Reservoir

Map 2.3, page 83

Set on the shores of the north end of the Piute Reservoir, this state park campground looks south to the distant Sevier Plateau to the east, the Tushar Mountains to the west, and rolling foothills around the lake. The park's recreational opportunities center on the lake and include boating, fishing, swimming, picnicking, and wildlife-viewing. Catchable fish include smallmouth bass and rainbow, cutthroat, and brown trout. At the boat launch area on the north end of the lake, a large, paved boat ramp offers easy boat access to the water and a floating dock. There's a day-use picnic area with six covered picnic tables. Long-eared jackrabbits hop through the sagebrush, tamarisk, and Mormon tea plants near the picnic tables. The primitive campground is separate from the picnic area and sits on the northwest shore of the lake. Big cottonwood trees provide shade for some of the sites. The lakeshore sites have flat areas for tents. The camping facilities are bare bones, with a handful of picnic tables scattered around the eight sites. Otherwise, the sites are simply open ground on the lakeshore. For $9 a night, it doesn't feel like a very good deal.

Campsites, facilities: There are eight sites. Vault toilets, fire rings, a handful of picnic tables, and some fire grills are provided. Leashed pets permitted.

Reservations, fees: Reservations are not accepted. The fee is $9 per site, $8 for an extra vehicle, and $5 for day use. Open year-round.

Directions: From Junction, drive north on Hwy. 89 for 5.3 miles, turn right, and continue 0.8 mile to the gravel road, which leads down to the lake and campground.

GPS Coordinates: N 38° 19.451' W 112° 12.534'

Contact: Piute State Park, 435/624-3268, http://stateparks.utah.gov/stateparks/parks/piute/

27 MINERSVILLE LAKE PARK

Scenic rating: 5

on the Minersville Reservoir, west of Beaver

Map 2.3, page 83

Minersville Lake Park used to be owned and operated as a state park, but in 2005 the facility was transitioned to Beaver County. It sits on the southeast shore of the Minersville Reservoir. The lake offers activities such as boating, fishing, and swimming on its waters. Fish species in the reservoir include smallmouth bass and cutthroat and rainbow trout. Trout must be over 20 inches long in order to be taken. A paved, wide boat ramp makes for easy lake access. The lake is surrounded by brown desert hills spotted with sporadic juniper trees. The campground has a single loop leading to sites with covered picnic tables and a large covered group pavilion. Some of the sites have built up gravel tent pads. Aside from the covered tables, the sites have an open feel, with views of the lake and the surrounding Tushar Mountains. Sagebrush and cottonwood trees grow around the sites. After a busy weekend the campground looked a little abused. Trash cans overflowed with litter, and beer cans were strewn around the sites. The campground appears a bit neglected and needs to be respected by its users.

Campsites, facilities: There are 29 RV sites with electric hook-ups, 18 tent sites, a group area, and a picnic area. Covered picnic tables with storage shelves, modern restrooms with showers, fire grills, drinking water, garbage service, boat dock, boat ramp, and dump station are provided. Leashed pets permitted.

Reservations, fees: Reservations are not accepted. Sites are $17, extra vehicles are $9, and day use is $5 per vehicle and $2 per bicycle. Open April 1 through November 1.

Directions: From Beaver, drive west on Rte. 21 for 12 miles. Turn right into the Minersville Lake campground.

GPS Coordinates: N 38° 13.129' W 112° 49.646'

Contact: Beaver County, 435/438-5472.

28 UNITED BEAVER CAMPERLAND

Scenic rating: 5

in Beaver

Map 2.3, page 83

United Beaver Campground is in a country setting in Beaver with distant views of the Tushar Mountains. Located just off the highway exit, the campground is within earshot of the rumbling interstate. Open fields of sagebrush surround the yard. Large trees provide shade for the grass campsites. The sites are tightly spaced. There are some pull-through sites for big rigs, and permanent trailers share the campground with visitors.

Campsites, facilities: There are 88 full hook-up (30- and 50-amp) RV sites and 30 tent sites. Amenities include picnic tables, barbeque pit, horseshoe pit, swimming pool, laundry, playground, modern restrooms with showers, drinking water, garbage service, and a game room. Leashed pets permitted.

Reservations, fees: Reservations are accepted

at 877/438-2808. Full hook-up sites with 30 amps are $24.95, full hook-up sites with 50 amps are $29.95, and tent sites are $19.50. Open year-round.

Directions: From I-15, take Exit 109, drive one block east, turn right and continue one block to the United Beaver Camperland, on the left side of the road.

GPS Coordinates: N 38° 14.880' W 112° 38.761'

Contact: United Beaver Camperland, 877/438-2808, www.unitedbeavercamperland.com/

29 BEAVER KOA

Scenic rating: 5

in Beaver

Map 2.3, page 83

The town of Beaver is the birthplace of Butch Cassidy, the infamous outlaw of the Wild West. It's also surrounded by wonderful outdoor recreation. Rockhounds like to explore the nearby Mineral Mountains to the west, and in the east the Tushar Mountains offer hiking and mountain biking opportunities. The nine-hole Canyon Breeze Golf Course is only two miles away. Beaver KOA has views up to both the Tushar and Mineral Mountain Ranges. The RV park occupies a quiet setting a good distance off the highway and away from the town of Beaver. RV campsites are lined up close together in orderly rows. The sites feature gravel parking aprons, and scattered trees provide shade. A fence surrounds and protects the campground.

Campsites, facilities: There are 70 RV sites, 25 with full hook-ups (20-, 30-, and 50-amp), as well as three cabins, 10 tent sites, and one group tent area for up to 50 people. Picnic tables, fire grills, a swimming pool (open seasonally), playground, game room, horseshoe pit, volleyball court, WiFi, cable TV, drinking water, garbage service, dump station, and modern restrooms with showers are provided. Firewood, laundry, and a convenience store are available. Leashed pets permitted.

Reservations, fees: Reservations can be made at 800/562-2912 or online at https://koa.com/where/ut/44102/reserve/. Full hook-up sites are $33, partial hook-up sites are $30, tent sites are $20, and cabins are $39–59. Open March through October.

Directions: From I-15, take Exit 112, turn left, and continue 0.5 mile to Manderfield Road. Turn left onto Manderfield Road and drive 0.25 mile to the Beaver KOA on the right side of the road.

GPS Coordinates: N 38° 17.668' W 112° 38.298'

Contact: Beaver KOA, 435/438-2924, www.koa.com/where/ut/44102/

30 BEAVER CANYON CAMPGROUND

🏠 🏇 ♿ 🚐 ⛺

Scenic rating: 5

in Beaver

Map 2.3, page 83

The Beaver Canyon Campground is on the Beaver Canyon Scenic Byway (Route 153) as it heads toward the Tushar Mountains east of Beaver. You'll be greeted by carved totem poles and intricate country-western-style timber latticework at the campground entrance office. Neatly trimmed grass lawns around the office create a good first impression. The well-maintained campground is in a peaceful rural setting bordered by farmland and occasional houses. Sites are close together and don't offer much privacy. The campground has a unique, hand-built, homegrown feel to it. Sites have a covered eating area, and fences create visual barriers. While Beaver Canyon Campground isn't actually in the canyon, it's only a short drive from great fishing opportunities farther up Beaver Canyon. It is near a golf course and a horse-racing track.

Campsites, facilities: There are 52 full hookup (30-amp), pull-through RV sites and 54 tent sites. Covered eating areas with picnic tables, fire rings, modern restrooms with showers,

drinking water, a playground, and garbage service are provided. Laundry, ice, firewood, and a Mexican restaurant are available. Leashed pets permitted.

Reservations, fees: Reservations are not accepted. RV and tent sites are both $19. Open May 1 to November 1.

Directions: From 1-15, take Exit 109 (Business I-15), drive two miles north on Business I-15, and turn right onto Rte. 153. Continue 1.6 miles east on Rte. 153 to the Beaver Canyon Campground on the left side of the road.

GPS Coordinates: N 38° 16.633' W 112° 36.938'

Contact: Beaver Canyon Campground, 435/438-5654.

31 LITTLE COTTONWOOD

🏊 🏠 ♿ 🚐 ⛺

Scenic rating: 7

in the Tushar Mountains in Fishlake National Forest

Map 2.3, page 83

Little Cottonwood is the first Forest Service Campground along the Beaver Canyon Scenic Byway in the Tushar Mountains. The Tushar Range runs from north to south at the western edge of the Fishlake National Forest. It features lovely, lush alpine meadows and high mountain reservoirs. Little Cottonwood campground is set on the valley floor among a mixed forest of ponderosa pine, juniper, pinyon pine, and cottonwood trees. The Beaver River flows through the campground and offers fishing for rainbow and cutthroat trout, as well as providing a refreshing vitality to the sites. However, keep in mind the fishing is better farther up the canyon in places like Kent's Lake, Little Reservoir, and Anderson Meadow Reservoir. The camp loop and parking spaces are paved. Conglomerate rock cliffs rise above the campground to the north.

Campsites, facilities: There are 13 sites for tents and RVs up to 40 feet in length. Sites 8 and 9 are wheelchair accessible. Picnic tables, fire grills, drinking water, vault toilets, and garbage service are provided. Firewood is available. Leashed pets permitted.

Reservations, fees: Reservations are accepted for the two wheelchair-accessible sites at 435/438-2436. The fee is $14, extra vehicles are $7, and the day-use fee is $5. Open May through October, weather permitting.

Directions: From Beaver, drive east on Rte. 153 for 6.8 miles; Little Cottonwood Campground is on the right side of the road.

GPS Coordinates: N 38° 15.420' W 112° 32.604'

Contact: Beaver Ranger District, 435/438-2436, www.fs.fed.us/r4/fishlake/recreation/camping/littlecottonwood.htm

32 TUSHAR LAKESIDE
🛶 🏕 🚐 ⛰

Scenic rating: 8

in the Tushar Mountains in Fishlake National Forest

Map 2.3, page 83

Tushar Lakeside is a unique campground below Tushar Reservoir that caters to large groups, particularly Girl Scouts, family reunions, and 4-H groups. If the campground isn't reserved for a group, it's open to the public on a first-come, first-served basis. There's good trout fishing on Tushar Reservoir, which is stocked annually with fingerling rainbow. Native brown trout also live in the lake. The campground is below the earthen dam that holds back the reservoir in a mixed forest of aspen, spruce, and fir. The sites are well spread out among the forest along the loop, especially considering its frequent use as a group campground. Views are mostly limited to the forest, but the Tushar Mountains climb quickly from around the shores of the lake.

Campsites, facilities: There are 24 individual sites, and the entire campground can be reserved as a group area for up to 200 people. Picnic tables, fire grills, a group pavilion with electricity, a volleyball court (bring your own net and ball), a horseshoe pit, drinking water,

and flush toilets are provided. Leashed pets permitted.

Reservations, fees: Reservations are accepted at 435/438-2642. Individual sites are $10, and reserving the entire campground for a group costs $100. Open June through September, weather permitting.

Directions: From Beaver, drive east on Rte. 153 for 10.8 miles and turn right onto Forest Road 137. Continue 4.1 miles and turn right into the Tushar Lakeside Group Site.

GPS Coordinates: N 38° 14.377' W 112° 28.179'

Contact: Beaver County, 435/438-2642.

33 LITTLE RESERVOIR
🛶 🏕 ♿ 🚐 ⛰

Scenic rating: 8

in the Tushar Mountains in Fishlake National Forest

Map 2.3, page 83

Little Reservoir Campground sits above an appealing mountain lake in the Tushar Mountains. The loop weaves through a mixed forest of ponderosa pine, spruce, and juniper trees above the lake. Lupine wildflowers bloom in the long grass around the sites and in a lovely meadow above the reservoir. The lake offers great fishing for families and serious anglers, with stocked rainbow trout. The sites on the small paved loop are fairly tightly spaced, but the forest setting and sloping hillside affords some privacy. The campground host was both friendly and accommodating. At 7,000 feet, this campground is lower and warmer than Anderson Meadow, Kent's Lake, and Tushar Lakeside Campgrounds farther up the road.

Campsites, facilities: There are eight sites for tents and RVs up to 40 feet in length. Site 4 is wheelchair accessible. Picnic tables, fire grills, drinking water, and vault toilets are provided. Firewood and bait worms for fishing are available. Leashed pets permitted.

Reservations, fees: Reservations are not

accepted. Sites are $12 and day use is $5. Open June through October, weather permitting.

Directions: From Beaver, drive east on Rte. 153 for 10.8 miles and turn right onto Forest Road 137. Continue 0.8 mile and turn right into the Little Reservoir Campground.

GPS Coordinates: N 38° 15.589' W 112° 29.307'

Contact: Beaver Ranger District, 435/438-2436, www.fs.fed.us/r4/fishlake/recreation/camping/littleres.htm

34 KENT'S LAKE

🚶 🚴 ⛵ 🎣 🛶 🐎 ♿ 🚗 ⛺

Scenic rating: 9

in the Tushar Mountains in Fishlake National Forest

Map 2.3, page 83

This Forest Service Campground is built on the North Shore of Kent's Reservoir, the middle of a series of three reservoirs on the South Fork of the Beaver River. The reservoir was created by an earthen dam built in 1928. The lake is also fed by a series of small natural springs. Kent's Lake is a small reservoir in a high meadow on the lower slopes of Birch Creek Mountain. The lake offers great fishing, especially for families with kids. The reservoir is typically stocked with 2,000 fingerling brook trout and 4,000 rainbow trout each spring. The campground is set in a beautiful aspen, spruce, and fir forest. Open meadows spread down from the campground to the shore of the lake. Views look across the lake at the rocky peaks of the Tushar Mountains. Woodpeckers can be heard industriously knocking on the trees. There's an open, sturdy rock building for a picnic area right above the lake. Sites are well dispersed, with some tucked into the security of the forest and others open on the shore of the lake. The loop and parking aprons are gravel. Below the campground are the trailheads for the Birch Lake, Patterson Hollow, and South Creek ATV Trails.

Campsites, facilities: There are 30 single sites and two family sites (for up to 16 people) for tents and RVs up to 60 feet in length. Sites 2, 8, and 32 are wheelchair accessible. Picnic tables, fire grills, fire rings, and vault toilets are provided. Firewood is available. Leashed pets permitted.

Reservations, fees: Reservations are not accepted. Single sites are $12, family sites are $42, extra vehicles are $6, and day use is $5. Open June through September, weather permitting.

Directions: From Beaver, drive east on Rte. 153 for 10.8 miles and turn right onto Forest Road 137. Continue 4.5 miles and turn right into the Kent's Lake Campground.

GPS Coordinates: N 38° 14.247' W 112° 27.518'

Contact: Beaver Ranger District, 435/438-2436, www.fs.fed.us/r4/fishlake/recreation/camping/kentslake.htm

35 ANDERSON MEADOW

⛵ 🐎 🚗 ⛺

Scenic rating: 9

in the Tushar Mountains in Fishlake National Forest

Map 2.3, page 83   **BEST (**

Anderson Meadow is perched on a hillside above Anderson Meadow Reservoir in the Tushar Mountains. The reservoir looks almost like a natural alpine lake and is fed by the meandering South Fork of the Beaver River. Anderson Meadow itself has been mostly engulfed by the lake, but the upper end offers a pretty wetland and bog area. Cool evenings and mornings are ideal for fly fishing, with the calm water surface broken only by the concentric circles created by jumping trout. The reservoir is stocked annually with rainbow and fingerling cutthroat trout, providing good fishing opportunities. Boating is possible on the lake, although there is no developed boat ramp. Anderson Meadow is one of the best campgrounds in the state for wildlife-viewing. Watch for the deer and moose that frequent the meadow at the edges of the day when the fishing is best. Mountain goats can also be seen near the campground, on the craggy peaks of the Tushar Mountains. The campground is tucked into a forest of noble fir, aspen, and spruce trees. The loop is gravel and leads to well-spaced sites that offer privacy and limited views down to the meadow and reservoir. Flat gravel tent pads and paved walkways to the toilets give the campground a tidy, classy feel. The campground is not recommended for trailers longer than 30 feet.

Campsites, facilities: There are 10 sites for tents and RVs up to 30 feet in length. Picnic tables, fire grills, vault toilets, and drinking water are provided. Leashed pets permitted.

Reservations, fees: Reservations are not accepted. The fee is $12 per site and $6 for extra vehicles. Open June through September, weather permitting.

Directions: From Beaver, drive east on Rte. 153 for 10.8 miles and turn right onto Forest Road 137. Continue eight miles and turn left into the Anderson Meadow Campground. GPS Coordinates: N 38° 12.581' W 112° 25.873'

Contact: Beaver Ranger District, 435/438-2436, www.fs.fed.us/r4/fishlake/recreation/camping/andersonmeadow.htm

36 MAHOGANY COVE

Scenic rating: 7

in the Tushar Mountains in Fishlake National Forest

Map 2.3, page 83

Mahogany Cove is a group campground along the Beaver River in the Tushar Mountains. The campground occupies a forested slope below a steep switchback in the Beaver Canyon Scenic Byway. Sites are carved out of a forest of mahogany, juniper, ponderosa pine, and gambel oak trees. Small moss- and lichen-painted boulders sit among the pinecones and pine needles scattered on the forest

floor around the sites. The sites have a peaceful feeling and offer good privacy, especially for a group-style campground. Birds chirp in the diverse forest canopy above the sites, and, despite the nearby road, the site feels secluded and protected. The loop and parking areas are gravel. The seven campsites can be reserved as a group area or can be used as individual sites if it's not reserved. Good trout fishing is possible about a mile downstream on the Beaver River or up the canyon in a series of alpine reservoirs.

Campsites, facilities: There are seven sites, which can serve as one group area (up to 75 people), for tents and RVs up to 24 feet in length. Picnic tables, fire grills, drinking water, and vault toilets are provided. Leashed pets permitted.

Reservations, fees: Reservations are accepted for the group site only at 877/444-6777 or online at www.recreation.gov and must be made a minimum of four days in advance. The fee is $10 per site, reserving the entire campground is $50, and day use is $5. Open May through October, weather permitting.

Directions: From Beaver, drive east on Rte. 153 for 12 miles and Mahogany Cove Campground is on the right side of the road. GPS Coordinates: N 38° 16.144' W 112° 29.147'

Contact: Beaver Ranger District, 435/438-2436, www.fs.fed.us/r4/fishlake/recreation/camping/mahoganycove.htm

37 TIMID SPRINGS

Scenic rating: 7

east of Beaver in the Tushar Mountains

Map 2.3, page 83

This is a relatively primitive Forest Service campground on the east side of the Tushar Mountains. The alpine campground is at 10,330 feet and is close to the Elk Meadows Ski Area. Nearby is the state-managed Puffer Lake. This alpine reservoir can be reached on Cullen Creek Road from Timid Springs Campground. Fishing is popular here. A meager loop of sites is tucked into a tall stand of fir trees. The sites are undeveloped and slope downhill. There are no facilities except for a vault toilet. Sites are shaded by the forest, and summer temperatures are cool. The camp loop is near Pauite ATV trail and the Skyline National Recreation Trail, which is closed to motorized vehicles but open to hikers, mountain bikers, and horseback riders.

Campsites, facilities: There are about a dozen campsites. Fire rings and a vault toilet are provided. Leashed pets permitted.

Reservations, fees: Reservations are not accepted. There is no fee. Open June through October, weather permitting.

Directions: From Circleville drive northeast on Hwy. 89 for six miles. At the town of Junction, turn west (left) onto Rte. 153 and continue 16 miles to Timid Springs on the right side of the road.

GPS Coordinates: N 38° 18.066' W 112° 21.548'

Contact: Beaver Ranger District, 435/438-2436, www.fs.fed.us/r4/fishlake/recreation/camping/timidsprings.htm

38 CITY CREEK
🏃 🛶 🏠 🚐 ⛰

Scenic rating: 7

eastern edge of Tushar Mountains

Map 2.3, page 83

City Creek Campground is located at the base of the eastern edge of the Tushar Mountains. The campground has an abandoned, forgotten feel. There's litter scattered around the sites and empty beer bottles thrown in the bushes. The water spigots haven't been turned on, adding to the aura of neglect. A canopy of ponderosa pine, cottonwood, pinyon pine, and juniper trees creates a comfortable, shaded environment for the campsites. While the sites have huge picnic tables, they sorely lack areas for pitching tents. As the name suggests,

City Creek runs by the campground. Both forks of the creek are stocked occasionally with rainbow trout, creating the best fishing on the south fork. There are trails, open to hikers and horses, leading up both the north and south fork of the creek. There's free dispersed camping along the road right below the campground.

Campsites, facilities: There are five sites for tents and RVs up to 24 feet in length. Picnic tables, fire grills, and vault toilets are provided. Leashed pets permitted.

Reservations, fees: Reservations are not accepted. Camping is free. Open May through October.

Directions: From Circleville, drive northeast on Hwy. 89 for six miles. At the town of Junction turn west (left) onto Rte. 153 and travel 5.6 miles. Turn right and continue 0.5 mile to the City Creek Campground.

GPS Coordinates: N 38° 16.203' W 112° 18.682'

Contact: Beaver Ranger District, 435/438-2436, www.fs.fed.us/r4/fishlake/recreation/camping/citycreek.htm

39 CIRCLEVILLE RV PARK
🏠 🏕 🚐 ⛰

Scenic rating: 4

in Circleville

Map 2.3, page 83

Circleville RV is a full-service, ATV-friendly RV park conveniently located in the middle of the Paiute ATV Trail. The trail is widely considered by the off-road community to be one of the best in the country. Circleville RV has views of the Tushar Mountains to the west and the Sevier Plateau to the east. The RV park is an open gravel yard with very little shade. A small tenting area is available with grass lawns, fire grills, and picnic tables.

Campsites, facilities: There are 25 full hook-up (25-, 30-, and 50-amp) sites, eight partial hook-up sites, and 16 tent sites. Amenities include picnic tables, fire grills, modern restrooms with showers, drinking water, WiFi, laundry, a dump station, garbage service, a playground, a horseshoe pit, ATV and RV supplies, fishing licenses, and firewood. Leashed pets permitted.

Reservations, fees: Reservations are accepted at 888/978-7275. Full hook-up sites are $24, partial hook-up sites are $18, and tent sites are $12. Open year-round.

Directions: From the southern limits of Circleville, drive north 0.5 mile on Hwy. 89. The Circleville RV Park is on the right side of the road.

GPS Coordinates: N 38° 10.279' W 112° 16.666'

Contact: Circleville RV Park, 888/978-7275, www.campatvplay.com/

40 OTTER CREEK STATE PARK

Scenic rating: 7

north of Circleville on the Otter Creek Reservoir

Map 2.3, page 83

This state park campground flanks the south beach of Otter Creek Reservoir and is set at 6,732 feet above sea level. The lake is popular for boating, fishing, swimming, canoeing, and wildlife viewing. Sport-fishing species include smallmouth bass and cutthroat, rainbow, and brown trout. A paved boat ramp and floating dock provide easy access to the lake. Hikers will enjoy the Otter Walk Nature Trail, and off-road vehicle users can access the 600-mile Paiute Trail directly from the state park. Birders may sight raptors like osprey, bald eagles, and great horned owls, as well as smaller avian species such as the Clark's nuthatch, black-billed magpie, and several species of blackbird (yellow-headed, red-winged, and Brewer's). Great blue herons and American white pelicans can also be spotted fishing the lake's waters. Mammals that occasionally visit the park include coyotes, red fox, Rocky Mountain elk, mule deer, and

mountain lions. The campground combines the amenities of an RV park with the ambience of lakefront camping. Sites are tightly packed along the lakeshore, with additional rows to the south. Short green dividing walls provide some shade and privacy for the picnic tables at the sites. Mature cottonwood trees offer shade from above. The friendly park ranger is excited about his job and offers a wealth of information.

Campsites, facilities: There are 24 RV sites, 10 overflow campsites, and six tent sites with developed tent pads. Picnic tables, barbeque grills, fire grills, drinking water, garbage service, dump station, paved parking, pull-through sites, a fish-cleaning station, modern restrooms with showers, and vault toilets are provided. Firewood and ice are available. Leashed pets permitted.

Reservations, fees: Reservations are accepted at 800/322-3770 or online at www.reserveamerica.com; they must be made a minimum of two days in advance and can be arranged up to 16 weeks in advance. There is an $8 non-refundable reservation fee for individual sites. The camping fee is $16 per site and $8 for an extra vehicle. Open year-round.

Directions: From Circleville, drive north on Hwy. 89 for four miles, turn right onto Rte. 62, and continue 11 miles. At the junction of with Rte. 62, stay right and drive 0.5 mile to the Otter Creek State Park entrance on the left.

GPS Coordinates: N 38° 10.001' W 112° 01.088'

Contact: Otter Creek State Park, 435/624-3268, http://stateparks.utah.gov/stateparks/parks/otter-creek/

41 OTTER CREEK RV AND MARINA

Scenic rating: 5

next to Otter Creek State Park and Reservoir

Map 2.3, page 83

Otter Creek RV and Marina is located across the street from the Otter Creek Reservoir.

While the RV park isn't right on the lake like the State Park Campground, it does offer a scenic setting overlooking Otter Creek. A wide variety of recreation opportunities await at the state park, including boating, canoeing, fishing, hiking, and wildlife-viewing. Anglers can expect to find smallmouth bass and cutthroat, rainbow, and brown trout. The state park has a paved boat ramp accessing a large reservoir and hiking trails. An ATV trail leads directly from the RV park to the Paiute ATV Trail, making it possible for ATVs to reach the trail without using the main road. Hunting for cougar, bobcat, elk, and deer is popular in the area. Fishing and hunting licenses can be purchased at the RV park store. The campground has a gravel yard with small fences separating tightly spaced sites. There is very little shade, and most sites are completely open and exposed.

Campsites, facilities: There are 31 full hook-up sites (30-amp) and four tent sites. Modern restrooms with showers, picnic tables, fire grills, a fish-cleaning station, drinking water, garbage service, and horseshoe pits are provided. Laundry, a general store, and a café are available. Leashed pets permitted.

Reservations, fees: Reservations are accepted at 435/624-3292 or online at www. ottercreekrv.com/reservations.htm. RV sites are $22 and tent sites are $17. Open year-round.

Directions: From Circleville, drive north on Hwy. 89 for four miles, turn right onto Rte. 62, and continue 11 miles. At the junction with Rte. 62, stay right and drive 0.5 mile to the Otter Creek RV and Marina on the right side of the road.

GPS Coordinates: N 38° 10.021' W 112° 01.215'

Contact: Otter Creek RV and Marina, 435/624-3292, www.ottercreekrv.com/

WASATCH RANGE AND CENTRAL UTAH

© MIKE MATSON

BEST CAMPGROUNDS

Like the spine of a dragon sleeping below the

earth's crust, Central Utah's landscape is dominated by a series of mountain ranges and plateaus pushing skyward. The state's backbone starts with the dramatic uplift of the Wasatch Range in the north and gradually mellows to the gentle rise of the Aquarius Plateau in the south. Between these benchmarks is a whole series of upland features, including the Wasatch Plateau, the Pavant Mountains, the Sevier Plateau, the Tushar Mountains, the Canyon Mountains, and the San Pitch Mountains. Utah's mountains are what make the state green. They are the catch basin for the state's freshwater, in the form of winter snow and summer thunderstorms. Great effort has been made to capture these valuable water sources, and reservoirs dot the landscape, preserving water not only for drinking and irrigation but also fish habitat and recreation. Forests of aspen, oak, maple, and spruce trees blanket the slopes and provide shelter for much of the state's wildlife. The timbered hills also offer a vast opportunity for outdoor adventures. From anglers casting for trout in mountain streams to ATV riders buzzing along backcountry byways to rock climbers scaling vertical cliffs, there's something for everyone to enjoy in Utah's national forests. And camping is at the heart of all these mountain adventures.

Two dominant upland features characterize Central Utah's landscape: the Wasatch Mountains and the Wasatch Plateau. The Wasatch Mountains are Utah's most striking and recognizable range. The chain is the westernmost range of the greater Rocky Mountains and marks the boundary between the Rockies and the Great Basin Desert. In total, the Wasatch Mountains stretch 160 miles from the Idaho border in the north to Mount Nebo, near the town of Nephi, in the south. While the Wasatch isn't the highest range in the state, it rises abruptly from around 4,500 feet in the Salt Lake Valley to heights above 11,000 feet. The range's dramatic relief, striking beauty, and proximity to Utah's largest urban center make it one of the most heavily used alpine environments in the country. The recreation centers of the Wasatch Range are two steep, narrow canyons that empty out into the suburbs south of Salt Lake. Little and Big Cottonwood Canyon each contain two ski resorts and a host of summer recreational opportunities including hiking, mountain biking, road biking, rock climbing, fly fishing, and camping. The five developed Forest Service campgrounds in the canyons of the alpine forests and meadows are just a fraction of the campgrounds spread across the Wasatch Range. Dense concentrations of campgrounds can also be found near Mount Timpanogos and Mount Nebo near the southern end of the range.

Directly south of the Wasatch Mountains is a broad, elevated highland known as the Wasatch Plateau. The plateau stretches roughly 65 miles from north to south and 25 miles across. While it doesn't have the razor-sharp vertical drama of the peaks to the north, its ridges still top out at over 11,000 feet. The Wasatch Plateau is a land of open alpine meadows, snow-fed mountain lakes, and aspen-blanketed hillsides. During the summer months, wildflowers bloom a pleasing palette of red, pink, purple, and blue. And in the fall, the aspen leaves burn a brilliant gold. But unlike the mountains to the north, the Wasatch Plateau is challenging to access. There are very few paved roads and those that exist are twisted and convoluted. For some, this only adds to the region's appeal. ATV riders prefer the curvy, dust-choked network of gravel roads and love the absence of RV drivers. Hearty anglers search out the tiny, lonesome fishing holes and carefully guard their secret honey pots. Campers have their special corners of the Wasatch Plateau, too. In addition to a wide variety of developed campgrounds, the plateau holds many secret stashes of dispersed undeveloped camping. Without giving out all the secrets, I've tried to include a smattering of undeveloped camping on the plateau for everyone to explore.

While this region is defined by its highest places, it should be noted that Central Utah has more to offer campers than just mountains. A collection of reservoirs, both large and small, has been established with earthen dams on almost every major watercourse in Central Utah. While these lakes have been created for practical purposes, the end result is a wonderful opportunity for water recreation. Sailing, windsurfing, waterskiing, and fishing are great ways to beat the summer heat and spend time at these lakes. Shining examples include the beautiful state park campgrounds that line the shores of the Jordanelle, Deer Creek, and East Canyon Reservoirs in the eastern Wasatch Mountains.

Regardless of your recreational preferences, Utah's high country offers something for you. This chapter should help determine where to stay as you explore the backbone of the state. So go get lost on the Wasatch Plateau, find those places that feel like they belong only to you...and do it with the confidence that great camping is always near.

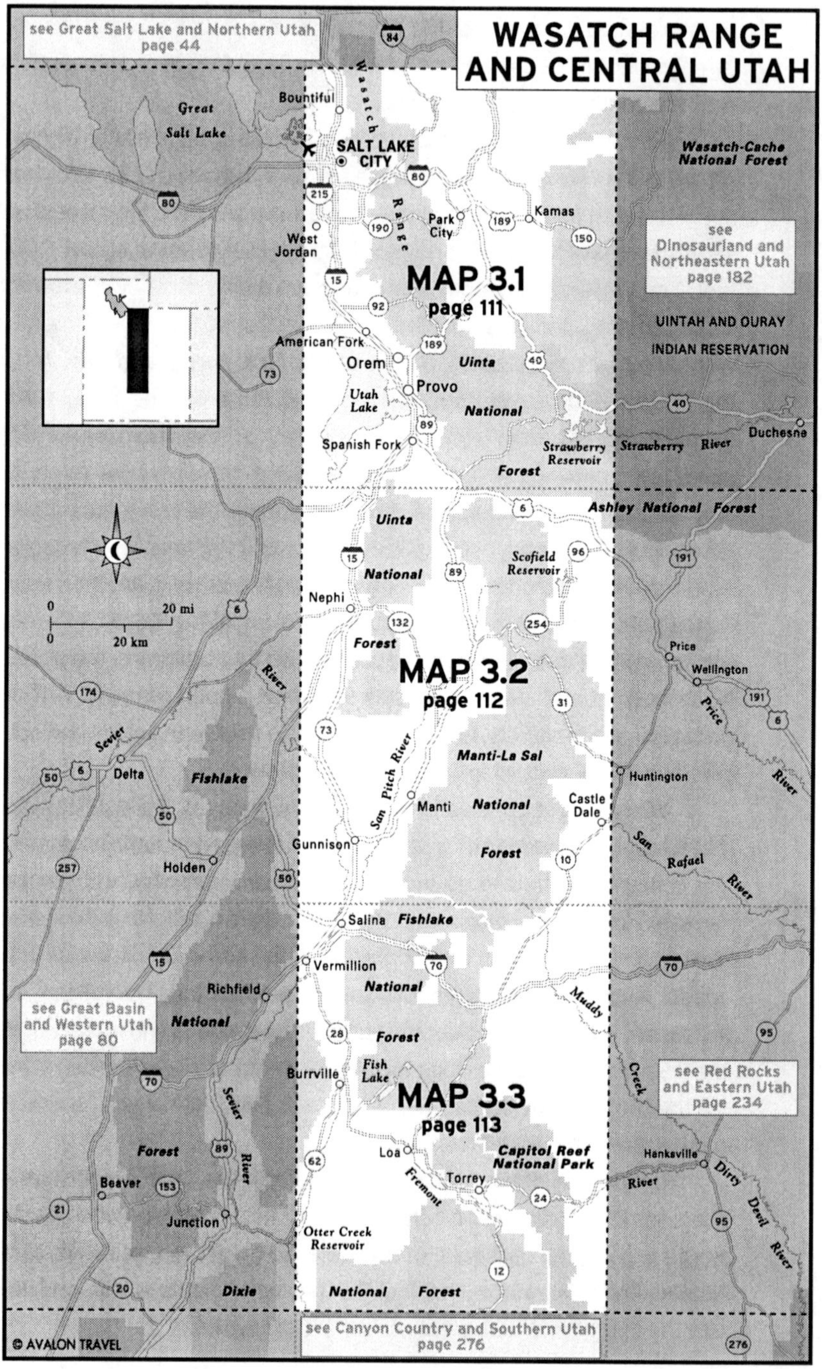
WASATCH RANGE AND CENTRAL UTAH
see Great Salt Lake and Northern Utah page 44
see Dinosaurland and Northeastern Utah page 182
see Great Basin and Western Utah page 80
see Red Rocks and Eastern Utah page 234
see Canyon Country and Southern Utah page 276
MAP 3.1 page 111
MAP 3.2 page 112
MAP 3.3 page 113
Great Salt Lake
Wasatch Range
Bountiful
SALT LAKE CITY
West Jordan
Park City
Kamas
Wasatch-Cache National Forest
UINTAH AND OURAY INDIAN RESERVATION
American Fork
Orem
Provo
Utah Lake
Uinta National Forest
Spanish Fork
Strawberry Reservoir
Strawberry River
Duchesne
Ashley National Forest
Scofield Reservoir
Nephi
Price
Wellington
Price River
Sevier River
Delta
Fishlake
San Pitch River
Manti-La Sal National Forest
Manti
Castle Dale
Huntington
San Rafael River
Holden
Gunnison
Salina
Fishlake National Forest
Vermillion
Richfield
Muddy Creek
Fish Lake
Burrville
Loa
Capitol Reef National Park
Torrey
Fremont River
Hanksville
Dirty Devil River
Otter Creek Reservoir
Beaver
Junction
Sevier River
Dixie National Forest
0 20 mi
0 20 km
© AVALON TRAVEL

Map 3.1

Campgrounds 1-58

Pages 114-149

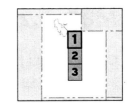

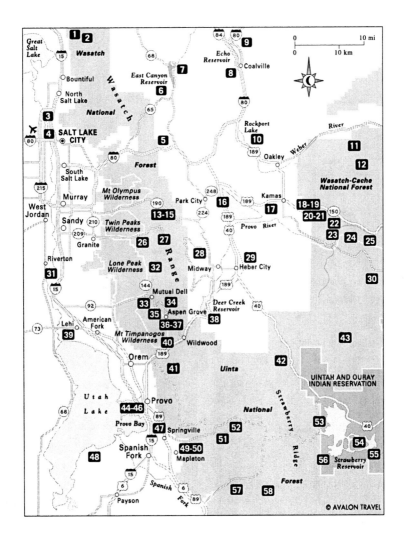

Map 3.2

Campgrounds 59-87

Pages 150-165

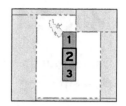

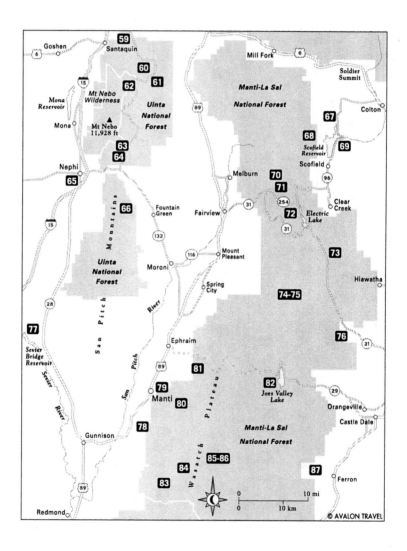

Map 3.3

Campgrounds 88-108
Pages 166-176

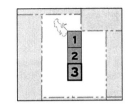

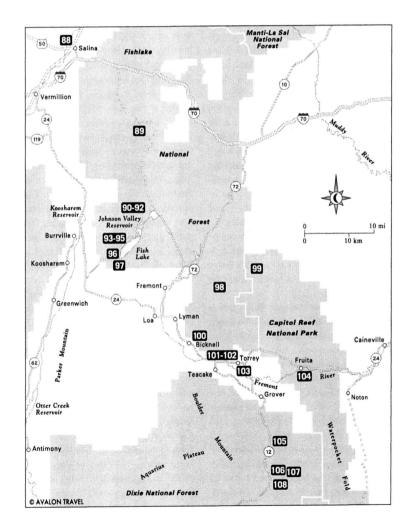

1 SUNSET

Scenic rating: 6

in Farmington Canyon below Bountiful Peak in the Wasatch-Cache National Forest

Map 3.1, page 111

Sunset Campground is located up a winding, rutted gravel road in Farmington Canyon under the massive Bountiful Peak. While the campground isn't far from the town of Farmington, the condition of the road certainly weeds out any casual explorers. This leaves the campground relatively quiet for off-road enthusiasts and campers who don't mind a little bit of driving adventure. There are awesome views down the canyon across the northern Salt Lake Valley, with sunsets standing out as particularly memorable. The views are better on the drive up than from the campground itself, as the sites are tucked into a Rocky Mountain maple forest with the broad deciduous leaves blocking most of the views. The camp loop is gravel, but if you've made it this far, that won't be an inconvenience. The parking slips are sloped with the hill, but the sites feature level tent pads, making the campground better for tent camping than for RVs or trailers. Farmington Creek Trail starts at the campground and is a three-mile roundtrip trail open to hikers, mountain bikers, and horses.

Campsites, facilities: There are 16 single sites and one double site. Picnic tables, fire rings, drinking water, and vault toilets are provided. Leashed pets permitted.

Reservations, fees: Reservations are not accepted. Single sites are $10, the double site is $20, day use and extra vehicles are $6. Open June through October, weather permitting.

Directions: From I-15, take Exit 327 toward Farmington. Drive east on Rte. 225 for 0.5 mile. Turn right on Main Street and drive 0.3 mile. Turn left onto 600 N, travel 0.1 mile, and turn left at the junction onto 100 E, which turns into Farmington Canyon Road. Continue 5.3 miles and turn right into Sunset Campground.

GPS Coordinates: N 41° 00.182' W 111° 50.370'

Contact: Salt Lake Ranger District, 801/466-6411, www.fs.fed.us/r4/uwc/recreation/wcnf/camping/slrd/davis_county_cg.shtml#sunset-cg

2 BOUNTIFUL PEAK

Scenic rating: 8

on Bountiful Peak east of Farmington in the Wasatch-Cache National Forest

Map 3.1, page 111

Bountiful Peak Campground is located on the flanks of Bountiful Peak east of Farmington on the Bountiful-Farmington Loop Road. The campground is set at 7,520 feet in an quaking aspen and Engelmann spruce forest and views up to Bountiful Peak and out to the surrounding Wasatch Mountains. The campground has lovely sites tucked into the trees with level gravel tent pads. The more open sites are surrounded by tall grass. Some sites have paths with steps leading from the parking spots to the picnic tables. Bountiful Peak Campground is reached via a long, winding road. High-clearance, four-wheel-drive vehicles are recommended.

Campsites, facilities: There are 34 single sites for tents and RVs up to 20 feet in length and one group site for up to 100 people. Picnic tables, fire rings, drinking water, and vault toilets are provided. Leashed pets permitted.

Reservations, fees: Reservations are accepted for the group site only at 877/444-6777 or online at www.recreation.gov and must be made a minimum of seven days in advance. Single sites are $12, the group site is $120, and day use and extra vehicles are $6.

Directions: From I-15, take Exit 327 toward Farmington. Drive east on Rte. 225 for 0.5 mile. Turn right on Main Street and drive 0.3 mile. Turn left onto 600 N, travel 0.1 mile, and turn left at the junction onto 100 E, which turns into Farmington Canyon Road. After

8.1 miles, take the right fork and continue 0.7 mile to Bountiful Peak Campground.
GPS Coordinates: N 40° 58.834' W 111° 48.276'
Contact: Salt Lake Ranger District, 801/466-6411, www.fs.fed.us/r4/uwc/recreation/wcnf/camping/slrd/davis_county_cg.shtml#bountiful-peak-cg

▣ PONY EXPRESS

Scenic rating: 2

north of Salt Lake City
Map 3.1, page 111

The Pony Express RV park is conveniently located near I-15 and downtown Salt Lake City. The campground is a good place to stop over on cross-country road trips or if you'll be spending some time exploring Salt Lake City. This RV park caters to overnight guests and not to permanent residents, which sets it apart from the other RV park options in Salt Lake City. The facilities are modern and well cared for, and the grounds have an inviting, safe feel. The sites are tightly spaced and don't offer much privacy, but they do have paved parking and grass lawns. The campground is open and exposed to the elements; though there are a few small trees, they provide very little shade.

Campsites, facilities: There are 173 full hookup (20-, 30-, and 50-amp) RV sites, a tent area, and 10 cabins. Picnic tables, playground, swimming pool, basketball court, horseshoes, billards, dog run, WiFi, cable TV, business office, security gate, modern restrooms with showers, garbage service, and drinking water are provided. Laundry and a convenience store are available. Leashed pets permitted.

Reservations, fees: Reservations are accepted at 800/780-0170 or online at http://host7.adventgx.com/vestivoolrs/ponyexpress/. RV sites are $29–42, tent sites are $22, and cabins are $46–52. Open year-round (tent camping is available seasonally).

Directions: From the junction of I-80 and I-215 (Exit 117) in Salt Lake City, travel north on I-215 for five miles. Take Exit 28 and turn right onto Redwood Road. Continue 0.2 mile and turn right into Pony Express RV Resort. GPS Coordinates: N 40° 49.849' W 111° 56.317'
Contact: Pony Express RV Resort, 801/355-1550, www.ponyexpressrvresort.com/

▣ SALT LAKE CITY KOA

Scenic rating: 2

in Salt Lake City
Map 3.1, page 111

The Salt Lake KOA is conveniently located between downtown Salt Lake City and the airport. It's near the Utah State Fair Grounds and the State Department of Natural Resources Office. The trade-off for the convenience of this location is a distinctly urban environment. The neighborhood is not appealing and certainly isn't what I think of when I imagine a camping trip. The KOA is bordered by a bar named The Old Bottling Club, a trailer park, and lots of airport motels. The RV park loop has a narrow grass lawn, a ponderosa pine, and a single deciduous tree in each slip. The sprawling campground driveways merge seamlessly with the permanent-residence trailer park bordering the KOA to the east.

Campsites, facilities: There are 226 full hookup (30, 50 amps) RV sites, two group tent areas, 18 tent sites, and two cabins. Amenities include picnic tables, WiFi, a playground, volleyball court, basketball court, game room, swimming pools, hot tub, garbage service, drinking water, and modern restrooms with showers. Laundry, RV and car wash, restaurants, barbershop, and a convenience store are available. Leashed pets permitted (there are breed restrictions, and dogs must be under 30 pounds).

Reservations, fees: Reservations are accepted at 800/226-7752 or online at https://koa.com/where/ut/44143/reserve/. RV sites are $42, group tent areas are $3 pp, tent sites are $30, and cabins are $55. Open year-round.

Directions: From I-80 eastbound, take Exit 115 for North Temple and merge onto Rte. 186 toward North Temple. Continue 3.5 miles and turn left into Salt Lake City KOA.

GPS Coordinates: N 40° 46.171' W 111° 56.056'

Contact: Salt Lake City KOA, 801/328-0224, www.campvip.com/

5 PARK CITY RV RESORT
⛵ 🏕 🚐 ⛺

Scenic rating: 6

in Park City

Map 3.1, page 111

The Park City RV Resort is a small, upscale campground off I-80 near the community of Jeremy Ranch. The RV park is near a staggering assortment of recreation, as well as the resort town of Park City and all its charm. A vast network of mountain bike trails dot the hills around Park City. Notable single-track rides near the RV park include the Pioneer Trail, which climbs up Little Immigration Canyon via the route the original Mormon settlers used. The Jeremy Ranch trail network and Deer Valley, Park City, and The Canyons Resorts all offer chair lift access trails. Other unique Park City summer recreation opportunities include hot air balloon rides, checking out the Utah Olympic Park, and a Frisbee golf course at The Canyons Resort. Park City RV has a paved driveway leading to flat, paved RV parking slips. There's not much shade, and sites are packed together like sardines. The landscaping and facilities are immaculate, and the place reflects Park City's upscale decor. The interstate is in plain view and definitely within earshot.

Campsites, facilities: There are 89 RV sites with full hook-ups and an unlimited amount of tent space on eight acres of land. Amenities include picnic tables, a game room, WiFi, drinking water, modern restrooms with showers, mini climbing wall, swimming pool, hot tub, a dog run, garbage service, and dump station. Ice and laundry are available. Leashed pets permitted.

Reservations, fees: Reservations are accepted at 435/649-2535 or online at www. parkcityrvresort.com/reservations.html#. Full hook-up sites are $35–45, partial hook-up sites are $30, and tent sites are $20. Open year-round.

Directions: From I-80, take Exit 141 for Jeremy Ranch. Turn right at the four-way stop onto Rasmussen Road. Drive 1.5 miles to the Park City RV Resort on the left side of the road.

GPS Coordinates: N 40° 44.241' W 111° 33.291'

Contact: Park City RV Resort, 435/649-2535, www.parkcityrvresort.com/

6 MORMON FLAT
🏃 🚴 🛶 🏕 ⛺

Scenic rating: 8

northeast of Park City

Map 3.1, page 111

Mormon Flat is a relatively primitive group area near the Jeremy Ranch community northeast of Park City. The campground sits at the base of Little Reservoir Canyon, which is part of the original trail pioneers used to immigrate to the Salt Lake Valley. The ill-fated Donner Party cut the trail on the way to their eventual long winter in the mountains of California. The next year, Mormon settlers led by Brigham Young followed the same route on their way to establishing the settlement in Salt Lake known then as Deseret. At the top of Little Immigration Canyon, Brigham Young's party got its first glimpse of the Salt Lake Valley, and he declared it would be the place to establish a new community for the Church of Jesus Christ of Latter-day Saints. The campground sits among waist-high grass in an open meadow. There's hiking and great mountain biking on the modern-day Little Immigration Trail; it now takes about an hour to ride the same distance that took the pioneers several days to negotiate. The single-track trail is popular for its gentle climb and smooth downhill slope. The group site is popular on weekends with Park City and Salt Lake locals looking to make a quick retreat into nature. The campground is open and exposed with good flat areas to pitch tents. Dense tamarisk and willow trees grow along the river but don't offer any shade for the sites. The campground is administered by East Canyon State Park.

Campsites, facilities: There is one group site for up to 100 people. Picnic tables and a vault toilet are provided. There is no drinking water. Leashed pets permitted.

Reservations, fees: Reservations are required at 800/322-3770 or online at www.reserveamerica.com. Group site reservations can be arranged up to 11 months in advance with a $10.25 nonrefundable reservation fee. The site costs $75. Open April through October, weather permitting.

Directions: From Salt Lake, drive east on I-80. Take the Jeremy Ranch Exit, turn left, and go under the freeway. At the stop sign, turn left and take the next right onto Jeremy Ranch Drive. Continue on this road until a fork and stay left on the East Canyon Road. Drive 4.9 miles and turn left into Mormon Flat.
GPS Coordinates: N 40° 48.931' W 111° 35.095'

Contact: East Canyon State Park, 801/829-6866, http://stateparks.utah.gov/stateparks/parks/east-canyon/

⁊ DIXIE CREEK AT EAST CANYON STATE PARK
🏊 🚣 🛶 🏠 ♿ 🚐 ⛺

Scenic rating: 7

on the East Canyon Reservoir

Map 3.1, page 111

East Canyon State Park is located on the East Canyon Reservoir west of Coalville. East Canyon is part of the historic Mormon Pioneer Trail, the path that brought the area's most influential early settlers. Trappers and native tribes also used the sheltered canyon for hunting and trapping because of its abundance of wildlife. The reservoir is a smaller, quieter version of the popular lakes at many of the state parks in the region. Swimming, boating, and fishing are popular pursuits on the lake. The park features a paved boat ramp with floating docks for swimmers and for docking boats. The reservoir has rainbow, tiger, and brown trout, as well as black crappie and smallmouth bass for anglers. The Dixie Creek Campground overlooks the beach, marina, and lake. It has great views down the valley and of the surrounding mountains. The campground is open and breezy, and the vegetation is limited to sagebrush and grass. Sites don't have specific tent pads, but most have flat spots where you could comfortably pitch a shelter. They are well spaced, but because the whole area is open, everything is in plain view. Yurts are available for those interested in camping in luxury or a little more privacy. They sit on wood deck platforms with barbecues, picnic tables, and benches.

Campsites, facilities: There are 33 RV and tent sites (15 full hook-ups and 18 partial hook-ups), four yurts, and one group site. The Large Spring group area can accommodate up to 25 people, and there are two day-use-only group areas. Sites 11 and 17 are wheelchair accessible. Boat-in camping is available. Covered picnic tables on cement pads, fire grills, a boat ramp, a dump station, garbage service, modern restrooms with showers, and drinking water are provided at the main campground. Leashed pets are permitted but not allowed in the yurts.

Reservations, fees: Reservations are accepted at 800/322-3770 or online at www.reserveamerica.com; they must be made a minimum of two days in advance and can be arranged up to 16 weeks in advance. Group reservations can be arranged up to 11 months in advance and require a $10.25 nonrefundable reservation fee. Full hook-up sites are $25, partial hook-up sites are $20, yurts are $60, the group site is $50, boat-in camping sites are $20, extra vehicles are $10–13, and day use is $9. Open year-round.

Directions: From Coalville, take I-84 north to Exit 115. Head south on Rte. 65. After one mile, turn left following Rte. 65. Drive eight miles and turn right onto Rte. 66. Continue 1.3 miles to entrance for East Canyon State Park. Turn left into the park.

GPS Coordinates: N 40° 55.432' W 111° 35.487'

Contact: East Canyon State Park, 801/829-6866, http://stateparks.utah.gov/stateparks/parks/east-canyon/

8 HOLIDAY HILLS RV PARK

Scenic rating: 5

in Coalville

Map 3.1, page 111

Holiday Hills RV Park is located along the Weber River off I-80. It's neighbored by a motel and gas station on one side and rolling hills on the other. The Rail Trail, which starts in Park City and runs 30 miles to Echo Junction, comes through Coalville and is a half mile away from Holiday Hills. Because the trail is converted from a railroad track, it's a flat, easy walk or bike ride. The campground yard is grass and is pleasantly shaded by large trees. Some sites border the river, where fly fishers cast for trout. A small footbridge leads across lazy Holiday Creek to a large field with a volleyball court and a covered group pavilion. This day-use area sits in a natural island between Holiday Creek and the Weber River. The parking slips and camp spots are packed tightly together. Privacy is hard to find, except maybe in the cabins set off to themselves. Check in and register at the Phillips 66 gas station.

Campsites, facilities: There are 42 full hook-up (30- and 50-amp) sites and two cabins. There are six designated tent sites. Some picnic tables, modern restrooms with showers, drinking water, and garbage service are provided. A day-use group pavilion, dump station, laundry, and a convenience store are available. Leashed pets permitted.

Reservations, fees: Reservations are accepted at 435/336-4421. RV sites with full hook-ups are $23, sites without hook-ups are $18, tent camping sites are $14, and cabins are $29. The group day-use pavilion is $50. Open year-round.

Directions: From I-80, take Exit 162 for Coalville. Turn west, cross the highway overpass, and continue 0.1 mile to Holiday Hills RV Park.

GPS Coordinates: N 40° 54.713' W 111° 24.294'

Contact: Holiday Hills RV Park, 435/336-4421.

9 ECHO RESORT

Scenic rating: 6

on Echo Reservoir in Coalville

Map 3.1, page 111

Echo Resort overlooks the Echo Reservoir north of the small town of Coalville. Echo Reservoir is a large lake on the Weber River. I-80 follows the reservoir's southwestern shore for several miles and has a scenic overlook where travelers can take in the lake. Echo Resort is the conspicuous resort directly across the lake from the overlooks. The lake offers boating, waterskiing, fishing, and swimming. Anglers will find brown trout, largemouth bass, channel catfish, and carp. Campsites at the resort vary tremendously. There is everything from beachfront sites with grass lawns to no-frills gravel parking spaces. There's a large parking lot for trucks, boats, trailers, and extra cars. Tall trees line the lakeshore and provide shade for the RV slips. The campsites are not extensively developed. In fact, the whole layout is sort of a free-for-all. Above the campground a collection of rusting trash, buoys, and old vehicles gives the resort a bit of a junkyard feel. On the road to the resort, look for the osprey—its big stick nest is on the right side.

Campsites, facilities: There are around 100 sites. The owners couldn't provide a specific number of sites but insisted there is plenty of room for everyone. Amenities include a small store, restaurant, picnic tables, boat launch, modern restrooms, drinking water, and garbage service. Leashed pets permitted.

Reservations, fees: Reservations are not accepted. The fee is $20 per vehicle. There is a $15 boat-launch fee, and the day-use fee is $10 per vehicle. Open May through September.

Directions: From I-80, take Exit 162 for Coalville. Turn east of the exit ramp on 100 S and drive 0.2 mile to Main Street. Turn left on Main Street. Follow Main Street north for 3.8 miles and take a sharp left down a hill into Echo Resort.

GPS Coordinates: N 40° 57.505' W 111° 24.468'

Contact: Echo Resort, 435/336-9894.

10 ROCKPORT STATE PARK
🧗 🏊 🚤 🚣 🏕 ♿ 🚗 ⛰

Scenic rating: 7

on the Rockport Reservoir, north of Kamas

Map 3.1, page 111   **BEST(**

Rockport State Park has an unique campground layout. Four camp areas are spread out along the shore of Rockport Reservoir. The lake is three miles long and narrow, and it offers boating and fishing as its most popular activities. Anglers can expect to find brown, cutthroat, and rainbow trout, as well as mountain whitefish, smallmouth bass, and yellow perch. The park has a broad concrete boat ramp with docks to tie up to and plenty of parking for big rigs with trailers. There's also a yurt store near the boat ramp for last-minute purchases. Juniper trees and sagebrush are the predominant plants in the park, and cottonwood trees grow near the water, especially along the Weber River. Visitors may spot a variety of mammals near the lake, including mule deer, chipmunks, jackrabbits, yellow-bellied marmots, badgers, raccoons, weasels, and foxes. Around the water, birders may spot Western grebes, whistling swans, and great blue herons. Large raptors like red-tailed hawks, golden eagles, bald eagles, and great

horned owls visit the park as well. The paved camp loops generally look down on the lake from above. The sites, for the most part, are open and exposed to the elements. Covered picnic tables on concrete pads help provide shade and give the sites a very tidy feeling. The facilities are top rate, and the park offers one of the state's best campgrounds on a reservoir and a great quick escape from Salt Lake City. At one time it was a private resort, and it has maintained its appeal.

Campsites, facilities: There are five developed campgrounds and three yurts. Cottonwood Campground has 17 sites, with three walk-in tent sites. Sites 7 and 15 are wheelchair accessible. Crandall Cove Campground has 10 sites; site 3 is wheelchair accessible. Twin Coves Campground has 24 sites; sites 7 and 22 are wheelchair accessible. Juniper Campground has 34 sites; sites 19, 20, 25, and 26 are wheelchair accessible. Cedar Point has four walk-in tent sites that are available by reservation only. Juniper Campground has shelters, modern restrooms with showers, garbage service, drinking water, and electric hook-ups. The other campgrounds provide picnic tables, garbage service, drinking water, vault toilets, and fire grills. A boat ramp, fish-cleaning station, small store, and dump station are available. Leashed pets are permitted, but not in the yurts.

Reservations, fees: Reservations are accepted at 800/322-3770 or online at www.reserveamerica.com; they must be made a minimum of two days in advance and can be arranged up to 16 weeks in advance. There is an $8 nonrefundable reservation fee for individual sites. Cottonwood, Crandall Cove, Twin Coves, and Cedar Point are $10 per site, and Juniper is $20 per site. Yurts are $60, and the day-use fee is $9. Open year-round.

Directions: From Kamas, drive north on Rte. 32 for 11.4 miles. Turn right on Rte. 302 and continue 0.2 mile to the park entrance. The different camping areas stretch north along the park drive and lakeshore.

GPS Coordinates: N 40° 45.207' W 111° 22.356'

Contact: Rockport State Park, 435/336-2241, http://stateparks.utah.gov/stateparks/parks/rockport/

11 SMITH AND MOREHOUSE
🥾 🚴 ⛵ 🛶 🚤 🏕 ♿ 🚐 ⛺

Scenic rating: 8

in Weber Canyon

Map 3.1, page 111   **BEST (**

The Smith and Morehouse Campground is set in an open forest in Weber Canyon. The campground is a quarter-mile from the Smith and Morehouse Reservoir. The small scenic lake is popular for fishing and nonmotorized boating. A boat ramp facilitates easy access to the lake. A few miles farther up Forest Road 33, at the Ledgefork Campground, is the trailhead for the Smith and Morehouse Trail. The trail leads to the Erickson Basin (five miles), Island Lake (seven miles), and Crystal Lake Trailhead (10 miles). It's open to hikers, mountain bikers, and horses. In the Smith and Morehouse Campground, aspen, spruce, and pine trees shade campsites, and polished boulders line the paved access loop and parking areas. Clumps of grass grow on the forest floor between the sites. Some sites on the loop feature paved pull-through parking for big vehicles. On the downside, other sites lack tent pads or any flat area to pitch a tent. In early August, temperatures in the forest were around 75°F at midday, when it was nearly 100°F in Salt Lake City. A gentle breeze rustled the aspen trees, tempering the heat even more. The sound of Smith and Morehouse Creek can be heard rushing down the canyon below from some of the sites. Intermittent trees allow peek-a-views up to the mountains above the campground. The cool forest atmosphere and access to good hiking and an alpine reservoir make Smith and Morehouse a great, easy escape from Salt Lake City.

Campsites, facilities: There are 34 sites for tents and RVs up to 35 feet in length. All sites are wheelchair accessible, but none are specifically designated. Picnic tables, fire grills, vault toilets, garbage service, and drinking water are provided. Firewood is available. Leashed pets permitted.

Reservations, fees: Reservations are accepted at 877/444-6777 or online at www.recreation.gov and must be made a minimum of five days in advance. Individual sites are $17 and extra vehicles are $6. Open May through October.

Directions: From Kamas, drive north on Rte. 32 for 5.9 miles. Turn right onto the Weber Canyon road and continue 11.8 miles to the sign for Smith and Morehouse Campground. Turn right onto Forest Road 33 and drive 1.8 miles to the campground on the left side of the road.

GPS Coordinates: N 40° 46.137' W 111° 06.444'

Contact: Heber-Kamas Ranger District, 435/783-4338, www.fs.fed.us/r4/uwc/recreation/wcnf/camping/kamas-camping.shtml#smithmorehouse

12 LEDGEFORK
🥾 🚴 ⛵ 🛶 🚤 ⛴ 🏕 ♿ 🚐 ⛺

Scenic rating: 8

in Weber Canyon

Map 3.1, page 111   **BEST (**

Ledgefork Campground is a Forest Service Campground near the Smith and Morehouse Reservoir in Weber Canyon. The reservoir is small but beautiful, with views down the canyon and of the surrounding mountains. The lake is popular with anglers and nonmotorized boats like canoes, rafts, and float tubes. Ledgefork is the trailhead for the Smith and Morehouse Trail, which leads to the Erickson Basin (five miles), Island Lake (seven miles), and Crystal Lake Trailhead (10 miles). The trail is open to hikers, mountain bikers, and horses. The campground is similar to Smith and Morehouse, about two miles down-canyon. The sites occupy a combination of spruce, aspen, and pine forest, bordered by open meadows and split by Weber Creek. Some sites are set right next to the gently flowing creek. Hummingbirds, squirrels, butterflies, and deer frequent the meadows in and around the campground. Signs explaining how to avoid bears are nailed to every picnic table, so be careful with food and don't do anything to habituate the bears to humans. Their lives and your safety depend upon your actions. The access loop is paved, and many of the sites have paved pads under the picnic tables. Like Smith and Morehouse, the tent pads aren't the best. Even in mid-summer the temperatures here are pleasant, but in the fall, when the aspen leaves change colors, the place truly shines. The quality facilities and relaxing forest setting with lots of kid-friendly activities like paddling on the reservoir, fishing, and hiking make Ledgefork one of the best campgrounds for families in Utah. Both Ledgefork and Smith and Morehouse are very popular, so making reservations is highly recommended by the campground hosts.

Campsites, facilities: There are 72 single sites and two double sites for tents and RVs up to 50 feet in length. Picnic tables, fire grills, vault toilets, drinking water, and garbage service are provided. Leashed pets permitted.

Reservations, fees: Reservations are accepted at 877/444-6777 or online at www.recreation.gov and must be made a minimum of five days in advance. Single sites are $17, double sites are $34, and extra vehicles are $6. Open May through October.

Directions: From Kamas, drive north on Rte. 32 for 5.9 nine miles. Turn right onto the Weber Canyon road and continue 11.8 miles to the sign for Ledgefork Campground. Turn right onto Forest Road 33 and drive 3.8 miles to Ledgefork on the left side of the road.

GPS Coordinates: N 40° 44.526' W 110° 05.959'

Contact: Heber-Kamas Ranger District, 435/783-4338, www.fs.fed.us/r4/uwc/recreation/wcnf/camping/kamas-camping.shtml#ledgefork

13 JORDAN PINES

Scenic rating: 7

east of Salt Lake City in Big Cottonwood Canyon in the Wasatch-Cache National Forest

Map 3.1, page 111

Jordan Pines is a group campground located at the entrance to Cardiff Fork in Big Cottonwood Canyon. Here you'll find a plethora of recreational opportunities. Large groups may enjoy the mellow hikes into Cardiff Fork (also known as Mill D). The trail leads to old mine tailings and a nice waterfall. Fly fishing can be found on Big Cottonwood Creek, and rock climbing is available on a variety of crags down-canyon from Jordan Pines. An abundance of wildlife can be seen around the campground including moose, deer, and beaver. Beaver ponds are visible below the campground on the creek. The campground is tucked into a forest of spruce trees that provides some shade for the group areas. The group sites are located on a spur road leading to a small community at the base of Cardiff Fork. The campground is a bit farther off busy Big Cottonwood Road than Spruces. The sites are equipped with picnic tables and benches sufficient for large groups.

Campsites, facilities: There are four group areas and one day-use area. Pinyon Grove is for day use only for up to 50 people; Ponderosa, Lodgepole and Limber Groves are for up to 100 people; and Pine Grove is for up to 125 people. Picnic tables, fire rings, barbeque grills, drinking water, garbage service, and vault toilets are provided. Pets are not permitted in the Big Cottonwood Canyon because it's a watershed.

Reservations, fees: Reservations are required for the group sites at 877/444-6777 or online at www.recreation.gov and must be made a minimum of three days in advance. The fees for the group sites are $138–205. Open late May through mid-October, weather permitting.

Directions: From Salt Lake City, take I-15 south and then I-215 east. Take Exit 6 (6200 S) for Wasatch Boulevard. Follow Wasatch Boulevard to the Big Cottonwood Road (Rte. 190) and turn left at the mouth of the canyon. Follow the winding road 8.8 miles up Big Cottonwood Canyon and turn right onto Cardiff Fork Road and continue 0.2 mile to Jordan Pines Campground.

GPS Coordinates: N 40° 38.773 W 111° 38.878

Contact: Salt Lake Ranger District, 801/466-6411, www.fs.fed.us/r4/uwc/recreation/wcnf/camping/slrd/big_cottonwood_canyon_cg.shtml#jordan-pines-cg

14 SPRUCES

Scenic rating: 8

east of Salt Lake City in Big Cottonwood Canyon in the Wasatch-Cache National Forest

Map 3.1, page 111   **BEST (**

Spruces is located in Big Cottonwood Canyon less than a half-hour drive from Salt Lake City. Big Cottonwood Canyon is one of the recreation jewels of the Wasatch Mountains and the Salt Lake area in general. Steep, craggy peaks rise quickly from the canyon floor, beckoning campers to come out and explore. Many popular hiking trails of varying length and difficulty leave from the Big Cottonwood Road and make Spruces one of the best campgrounds for hiking in Utah. The 3.5-mile Days Fork Trail leaves directly from the campground and accesses a beautiful canyon with old mining camps. Hundreds of easily accessible rock-climbing routes have been established at cliffs up and down the canyon. Some of the most concentrated and popular collections of routes are at crags like Storm Mountain, the S Curve, and the Salt Lake Slips. Excellent single-track mountain biking trails are located near the top of Big Cottonwood at Guardsman Pass, and via chairlift at Solitude Mountain Resort. For being this close to such a big city, the wild character this campground maintains is remarkable. Stately spruce and Douglas fir trees shade many of the campsites and give the area a lush, alpine feel. Big Cottonwood Creek runs quietly through the campground and attracts fly fishers to the open meadows downstream from the camping. Moose frequent these wetlands, providing a good chance for a sighting. The loops and parking areas are paved, and the facilities are well maintained. Thick trees provide good separation between sites. Spruces is a huge campground and is almost always busy.

Campsites, facilities: There are 97 sites for tents and RVs and three group sites for up to 50 people. Individual sites 10, 35, and the three group sites are wheelchair accessible. Picnic tables, barbeque grills, fire pits, drinking water, modern restrooms, and garbage service are provided. Firewood and ice are available. Pets are not permitted in Big Cottonwood Canyon because it's a watershed.

Reservations, fees: Reservations are accepted at 877/444-6777 or online at www.recreation.gov and must be made a minimum of three days in advance. Single sites are $18, double sites are $36, triple sites are $54, group sites are $120, and extra vehicles and day use are $6. Open late May through mid-October, weather permitting.

Directions: From Salt Lake City, take I-15 south to I-215 east. Take Exit 6 (6200 S) for Wasatch Boulevard. Follow Wasatch Boulevard to the Big Cottonwood Road (Rte. 190) and turn left at the mouth of the canyon. Follow the winding road 10.1 miles up Big Cottonwood Canyon to Spruces Campground on the right side of the road.

GPS Coordinates: N 40° 38.546' W 111° 38.244'

Contact: Salt Lake Ranger District, 801/466-6411, www.fs.fed.us/r4/uwc/recreation/wcnf/camping/slrd/big_cottonwood_canyon_cg.shtml#spruces-cg

15 REDMAN

Scenic rating: 8

east of Salt Lake City in Big Cottonwood
Canyon in the Wasatch-Cache National Forest

Map 3.1, page 111   **BEST**

Redman Campground is a smaller Forest Service campground in the upper reaches of Big Cottonwood Canyon. Redman is between Brighton and Solitude Resorts and surrounded by recreation opportunities: Hiking, mountain biking, road biking, fishing, and rock climbing are all possible within a short drive of Redman. The Silver Lake Loop (great for families) and Brighton Lakes Trails both begin within a mile of the campground. More ambitious hikers may want to try the Lake Blanche trail in Mill B or the Twin Lakes Pass Trail. Single-track mountain biking trails can be accessed via chairlifts at Solitude, or by earning the downhill at Guardsman Pass on the Wasatch Crest Trail. There's a whole series of cliffs with rock climbing in Big Cottonwood Canyon. Climbers will find both bolted sport climbing routes and those requiring traditional protection. Fly fishing for trout is possible at many places along Big Cottonwood Creek as it cascades down the canyon. Redman Campground is set down in the creek bottom among an aspen and spruce forest. Views from the campground look up to the surrounding mountains, including USA Bowl and Guardsman Pass. Granite boulders are scattered around the campground, especially in the upper part of the loop. The campground has a distinctly alpine feel, even more so than Spruces and Jordan Pines farther down-canyon. Redman is considerably smaller and has more a rustic feel than Spruces. It's also farther off the busy Big Cottonwood Road, making it noticeably quieter. Temperatures are cool and pleasant, and it even gets a little chilly at night in the summer. The loop and parking aprons are gravel. Some of the sites are right on Big Cottonwood Creek. The overall quality of Redman and excellent access to the recreation in Big Cottonwood Canyon make Redman one of the best quick camping escapes from Salt Lake City.

Campsites, facilities: There are 38 single sites, one double site, two triple sites for tents and RVs up to 30 feet in length, and two group sites. Group site 24 can accommodate up to 50 people and group site 28 up to 35 people. Picnic tables, fire grills, wood cooking stoves, garbage service, modern restrooms, and drinking water are provided. Firewood is available. Pets are not permitted in the Big Cottonwood Canyon because it's a watershed.

Reservations, fees: Reservations are accepted for the group sites only at 877/444-6777 or online at www.recreation.gov and must be made a minimum of three days in advance. Single sites are $17, double sites are $34, triple sites are $51, group sites are $75–110, and extra vehicles are $6. Open mid-June through late September, weather permitting.

Directions: From Salt Lake City, take I-15 south and then I-215 east. Take Exit 6 (6200 S) for Wasatch Blvd. Follow Wasatch Blvd. to the Big Cottonwood Road (Rte. 190) and turn left at the mouth of the canyon. Follow the winding road 13 miles up Big Cottonwood Canyon to Redman Campground on the right side of the road.

GPS Coordinates: N 40° 36.917' W 111° 35.354'

Contact: Salt Lake Ranger District, 801/466-6411, www.fs.fed.us/r4/uwc/recreation/wcnf/camping/slrd/big_cottonwood_canyon_cg.shtml#redman-cg

16 HAILSTONE AT JORDANELLE STATE PARK

Scenic rating: 7

on the west side of the Jordanelle Reservoir,
southeast of Park City

Map 3.1, page 111   **BEST**

The Jordanelle Reservoir is a huge, popular recreation site on the east side of the Wasatch

Mountain Range. During summer months the lake's surface is busy with boat traffic, as Salt Lake Valley locals bring up their ski boats and Jet Skis to cool off in the reservoir. Fishing is also popular on the reservoir for rainbow, brown, and cutthroat trout, as well as smallmouth and large-mouth bass, yellow perch, and walleye. The park is also frequented by wildlife including red fox, mule deer, and muskrats. The sprawling Hailstone facility is on the northwest arm of the lake and offers a visitors center, public beach, beach house, and two boat ramps (one for personal watercraft), in addition to seven camping loops. The landscape at Hailstone is mostly open, with clumps of grass and sagebrush between camp-sites. Most camp loops offer views down to the reservoir and up to the southeastern slopes of the Wasatch Mountains, including Deer Valley Resort. Only a few loops are right on the water. Pinyon pine, blue spruce, and gambel oak trees grow in some of the camp loops. McHenry Loop (B) is a tent-only area with paved parking and natural tent pads. From McHenry Loop (B), look for a pair of ospreys nesting on a power pole near Highway 40. Murdoch Way Loop has waterfront sites. The campground's wheelchair-accessible sites have paved cement paths circling tent pads and paved access to drinking water. Hailstone is a first-rate facility and one of the best public campgrounds for RVs in Utah.

Campsites, facilities: There are 103 RV sites in the Murdoch Way Area (sites 47, 68, 70, and 72–74 are wheelchair accessible), McHenry Tent Camping Area has 40 tent sites (sites 122 and 124 are wheelchair accessible) and the hike-in/boat-in camping area has 39 sites. Amenities include picnic tables on concrete slabs, playgrounds, modern restrooms with showers, aluminum recycling, barbeque grills, fire grills, drinking water, a fish-cleaning station, general store, boat ramps, public docks (wheelchair accessible), garbage service, and dump station. Leashed pets are permitted only in the campground area.

Reservations, fees: Reservations are accepted at 800/322-3770 or online at www.reserveamerica.com; they must be made a minimum of two days in advance and can be arranged up to 16 weeks in advance. There is an $8 non-refundable reservation fee for individual sites. McHenry Loop sites are $16, Hailstone RV sites are $20, Keetley walk-in/boat-in sites are $16, and the day-use fee is $10. Open year-round.

Directions: From Heber City, drive north 8.0 miles on Hwy. 40 and take Exit 8. Drive over the freeway overpass and follow Rte. 313 for 1.2 miles to the Jordanelle State Park entrance station.

GPS Coordinates: N 40° 37.184' W 111° 25.463'

Contact: Jordanelle State Park, 435/649-9540, http://stateparks.utah.gov/stateparks/parks/jordanelle/

17 ROCK CLIFF RECREATION AREA AT JORDANELLE STATE PARK

Scenic rating: 7

on the southeast corner of the Jordanelle Reservoir

Map 3.1, page 111

The Rock Cliff Recreation Area is a wetland area on the southeast arm of the Jordanelle Reservoir. The wetland is a low, flat marsh where the Upper Provo River feeds into the reservoir. Camping at Rock Cliff is a quiet, low-key experience, especially when compared with the massive facilities at the other campground in this state park. The campsites are walk-in only, attracting different users than the powerboat-loving crowd normally associated with the Jordanelle Reservoir. Tall grass and small trees surround the sites set very close to the river (5–7 are right by the water). In fact, you'll hear the sound of the river flowing by from the sites. Keep your eyes open for wildlife; we spotted a garter snake and a red-tailed hawk during our visit. The facilities are very nice, with elevated wood tent pads and cement paths leading to the sites. There's also a nature center near the campground overlooking a small pond, with a stuffed black bear and cougars hanging out in the entry. Both the nature center and Rock Cliff

Recreation Area are great places for kids to learn about the outdoors.

Campsites, facilities: There are four walk-in camping areas with a total of 51 tent sites. Sites 1–4 and Site 37 are wheelchair accessible. A fish-cleaning station, nature center, picnic tables, wood platform tent pads, fire grills, modern restrooms with showers, and a day-use pavilion are provided. Pets are not permitted.

Reservations, fees: Reservations are accepted at 800/322-3770 or online at www.reserveamerica.com; they must be made a minimum of two days in advance and can be arranged up to 16 weeks in advance. There is an $8 nonrefundable reservation fee for individual sites. Sites are $16, and the day-use fee is $7. Open year-round.

Directions: From Heber City, drive three miles north on Hwy. 40 and turn right at the intersection of Hwy. 40 and Hwy. 32. Travel 7.7 miles east on Hwy. 32, turn left, and continue 0.8 mile to the entrance station.

GPS Coordinates: N 40° 36.229' W 111° 20.653'

Contact: Jordanelle State Park, 435/782-3030, http://stateparks.utah.gov/stateparks/parks/jordanelle/

18 PONDEROSA GROUP AREA

🏃 🚴 🏊 🏕 🚐 ⛺

Scenic rating: 8

on the Mirror Lake Scenic Byway in the Wasatch-Cache National Forest

Map 3.1, page 111

Ponderosa group area is the first campground encountered driving northeast from Kamas on the Mirror Lake Highway on the western slopes of the Uinta Mountains. The group site is found under a grove of mature ponderosa pines several hundred yards off the scenic byway. Views from the campground look up to rolling hills and the aspen-painted slopes of the Uintas. The site is quiet and secluded and offers a nice private spot for family reunions and other group functions.

The group site offers level tenting areas and a flat gravel parking area for RVs and trailers. The campground is close to both the Slate Creek horse trail and the Yellow Pine Trailhead. The Yellow Pine Trail is open to hikers, mountain bikers, and horses.

Campsites, facilities: There is one group site for up to 100 people and for tents and RVs up to 37 feet in length. Picnic tables, portable toilets, and fire grills are provided. There is no drinking water. Leashed pets permitted.

Reservations, fees: Reservations are required at 877/444-6777 or online at www.recreation.gov and must be made a minimum of five days in advance. The group site is $80. Open May through October, weather permitting.

Directions: From the intersection of Main Street (Rte. 32) and 200 S (Rte. 248) in Kamas, head north on Rte. 32 and turn east (right) after one block onto Rte. 150. Continue east on Rte. 150 for six miles, turn left, and after 100 feet turn left again and continue 0.2 mile to the Ponderosa Group Area.

GPS Coordinates: N 40° 37.802' W 111° 11.853'

Contact: Kamas Ranger District, 435/783-4338, www.fs.fed.us/r4/uwc/about/districts/kamas/index.shtml.

19 YELLOW PINE CREEK

🏃 🚴 🏊 🏕 🚐 ⛺

Scenic rating: 8

on the Mirror Lake Scenic Byway in the Wasatch-Cache National Forest

Map 3.1, page 111

The Yellow Pine Creek Campground is located just past the entrance booth for the Mirror Lake Highway on the western side of the Uinta Mountains. The campground sits above the road in a stand of lodgepole and ponderosa pines accented with aspens and the occasional willow tree. The camp loops lead to sites set on a gently sloping hill. While views are limited by the forest, you'll be able to catch glimpses of the surrounding sagebrush-dotted hills and aspen groves. Plan a trip here in early fall to experience the spectacular show of changing colors. There's trout fishing on Yellow Pine Creek, and the Slate Creek Horse Trail is nearby. The Yellow Pine Trailhead, open to hikers, mountain bikers, and horseback riders, is close to the campground as well.

Campsites, facilities: There are 33 sites for tents and RVs up to 25 feet in length. Picnic tables, fire grills, garbage service, and vault toilets are provided. There is no drinking water. Leashed pets permitted.

Reservations, fees: Reservations are not accepted. Sites are $10; extra vehicles and day use are $6. Open May through October, weather permitting.

Directions: From the intersection of Main Street (Rte. 32) and 200 S (Rte. 248) in Kamas, head north on Rte. 32 and turn east (right) after one block onto Rte. 150. Continue east on Rte. 150 for 6.9 miles, and turn right into the Yellow Pine Creek Campground.

GPS Coordinates: N 40° 37.725' W 111° 10.665'

Contact: Kamas Ranger District, 435/783-4338, www.fs.fed.us/r4/uwc/recreation/wcnf/camping/kamas-camping.shtml#yellowpine

busy. Sites enjoy both shade from the trees and views across the meadows. There are some pull-through parking slips for small RVs and campers, and good level tenting ground.

Campsites, facilities: There are 11 sites for tents and RVs up to 25 feet in length. Picnic tables, fire grills, garbage service, drinking water, pull-through sites, and vault toilets are provided. Leashed pets permitted.

Reservations, fees: Reservations are not accepted. Sites are $12; extra vehicles and day use are $6. Open May through October, weather permitting.

Directions: From the intersection of Main Street (Rte. 32) and 200 S (Rte. 248) in Kamas, head north on Rte. 32 and turn east (right) after one block onto Rte. 150. Continue east on Rte. 150 for 9.3 miles, and turn right into the Taylors Fork Campground.

GPS Coordinates: N 40° 37.169' W 111° 08.112'

Contact: Kamas Ranger District, 435/783-4338, www.fs.fed.us/r4/uwc/recreation/wcnf/camping/kamas-camping.shtml#taylorsforkatv

20 TAYLORS FORK
🚶 🛶 🐕 🚐 ⛺

Scenic rating: 8

on the Mirror Lake Scenic Byway in the Wasatch-Cache National Forest

Map 3.1, page 111

Taylors Fork Campground is part of a double campground and ATV staging area on the Mirror Lake Highway in the western Uinta Mountains. Taylors Fork is the trailhead for the Cedar Loop (rocky and rough) and Beaver Creek (easier) ATV Trails. The campground sits in a transition zone between lodgepole forest and open grass meadows. Beaver ponds line the stream running through the meadows, and gnawed-off aspen stumps poke up through the grass everywhere. These beavers have been

21 SHINGLE CREEK
🚶 🛶 🐕 🚐 ⛺

Scenic rating: 8

on the Mirror Lake Scenic Byway in the Wasatch-Cache National Forest

Map 3.1, page 111

Shingle Creek is the other half of the dual campground and trailhead facility coupled with the Taylor's Fork. The campground is named after a shingle mill that operated in the area in the 1870s. Like the Taylors Fork Loop, Shingle Creek borders a long grass meadow dotted with beaver ponds. The sites sit under the protection of an open stand of aspen, lodgepole, and small ponderosa pine trees. The sites are flat and offer good tenting on the level forest floor. The long narrow layout allows for well-spaced, private sites. Views from the sites look out to the beaver ponds, rimmed with willow trees and tall grasses. Piles of dead branches and thinned lodgepole are stacked around the loop, left over from thinning out trees killed by pesky pine bark beetles. The campground is near the trailhead for Shingle Creek Trail, open to horses and hikers. It's also within several hundred yards of the Cedar Loop and Beaver Creek ATV Trails.

Campsites, facilities: There are 21 sites for tents and RVs up to 25 feet in length. Picnic tables, fire grills, garbage service, drinking water, pull-through sites, and vault toilets are provided. Firewood is available. Leashed pets permitted.

Reservations, fees: Reservations are not accepted. Sites are $12; extra vehicles and day use are $6. Open May through October, weather permitting.

Directions: From the intersection of Main Street (Rte. 32) and 200 S (Rte. 248) in Kamas, head north on Rte. 32 and turn east (right) after one block onto Rte. 150. Continue east on Rte. 150 for 9.7 miles, and turn right into the Shingle Creek Campground.

GPS Coordinates: N 40° 36.856' W 111° 07.825'

Contact: Kamas Ranger District, 435/783-4338, www.fs.fed.us/r4/uwc/recreation/wcnf/camping/kamas-camping.shtml#shinglecreekatv

22 PINE VALLEY GROUP AREA
🏊 🏠 🚐 ⛰️

Scenic rating: 8

on the Mirror Lake Scenic Byway in the Wasatch-Cache National Forest

Map 3.1, page 111

The Pine Valley Group Area is a large group campground a short distance off the Mirror Lake Highway. Three group areas with paved loops are tucked into the aspen, lodgepole, and ponderosa pine forest. Each of the three camps—Laurel, Mahonia, and Snowberry—has its own driveway, offering lots of separation and privacy. The loops have parallel parking for RVs. There are views of the surrounding

Uinta Mountains and tall grass meadows. In winter, there are opportunities for cross-country skiing and snowshoeing at Pine Valley.

Campsites, facilities: There are three group sites. Group A is for up to 120 people, Group B is for up to 60 people, and Group C is for up to 140 people. Picnic tables, fire grills, barbeque grills, garbage service, drinking water, and vault toilets are provided.

Reservations, fees: Reservations are required at 877/444-6777 or online at www.recreation.gov and must be made a minimum of five days in advance. The group sites are $150–250. Open May through October, weather permitting.

Directions: From the intersection of Main Street (Rte. 32) and 200 S (Rte. 248) in Kamas, head north on Rte. 32 and turn east (right) after one block onto Rte. 150. Continue east on Rte. 150 for 11 miles, turn right and continue 0.1 mile, and turn left into the Pine Valley Group Area.

GPS Coordinates: N 40° 35.951' W 111° 06.864'

Contact: Kamas Ranger District, 435/783-4338, www.fs.fed.us/r4/uwc/recreation/wcnf/camping/kamas-camping.shtml#pinevalley

23 LOWER PROVO RIVER
🏊 🏠 🚐 ⛰️

Scenic rating: 7

on the Mirror Lake Scenic Byway in the Wasatch-Cache National Forest

Map 3.1, page 111

The Lower Provo River Campground is a quiet alternative to the campgrounds right on the Mirror Lake Highway. Down a short spur road, the campground enjoys relative peace and quiet compared to the sites right along the main road. The only noises you'll hear at Lower Provo River are the other campers around you and the breeze in the pine trees. The gravel camp loop wanders through aspen, Douglas fir, lodgepole pine, and spruce trees, which shade flat sites with great spots for tents and flat parking for campers and RVs. There's dispersed camping near the Lower Provo River Campground if you're looking for a free alternative.

Campsites, facilities: There are 10 sites for tents and RVs up to 30 feet in length. Picnic tables, fire grills, drinking water, garbage service, and vault toilets are provided. Firewood is available. Leashed pets permitted.

Reservations, fees: Reservations are accepted at 877/444-6777 or online at www.recreation.gov and must be made a minimum of five days in advance. To make a reservation, Lower Provo River Campground requires a two-night minimum stay on weekends and three nights on holiday weekends. Sites are $12; extra vehicles are $6. Open May through October, weather permitting.

Directions: From the intersection of Main Street (Rte. 32) and 200 S (Rte. 248) in Kamas, head north on Rte. 32 and turn east (right) after one block onto Rte. 150. Continue east on Rte. 150 for 11 miles, turn right, and continue 0.6 mile to the Lower Provo River Campground.

GPS Coordinates: N 40° 35.600' W 111° 07.082'

Contact: Kamas Ranger District 435/783-4338, www.fs.fed.us/r4/uwc/recreation/wcnf/camping/kamas-camping.shtml#lowerprovo

24 SOAPSTONE

🚲 🏊 🏕 🚙 ⛰

Scenic rating: 8

on the Mirror Lake Scenic Byway in the Wasatch-Cache National Forest

Map 3.1, page 111

Soapstone Campground is one of the most attractive campgrounds along the lower part of the Mirror Lake Highway. The Soapstone loop is paved and leads to sites next to the Provo River. These riverbed sites offer level areas to pitch a tent under a canopy of lodgepole pines and aspen trees. The sites are well spread out in the forest and offer good privacy, though some road noise from the highway makes its way into the sites. The sites have views up to the forested

slopes of the Uinta Mountains. Trout fishing is possible in the Provo River. Keep an eye out for wildlife along the river, including moose. The campground is near the Soapstone Basin Mountain Bike Trail. This mostly double-track trail offers a good, nontechnical mountain bike ride through open wildflower and grass meadows. The loop trail is 15 miles long. Soapstone Campground is one of the busiest along this stretch of the road, so make a reservation.

Campsites, facilities: There are 31 single sites, two double sites, and one triple site for tents and RVs up to 80 feet in length. Picnic tables, fire grills, drinking water, garbage service, and vault toilets are provided. Firewood is available. Leashed pets permitted.

Reservations, fees: Reservations are accepted at 877/444-6777 or online at www.recreation.gov and must be made a minimum of five days in advance. To make a reservation, Soapstone Campground requires a two-night minimum stay on weekends and three nights on holiday weekends. Sites are $16; extra vehicles and day use are $6. Open May through October, weather permitting.

Directions: From the intersection of Main Street (Rte. 32) and 200 S (Rte. 248) in Kamas, head north on Rte. 32 and turn east (right) after one block onto Rte. 150. Continue east on Rte. 150 for 16 miles and turn right into Soapstone Campground.

GPS Coordinates: N 40° 34.716' W 111° 01.673'

Contact: Kamas Ranger District 435/783-4338, www.fs.fed.us/r4/uwc/recreation/wcnf/camping/kamas-camping.shtml#soapstone

25 SHADY DELL

🏊 🏕 🚙 ⛰

Scenic rating: 8

on the Mirror Lake Scenic Byway in the Wasatch-Cache National Forest

Map 3.1, page 111

Shady Dell Campground is another very popular campground along the Mirror Lake

Highway in the Uinta Mountains. The campground is set in a stand of aspen, lodgepole pine, and willow trees. There's trout fishing in the Provo River. At around 8,000 feet in elevation, Shady Dell offers a good summer escape during hot weather and a place to spot wildlife like deer and moose. In the early fall it becomes a convenient base camp for hunters or a beautiful place to take in the autumn colors.

Campsites, facilities: There are 19 sites for tents and RVs up to 25 feet in length. Picnic tables, fire grills, drinking water, garbage service, and vault toilets are provided. Firewood is available. Leashed pets permitted.

Reservations, fees: Reservations are not accepted. Sites are $14; day use and extra vehicles are $6. Open May through October, weather permitting.

Directions: From the intersection of Main Street (Rte. 32) and 200 S (Rte. 248) in Kamas, head north on Rte. 32 and turn east (right) after one block onto Rte. 150. Continue east on Rte. 150 for 17 miles and turn right into Shady Dell Campground.

GPS Coordinates: N 40° 35.419' W 111° 00.879'

Contact: Kamas Ranger District, 435/783-4338, www.fs.fed.us/r4/uwc/about/districts/kamas/index.shtml.

26 TANNER'S FLAT

Scenic rating: 9

east of Salt Lake City in Little Cottonwood Canyon

Map 3.1, page 111   BEST

Tanner's Flat is located in the heart of Little Cottonwood Canyon, a recreation hot spot in the Wasatch Mountains and one of the most popular ski destinations in the world. Little Cottonwood is home to Alta and Snowbird Ski Resorts, both of which are consistently rated in the top 10 ski destinations in North America. While the light powder snow that makes Little Cottonwood so universally loved is long gone

in the summer, the beauty and accessibility of the canyon remain. Rock climbing, bouldering, hiking, trail running, and road biking are all popular pursuits during the warmer months. Tanner's Flat Campground is located midway up Little Cottonwood, before the ski resorts and town of Alta. Its location allows a wild feel, despite heavy traffic on Little Cottonwood Road and a constant buzz of outdoor enthusiasts recreating in the canyon. Many of the sites are set right on Little Cottonwood Creek, which roars by in early summer and quiets to a trickle in August and September. Huge gray granite boulders are strewn between aspen, maple, spruce, and fir trees. The sites find a good balance between development and maintaining the grounds' natural character. Picnic tables are set on concrete pads, but tent areas are simply dirt patches between thick undergrowth. Tanner's Flat is just a half-hour drive from Salt Lake City, making it one of the best campgrounds for an easy escape into the mountains.

Campsites, facilities: There are 38 campsites and four group sites. Group sites A, B, and C are for up to 25 people, and group site 23 is for up to 50 people. Wheelchair-accessible sites are 6, 10 16–19, 26, and the group sites. Picnic tables on concrete pads, fire rings, volleyball court (bring your own net/ball), flush toilets, drinking water, and garbage service are provided. Firewood and ice are available. Pets are not permitted because Little Cottonwood Canyon is a watershed.

Reservations, fees: Reservations are accepted at 877/444-6777 or online at www.recreation.gov and must be made a minimum of three days in advance. Single sites are $18, double sites are $36, group sites A, B, and C are $61, and group site 23 is $97. Open mid-May through mid-October, weather permitting.

Directions: From Salt Lake City, take I-215 south to Exit 6 (6200 S), drive east for one mile to Wasatch Boulevard. Continue driving south on Wasatch Boulevard for three miles to the base of Little Cottonwood Canyon. Turn left on Rte. 210 (Little Cottonwood Road) and drive 4.3 miles to campground entrance on the right side of the road.

GPS Coordinates: N 40° 34.340' W 111° 42.013'

Contact: Salt Lake Ranger District, 801/466-6411, www.fs.fed.us/r4/uwc/recreation/wcnf/camping/slrd/little_cottonwood_canyon_cg.shtml#tanners-flat-cg

27 ALBION BASIN

Scenic rating: 9

east of Salt Lake City in Little Cottonwood Canyon

Map 3.1, page 111   BEST (

Albion Basin is a breathtaking alpine basin located within the boundaries of Alta Ski Resort in Little Cottonwood Canyon. Alta is famous for being the epicenter of the Utah ski community and a mecca for hard-core skiers from around the globe. Summertime in Albion Basin brings open fields of wildflowers too numerous to count. Splashes of pink, purple, yellow, and white highlight the lush carpet of green shrubs and grass in the tundralike cirque. Hikes to Catherine Pass and Cecret Lake leave from near the campground, leading to bird's-eye views of the mountainous wonderland. The campground sits in the middle of all this glory, below a chairlift, on a gently sloping hillside. The access loop is unpaved but well graded and leads to simple yet functional sites. Sites on the steepest slopes even have granite boulder retaining walls to level off sleeping and eating areas. The headwaters of Little Cottonwood creek flow through the silver firs and spruce trees, which provide shade and shelter in the alpine environment.

Campsites, facilities: There are 22 single sites, two double sites, and one triple site. Picnic tables, fire grills, garbage service, vault toilets, and drinking water are provided. Recycling containers are available down the road, in the town of Alta. Pets are not permitted because Little Cottonwood Canyon is a watershed.

Reservations, fees: Reservations are accepted at 877/444-6777 or online at www.recreation.gov and must be made a minimum of three days in advance. Single sites are $15, double sites are $30, triple sites are $45, extra vehicles are $6, and day use is $8. Open late June through mid-September, weather permitting.

Directions: From Salt Lake City, take I-15 south and then I-215 east to Exit 6 (6200 S), drive east for one mile to Wasatch Boulevard. Continue driving south on Wasatch Boulevard for three miles to the base of Little Cottonwood Canyon. Turn left on Rte. 210 (Little Cottonwood Road) and drive 11.3 miles to campground entrance at the end of the road.

GPS Coordinates: N 40° 34.659' W 111° 36.786'

Contact: Salt Lake Ranger District, 801/466-6411, www.fs.fed.us/r4/uwc/recreation/wcnf/camping/slrd/little_cottonwood_canyon_cg.shtml#albion-basin-cg

28 WASATCH MOUNTAIN STATE PARK

Scenic rating: 7

north of Midway

Map 3.1, page 111

Wasatch Mountain State Park protects a huge tract of land on the east side of the Wasatch Mountain Range. It's also home to two scenic golf courses, and a not-so-scenic hot springs. Well, the hot springs themselves aren't bad, but the surroundings are a bit of an eyesore. If you're interested in unique hot springs, check out the Midway Hot Pots (a private resort) and scuba diving pools a bit farther downstream. If golfing is your priority, there's no better place to camp and play in the state of Utah. The state park features two different 18-hole layouts, the Mountain Course and the Lakes Course.

© MIKE MATSON

Gambel oak leaves turning in autumn over the Jordanelle Reservoir

The courses incorporate the beautiful natural landscape into their design and are often visited by resident moose, elk, and deer in addition to golfers. The camping at Wasatch Mountain is next to the golf course among gambel oak trees and sagebrush flats. The facilities are modern, well kept, and spread out over four different loops. Most sites share views up to the Wasatch Mountains. There are separate loops for RV and for tent campers. The Little Deer Creek area offers more a primitive and solitary experience. The Pine Creek Nature Trail leaves directly from the campground.

Campsites, facilities: There are 47 RV-only sites in the Cottonwood Loop, 31 with full hook-ups and 16 with partial hook-ups. Mahogany Loop has 35 RV-only sites, all with full hook-ups. Oak Hollow Loop has 40 tent-only sites. There are 17 sites in the Little Deer Creek Area. Picnic tables, fire grills, drinking water, and garbage service are provided at both campgrounds. Modern restrooms

with showers, day-use group areas, and a dump station are provided at the Pine Creek Campground. Firewood and ice are available. Leashed pets permitted.

Reservations, fees: Reservations are accepted at 800/322-3770 or online at www.reserveamerica.com; they must be made a minimum of two days in advance and can be arranged up to 16 weeks in advance. There is an $8 non-refundable reservation fee for individual sites. Full hook-up sites are $25, and partial hook-up and tent sites are $20. Little Deer Creek sites are $13. Open April through October, weather permitting.

Directions: From Heber City, drive three miles north on Hwy. 40. Turn left at the stoplight onto River Road. After 2.9 miles stay right at the roundabout. Continue one mile and turn right on Pine Canyon Road. Drive 1.1 miles and turn left into the campground entrance. GPS Coordinates: N 40° 32.659' W 111° 29.177'

Contact: Wasatch Mountain State Park, 435/654-1791, http://stateparks.utah.gov/stateparks/parks/wasatch/

29 HEBER VALLEY RV PARK RESORT

Scenic rating: 6

in Heber City

Map 3.1, page 111

The Heber Valley RV Park Resort sits in a deep valley in the shadow of the mighty rock dam that holds back the Jordanelle Reservoir. The Provo River escapes from an aqueduct in the dam and runs clear and cold by the Heber Valley Resort. The highlight of the resort is a collection of red-roofed yurts and a matching covered group pavilion. The RV side of the campground is pleasant but lacks shade, with few trees that actually shield sites from the sun. There are cottonwood trees down by the creek, but these contribute little more than scenic value. And the scenery isn't bad, especially for an RV park.

Small touches like the log cabin office and the oft-visited collection of hummingbird feeders in the front garden help add character. Robins and swallows are everywhere, and more wildlife can be seen on the riverside trail near the campground. The resort's only real shortcoming is tightly spaced sites with little privacy.

Campsites, facilities: There are 34 full hookup sites, 46 partial hook-up sites, and nine yurts. Tents are only allowed with a registered RV guest. Amenities include picnic tables, rock fire rings, modern restrooms with showers, drinking water, horseshoe pit, playground, volleyball court, WiFi, satellite TV, garbage service, and dump station. Firewood and ice are available. Leashed pets permitted.

Reservations, fees: Reservations are accepted at 435/654-4049 or online at www.hebervalleyrvpark.com/reservation_form.php. Full hook-ups are $39.95, partial hook-ups are $36.95, cabins are $79.95–179.95, and yurts are $79.95. Open year-round.

Directions: From Heber City, drive three miles north on Hwy. 40 to the first stop light and turn east (right) onto Hwy. 32. After 0.2 mile, turn left onto Old Hwy. 40 and travel two miles to the Heber Valley RV Park Resort, on the right side of the road.

GPS Coordinates: N 40° 35.603' W 111° 25.652'

Contact: Heber Valley RV Park Resort, 435/654-4049, www.hebervalleyrvpark.com/

30 WOLF CREEK

Scenic rating: 8

in the Uinta National Forest at Wolf Creek Summit

Map 3.1, page 111

Wolf Creek Campground is located right on the Wolf Creek Summit at 9,485 feet. An alpine spruce forest surrounds the sites and the pine needle–padded forest floor offers excellent tent-pitching options. The campground is flat for being located on a mountain pass.

Grass grows in an open meadow near the perimeter of the campground and around the sites. Spruce trees provide shade for most of the picnic tables and tenting areas, except in the open group areas. The picnic tables are set on gravel pads. A trail leads from the campground to the West Fork of Duchesne River.

Campsites, facilities: There are three single sites and two group sites. One group site accommodates up to 30 people, the other up to 60 people. Picnic tables, barbeque grills, vault toilets, fire rings, and drinking water are provided. Leashed pets permitted.

Reservations, fees: Reservations are accepted for the group sites only at 877/444-6777 or online at www.recreation.gov and must be made a minimum of five days in advance. Sites are $14, and the group sites are $75–150. Open July through October, weather permitting.

Directions: From Kamas, drive south on Rte. 35 for two miles. Continue east on Rte. 35 for 19.6 miles. Turn right into Wolf Creek Campground.

GPS Coordinates: N 40° 28.909' W 111° 01.939'

Contact: Heber Ranger District, 435/654-0470, www.fs.fed.us/r4/uwc/recreation/uinta/camping/heber/index.shtml#wolf_creek

31 MOUNTAIN SHADOWS RV PARK

Scenic rating: 4

in Draper

Map 3.1, page 111

The Mountain Shadows RV park is a large, convenient RV park for travelers passing through the Salt Lake Valley. It's right off I-15, where lanes are four deep in both directions. If you stay here, you'll hear traffic. On the other hand, the location is easy to get in and out of, and if you have a big rig and want to stay in the southern suburban valley, this is a good option. Despite its urban surroundings, Mountain Shadows does live up to its name with views of the spectacular

Wasatch Mountains. The gray granite of Lone Pine Cirque looks particularly appealing from this angle. The campground has inviting, well-cared-for facilities. A welcoming rock waterfall fountain greets visitors at the front gate, and kids play in the pool near the entrance. Like a busy restaurant, all the activity makes the place feel enticing. Sites are tightly packed into the lot but are shaded by broad-leaved trees. Expect to share the place with the whole gamut of camping characters, including retired, full-time road veterans and trailer park residents.

Campsites, facilities: There are 110 full hook-up sites (30, 50 amps), 13 partial hook-up sites, and 20 tent sites. Amenities include picnic tables, a swimming pool, WiFi, playground, basketball court, volleyball court, dog walk, laundry, pull-through sites, a convenience store, drinking water, modern restrooms with showers, garbage service, and two dump stations. Leashed pets permitted.

Reservations, fees: Reservations are accepted at 801/571-4024 or online at www.mountain-shadows.com/reserve.html. Full hook-up sites are $39.25, partial hook-up sites are $34.25, and tent sites are $18. Open year-round.

Directions: From I-15, take Exit 291. Take the ramp toward Draper. Turn left on 12300 S and drive 0.1 mile to Minuteman Drive. Turn right onto Minuteman Drive and continue 1.2 miles to the Mountain Shadows RV Park on the left side of the road.

GPS Coordinates: N 40° 30.623' W 111° 53.424'

Contact: Mountain Shadows RV Park, 801/571-4024, www.mountain-shadows.com/

32 GRANITE FLAT

Scenic rating: 9

in American Fork Canyon

Map 3.1, page 111   BEST (

Granite Flat Campground is one of the crown jewels of the Wasatch campgrounds. It was the first campground built in Utah by Franklin Roosevelt's New Deal Civilian Conservation Corps in the early 1930s. It was a headquarters of sorts for the "Tree Army," complete with barracks, a mess hall, a hospital, and an amusement room. Most of these original facilities are gone, and what remains is simply one of the most scenic campgrounds in the state of Utah. The campground is located at the very top of American Fork Canyon. Above camp is Box Elder Peak. During winter the 11,100-foot hunk of gray granite offers one of the longest vertical ski chutes in the Wasatch down its northwest couloir. The peak is also the source of many of the car-sized boulders that give the campground its unique character. Granite Flat is near the Tibble Fork Reservoir, a popular spot to fly fish for brown and rainbow trout and for nonmotorized boating. The campground itself is large and easy to get lost in—so large it even has an alpine baseball field. The paved loops are all named after the campground's storied history and maintained by a small army of golf cart–driving campground hosts. Sites are tucked in between aspen, spruce, fir, maple, and willow trees. The thick woods and dispersed spacing make sites quiet and private. Granite Flat's alpine splendor, quality facilities, and close proximity to the city make it one of the best escapes from Salt Lake.

Campsites, facilities: There are 44 single sites, eight double sites, and three group areas. Stonemason and Handshaker Group Areas are for up to 100 people, and Sandwagon Group Area is for up to 125 people. Over 20 of the single sites are wheelchair accessible, as are four of the double sites and two of the group sites. Picnic tables, flush toilets, drinking water, a baseball field, and fire grills are provided. Firewood is available. Leashed pets permitted.

Reservations, fees: Reservations are accepted at 877/444-6777 or online at www.recreation.gov and must be made a minimum of five days in advance. Single sites are $13, double sites are $26, group sites are $150–175, extra vehicles are $5, and the day-use fee is $6. Open June through October, weather permitting.

Directions: From I-15, take Exit 284 (Alpine-Highland) and drive east on Hwy. 92 for eight miles to the base of American Fork Canyon. Continue five miles and turn left at the junction onto Forest Road 85, and travel 3.2 miles to the campground.

GPS Coordinates: N 40° 29.386' W 111° 39.186'

Contact: Pleasant Grove Ranger District, 801/785-3563, www.fs.fed.us/r4/uwc/recreation/uinta/camping/pleasant_grove/index.shtml#granite_flat

33 LITTLE MILL

Scenic rating: 8

in American Fork Canyon in the Uinta National Forest

Map 3.1, page 111

Little Mill Campground is a brand-new Forest Service facility in the American Fork Canyon. The previous campground was destroyed by rockfall, which is easy to imagine considering the steep, often overhanging limestone cliffs towering on both sides of the canyon. These same cliffs are also what make American Fork such a fun place to visit. There's excellent and difficult rock climbing on the limestone and the Timpanogos Cave tunnels through the rock itself. Timpanogos Cave National Monument offers tours of the cave and a paved trail accessing it. The Little Mill Campground has a paved central parking area accessing forest sites. The newly paved loop makes for excellent wheelchair accessibility. The sites are sheltered by a mix of Rocky Mountain Maple, box elder, cottonwood, and evergreen trees. While the central layout makes most sites visible to one another, the forest provides some separation. The America Fork Creek runs by the campground, offering trout fishing and adding a refreshing quality. Bighorn sheep and mountain goats are frequently sighted foraging among the crags.

Campsites, facilities: There are 74 sites for tents and RVs up to 30 feet in length. Picnic tables, fire pits, barbeque grills, drinking water, and vault toilets are provided. Leashed pets permitted.

Reservations, fees: Reservations are accepted at 877/444-6777 or online at www.recreation.gov and must be made a minimum of five days in advance. Sites are $13. Open May through October, weather permitting.

Directions: From I-15, take Exit 284 (Alpine-Highland) and drive east on Hwy. 92 for eight miles to the base of American Fork Canyon. Continue 3.8 miles and turn right into Little Mill Campground.

GPS Coordinates: N 40° 26.901' W 111° 40.665'

Contact: Pleasant Grove Ranger District, 801/785-3563, www.fs.fed.us/r4/uwc/recreation/uinta/camping/pleasant_grove/index.shtml#little_mill.

34 ALTAMONT

Scenic rating: 8

in American Fork Canyon

Map 3.1, page 111

Altamont is a Forest Service group campground on the Alpine Loop Scenic Byway set on the lower flanks of the mighty Mount Timpanogos. The group area offers undeniable views of the upper mountain and alpine cirque which holds snow into August. Layers of wildly twisted gray, brown, and white rock call to you from the campground, begging campers to come take a closer look. The campground has a peaceful, secluded feel with its own spur road branching off the scenic byway. It's easily accessible and has a paved loop and large parking lot. There's a large covered pavilion with picnic tables and barbeque grills that can accommodate groups up to 150 people. Tent areas are dispersed in the forest beside the pavilion. Aspen, fir, and spruce trees grow between the tent pads and add to the lush, green feel of the place. Expect a forest you'd associate more with the dripping Pacific Northwest than arid Utah.

Campsites, facilities: There is one group area that accommodates up to 150 people (wheelchair accessible). Picnic tables, a covered pavilion, drinking water, flush toilets, and fire grills are provided. Leashed pets permitted.

Reservations, fees: Reservations are accepted at 877/444-6777 or online at www.recreation.gov and must be made a minimum of five days in advance. The fee is $150. Open June through September, weather permitting.

Directions: From I-15 take Exit 284 (Alpine-Highland) and drive east on Hwy. 92 for eight miles to the base of American Fork Canyon. Continue for five miles, stay right at the junction on the Alpine Scenic Loop (Rte. 92), and travel 3.5 miles to the campground on the left side of the road.

GPS Coordinates: N 40° 26.081' W 111° 38.123'

Contact: Pleasant Grove Ranger District, 801/785-3563, www.fs.fed.us/r4/uwc/recreation/uinta/camping/pleasant_grove/index.shtml#altamont

35 TIMPOONEKE

Scenic rating: 8

In American Fork Canyon

Map 3.1, page 111   BEST (

Timpooneke Campground is located high in the alpine forest of Mount Timpanogos. Incredible views from the campground look up to the Lone Peak Wilderness Area, topped by peaks carved from distinctly gray granite at the ceiling of the Wasatch Range. Hikers and horseback riders looking for a challenging day can hike up Mount Timpanogos via the glacial valley dubbed the Giant Staircase (15 miles round-trip). Much of Mount Timpanogos is above the tree line, where wildflowers grow thick in the tundralike environment, making it one of the best spots for wildflowers in the Wasatch Mountains. There's also access to the Great Western Trail from the campground. Keep a watchful eye out for deer in the area, especially while you're driving the winding Alpine Loop Scenic Drive. The campground is spread out on gravel loops. Sites are relatively far apart, and thick trees provide lots of shade and privacy. In Loop A there are horse corrals and water troughs to accommodate equestrians. The forest and vegetation are thick and green, a far cry from the arid valleys below.

Campsites, facilities: There are 20 single sites, seven double sites, and one group area for up to 40 people. Vehicles over 30 feet are not permitted on the Alpine Scenic Loop. Picnic tables on concrete pads, concrete fire rings, drinking water, horse corrals (Loop A), and vault toilets are provided. Leashed pets permitted.

Reservations, fees: Reservations are accepted at 877/444-6777 or online at www.recreation.gov and must be made a minimum of five days in advance. Single sites are $13, double sites are $26, extra vehicles are $5, and the day-use fee is $6. Open June through October, weather permitting.

Directions: From I-15, take Exit 284 (Alpine-Highland) and drive east on Hwy. 92 for eight miles to the base of American Fork Canyon. Continue for five miles, stay right at the junction on the Alpine Scenic Loop (Rte. 92), and travel 3.5 miles to the campground on the right side of the road.

GPS Coordinates: N 40° 26.026' W 111° 38.262'

Contact: Pleasant Grove Ranger District, 801/785-3563, www.fs.fed.us/r4/uwc/recreation/uinta/camping/pleasant_grove/index.shtml#timpooneke

36 MOUNT TIMPANOGOS

Scenic rating: 7

In American Fork Canyon

Map 3.1, page 111

Like the Theater in the Pines Group Area, this Forest Service campground sits under

the trail on Mount Timpanogos, Wasatch Mountains

toilets are provided. Firewood is available. Leashed pets permitted.

Reservations, fees: Reservations are accepted at 877/444-6777 or online at www.recreation.gov and must be made a minimum of five days in advance. Single sites are $13, double sites are $26, extra vehicles are $5, and the day-use fee is $6. Open June through October, weather permitting.

Directions: From Provo, drive northeast on Hwy. 189 for seven miles and turn left on Rte. 92. Travel 5.5 miles to the campground on the right side of the road.

GPS Coordinates: N 40° 24.339' W 111° 36.401'

Contact: Pleasant Grove Ranger District, 801/785-3563, www.fs.fed.us/r4/uwc/recreation/uinta/camping/pleasant_grove/index.shtml#timp

37 THEATER IN THE PINES GROUP AREA

Scenic rating: 8

in American Fork

Map 3.1, page 111

Theater in the Pines Group Area is the first Forest Service campground you'll encounter along the Alpine Loop Scenic Byway from the east. It's named after an old amphitheater (built by the Civilian Conservation Corps in 1935) that nature is starting to reclaim. The campground is at the entrance to the Uinta National Forest, just beyond the hustle and bustle of Robert Redford's Sundance Ski Resort. Campers may be more entertained by the Sundance's Summer Outdoor Theater than what they'll find at the decaying Theater in the Pines. However, it's still a good place to camp. The campground sits beneath the eastern face of the inspiring Mount Timpanogos. The multilayered mountain is one of the Wasatch's most recognized and distinctive mountains and is worth a visit at any time of the year. The Theater Group Area

the hulk of the inspiring Mount Timpanogos. While views of the mountain are mostly blocked by a dense forest canopy of aspen, fir, gambel oak, and maple trees, the campground has a wonderful peaceful feel. Midsummer thundershowers and runoff from Timpanogos provide enough moisture to keep the grounds lush and green. There's even a blanket of ferns growing along the road. The campground is older, and the facilities show their age, but that doesn't make it a bad place to stay. You'll find hillside sites on the outside of the campground loop and flat ones in the middle, with good sites for tents and pull-through parking for RVs. There's enough variety to please everyone. And if you're lucky enough to get site 5, the views up to the mountain are incredible.

Campsites, facilities: There are 27 sites. Maximum vehicle length is 20 feet. Picnic tables, concrete fire rings, drinking water, and flush is an opportunity for large groups to camp in the shadow of the beautiful mountain. Recreation around the campground ranges from scenic drives to climbing the peak itself (the trailhead leaves from the campground) to fishing in the creek. The campground is set in a forest of maple, aspen, gambel oak, and fir trees. Keep an eye out for deer, moose, and elk, which visit the area in different seasons.

Campsites, facilities: There is one group area that accommodates up to 150 people. Picnic tables, barbeque grills, and a vault toilet are provided. Leashed pets permitted.

Reservations, fees: Reservations are accepted at 877/444-6777 or online at www. recreation.gov and must be made a minimum of five days in advance. The fee is $240. Open June through September, weather permitting.

Directions: From Provo, drive northeast on Hwy. 189 for seven miles and turn left on Rte. 92. Travel 5.3 miles to the campground on the left side of the road.

GPS Coordinates: N 40° 24.272' W 111° 36.203'

Contact: Pleasant Grove Ranger District, 801/785-3563, www.fs.fed.us/r4/uwc/recreation/uinta/camping/pleasant_grove/index.shtml#theater_camp

38 CHOKE CHERRY AND GREAT HORNED OWL LOOPS AT DEER CREEK STATE PARK

🏊 🚤 🚗 🎣 ♿ 🚐 ⛺

Scenic rating: 7

south of Heber

Map 3.1, page 111

Deer Creek State Park is a popular boating and fishing destination in the Heber Valley on the eastern side of the Wasatch Mountains. The Deer Creek Reservoir is the second largest reservoir on the Provo River downstream from the Jordanelle. Consistent winds

blowing up from Provo Canyon make the lake a great spot for windsurfing and sailing. Sport-fishing species in the reservoir include trout, perch, walleye, and smallmouth bass. Trout anglers report success early and late in the day when the winds are calm. The camping at Deer Creek is spread out in two loops: Choke Cherry is the upper loop designed for RV users (sites have hook-ups), and the Great Horned Owl Loop caters to tent campers. Both loops are paved and feature new, quality facilities. The campground has views down to the reservoir, and the nearby boat ramp provides direct access to the water. The campsites are fairly tightly spaced, and the small trees and scrubs don't offer much privacy or shade.

Campsites, facilities: There are 40 sites in the Choke Cherry Loop and 23 sites in the Great Horned Owl Loop. Wheelchair-accessible sites 8, 23, and 38 are located in the Choke Cherry Loop. Sites 31–36 are walk-in tent sites. Covered picnic tables, modern restrooms with showers, fire grills, barbeque grills, drinking water, four day-use areas, pull-through sites, garbage service, and a dump station are provided. Leashed pets are permitted only in the campgrounds.

Reservations, fees: Reservations are accepted at 800/322-3770 or online at www.reserveamerica.com; they must be made a minimum of two days in advance and can be arranged up to 16 weeks in advance. There is an $8 nonrefundable reservation fee for individual sites. Choke Cherry fees are $25 for full hook-ups, and extra vehicles are $13. Great Horned Owl fees are $16 (without hook-ups), and extra vehicles are $8. The day-use fee is $10. Open year-round.

Directions: From Heber City, drive eight miles southwest on Hwy. 189 and turn right into the campground entrance.

GPS Coordinates: N 40° 24.700' W 111° 30.270'

Contact: Deer Creek State Park, 435/654-0171, http://stateparks.utah.gov/stateparks/parks/deer-creek/

39 WILLOW PARK

Scenic rating: 7

in Lehi

Map 3.1, page 111

Willow Park is a Utah County Park located along the Jordan River on the west side of Lehi. The campground has a city park look and feel, with large open fields for sporting activities. There are opportunities for canoeing and fishing on the lazy Jordan River, and the Jordan River Parkway Trail runs by the campground. The parkway trail system weaves through a cattail-filled wetland and is popular with cyclists, joggers, and walkers. Some sections of this trail are paved and others are gravel. The marsh ecosystem is an excellent bird habitat and home to small mammals like foxes. The sites at Willow Park are shaded by cottonwood and willow trees and are divided into clusters that can be reserved as group sites or used as individual sites. The grounds are flat and offer good, level tenting options. There are scenic views up to rolling hills and the distant Wasatch Mountains.

Campsites, facilities: There are 12 group camping areas for up to 150 people. Sites 2, 3, 7, 11, and 12 have covered pavilions. If the group areas are not reserved, single sites are available. Picnic tables, fire grills, drinking water, garbage service, flush toilets and portable toilets, a volleyball net, and a playground are provided. Leashed pets permitted.

Reservations, fees: Reservations are not accepted for single sites. Reservations are required for the group sites and can be arranged at 801/851-8640. Single sites are $10; group sites with pavilions are $85–95 and an additional $2 pp for groups larger than 45 people; and all other group sites cost $2 pp with a $50 minimum. Open April through October, weather permitting.

Directions: From I-15, take Exit 279 in Lehi. Drive west on Main Street (Rte. 73). After 3.1 miles, turn right and continue 0.2 mile, then turn left into Willow Park.

GPS Coordinates: N 40° 23.483' W 111° 53.930'

Contact: Utah County Parks, 801/851-8640, www.utahcountyonline.org/Dept/PubWrks/Parks/ParkDetails.asp?IDNO=11

40 NUNN'S PARK

Scenic rating: 7

in Provo Canyon

Map 3.1, page 111

Nunn's Park is a Utah County–run facility that has a city park feel, but it is set in Provo Canyon among soaring peaks and tumbling waterfalls. Bridal Veil Falls in particular is one the Provo area's most easily accessed and picturesque attractions. The falls is within walking distance of Nunn's Park. The park is named after hydroelectric pioneer L. L. Nunn, who in 1897 built what was at the time America's most powerful hydroelectric project. The power was used to fuel mining operations near Mercur, Utah. The property has since been acquired by the county and transformed into a park. The campground at Nunn's Park sits along the banks of the Provo River. It's also within spitting distance of the freeway, which rolls by overhead. The campsites are tightly packed into a small loop area. Some sites border the river, while others look out across a grass lawn. There are flat spaces for tents at most sites. Recreational activities at Nunn's park include trout fishing in the Provo River, hiking and biking on the Provo River Parkway (paved for 14 miles), and photographing the multitiered Bridal Veil Falls.

Campsites, facilities: There are 16 campsites. Picnic tables, flush toilets, drinking water, barbeque grills, a playground, horseshoe pits, fire pits, and garbage service are provided. Leashed pets permitted.

Reservations, fees: Reservations are accepted only for the day-use pavilions at 801/851-

8640. Sites are $10, and day-use pavilions are $40–95. Open April through October, weather permitting.

Directions: From Provo, drive northeast on Hwy. 189 for 3.3 miles and turn left into Nunn's Park.

GPS Coordinates: N 40° 20.178' W 111° 36.740'

Contact: Utah County Government, 801/851-8600, www.utahcountyonline.org/Dept/Pub-Wrks/Parks/ParkDetails.asp?IDNO=1

41 HOPE

Scenic rating: 8

in Provo Canyon in the Uinta National Forest

Map 3.1, page 111

Hope Campground is perched at nearly 7,700 feet on a hillside above the dramatic Provo Canyon. Views from the campground look east to the crumbling gray rock walls of Provo Peak and north to the southern reaches of Mount Timpanogos. Maple, gambel oak, willows, and other broad-leaved deciduous trees create a cool, shady camping environment. Orange-and-black variegated fritillary butterflies visit the long grass and dense understory of brush growing between sites. The sites are well spaced and offer some privacy from other campers. The Squaw Peak access road is paved but turns to gravel as it enters the campground. The campground speed limit is posted as No Dust, implying it can be a problem when things dry out. The views from Squaw Peak Road are even better than those in the campground and are worth the journey on their own.

Campsites, facilities: There are 24 single sites and two double sites for tents and RVs up to 20 feet in length. Picnic tables, concrete fire grills, barbeque grills, drinking water, and vault toilets are provided. Firewood is available. Leashed pets permitted.

Reservations, fees: Reservations are accepted at 877/444-6777 or online at www.recreation.

gov and must be made a minimum of five days in advance. Single sites are $13, double sites are $26, extra vehicles are $5, and day use is $5 (three hours). Open June through September, weather permitting.

Directions: From Provo, drive northeast on Hwy. 189 and turn right onto Squaw Peak Road. Continue 4.0 miles to a fork in the road. Take the left fork and drive 0.5 mile, turn left and drive 0.3 mile to the Hope Campground.

GPS Coordinates: N 40° 18.185' W 111° 36.993'

Contact: Pleasant Grove Ranger District, 801/785-3563, www.fs.fed.us/r4/uwc/recreation/uinta/camping/pleasant_grove/index.shtml#hope

42 LODGEPOLE

Scenic rating: 8

east of Heber City in the Uinta National Forest

Map 3.1, page 111

Tucked into the Daniels Canyon, this campground is named for its rail-straight lodgepole pine trees that ranchers traditionally used for building fences. It could easily be called Aspen, however, as groves blanket the gently rolling Uinta Mountains in every direction. In autumn, the aspens are a sight to be seen, with quaking leaves contrasting fiery hues of yellow and orange against gleaming white bark. The modern, swanky campground is well dispersed among its namesake trees. Sites feature clean concrete eating areas next to level tent pads. Long grass grows between sites, and despite the abundance of trees, the grounds have an open, meadowlike feel. RV users will appreciate the adequate, paved parking. Two large, sheltered group areas provide plenty of shade and protection from summer thunderstorms. The 3.8-mile Foreman Hollow Trail begins in Loop A. The trail has interpretive signs describing the area's plants and animals along the way to an overlook of scenic Daniels Canyon.

The friendly camp host, who asked to be called only "The President," mentioned there is a herd of over 100 deer living in the surrounding hills. Moose have also been spotted in the area. The President also recommended making reservations, citing busy weekdays and packed weekends.

Campsites, facilities: There are 23 family sites and two group sites for tents and RVs up to 70 feet in length. Group site B1 can accommodate up to 50 people and group site B2 up to 100 people; both sites are wheelchair accessible. Picnic tables on concrete slabs, fire pits, drinking water, flat tent pads, and vault toilets are provided. Firewood and a dump station are available. Leashed pets permitted.

Reservations, fees: Reservations are accepted at 877/444-6777 or online at www.recreation. gov and must be made a minimum of five days in advance. Single sites are $14, double sites are $28, group sites are $135–228, extra vehicles are $6, dump station is $6, and day use is $5. Open May through October.

Directions: From Heber City, drive east 15.7 miles on Hwy. 40. Turn right and enter Lodgepole Campground on the right.

GPS Coordinates: N 40° 18.653' W 111° 15.555'

Contact: Heber Ranger District, 435/654-0470.

43 CURRANT CREEK RESERVOIR

🚶‍♂️ 🏊 🎣 ⛴ 🏍 🐕 🚣 ♿ 🚐 ⛺

Scenic rating: 9

in the Uinta National Forest

Map 3.1, page 111

Currant Creek is a Forest Service campground perched above a large reservoir. The lake and campground are set deep in the mountains, with the bald-topped Currant Creek Peak (10,554 feet) standing guard over the area. Signs of beaver activity are apparent along the creek, which flows by the campground. Look for telltale chewed-off aspen stumps. Four camp loops are cut out of an aspen and lodgepole pine forest. Pine bark beetles have killed many of the trees in the area, and dead wood is being actively thinned in some sites. The facilities find a good balance between being functional while still maintaining a natural feel. Sites have concrete pads for picnic tables, while tents must be pitched on the forest floor. The sites are well spread out in the thin forest but are within sight of one another. Some sites offer views down to the Currant Creek Reservoir and the surrounding ridges that sometimes hold snow into early August. Boating and fishing for rainbow, cutthroat, and brook trout are popular on the reservoir. A one-mile nature trail heads up into the forest, leaving from the playground in Loop D. There are also trails down to the reservoir from Loop D. Multiple sites are wheelchair accessible, especially those nearest to the restrooms, with paved paths from the parking area to the site, drinking water, and the restrooms.

Campsites, facilities: There are four separate loops. Loop A has 22 sites, Loop B has 23 sites (or four group sites), Loop C has 33 sites, and Loop D has 21 sites. Picnic tables on concrete slabs, drinking water, garbage service, barbeque grills, fire pits, flush toilets, aluminum recycling, a boat launch, a fish-cleaning station, and a playground (Loop D) are provided. Firewood is available. Leashed pets permitted.

Reservations, fees: Reservations are accepted for Loops A and C (horse units) and the four group sites in Loop B at 877/444-6777 or online at www.recreation.gov and must be made a minimum of five days in advance. Single sites are $14, double sites are $28, group sites are $75–100, and the day-use fee is $5. Open May through October.

Directions: From Heber City, drive east on Hwy. 40 for 24 miles, then turn left and follow signs to Co-op Creek. Drive 10.1 miles on a gravel road and follow the right fork on

Forest Road 082. Continue 3.9 miles and turn right on Forest Road 471. Drive 1.8 miles to the campground entrance station.

GPS Coordinates: N 40° 19.853' W 111° 04.079'

Contact: Heber Ranger District, 435/654-0470, www.fs.fed.us/r4/uwc/recreation/uinta/camping/heber/index.shtml#currant_creek

44 PROVO KOA

Scenic rating: 5

in Provo

Map 3.1, page 111

The Provo KOA is set between two ribbons of freshwater, the Provo River and a small canal. Ducks and geese hang out on the canal and give the RV park a natural, kid-friendly feel. Fishing is possible in the Provo River or nearby in Utah Lake. The Provo River Parkway Trail offers hiking or biking near the KOA. Large cottonwood trees shade most of the yard and help keep the place cool. The facilities are nice and clean, with a paved loop, parking, and sparkling bathrooms. In the center of the loop are pull-through sites for big rigs. The campground is next to a city park with baseball diamonds, open fields, and historic Fort Utah. The fort was established in 1849 to protect early Mormon settlers.

Campsites, facilities: There are 40 full hook-up (30 amps) sites, 36 partial hook-up sites, four tent sites, and two cabins. Picnic tables, modern restrooms with showers, drinking water, playground, game room, garbage service, dump station, dog walk, WiFi, and a swimming pool (open seasonally) are provided. Propane and laundry are available. Leashed pets are permitted, but not in the pool area or inside the buildings.

Reservations, fees: Reservations are accepted at 800/562-1894. RV sites are $26–40, tent sites are $22–26, and cabins are $38–45. Open year-round.

Directions: From I-15, take Exit 265 (northbound I-15 take Exit 265B); stay right as you exit and turn right onto Center Street. Drive 0.5 mile west on Center Street and turn north (right) onto 2050 West (Geneva Road). Continue 0.2 mile and turn right into Provo KOA.

GPS Coordinates: N 40° 14.259' W 111° 41.590'

Contact: Provo KOA, 801/375-2994, www.koa.com/where/ut/44108/

45 LAKESIDE RV AND CAMPGROUND

Scenic rating: 6

near Provo

Map 3.1, page 111

Lakeside RV and Campground is a great alternative to camping in Utah Lake State Park. Located literally right outside the park's entrance, this is one instance where the scenic value and quality of a RV park outshines the campground at the state park. It's close enough to the park to use the lake during the day, yet far enough away to feel like a different environment. While you can't sail or water ski in the RV park, you might find swimming in the pool a lot more appealing than the murky, wind-churned waters of Utah Lake. There are lots of big trees for shade, green grass lawns, a covered picnic area, and even a basketball hoop. The driveway loop is paved and offers pull-through sites in the center. There are some permanent residents here, but they don't make the place feel like a trailer park.

Campsites, facilities: There are 96 full hook-up (20-, 30-, and 50-amp) sites, 32 partial hook-up sites, eight tent sites, and two large group areas. Amenities include WiFi, a swimming pool (open seasonally), drinking water, barbeque grills, picnic tables, game room, horseshoe pit, playground, basketball hoop, modern restrooms with showers, covered picnic area, garbage service, and dump station. Laundry, a convenience store, bicycle rentals, and propane are available. Leashed pets are permitted, but not in the tent sites.

Reservations, fees: Reservations are accepted at 800/906-5267 or online at www.lakesidervcampground.com/Make_a_reservation.html. Full hook-up, pull-through sites are $28–29.50, partial hook-up sites are $26, and tent sites are $23. Open year-round.

Directions: From I-15, take Exit 265B (for Provo Center) and drive two miles west on Center Street. Lakeside RV is on the right side of the road.

GPS Coordinates: N 40° 14.143' W 111° 43.686'

Contact: Lakeside RV and Campground, 801/373-5267, www.lakesidervcampground.com/

46 UTAH LAKE STATE PARK

Scenic rating: 5

on Utah Lake in Provo

Map 3.1, page 111

Utah Lake is the largest freshwater lake in Utah. Like the Great Salt Lake, Utah Lake is a remnant of the historical Lake Bonneville, which covered much of northwestern Utah and northeastern Nevada. The lake has a huge surface area but is very shallow, with a maximum depth of only 14 feet. The lake's shallow nature, combined with an open landscape and prevailing strong winds, leads to sediment being stirred up from the lake's bottom. The result is that the lake's water is commonly a turbid, light green. Located east of Provo, the lake is popular with Salt Lake Valley residents for waterskiing, sailing, canoeing, kayaking, and fishing. Fishing species include channel catfish, walleye, white bass, and black bass. The state park has a beautiful day-use area with broad grass lawns and covered picnic areas. Between the campground and the lakeshore is a wetland

and bird-watching area. Raptors like bald eagles, northern harriers, red-tailed hawks, and American kestrels have been spotted here. Also look for smaller species like the marsh wren, red-winged blackbird, northern flicker, and downy woodpecker. The campground at Utah Lake isn't the best part of the park. It isn't that the campground is in bad shape or the facilities are inadequate, but the campground has sort of an overlooked, underutilized feel to it. Perhaps it's because the majority of the park's visitors just come for the day, or maybe it's that the campground is not on the actual shore of the lake. On a gorgeous midsummer weekend afternoon, the campground was almost empty while the rest the of the park was packed. The paved loop is large and open, so expect to hear and see other campers at the campground. The lack of trees leaves clear but distant views of Mount Timpanogos and the Wasatch Mountains. Between sites there are clumps of dried-out grass growing in the gravel and dirt. Covered picnic tables provide some shade and relief from the sun, but otherwise the whole campground is open and exposed. The two RV parks nearby in Provo offer a more appealing atmosphere and are more popular.

Campsites, facilities: Loop A has 23 partial hook-up sites, and Loop B has 32 sites. Amenities include covered picnic tables, pull-through sites, modern restrooms with showers, drinking water, fire pits, a fish-cleaning station, garbage service, and dump station. There is a playground and open grass fields in the day-use area. Leashed pets permitted.

Reservations, fees: Reservations are accepted at 800/322-3770 or online at www.reserveamerica.com; they must be made a minimum of two days in advance and can be arranged up to 16 weeks in advance. There is an $8 non-refundable reservation fee for individual sites. The camping fee is $20, extra vehicles are $10, and day use is $9. Open year-round.

Directions: From I-15, take Exit 265B (Provo-Center Street) and drive three miles west on Center Street to Utah Lake State Park.

GPS Coordinates: N 40° 14.233' W 111° 44.022'

Contact: Utah Lake State Park, 801/375-0731, http://stateparks.utah.gov/stateparks/parks/utah-lake/

47 EAST BAY RV PARK

🏊 🏕 👫 🚐

Scenic rating: 7

in Springville

Map 3.1, page 111

East Bay RV Park is in Springville at the base of the Wasatch Mountains, which rise dramatically over the campground. The RV park is a well-kept, upscale facility with paved loops and parking slips leading to manicured grass lawn strip sites. The sites extend away from the office in long, neat rows in typical RV-park style. The slips are close together, so privacy is limited. Views from the sites look up to the peaks above and out to its urban surroundings. You won't have a "nature" experience at East Bay, but Provo Canyon and Mount Timpanogos are nearby, and you can find plenty of adventure at both. There is a private trout pond at the campground for kids who want to fish.

Campsites, facilities: There are 155 pull-through, full hook-up (20-, 30-, and 50-amp) sites for RVs up to 60 feet in length. Tents are not permitted. Picnic tables, WiFi, cable TV, a playground, swimming pool (open seasonally), miniature golf, trout pond, modern restrooms with showers, garbage service, and drinking water are provided. Laundry, a convenience store, a gift shop, and RV wash are available. Leashed pets permitted.

Reservations, fees: Reservations are accepted at 801/491-0700. RV sites are $30.95. Open year-round.

Directions: From I-15, take Exit 261 (Rte. 75) in Springville. Drive east on Rte. 75 for 0.1 mile and turn left at the first light at 1600 North Street. Turn right into East Bay RV Park.

GPS Coordinates: N 40° 11.360' W 111° 38.513'

Contact: East Bay RV Park, 801/491-0700, www.eastbayrvpark.com/

48 LINCOLN BEACH

🏊 🚣 🚐 🐕 🚐 ⛺

Scenic rating: 8

on the south shore of Utah Lake

Map 3.1, page 111

Lincoln Beach is a Utah County park located on the southeast shore of Utah Lake. Utah Lake is a freshwater remnant of the ancient Lake Bonneville. The lake is extremely shallow, with a maximum depth of around 14 feet, and typically murky. So while the lake's waters may offer more attractive swimming conditions than the Great Salt Lake, don't come here expecting to see your toes as you wade in. Utah Lake still has plenty to offer in the way of recreation. Persistent winds make for good sailing, windsurfing, and kiteboarding. Powerboating and fishing for white bass, black bass, walleye, and channel catfish are also popular. Lincoln Beach Campground has a city-park feel, with open campsites surrounding a paved loop. The sites don't have much privacy but are clean and well taken care of. There are views out to the lake and of the Wasatch Front in the distance.

Campsites, facilities: There are eight sites and one pavilion available for day use only. Picnic tables, barbeque grills, fire grills, a sand volleyball court, fish-cleaning station, boat ramp, floating dock, drinking water, garbage service, and flush toilets are provided. Leashed pets permitted.

Reservations, fees: Reservations are not accepted for single sites. They are accepted for the day-use pavilion at 801/851-8640. Sites are $10 and the day-use pavilion is $30–50 for up to 100 people. Open April through October, weather permitting.

Directions: From I-15, take Exit 257 in Spanish Fork and drive south on Main Street (Rte. 156) to Rte. 147. Turn west (right) onto Rte. 147 and continue for four miles and stay straight onto 6400 S. After 0.2 mile 6400 S becomes 4800 W. Turn left onto 6300 S and continue 0.5 mile. The road now becomes 6400 S. Continue 1.3 miles and the road becomes Lincoln Beach Road. Lincoln Beach Campground will be on the right side of the road.

GPS Coordinates: N 40° 08.477' W 111° 48.203'

Contact: Utah County Parks, 801/851-8640, www.utahcountyonline.org/Dept/PubWrks/Parks/ParkDetails.asp?IDNO=9

49 JOLLEY'S RANCH

Scenic rating: 6

east of Provo in the Uinta National Forest

Map 3.1, page 111

Jolley's Ranch Campground is run by the city of Springville at the entrance to Hobble Creek Canyon. The park is bordered by the Hobble Creek Golf Course on the west and the Uinta National Forest to the east. Sites are set under gambel oak and maple trees. The forest floor is mostly dirt but is becoming overgrown with weeds. The park feels like a city park that added a campground as an afterthought. It isn't particularly popular and is mostly used by local residents, who pay less to camp than the general public. With two Forest Service campgrounds a little farther up the canyon, it is probably worth the drive to see all your options before staying here.

Campsites, facilities: There are 45 sites with partial hookups. Picnic tables, barbeque grills, modern restrooms with showers, drinking water, garbage service, and a playground are provided. Leashed pets permitted.

Reservations, fees: Reservations are not accepted for individual sites. They are accepted for the group pavilions. The fee for individual sites is $12 for Springville residents and $18 for nonresidents. The pavilions are $170.50–264 for overnight use, and the day-use-only fee is $100–132. An extra tent or extra vehicle is $6. Open April through October, weather permitting.

Directions: From I-15, take exit 260. Drive east on Rte. 77 (400 S) for three miles, bend right at the four-way stop, and stay on the main arterial. After 8.2 miles take the right fork and continue 0.2 miles to the Jolley's Ranch Campground on the right side of the road. The campground entrance is just past the Hobble Creek Golf Course.

GPS Coordinates: N 40° 09.997' W 111° 29.715'

Contact: Springville City, 801/489-2700, http://pbw.co.utah.ut.us/Visguide/campgrnd/jolleys.htm

50 WHITING

Scenic rating: 7

east of Spanish Fork in the Uinta National Forest

Map 3.1, page 111

Whiting is a Forest Service campground located in a narrow, winding canyon. The canyon is carved from the Wasatch Mountains east of the suburban community of Mapleton. Literally at the end of the road, Whiting is the trailhead for the Maple Canyon horse and hiking trail leading up into the Wasatch Range. Fishing is popular at Whiting in a small creek that flows through the north side of the campground. The creek is seasonal and dries out in mid- to late summer. The sites at Whiting are spread out in a maple and gambel oak forest. The broad-leaved trees provide plenty of shade for the sites and some relief from summer heat. With Whiting at around 5,400 feet in elevation, summer temperatures are not much cooler than on the valley floor. Sites are packed earth, with tall waving grass surrounding them. Some sites have hitching posts to accommodate equestrians using the Maple Canyon Trail. Aside from the trail, there's no real destination appeal to the campground. Whiting is an easy campground to access, with a paved loop and parking. It's only a couple of miles on a paved road from the towns of Mapleton, Springville, and Spanish Fork.

Campsites, facilities: There are 18 single sites, eight double sites, and two group sites. Group area A is for up to 200 people, and group area B is for up to 100 people. Picnic tables on cement pads, fire rings, vault toilets, and drinking water are provided. Leashed pets permitted.

Reservations, fees: Reservations are accepted at 877/444-6777 or online at www.recreation. gov and must be made a minimum of five days in advance. Single sites are $14, double sites are $28, group areas are $150–300, and extra vehicles and day use are $5. Open May through September.

Directions: From Main Street and 400 N in Mapleton, drive east on 400 N for 2.6 miles to the campground.

GPS Coordinates: N 40° 07.904' W 111° 31.730'

Contact: Spanish Fork Ranger District, 801/798-3571, www.fs.fed.us/r4/uwc/recreation/uinta/camping/spanish_fork/index. shtml#whitting

51 CHERRY

Scenic rating: 6

in Hobble Creek Canyon east of Provo in the Uinta National Forest

Map 3.1, page 111

Cherry Campground is the first of two Forest Service campgrounds in Hobble Creek Canyon. The scenic canyon cuts into the western base of the Wasatch Mountains east of Mapleton, Springville, and Provo. The right fork of Hobble Creek runs through the campground and offers fishing for native brown

and stocked rainbow trout. The creek is reduced to a gentle trickle in summer while water is diverted for irrigation, but during winter and spring the fishing can be quite good. Even at its reduced summer volume it still adds character and a refreshing quality to the Cherry Campground. The paved loop and parking aprons lead to a combination of individual and group sites set under the shade of deciduous trees like maple and gambel oak. The shade offers some relief from summer heat, but because the campground is at a relatively low elevation, expect it to be hot. Fall is a great season to visit the Hobble Creek Canyon, when the variety of broad-leaved trees show their best colors.

Campsites, facilities: There are 10 single sites, four double sites, and four tent-only group sites. Maximum RV length is 35 feet. Group areas A and B are wheelchair accessible. Group areas A, C and D can accommodate up to 75 people and group area B up to 50 people. Picnic tables on concrete pads, fire grills, garbage service, vault toilets, and drinking water are provided. There is a volleyball court for the group areas to share (bring your own net and volleyball). Firewood is available. Leashed pets permitted.

Reservations, fees: Reservations are accepted at 877/444-6777 or online at www.recreation. gov and must be made a minimum of five days in advance. Single sites are $14, double sites are $28, group sites are $75–100, and extra vehicles and day use are $5. Open May through October.

Directions: From I-15, take Exit 260. Drive east on Rte. 77 (400 S) for three miles, then bend right at the four-way stop and stay on the main arterial. After 8.2 miles, take the right fork and continue 1.4 miles to the Cherry Campground.

GPS Coordinates: N 40° 10.114' W 111° 28.615'

Contact: Spanish Fork Ranger District, 801/798-3571, www.fs.fed.us/r4/uwc/recreation/uinta/camping/spanish_fork/index. shtml#cherry

52 BALSAM

Scenic rating: 7

east of Provo in the Uinta National Forest

Map 3.1, page 111

Balsam is a small Forest Service campground on the gentle Hobble Creek. The creek and campground are in a lovely canyon east of the town of Springville near Provo and the I-15 corridor. The campground is accessed via a narrow, twisting, paved road. The paved loop leads to shaded, quiet sites under a canopy of maple, oak, and cottonwood trees. The trees block views up to the Wasatch Mountains above, but they help keep the place cool during the popular summer camping season. There's fishing for brown (native) and rainbow (stocked) trout in Hobble Creek; several footbridges cross the creek to provide easy access to either bank. Traditional bait and spinners work better than fly fishing because of the dense vegetation along the streams banks. The footbridges also lead to walk-in tent sites. For the most part the sites are well spaced and offer a little privacy, with thick stands of trees acting as a visual dividers.

Campsites, facilities: There are 24 single sites, one triple site, and a group area for up to 100 people. Maximum RV length is 35 feet. Picnic tables on cement pads, drinking water, fire grills, and vault toilets are provided. Leashed pets permitted.

Reservations, fees: Reservations are accepted at 877/444-6777 or online at www.recreation. gov and must be made a minimum of five days in advance. Single sites are $14, double sites are $28, the group site is $150, and extra vehicles and day use are $5. Open May through September.

Directions: From I-15, take Exit 260. Drive east on Rte. 77 (400 S) for three miles, then bend right at the four-way stop and stay on the main arterial. After 8.2 miles, take the right fork and continue 6.8 miles to the Balsam Campground.

GPS Coordinates: N 40° 11.88' W 111° 24.129'

Contact: Spanish Fork Ranger District, 801/798-3571, www.fs.fed.us/r4/uwc/recreation/uinta/camping/spanish_fork/index. shtml#balsam

53 STRAWBERRY BAY

Scenic rating: 7

on Strawberry Reservoir in the Uinta National Forest

Map 3.1, page 111

The Strawberry Bay Campground occupies a peninsula jutting out into Strawberry Reservoir. The reservoir is a large, man-made lake created by a tall earthen dam on the Strawberry River and fed by other tributaries like Currant Creek. The lake maintains a reputation as being Utah's premier cold-water fishery for large cutthroat and rainbow trout. In fact, a 27-pound cutthroat caught in 1930 still holds the official state record. Summer weather at the reservoir is typically hot and breezy, making the waters a nice place to swim and boat. The campground has commanding views down to Strawberry Bay. Sites are surrounded by tall waving grasses sprinkled with red Indian paintbrush and purple lupine wildflowers. Sagebrush and the occasional small pine tree round out the vegetation in the mostly open landscape. The facilities are modern and well cared for. Their only shortcoming is their lack of tent pads. The huge campground has seven individual loops, plus an overflow camping area. All the sites in the Cutthroat Loop have full hookups, which you'll hardly ever find in a Forest Service campground.

Campsites, facilities: There are 249 single/ double sites, 26 single sites with full hookups, and seven group areas (six for up to 50 people and one for up to 60 people). Amenities include picnic tables on concrete pads (some are covered), pull-through sites, fire grills, flush toilets, drinking water, garbage service, and a dump station. Leashed pets permitted.

Reservations, fees: Reservations are accepted at 877/444-6777 or online at www.recreation.gov and must be made a minimum of five days in advance. To make a reservation, Strawberry Bay Campground requires a two-night minimum stay on weekends and three nights on holiday weekends. Single sites are $14, single sites with full hook-ups are $14 plus a $10 utility fee, double sites are $28, group sites are $135–150, day use is $5, and extra vehicles are $6. Open May through October.

Directions: From Heber City, drive 22.6 miles east on Hwy.40 and turn right at the sign for the Strawberry Recreation Area Visitor Center. Continue 3.8 miles on Forest Road 452 toward Strawberry Bay. Drive one mile and turn right into the campground.

GPS Coordinates: N 40° 10.680 ' W 111° 11.385'

Contact: Heber Ranger District, 435/654-0470, www.fs.fed.us/r4/uwc/recreation/uinta/camping/heber/index.shtml#strawberry_bay

54 SOLDIER CREEK

Scenic rating: 7

on Strawberry Reservoir in the Uinta National Forest

Map 3.1, page 111

The Soldier Creek Campground overlooks the eastern side of the massive Strawberry Reservoir. Strawberry Reservoir is renowned for its cutthroat and rainbow trout fishery, and it receives as much fishing pressure as Lake Powell, whose surface area is many times its size. Kokanee (Canadian landlocked salmon) and cutthroat trout have been introduced to the reservoir. The cutthroat trout are from hardy Bear Lake stock. The campground is open, with a sprinkling of small pine and aspen trees mixed in with sagebrush and lupine flowers. The facilities are older but in

excellent shape. Each site has a covered picnic table on cement slabs and many have second tables out in the open. There are paved parking areas and loops with pull-through sites for RVs. Swallows swoop through campsites while turkey vultures and red-tailed hawks soar on thermals high above.

Campsites, facilities: There are 163 sites and one group area for up to 100 people and 15 RVs. Covered picnic tables, fire grills, flush toilets, drinking water, garbage service, fish-cleaning station, dump station, and boat ramp are provided. Leashed pets permitted.

Reservations, fees: Reservations are accepted at 877/444-6777 or online at www.recreation.gov and must be made a minimum of five days in advance. To make a reservation, Soldier Creek Campground requires a two-night minimum stay on weekends and three nights on holiday weekends. Single sites are $14, double sites are $28, the group area is $225, extra vehicles are $6, and day use is $4. Open May through October.

Directions: From Heber City, drive east on Hwy. 40 for 32 miles. Turn right onto Forest Road 480 and travel 2.6 miles to the campground entrance.

GPS Coordinates: N 40° 09.276' W 111° 03.318'

Contact: Heber Ranger District, 435/654-0470, www.fs.fed.us/r4/uwc/recreation/uinta/camping/heber/index.shtml#soldier_creek

55 ASPEN GROVE

Scenic rating: 7

on Strawberry Reservoir in the Uinta National Forest

Map 3.1, page 111

The Aspen Grove Campground is on the southeast arm of Strawberry Reservoir near the huge earthen dam that creates the lake. Hummingbirds feed at the colorful red begonia bush by the entrance sign. The campsites are set among aspen groves, though the campground is not as forested as you might expect from the name. Loop A offers views across the reservoir to distant hills and a small community by the Solider Creek Campground. From Loop B you can look down to the lake or up to the forested hills behind the campground, where bark beetles have killed off about half of the evergreen trees. Loop B is the more open of the two loops, with fewer aspens and more sagebrush surrounding sites. The walk-in tent sites have mediocre tent pads that are simply sloped patches of dirt. It would be difficult to spend a comfortable night in these sites. Otherwise the campground offers good facilities. When we visited in August, temperatures were in the mid-80s and a gentle breeze blew through the campground.

Campsites, facilities: There are 60 sites; sites 12–14 are walk-in tent sites. Sites 31–34 are wheelchair accessible. Covered picnic tables on concrete pads in Loop A, uncovered picnic tables in Loop B, garbage service, drinking water, fire grills, boat ramp, fish-cleaning station, and pull-through sites are provided. Firewood is available. Leashed pets permitted.

Reservations, fees: Reservations are accepted at 877/444-6777 or online at www.recreation.gov and must be made a minimum of five days in advance. To make a reservation, Aspen Grove Campground requires a two-night minimum stay on weekends and three nights on holiday weekends. Single sites are $14, double sites are $28, extra vehicles are $6, and day use is $5. Open May through October.

Directions: From Heber City, drive east on Hwy. 40 for 33.2 miles. Turn right onto Forest Road 90 and drive 5.3 miles, turn left onto Forest Road 482 and continue 0.3 mile to the Aspen Grove Campground on the right. GPS Coordinates: N 40° 07.259' W 111° 02.203'

Contact: Heber Ranger District, 435/654-0470, www.fs.fed.us/r4/uwc/recreation/uinta/camping/heber/index.shtml#aspen_grove

56 RENEGADE

Scenic rating: 7

on Strawberry Reservoir

Map 3.1, page 111

Renegade is the farthest south and most remote of the Forest Service campgrounds on Strawberry Reservoir. The campground enjoys distant views of the lake and the surrounding red-tinted hills. Sagebrush, grass, lupine, and Indian Paintbrush wildflowers surround the open, breezy campsites. Aspen trees blanket the ridge to the south. The campground has a wide-open, big sky feel to it, like there is nobody around for miles. Well, except your fellow campers. Yellow and white butterflies flit between the flowers. Ground squirrels scurry quickly from burrow to burrow, and small birds land right on the picnic tables. Unfortunately, the sites lack tent pads. You'd be hard pressed to pitch a tent anywhere in the brush and grasses. Besides this oversight, the facilities are nice, with a paved access loop and paths leading to the bathrooms.

Campsites, facilities: There are 66 for tents and RVs up to 30 feet in length. Picnic tables on cement pads, fire grills, flush toilets, drinking water, boat ramp, garbage service, and fish-cleaning station are provided. Firewood is available. Leashed pets permitted.

Reservations, fees: Reservations are accepted at 877/444-6777 or online at www.recreation.gov and must be made at least five days in advance. To make a reservation, Renegade Campground requires a two-night minimum stay on weekends and three nights on holiday weekends. Single sites are $14, double sites are $28, extra vehicles are $6, and day use is $5. Open May through October.

Directions: From Heber City, drive east on Hwy. 40 for 22.6 miles. Turn right at the information station and continue 13.7 miles to Renegade Campground. The campground is on the right side of the road. GPS Coordinates: N 40° 07.246' W 111° 09.532'

Contact: Heber Ranger District, 435/654-

0470, www.fs.fed.us/r4/uwc/recreation/uinta/camping/heber/index.shtml#renegade

57 DIAMOND

Scenic rating: 7

in the southern Wasatch Mountains in the Uinta National Forest

Map 3.1, page 111

Diamond Campground is a quiet river-bottom site in the southern reaches of the Wasatch Mountains. Little Diamond Creek is lined with tall cottonwood trees and a dense understory of willow and other deciduous trees. The creek offers good fishing for brown and cutthroat trout. The campground features a nice collection of walk-in tent sites along the banks of the creek. These sites have decent tent spots tucked under and around the thick trees. The main loop sites are surrounded by tall grass and sagebrush and have limited tent pad options. The loop is paved, and sites are well maintained and shaded. Open sites have covered picnic tables, making this a nice hot-weather spot. Keep a wary eye out for the Great Basin rattlesnakes that live in and around the campground. Other likely wildlife encounters include deer and nighthawks.

Campsites, facilities: There are 38 single sites, 22 double sites, and seven group sites. Sites 27–29 and 58–61 are walk-in tent sites. Group sites 1A and 1B are for up to 25 people, group sites 2 and 4–6 are for up to 75 people, and group site 3 is for up to 125 people. Group sites 1A, 1B, and 2 are wheelchair accessible. Covered picnic tables on concrete pads, garbage service, fire rings, fire grills, vault toilets, and drinking water are provided. Leashed pets permitted

Reservations, fees: Reservations are accepted at 877/444-6777 or online at www.recreation. gov and must be made at least five days in advance. Single sites are $14, double sites are $28, group sites are $40–175, and day use is $5. Open year-round.

Directions: From Spanish Fork, drive 10 miles south on Hwy. 89, then turn left onto Forest Road 29 and continue 5.3 miles to the Diamond Campground on the right side of the road.

GPS Coordinates: N 40° 04.320' W 111° 25.805'

Contact: Spanish Fork Ranger District, 801/798-3571, www.fs.fed.us/r4/uwc/recreation/uinta/camping/spanish_fork/index.shtml#diamond

58 UNICORN RIDGE

Scenic rating: 8

in the Uinta National Forest

Map 3.1, page 111

Unicorn Ridge is a tiny Forest Service site on the western slopes of the Wasatch Mountains. The campground is a simple extension of a gravel parking lot, with five well-defined sites overlooking a beautiful valley. Despite being right off a paved road, the campground has the distinct feeling of being in the middle of nowhere. Sites are simple but functional with long gravel parking areas for big rigs. Grass and small shrubs grow between sites, and gambel oak trees grow along the ridge. ATV roads leave directly from the campground. This is a simple, functional, free camping area.

Campsites, facilities: There are five sites. Picnic tables, fire rings, barbeque grills, and a vault toilet are provided. There is no drinking water. Leashed pets permitted.

Reservations, fees: Reservations are not accepted. There is no fee. Open May through October, weather permitting.

Directions: From Tucker, drive nine miles west on Hwy. 6, turn north (right) onto Sheep Pass Road, and drive 7.3 miles to the Unicorn Ridge Campground.

GPS Coordinates: N 40° 01.743' W 111° 16.923'

Contact: Spanish Fork Ranger District, 801/798-3571.

59 MAPLE BENCH
🏕 �caravan 🏕

Scenic rating: 7

east of Santaquin on the Nebo Loop Scenic Byway in the Uinta National Forest

Map 3.2, page 112

This campground sits perched on a dramatic bench overlooking the Nebo Loop Scenic Byway in the Uinta National Forest. The campground's unusual position isn't apparent when you first drive into the place. However, an abrupt edge drops off into the deep Payson Canyon carved by Peteeneet Creek. Views from the edge of the drop-off look all the way down the valley to the distant town of Payson. The creek below is home to rainbow, brook, and Bonneville trout. White fir, pinyon pine, gambel oak, and maple trees grow in an open forest that provides shade and shelter for sites. The once-paved loop has deteriorated to something closer to a gravel surface, but it is still adequate. The campground is small, quiet, and peaceful, especially when compared to some of the sprawling campgrounds on the Nebo loop road.

Campsites, facilities: There are 10 sites for tents and RVs up to 35 feet in length. Picnic tables, fire grills, drinking water, garbage service, and vault toilets are provided. Firewood is available. Leashed pets permitted.

Reservations, fees: Reservations are not accepted. Sites are $14 and extra vehicles are $5. Open Memorial Day through Labor Day, weather permitting.

Directions: From Payson, drive five miles south on the Nebo Loop Scenic Byway. Turn right, continue 0.3 mile, and then turn left into the Maple Bench Campground.

GPS Coordinates: N 39° 57.764' W 111° 41.526'

Contact: Spanish Fork Ranger District, 801/798-3571, www.fs.fed.us/r4/uwc/recreation/uinta/camping/spanish_fork/index.shtml#maple

60 PAYSON LAKES
🚶 🏊 🚴 🏕 ♿ �caravan 🏕

Scenic rating: 7

east of Santaquin on the Nebo Loop Scenic Byway in the Uinta National Forest

Map 3.2, page 112

Payson Lakes is a huge, popular campground along the Nebo Loop Scenic Byway in the Uinta National Forest. The campground is near three small mountain lakes named McClellan, Box, and Big East. In addition to camping, the lakes are a great place for hiking, swimming, picnicking, and fishing. A hiking trail to the lakes starts near the entrance to Loop B. The lakes are popular with anglers and perfect for kids because the brook and rainbow trout bite fast and furious. Inflatable float tubes and small rafts dot the lake's surface during summer months. The paved camp loops wind through an open, alpine forest of aspen, spruce, and white fir, with dense thickets of brush, shrubs, and long grass crowding in where the trees don't grow. With such prolific underbrush, many sites don't have anywhere to pitch a tent and therefore are much more suitable for RVs, vans, or pickup truck campers. If you're looking for good tenting sites check out Loop C first, where the most tent-friendly sites are located. Most of the visitors here are locals from along the Wasatch Front, but the Nebo Loop Scenic Byway is a worthy destination for other travelers as well. Mount Nebo climbs to 11,928 feet and is both the southernmost and highest peak in the Wasatch Mountain Range. Its barren, tundralike slopes are both striking and beautiful; it draws comparisons to its northern neighbor, Mount Timpanogos.

Campsites, facilities: There are 98 single sites, 10 double sites, and three group sites for tents and RVs up to 45 feet in length. Group site A is for up to 100 people, and group sites B and C are for up to 75 people. All sites are wheelchair accessible. Picnic tables on cement pads, fire grills, vault toilets, and drinking water are provided. Firewood is available. Leashed pets permitted.

Reservations, fees: Reservations are accepted

at 877/444-6777 or online at www.recreation.gov and must be made a minimum of five days in advance. Single sites are $14, double sites are $28, group sites are $100–150, and extra vehicles and day use are $5. Open Memorial Day through Labor Day, weather permitting.

Directions: From Payson, drive 12 miles south on the Nebo Loop Scenic Byway. Turn right and continue 0.4 mile to the Payson Lakes Campground.

GPS Coordinates: N 39° 55.847' W 111° 38.416'

Contact: Spanish Fork Ranger District, 801/798-3571, www.fs.fed.us/r4/uwc/recreation/uinta/camping/spanish_fork/index.shtml#payson

61 BLACKHAWK

Scenic rating: 7

east of Santaquin on the Nebo Loop Scenic Byway in the Uinta National Forest

Map 3.2, page 112

Blackhawk Campground is a sprawling, group-oriented campground on the Nebo Loop Scenic Byway in the Uinta National Forest. The campground is named after one of the great leaders of the native Ute Nation, known as Chief Noonch, or Black Hawk. The paved loops are spread out over a large area, with Loops A, B, C, and D designated for groups only. The campground is designed to accommodate horses and horseback riders. Specific horse facilities include a horse unloading ramp and hitching posts. The Blackhawk Loop Trail and Blackhawk Trail lead through and out of the campground connecting to the Nebo Wilderness Area. The trail is open to hikers, mountain bikers, and horseback riders. Many variations on the 18-mile trail are possible. All descriptions note the trail is long and strenuous. Consider riding or hiking the trail in the fall when the surrounding aspens are turning their fiery autumn colors. The campground's alpine landscape is similar in all the loops, with patches of aspen, fir, and gambel oak forest broken up by open, long-grass meadows. Near the crest of the Nebo Loop Scenic Byway, the campground is at around 8,000 feet in elevation, which keeps temperatures cool even during the summer months.

Campsites, facilities: There are 12 single horse sites, three double horse sites, two group sites for up to 50 people with horses, and 21 group sites for up to 50 or 100 people, depending on the site. All sites are wheelchair accessible. Picnic tables, fire pits, flush toilets, drinking water, hitching posts, a horse-loading ramp, and a dump station are provided. Firewood is available. Leashed pets permitted.

Reservations, fees: Reservations are accepted at 877/444-6777 or online at www.recreation.gov and must be made a minimum of five days in advance. Single sites are $14, double sites are $28, group sites are $75–150, and extra vehicles and day use are $5. Open Memorial Day through Labor Day, weather permitting.

Directions: From Payson, drive 16 miles south on the Nebo Loop Scenic Byway. Turn left and continue 1.6 miles to Blackhawk Campground.

GPS Coordinates: N 39° 53.876' W 111° 37.855'

Contact: Spanish Fork Ranger District, 801/798-3571, www.fs.fed.us/r4/uwc/recreation/uinta/camping/spanish_fork/index.shtml#blackhawk

62 TINNEY FLAT

Scenic rating: 7

east of Santaquin on the Nebo Loop Scenic Byway in the Uinta National Forest

Map 3.2, page 112

Tinney Flat is along Santaquin Creek near the Nebo Wilderness Area. The area is popular with anglers who line the creek and road on summer weekends. The campground, with access to the nearby Monument Trailhead, is a

favorite of horseback riders. The trail leads to
the Nebo Peak Trail and into the 27,000-acre
Nebo Wilderness Area. The trail is long and
strenuous and can be challenging for horses
where the tread is rocky and where it crosses
steep shale slopes. The campground is set in a
beautiful, dense forest of maple and white fir.
The trees provide plentiful shade in and around
the sites and Santaquin Creek helps add to the
campground's refreshing feel. The camp loop
and parking aprons are paved, and the picnic
tables sit on cement pads. There are three group
areas, which feature horseshoe pits.

Campsites, facilities: There are 11 single sites,
two double sites, and three group sites for up
to 50 people. Sites 1, 2, 10–13, and two of the
group sites are wheelchair accessible. Picnic
tables on cement pads, fire grills, horseshoe
pits, vault toilets, drinking water, and garbage
service are provided. Leashed pets permitted.

Reservations, fees: Reservations are accepted
at 877/444-6777 or online at www.recreation.
gov and must be made a minimum of five days
in advance. Single sites are $14, double sites are
$28, group sites are $75, and extra vehicles and
day use are $5. Open Memorial Day through
Labor Day, weather permitting.

Directions: From Santaquin, drive nine miles
up the Santaquin Canyon Road (Forest Road
14). Tinney Flat Campground will be on the
right side of the road.

GPS Coordinates: N 39° 54.100' W 111°
43.678'

Contact: Spanish Fork Ranger District, 801/798-
3571, www.fs.fed.us/r4/uwc/recreation/uinta/
camping/spanish_fork/index.shtml#tinney

campground is located on a short spur road
near the southern end of the Nebo Loop
Scenic Byway. The campground sits in a
deciduous forest of maple and gambel oak
trees. There's trout fishing on Salt Creek by
the campground. Group areas feature raised,
paved eating areas and central fire rings with
benches. The concrete pads built have been
built up with rock mason work.

Campsites, facilities: There are six single sites
for tents and RVs up to 35 feet in length and
three group sites. Group sites A and B can accommodate up to 75 people and group site C
up to 50 people. All group sites are wheelchair
accessible. Picnic tables on cement pads, fire
rings, barbeque grills, drinking water, and flush
toilets are provided. Leashed pets permitted.

Reservations, fees: Reservations are accepted
for the group sites only at 877/444-6777 or online at www.recreation.gov and must be made a
minimum of five days in advance. Single sites
are $14, group sites are $65–100, and extra vehicles and day use are $5. Open Memorial Day
through Labor Day, weather permitting.

Directions: From 100 N and Main Street in
Nephi, drive six miles east on Main Street
(Rte. 132). Turn left onto the Nebo Loop Sce-
nic Byway and travel 3.4 miles. Turn left into
Bear Canyon, continue about one mile to the
Bear Canyon Campground.

GPS Coordinates: N 39° 47.164' W 111°
43.492'

Contact: Spanish Fork Ranger District,
801/798-3571, www.fs.fed.us/r4/uwc/rec-
reation/uinta/camping/spanish_fork/index.
shtml#bear

63 BEAR CANYON

Scenic rating: 7

north of Nephi on the Nebo Loop Scenic
Byway in the Uinta National Forest

Map 3.2, page 112

Bear Canyon is a small Forest Service campground in the Uinta National Forest. The

64 PONDEROSA

Scenic rating: 7

north of Nephi on the Nebo Loop Scenic
Byway in the Uinta National Forest

Map 3.2, page 112

Ponderosa is the first Forest Service campground encountered if you're driving the

Nebo Loop Scenic Byway from south to north. The scenic byway is a gorgeous high country route that traverses the Uinta National Forest near the massive and beautiful Mount Nebo. Mount Nebo is the highest peak in the Wasatch Mountains and marks the southern boundary of the range. Trails leaving from the byway access the Mount Nebo Wilderness Area, and wildlife-viewing possibilities are plentiful. Wildlife lovers should bring binoculars and keep their eyes peeled for birds like red-tailed hawks, golden eagles, and mountain bluebirds. Large animals like elk and mule deer are common; harder-to-spot mammals like mountain lions, badgers, and black bears also call the area home. The Ponderosa Campground sits in a grove of its namesake trees, with tall grass growing on the forest floor. The paved loop has well-spaced sites with paved parking and cement pads for the eating areas. Sites 2 and 3 share the best views up to Mount Nebo. There are a handful of pull-through sites for easy RV egress. Fishing for rainbow trout is possible in Salt Creek, which flows by the campground.

Campsites, facilities: There are 23 campsites for tents and RVs up to 40 feet in length. Picnic tables on cement pads, fire grills, vault toilets, and drinking water are provided. Leashed pets permitted.

Reservations, fees: Reservations are accepted at 877/444-6777 or online at www.recreation. gov and must be made a minimum of five days in advance. Single sites are $14; extra vehicles and day use are $5. Open Memorial Day through Labor Day, weather permitting.

Directions: From 100 N and Main Street in Nephi, drive six miles east on Main Street (Rte. 132). Turn left onto the Nebo Loop Scenic Byway and travel 3.4 miles. Turn left into Bear Canyon, and continue 0.4 mile to the Ponderosa Campground on the left side of the road.

GPS Coordinates: N 39° 46.071' W 111° 42.946'

Contact: Spanish Fork Ranger District, 801/798-3571, www.fs.fed.us/r4/uwc/ recreation/uinta/camping/spanish_fork/index. shtml#ponderosa

65 HIGH COUNTRY RV CAMP

Scenic rating: 4

in Nephi

Map 3.2, page 112

High Country RV is in the town of Nephi with views up to the most dominant feature of the southern Wasatch Range, Mount Nebo. The RV park is a full-service spot to stay before starting out on the Mount Nebo National Scenic Byway, which is worthy of at least a day of your time. The high country drive is extremely popular with ATV users, and the trails it accesses see lots of hiker and horse traffic. Trout fishing is available along the parkway in the mountain lakes and streams. The RV park is within view of I-15, but far enough away that road noise isn't really an issue. With a Best Western Motel on one side and an industrial yard on the other, it has an urban-meets-rural feel. The grounds are gravel with a few islands of grass. Sites are shaded by large trees, and there is a sprinkling of picnic tables available for use.

Campsites, facilities: There are 42 full hook-up (30, 50 amps) sites, six partial hook-up sites, and 10 tent sites. Amenities include a dump station, picnic tables (at some sites), pull-through sites, WiFi, modern restrooms with showers, and laundry. Leashed pets permitted.

Reservations, fees: Reservations are accepted at 800/379-2624. RV sites are $25 (50 amps) and $20 (30 amps), and tent sites are $15. Open year-round.

Directions: From I-15, take Exit 222 and drive 0.5 mile on Business I-15. High Country RV Camp is on the right side of the road.

GPS Coordinates: N 39° 41.739' W 111° 50.106'

Contact: High Country RV Camp, 435/623-2624.

66 MAPLE CANYON

Scenic rating: 8

south of Nephi in the San Pitch Mountains

Map 3.2, page 112

Maple Canyon is a narrow, winding canyon penetrating the western slopes of the San Pitch Mountains. The canyon is noteworthy for its beautiful conglomerate rock walls, towers, and fins, which rise hundreds of feet above the canyon's floor. Cottonwoods, gambel oak, and—you guessed it—maple trees choke the creek bed at the base of the canyon and contribute to the area's lush, cool feel. The steep conglomerate walls look like a riverbed turned on its side, with rocks ranging in size from pebbles to boulders embedded in concrete like limestone rock. Understandably, rock climbers have been drawn to the canyon's unique geology, mild temperatures, and summer shade, and hundreds of routes have been established on a cluster of walls near the end of the Forest Service road. The small campground is mostly used by climbers on weekend trips from Salt Lake or passing through on longer road trips. Low-profile campsites have been established beneath the forest canopy, shaded by the trees and off to both sides of the gravel road. The sites are well spread out and private, though sound travels easily up and down the canyon so you're likely to hear your neighbors. Sites 2, 3, and 4 are walk-in tent sites and all the sites are designed for tent camping. The Middle Fork, Arch, and Right Fork Trails start from the walk-in sites, and there's also the Box Canyon Trail farther down-canyon.

Campsites, facilities: There are 12 sites and one group site for up to 40 people. In the main campground, picnic tables, fire grills, and vault toilets are provided. The sites along the road before entering the campground are primitive, with fire rings and tree stump chairs. There is no drinking water. Leashed pets permitted.

Reservations, fees: Reservations are accepted at 877/444-6777 or online at www.recreation. gov and must be made a minimum of four days in advance. Individual sites are $8, the group site is $40 (if the group site is not reserved the fee is $15), and the day-use fee is $3. Open May through October.

Directions: From Nephi, drive 14 miles southeast on Rte. 132 and turn right on 400 S in the town of Fountain Green. Continue six miles, turn right on Freedom Road, and travel 1.9 miles to the base of Maple Canyon. The campground is 1.8 miles up Maple Canyon.

GPS Coordinates: N 39° 33.355' W 111° 41.195'

Contact: Sanpete Ranger District, 435/283-4151.

67 MADSEN BAY AT SCOFIELD STATE PARK

Scenic rating: 6

west of Price on the Scofield Reservoir

Map 3.2, page 112

Scofield State Park is located on the east shore of the Scofield Reservoir in the Manti-La Sal Mountains. The lake is surrounded by hills forested with groves of aspen. In summer, the lake is popular for boating and fishing for rainbow and cutthroat trout. Ice fishing is good during the winter. The state park has two campgrounds above the reservoir's waters. The Madsen Bay Campground on the lake's northern tip is the more primitive of the two campgrounds, with a gravel loop leading to sites on a gently rising hill. The sites have cement pads around the picnic tables, but are completely devoid of tent areas. The ground around the tables is covered with dense sagebrush, so we ended up pitching our tent in the gravel parking spot. A few trees have been planted in the center of the loop, but they provide little shade for campers. Some sites have views down to the lake, but others don't. The campground is open and sound carries easily between sites. Truck traffic from Route 96 can be heard in the campground.

Campsites, facilities: There are 36 sites for tents and RVs up to 35 feet in length. Picnic tables, barbeque grills, flush toilets, drinking water, a fish-cleaning station, pull-through sites, garbage service, and a dump station are provided. Leashed pets permitted.

Reservations, fees: Reservations are accepted at 800/322-3770 or online at www.reserveamerica.com; they must be made a minimum of two days in advance and can be arranged up to 16 weeks in advance. There is an $8 nonrefundable reservation fee for individual sites. Sites are $13, extra vehicles are $6, and the day-use fee is $7. Open May through October.

Directions: From Price, drive north 24 miles on Hwy. 6 and turn west (left) on Rte. 96. Continue nine miles to the Mountain View Campground on the right side of the road. GPS Coordinates: N 39° 48.946' W 111° 08.211'

Contact: Scofield State Park, 435/448-9449 (summer) and 435/687-2491 (winter), http://stateparks.utah.gov/stateparks/parks/scofield/

68 FISH CREEK

Scenic rating: 7

near Scofield

Map 3.2, page 112

Fish Creek Campground is more of a glorified trailhead than a campground. It's the trailhead for the Fish Creek National Recreation Trail. The trail is open to hiking, biking, and horses and runs for 15 miles from Skyline Drive to Scofield Reservoir, following a beautiful canyon and Fish Creek most of the way. The area is known for its abundant wildlife populations and holds a reputation with anglers and hunters for its bounty. There's great fly fishing on the lower part of Fish Creek, and wildlife seekers can expect to see deer and elk foraging in the area. Beaver and fox are typically more difficult to spot, but they live in the valley as well. The campsites have views up Fish Creek and its canyon, a wide river plain filled with dense brush and beaver ponds. Aspen and spruce forests blanket the hills rising above the creek. The sites are

very minimal, with small gravel parking spots and sloping ground. Some sites lack parking and don't even have a flat spot to pitch a tent. The campground looks a bit overgrown. There are many undeveloped dispersed sites along the road out to the campground.

Campsites, facilities: There are seven sites. Picnic tables, fire grills, and vault toilets are provided. There is no drinking water. Leashed pets permitted.

Reservations, fees: Reservations are not accepted. The fee is $7 per site. Open Memorial Day through Labor Day, weather permitting.

Directions: From Scofield, turn right on Myrtle Street, turn right again on Church Street, and drive 3.7 miles to a junction. At the junction, take the left fork on Forest Road 123 and travel 1.5 miles to the campground following the brown arrow signs. GPS Coordinates: N 39° 46.469' W 111° 12.188'

Contact: Ferron-Price Ranger District, 435/637-2817.

69 MOUNTAIN VIEW AT SCOFIELD STATE PARK

Scenic rating: 6

west of Price on the Scofield Reservoir

Map 3.2, page 112

The Mountain View Campground at Scofield is located on the lake's eastern shore. Mountain View is the place to stay if you'd like direct access to the reservoir. There's a paved boat ramp and floating docks next to the campground. The sites at Mountain View feel like an RV park, placed in long, straight rows, each with a single spruce tree for shade. They're tightly packed and all within sight and shouting distance of each other. Expect to hear and get to know your neighbors. Like Madsen Bay, this campground suffers from road noise created by a steady stream of trucks passing by on Route 96.

Campsites, facilities: There are 34 sites for tents and RVs up to 30 feet in length. Picnic tables, barbeque grills, modern restrooms with showers, drinking water, fish-cleaning station, fishing pier, boat ramp, day-use pavilion, garbage service, and a dump station are provided. Leashed pets permitted.

Reservations, fees: Reservations are accepted at 800/322-3770 or online at www.reserveamerica.com; they must be made a minimum of two days in advance and can be arranged up to 16 weeks in advance. There is an $8 nonrefundable reservation fee for individual sites. Sites are $16, extra vehicles are $6, and the day-use fee is $7. Open May through October.

Directions: From Price, drive north 24 miles on Hwy. 6 and turn west (left) on Rte. 96. Continue 10 miles to the Mountain View Campground on the right side of the road. GPS Coordinates: N 39° 47.445' W 111° 07.803'

Contact: Scofield State Park, 435/448-9449 (summer) and 435/687-2491 (winter), http://stateparks.utah.gov/stateparks/parks/scofield/

70 GOOSEBERRY RESERVOIR

Scenic rating: 7

in the Manti-La Sal National Forest

Map 3.2, page 112

Gooseberry Reservoir is a small reservoir in a sagebrush and grass meadow on Gooseberry Creek in the Manti-La Sal National Forest. Wildflowers add splashes of color to the landscape. The lake is used for fishing, and to a lesser extent for boating and swimming. In winter the area is visited by snowmobilers and cross-country skiers. The reservoir is particularly beautiful where Gooseberry Creek enters the lake, its meandering course snaking through a lush green wetland delta. When we visited, we saw sandhill cranes feeding in the wetlands. The lake and campground are surrounded by rolling hills blanketed in dense aspen stands. The gravel campground loop is open and exposed to the sun and wind.

Campsites, facilities: There are 16 sites for tents and RVs up to 40 feet in length. Picnic tables, fire grills, and vault toilets are provided. There is no drinking water in the campground (it is available one mile up the road from the reservoir). Leashed pets permitted.

Reservations, fees: Reservations are accepted at 877/444-6777 or online at www.recreation.gov and must be made a minimum of four days in advance. The fee is $10. Open May through September.

Directions: From Fairview, drive eight miles east on Rte. 31 and turn left onto Forest Road 124. Continue 2.6 miles to the Gooseberry Reservoir Campground. GPS Coordinates: N 39° 42.622' W 111° 17.660'

Contact: Ferron-Price Ranger Districts, 435/637-2817.

71 GOOSEBERRY

Scenic rating: 7

in the Manti-La Sal National Forest

Map 3.2, page 112

Gooseberry Campground is a minimally developed forest facility in the Manti-La Sal National Forest. With adequate shade and an elevation of around 8,500 feet, the campground is cool and comfortable, even in midsummer. The campground is popular with ATV aficionados, who use it as a base camp for local trails like Skyline Drive. A gravel loop leads to simple sites cut out of the forest. Soft sunlight filters down through the trees, and butterflies flutter from wildflowers to pine needles on the forest floor. Watch for deer foraging in the forest. The well-dispersed sites are simple but functional and offer plenty of privacy. This isn't the flashiest campground in the world, but it does offer a quiet place to relax and get away from it all.

Campsites, facilities: There are eight single sites for tents and RVs up to 25 feet in length and two group sites for up to 40 people. Picnic tables, fire grills, vault toilets, and drinking water are provided. Leashed pets permitted.

Reservations, fees: Reservations are accepted for the group sites only at 877/444-6777 or online at www.recreation.gov and must be made a minimum of four days in advance. Single sites are $10, and the group sites are $40. Open May through September.

Directions: From Fairview, drive eight miles east on Rte. 31 and turn left onto Forest Road 124. After 1.2 miles, turn right onto Forest Road 224 and continue 0.5 mile to the campground.

GPS Coordinates: N 39° 41.268' W 111° 17.946'

Contact: Ferron-Price Ranger Districts, 435/637-2817.

72 LAKE CANYON RECREATION AREA

Scenic rating: 7

in the Manti-La Sal National Forest

Map 3.2, page 112

The Lake Canyon Recreation Area is an ATV playground on the Wasatch Plateau in the Manti-La Sal National Forest. The recreation site is situated between the Huntington and Cleveland Reservoirs. The Lake Canyon Multi-Use Trail system was built specifically for the four-wheeling off-road riders and features three learning loops. Additionally, it provides access to a seemingly endless system of backwoods byways. Sagebrush and fields of wildflowers grow between the intertwining trails and campsites. Widely spaced sites have plenty of room for privacy and everyone's vehicles. The campsites are tucked in among stands of spruce and aspen trees. The sites are relatively primitive; some have only cement fire rings, while others have picnic tables. Nonetheless, this area is very popular.

Campsites, facilities: There are 50 sites and five group sites. Miller A group site can accommodate up to 80 people, Lake A up to 100 people, Rolfson A up to 50 people, Rolfson B up to 150 people, and Rolfson C up to 30 people. Picnic tables (at some sites), vault toilets, pull-through

sites, and fire rings are provided. There is no drinking water. Leashed pets permitted.

Reservations, fees: Reservations are accepted at 877/444-6777 or online at www.recreation. gov and must be made a minimum of four days in advance. Single sites are $5 per vehicle, and group sites are $40–60. Open May through October.

Directions: From Fairview, drive 18 miles east on Hwy. 31 and turn right onto Miller Flat Road (Forest Road 14). The Lake Canyon Recreation Area is a short distance beyond the large parking lot.

GPS Coordinates: N 39° 34.750' W 111° 15.001'

Contact: Ferron-Price Ranger Districts, 435/637-2817.

73 HUNTINGTON CANYON RECREATION SITES

Scenic rating: 7

in the Manti-La Sal National Forest

Map 3.2, page 112

Huntington Canyon is a general name for a group of dispersed campsites along what is known as the Energy Loop: Huntington and Eccles Canyon National Scenic Byway (Route 31), north of the town of Huntington. The byway gets its name from several conspicuous coal-fired power plants in the region (including one in Huntington), and a working coal mine along the road. The deep Huntington Canyon is carved out of aesthetic, hueco-textured brown rock spilling down from Gentry Ridge on the Wasatch Plateau. Huntington Creek offers good fly fishing for trout and a peaceful atmosphere by which to camp. Ten different Forest Service sites, each with its own name, line the creek as it flows down-canyon. The sites are dispersed in approximately half-mile increments along the canyon. Cottonwood trees line the creek and provide shade for the simple sites. The facilities vary at each site but are generally primitive, so come prepared. The most developed area is at the Forks of the Huntington, where the Left Fork of Huntington Creek unites with the main creek. There's a group site and several walk-in sites at the trailhead for the Left Fork of Huntington National Recreation Trail. Be aware the access driveways to the some of the sites drop off quickly from the main highway and are deeply rutted.

Campsites, facilities: There are dispersed sites along Rte. 31. At the Fork of Huntington there are five walk-in sites and one group site for up to 40 people. Some of the dispersed sites have picnic tables and fire rings. Drinking water is only available at Forks of Huntington. Leashed pets permitted.

Reservations, fees: Reservations are accepted for the group area at Forks of the Huntington only at 877/444-6777 or online at www. recreation.gov and must be made a minimum of four days in advance. Sites are $3, and the group site is $40. Open year-round.

Directions: From Huntington, drive northwest 12.4 miles on Rte. 31 to the brown tent sign on the left side of the road. More sites are dispersed along the road over the next 12 miles.

GPS Coordinates: N 39° 25.861' W 111° 07.791'

Contact: Ferron-Price Ranger District, 435/637-2817.

74 INDIAN CREEK

Scenic rating: 7

in the Manti-La Sal National Forest
Map 3.2, page 112

This Indian Creek Campground is not to be confused with the famous rock-climbing destination near Canyonlands National Park. You won't find any sandstone crack climbing here. What you will find is a quiet, peaceful setting among a lovely aspen and spruce forest. Wildlife is abundant in this part of the Wasatch Plateau; we saw a spotted fawn grazing under an aspen grove and hummingbirds and butterflies buzzing in the wildflowers around the sites. Aspen-covered

hills rise above the campground on both sides. The campground is popular with ATV enthusiasts who access the nearby Miller's Flat and Arapeen OHV Trail Systems. The camp loop, parking, and roads leading to the campground are all gravel. Your vehicle will be covered in a thick layer of dust when you leave.

Campsites, facilities: There are seven group sites for up to 30, 50, or 70 people depending on the site. Sites 1, 3, 4, 6, and 7 are wheelchair accessible. Picnic tables, concrete fire rings, drinking water, and vault toilets are provided. Leashed pets permitted.

Reservations, fees: Reservations are accepted at 877/444-6777 or online at www.recreation. gov and must be made a minimum of four days in advance. Group sites are $30–50. If the group sites have not been reserved, they are available on a first come, first served basis, and the fee is $3 per vehicle. Open June through October, weather permitting.

Directions: From Fairview, drive 18 miles east on Hwy. 31 and turn right onto Miller Flat Road (Forest Road 14). Travel 14.4 miles and turn left onto Forest Road 40; after 0.6 mile turn left again onto Forest Road 17 and continue 1.2 miles to the campground.

GPS Coordinates: N 39° 26.518' W 111° 14.271'

Contact: Ferron-Price Ranger District, 435/637-2817.

75 POTTER'S PONDS

Scenic rating: 7

in the Manti-La Sal National Forest
Map 3.2, page 112

Potter's Pond is a scenic little fishing hole in the Upper Joe's Valley–Miller Flat area of the Wasatch Plateau. The area is popular with anglers and ATV enthusiasts who ride on the Arapeen OHV Trail System. The trail system includes 350 miles of dirt road and 4-by-4 track, including the ultra-scenic South Skyline Drive. South Skyline Drive follows the crest of the plateau, riding the backbone of the range from as far north as Highway 6 all the way south to I-70. Potter's Pond itself is a good-sized pond created by a small earthen dam. Fisherfolk line the top of the dam in lawn chairs as they cast for trout. A wetland borders the campground, where frogs croak at night and mosquitoes breed in the early season. The minimally developed campground fills to capacity with RVs, trailers, ATVs, and big rigs. Aspen and spruce trees grow in bunches and break up the meadow setting. Most of the sites are large and function as group or large family units. Be aware it's a long haul on gravel roads to reach the campground. Driving on unpaved terrain is part of the appeal!

Campsites, facilities: There are 19 sites; sites 16–19 are equestrian-only units, and site 6 is a group site for up to 50 people. The only amenity is vault toilets. There is no drinking water. Leashed pets permitted.

Reservations, fees: Reservations are accepted at 877/444-6777 or online at www.recreation.gov. Sites are $3 per vehicle, reserved sites are $10, reserved equestrian sites are $15, and the group site is $40. Open June through October, weather permitting.

Directions: From Fairview, drive 18 miles east on Hwy. 31 and turn right onto Miller Flat Road (Forest Road 14). Travel 12.5 miles and turn right onto Forest Road 271. After 100 yards, bear right and continue one mile to Potter's Pond Campground.

GPS Coordinates: N 39° 27.024' W 111° 16.132'

Contact: Ferron-Price Ranger District, 435/637-2817.

76 BEAR CREEK

Scenic rating: 6

northwest of Huntington in Huntington Canyon

Map 3.2, page 112

Bear Creek Campground sits at the entrance to Huntington Canyon and is managed by Emery County. The campground is nestled down in a gully by Huntington Creek but has decent views up to the pink cliffs of Huntington Canyon. Cottonwood, juniper, cedar, and spruce trees provide shade for the campers. Tangled trees and underbrush grow thick around all of the sites. Small boulders line the access loop, and a pond decorates the campground. There is a large group pavilion with picnic tables and grills next to an open grass field and volleyball court. The county-run facility has a unique feel to it. Signs warned that bears frequent the campground, yet there was an open garbage can at each site—go figure.

Campsites, facilities: There are 27 campsites. Picnic tables, barbeque grills, fire pits, drinking water, garbage service, two day-use pavilions, a volleyball court, horseshoe pits, and flush toilets are provided. Leashed pets permitted.

Reservations, fees: Reservations are accepted at 435/381-2108, or download forms to mail at www.emerycounty.com/rec/2007/campground_res_form.PDF. Sites are $7. Open May 1 through October 1.

Directions: From Huntington, drive west for 8.7 miles on Rte. 31 to the Bear Creek Campground on the left side of the road.

GPS Coordinates: N 39° 23.564' W 111° 05.959'

Contact: Emery County, 435/381-2108, www.emerycounty.com/rec/campground.htm

77 PAINTED ROCKS AT YUBA STATE PARK

Scenic rating: 7

on Yuba Reservoir

Map 3.2, page 112

Painted Rocks Campground is set off by itself on the eastern shore of Yuba Reservoir. The campground is named after rock pictographs made by people of ancient cultures who camped by the Sevier River. The rock art can be seen near the boat ramp west of the campground. The Painted Rocks Campground sits on the hillside above the lake. The surface of the lake is just visible from most of the sites. The campground is exposed to the elements and can be hot. The facilities are immaculate, with a paved loop leading to picnic tables on cement pads accompanied by raised food-preparation tables. Vegetation in the campground is sparse, but Utah juniper, sagebrush, and rabbit brush surround the reservoir. Many animals utilize the immediate reservoir environment, including mammals like mule deer, cottontail rabbits, jackrabbits, and coyotes; raptors such as golden eagles, red-tailed hawks, and great horned owls; and waterfowl like western grebes, ducks, Canadian geese, and pelicans.

Campsites, facilities: There are 38 campsites, three tent-only sites, and a group area for up to 150 people. Covered picnic tables, fire grills, food-preparation table, vault toilets, garbage service, dump station, and drinking water are provided. Leashed pets permitted.

Reservations, fees: Reservations are accepted at 800/322-3770 or online at www.reserveamerica.com; they must be made a minimum of two days in advance and can be arranged up to 16 weeks in advance. Group site reservations can be arranged up to 11 months in advance. There is a nonrefundable reservation fee of $8 for individual sites and $10.25 for group sites. Sites are $10, the group area is $100, extra vehicles are $10, and day use is $7. Open year-round.

Directions: From Nephi, drive south on I-15 to Exit 222 for Rte. 28. Travel south for 24 miles, turn right, and after 0.2 mile take the left branch and continue to the campground.

GPS Coordinates: N 39° 21.169' W 111° 56.542'

Contact: Yuba State Park, 435/758-2611, http://stateparks.utah.gov/stateparks/parks/yuba/

78 PALISADE STATE PARK

Scenic rating: 7

south of Manti on the Palisade Reservoir

Map 3.2, page 112

Weekends at Palisade State Park are busy! Kids biking around the parking lot, canoeists paddling across the lake, groups picnicking in the pavilions, golfers smashing drives off the tee... everywhere you look there are people having fun. If you didn't know better, you might think you were near a big city. The green waters of the lake are surrounded by brown, juniper-dotted hills, and huge cottonwood trees dominate the shoreline. Sandy beaches make for enjoyable swimming, even if you can't see your feet in the lake's milky water. The park has a boat ramp to facilitate easy access for boaters and anglers. Sportfishing species include rainbow, tiger, and brown trout. There are also ATV trails nearby in Six Mile Canyon. The campground has tightly packed sites along the lakeshore and a full-hookup loop overlooking the lake from above. The upper loop also features covered picnic tables.

Campsites, facilities: Arapeen Loop has 22 sites, Pioneer Loop has 13 sites (tents are not allowed in Sites 27–35), Sanpitch Loop has 20 sites (eight with hook-ups), Wakara Loop has 20 sites (all with full or partial hook-ups), and there are four group sites for up to 150 people (one in each loop). Site 7 in the Arapeen Loop, site 20 in the Wakara Loop and sites 40, 47, and 53 in the Sanpitch Loop are wheelchair accessible. Amenities include picnic tables, barbeque grills, modern restrooms with showers, drinking water, floating swim platforms, a dock, boat ramp (non-motorized use only), dump station, and garbage service. Canoe and pedal boat rentals are available. Leashed pets permitted.

Reservations, fees: Reservations are accepted at 800/322-3770 or online at www.reserveamerica.com; they must be made a minimum of three days in advance and can be arranged up to 16 weeks in advance.

Group site reservations can be arranged up to 11 months in advance. There is a nonrefundable reservation fee of $8 for individual sites and $10.25 for group sites. Single sites are $16, full hook-up sites are $25, group sites are $75–87.50 and $3 pp over 25 people, extra vehicles are $8, and day use is $6. Open May through September.

Directions: From Manti, drive 5.0 miles south on Hwy. 89, turn east (left) following signs to Palisade State Park, and continue 1.6 miles to the campground entrance.

GPS Coordinates: N 39° 12.135' W 111° 39.939'

Contact: Palisade State Park, 435/835-7275, http://stateparks.utah.gov/stateparks/parks/palisade/

79 TEMPLE HILL RV RESORT
🏊 🏠 ♿ 🚐 ⛰️

Scenic rating: 5

In the town of Manti

Map 3.2, page 112

Temple Hill RV Resort is located at the north end of the town of Manti. The Manti Utah Temple is one of the first temples built by the Church of Jesus Christ of Latter-day Saints in Utah; it is perched on a hilltop south of the campground. Manti is also the headquarters of a polygamist sect of the LDS faith, The True and Living Church of Jesus Christ and Saints of the Last Days. Each year the town of Manti hosts the Mormon Miracle Pageant. There's no closer place to stay to the temple than the Temple Hill RV Resort. The entrance to this kid-friendly RV park is decorated with a bear statue and historic wagon parts. Pleasant views from the yard look up to the rolling hills of the Wasatch Plateau. Campsites have strips of grass lawn and are shaded by a mix of cottonwood and spruce trees.

Campsites, facilities: There are 97 RV sites, 19 tent sites, one yurt, and a wagon tent. Amenities include modern restrooms with showers,

a swimming pool, hot tub, WiFi, complimentary Saturday morning chuck wagon breakfast, a sand volleyball court, horseshoe pits, playground, general store, dump station, and campfire pits. Leashed pets are permitted for a fee.

Reservations, fees: Reservations are accepted at 435/835-2267 or online at https://templehillrv.com/contact/reserve.shtml. RV sites are $25, tent sites are $18, the Wagon Tent is $25, the Pacific Yurt Tent is $30, and pets are $2 per day. Open year-round.

Directions: From Manti, drive north for 0.2 mile on Hwy. 89, turn right, and continue 0.5 mile to the Temple Hill RV Resort entrance.

GPS Coordinates: N 39° 16.670' W 111° 37.764'

Contact: Temple Hill RV Resort, 435/835-2267, www.templehillrv.com/

80 MANTI COMMUNITY
🚶 ⛵ 🏠 🚐 ⛰️

Scenic rating: 7

on the Wasatch Plateau in the Manti-La Sal National Forest

Map 3.2, page 112

Manti Community Campground is a little Forest Service camp loop near a small pond named Yearns Reservoir. The pond is a popular fishing hole, where a line of anglers cast from the shore. The campsite is part of a natural creek and wetland system created and maintained by the local beaver population. Beaver ponds dot the area, and a lush forest of juniper, aspen, spruce, and fir trees shade the campsites. The campground loop and parking spots are gravel. A short trail leads from the sites to the pond.

Campsites, facilities: There are nine sites and one group area for up to 30 people. Picnic tables, fire grills, some barbeque grills, drinking water, and vault toilets are provided. Leashed pets permitted.

Reservations, fees: Reservations are accepted for the group sites only at 877/444-6777 or online at www.recreation.gov and must be made a minimum of four days in advance. Sites are $10, the group site is $40 (if the group site is not reserved the fee is $15), and extra vehicles are $3. Open June through October.

Directions: From the intersection of Main Street and 500 S in Manti, turn east (left) on 500 S and drive 6.0 miles on Forest Road 045 to the campground.

GPS Coordinates: N 39° 15.283' W 111° 32.419'

Contact: Sanpete Ranger District, 435/283-4151.

81 LAKE HILL

Scenic rating: 6

east of Ephraim in the Manti-La Sal National Forest

Map 3.2, page 112

Lake Hill Campground is a forest site on the western slopes of the Wasatch Plateau east of the town of Ephraim. The drive to the campground has noteworthy views of the Sanpete Valley, but the campground itself is tucked into the forest and doesn't share the same panoramas. The forest is dominated by aspen and spruce, which shade sites and provide relief from hot summer temperatures. The ample shade combined with an altitude of around 8,500 feet make it a good place to camp in July and August. The access loop is gravel, as is the road approaching the campground. The sites are well distributed and the campground is not busy, offering an opportunity for solitude. Also of interest in Ephraim Canyon is the Experimental Station Trail. The Great Basin Experimental Station researches different methods of land management in an effort to better conserve the environment. Ephraim Canyon offers a self-guided auto tour detailing the parts of the canyon under experimental research.

Campsites, facilities: There are 11 single sites and two group sites for up to 30 or 75 people,

depending on the site. Picnic tables, barbeque grills, fire grills, drinking water, and vault toilets are provided. Leashed pets permitted.

Reservations, fees: Reservations are accepted at 877/444-6777 or online at www.recreation.gov and must be made a minimum of five days in advance. Single sites are $10, group sites are $30–40, and the day-use fee is $3. Open June through October.

Directions: From Ephraim (intersection of Main Street and 400 S), turn east on 400 S, after 0.3 miles turn right on 300 E. Drive 7.2 miles, turn right onto campground access road and continue 0.3 mile to the campground.

GPS Coordinates: N 39° 19.663' W 111° 29.933'

Contact: Sanpete Ranger District, 435/283-4151.

82 JOE'S VALLEY

Scenic rating: 8

in the Manti-La Sal National Forest

Map 3.2, page 112

The campground at Joe's Valley overlooks a large reservoir built on Cottonwood Creek. The reservoir sits in a natural basin on the eastern slope of the Wasatch Plateau. The reservoir is used for boating and fishing. The campground is popular with ATV riders who access a vast trail system in Upper Joe's Valley and at Miller's Flat. Fish species include albino, splake, and rainbow trout, as well as largemouth bass. The Forest Service campground is mostly open, taking advantage of expansive views down to the water and beyond to Gentry Ridge and the surrounding plateau. The landscape is dotted with occasional small trees, mostly pinyon pine and juniper. Sagebrush, grass, and small shrubs blanket the campground floor. The sites are very spread out, so those campers who enjoy privacy will appreciate the layout. The facilities are nice and well maintained, with a paved loop and parking areas. The campground is busy, even mid-week, so make reservations. Compared to other campgrounds in the area, this spot is hot and exposed to the sun, so be ready for summer heat!

Campsites, facilities: There are 49 sites and one group site for up to 100 people. Sites 8, 19, 24, 25, 27–36, 43, 48, and 49 are wheelchair accessible. Picnic tables, fire grills, drinking water, vault toilets, boat ramp, and fish-cleaning station are provided. Leashed pets permitted.

Reservations, fees: Reservations are accepted at 877/444-6777 or online at www.recreation.gov and must be made a minimum of four days in advance. Single sites are $10, double sites are $18, and the group site is $50. Open May through October.

Directions: From Orangeville, drive 17.5 miles west on Rte. 29. Turn left onto Forest Road 170, drive 0.1 mile, and turn left into the Joe's Valley Campground.

GPS Coordinates: N 39° 17.494' W 111° 17.709'

Contact: Ferron-Price Ranger District, 435/384-2372.

83 TWIN LAKES
🏕 🚙 ⛰

Scenic rating: 7

near Twelvemile Creek on the Wasatch Plateau
Map 3.2, page 112

Twin Lakes Campground is located near Twelvemile Creek on the Wasatch Plateau. The campground is popular with ATV riders who buzz around the extensive network of dirt roads and trails in this beautiful, mountainous region. The campground features a learner's loop for budding ATVers. A gravel loop leads to dispersed, relatively primitive sites in a juniper forest. The sites are tucked in among the trees, but look out to open meadows. There are limited views up to the Wasatch Plateau and its gray-ridged peaks. Unfortunately, a web of unnecessary trails crisscrosses the

campground, putting a damper on the scenic character of the place.

Campsites, facilities: There are 21 sites and one group site. Vault toilets and concrete fire rings are provided. There is no drinking water. Leashed pets permitted.

Reservations, fees: Reservations are not accepted. The fee is $5 per vehicle. Open June through October.

Directions: From Main Street and Canyon Road in Mayfield, turn left on Canyon Road and drive east for 7.6 miles on Forest Road 22. The campground will be on the left side of the road.

GPS Coordinates: N 39° 07.255' W 111° 36.072'

Contact: Sanpete Ranger District, 435/283-4151.

84 TWELVEMILE FLAT
🏕 🚙 ⛰

Scenic rating: 9

east of Mayfield in the Manti-La Sal National Forest
Map 3.2, page 112

High on the Wasatch Plateau, Twelvemile Flat Campground is set in a wide, scenic meadow among clusters of fir, aspen, and spruce trees. The meadow has a tundralike feel, with short grass and small, white wildflowers spreading out across the landscape. Views from the campground look up to the gray rock peaks and ridgelines topping out well above 10,000 feet. This area is ATV heaven. Starting near the campground, Forest Road 022 becomes a four-wheel-drive road, heading west into the Grove of the Aspen Giants Scenic Area. The Black Mountain Trail, which ascends to the summit of the 10,632-foot peak, can also be accessed directly from the campground. The campground is primitive but adequate, with a gravel loop and parking slips. Sites are tucked into clumps of trees and have rocky alpine soil. Even if you don't stay at the campground, this part of the Wasatch Plateau is worth your time. Canyon Road (Forest Road 22) is a great scenic drive on an unpaved but well-maintained road suitable for normal passenger cars.

Campsites, facilities: There are 16 single sites and three group sites for up to 50 or 75 people, depending on the site. Picnic tables, fire rings, drinking water, and vault toilets are provided. Leashed pets permitted.

Reservations, fees: Reservations are accepted at 877/444-6777 or online at www.recreation. gov and must be made a minimum of four days in advance. Sites are $7 and the group sites are $40. Open June through October.

Directions: From Main Street and Canyon Road in Mayfield, turn left on Canyon Road and drive east for 19.1 miles on Forest Road 22. The campground will be on the right side of the road.

GPS Coordinates: N 39° 07.394' W 111° 29.217'

Contact: Sanpete Ranger District, 435/283-4151.

85 FERRON RESERVOIR

🏃 🏊 🏕 🚐 ⛺

Scenic rating: 9

east of Manti in the Manti-La Sal National Forest

Map 3.2, page 112   **BEST (**

Ferron Reservoir (sometimes called Indian Creek Reservoir) is located in the highlands of the Wasatch Plateau in a glacier-carved cirque overflowing with blooming wildflowers. Purple lupine, pink fireweed, red Indian paintbrush, and wild blue flax paint the lake shore and surrounding valley a beautiful rainbow of color. The basin is a wildflower lover's dream! The campground enjoys panoramic views of the surrounding mountains, with their chalk gray rock and green blanket of trees. The lake fits into the landscape as though it were natural, and the low-profile dam does little to take away from

Indian paintbrush above Ferron Reservoir

this perception. The campground has sites on two sides of the lake, with one loop overlooking the water and another off to the side in an intermittent forest. The loop and parking are gravel and lead to simple yet functional sites. A nature trail leaves from the campground and loops through the wetland area at the lake's outlet. Cutthroat trout spawn in Ferron Creek where it drains out of the lake. The campground is popular with the fishing and ATV crowds, which come to sample the area's ample trails and lakes.

Campsites, facilities: There are 30 sites and one group site for up to 50 people. Picnic tables, fire grills, drinking water, and vault toilets are provided. Leashed pets permitted.

Reservations, fees: Reservations are accepted at 877/444-6777 or online at www.recreation. gov and must be made a minimum of four days in advance. Sites are $7 and the group site is $40. Open May through October.

Directions: From State Street in Ferron, turn west (right) on 100 S (Canyon Road) and drive

26.6 miles on Forest Road 022, then bear left and continue 0.1 mile to the first entrance to the campground.

GPS Coordinates: N 39° 08.299' W 111° 27.121'

Contact: Ferron-Price Ranger District, 435/384-2372.

86 WILLOW LAKE

Scenic rating: 8

in the Manti-La Sal National Forest

Map 3.2, page 112

Willow Lake Campground is a small, minimally developed camping area high on the Wasatch Plateau. The lake fills a natural depression in the almost tundralike high country. While it appears to be natural, closer inspection reveals a short earthen dam holding the lake's water in place and creating a quaint little fishing hole. The pond-sized lake is too small for any real boating. The gravel camp loop dips into a spruce and aspen forest and accesses meadowlike campsites. Most sites have grass areas where you may pitch a tent, but they are not perfectly flat. A recent forest fire has burned the forest above the campground, but not the trees in the sites. Look for mountain bluebirds and deer around camp.

Campsites, facilities: There are 10 sites. Vault toilets and fire grills are provided. There is no drinking water. Leashed pets permitted.

Reservations, fees: Reservations are accepted at 877/444-6777 or online at www.recreation.gov. Sites are $3 per vehicle. Open May through October.

Directions: From State Street in Ferron, turn west (right) on 100 S (Canyon Road) and drive 22.2 miles on Forest Road 022. Willow Lake Campground will be on the left side of the road.

GPS Coordinates: N 39° 08.116' W 111° 22.757'

Contact: Ferron-Price Ranger District, 435/384-2372.

87 MILLSITE STATE PARK

Scenic rating: 8

west of Ferron on the Millsite Reservoir

Map 3.2, page 112

Millsite is located on a reservoir at the base of Ferron Canyon. The reservoir is surrounded by wild, brown mesas and buttes. The soft, brown soils have been sculpted by eons of erosion into intriguing and wonderful landscape. Boating, kayaking, swimming, and fishing are all popular in the state park. Tiger, cutthroat, and rainbow trout can be caught on the lake. Deer, elk, and moose feed on the vegetation around the reservoir, and large raptors like bald eagles, osprey, and red-tailed hawks visit the lake. Blue herons and many species of ducks can be spotted on the water. Wild mustangs also live in the area. For those not interested in playing on the lake, the links of the Millsite Golf Course are just down the road. In typical Utah state park style, Millsite Campground is in great shape. A paved loop leads to sites with gravel pull-through parking slips, paved cement eating areas, and trees for shade. The sites are right on the shore of the lake, giving campers a front-row seat to the action.

Campsites, facilities: There are 20 sites and an overflow camping area. Site 19 is wheelchair accessible. Picnic tables on cement pads, barbeque grills, pull-through sites, modern restrooms with showers, a boat ramp, drinking water, garbage service, and a dump station are provided. Leashed pets permitted.

Reservations, fees: Reservations are accepted at 800/322-3770 or online at www.reserveamerica.com; they must be made a minimum of two days in advance and can be arranged up to 16 weeks in advance. There is an $8 nonrefundable reservation fee for individual sites. Sites are $16, extra vehicles are $8, and day use is $5. Open year-round.

Directions: From State Street in Ferron, turn west (right) on 100 S (Canyon Road). Drive 4.2 miles and turn right into the Millsite State Park entrance.

GPS Coordinates: N 39° 05.483' W 111° 11.606'
Contact: Millsite State Park, 435/687-2491, http://stateparks.utah.gov/stateparks/parks/millsite/

88 BUTCH CASSIDY RV PARK

Scenic rating: 4

in Salina

Map 3.3, page 113

Butch Cassidy RV Park is named after the infamous train robber, bank robber, and leader of the Hole in Wall Gang, who was born in Beaver, Utah, and grew up south of Salina on his parents' ranch near Circleville. His legend was forever imprinted in the American public's mind by the Hollywood film *Butch Cassidy and the Sundance Kid,* featuring Robert Redford, who turned out to be another influential Utah personality. The RV park is on State Street as you drive into town from the interstate. The campground loop is gravel and leads to an interesting mix of permanent trailers and visiting RVs. Trees provide some shade for the sites. There's a large separate tent area, which is set down by State Street. The tent area offers green lawns and adequate shade. Unfortunately, it's right on the road.

Campsites, facilities: There are 40 RV sites and an open grass tent area. Amenities include WiFi, a game area, a swimming pool, a playground, modern restrooms with showers, drinking water, and garbage. The tent area amenities include picnic tables and fire grills. Leashed pets permitted.

Reservations, fees: Reservations are accepted at 800/551-6842. Full hook-up sites are $20.50–21.95, sites without hook-ups are $17, tent sites are $6 per adult and $2 per child, and a family tent site is $18 (no charge for children six and under). Open year-round.

Directions: From I-70, take Exit 56 and drive

0.5 mile north on State Street. Butch Cassidy RV Park will be on the left side of the road.
GPS Coordinates: N 38° 56.604' W 111° 51.333'
Contact: Butch Cassidy RV Park, 800/551-6842.

89 GOOSEBERRY

Scenic rating: 7

in the Fishlake National Forest

Map 3.3, page 113

Gooseberry Campground is located on Gooseberry Creek in the Fishlake National Forest. Gooseberry is close to a wide variety of trails popular with ATV and horseback riders, hikers, and anglers. There is a footpath leading to nine backcountry lakes with trout fishing, the Equestrian Trail, and a whole network of ATV tracks, including the Great Western Trail. Campers with horses will appreciate the corrals at the campground. Gooseberry has sites both out in the open and tucked into an aspen forest. Sites have gravel parking areas and views down the scenic valley. Blue wildflowers decorate the meadows around the sites. The unique group area, known as the Gooseberry Administrative Site, features bunkhouses that can be reserved in advance.

Campsites, facilities: There are 13 individual sites, one group site, and three bunk cabins. Picnic tables, fire rings, drinking water, garbage service, and vault toilets are provided. Leashed pets permitted.

Reservations, fees: Reservations are accepted for the bunk houses only at 877/444-6777 or online at www.recreation.gov and must be made a minimum of seven days in advance. Individual sites are $5, the group site is $20, and the bunkhouses are $300. Open May through November.

Directions: From Salina, drive east on I-70 for seven miles. Take Exit 63 and drive south on Gooseberry Road for 9.3 miles to the campground on the right side of the road. The bunkhouses are just past the campground on the right side of the road.

GPS Coordinates: N 38° 48.210' W 111° 40.991'

Contact: Richfield Ranger District, 435/896-9233, www.fs.fed.us/r4/fishlake/recreation/camping/gooseberry.shtml, for the bunkhouses www.fs.fed.us/r4/fishlake/recreation/rentals/gbadminsite.shtml.

90 PIUTE

Scenic rating: 7

on Fish Lake in the Fishlake National Forest

Map 3.3, page 113

Piute Campground overlooks the Johnson Valley Reservoir from a sagebrush hillside in the Fishlake National Forest. The lake is popular for swimming, boating, and fishing. Rainbow, cutthroat, and brook trout can all be caught in the lake's shallow, turbid waters. Conspicuous American white pelicans can be spotted floating lazily on the surface of the reservoir. The Fishlake National Forest is home to two long-distance ATV trails, the Great Western Trail and the Paiute ATV Trail. The campground is open and exposed to the sun, with little more than grass, wildflowers, and sage for vegetation. Small, lichen-covered lava rocks are strewn between the campsites. The paved camping loop is designed to incorporate as many pull-through parking slips as possible. Tiers of sites stretch up the hill away from the road toward a backdrop of aspen and spruce.

Campsites, facilities: There are 47 sites. Picnic tables, fire grills, drinking water, pull-through sites, and vault toilets are provided. Leashed pets permitted.

Reservations, fees: Reservations are not accepted. Sites are $10; extra vehicles and day use are $5. Open May through September.

Directions: From Loa, drive west on Rte. 24 for 13 miles and turn east (right) onto Rte. 25.

Continue 15 miles and the Piute Campground will be on the left side of the road.

GPS Coordinates: N 38° 37.102' W 111° 39.115'

Contact: Fremont River/Loa Ranger District, 435/836-2800, www.fs.fed.us/r4/fishlake/recreation/camping/fishlake.shtml

91 TASHA EQUESTRIAN

Scenic rating: 7

on Fish Lake in the Fishlake National Forest

Map 3.3, page 113

Tasha Equestrian Campground is reserved for horseback riders and their animals. The campground is near Fish Lake and the Johnson Valley Reservoir in the green aspen groves of the Fishlake National Forest. A horse trail to Mytoge Mountain and the Fishlake Hightop Plateau along Tasha Creek leaves directly from the campground. The sites are set in an aspen and spruce forest and feature green metal horse corrals in addition to picnic tables and fire grills. Overall, the sites feel simple if not primitive, but modern restrooms give the campground a luxurious touch. The facilities include horse-loading ramps.

Campsites, facilities: There are 10 single sites with a minimum of one horse per site and a group site for up to 25 people with a minimum of four horses. Picnic tables, fire grills, flush toilets, drinking water, hitching posts, horse corrals, and a loading ramp are provided. Leashed pets permitted.

Reservations, fees: Reservations are accepted at 877/444-6777 or online at www.recreation.gov and must be made a minimum of four days in advance. Single sites are $10, and the group site is $35. Open Memorial Day through Labor Day, weather permitting.

Directions: From Loa, drive west on Rte. 24 for 13 miles and turn east (right) onto Rte. 25. Travel 14 miles and turn left onto Forest Road 1458 and continue 0.5 mile to the campground.

GPS Coordinates: N 38° 37.237' W 111° 39.770'

Contact: Fremont River/Loa Ranger District, 435/836-2800, www.fs.fed.us/r4/fishlake/recreation/camping/fishlake.shtml

92 FRYING PAN

Scenic rating: 7

on Fish Lake in the Fishlake National Forest

Map 3.3, page 113

Frying Pan Campground rests between Fish Lake and Johnson Reservoir in the Fishlake National Forest. Fish Lake offers a rare opportunity to fish in one of Utah's only natural mountain lakes. The campground is a small, intimate facility with just 11 sites. There's an aspen and spruce forest blanketing the hills above the sites. The camp loop features views down to an open valley below, where the road winds through a lovely mosaic of lupine wildflowers and sagebrush. The loop and parking spaces are paved, and the campground is well maintained. The sites are fairly close together, so generators are not allowed between 10 P.M. and 6 A.M. If you are looking for some privacy, site 11 is set off by itself. The sites don't offer much room to pitch a tent.

Campsites, facilities: There are 11 sites and a group site for up to 100 people. Picnic tables, fire grills, drinking water, and flush toilets are provided. Firewood is available. Leashed pets permitted.

Reservations, fees: Reservations are accepted at 877/444-6777 or online at www.recreation.gov and must be made a minimum of four days in advance. Single sites are $12, the group site is $60, and extra vehicles are $6. Open Memorial Day through Labor Day, weather permitting.

Directions: From Loa, drive west on Rte. 24 for 13 miles and turn east (right) onto Rte. 25. Continue 13 miles and the Frying Pan Campground will be on the left side of the road.

GPS Coordinates: N 38° 36.496' W 111° 40.765'

Contact: Fremont River/Loa Ranger District, 435/836-2800, www.fs.fed.us/r4/fishlake/recreation/camping/fishlake.shtml

93 BOWERY HAVEN RESORT

Scenic rating: 6

on the north shore of Fish Lake

Map 3.3, page 113

Fish Lake is the largest natural mountain lake in Utah, stretching five miles long and a half mile wide. It's also quite deep and located at around 8,800 feet on the Fish Lake Hilltop Plateau. The lake's lofty elevation combined with its large size keeps the water a bit chilly for swimming. However, the cold water makes it an excellent fishery. Fish Lake is one of the better destinations for anglers in Utah, who ply the lake's waters for rainbow trout, yellow perch, and splake (a trout/brook trout hybrid). Bowery Haven Resort is located near the north end of Fish Lake. The Bowery Haven Resort offers a boat marina, small grocery store, a good café, and a gas station in addition to a busy RV park. The RVs are tightly packed into neat, long rows working uphill away from Fish Lake. The sites have limited views of the lake over the other trailers, and the gravel loop and parking spaces are well maintained and graded. If you're looking for a social camping atmosphere at a full-service RV park with easy access to the lake, Bowery Haven Resort is a good choice.

Campsites, facilities: There are 90 full hookup RV sites and a selection of cabins. Amenities include picnic tables, modern restrooms with showers, laundry, drinking water, garbage service, marina, café, boat ramp, fish-cleaning station, and convenience store. Leashed pets permitted.

Reservations, fees: Reservations are accepted at 435/638-1040 or 866/708-6007. RV sites are $22 and cabins are $49–125. Open May through early October.

Directions: From Loa, drive west on Rte. 24 for 13 miles and turn east (right) onto Rte. 25. Travel approximately 11 miles to Bowery Haven Resort on the left side of the road.
GPS Coordinates: N 38° 33.791' W 111° 42.331'
Contact: Bowery Haven Resort, 435/638-1040 (May 1–October 1) and 435/638-7525 (October 1–May 1), www.boweryhaven.com/

94 BOWERY CREEK

Scenic rating: 7

on Fish Lake in the Fishlake National Forest

Map 3.3, page 113

Bowery Creek is just south of the Bowery Haven Resort above Fish Lake. This can be a good or bad thing, depending on your perspective. On the positive side, it's near a marina, gas station, convenience store and a tasty café. On the other hand, the level of development at the resort and on this end of Fish Lake in general leaves a wilderness experience out of the question. Bowery Creek is a Forest Service campground that feels a lot like an RV park. Sites are more spread out than what you'd find at an RV park, and stands of aspens provide nice visual barriers between each pull-through site. There are views down to the lake from the campground, and lupine wildflowers add color to the natural setting.
Campsites, facilities: There are 33 single sites, seven double sites, and three triple sites. Sites 5 and 6 are wheelchair accessible. Picnic tables, fire grills, drinking water, day-use picnic area, and flush toilets are provided. Firewood is available. Leashed pets permitted.
Reservations, fees: Reservations are accepted at 877/444-6777 or online at www.recreation.gov and must be made a minimum of five days in advance. Single sites are $14, double sites are $28, triple sites are $42, and extra vehicles are $7. Open Memorial Day through Labor Day, weather permitting.
Directions: From Loa, drive west on Rte. 24

for 13 miles and turn east (right) onto Rte. 25. Travel approximately 11 miles to Bowery Creek Campground, on the left side of the road.
GPS Coordinates: N 38° 33.751' W 111° 42.435'
Contact: Fremont River/Loa Ranger District, 435/836-2800, www.fs.fed.us/r4/fishlake/recreation/camping/fishlake.shtml

95 MACKINAW

Scenic rating: 7

on Fish Lake in the Fishlake National Forest

Map 3.3, page 113

Mackinaw Campground is a sprawling Forest Service facility, climbing up a gently rising hillside on the northwest shore of Fish Lake. The campground is named after trophy Mackinaw trout that have been caught on Fish Lake. The campground is one of the largest campgrounds along Fish Lake and has a variety of sites with different looks and feels. Paved loops and parking spaces add to the campground's clean, attractive quality. The upper loop (sites 60–67) has particularly good views down to the waters of Fish Lake. Mackinaw is the closest campground to the Twin Creeks Picnic Area and Amphitheater, as well as the Lakeview Nature Trail.
Campsites, facilities: There are 58 single sites and nine double sites. Sites 13 and 14 are wheelchair accessible. Modern restrooms with showers, picnic tables, barbeque grills, drinking water, and garbage service are provided. Leashed pets permitted.
Reservations, fees: Reservations are accepted at 877/444-6777 or online at www.recreation.gov and must be made a minimum of five days in advance. Single sites are $14, double sites are $28, and extra vehicles are $7. Open Memorial Day through Labor Day, weather permitting.
Directions: From Loa, drive west on Rte. 24 for 13 miles and turn east (right) onto Rte. 25.

Continue approximately seven miles to the Mackinaw Campground on the left side of the road.

GPS Coordinates: N 38° 33.372' W 111° 42.927'

Contact: Fremont River/Loa Ranger District, 435/836-2800, www.fs.fed.us/r4/fishlake/recreation/camping/fishlake.shtml

96 LAKESIDE RESORT

Scenic rating: 7

on Fish Lake

Map 3.3, page 113

The Lakeside Resort is a full-service resort on the western shore of Fish Lake. This RV park is part of a greater Lakeside Resort complex that offers lodging, cabins, a grocery store, and boat rentals, in addition to RV sites. The RV section of the resort is relatively small, offering only 24 sites in a tight loop. The complex has excellent views down to Fish Lake from open campsites. Sites are surrounded by shrubs, namely sagebrush, rabbitbrush, and wild grasses. The loop and parking areas are unpaved but well graded, and there are pull-through sites available for easy parking.

Campsites, facilities: There are 24 RV sites and a wide selection of cabin options. Picnic tables, modern restrooms with showers, drinking water, a dump station, and garbage service are provided. Laundry, a convenience store, and boat rentals are available. Leashed pets permitted.

Reservations, fees: Reservations are accepted at 435/638-1000. RV sites are $20 per night, and cabins are $100–725. Open May through October, weather permitting.

Directions: From Loa, drive west on Rte. 24 for 13 miles and turn east (right) onto Rte. 25. Travel approximately eight miles to the Lakeside Resort on the left side of the road.

GPS Coordinates: N 38° 32.116' W 111° 44.292'

Contact: Lakeside Resort, 435/638-1000, www.fishlake.com/rv-park.html

97 DOCTOR CREEK

Scenic rating: 8

on Fish Lake in the Fishlake National Forest

Map 3.3, page 113

Doctor Creek Campground is located at the southern end of Fish Lake. This campground is one of the best in this group of Fish Lake–area campgrounds. It's on the valley floor and has a more intimate feel than some of the other public campgrounds in the area. The loop overlooks a marshy wetland called Coots Slough from a grove of mature aspens. The wetland is a good place to spot waterfowl. The loop is small and appears well kept and cared for. It seems to be the preferred public campground for RVs at this end of the lake and is the busiest in the area. Interpretive Ranger Programs are held on weekends during the summer. A trail leading to the Mytoge Mountains leaves from the east side of the lake.

Campsites, facilities: There are 27 sites for tents and RVs up to 22 feet in length and two group sites for up to 150 people. Site 5 is wheelchair accessible. Amenities include picnic tables, fire grills, a covered picnic area, barbeque grills, drinking water, garbage service, and a dump station. Firewood is available. Leashed pets permitted.

Reservations, fees: Reservations are accepted at 877/444-6777 or online at www.recreation.gov and must be made a minimum of four days in advance. Single sites are $14, group sites are $92, and extra vehicles are $7. Open Memorial Day through Labor Day, weather permitting.

Directions: From Loa, drive west on Rte. 24 for 13 miles and turn east (right) onto Rte. 25. Travel approximately seven miles to Doctor Creek Campground on the right side of the road.

GPS Coordinates: N 38° 31.725' W 111° 44.403'

Contact: Fremont River/Loa Ranger District, 435/836-2800, www.fs.fed.us/r4/fishlake/recreation/camping/fishlake.shtml

98 CATHEDRAL

Scenic rating: 8

in the Cathedral Valley of Capitol Reef National Park

Map 3.3, page 113   **BEST(**

Cathedral Campground is tucked away in Cathedral Valley, a little-seen corner of Capitol Reef National Park. Cathedral Valley sees few visitors because it takes significant effort to reach. The valley is accessible via a series of gravel roads of varying quality. While the roads would be nasty for RVs or trucks with trailers, they're not unreasonable for trucks with high clearance or cars with four-wheel drive. The rewards for driving out to Cathedral Valley are twofold: scenery and solitude. The campground is a small dirt loop with six campsites. The sites sit on the desert floor between scattered juniper and pinyon pine trees. Brown dirt, small lava rocks, and ghostly juniper skeletons round out the immediate camp surroundings. Off in the distance, views open up to the rock fins and deep-cut canyons of Cathedral Valley. During the muggy heat of the afternoon following a thunderstorm, we were attacked by a relentless swarm of tiny black flies and no-see-um flies. That encounter aside, the Cathedral Valley is a great place to experience Capitol Reef National Park's amazing geology without encountering an onslaught of other tourists. A short walk from the campground leads to the Cathedral Valley Overlook, which provides panoramic views of the red rock fins and towers of the Temple of the Sun and Gypsum Sink Hole. This is one of the quietest campgrounds in Utah's least-traveled national park, and it's free!

Campsites, facilities: There are six campsites. Picnic tables, fire grills, and vault toilets are provided. There is no drinking water. Leashed pets permitted.

Reservations, fees: Reservations are not accepted. There is no fee. Open year-round.

Directions: From Fremont, drive seven miles north on Rte. 72 and turn east (right) onto Thousand Lakes Mountain Road. Continue 4.6 miles and take the right fork onto Forest Road 206. After 0.7 mile, turn left and continue 6.9 miles on Forest Road 022. Turn left again and continue 0.3 mile to the campground.

GPS Coordinates: N 38° 28.457' W 111° 22.044'

Contact: Capitol Reef National Park, 435/425-3791, www.nps.gov/care/planyourvisit/primitivecampsites.htm

99 ELKHORN

Scenic rating: 7

in Fishlake National Forest

Map 3.3, page 113   **BEST(**

Elkhorn Campground is a Forest Service campground in a remote forest, perched above Capitol Reef's Cathedral Valley. Across an open meadow, Elkhorn Ranger Station is visible from the campground. The gravel loop is set in a meadow and spruce forest transition zone, where clumps of trees give way to open fields of lupine and Indian Paintbrush wildflowers. These displays of flowers make Elkhorn one of the best campgrounds in Utah for wildflowers. Grass grows in the relatively primitive sites. The sites are well spaced for solitude and privacy, adding to the small campground's remote feel. Deer graze in the meadows and visit the campground around dusk. Both the Riley Spring and Great Western Trails are accessible from Elkhorn. The Great Western Trail is open to ATVs, horses, mountain bikes, and hikers. A short distance from camp, an open meadow offers views down to Capitol Reef National Park's little-visited Cathedral Valley.

Campsites, facilities: There are five individual sites and one group site for up to 75 people. Picnic tables, vault toilets, nonpotable water, fire grills, and fire pits are provided. Leashed pets permitted.

Reservations, fees: Reservations are accepted for the group sites only at 877/444-6777 or online at www.recreation.gov and must be made a minimum of four days in advance. Individual sites are $8, and group sites are $35. Open mid-June through October.

Directions: From Fremont, drive seven miles north on Rte. 72 and turn east (right) onto the Thousand Lakes Mountain Road. Continue 4.6 miles and take the right fork onto Forest Road 206 and continue 3.2 miles to Elkhorn Campground.

GPS Coordinates: N 38° 27.825' W 111° 27.415'

Contact: Fremont River/Loa Ranger District, 435/836-2800.

100 SUNGLOW
🏠🚐⛺️

Scenic rating: 7

in Fishlake National Forest

Map 3.3, page 113

Sunglow Campground is located below Thousand Lake Mountain at the very southeastern tip of the Fishlake National Forest. The campground is a convenient place to stay to explore Cathedral Valley in the desolate northern reaches of Capitol Reef National Park. It's also near the Ke Bullock Waterfowl Management Area. Red cliffs surround the campground in a natural amphitheater. A small, clear creek runs through the campground in the otherwise dry environment. Juniper trees, shrubs, and common prickly pear grow in red-brown dirt around the campsites. Sandstone and basalt boulders are scattered between the desert flora. Sites are well spaced and offer privacy, peace, and quiet.

Campsites, facilities: There are seven individual sites and two group sites for up to 20 people. Picnic tables, fire grills, garbage service, drinking water, and vault toilets are provided. Group sites have a large picnic table, food preparation table, and benches around a fire pit. Leashed pets permitted.

Reservations, fees: Reservations are accepted for the group sites only at 877/444-6777 or online at www.recreation.gov and must be made a minimum of four days in advance. Individual sites are $8, and group sites are $20. Open May through October.

Directions: From Bicknell, drive 0.5 mile south on Rte. 24, turn left on Forest Road 143, and continue one mile to the campground.

GPS Coordinates: N 38° 20.506' W 111° 31.236'

Contact: Fremont River/Loa Ranger District, 435/836-2800.

101 THOUSAND LAKES RV PARK
🏊🐕♿🚐⛺️

Scenic rating: 7

west of Torrey near Capitol Reef National Park

Map 3.3, page 113

Thousand Lakes RV Park is located west of Capitol Reef National Park outside the small town of Torrey. It's a large, full-service RV park that offers a restaurant, gift shop, swimming pool, and even cabins for those who like a little luxury and civilization along with nature. Monday through Friday there's a Western-style cookout in the RV park pavilion. The cookout menu includes Dutch oven potatoes, cowboy beans, and homemade scones to accompany a main dish of your choice. The cottonwood trees between the sites provide shade, while not blocking the views out to the beautiful red rock mesa north of the campground. RV sites have small grass lawns and gravel parking slips accessed via a gravel loop. The tent camping area is on a large grass lawn away from the RV sites.

Campsites, facilities: There are 46 full-hook up (20-, 30-, and 50- amp) sites, 16 partial hook-up sites, nine tent sites, five camping cabins, and three deluxe cabins. Amenities include picnic tables, fire pits, a swimming pool, WiFi, modern restrooms with showers, drinking water, garbage service, horseshoe pits, and a covered picnic area. A restaurant, a convenience store, a gift shop, laundry, and 4WD rentals are available. Leashed pets permitted (only allowed in certain cabins).

Reservations, fees: Reservations are accepted at 800/355-8995. Full hook-up sites are $24.50, partial hook-up sites are $23.50, tent sites are $16, the group tent area is $7.50 pp, and cabins are $32.50–95. Open late March through October.

Directions: From the junction of Rte. 12 and Rte. 24, drive two miles west on Rte. 24. The Thousand Lakes RV Park is on the right side of the road.

GPS Coordinates: N 38° 18.047' W 111° 26.697'

Contact: Thousand Lakes RV Park, 435/425-3500, www.thousandlakesrvpark.com/

102 SAND CREEK RV PARK

Scenic rating: 7

west of Torrey near Capitol Reef National Park

Map 3.3, page 113

Sand Creek RV Park is west of the small town of Torrey near the southern entrance to Capitol Reef National Park. Tucked behind an office with a country-western motif, this little RV park has the most intimate feel of the RV parks in and around Torrey. The grounds are open and breezy, and the lack of trees leaves good views of the red rocks to the north. Sites are simple and tightly packed together. The tent sites have short fences separating them in an effort to provide a little sense of personal space. The place might feel a bit claustrophobic, but then again, so does Fruita Campground in the

national park. Horses are welcome at Sand Creek, and there's a fenced 1.5-acre field and a corral to accommodate them.

Campsites, facilities: There are 12 pull-through, full hook-up (30, 50 amps) sites, three tent sites, two group tenting areas, and two cabins. Picnic tables, barbeque grills, fire pits, drinking water, modern restrooms, a horseshoe pit, and garbage service are provided. Laundry, a dump station and showers are available. Leashed pets permitted.

Reservations, fees: Reservations are accepted at 435/425-3577 or online at www. sandcreekrv.com/reservations.htm. Full hook-ups (30 amps) are $17, full hook-ups (50 amps) are $21, tent sites are $13, cabins are $28, dump station is $5, showers are $4, and horses are $5 per night. Open late March through October.

Directions: From the junction of Rte. 12 and Rte. 24, drive one mile west on Rte. 24. The Sand Creek RV Park is on the right side of the road.

GPS Coordinates: N 38° 17.951' W 111° 25.987'

Contact: Sand Creek RV Park, 435/425-3577, www.sandcreekrv.com/

103 WONDERLAND RV PARK

Scenic rating: 7

in Torrey at the intersection of Rte. 12 and Rte. 24 near Capitol Reef National Park

Map 3.3, page 113

Wonderland RV Park is in the small town of Torrey outside Capitol Reef National Park. Wonderland is the closest full-service RV park to the national park, making a good base camp for those who plan on leaving their rig and driving something smaller into the park. The yard is well maintained, clean, and inviting. It also has views of the red rock landscape to the east. The RV park's only major drawback: no shade. The sites are completely open and exposed, both to the sun and one another. The camp host is friendly and helpful.

Campsites, facilities: There are 31 RV sites and nine tent sites. Amenities include picnic tables, pull-through sites, modern restrooms with showers, drinking water, cable TV, WiFi, a covered shelter/cooking area, basketball court, and garbage service. Firewood, a dump station, and laundry are available. Leashed pets permitted.

Reservations, fees: Reservations are accepted at 877/854-0184. RV sites are $21.50–24, tent sites are $20, and there is a $7 charge for the dump station. Open April through November, weather permitting.

Directions: From the intersection of Rte. 12 and Rte. 24 in Torrey, drive south on Rte. 12 and immediately turn right into the Wonderland RV Park.

GPS Coordinates: N 38° 17.889' W 111° 24.133'

Contact: Wonderland RV Park, 435/425-3665, http://wonderland.rvpark.googlepages.com/

104 FRUITA

Scenic rating: 6

in Capitol Reef National Park

Map 3.3, page 113

For campers who enjoy history, Fruita is the place to stay. Fruita was actually a Mormon pioneer community established in 1880. Extensive orchards of around 2,700 cherry, apricot, peach, pear, and apple trees provided sustenance for the early settlers. These orchards are still here and are within walking distance of the campground. Visitors may stroll through the orchards and sample the fruit they produce. During designated harvest times it's also possible to pick and take home a basket of the bounty—for a small fee, of course. The camping is in a pleasant but tightly spaced configuration. RV and tent campers are intermixed in a hodgepodge of different styles. Loop B feel is a bit more spread out than Loop A. If you're lucky enough to secure a site on the outside

of the loop you'll have views out to the surrounding scenery rather than of your neighbors. Plan ahead, as the campground fills up quickly during the summer months. This is the only developed campground in the southern part of Capitol Reef National Park.

Campsites, facilities: There are 71 tent and RV sites and one group site for up to 40 people. Picnic tables, flush toilets, fire grills, drinking water, garbage service, aluminum recycling, and a dump station are provided. Leashed pets permitted.

Reservations, fees: Reservations are not accepted for the individual sites. The group site can be reserved for April 1–October 20 by faxing or mailing in a request. Mail reservation requests to:

Group Campsite Reservations
HC 70, Box 15
Torrey, UT 84775
fax 435/425-3026

The opening day for reservations is the first Monday of February. Faxes received or mail postmarked prior to this date will be rejected. More information is available at www.nps.gov/care/planyourvisit/groupcampsite.htm. Individual sites are $10 per night and the group site is $3 pp ($50 minimum). Open year-round.

Directions: From Torrey, drive east on Rte. 24 for 10.5 miles, turn right at the visitors center, and continue one mile to the Fruita Campground on the right side of the road.

GPS Coordinates: N 38° 16.951' W 111° 14.827'

Contact: Capitol Reef National Park, 435/425-3791, www.nps.gov/care/planyourvisit/fruita-campground.htm

105 SINGLETREE

Scenic rating: 8

in the Fishlake National Forest

Map 3.3, page 113

This is the best and largest of the Forest Service campgrounds on Boulder Mountain along State Route 12. Consider cruising this section of road in the early morning or before sunset to enjoy views of the expansive landscape below. The scene stretches out over much of the eastern part of Southern Utah, including an area larger than the entire state of Connecticut. More specifically, views from Singletree Campground look down to the colorful Capitol Reef National Park, with the dark mass of the Henry Mountains looming behind. Throw in mature ponderosa pine trees in an otherwise open meadow and you have a perfect setting for a campground. The paved drive leads to well-spaced sites with adequate parking for big rigs, although there are no pull-through sites for RVs. The campground is designed to accommodate groups, with two designated large group areas and double sites for smaller parties. A sand volleyball court and horseshoe pits add a parklike dynamic to the forest. A half-mile hiking trail to Singletree Falls starts in the campground. This is certainly the best maintained of the Forest Service campgrounds in the area and is the most convenient for larger vehicles as well.

Campsites, facilities: There are 31 individual sites and two group areas for up to 50 people. Sites 12 and 31 are wheelchair accessible. Picnic tables, barbeque grills, fire grills, drinking water, flushing toilets, vault toilets, garbage service, a dump station, a sand volleyball court, and horseshoe pits are provided. Firewood is available. Leashed pets permitted.

Reservations, fees: Reservations are accepted at 877/444-6777 or online at www.recreation.gov and must be made a minimum of four days in advance. Single sites are $10, double sites are $20, the group areas are $35, and extra vehicles are $5. Open May through September.

Directions: From Torrey, drive south on Rte. 12 for 12.1 miles and turn right into Single Tree Campground.

GPS Coordinates: N 38° 09.682' W 111° 20.055'

Contact: Fremont River Ranger District, 435/836-2800, www.fs.fed.us/r4/fishlake/recreation/camping/singletree.html

106 OAK CREEK

Scenic rating: 7

in the Fishlake National Forest

Map 3.3, page 113

Oak Creek Campground sits on the east slope of Boulder Mountain, just north of the neighboring Pleasant Creek Campground. Nearby on the scenic byway are beautiful views at Steep Creek Overlook of Capitol Reef National Park, the Henry Mountains, and Navajo Mountain. In total, the overlook gazes down upon an area larger than the state of Connecticut. The bird's-eye view of the undulating topography of the Colorado Plateau is so sweeping in scope it's akin to studying a three-dimensional map. Even if you don't end up staying in the area, the drive is a scenic experience in itself. Oak Creek is a forested campground, with mature spruce, Douglas fir, and aspen trees sheltering sites. The presence of scattered gas-pocketed lava boulders will remind campers of Boulder Mountain's volcanic past. The loops are close enough to State Route 12 that road noise can be heard from some of the sites. The campground is most popular with ATV users, but it also features a hiking trail leading to Long Lake, Scout Lake, Round Lake, and finally Oak Creek Reservoir. The paved loops are tight; trailers over 20 feet are not recommended. This campground is very close and similar to the Pleasant Creek Campground. You may want to take the time to check out both campgrounds before selecting a site.

Campsites, facilities: There are nine sites. Picnic tables, barbeque grills, drinking water, and vault toilets are provided. Leashed pets permitted.

Reservations, fees: Reservations are not accepted. Single sites are $9, double sites are $18, extra vehicles are $5, and the day-use fee is $5. Open May through October.

Directions: From Torrey, drive south on Rte. 12 for 18.4 miles and turn right into Oak Creek Campground.

GPS Coordinates: N 38° 05.346' W 111° 20.531'

Contact: Fremont River Ranger District, 435/836-2800, www.fs.fed.us/r4/fishlake/recreation/camping/oakcreekfr.htm.

107 LOWER BOWNS

Scenic rating: 6

in the Fishlake National Forest

Map 3.3, page 113

Lower Bowns Reservoir (sometimes spelled "Browns") is a small reservoir in a desert setting among gently rolling forested hills. The campground is even smaller than the reservoir, a gravel loop with sites set among shrubs and bushes near the lake. Sites are new and well built with concrete pads and gravel parking areas. The campground has an open, exposed feel to it and doesn't provide any shade or shelter from the wind. The reservoir is frequently used by boaters and anglers. While the lake is open to boating, there is no developed boat ramp, and the reservoir is too small for waterskiing. Nearby trails cater to off-road vehicle users and horseback riders; there's even an ORV-specific trail that leads to Lower Bowns from the highway. Free dispersed camping is also available along a fork of Pleasant Creek running down to the lake. These sites are simply open spaces near the gently flowing stream, but they are well shaded by pine trees and offer an opportunity for free camping. If you don't need a picnic table, or prefer the protection of the forest, these sites might be more appealing than Lower Bowns.

Campsites, facilities: There are four sites and one group site for up to 50 people. Picnic tables, fire grills, and vault toilets are provided. There is no drinking water. Leashed pets permitted.

Reservations, fees: Reservations are accepted at 877/444-6777 or online at www.recreation.gov and must be made a minimum of four days in advance. Individual sites are $8, extra vehicles are $4, and the group site is $35. The dispersed sites are free and are first come, first served. Open May through October.

Directions: From Torrey, drive south on Rte. 12 for 17.3 miles and turn east (right) onto Forest Service Road 181. Continue 3.7 bumpy miles down to Bowns Reservoir Recreation Area.

GPS Coordinates: N 38° 06.365' W 111° 16.630'

Contact: Fremont River Ranger District, 435/836-2800, www.fs.fed.us/r4/fishlake/recreation/camping/lowerbowns.html

108 PLEASANT CREEK

Scenic rating: 7

in the Fishlake National Forest

Map 3.3, page 113

Pleasant Creek is a small Forest Service campground on State Route 12 as it climbs over the plateaulike Boulder Mountain. The highlight of this area is the view from overlooks like Larb Hollow and Steep Creek, which look east down to the wonders of Capitol Reef National Park and its defining crinkle in the earth's crust, Waterpocket Fold. The campground is located at the turnoff for Lower Bowns Reservoir. Bowns, or Browns, depending on which sign you see, is a popular fishing spot for brook trout and is heavily used by ATV riders. The small Pleasant Creek campground is right off the scenic byway and is shaded by big pine trees. Copious pinecones and pine needles litter the forest floor. There are two loops, Upper Pleasant Creek, and Lower Pleasant Creek. The upper loop is the second entrance to the campground, about 0.1 mile farther up the highway. Some sites have nice views down to an open meadow below the campground. Both access loops are paved. The Rosebud OHV Trail leaves from the campground and accesses the Lower Bowns Reservoir. Larger vehicles and trailers over 20 feet are not recommended in this little campground.

Campsites, facilities: There are 17 sites, five at Lower Pleasant Creek and 12 at Upper Pleasant Creek. Picnic tables, barbeque grills, drinking water, and vault toilets are provided. Leashed pets permitted.

Reservations, fees: Reservations are not accepted. The fee is $9 and extra vehicles are $5. Open May through October.

Directions: From Torrey, drive south on Rte. 12 for 17.3 miles and turn right into Pleasant Creek Campground.

GPS Coordinates: N 38° 06.052' W 111° 20.206'

Contact: Fremont River Ranger District, 435/836-2800, www.fs.fed.us/r4/fishlake/recreation/camping/pleasantcreek.html

DINOSAURLAND AND NORTHEASTERN UTAH

© MIKE MATSON

BEST CAMPGROUNDS

Jurassic Park, the 1990 science fiction novel by
Michael Crichton, captured the imagination of the American public by
inventing a world where dinosaurs were brought back to life in a larger-
than-life theme park. Crichton's convincing scientific explanations of the
possibility of cloning prehistoric creatures – and the man vs. beast thrill
ride that followed – rekindled an interest in dinosaurs not only in kids, but
in adults as well. While the Steven Spielberg movie left the intriguing science behind, it expanded Crichton's audience considerably. Ask a modern
teenager to name any prehistoric period, and the first answer will almost
certainly be the Jurassic Period. What does Jurassic Park have to do with
camping in Utah, you ask?

Northeastern Utah is the real Jurassic Park. Dinosaur National
Monument in Utah's northeastern corner protects the largest Jurassic
dinosaur quarry in the world. Earl Douglas discovered the quarry in 1909
while searching out fossils for the Carnegie Museum. In 1915, Dinosaur
National Monument was created to protect the bones and fossils from
looters. The monument has since expanded from its original 80 acres
to a 210,844-acre park that encompasses the amazing geology of Split
Mountain and beautiful meandering stretch of the Green River in addition
to the dinosaur fossils. Partially unearthed bones have been preserved
for visitors to see in the park's visitors center. The Utah side of the monument has three incredibly scenic campgrounds set on the banks of the
Green River. If you have the time and the means, perhaps the best way
to see Dinosaur National Monument is on a multi-day river-rafting trip
down the Green River, right through Split Mountain.

Dinosaur National Monument is not all northeastern Utah has to
offer campers. The most striking natural feature in the region is the Uinta
Mountain Range. The Uinta Mountains are Utah's tallest mountains and
the only prominent range in the Rocky Mountains to run from west to

east rather than north to south. The range is capped by the High Uinta Wilderness Area, protecting countless high mountain lakes, open grass meadows, and glacier-carved basins. At 13,528 feet, Kings Peak is the state's tallest mountain and attracts peak baggers from all over. Unlike many of Colorado's "fourteeners" (peaks taller than 14,000 feet), Kings Peak is not easily accessible. While it can be climbed in a day, it is better done as a two-day backpacking trip. Much of the Uintas have a remote feel, and reaching them requires driving on gravel and dirt roads. The range's only major paved road, the Mirror Lake Highway is lined with popular campgrounds and offers direct access to the alpine lake-dotted high country. The road climbs over Bald Mountain pass and provides an easy approach to the 60-mile Highline Trail, one of the best long back-packing trails in the Rockies, if not the entire country. There's no better backcountry camping experience in Utah.

An overview of northeastern Utah would not be complete without mentioning The Flaming Gorge National Recreation Area. The recreation area surrounds the 91-mile-long Flaming Gorge Reservoir, created by a massive concrete dam on the Green River. Most of the lake is actually in Wyoming, but the most spectacular scenery, in the actual Flaming Gorge, is in Utah at the lake's southern end. The Flaming Gorge is a steep-sided, brightly colored sandstone gorge that rises above the lake for thousands of feet. When John Wesley Powell and his men first braved the rapids of the Green River in their wooden dories in the spring of 1969, they named the narrow canyon for its colorful wall burning in the warm glow of sunset. The lake is known for its trophy mackinaw trout and kokanee (landlocked salmon) fishery. The recreation area around the reservoir has an impres-sive collection of campgrounds offering something for every type of camper. From boat launches with full-service marinas to breathtakingly beautiful scenic overlooks, the Flaming Gorge won't disappoint.

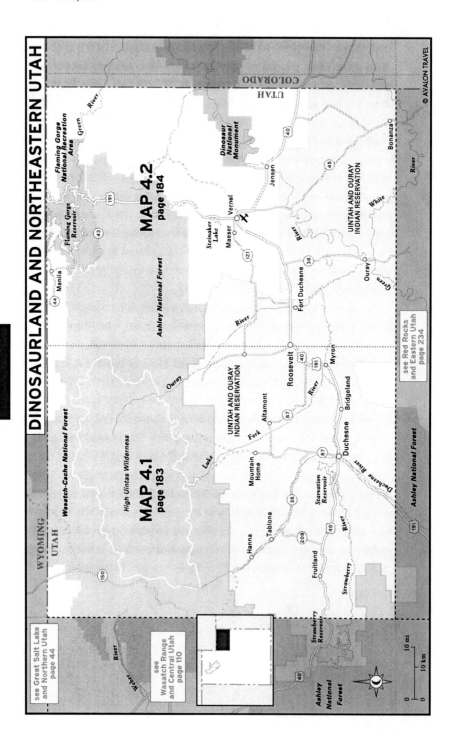

DINOSAURLAND AND NORTHEASTERN UTAH

Map 4.1

Campgrounds 1-44
Pages 185-210

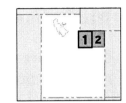

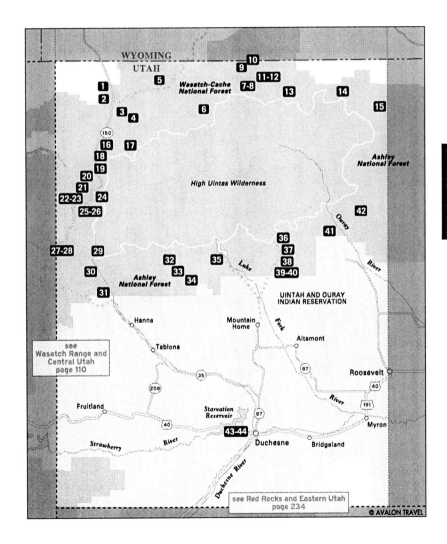

Map 4.2

Campgrounds 45-81
Pages 211-230

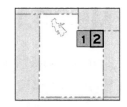

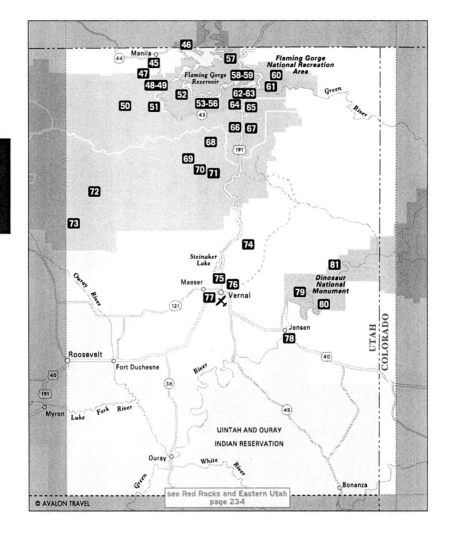

1 EAST FORK BEAR RIVER
🛶 🐴 �e 🏕

Scenic rating: 7

on the Mirror Lake Scenic Byway in the
Wasatch-Cache National Forest

Map 4.1, page 183

The East Fork Bear River is a humble little campground on the banks of the Bear River. The campground is close neighbors with Bear River Campground, and they can effectively be thought of as one campground. The sites at East Fork stretch out single file along the river, offering prime doorstep fishing for rainbow, cutthroat, and brook trout. Sagebrush and grass grow thick around the sites and blanket the hills on both sides of the river. A small meadow separates the campground from the Mirror Lake Highway, providing enough of a buffer to effectively reduce road noise. The gently flowing stream helps drown out the passing traffic noise as well. A sprinkling of lodgepole pines and aspens provide some shade and cover for the campsites.

Campsites, facilities: There are seven sites for tents and RVs up to 20 feet in length. Picnic tables, fire grills, drinking water, and a vault toilet are provided. Leashed pets permitted.

Reservations, fees: Reservations are not accepted. The camping fee is $12; day use and extra vehicles are $5. Open June through October, weather permitting.

Directions: From the intersection of Main Street (Rte. 32) and 200 S (Rte. 248) in Kamas, head north on Rte. 32 and turn east (right) after one block onto Rte. 150. Continue east on Rte. 150 for 48.3 miles and turn left into the East Fork Bear River Campground.

GPS Coordinates: N 40° 54.716' W 110° 49.767'

Contact: Evanston Ranger District, 307/789-3194, www.fs.fed.us/r4/uwc/recreation/wcnf/camping/evanston-campgrounds.shtml#eastforkbearriver

2 BEAR RIVER
🛶 🐴 🏕

Scenic rating: 7

on the Mirror Lake Scenic Byway in the
Wasatch-Cache National Forest

Map 4.1, page 183

Bear River Campground is located at the very northern end of the Mirror Lake Highway, near the Wyoming border. There's fishing on the river for rainbow, cutthroat, and brook trout. The sites line the water and offer a quiet, low-key camping experience. Lodgepole pines and aspen trees grow around the tent pads, with sagebrush and long grass growing up the gentle hills on either side of the stream. The gravel loop is small, so large trailers and RVs are not recommended. There's a tight hairpin turn on the short gravel driveway, further restricting access for large vehicles. Tent campers will be happier here anyway, as the sites are small and the parking slips are short. The sites are close together but enjoy some separation courtesy of dense willows and other vegetation along the river.

Campsites, facilities: There are four tent sites. RVs and trailers are not recommended. Picnic tables, fire grills, drinking water, and a vault toilet are provided. Leashed pets permitted.

Reservations, fees: Reservations are not accepted. The camping fee is $12; day use and extra vehicles are $5. Open June through October, weather permitting.

Directions: From the intersection of Main Street (Rte. 32) and 200 S (Rte. 248) in Kamas, head north on Rte. 32 and turn east (right) after one block onto Rte. 150. Continue east on Rte. 150 for 48.2 miles and turn left into the Bear River Campground.

GPS Coordinates: N 40° 54.672' W 110° 49.835'

Contact: Evanston Ranger District, 307/789-3194, www.fs.fed.us/r4/uwc/recreation/wcnf/camping/evanston-campgrounds.shtml#Bearriver

3 STILLWATER

Scenic rating: 7

on the Mirror Lake Scenic Byway in the Wasatch-Cache National Forest

Map 4.1, page 183

Stillwater Campground offers riverside sites along the Bear River near the Wyoming border in the northern Uinta Mountains. The gravel camp loop leads through stands of lodgepole pine and quaking aspen to grassy sites. Piles of dead limbs and slash from thinned lodgepole are stacked around the campground in an effort to reduce the potential fuel for future forest fires. Up to half the trees in this part of the forest have been killed by pine bark beetles. The river adds a peaceful feel to the campground. Flat tent pads provide good tenting within earshot of the water. Sagebrush and grass grow around the sites, and the trees offer plenty of shade.

Campsites, facilities: There are 18 single sites for tents and RVs up to 30 feet in length. There are four group sites for up to 25 to 50 people, depending on the site. Picnic tables, fire grills, pull-through sites, tent pads, drinking water, and vault toilets are provided. Leashed pets permitted.

Reservations, fees: Reservations are accepted at 877/444-6777 or online at www.recreation.gov and must be made a minimum of four days in advance. To make a reservation, Stillwater Campground requires a two-night minimum stay on weekends and three nights on holiday weekends. Single sites are $14, group sites are $40–55, and day use and extra vehicles are $5. Open June through October, weather permitting.

Directions: From the intersection of Main Street (Rte. 32) and 200 S (Rte. 248) in Kamas, head north on Rte. 32 and turn east (right) after one block onto Rte. 150. Continue east on Rte. 150 for 45.6 miles and turn right into the Stillwater Campground.

GPS Coordinates: N 40° 52.258' W 110° 49.998'

Contact: Evanston Ranger District, 307/789-3194, www.fs.fed.us/r4/uwc/recreation/wcnf/camping/evanston-campgrounds.shtml#stillwater

4 WOLVERINE

Scenic rating: 7

on the Mirror Lake Scenic Byway in the Wasatch-Cache National Forest

Map 4.1, page 183

Wolverine is a trailhead-campground hybrid near the Wyoming border in the northern Uinta Mountains. The Wolverine Exploration Company drilled an exploratory oil well on the site in 1984. The company converted the site into an ATV trailhead and built a trail with matching funds from a State of Utah Off-Highway Vehicle grant. The loop trail leads up into the Uinta Mountains to Lily Lake. Wolverine is plainly an effort to salvage a disturbed site and isn't the prettiest or most user-oriented campground. It does, however, offer convenient access to a cool ATV trail. The sites run in a straight row along one side of a gravel parking lot. The lot is surrounded by a lodgepole and aspen forest, and there are limited views to the valley below the campground. The sites are close together and open with very little shade. Privacy between sites doesn't exist.

Campsites, facilities: There are six sites. Picnic tables, fire grills, and a vault toilet are provided. There is no drinking water. Leashed pets permitted.

Reservations, fees: Reservations are not accepted. The fee is $10; day use and extra vehicles are $5. Open June through October, weather permitting.

Directions: From the intersection of Main Street (Rte. 32) and 200 S (Rte. 248) in Kamas, head north on Rte. 32 and turn east (right) after one block onto Rte. 150. Continue east on Rte. 150 for 45.8 miles and turn right onto Forest Road 57. After 1.6 miles, take the left fork and continue 1.2 miles to the Wolverine Campground.

GPS Coordinates: N 40° 50.785' W 110° 48.877'

Contact: Evanston Ranger District, 307/789-3194.

5 LITTLE LYMAN LAKE

Scenic rating: 7

in the northern Uinta Mountains in the
Wasatch-Cache National Forest

Map 4.1, page 183

Little Lyman Lake is a small, shallow lake on the northern slopes of the Uinta Mountains. The lake and campground are tucked away in a quiet, peaceful spot of the Blacks Fork River over 15 miles from the nearest paved road. The lake is formed by a natural dam of the glacial till of a terminal moraine, where a glacier ended and dumped its sediment load. A short, man-made dam has been added to conserve water for irrigation. Ducks frequent the secluded fishing hole. The lake is stocked with a combination of albino, brook, and rainbow trout. Hiking, horseback riding, and mountain biking are popular on the nearby West Fork Black Forks Trail. The surrounding system of bumpy dirt roads and trails is also popular with ATV riders. The campsites sit above the lake in an open lodgepole pine forest. The campground enjoys a nice combination of sun and shade and offers good, flat, forest-floor spots to pitch a tent. While most of the sites have views of the lake, site 4 stands out as particularly scenic. The camp loop and parking areas are gravel, as is the long, winding approach road.

Campsites, facilities: There are 10 sites for tents and RVs up to 20 feet in length. Picnic tables, fire grills, pull-through sites, drinking water, and vault toilets are provided. Leashed pets permitted.

Reservations, fees: Reservations are not accepted. Single sites are $10, double sites are $20, and extra vehicles and day use are $5. Open June through September.

Directions: From the intersection of Main Street (Rte. 32) and 200 S (Rte. 248) in Kamas, head north on Rte. 32 and turn east (right) after one block onto Rte. 150. Continue east on Rte. 150 for 49 miles. Turn east (right) onto North Slope Scenic Byway/Forest Road 58 and travel 16 miles. Turn left and continue 0.3 mile to the Little Lyman Lake Campground.

GPS Coordinates: N 40° 56.091' W 110° 36.769'

Contact: Evanston Ranger District, 307/789-3194, www.fs.fed.us/r4/uwc/recreation/wcnf/camping/evanston-campgrounds.shtml#littlelymanlake

6 EAST FORK OF THE BLACKS FORK

Scenic rating: 8

in the northern Uinta Mountains in the
Wasatch-Cache National Forest

Map 4.1, page 183

The East Fork of the Blacks Fork Campground is a trailhead campground in the upper elevations of the northern Uinta Mountains. The campground has horse facilities to accommodate packers heading on the 30-mile loop trail that leaves from the campground. The loop trail heads south over Red Knob Pass and Squaw Pass to Lambert Meadows. The unpaved campground loop is small and leads to sites sheltered by a lodgepole pine forest. There are flat spots on the pine-needle floor to pitch tents, and there's room to park horse trailers. Expansive grassy meadows stretch away from the campground and toward the rocky summits of the Uintas. There are views to forested hills above and the wide, shallow East Fork of the Blacks Fork River below. Fishing for trout is possible in the river. This campground is also near the Bear River–Smith Forks Trail leading to the Hewinta Guard Station (eight miles), Red Castle Lake (10 miles), West Fork of the Black Fork River (10 miles), and the Bear River (22 miles). The trail is open to horses, mountain bikes, and hikers.

Campsites, facilities: There are eight sites for tents and RVs up to 20 feet in length. Picnic tables, fire grills, vault toilets, horse troughs, and hitching posts are provided. There is no drinking water. Leashed pets permitted.

Reservations, fees: Reservations are not accepted. There is no fee. Open June through September, weather permitting.

Directions: From the intersection of Main Street (Rte. 32) and 200 S (Rte. 248) in Kamas, head north on Rte. 32 and turn east (right) after one block onto Rte. 150. Continue east on Rte. 150 for 49 miles. Turn east (right) onto North Slope Scenic Byway/Forest Road 58 and travel 19 miles. Turn right onto Forest Road 65 and continue 5.5 miles to the campground.

GPS Coordinates: N 40° 53.083' W 110° 32.310'

Contact: Evanston Ranger District, 307/789-3194.

7 CHINA MEADOWS
🚶 🚴 🛶 🚐 ⛵ 🐴 🚙 ⛺

Scenic rating: 8

in the northern Uinta Mountains in the Wasatch-Cache National Forest

Map 4.1, page 183

China Meadows is a Forest Service campground next to a pond-sized lake in the East Fork of the Clark Fork drainage in the northern Uinta high country. Sites are in an open stand of lodgepole pines that provide intermittent shade. Three sites sit right on the shore of China Lake and offer views up to the table-top ridges of the Uinta Range's highest peaks. The lake offers trout fishing and non-motorized boating, like canoeing. Meadows

surround the campground and lake. Robins fly back and forth between the pine trees, and waterfowl can be spotted on the surface of the pond. Trailhead Campground and the China Meadows Trail are less than a half mile away. China Meadows is a good place to stay if you're interested exploring the trail on foot, horseback, or a mountain bike but are trying to avoid the flies associated with the horses at Trailhead Campground.

Campsites, facilities: There are nine sites for tents and RVs up to 20 feet in length. Picnic tables, fire grills, and a vault toilet are provided. There is no drinking water. Leashed pets permitted.

Reservations, fees: Reservations are not accepted. The fee is $10 per site, and extra vehicles and day use are $5. Open June through September.

Directions: From Mountain View, Wyoming, drive south on Rte. 410. After six miles turn left onto Uinta County Road 246. Follow this dirt road, which becomes Forest Road 72, for 18.5 miles. Turn left, cross the bridge, and turn right into the China Meadows Campground.

GPS Coordinates: N 40° 55.878' W 110° 24.218'

Contact: Mountain View Ranger District, 307/782-6555.

8 TRAILHEAD
🚶 🚴 🐴 🚙 ⛺

Scenic rating: 7

in the northern Uinta Mountains in the Wasatch-Cache National Forest

Map 4.1, page 183

The China Meadows Trail leads into the heart of the northern Uinta Mountains. The trail is popular with horseback riders and is open to hikers and mountain bikers as well. At the China Meadows Trailhead is a campground with horse corrals and facilities. The campground is partitioned into two areas, with one side (sites 9–13) catering to campers with horses. The sites are dispersed in an open lodgepole pine forest and offer good tent camping on the forest floor. The trees offer some shade for the sites but don't block views of the gorgeous surroundings. A lodgepole fence surrounds the grounds to keep the cows out (and horses in). The loop, parking spaces, and access road are all gravel and dirt.

Campsites, facilities: There are 13 sites. Picnic tables, fire grills, vault toilets, a horse corral, and hitching posts are provided. There is no drinking water. Leashed pets permitted.

Reservations, fees: Reservations are not accepted. Sites are $8. Open June through September, weather permitting.

Directions: From Mountain View, Wyoming, drive south on Rte. 410. After six miles turn left onto Uinta County Road 246. Follow this dirt road, which becomes Forest Road 72, for 18.5 miles. Turn left, cross the bridge, and continue 0.5 mile to the Trailhead Campground. GPS Coordinates: N 40° 55.451' W 110° 24.356'

Contact: Mountain View Ranger District, 307/782-6555.

9 BRIDGER LAKE

Scenic rating: 8

In the northern Uinta Mountains in the Wasatch-Cache National Forest

Map 4.1, page 183   BEST (

Bridger Lake is one of the small, shallow lakes formed by a glacial moraine in the Smith's Fork drainage in the high Uinta Mountains. The lake is surrounded by a pleasant ponderosa pine forest, where you'll find the Forest Service–owned Bridger Lake Campground. Long lush grass grows around the open campsites, and the forest floor, covered with flat pine needles, makes for great tent camping. There are nice views of the lake from about half the campground loop. The trees provide plenty of shade for the gravel loop. The lake is a great place for nonmotorized boating like canoeing or kayaking. There's fishing for stocked rainbow and brook trout. The area is also good moose habitat; these awkward wetland beauties are frequently seen in the lake and the surrounding marshes. Lily pads grow on the surface of the water, adding to its pondlike feeling.

Campsites, facilities: There are 28 single sites and two double sites for tents and RVs up to 95 feet in length. Sites 10 and 22 are wheelchair accessible. Picnic tables, fire grills, drinking water, pull-through sites, garbage service, and vault toilets are provided. Leashed pets permitted.

Reservations, fees: Reservations are accepted at 877/444-6777 or online at www.recreation.gov and must be made a minimum of four days in advance. To make a reservation, Bridger Lake Campground requires a two-night minimum stay on weekends and three nights on holiday weekends. Single sites are $14, double sites are $28, and extra vehicles and day use are $5. Open June through September, weather permitting.

Directions: From Mountain View, Wyoming, drive south on Rte. 410. After six miles turn left onto Uinta County Road 246. Follow this dirt road, which becomes Forest Road 72, for 16 miles, turn left and continue 0.5 mile to the campground. GPS Coordinates: N 40° 58.014' W 110° 23.279'

Contact: Mountain View Ranger District, 307/782-6555.

10 STATELINE RESERVOIR

Scenic rating: 7

In the northern Uinta Mountains in the Wasatch-Cache National Forest

Map 4.1, page 183

Stateline Reservoir is a large reservoir in the Uinta high country on the Utah/Wyoming border. The reservoir was built in 1979 by the Bureau of Reclamation, which developed this campground on the lake as well. The lake offers boating, fishing, and swimming, though at about 9,200 feet in elevation, the water temperature stays chilly for swimming. The lake has a great diversity of fish species, including rainbow and cutthroat trout, kokanee, mountain whitefish, and mountain suckers. The paved campground loop is carved out of a dense grove of quaking aspen and lodgepole pine. The unique layout has sites in long rows touching back to back. There are nice, long, paved parking slips for RVs and trailers. The picnic tables and tent pads are gravel strips that are simple extensions of the parking spots. If the campground is full, expect to get to know your neighbor behind your site. The lake has a boat ramp that is easily accessible via a short trail or gravel driveway from the campground.

Campsites, facilities: There are 41 sites for tents and RVs up to 40 feet in length. Site 25 is wheelchair accessible. Picnic tables, barbeque grills, fire pits, drinking water, garbage service, wastewater disposal stations, and vault toilets are provided. Leashed pets permitted.

Reservations, fees: Reservations are accepted at 877/444-6777 or online at www.recreation.gov and must be made a minimum of four days in advance. To make a reservation, Stateline Reservoir Campground requires a two-night minimum stay on weekends and three nights on holiday weekends. Sites are $14; extra vehicles and day use are $5. Open June through September, weather permitting.

Directions: From Mountain View, Wyoming, drive south on Rte. 410. After six miles turn left onto Uinta County Road 246. Follow this dirt road, which becomes Forest Road 72, for 15 miles to Stateline Reservoir on the right side of the road.

GPS Coordinates: N 40° 58.915' W 110° 23.124'

Contact: Mountain View Ranger District, 307/782-6555.

11 WEST MARSH LAKE

Scenic rating: 8

in the northern Uinta Mountains in the Wasatch-Cache National Forest

Map 4.1, page 183

West Marsh Campground occupies the opposite side of the lake from its East Marsh Lake neighbor. There are a few noticeable differences between the campgrounds. West Marsh offers direct access to the lake for fishing, canoeing, and other nonmotorized boats. It's also more accommodating for RV and long trailers because the parking slips have more space. While there are tent pads here, East probably offers more choices for tent campers. Like its neighbor across the lake, West Marsh Lake is shaded by lodgepole pine trees. However, the forest is much more open on this side, offering a pleasant mix of shade and sun. The campground's open nature also provides better views of the lake on one side and a marshy wetland on the other. A mountain bike trail leaves from the entrance to the campground. The area is also popular with ATV riders. The access loop, parking spots, and approach road are gravel. Expect a long bumpy ride to get to Marsh Lake.

Campsites, facilities: There are 17 individual sites and one group site for tents and RVs up to 60 feet in length. Picnic tables, fire grills, drinking water, stove stands, vault toilets, garbage service, and a boat ramp are provided. Leashed pets permitted.

Reservations, fees: Reservations are accepted at 877/444-6777 or online at www.recreation.gov and must be made a minimum of four days in advance. To make a reservation, Marsh Lake Campground requires a two-night minimum stay on weekends and three nights on holiday weekends. Open June through September, weather permitting.

Directions: From Mountain View, Wyoming, drive south on Rte. 410. After six miles turn left onto Uinta County Road 246. Follow this dirt road, which becomes Forest Road 72, for

17.5 miles and West Marsh Lake Campground will be on the right side of the road.
GPS Coordinates: N 40° 57.113' W 110° 23.894'
Contact: Mountain View Ranger District, 307/782-6555.

12 EAST MARSH LAKE

Scenic rating: 8

in the northern Uinta Mountains in the Wasatch-Cache National Forest

Map 4.1, page 183

There are two campgrounds on opposite shores of the little Marsh Lake in the Uinta Mountains. Marsh Lake is a high mountain lake only four miles from the Wyoming border. The natural lake offers good fishing on float tubes and canoeing. The lake is stocked by the Utah State Department of Natural Resources with brook and rainbow trout. Stands of lodgepole pine, interspersed with an occasional subalpine fir and Engelmann spruce, grow around the lake. East Marsh Lake Campground is set in a thick, shaded grove on the east side of the lake. The gravel loop accesses sites with nice tent pads, some built up and others on the pine needle–blanketed forest floor. There are also adequate parking options for midsize RVs and trailers, though West Marsh Lake's sites are better equipped for larger rigs.

Campsites, facilities: There are 29 sites for tents and RVs up to 40 feet in length. Picnic tables, fire grills, stove stands, drinking water, vault toilets, and garbage service are provided. Leashed pets permitted.

Reservations, fees: Reservations are accepted at 877/444-6777 or online at www.recreation. gov and must be made a minimum of four days in advance. To make a reservation, Marsh Lake Campground requires a two-night minimum stay on weekends and three nights on holiday weekends. Sites are $14, and extra vehicles and day use are $5. Open June through September, weather permitting.

Directions: From Mountain View, Wyoming, drive south on Rte. 410. After six miles turn left onto Uinta County Road 246. Follow this dirt road, which becomes Forest Road 72, for 17.5 miles and East Marsh Lake Campground will be on the right side of the road.
GPS Coordinates: N 40° 57.134' W 110° 23.719'
Contact: Mountain View Ranger District, 307/782-6555.

13 HENRY FORK CAMPGROUND

Scenic rating: 7

in the northern Uinta Mountains in the Wasatch-Cache National Forest

Map 4.1, page 183

The Henry Fork Campground is located at the trailhead for the Henry Fork Trail. The trail is open to hikers and horses. The 32-mile loop trail leads up the Henry Fork Basin and through the Red Castle Area. It's also the approach to the summit trail for Kings Peak, the tallest peak in both the Uinta Range and the state of Utah. This, combined with stellar scenery, makes this trail very busy. While the trailhead campground isn't as pretty as the hike itself, it isn't a bad place to stay for access to the Kings Peak Wilderness. The campground and trailhead is divided into two areas, one designed specifically for horses and one for all other users. There are four sites by the hiking trailhead and three sites for horses. The sites, shaded by lodgepole pines and a few aspens, sit off to the side of two large, gravel parking areas. Sagebrush and grass fill in where the forest leaves off. Views look out beyond the parking areas to open alpine meadows with long grass and wildflowers.

Campsites, facilities: There are seven sites for tents and RVs up to 20 feet in length. Picnic tables, fire grills, a vault toilet, horse corrals, and hitching posts are provided. There is no drinking water. Leashed pets permitted.

Reservations, fees: Reservations are not accepted. There is no fee. Open June through September, weather permitting.

Directions: From Mountain View, Wyoming, drive south on Rte. 410. After six miles turn left onto Uinta County Road 246. Follow this dirt road, which becomes Forest Road 72, for 12 miles and turn left. Travel seven miles to an intersection and stay right (straight). Continue three miles to the Henry Fork Campground.

GPS Coordinates: N 40° 54.731' W 110° 19.692'

Contact: Mountain View Ranger District, 307/782-6555.

14 HOOP LAKE

Scenic rating: 8

in the northern Uinta Mountains in the Wasatch-Cache National Forest

Map 4.1, page 183

Hoop Lake is a high mountain lake in a open meadow of the Uinta Mountains. The level of the lake was raised from 11 feet in depth to around 25 feet by an earthen dam in 1948. The water is used for irrigation in southern Wyoming and lowers as the summer progresses. Despite the sometimes-depleted look of the lake, the area has a lovely feel. The lake gets heavy use by anglers who fish for brook, rainbow, and cutthroat trout. Boating and swimming is also possible in the lake. Sagebrush hills surround the campground, which is tucked into a thick aspen and lodgepole pine forest. In fact some of the parking spots are on their way to being reclaimed by sprouting aspen shoots. Sites 24, 25, 28, 29, 33, and 34 offer the best views of the lake. A road leads across the earthen dam on the lake to sites 37–42 right on the lakeshore. These offer unbeatable lake access but are out in the open.

Campsites, facilities: There are 44 sites for tents and RVs up to 25 feet in length. Picnic tables, fire grills, pull-through sites, and vault toilets are provided. There is no potable water. Leashed pets permitted.

Reservations, fees: Reservations are not accepted. Sites are $12; day use and extra vehicles are $5. Open June through October, weather permitting.

Directions: From Lonetree, Wyoming, drive east on Rte. 414 for 1.5 miles and turn south (right) onto Cedar Basin Road. After 4.5 miles, turn left and continue 2.6 miles to a fork in the road. Take the left fork, drive 3.7 miles, and turn right into the Hoop Lake Campground.

GPS Coordinates: N 40° 55.589' W 110° 07.242'

Contact: Mountain View Ranger District, 307/782-6555.

15 SPIRIT LAKE

Scenic rating: 9

northern Uinta Mountains in the Ashley National Forest

Map 4.1, page 183   BEST (

Spirit Lake is one of prettiest alpine lakes in all of Utah. The lake sits in a glacier-carved valley of the Uinta Mountains near the Daggett/Summit County line. At around 10,000 feet in elevation, the large alpine lake is surrounded by a forest of lodgepole pine, Engelmann spruce, and subalpine fir growing out of nutrient-poor rocky soil. The campground is set slightly above the lake in this lovely forest. Small red boulders dot the forest floor, and a slope of loose talus rises above the campground opposite the lake. The unpaved loop leads to well-spaced sites tucked into the evergreen trees. There are limited views from the sites down to the lake. The campground offers incredible high-country hiking from a web of trails leading through the alpine meadows to a series of wonderful mountain lakes. The Spirit-Tamarack Trail leads to Jessen Lake (1.5 miles), Tamarack Lake (two miles), and Fish Lake (five miles). The longer Browne-Spirit Lake Trail will take you

© MIKE MATSON

Spirit Lake in the Uinta Mountains

to Daggett Lake (four miles), Weyman Park (six miles), Anson Lake (eight miles), and Browne Lake (15 miles). The area has abundant wildlife. Ospreys are easy to spot fishing the lake's waters, and other visible wildlife includes moose, elk, and deer. Black bears, bighorn sheep, coyotes, and mountain lions frequent the area as well but are less likely to be seen.

Campsites, facilities: There are 24 sites for tents and RVs up to 30 feet in length. Picnic tables, fire grills, and vault toilets are provided. There is no drinking water. Cabins, a restaurant, and a limited grocery store are available at the Spirit Lake Lodge next to the campground. Leashed pets permitted.

Reservations, fees: Reservations are not accepted. The fee is $10 per night. Open mid-May through mid-September.

Directions: From Manila, drive south on Hwy. 44 for 13 miles. Turn right onto the southern entrance of the Sheep Creek Geologic Loop Road. After three miles turn left (continue straight) onto Forest Road 221 and travel on

this road for 10.6 miles. Turn left onto Forest Road 01 and continue 6.1 miles to the Spirit Lake Campground.

GPS Coordinates: N 40° 50.248' W 109° 59.957'

Contact: Flaming Gorge Ranger District, 435/784-3445.

16 HAYDEN FORK

Scenic rating: 7

on the Mirror Lake Scenic Byway in the Wasatch-Cache National Forest

Map 4.1, page 183

The Hayden Fork of the Bear River runs north from Bald Mountain Pass through the northern Uinta Mountains toward Wyoming. This beautiful mountain stream is fed by snowmelt from the Uinta crest and heavily fortified with beaver ponds and marshy wetlands, making it a relatively pristine and intact natural water system. This makes it an excellent place to fish for trout or get away from the crowds on the southern side of the Mirror Lake Highway. The campground environment is a combination of lodgepole pines, aspens, open sagebrush, and grass meadows. An upper loop has a steep gravel road leading to it, making the approach difficult for trailers or RVs. The flat lower loop offers a good alternative. Expect fairly well-spaced sites, few crowds, and privacy.

Campsites, facilities: There are nine sites for tents and RVs up to 26 feet in length. RVs and trailers are not recommended in the upper loop due to a steep road. Picnic tables, fire grills, and vault toilets are provided. There is no potable water. Leashed pets permitted.

Reservations, fees: Reservations are not accepted. Sites are $12; day use and extra vehicles are $5. Open June through October, weather permitting.

Directions: From the intersection of Main Street (Rte. 32) and 200 S (Rte. 248) in Kamas, head north on Rte. 32 and turn east (right) after one block onto Rte. 150. Continue east on Rte. 150 for 42.5 miles and turn right into the Hayden Fork Campground.

GPS Coordinates: N 40° 49.814' W 110° 51.215'

Contact: Evanston Ranger District, 307/789-3194, www.fs.fed.us/r4/uwc/recreation/wcnf/camping/evanston-campgrounds.shtml#haydenfork

17 CHRISTMAS MEADOWS
🏃 🛶 🏕 🚐 ⛺

Scenic rating: 8

on the Mirror Lake Scenic Byway in the Wasatch-Cache National Forest

Map 4.1, page 183

Christmas Meadows is a huge alpine meadow on the Stillwater Fork of the Bear River in the northern Uinta Mountains. The beauty of the meadow and river are breathtaking with distant but dramatic views up to the High Uinta Wilderness. The Christmas Meadows Trail leaves from near the campground, leading up into the wilderness area and looping back to a series of alpine lakes in the Middle Basin. Fly fishing is good along the Stillwater Fork or in the lakes reached along the trail. The small, gravel campground loop is minimally developed but has all the necessities you'll need. The sites sit under a canopy of lodgepole pine and aspen trees with views out to inspiring peaks. The sites are relatively close together and don't offer much privacy.

Campsites, facilities: There are 11 sites for tents and RVs up to 45 feet in length. Picnic tables, fire grills, garbage service, vault toilets, and drinking water are provided. Leashed pets permitted.

Reservations, fees: Reservations are accepted at 877/444-6777 or online at www.recreation.gov and must be made a minimum of four days in advance. To make a reservation, Christmas Meadows Campground requires a two-night minimum stay on weekends and three nights on holiday weekends. Sites are $14; day use and extra vehicles are $5. Open June through September, weather permitting.

Directions: From the intersection of Main Street (Rte. 32) and 200 S (Rte. 248) in Kamas, head north on Rte. 32 and turn east (right) after one block onto Rte. 150. Continue east on Rte. 150 for 45.8 miles and turn right onto Forest Road 57. Continue 4.1 miles and turn right into the Christmas Meadows Campground.

GPS Coordinates: N 40° 49.502' W 110° 48.115'

Contact: Evanston Ranger District, 307/789-3194, www.fs.fed.us/r4/uwc/recreation/wcnf/camping/evanston-campgrounds.shtml#christmasmeadows

18 BEAVER VIEW
🛶 🏕 🚐 ⛺

Scenic rating: 7

on the Mirror Lake Scenic Byway in the Wasatch-Cache National Forest

Map 4.1, page 183

Beaver View Campground is set along the beaver pond–choked waters of the Hayden Fork of the Bear River. Grassy meadows and wetlands, augmented by the constantly evolving system of beaver dams, stretch away for the campground. It's easy to see why this was once a popular area for mountain men to trap and collect pelts. In addition to sustaining the beaver population, the ponds and river make excellent trout habitat; fishing is possible for cutthroat and rainbows. The campground at Beaver View sits under a canopy of dying lodgepole pine trees. The trees have been hit hard by the pine bark beetle, and dead trees are being thinned out of the campground. This project takes away from the wild character of the place, but it is understandable considering how much dead wood (fuel for potential forest fires) is standing around the sites. Big boulders and polished river stones left by the long-since-receded glaciers are scattered around the sites. The campground loop and parking slips are gravel.

Campsites, facilities: There are 17 sites for tents and RVs up to 22 feet in length. Picnic tables, fire grills, pull-through sites, drinking water, garbage service, and vault toilets are provided. Leashed pets permitted.

Reservations, fees: Reservations are not accepted. Single sites are $14; day use and extra vehicles are $5. Open June through September, weather permitting.

Directions: From the intersection of Main Street (Rte. 32) and 200 S (Rte. 248) in Kamas, head north on Rte. 32 and turn east (right) after one block onto Rte. 150. Continue east on Rte. 150 for 42 miles and turn right into the Beaver View Campground.

GPS Coordinates: N 40° 49.480' W 110° 51.780'

Contact: Evanston Ranger District, 307/789-3194, www.fs.fed.us/r4/uwc/recreation/wcnf/camping/evanston-campgrounds.shtml#beaverview

19 SULPHUR

Scenic rating: 8

on the Mirror Lake Scenic Byway in the Wasatch-Cache National Forest

Map 4.1, page 183

Sulphur Campground is located on the Hayden Fork of the Bear River in the northwestern Uinta Mountains. The campground is in a lodgepole pine and Engelmann spruce forest with large river rocks scattered around the sites and forest floor. Long grass crowds in around the trees and creeps into the sites. There's fishing for trout on Hayden Fork. Views from the campground peer out to the wildflower-painted meadows and up to steep talus slopes of the Uintas. The flat landscape makes for good tent sites. The loop and parking spaces are gravel. The campgrounds north of Bald Mountain Pass are much quieter than those on the other side of the Mirror Lake Highway. Sulphur is a good place to experience this part of the Uintas without the crowds.

Campsites, facilities: There are 17 single sites and four double sites for tents and RVs up

to 22 feet in length. Picnic tables, fire grills, pull-through sites, drinking water, garbage service, and vault toilets are provided. Leashed pets permitted.

Reservations, fees: Reservations are not accepted. Single sites are $14, double sites are $28, and day use and extra vehicles are $5. Open June through September, weather permitting.

Directions: From the intersection of Main Street (Rte. 32) and 200 S (Rte. 248) in Kamas, head north on Rte. 32 and turn east (right) after one block onto Rte. 150. Continue east on Rte. 150 for 39 miles and turn right into the Sulphur Campground.

GPS Coordinates: N 40° 47.267' W 110° 53.115'

Contact: Evanston Ranger District, 307/789-3194, www.fs.fed.us/r4/uwc/recreation/wcnf/camping/evanston-campgrounds.shtml#sulphur

20 BUTTERFLY LAKE

Scenic rating: 9

on the Mirror Lake Scenic Byway in the Wasatch-Cache National Forest

Map 4.1, page 183

Butterfly Lake is a small mountain lake north of Bald Mountain Pass on the Mirror Lake Scenic Byway. The lily pad–dotted lake sits at 10,360 feet and offers good trout fishing on its calm waters. The campground is a short distance from the lake in an open spruce and fir forest. The loop and parking aprons are gravel. The sites cozy up to bunched evergreen trees and are decorated with red and brown boulders. There's a beautiful meadow of grass and wildflowers separating the camp loop from the lake. Deer frequent the meadow, especially in the late evening. The campground has views down to the lake and up to the Uinta Mountains. Butterfly Lake is the closest campground to the trailhead for the Highline Trail. The 60-mile Highline Trail is one of the best long backpacking trips in the Rocky Mountains. It winds through the High Uinta Wilderness Area and along the crest of this unique west-to-east range, staying above 10,000 feet and above timberline for almost all of its length. Butterfly Lake is also near the Ruth Lake Trail, which accesses the Ruth Lake rock climbing area. This recently developed sport climbing area offers cool climbing in midsummer, when most of the state is experiencing triple-digit temperatures.

Campsites, facilities: There are 20 sites for tents and RVs up to 30 feet in length. Picnic tables, fire grills, pull-through sites, drinking water, garbage service, and vault toilets are provided. Firewood is available. Leashed pets permitted.

Reservations, fees: Reservations are not accepted. Single sites are $14; day use and extra vehicles are $6. Open June through September, weather permitting.

Directions: From the intersection of Main Street (Rte. 32) and 200 S (Rte. 248) in Kamas, head north on Rte. 32 and turn east (right) after one block onto Rte. 150. Continue east on Rte. 150 for 34 miles and turn left into the Butterfly Lake Campground. GPS Coordinates: N 40° 43.264' W 110° 52.045'

Contact: Kamas Ranger District, 435/783-4338, www.fs.fed.us/r4/uwc/recreation/wcnf/camping/kamas-camping.shtml#butterfly

21 MOOSEHORN
🏃 ⛷ 🚣 🎣 🐴 🚐 ⛺

Scenic rating: 9

on the Mirror Lake Scenic Byway in the Wasatch-Cache National Forest

Map 4.1, page 183

Moosehorn Campground sits beneath the towering beauty of Bald Mountain on the shores of Moosehorn Lake. There couldn't be a more classic Uinta setting than this. Imagine the raw beauty of one of the Uinta's highest and most recognizable peaks, Bald Mountain (11,943 feet), coupled with the sublime calm of alpine lake surrounded by spruce trees and cascading rock talus slopes. Pikas and marmots peek out of the steep rock fields and whistle at the people on the lake below. The campground at Moosehorn is on the opposite side of the lake from Bald Mountain, the layout taking advantage of the relatively gentle terrain among the trees. Spruce and sub-alpine firs grow in dense pockets out of the rocky alpine soil during a painfully short growing season. Imagine how many short summers it took for these trees to reach their modest height. The sites have amazing views of the lake and its surrounding glory and offer decent tent pads, considering the rocky soil. Picnic tables have gravel pads to minimize the impact and keep the dust down. The sites are well spread out, and the trees help with separation from other campers. There is fishing for stocked trout on the lake and hiking on the nearby Fehr Lake Trail. Canoeing is possible on the calm lake. Expect cold nights and be prepared for inclement weather any time of the year.

Campsites, facilities: There are 33 sites for tents and RVs up to 90 feet in length. Picnic tables, fire grills, drinking water, pull-through sites, garbage service, and vault toilets are provided. Firewood is available. Leashed pets permitted.

Reservations, fees: Reservations are accepted at 877/444-6777 or online at www.recreation.gov and must be made a minimum of five days in advance. To make a reservation, Moosehorn Campground requires a two-night minimum stay on weekends and three nights on holiday weekends. Sites are $16; day use and extra vehicles are $6. Open June through September, weather permitting.

Directions: From the intersection of Main Street (Rte. 32) and 200 S (Rte. 248) in Kamas, head north on Rte. 32 and turn east (right) after one block onto Rte. 150. Continue east on Rte. 150 for 30.2 miles and turn left into the Moosehorn Campground. GPS Coordinates: N 40° 41.634' W 110° 53.531'

Contact: Kamas Ranger District, 435/783-4338, www.fs.fed.us/r4/uwc/recreation/wcnf/camping/kamas-camping.shtml#moosehorn

22 WASHINGTON LAKE

Scenic rating: 9

on the Mirror Lake Scenic Byway in the
Wasatch-Cache National Forest

Map 4.1, page 183   **BEST (**

Washington Lake is the close neighbor of Trial
Lake, below Bald Mountain Pass on the Mirror Lake Highway. This high Uinta lake is surrounded by dramatic, glacier-polished peaks
like Mount Watson (11,521 feet) and Notch
Mountain (11,263 feet). Like many of the lakes
in the Uintas, this originally natural lake has
been supplemented with a man-made dam to
conserve water for the Provo River watershed.
The reservoir offers fishing for brook, rainbow,
and cutthroat trout and rainbow chub. There's
an excellent system of trails near the lake including the Crystal Lake Trail, which leads to Long
Lake (two miles), Island Lake (three miles), and
the Big Elk area (six miles). The campground is
set among clumps of spruce and lodgepole pine
trees. Red boulders dot the campground among
patches of native grass and stunted trees. The
sites have views of the lake, meadows, and surrounding peaks. Watch for deer in the meadows
and around camp. There's a large group area
featuring five different units above the lake in
an alpine meadow. This is one of the prettiest
campgrounds in the state and offers a quick
escape from Salt Lake City via the beautiful
Mirror Lake Scenic Byway.

Campsites, facilities: There are 38 single sites,
four double sites, and five group sites for tents
and RVs up to 100 feet. The group sites are
all wheelchair accessible. Picnic tables on
concrete pads, fire pits, stove stands, garbage
service, and vault toilets are provided. There
is no drinking water. Firewood is available.
Leashed pets permitted.

Reservations, fees: Reservations are accepted
at 877/444-6777 or online at www.recreation.
gov and must be made a minimum of five days
in advance. To make a reservation, Washington Lake Campground requires a two-night
minimum stay on weekends and three nights
on holiday weekends. Sites are $16; day use
and extra vehicles are $6. Open June through
September, weather permitting.

Directions: From the intersection of Main Street
(Rte. 32) and 200 S (Rte. 248) in Kamas, head
north on Rte. 32 and turn east (right) after one
block onto Rte. 150. Continue east on Rte. 150
for 25.1 miles, turn left, and after 0.1 mile take
the left fork onto Forest Road 41. After 0.7 mile
turn right, continue 0.3 mile, and turn left into
the Washington Lake Campground.

GPS Coordinates: N 40° 40.809' W 110°
57.685'

Contact: Kamas Ranger District, 435/783-
4338, www.fs.fed.us/r4/uwc/recreation/wcnf/camping/kamas-camping.
shtml#washingtonlake

23 TRIAL LAKE

Scenic rating: 8

on the Mirror Lake Scenic Byway in the
Wasatch-Cache National Forest

Map 4.1, page 183

Trial Lake is a beautiful alpine reservoir in the
shadow of two dramatic Uinta peaks, Mount
Watson (11,521 feet) and Notch Mountain
(11,263 feet). The scenery is gorgeous, and the
recreation opportunities in the area are limited
only by your imagination. The lake is stocked
with albino, rainbow, and brook trout and offers picturesque fishing. The trailhead for the
Crystal Lake Trail is nearby, and there are many
other excellent trails in the immediate vicinity.
The lake and campground are at 9,840 feet and
have a distinctly alpine feel. The paved camp
loop leads through a lodgepole pine, spruce, and
sub-alpine fir forest. Many of the spruce trees
have died from bark beetle infestation, but that
doesn't diminish the area's natural beauty. The
sites feature raised tent pads with views down
to the lake and up to the surrounding glacier-
scoured peaks. A short trail leads from the camp
loop to the lake shore. The campground is large
and many of the sites are close together, but

this seems inevitable in an area as popular as the Mirror Lake Highway.

Campsites, facilities: There are 60 sites for tents and RVs up to 100 feet in length. Picnic tables, fire grills, tent pads, drinking water, pull-through sites, garbage service, and vault toilets are provided. Leashed pets permitted.

Reservations, fees: Reservations are accepted at 877/444-6777 or online at www.recreation. gov and must be made a minimum of five days in advance. To make a reservation, Trial Lake Campground requires a two-night minimum stay on weekends and three nights on holiday weekends. Sites are $16; day use and extra vehicles are $6. Open June through September, weather permitting.

Directions: From the intersection of Main Street (Rte. 32) and 200 S (Rte. 248) in Kamas, head north on Rte. 32 and turn east (right) after one block onto Rte. 150. Continue east on Rte. 150 for 25.1 miles, turn left, and after 0.1 mile turn right and continue 0.2 mile to the Trial Lake Campground.

GPS Coordinates: N 40° 40.867' W 110° 57.215'

Contact: Kamas Ranger District, 435/783-4338, www.fs.fed.us/r4/uwc/recreation/wcnf/camping/kamas-camping.shtml#triallalke

24 MIRROR LAKE

Scenic rating: 9

on the Mirror Lake Scenic Byway in the Wasatch-Cache National Forest

Map 4.1, page 183

Mirror Lake is the poster child for one of the most beloved and popular camping destinations in northern Utah, the high Uintas. A paved road leads down to Mirror Lake from the highway, and its easy accessibility makes it probably the best-known natural mountain lake in the state. Its appeal is obvious: a large natural lake offering boating, fishing, hiking, and horseback riding under the impressive bulk of Bald Mountain. Brook, rainbow, and albino trout are stocked in the lake. A paved boat launch facility provides easy access. The large campground isn't on the lake itself but is set back among a stand of spruce and fir trees. Huge green boulders are scattered between well-designed campsites. The trees provide some privacy for tightly spaced sites. Some sites feature horse facilities, and others have large parking slips for RVs. The loop and parking slips are gravel but well graded and maintained. The sites offer level tenting and picnic tables on gravel pads. There's a short trail leading to the lake and an amphitheater; check to see what ranger programs are offered at the amphitheater. When we visited there was a presentation on red-tailed hawk migrations. Mirror Lake is the trailhead for two trails leading into the High Uinta Wilderness Area.

Campsites, facilities: There are 85 sites for tents and RVs up to 78 feet in length. Sites 67, 68, 70–74, and 76 are equestrian sites, and sites 65, 66, 69, and 75 are wheelchair-accessible equestrian sites. Sites 1, 3, 6, 26, 32, 47, 48, 52, 55, and 61 are also wheelchair accessible. Picnic tables, fire pits, stove stands, drinking water, horse troughs, tent pads, pull-through sites, a boat launch, garbage service, aluminum recycling, vault toilets, and a picnic area are provided. Leashed pets permitted.

Reservations, fees: Reservations are accepted at 877/444-6777 or online at www.recreation. gov and must be made a minimum of five days in advance. To make a reservation, Mirror Lake Campground requires a two-night minimum stay on weekends and three nights on holiday weekends. Sites are $16; day use and extra vehicles are $6. Open June through September, weather permitting.

Directions: From the intersection of Main Street (Rte. 32) and 200 S (Rte. 248) in Kamas, head north on Rte. 32 and turn east (right) after one block onto Rte. 150. Continue east on Rte. 150 for 31 miles, turn right, and continue 0.4 mile to the Mirror Lake Campground.

GPS Coordinates: N 40° 42.006' W 110° 53.206'

Contact: Kamas Ranger District, 435/783-4338, www.fs.fed.us/r4/uwc/recreation/wcnf/camping/kamas-camping.shtml#mirrorlake

25 LOST CREEK

Scenic rating: 8

on the Mirror Lake Scenic Byway in the
Wasatch-Cache National Forest

Map 4.1, page 183

Lost Creek Campground is located on the Mirror Lake Highway below Bald Mountain Pass and the crest of the Uinta Range. The campground is surrounded by Lost, Teapot, and Lily Lakes, offering excellent trout fishing in a beautiful alpine environment. At nearly 10,000 feet, these lakes melt out late in the season and can get snow as early as August. Lost Creek and the surrounding campgrounds are open for only 2–3 months—from late June or early July through the first week of September—so enjoy them while you can. Expect cool temperatures and breathtaking scenery. In addition to fishing, there's great hiking nearby and excellent high-country rock climbing. The Lost Creek campsites are set in a mix of meadows and alpine forest. Spruce and sub-alpine fir trees shade many of the sites, and wildflowers among long sedges crowd in where the trees leave off. Lost Creek flows through the campground before emptying into Lost Lake. While autumn can bring early snow, it is also the time of wonderful fall colors, when the meadows burn red and yellow as the spent deciduous leaves say goodbye with a final splash of color.

Campsites, facilities: There are 35 sites for tents and RVs up to 40 feet in length. Picnic tables, fire grills, pull-through sites, drinking water, dump station, garbage service, and vault toilets are provided. Firewood is available. Leashed pets permitted.

Reservations, fees: Reservations are accepted at 877/444-6777 or online at www.recreation.gov and must be made a minimum of five days in advance. To make a reservation, Lost Creek Campground requires a two-night minimum stay on weekends and three nights on holiday weekends. Sites are $16; day use and extra vehicles are $6. Open June through September, weather permitting.

Directions: From the intersection of Main Street (Rte. 32) and 200 S (Rte. 248) in Kamas, head north on Rte. 32 and turn east (right) after one block onto Rte. 150. Continue east on Rte. 150 for 26.4 miles and turn right into the Lost Creek Campground.

GPS Coordinates: N 40° 40.863' W 110° 56.064'

Contact: Kamas Ranger District, 435/783-4338, www.fs.fed.us/r4/uwc/recreation/wcnf/camping/kamas-camping.shtml#lostcreek

26 LILY LAKE

Scenic rating: 8

on the Mirror Lake Scenic Byway in the
Wasatch-Cache National Forest

Map 4.1, page 183

Lily Lake is a midsize alpine lake at 9,900 feet, right off the Mirror Lake Highway near the crest of the Uinta Mountains. Lily sits at the center of a cluster of mountain lakes, including its immediate neighbor, Teapot Lake. The scenic byway has parking for the lakes at a turnoff, so these lakes get as much traffic as any in the heavily used upper basin. There is fishing for brook and rainbow trout on the lake. The small campground loop at Lily Lake leads to sites tucked into the spruce trees. Grass meadows spread out around the timber and down to the lake. The sites offer good camping for RVs, with some pull-through parking slips, or tents, with level tent spots found on the dirt and rock forest floor. Views from the sites look down to the lovely lake and up to the Uinta Mountains.

Campsites, facilities: There are 14 sites for tents and RVs up to 30 feet in length. Picnic tables, fire grills, drinking water, garbage service, and vault toilets are provided. Leashed pets permitted.

Reservations, fees: Reservations are not accepted. Sites are $16; day use and extra vehicles are $6. Open June through September, weather permitting.

Directions: From the intersection of Main Street (Rte. 32) and 200 S (Rte. 248) in Kamas, head north on Rte. 32 and turn east (right) after one block onto Rte. 150. Continue east on Rte. 150 for 26.2 miles and turn left into the Lily Lake Campground.

GPS Coordinates: N 40° 40.838' W 110° 56.311'

Contact: Kamas Ranger District, 435/783-4338, www.fs.fed.us/r4/uwc/recreation/wcnf/camping/kamas-camping.shtml#lilylake

27 COBBLEREST

Scenic rating: 8

on the Mirror Lake Scenic Byway in the Wasatch-Cache National Forest

Map 4.1, page 183

Cobblerest Campground is one of the better Forest Service campgrounds on the south side of Bald Mountain Pass on the Mirror Lake Highway. Cobblerest sits at 8,280 feet in elevation, on the banks of the Provo River as it tumbles down from the Uinta high country. The campground enjoys the protection of an Engelmann spruce, lodgepole pine, and aspen forest. These trees provide shade for flat sites offering tent camping on the level forest floor, among the cobbles and polished river rocks that lend the campground its name. The paved loop has nice, flat parking slips for RV and trailers. The trees create some degree of privacy and separation between sites, despite their relatively tight spacing. Views from camp look out to talus slopes tumbling down from craggy cliffs on the opposite side of the canyon. Trout fishing is possible on the Provo River.

Campsites, facilities: There are 18 sites for

tents and RVs up to 30 feet in length. Picnic tables, fire grills, garbage service, pull-through sites, and vault toilets are provided. There is no drinking water. Leashed pets permitted.

Reservations, fees: Reservations are not accepted. Sites are $12. Open May through October, weather permitting.

Directions: From the intersection of Main Street (Rte. 32) and 200 S (Rte. 248) in Kamas, head north on Rte. 32 and turn east (right) after one block onto Rte. 150. Continue east on Rte. 150 for 18.6 miles and turn right into the Cobblerest campground.

GPS Coordinates: N 40° 35.685' W 110° 58.513'

Contact: Kamas Ranger District, 435/783-4338, www.fs.fed.us/r4/uwc/recreation/wcnf/camping/kamas-camping.shtml#cobblerest

28 DUCHESNE TUNNEL

Scenic rating: 8

on the Mirror Lake Scenic Byway in the Wasatch-Cache National Forest

Map 4.1, page 183

The Duchesne Tunnel is an important aqueduct in the Provo River Project, a Bureau of Reclamation project designed to secure irrigation water for farmland in much of Utah, Salt Lake, and Wasatch Counties. The tunnel is six miles long and transports water from the Duchesne River (a tributary to the Colorado River) to the Provo River (part of the great basin drainage that eventually empties into the Great Salt Lake). The tunnel emerges from underground and flows into an open aqueduct at the West Portal and the entrance to the camping area. The Duchesne Tunnel camping area is a large, well-established "dispersed" campground, perhaps better described as a campground without facilities. There's room for dozens of campers, trailers, and tents. The ground is rocky but offers spots to pitch tents on gravel or dirt among lodgepole pine trees and spaces to park trailers in the large-gauge gravel parking lot. The ATV crowd rules the campground, but anyone is welcome to use the facility, free of charge. The camping area is near the turn for the road leading to Lambert Meadows, Alexander Lake, and Trial Lake.

Campsites, facilities: This is an open, dispersed camping area. The only facilities are rock fire rings. There is no drinking water. Leashed pets permitted.

Reservations, fees: Reservations are not accepted. There is no fee. Open May through October, weather permitting.

Directions: From the intersection of Main Street (Rte. 32) and 200 S (Rte. 248) in Kamas, head north on Rte. 32 and turn east (right) after one block onto Rte. 150. Continue east on Rte. 150 for 17.5 miles and turn right into the camping area.

GPS Coordinates: N 40° 35.578' W 110°59.938'

Contact: Kamas Ranger District, 435/783-4338.

29 IRON MINE

🏃 🏊 🏕 🚐 ⛺

Scenic rating: 8

in the North Fork Valley in the southern Uinta Mountains in Ashley National Forest

Map 4.1, page 183

Iron Mine Campground is located along the North Fork of the Duchesne River under Iron Mine Mountain (10,465 feet) in the southern Uintas. Trout fishing is possible in the river. The campground is sheltered by a forest of lodgepole and ponderosa pines, aspen, and spruce and surrounded by long grassy meadows. The sites are well spaced and branch off a gravel loop. Some of the picnic tables have gravel pads to reduce dust. Views from the sites look up toward the local peaks to both the west and the east. Nearby at the end of the road, the Grandview Trail leads up into the alpine lake dotted Granddaddy

Basin in the remote and beautiful High Uinta Wilderness.

Campsites, facilities: There are 23 single sites and two double sites for tents and RVs up to 60 feet in length. There is one group site for up to 50 people. Picnic tables, fire grills, pull-through sites, garbage service, drinking water, and vault toilets are provided. Firewood is available. Leashed pets permitted.

Reservations, fees: Reservations are accepted at 877/444-6777 or online at www.recreation. gov and must be made a minimum of five days in advance. Single sites are $10, and double sites are $16. Open May through September, weather permitting.

Directions: From Fruitland, drive six miles east on Hwy. 40, turn north (left) on Rte. 208 and continue 10 miles. Turn north (left) on Rte. 35 and drive 13 miles northwest. Turn right onto the North Fork Road and drive 6.4 miles. At the fork, continue 1.5 miles and look carefully for a sharp right turn into Iron Mine Campground.

GPS Coordinates: N 40° 33.317' W 110° 53.264'

Contact: Duchesne Ranger District, 435/738-2482.

30 HADES

🏃 🏊 🏕 🚐 ⛺

Scenic rating: 8

in the southern Uinta Mountains in Ashley National Forest

Map 4.1, page 183

Hades Campground is the second Forest Service campground encountered along the North Fork of the Duchesne River in the southern Uinta Mountains. Site 8 is the trailhead for an eight-mile path leading up Trail Hollow into the Uinta Mountains. This trail is open to hikers and horseback riders. The nearby Grandview Trail leads up into the remote High Uinta Wilderness Area. Hades Campground is set on the valley floor among aspen and spruce trees under green, forested hills.

The sites allow great views up to Lightning Ridge and Castle Rock. The camp loop and parking slips are gravel, and a lodgepole fence circles the campground to keep the cattle at bay. There's fly fishing for rainbow, brown, and brook trout on the North Fork of the Duchesne River. Next to Hades you'll find Defa's Dude Ranch, a resort with cabins, a café, a saloon, and horse rentals. Keep an eye out for the "stone face" in a large boulder along the road.

Campsites, facilities: There are 12 single sites and two double sites for tents and RVs up to 30 feet in length. Picnic tables, fire grills, pull-through sites, garbage service, drinking water, and vault toilets are provided. Leashed pets permitted.

Reservations, fees: Reservations are accepted at 877/444-6777 or online at www.recreation. gov and must be made a minimum of five days in advance. Single sites are $10, and double sites are $16. Open May through September, weather permitting.

Directions: From Fruitland, drive six miles east on Hwy. 40, turn north (left) on Rte. 208, and continue 10 miles. Turn north (left) on Rte. 35 and drive 13 miles northwest. Turn right onto the North Fork Road, drive 5.9 miles, and turn left into Hades Campground. GPS Coordinates: N 40° 32.049' W 110° 52.336'

Contact: Duchesne Ranger District, 435/738-2482.

31 ASPEN

Scenic rating: 9

in the southern Uinta Mountains in Ashley National Forest

Map 4.1, page 183

Aspen Campground sits at the base of a steep-sided canyon along the North Fork of the Duchesne River. Light-brown rock cliffs rise above the campground on both sides of the valley. Open fields of sagebrush greet campers at the entrance to the camp loop, but a mixed forest of aspen, juniper, ponderosa pine, lodgepole pine, and spruce trees shelter the sites themselves. The lodgepole pines and spruce trees are showing signs of infestation by bark beetles. It's easy to spot infested trees by their browning tops—the afflicted trees appear to die from the top down. In spruce trees, an abundance of cones near the top of the trees indicates they are stressed from fending off the beetles. In lodgepoles, excessive sap dripping down the trunk is the most apparent sign the tree is in trouble. Northern flickers and downy woodpeckers can be spotted working over the dead pine trees for bugs. They are joined by rowdy, gray stellar jays. The sites offer good level tent spots and long, flat parking spaces for trailers and RVs. The thick, lush forest provides good privacy between sites. Aspen Campground offers an excellent mix of densely forested sites and more open, meadowlike sites. Fishing for rainbow, brook, and brown trout is possible on the North Fork.

Campsites, facilities: There are 28 single sites and two double sites for tents and RVs up to 60 feet in length. There is one group site for up to 32 people. Picnic tables, fire grills, drinking water, garbage service, and vault toilets are provided. Leashed pets permitted.

Reservations, fees: Reservations are accepted at 877/444-6777 or online at www.recreation. gov and must be made a minimum of five days in advance. Single sites are $10, double sites are $16, and the group site is $30. Open May through September, weather permitting.

Directions: From Fruitland, drive six miles east on Hwy. 40, turn north (left) on Rte. 208, and continue 10 miles. Turn north (left) on Rte. 35 and drive 13 miles northwest. Turn right onto the North Fork Road, drive 2.7 miles, and turn left into Aspen Campground. GPS Coordinates: N 40° 29.746' W 110° 50.706'

Contact: Duchesne Ranger District, 435/738-2482.

32 UPPER STILLWATER

Scenic rating: 8

in the southern Uinta Mountains in Ashley National Forest

Map 4.1, page 183

The Upper Stillwater Reservoir is created by a tall concrete dam on Rock Creek. Rock Creek drains out of the High Uinta Wilderness watershed and the countless tiny alpine lakes found there. The reservoir is popular for boating, fishing, and swimming, especially early in the summer before the water is drawn down for irrigation. The lake is stocked annually with rainbow trout. Upper Stillwater Campground sits below the dam in a forest of aspen, lodgepole pine, and spruce trees. Views from the campground look across the valley to steep red cliffs and to the huge concrete wall of the Upper Stillwater Dam. The campsites have picnic tables on paved pads and long paved parking aprons that can accommodate midsize RVs; the loop is also paved. This very nice campground is managed in cooperation with the Bureau of Reclamation. Nearby is the trailhead for the Rock Creek Trail, leading up into the High Uinta Wilderness and accessing Brown Duck Mountain, the Clements Lakes, and the East Basin.

Campsites, facilities: There are 19 sites for tents and RVs up to 30 feet in length. Picnic tables on paved pads, garbage service, drinking water, fire pits and grills, flush toilets, and aluminum recycling are provided. Leashed pets permitted.

Reservations, fees: Reservations are accepted at 877/444-6777 or online at www.recreation.gov and must be made a minimum of five days in advance. Single sites are $10, double sites are $16, and the group site is $30. Open May through September, weather permitting.

Directions: From Duchesne, drive north on Rte. 87 for 16 miles and turn left (north) onto 21000 W toward Mountain Home. Continue north three miles on 21000 W to Mountain Home. From Mountain Home, turn west (left) and travel northwest on Forest Road 134 for 10 miles, take the right fork, and continue 12 miles to the Upper Stillwater Campground.

GPS Coordinates: N 40° 33.302' W 110° 41.945'

Contact: Duchesne Ranger District, 435/738-2482.

33 YELLOWPINE

Scenic rating: 8

in the southern Uinta Mountains in Ashley National Forest

Map 4.1, page 183

Yellowpine Campground occupies a mature grove of ponderosa pine trees along Rock Creek in the southern Uinta Mountains. The campground is set in a flat wooded valley below the Upper Stillwater Reservoir and Dam. Yellowpine has inviting facilities in a pretty setting. The paved loop accesses sites well shaded by a combination of aspen and ponderosa and lodgepole pine. Rock Creek runs through the campground, providing an opportunity for fishing and adding a refreshing quality to the forest. A paved, level (wheelchair- and kid-friendly) nature trail follows along the creek and loops through the forest. A series of black-and-silver signs describe the forest in broad strokes and help identify the flora and fauna. Yellowpine campground feels well cared for, in everything from the nature trail to the tidy sites with built-up, level tent pads. The layout does a nice job of dispersing the sites among the forest to provide privacy for campers. There's fishing for rainbow trout on Rock Creek.

Campsites, facilities: There are 23 single sites, four double sites, and two triple sites (for up to 32 people) for tents and RVs up to 30 feet in length. Picnic tables, fire grills, drinking water, barbeque grills, flush toilets, pull-through sites, and a dump station are provided. Leashed pets permitted.

Reservations, fees: Reservations are accepted at 877/444-6777 or online at www.recreation. gov and must be made a minimum of five days in advance. Single sites are $10, double sites are $16, and triple sites are $30. Open mid-May through September.

Directions: From Duchesne, drive north on Rte. 87 for 16 miles and turn left (north) onto 21000 W toward Mountain Home. Continue north three miles on 21000 W to Mountain Home. From Mountain Home, turn west (left) and travel northwest on Forest Road 134 for 10 miles, then take the right fork and continue 8.5 miles to the Yellowpine Campground on the right side of the road.

GPS Coordinates: N 40° 32.130' W 110° 338.251'

Contact: Duchesne Ranger District, 435/738-2482.

34 MINER'S GULCH

Scenic rating: 8

in the southern Uinta Mountains in Ashley National Forest

Map 4.1, page 183

Miner's Gulch is located in the southwestern Uinta Mountains near Rock Creek. The gulch is just south of the boundary for the High Uinta Wilderness Area. Miner's Gulch Campground is a group campground, with individual sites available when no group has reserved the campground. The campground is small and private, in a sparse stand of aspen and juniper trees. Sagebrush and grass meadows spread out around the campground. A lodgepole fence circles the sites to keep the cows out. The camp loop and parking aprons are paved. Fishing is available nearby on Rock Creek and just down the road is the parking lot and picnic area for anglers.

Campsites, facilities: There are five sites for tents and RVs up to 24 feet in length; all

five can be reserved together as a group site for up to 40 people. Picnic tables, fire pits, garbage service, and a vault toilet are provided. There is no drinking water. Leashed pets permitted.

Reservations, fees: Reservations are accepted at 877/444-6777 or online at www.recreation. gov and must be made a minimum of four days in advance. Individual sites are $5, and the entire campground is $25. Open mid-May through September, weather permitting.

Directions: From Duchesne, drive north on Rte. 87 for 16 miles and turn left (north) onto 21000 W toward Mountain Home. Continue north three miles on 21000 W to Mountain Home. From Mountain Home, turn west (left) and travel northwest on Forest Road 134 for 10 miles, then take the right fork and continue 7.5 miles to the Miner's Gulch Campground on the right side of the road.

GPS Coordinates: N 40° 32.025' W 110° 37.410'

Contact: Duchesne Ranger District, 435/738-2482.

35 MOON LAKE

Scenic rating: 7

in the southern Uinta Mountains in Ashley National Forest

Map 4.1, page 183

Moon Lake is a long reservoir running from north to south in the Uinta Mountains. Moon is popular for boating and fishing, and the lake is stocked with rainbow, cutthroat, and brook trout. The campground at Moon Lake is carved out of a homogenous lodgepole pine forest. Unfortunately, it will soon be a dead forest because pine bark beetles are starting to get a foothold and there are no other species to survive the onslaught. A bumpy gravel road accesses the group area, a simple, open parking area with amenities around its periphery. The individual sites offer pull-through slips in an RV loop and good, flat tent-pitching opportunities in a tent-friendly area. The campground has nice views down to Moon Lake through the skinny tree trunks. Across from the campground is the Moon Lake Resort, offering trail rides, boat rentals, cabins, and a grocery store. Near the campground is the trailhead for the seven-mile Lake Fork Trail, which climbs into the High Uinta Wilderness and is open to hikers and horses.

Campsites, facilities: There are 56 sites for tents and RVs up to 22 feet in length and three group sites for up to 75 people. Picnic tables, fire grills, drinking water, pull-through sites, garbage service, and flush and vault toilets are provided. Leashed pets permitted.

Reservations, fees: Reservations are accepted for the group sites only at 877/444-6777 or online at www.recreation.gov and must be made a minimum of four days in advance. Sites are $10, and the group sites are $50. Open mid-May through September.

Directions: From Duchesne, drive north on Rte. 87 for 16 miles and turn left (north) onto 21000 W toward Mountain Home. Continue north three miles on 21000 W to Mountain Home. From Mountain Home, head north on Forest Road 131 (Moon Lake Road) for 14.8 miles to the Moon Lake Campground. The individual sites are on the left side of the road; the group area is on the right.

GPS Coordinates: N 40° 34.085' W 110° 30.406'

Contact: Roosevelt Ranger District, 435/722-5018.

36 SWIFT CREEK

Scenic rating: 8

in the southern Uinta Mountains in Ashley National Forest

Map 4.1, page 183

Swift Creek Campground is the trailhead for the Yellowstone Trail, which links up with four different trails in High Uinta Wilderness Area. The trails are popular with both hikers and horseback riders. From the trailhead, it is 0.2 mile to the Swift Creek Trail, nine miles to Garfield Creek Trail, 12 miles to Jackson Park Trail, and 15 miles to the Highline Trail. The campground is located at the end of the road in a pristine wooded valley at the confluence of Swift Creek and Yellowstone Creek. Views from the campsites look across the valley at green, forested hills. The sites are relatively open, with short grass around picnic tables and barbeque grills. Aspen and ponderosa pine trees offer some shade in the campground but also block the awesome views. The camp loop is gravel and provides some pull-through sites for big rigs and horse trailers. The sites themselves are level and offer good tenting, though there are no specifically developed tent pads. Be prepared for lots of flies because of the popular horse trail.

Campsites, facilities: There are 13 sites for tents and RVs up to 20 feet in length. Picnic tables, fire grills, barbeque grills, drinking water, aluminum recycling, garbage service, vault toilets, horse corrals, an unloading ramp, and water troughs are provided. Leashed pets permitted.

Reservations, fees: Reservations are not accepted. Sites are $8. Open mid-May through September.

Directions: From Duchesne, drive north on Rte. 87 for 16 miles and turn left (north) onto 21000 W toward Mountain Home. Continue north three miles on 21000 W to Mountain Home. From Mountain Home, drive north on Forest Road 131 (Moon Lake Road) for five miles and turn right toward the Yellowstone Recreation Area. Drive 11.5 miles on a bumpy road to Swift Creek Campground at the end of the road.

GPS Coordinates: N 40° 36.076' W 110° 20.908'

Contact: Roosevelt Ranger District, 435/722-5018.

37 RIVERVIEW

Scenic rating: 8

in the southern Uinta Mountains in Ashley National Forest

Map 4.1, page 183

Riverview Campground is located on Yellowstone Creek, just outside the southern border of the High Uinta Wilderness. The campground sits in an open woodland with shafts of light filtering through the trees' upper canopy. Flat riverside sites are shaded by aspen and ponderosa and lodgepole pine trees. The sites are excellent for tent camping, with level tent pads surrounded by tall seeding grass. Sites 13 and 14 stand out as my favorite sites, with the best views of the river and surrounding mountains. The road, camp loop, and parking spaces are gravel. The sites are well spaced, but privacy is limited because of the open nature of the forest. The campground's remoteness, however, makes crowds unlikely. There's fly fishing for trout on Yellowstone Creek. Nearby is the trailhead for the Yellowstone Trail, which leads up Swift Creek and the West Fork into the High Uinta Wilderness to quaint alpine lakes like Timothy and Five Point Lakes. The Yellowstone Trail connects with four backcountry trails.

Campsites, facilities: There are 19 sites for tents and RVs up to 20 feet in length. Picnic tables, fire grills, drinking water, garbage service, and vault toilets are provided. Leashed pets permitted.

Reservations, fees: Reservations are not accepted. Sites are $10. Open mid-May through September.

Directions: From Duchesne, drive north on Rte. 87 for 16 miles and turn left (north) onto 21000 W toward Mountain Home. Continue north three miles on 21000 W to Mountain Home. From Mountain Home, drive north on Forest Road 131 (Moon Lake Road) for five miles and turn right toward the Yellowstone Recreation Area. Drive 10.5 miles on a bumpy road to Riverview Campground on the left side of the road.

GPS Coordinates: N 40° 35.410' W 110° 20.190'

Contact: Roosevelt Ranger District, 435/722-5018.

38 RESERVOIR

Scenic rating: 8

in the southern Uinta Mountains in Ashley National Forest

Map 4.1, page 183

Reservoir Campground is set on a hillside above an overflowing reservoir in Cow Canyon. The small reservoir backs up Yellowstone Creek for about 200 yards before it pours over a short dam, built to provide hydroelectric power. A nice observation platform and dock is at the edge of the lake. The lake is just a short walk down stairs from the campground. The small loop includes sites that are mostly open, with minimal shade and shelter provided by aspen, ponderosa pine, and spruce trees. Grass and smooth brown boulders line the gravel parking slips. There are great vistas from the sites across the lake and up to the forested mountains on the far side. At the south end of the campground, views look down the valley over sagebrush flats. A beaver family has taken advantage of the man-made dam and built a huge beaver lodge at the north end of the reservoir.

Campsites, facilities: There are five sites. Picnic tables, fire grills, drinking water, garbage service, and a vault toilet are provided. Leashed pets permitted.

Reservations, fees: Reservations are not accepted. Sites are $5. Open mid-May through September.

Directions: From Duchesne, drive north on Rte. 87 for 16 miles and turn left (north) onto 21000 W toward Mountain Home. Continue north three miles on 21000 W to Mountain Home. From Mountain Home, drive north on Forest Road 131 (Moon Lake Road) for five miles and turn right toward the Yellowstone

Recreation Area. Drive 9.3 miles on a bumpy road to Reservoir Campground on the left side of the road.

GPS Coordinates: N 40° 34.552' W 110° 19.517'

Contact: Roosevelt Ranger District, 435/722-5018.

39 BRIDGE

Scenic rating: 7

in the southern Uinta Mountains in Ashley National Forest

Map 4.1, page 183

Bridge Campground is a small, primitive campground along Yellowstone Creek in the central Uinta Mountains. A narrow entrance through an old stone wall leads into the dirt-and-gravel campground loop. The crystal-clear creek flows right by sites 2 and 3. There's a small bridge leading across the stream to good trout fishing. Willows grow near the water, and a mix of ponderosa and lodgepole pines shade the campsites. The sites are flat with good, level spots to pitch tents. The campground is popular with ATV riders who access the nearby Yellowstone ATV trail. Expect a long, bumpy, rock-and-gravel road approach to Bridge Campground. The road doubles as a creek bed in one particularly nasty section where erosion seems to have gotten the better of it. Four-wheel-drive and high-clearance vehicles are recommended, if not required.

Campsites, facilities: There are five sites (RVs are not recommended due to the very narrow entrance into the campground). Picnic tables, fire grills, a vault toilet, garbage service, and drinking water are provided. Leashed pets permitted.

Reservations, fees: Reservations are not accepted. Sites are $8. Open June through September, weather permitting.

Directions: From Duchesne, drive north on Rte. 87 for 16 miles and turn left (north) onto 21000 W toward Mountain Home. Continue north three miles on 21000 W to Mountain Home. From Mountain Home, drive north on Forest Road 131 (Moon Lake Road) for five miles and turn right toward the Yellowstone Recreation Area. Drive 6.9 miles on a bumpy road to Bridge Campground on the right side of the road.

GPS Coordinates: N 40° 32.736' W 110° 20.027'

Contact: Roosevelt Ranger District, 435/722-5018.

40 YELLOWSTONE

Scenic rating: 7

in the southern Uinta Mountains in Ashley National Forest

Map 4.1, page 183

Utah's Yellowstone Campground is a far cry from Yellowstone National Park. Yellowstone Campground is located along Yellowstone Creek in the remote southern Uinta Mountains. The camp is located in a forest of aspens, cottonwoods, and ponderosa pine trees. This relatively minimally developed campground has a gravel loop and parking slips. The sites are mostly short grass with young aspen saplings sprouting up between the picnic tables and fire grills. A mix of sun and shade filters down through the trees. There's a dry creek bed of boulders running through the campground. A fence marks the southern boundary of the campground. Meadows extend south from the fence line in the privately owned Crystal Ranch. Fishing for rainbow, cutthroat, and brown trout is possible on Yellowstone Creek. The 41-mile-long Yellowstone ATV Trailhead is near the campground, making this area popular with ATVers. The road out to Yellowstone campground is extremely rough and bumpy over a several-mile stretch. Four-wheel-drive and high-clearance vehicles are strongly recommended.

Campsites, facilities: There are 11 sites for tents and RVs up to 22 feet in length and one group site for up to 80 people. Picnic tables, fire grills, pull-through sites, drinking water, and vault toilets are provided. Leashed pets permitted.

Reservations, fees: Reservations are accepted for the group site at 877/444-6777 or online at www.recreation.gov and must be made a minimum of five days in advance. Single sites are $10, and the group site is $50. Open mid-May through September.

Directions: From Duchesne, drive north on Rte. 87 for 16 miles and turn left (north) onto 21000 W toward Mountain Home. Continue north three miles on 21000 W to Mountain Home. From Mountain Home, drive north on Forest Road 131 (Moon Lake Road) for five miles and turn right toward the Yellowstone Recreation Area. Drive 6.6 miles on a bumpy road to Yellowstone Campground on the right side of the road.

GPS Coordinates: N 40° 32.398' W 110° 20.282'

Contact: Roosevelt Ranger District, 435/722-5018.

41 UINTA CANYON

Scenic rating: 8

in the southeastern Uinta Mountains in the Ashley National Forest

Map 4.1, page 183

Uinta Canyon is a lovely, remote canyon on the southeastern slopes of the Uinta Mountains with wooded hills and rocky peaks. The campground is set in an open stand of lodgepole and ponderosa pine trees. Aspen groves grow outside of the pines, and open fields of sagebrush and wild grass spread beyond that. The campground loop and parking slips are gravel. The Uinta River flows by the west side of the campground, offering fishing for rainbow, brown, and cutthroat trout. There are great sites along the river, with a grassy bench looking out across the water. A rocky, dry streambed cuts through the campground to the left of the loop. There are level tent sites and flat parking slips for campers. Look for the beaver pond along the road just past the entrance to the campground. One evening after sunset we watched a beaver put on quite a show swimming around

a beaver pond in the Uinta Mountains

the pond, repeatedly slapping the water with its tail before diving below the surface.

Campsites, facilities: There are 24 sites and one group site for up to 50 people. Picnic tables, fire grills, garbage service, and vault toilets are provided. There is no potable water. Leashed pets permitted.

Reservations, fees: Reservations are accepted for the group site at 435/722-5018. Sites are $5, and the group site is $50. Open mid-May through September.

Directions: From the intersection of Hwy. 40 and Rte. 121 in Roosevelt, head north on Rte. 121 for 10 miles to Neola. Continue north toward Uinta Canyon on 2000 W for eight miles, turn right, and continue four miles. Turn right again, travel 0.1 mile, and take the left fork onto Forest Road 118. Continue 2.5 miles on Forest Road 118 and enter the campground on the left side of the road.

GPS Coordinates: N 40° 37.343' W 110° 08.571'

Contact: Roosevelt Ranger District, 435/722-5018.

42 POLE CREEK LAKE

Scenic rating: 8

in the southern Uinta Mountains in the Ashley National Forest

Map 4.1, page 183

Pole Creek Lake Campground is set at what feels like the top of the world, at 10,200 feet in the Uinta Mountains. The surrounding plateau-like peaks rise to heights of 10,000–12,000 feet. Nearby, the alpine Pole Creek Lake is stocked with rainbow trout. A collection of other small lakes have also been stocked with cutthroats and rainbows and can be reached by an unofficial hiking trail marked by cairns. The trail leads to Lower Rock Lake; Middle and Upper Rock Lakes can also be reached by continuing off-trail. The campground hosts have created informative signs describing these trails. The campground loop leads to sites tucked into a stunted alpine

forest with spruce, lodgepole pine, and silver fir trees. The forest grows from rocky, tundralike soil, along with small clumps of native grasses. Reddish-brown boulders line the access loop to keep vehicles off the fragile soil. The sites are well spaced, and the trees provide good privacy. Be prepared for cool nights even in the summer.

Campsites, facilities: There are 19 sites for tents and RVs up to 22 feet in length. Picnic tables, fire grills, garbage service, vault toilets, and aluminum recycling are provided. There is no drinking water. Leashed pets permitted.

Reservations, fees: Reservations are not accepted. The fee is $5. Open July through September, weather permitting.

Directions: From the intersection of Hwy. 40 and Rte. 121 in Roosevelt, head north on Rte. 121 for 10 miles to Neola. Turn right, staying on Rte. 121, and continue five miles. Turn left and travel three miles to the town of Whiterocks. From Whiterocks, drive northwest for three miles, then turn right and continue 17 miles. At the fork, stay left and continue 0.5 mile and turn left into the Pole Creek Lake Campground.

GPS Coordinates: N 40° 40.728' W 110° 03.454'

Contact: Roosevelt Ranger District, 435/722-5018.

43 LOWER BEACH AT STARVATION STATE PARK

Scenic rating: 7

northwest of Duchesne

Map 4.1, page 183

Starvation Reservoir is a large, turquoise-blue reservoir north of Duchesne. There are conflicting legends about the origin of the name Starvation. One version of the story claims early settlers were starving during a harsh winter and stole Native American food stores to survive. Another version claims the opposite, that it was the Natives doing the stealing. Regardless of which story is true, this arid valley is certainly more appealing now than it was in the pioneer days. The elevation of the lake is 5,712 feet, and views from the campgrounds look north across the lake to distant peaks of the Uinta Mountains. The reservoir is fed by the Duchesne River (at the northeast end of the reservoir via a diversion tunnel) and Strawberry River. The water will eventually flow down the Strawberry, Duchesne, Green, and Colorado Rivers before making its way to the Gulf of Mexico. The lake offers boating, swimming, and fishing. Sport-fishing species in the lake include walleye, brown trout, smallmouth bass, and yellow perch. A wide variety of mammals including mule deer, mountain lions, coyotes, red foxes, cottontail rabbits, marmots, badgers, and minks all use the reservoir and surrounding lands. Birds like blue herons, western grebes, common loons, golden eagles, bald eagles, kestrels, and red-tailed hawks can be spotted here as well. The Lower Beach Campground at Starvation is next to a nice day-use area with a volleyball net and grass lawns with picnic tables. The Lower Beach camp loop and parking spots are paved. There are pull-through sites for RV and big rigs. Compared to the rest of the park, the Lower Beach camping area is a little disappointing. The sites are surrounded by weeds, dirt, and a few scattered deciduous trees that don't provide much shade. The whole loop is very open, and there is no privacy between sites.

Campsites, facilities: There are 24 sites for tents and RVs up to 60 feet in length and one group site for 25 to 75 people. Sites 49 and 50 are wheelchair accessible. Picnic tables on concrete pads, paved boat ramp with floating docks, flush toilets, fish-cleaning station, volleyball net (in day-use area), pull-through sites, barbeque grills, drinking water, and garbage service are provided. The day-use area has a covered pavilion. Leashed pets are permitted but are not allowed on the beaches.

Reservations, fees: Reservations are accepted at 800/322-3770 or online at www.reserveamerica.com. Single site reservations must be made a minimum of two days in advance and can be arranged up to 16 weeks in advance, and group site reservations can be arranged up to 11 months

in advance. There is a nonrefundable reservation fee of $8 for individual sites and $10.25 for group sites. Sites are $16, the group site is $3 pp, and day use is $7. Open May through September.

Directions: From Duchesne, drive four miles northwest on Rte. 311. Continue 0.5 mile past the entrance station down to the Lower Beach Camping Area.

GPS Coordinates: N 40° 11.480' W 110° 27.484'

Contact: Starvation Lake State Park, 435/738-2326, http://stateparks.utah.gov/stateparks/parks/starvation/

44 MOUNTAIN VIEW AT STARVATION LAKE STATE PARK

Scenic rating: 8

northwest of Duchesne

Map 4.1, page 183

The Mountain View Campground at Starvation State Park sits on a raised bluff above the lake. The campground lives up to its name, with incredible views down to the reservoir and beyond to a backdrop of layers of stratified red rock. Behind the rocky mesas and hills, the distant peaks of the eastern Uinta Mountains climb above it all. The sites at Mountain View are quite different from the wide-open loop at Lower Beach. Each site at Mountain View features a covered picnic table on a concrete pad, and there are wind blocks that double as a visual barrier from other sites. The sites are tightly spaced on the paved loop. There are also four primitive dispersed camping areas on the southwest side of Starvation Reservoir. There are no facilities besides vault toilets and garbage service at these dispersed areas.

Campsites, facilities: There are 30 sites for tents and RVs up to 36 feet in length. Sites 25 and 26 are wheelchair accessible. Covered picnic tables, barbeque grills, tent pads, flush toilets, garbage service, paved boat ramp with floating docks, fish-cleaning station, and drinking water are

Flaming Gorge Reservoir as seen from Red Canyon

provided. Leashed pets are permitted but are not allowed on the beaches.

Reservations, fees: Reservations are accepted at 800/322-3770 or online at www.reserveamerica.com. Single sites reservations must be made a minimum of two days in advance and can be arranged up to 16 weeks in advance. There is an $8 nonrefundable reservation fee for individual sites. Sites are $16, and day use is $7. Primitive sites are $10. Open year-round.

Directions: From Duchesne, drive four miles northwest on Rte. 311. Turn right after the entrance station into the Mountain View Campground.

GPS Coordinates: N 40° 11.454' W 110° 27.140'

Contact: Starvation Lake State Park, 435/738-2326, http://stateparks.utah.gov/stateparks/parks/starvation/

45 FLAMING GORGE KOA

Scenic rating: 5

in Manila

Map 4.2, page 184

The Flaming Gorge KOA is the only camping option in the small town of Manila on the Utah/ Wyoming border. Manila is an intersection town where Rte. 44 and Rte. 43 come together west of the Flaming Gorge Reservoir and National Recreation Area. The KOA is near the reservoir and the boat-friendly launching site at Lucerne Valley Marina and Campground. While Manila isn't a long drive from the lake, you'll find a much more scenic and convenient campground and full-service marina on the lake shore. The KOA offers an RV-park alternative, with more shade, a playground, and a swimming pool. Large cottonwood trees shade tightly spaced sites with gravel parking slips. The driveway loop is gravel as well. The campground is clean and meticulously kept, with abundant reminders of the house rules posted throughout the campground.

Campsites, facilities: There are 40 full hookup (20-, 30-, and 50-amp) sites and 10 partial hook-up sites for RVs up to 75 feet in length, 10 tent sites, and six cabins. Picnic tables, modern restrooms with showers, drinking water, WiFi, swimming pool (open seasonally), playground, basketball hoop, horseshoes, and garbage are provided. Firewood is available. Leashed pets permitted.

Reservations, fees: Reservations are accepted at 800/562-3254. RV sites are $30–35, tent sites are $20–25, and cabins are $40–60. Open April 15 through November 1.

Directions: From the intersection of Rte. 44 and Rte. 43 in Manila, drive west 0.5 mile on Rte. 43 and turn right into the Flaming Gorge KOA. GPS Coordinates: N 40° 59.318' W 109° 43.813'
Contact: Flaming Gorge KOA, 435/784-3184, www.koa.com/where/ut/44114/

46 LUCERNE VALLEY

Scenic rating: 7

on the western shore of Flaming Gorge Reservoir just south of the Wyoming/Utah border

Map 4.2, page 184   **BEST**

Lucerne is a sprawling campground on the shores of the Flaming Gorge Reservoir, a huge reservoir held back by a 502-foot-tall concrete dam on the Green River. The dam was completed in 1964, creating a 92-mile-long lake with over 300 miles of shoreline. The Flaming Gorge National Recreation Area is managed by the Forest Service, with over 35 different campgrounds and group sites in Utah and Wyoming. Lucerne Valley offers some of the best and easiest access to the reservoir south of the Wyoming border. There's a boat ramp, full-service marina with a grocery store, and a swimming beach north of the campground. The lake is known for producing enormous trout. Fish species include mackinaw, rainbow trout, cutthroat trout, kokanee, channel catfish, and smallmouth bass. Lucerne is straight across a narrow arm of the lake from Antelope Flat. The habitats are similar on both sides, and you're likely to spot pronghorn antelope in and around Lucerne Valley. The campground is big and open, with a few cottonwood trees providing a little relief from the sun. The easy access to the lake and RV-friendly facilities at Lucerne Valley make it one of the best public campgrounds for RVs in the state.

Campsites, facilities: There are 143 sites for tents and RVs up to 45 feet in length. There are four group sites for up to 80 people. Sites B6, B11, and D6 are wheelchair accessible.

Electricity hook-ups (50 amps) are available in the inside loops of Loops A, C, and D. Amenities include covered picnic tables on concrete pads, barbeque grills, fire grills, modern restrooms, drinking water, dump station, fish-cleaning station, garbage service, amphitheater, boat ramp, and marina. Leashed pets permitted.

Reservations, fees: Reservations are accepted at 877/444-6777 or online at www.recreation. gov and must be made a minimum of four days in advance. Sites are $15, group sites are $65, and electricity is available at some sites for a $4 fee. Open May through October.
Directions: From Manila, drive northeast on Rte. 43 for 3.2 miles. Turn east (right) and continue four miles to the Lucerne Valley Campground. GPS Coordinates: N 40° 59.206' W 109° 35.576'
Contact: Flaming Gorge Ranger District, 435/784-3445.

47 CARMEL

Scenic rating: 8

along Sheep Creek in the Flaming Gorge National Recreation Area

Map 4.2, page 184

Carmel Campground is along Sheep Creek, under dramatic golden cliffs of Navajo Sandstone. These walls are particularly beautiful at sunset, when they catch the warm evening light. The Forest Service protects this as the Sheep Creek Geologic Area for its amazing natural scenery and fascinating geology. More than a billion years of geologic time can be seen in the ancient rift zone. Carmel Campground offers the most secluded camping in this part of the Flaming Gorge Recreation Area. The short drive from the main road is well worth the trip. The flat, open campground loop leads to sites shaded by cottonwood and Engelmann spruce trees. Grass and Mormon tea shrubs grow around the sites. The sites don't offer much privacy but are adequately spread out. They also enjoy good views up to the cliffs across the river and rolling, sagebrush-blanketed hills in the other direction. Fishing is possible in Sheep Creek, but the fishery is closed August 15–October 31 to protect kokanee, the landlocked salmon that spawn in the creek during late summer. Sheep Creek is one of two main spawning streams for the kokanee.

Campsites, facilities: There are 15 sites for tents and RVs up to 25 feet in length. Picnic tables, fire grills, and vault toilets are provided. There is no potable water. Leashed pets permitted.

Reservations, fees: Reservations are not accepted. The fee is $10 per night. Open May 15 through September 15.

Directions: From Manila, drive south on Rte. 44 for 5.6 miles. Turn right onto the Sheep Creek Geological Loop Road (Forest Road 218). Continue 0.7 mile to the Carmel Campground on the right side of the road.

GPS Coordinates: N 40° 55.856' W 109° 43.947'

Contact: Flaming Gorge Ranger District, 435/784-3445.

48 WILLOWS

Scenic rating: 7

along Sheep Creek in the Flaming Gorge National Recreation Area

Map 4.2, page 184

Willows Campground is squeezed in between Sheep Creek and Rte. 44 in the Sheep Creek Canyon. The little campground occupies a creek-bottom environment with thickets of willow trees and other dense deciduous trees crowding around the stream. Fishing is possible in Sheep Creek except for August 15–October 31. Kokanee salmon spawn in the creek during late summer. The fishing closure helps ensure their reproductive success. The sites enjoy views up to the interesting Navajo Sandstone cliffs above Sheep Creek. These beautiful sandstone walls are the back side of the formation exposed in

Flaming Gorge. The gorge was named by John Wesley Powell and his men on their inaugural journey down the Green and Colorado Rivers on May 26, 1869. The highway is right next to the campground, making road noise inevitable. Luckily, it's not all that busy. The sites don't have designated numbers and offer flat spots of dirt to pitch a tent. Big cottonwood and willow trees provide some shade for the sites. The loop and parking spots are gravel. Watch for bighorn sheep in the steep, rocky canyon.

Campsites, facilities: There are eight sites for tents and RVs up to 40 feet in length. Picnic tables, fire grills, vault toilets, and garbage service are provided. There is no potable water. Leashed pets permitted.

Reservations, fees: Reservations are not accepted. Sites are $10. Open mid-May through mid-September.

Directions: From Manila, drive south on Rte. 44 for six miles. Turn left into Willows Campground.

GPS Coordinates: N 40° 55.563' W 109° 42.915'

Contact: Flaming Gorge Ranger District, 435/784-3445.

49 MANNS

Scenic rating: 8

along Sheep Creek in the Flaming Gorge National Recreation Area

Map 4.2, page 184

Manns Campground is located under the gold-and-red cliffs of Navajo Sandstone exposed by Sheep Creek near the shore of the Flaming Gorge Reservoir. There's fishing on Sheep Creek, but it's closed August 15–October 31 to protect spawning of the kokanee salmon. The sites at Manns have picnic tables on gravel pads surrounded by tall grass and sagebrush. Big cottonwood trees loom over the campground and offer some shade and relief from midsummer heat. Views from the sites include rocky crags to one side and open, rolling, sagebrush- and juniper-blanketed hills on the other. The campground is close to the Sheep Creek boat ramp on the Flaming Gorge Reservoir; it's close to Rte. 44, too, so don't expect a very remote experience.

Campsites, facilities: There are eight sites for tents and RVs up to 45 feet in length. Picnic tables, fire grills, vault toilets, and garbage service are provided. There is no potable water. Leashed pets permitted.

Reservations, fees: Reservations are not accepted. Single sites are $10 and double sites are $20. Open mid-May through mid-September.

Directions: From Manila, drive south on Rte. 44 for 6.4 miles. Turn left into Mann's Campground.

GPS Coordinates: N 40° 55.404' W 109° 42.526'

Contact: Flaming Gorge Ranger District, 435/784-3445.

50 BROWNE LAKE

Scenic rating: 8

in the northern Uinta Mountains in the Ashley National Forest

Map 4.2, page 184   **BEST (**

Browne Lake is a high alpine reservoir located in the northern Uinta Mountains. The lake is named after J. Allen Browne (pronounced Brownie), who was once the Fish and Game Commissioner of Utah. The reservoir was created in 1957 by construction of an earthen dam on Beaver Creek. The lake is maintained solely for recreation as a fishery and is home to a pure strain of cutthroat trout. Browne Lake Campground is the trailhead for a collection of trails leading into the surrounding Uinta Mountains, making it one of the best campgrounds for hiking in Utah. The Old Carter Trail leaves from the campground and leads to Young Spring Park (three miles), Summit Park (seven miles), Hacking Lake (seven miles),

and Elk Park (nine miles). Also the Browne–Spirit Lake Trail passes Potter Lake (eight miles) and Weyman Lake (nine miles) on the way to Spirit Lake (15 miles). The campground has two separate gravel loops weaving through open forests of lodgepole pine on either side of the lake. The upper loop does a better job of accommodating RVs, and the lower loop is more appropriate for tents. Open grassy meadows surround the lake and campground. The sites have views of the lake and up toward Half Moon Park and the upper Uinta Mountains.

Campsites, facilities: There are 20 sites and four group sites for up to 40 people. Picnic tables, fire grills, and vault toilets are provided. There is no drinking water. Leashed pets permitted.

Reservations, fees: Reservations are not accepted. Sites are $10 and the group sites are $50–55. Open mid-May through mid-September.

Directions: From Manila, drive south on Hwy. 44 for 13 miles. Turn right onto the southern entrance of the Sheep Creek Geologic Loop Road. After three miles take the left fork and continue 4.7 miles and turn left onto Forest Road 96 (Browne Lake Road). Travel 1.7 miles to the campground.

GPS Coordinates: N 40° 51.624' W 109° 49.068'

Contact: Flaming Gorge Ranger District, 435/784-3445.

51 DEEP CREEK

Scenic rating: 7

in the northern Uinta Mountains in the Ashley National Forest

Map 4.2, page 184

Deep Creek is located on the northeastern edge of the Ashley National Forest in the Uinta Mountains. The quiet canyon campground is split by a lovely fishing stream. The creek has had extensive habitat restoration improvements to increase the diversity and quality of the trout fishing. Wood debris has been strategically placed in the stream to provide deep, protected pools for the fish. The camp loop is in a forest of lodgepole and ponderosa pine, aspen, and Engelmann spruce. Some of the sites have shade, while others do not. The open sites are surrounded by grass and have the best views up to red rock cliffs. The forest creates good visual barriers between the well-spaced sites. The facility is small and remote and a good place to escape the crowds.

Campsites, facilities: There are 17 sites for tents and RVs up to 30 feet in length. Picnic tables, fire grills, and a vault toilet are provided. There is no drinking water. Leashed pets permitted.

Reservations, fees: Reservations are not accepted. Sites are $10. Open mid-May through mid-September.

Directions: From Manila, drive south on Rte. 44 for 17 miles and turn right onto Forest Road 218. After three miles take the left fork onto Forest Road 539, continue 2.6 miles, and turn left into the Deep Creek Campground. GPS Coordinates: N 40° 51.303' W 109° 43.772'

Contact: Flaming Gorge Ranger District, 435/784-3445.

52 SHEEP CREEK BAY

Scenic rating: 7

along Sheep Creek in the Flaming Gorge National Recreation Area

Map 4.2, page 184

Sheep Creek Bay is a small inlet on the southwestern arm of the Flaming Gorge Reservoir. The campground at the bay is more of an add-on to the boat ramp parking lot than a bona-fide campground. Four RV-only sites are located at the far end of the huge paved lot. A tall lodgepole fence makes a superficial barrier between the parking lot and the sites. A central site with two picnic tables sits right on the pavement, distinguished by a circular curb. The other three picnic tables are tucked into the dense willow trees on the outside of this little loop. There's plenty of room for RVs to park in the camping area. On the bright side, the campground has incredible views up to the Flaming Gorge geology above the lake. The stunning views, however, are diminished somewhat by the haphazard facilities. This campground is all about convenience. If you're trying to maximize time on the lake, there isn't anywhere closer to the Sheep Creek Bay boat ramp. If you'd like a more appealing place to camp or are tent camping, options a little farther west on Rte. 44 include Willow, Carmel, and Manns Campgrounds.

Campsites, facilities: There are four sites for RVs up to 45 feet in length. Picnic tables, fire grills, vault toilets, garbage service, and a boat ramp are provided. There is no drinking water. Leashed pets permitted.

Reservations, fees: Reservations are not accepted. The fee is $10 per night. Open mid-May through mid-September

Directions: From Manila, drive south on Rte. 44 for seven miles. Turn left and continue 0.5 mile to the Sheep Creek Campground. GPS Coordinates: N 40° 55.275' W 109° 40.504'

Contact: Flaming Gorge Ranger District, 435/784-3445.

53 RED CANYON

Scenic rating: 8

in the Red Canyon Recreation Area of the Flaming Gorge National Recreation Area

Map 4.2, page 184

Red Canyon Campground is perched on the edge of a beautiful canyon rim overlooking the Flaming Gorge Reservoir. The campground is next to a scenic overlook and the Red Canyon Visitor Center, so there's a lot of day-use traffic in the area. The paved loop winds through a sparse ponderosa grove and grassy meadow.

The sites alternate between shaded and sunny and offer level tenting and paved parking for RVs and trailers. Deer frequent the meadows and fields around the campground, grazing on long grass, small shrubs, and trees. The Canyon Rim Trailhead is at the visitors center; this hiking, mountain biking, and horseback riding trail leads one mile to Canyon Rim Campground, 2.5 miles to Green Lake Campground, three miles to Red Canyon Lodge, and 4.5 miles to the Greendale Overlook.

Campsites, facilities: There are eight sites for tents and RVs up to 35 feet in length. Picnic tables, fire grills, drinking water, garbage service, and vault toilets are provided. Leashed pets permitted.

Reservations, fees: Reservations are accepted at 877/444-6777 or online at www.recreation. gov and must be made a minimum of four days in advance. Sites are $15. Open mid-May through mid-September.

Directions: From Vernal, drive north on Hwy. 191 for 35 miles. Turn west (left) onto Rte. 44 and travel four miles. Turn right toward the Red Canyon Visitor Center and continue 2.4 miles to the Red Canyon Campground on the right side of the road.

GPS Coordinates: N 40° 53.408' W 109° 33.597'

Contact: Flaming Gorge Ranger District, 435/784-3445.

54 CANYON RIM

Scenic rating: 8

in the Red Canyon Recreation Area of the Flaming Gorge National Recreation Area

Map 4.2, page 184   BEST (

Canyon Rim Campground overlooks the rim of the spectacular Red Canyon in the Flaming Gorge National Recreation Area. The canyon drops precipitously thousands of feet to the waters of the reservoir. Camping near the edge of such a dramatic natural feature is a rare opportunity. The Canyon Rim Campground sits in an open ponderosa pine forest among tall grass. It has a paved loop and parking spaces and level spots to pitch tents. The campground is an excellent place for wildlife-viewing. Herds of deer can be spotted in and around the campground all day but are especially active in the evenings around sunset. Scrub jays and robins chirp in the ponderosas. The Canyon Rim Trail (open to hikers, horseback riders, and mountain bikers) passes through the campground and offers awesome views off the side of the breathtaking canyon rim.

Campsites, facilities: There are 18 sites for tents and RVs up to 45 feet in length. Picnic tables, fire grills, garbage service, vault toilets, and drinking water are provided. Leashed pets permitted.

Reservations, fees: Reservations are accepted at 877/444-6777 or online at www.recreation. gov and must be made a minimum of four days in advance. Sites are $15. Open mid-May through mid-September (seven sites remain open until it snows).

Directions: From Vernal, drive north on Hwy. 191 for 35 miles. Turn west (left) onto Rte. 44 and travel four miles. Turn right toward the Red Canyon Visitor Center, continue 1.6 miles, and turn right into Canyon Rim Campground.

GPS Coordinates: N 40° 53.070' W 109° 32.915'

Contact: Flaming Gorge Ranger District, 435/784-3445.

55 GREENS LAKE

Scenic rating: 7

in Red Canyon Recreation Area in the Flaming Gorge National Recreation Area

Map 4.2, page 184

Greens Lake Campground is located off by itself down a spur road in Red Canyon, above the south shore of the Flaming Gorge Reservoir. Greens Lake is a small, pond-sized lake. The campground isn't on the lake but occupies a tall grass meadow and open woodland. Ponderosa pines offer some shade for the sites, which have good level tent pads. The camp loop is paved but has gravel parking slips. The campground is surrounded by a fence and has views out to the adjacent meadows. Greens Lake Campground presents a quieter experience than the Canyon Rim and Red Canyon Campgrounds, which are right by the visitors center. The Canyon Rim Trail runs through Greens Lake Campground and continues one mile to Canyon Rim Campground, two miles to Skull Creek Campground, and three miles to Greendale. The trail is open to hikers, bikers, and horses.

Campsites, facilities: There are 20 sites for tents and RVs up to 45 feet in length and one group site for up to 40 people. Picnic tables, fire grills, drinking water, vault toilets, and garbage service are provided. Leashed pets permitted.

Reservations, fees: Reservations are accepted at 877/444-6777 or online at www.recreation. gov and must be made a minimum of four days in advance. Sites are $15 and the group site is $65. Open mid-May through mid-September.

Directions: From Vernal, drive north on Hwy. 191 for 35 miles. Turn west (left) onto Rte. 44 and travel 3.3 miles. Turn right, drive 0.5 mile, turn right again, and continue 0.6 mile to Greens Lake Campground.

GPS Coordinates: N 40° 52.400' W 109° 32.172'

Contact: Flaming Gorge Ranger District, 435/784-3445.

56 SKULL CREEK

Scenic rating: 7

in the Flaming Gorge National Recreation Area
Map 4.2, page 184

The Skull Creek Campground is located along Rte. 44 above the southern shore of the Flaming Gorge Reservoir. Skull Creek drops out of the Uinta Mountains, passes the campground and empties into the lake east of Red Canyon. The campground loop circles beneath old ponderosa pine and open aspen tree groves. The campsites get a mix of sun and shade through the open forest canopy. The forest floor sites are rocky but feature built-up, level tent pads. Long grass grows under the trees around the sites. The loop and parking slips are gravel. The Canyon Rim hiking trail leaves directly from camp and leads two miles to the Greens Lake and Canyon Rim Campgrounds, and three miles to Greendale Campground. The trail is open to hikers, bikers, and horses.

Campsites, facilities: There are 17 sites for tents and RVs up to 30 feet in length. Picnic tables, fire grills, vault toilets, garbage service, pull-through sites, and drinking water are provided. Leashed pets permitted.

Reservations, fees: Reservations are accepted at 877/444-6777 or online at www.recreation. gov and must be made a minimum of four days in advance. Sites are $15. Open mid-May through mid-September.

Directions: From Vernal, drive north on Hwy. 191 for 35 miles. Turn west (left) onto Rte. 44 and travel 2.6 miles. Skull Creek Campground will be on the right side of the road.

GPS Coordinates: N 40° 51.793' W 109° 31.702'

Contact: Flaming Gorge Ranger District, 435/784-3445.

57 ANTELOPE FLAT

Scenic rating: 8

in the Flaming Gorge National Recreation Area
Map 4.2, page 184   BEST (

Antelope Flat offers a wide-open camping environment on the eastern shore of the Flaming Gorge Reservoir, directly across the lake from the entrance to the actual Flaming Gorge formation. The campground is on gentle slope above the shore of the lake. As the name suggests, Antelope Flat offers great opportunities for viewing wildlife. The sagebrush and grassland is classic pronghorn antelope habitat, and they are easily spotted around the campground or resting in the open, sandy flats below. Ospreys frequent the area, capitalizing on the abundant fish in the reservoir; look for them in the dead snag just northeast of the camp loop. The camp loop offers sites with established gravel tent pads and cabana-style picnic tables offer shade from the sun. The sites are open and the loop is exposed, so there's not much privacy to be had. There's a boat ramp providing lake access not far from the camping area.

Campsites, facilities: There are 46 sites for tents and RVs up to 45 feet in length and four group sites for up to 50 or 80 people, depending on the site. Covered picnic tables, fire grills, barbeque grills, drinking water, flush toilets, boat ramp, dump station, garbage service, and aluminum recycling are provided. Leashed pets permitted.

Reservations, fees: Reservations are accepted at 877/444-6777 or online at www.recreation. gov and must be made a minimum of four days in advance. Sites are $14, and group sites are $85. Open mid-May through mid-September.

Directions: From Vernal, drive north on Hwy. 191 for 52 miles. Turn left and continue four miles to Antelope Flat Campground.

GPS Coordinates: N 40° 57.857' W 109° 33.231'

Contact: Flaming Gorge Ranger District, 435/784-3445.

⑤⑧ DUTCH JOHN DRAW

Scenic rating: 7

in the Flaming Gorge National Recreation Area
Map 4.2, page 184

Dutch John Draw features a dock and group area on the easternmost arm of the Flaming Gorge Reservoir. The facilities are accessed via a gravel road branching off Hwy. 191. Juniper,

pinyon pine, sagebrush, and wild grasses make up the varied plant community around the campground. Red-and-brown dirt hills rise quickly above the campground, closing the site in and giving it a secluded, private feel. A recent fire burned most of the surrounding forest, but in and around the campground the trees have been left standing. A series of sloping, bare dirt tent sites are tucked into the juniper trees across from the pavilion eating area. The trees offer some shade and protection for the tent pads.

Campsites, facilities: There is one group site for up to 50 people and tents and RVs up to 22 feet in length. A covered pavilion, picnic tables, barbeque grills, fire grills, a large group fire ring, vault toilets, garbage service, and a floating dock are provided. There is no drinking water. Leashed pets permitted.

Reservations, fees: Reservations are required and can be arranged at 877/444-6777 or online at www.recreation.gov and must be made a minimum of four days in advance. The group site is $85. Open mid-May through mid-September.

Directions: From Vernal, drive north on Hwy. 191 for 45 miles. Turn left and continue one mile to Dutch John Draw Campground.

GPS Coordinates: N 40° 56.074' W 109° 25.453'

Contact: Flaming Gorge Ranger District, 435/784-3445.

⑤⑨ MUSTANG RIDGE

Scenic rating: 8

in the Flaming Gorge National Recreation Area
Map 4.2, page 184

Mustang Ridge sits high above the Flaming Gorge Reservoir. The campground is set in a pygmy forest of pinyon pine and Utah juniper trees. Much of the surrounding forest burned recently in a fire, but the campground itself has been spared. Unlike most forest ecosystems that benefit from periodic fires, pinyon and juniper forests don't recover well after burns, so it's good this fire missed the Mustang Ridge sites. The paved camp loop leads to nice facilities tucked into the trees. The vegetation creates a visual barrier between sites, which adds privacy and shade. Some of the sites have views down to the reservoir. The campground has a nice group pavilion and amphitheater with metal benches. The sites' dirt floors offer good, flat tent pitching options.

Campsites, facilities: There are 73 sites for tents and RVs up to 45 feet in length and one group site for up to 50 people. Sites 53 and 54 are wheelchair accessible. Picnic tables, fire grills, drinking water, flush and vault toilets, showers, and garbage service are provided. Leashed pets permitted.

Reservations, fees: Reservations are accepted at 877/444-6777 or online at www.recreation. gov and must be made a minimum of four days in advance. Sites are $20, the group site is $105, and showers are $3 for noncampers. Open mid-May through mid-September.

Directions: From Vernal, drive north on Hwy. 191 for 49 miles. Turn left, continue 1.8 miles and turn left into the Mustang Ridge Campground.

GPS Coordinates: N 40° 55.630' W 109° 26.629'

Contact: Flaming Gorge Ranger District, 435/784-3445.

60 DRIPPING SPRINGS

Scenic rating: 7

In the Flaming Gorge National Recreation Area
Map 4.2, page 184

Dripping Springs Campground is set in a valley surrounded by rolling hills in the Flaming Gorge National Recreation Area. The campground is the closest campground to the put-in for rafting the Green River. It's popular with anglers who float the Green River from the dam to Little Hole. Dripping Springs burned in a forest fire in 2002; while the wild grasses

and rabbit brush shrubs have grown back, a skeleton forest of juniper and pinyon pine is anything but recovered. It looks like it burned just yesterday. The lack of living trees leaves the campground very open, with no shade. An effort has been made to plant ponderosa pine trees, with metal cages protecting the trees from foraging deer. The sites are all in plain view of each other, making privacy limited.

Campsites, facilities: There are 22 single sites and one double site for tents and RVs up to 45 feet in length. There are four group sites for up to 40 or 60 people, depending on the site. Sites 1, 3, 6, 9, 12, 15, 18, and one group site are wheelchair accessible. Picnic tables, fire grills, drinking water, and vault toilets are provided. Group sites have barbeque grills and picnic tables (three have covered pavilions). Leashed pets permitted.

Reservations, fees: Reservations are accepted at 877/444-6777 or online at www.recreation. gov and must be made a minimum of four days in advance. Single sites are $15, double sites are $30, and group sites are $75. Open mid-May through mid-September (in the winter, sites are $5 and there is no water).

Directions: From Vernal, drive north on Hwy. 191 for 45 miles to the town of Dutch John. Turn right, travel 3.1 miles, and turn right into Dripping Springs Campground.

GPS Coordinates: N 40° 55.363' W 109° 21.410'

Contact: Flaming Gorge Ranger District, 435/784-3445.

61 ARCH DAM

Scenic rating: 6

In the Flaming Gorge National Recreation Area
Map 4.2, page 184

Arch Dam is a group area near the Flaming Gorge Reservoir. The site is less than a mile from the impressive Arch Dam and good fishing and rafting on the Green River. The campground isn't on the lake but is located in a hill landscape above. The group sites feature good flat areas to pitch tents on the red earth under a mix of juniper, pinyon, and ponderosa pines. Mormon tea bushes and long waving grass fill out the vegetation in the otherwise open setting. There are limited views from the sites up to the surrounding hills. Considering its proximity to such beautiful scenery, this campground is lacking in visual appeal. The access road, loop, and parking are gravel and red dirt.

Campsites, facilities: There are three group sites for tents and RVs up to 35 feet in length and for up to 60 to 75 people, depending on the site. Picnic tables, large group fire pits, drinking water, and vault toilets are provided. Leashed pets permitted.

Reservations, fees: Reservations are required and can be arranged at 877/444-6777 or online at www.recreation.gov and must be made a minimum of four days in advance. The group sites are $75. Open mid-May through mid-September.

Directions: From Vernal, drive north on Hwy. 191 for 43 miles and the Arch Dam Campground will be on the right side of the road. GPS Coordinates: N 40° 54.703' W 109° 24.691'

Contact: Flaming Gorge Ranger District, 435/784-3445.

tables on paved pads and good, flat tent pads under the shade of the short, squat trees. There are beautiful views down to the reservoir and across to a red sandstone canyon. In addition to its easy lake access, Cedar Springs is also near Arch Dam and Green River. Green River offers recreational opportunities such as fishing and rafting.

Campsites, facilities: There are 21 sites for tents and RVs up to 45 feet in length. Picnic tables, fire grills, barbeque grills, drinking water, vault toilets, garbage service, paved boat ramp, marina, floating dock, and fish-cleaning station are provided. Leashed pets permitted.

Reservations, fees: Reservations are accepted at 877/444-6777 or online at www.recreation. gov and must be made a minimum of four days in advance. To make a reservation, Cedar Springs Campground requires a two-night minimum stay on weekends and three nights on holiday weekends. Sites are $20. Open mid-April through mid-September.

Directions: From Vernal, drive north on Hwy. 191 for 40 miles. Turn left and continue 0.5 mile to the Cedar Springs Campground. GPS Coordinates: N 40° 54.513' W 109° 27.012'

Contact: Flaming Gorge Ranger District, 435/784-3445.

62 CEDAR SPRINGS

Scenic rating: 8

in the Flaming Gorge National Recreation Area

Map 4.2, page 184

Cedar Springs Campground sits on a hillside right above the Flaming Gorge Reservoir. It offers doorstep access to a marina and paved boat ramp. The campground itself is very similar to its neighbor Deer Run, except it is a little closer to the lake facilities. Sites are accessed via a paved loop and sit in the protection of a juniper and pinyon pine forest. The facilities are nice and well kept and feature picnic

63 DEER RUN

Scenic rating: 7

in the Flaming Gorge National Recreation Area

Map 4.2, page 184

Deer Run Campground is located near Cedar Springs Marina above the Flaming Gorge Reservoir. The paved loop leads to sites tucked into large juniper and pinyon pine trees. Some of the sites offer good views out to the rolling hills above the lake. The layout provides some pull-through spaces for RVs, long vehicles, and boat trailers. There are flat parking spots and level tent pads for those sleeping out on the ground. Deer seem to be everywhere in the Flaming Gorge Recreation Area and can be easily spotted at Deer Run Campground. The campground provides convenient lake access but is also far enough from the marina to offer a natural if not wilderness feel. Fishing, boating, and swimming are all popular on the lake.

Campsites, facilities: There are 15 single sites and four double sites for tents and RVs up to 45 feet in length. Sites 8 and 9 are wheelchair accessible. Picnic tables, fire grills, modern restrooms with showers, drinking water, vault toilets, garbage service, aluminum recycling, fish-cleaning station, and dump station are provided. Firewood is available. Leashed pets permitted.

Reservations, fees: Reservations are accepted at 877/444-6777 or online at www.recreation. gov and must be made a minimum of four days in advance. Single sites are $20, double sites are $40, and showers for noncampers are $3. Open mid-April through mid-October.

Directions: From Vernal, drive north on Hwy. 191 for 40 miles. Turn left, drive 0.3 mile, and turn left into Deer Run Campground.

GPS Coordinates: N 40° 54.304' W 109° 26.663'

Contact: Flaming Gorge Ranger District, 435/784-3445.

64 GREENDALE

Scenic rating: 7

in the Flaming Gorge National Recreation Area
Map 4.2, page 184

Greendale Campground is a small campground well above the waters of the Flaming Gorge Reservoir. Greendale has two separate loops across the road from one another. Greendale West on the west side of the road offers individual and family sites, and Greendale East is a group site. The camp areas are sheltered by large ponderosa pine trees and surrounded by grassy meadows. The pines create a nice,

shady atmosphere, and the meadow attracts families of deer. The site's small size and large trees give it a private, comfortable feel despite being relatively close to the road. The facilities are not as nice as some in the area but are adequate for a good camping experience. There are pull-through parking slips for RVs. Bear Canyon Trail is nearby and offers mountain biking and hiking.

Campsites, facilities: There are eight sites for tents and RVs up to 45 feet in length in the Greendale West Area and two group sites for up to 40 or 50 people in the Greendale East Area. Picnic tables, fire grills, drinking water, vault toilets, and garbage service are provided. Leashed pets permitted.

Reservations, fees: Reservations are accepted at 877/444-6777 or online at www.recreation. gov and must be made a minimum of four days in advance. Single sites are $15, and group sites are $75. Open mid-May through mid-September.

Directions: From Vernal, drive north on Hwy. 191 for 36.8 miles and turn left for the individual sites at Greendale or right for the group area.

GPS Coordinates: N 40° 52.960' W 109° 27.567'

Contact: Flaming Gorge Ranger District, 435/784-3445.

65 FIREFIGHTERS MEMORIAL

Scenic rating: 9

in the Flaming Gorge National Recreation Area
Map 4.2, page 184

Firefighters Memorial Campground is perched on a hill above the Flaming Gorge Reservoir. The campground is named in honor of three firefighters who died battling the Cart Creek Fire in 1977. The paved campground loop circles a ponderosa pine and juniper forest. Patches of native grass and sagebrush grow between the well-spaced sites. There are good views from many of the sites, especially those on the outside of the loop, looking over a wide valley to distant forested hills and the Flaming Gorge Reservoir. Look for deer in the meadows around the campground in the morning and evening hours. Hiking is available on the Memorial Trail and the 1.5-mile Bear Canyon Trail starts across the road (Hwy. 191) from the campground. Bear Canyon Trail is open to mountain biking as well. The Bootleg Amphitheater is found here and presents a planned activity every Friday evening. This campground features some of the best wheelchair-accessible facilities we've seen in any campground in the state.

Campsites, facilities: There are 94 sites for tents and RVs up to 45 feet in length. Sites 12, 14, 15, 17, 71, and 91 are wheelchair accessible. Picnic tables, fire grills, drinking water, flush toilets, a dump station, garbage service, aluminum recycling, and an amphitheater are provided. Firewood is available. Leashed pets permitted.

Reservations, fees: Reservations are accepted at 877/444-6777 or online at www.recreation.gov and must be made a minimum of four days in advance. Single sites are $15, and double sites are $30. Open mid-May through early October.

Directions: From Vernal, drive north on Hwy. 191 for 37 miles and turn right into the Firefighters Memorial Campground.

GPS Coordinates: N 40° 53.479' W 109° 27.401'

Contact: Flaming Gorge Ranger District, 435/784-3445.

66 RED SPRINGS

Scenic rating: 7

in the eastern Uinta Mountains

Map 4.2, page 184

Red Springs Campground rests in a relatively thick lodgepole and aspen forest at around 8,100 feet in the Uinta Mountains. Long grass grows around the campsites, which are accessed via a gravel loop. The spring is at the center of the campground and trickles through red boulders. The campground is very close to Highway 191 but does enjoy some privacy provided by dense forest. Compared to Lodgepole Campground, across the street, Red Springs is the more primitive, natural campground. Red Springs is near a trailhead for the Highline Trail. This is the eastern terminus of the 60-mile Highline Trail, which traces the crest of the Uinta Mountains. The trail is one of the best long backpacking trips in the country. Watch for elk and deer in the meadows along the highway and around Red Springs Campground.

Campsites, facilities: There are 13 sites for tents and RVs up to 25 feet in length. Picnic tables, fire grills, drinking water, and vault toilets are provided. Garbage service and a dump station are available at the nearby Lodgepole Campground. Leashed pets permitted.

Reservations, fees: Reservations are not accepted. Single sites are $12, and double sites are $24. Open late May through early September.

Directions: From Vernal, drive north on Hwy. 191 for 29 miles and turn left into Lodgepole Campground.

GPS Coordinates: N 40° 48.512' W 109° 28.104'

Contact: Vernal Ranger District, 435/789-1181.

67 LODGEPOLE

Scenic rating: 7

in the eastern Uinta Mountains

Map 4.2, page 184

Lodgepole Campground sits across the highway from Red Springs south of the Flaming Gorge National Recreation Area. The small paved campground loop leads to level sites in a thick grove of quaking aspen and lodgepole pine. The sites on the east side of the loop sit above a small valley and Cart Creek.

Lodgepole Campground is at about 8,100 feet in elevation and is significantly cooler than many of the campgrounds in the Flaming Gorge. If you're looking to escape the heat, Lodgepole or Red Springs are a nice choice. The campground is very close to the highway, and road noise can be heard from the sites. Lodgepole is nearby the eastern end of the Highline Trail, a 60-mile traverse of the Uinta Mountains. Watch for elk in the meadows along the highway near the campground.

Campsites, facilities: There are 36 sites for tents and RVs up to 63 feet in length. Picnic tables on paved pads, fire grills, gravel tent pads, drinking water, pull-through sites, a dump station, and wastewater disposal stations are provided. Leashed pets permitted.

Reservations, fees: Reservations are accepted at 877/444-6777 or online at www.recreation. gov and must be made a minimum of four days in advance. To make a reservation, Lodgepole Campground requires a two-night minimum stay on weekends and three nights on holiday weekends. Sites are $14. Open mid-May through mid-September.

Directions: From Vernal, drive north on Hwy. 191 for 29 miles and turn right into Lodgepole Campground.

GPS Coordinates: N 40° 48.819' W 109° 27.937'

Contact: Vernal Ranger District, 435/789-1181.

68 EAST PARK

Scenic rating: 8

in eastern Uinta Mountains in the Ashley National Forest

Map 4.2, page 184

East Park Campground is located near the East Park Reservoir high in the northeastern Uinta Mountains. There's a boat ramp accessing the lake, which is popular for trout fishing and waterfowl hunting. The Utah State Department of Wildlife Resources stocks the

reservoir annually with 4,000 rainbow trout and 7,000 fingerling brook trout. The campground is set in an open lodgepole pine and spruce forest, with a fence to keep the grazing livestock out. The loop and long parking slips are gravel. There are some pull-through spots, and parking is adequate for midsize RVs or trailers. Views from the campground look out across the lake to the gently rising forested slopes of the Uinta Mountains.

Campsites, facilities: There are 21 sites for tents and RVs up to 25 feet in length. Picnic tables, fire grills, drinking water, flush toilets, and garbage service are provided. Leashed pets permitted.

Reservations, fees: Reservations are not accepted. Sites are $8. Open mid-May through mid-September.

Directions: From Vernal, drive north on Hwy. 191 for 21 miles and turn west (left) on the Red Cloud-Dry Fork Loop. Drive 3.2 miles and turn north (right); continue five miles. Turn right and continue 0.7 mile to the East Park Campground.

GPS Coordinates: N 40° 469.863' W 109° 33.152'

Contact: Vernal Ranger District, 435/789-1181.

69 OAKS PARK

Scenic rating: 7

in the eastern Uinta Mountains in the Ashley National Forest

Map 4.2, page 184

Oaks Park is a mix of beautiful high country meadows and lodgepole pine forest at around 9,000 feet in the Uinta Mountains. The high elevation makes for cool daytime temperatures and chilly nights. Expect inclement weather any time of year. The campground is used mostly by ATV riders and anglers who fish for rainbow trout in the nearby Oaks Park Reservoir. There is no developed boat ramp at the lake, but it is possible to launch a small boat near the dam.

The area is also known for its good waterfowl hunting. An undeveloped trail leaves from near the campground to the Big Brush Creek Cave. At five miles long, the Big Brush Creek Cave is a great opportunity for spelunkers. During spring runoff, the whole cave becomes a rushing river, often clogging the underground passage with wood debris. Explorers should contact the Forest Service and come prepared to cut through and clear away wood. The camp loop, parking spots, and access road are gravel. Lodgepole pine barriers keep vehicles on the road and out of the sites. The sites are well spread out and offer good privacy despite the open nature of the forest.

Campsites, facilities: There are 11 sites for tents and RVs up to 20 feet in length. Picnic tables, fire pits, drinking water, and vault toilets are provided. Leashed pets permitted.

Reservations, fees: Reservations are not accepted. Sites are $5. Open mid-May through mid-September.

Directions: From Vernal, drive north on Hwy. 191 for 21 miles and turn west (left) on the Red Cloud-Dry Fork Loop. After 3.2 miles, stay left on the Red Cloud Loop and continue 8.4 miles, then turn right and drive one mile to East Park Campground.

GPS Coordinates: N 40° 44.554' W 109° 37.421'

Contact: Vernal Ranger District, 435/789-1181.

70 KALER HOLLOW

Scenic rating: 7

in the eastern Uinta Mountains

Map 4.2, page 184

Kaler Hollow is a tiny Forest Service campground near the north end of the Taylor Mountain Plateau. The campground is accessed via the Red Cloud Loop Scenic Byway. Aspen and lodgepole pine trees grow in clumps around four campsites in an otherwise open alpine meadow. One site sits near a small parking spot,

and three sites branch off in walk-in style. The campground is simple, with picnic tables, fire pits, and a vault toilet, but otherwise could be described as undeveloped or dispersed camping. It's popular with ATV riders who access the Old Carter Military Trail and a web of spur trails and dirt roads. If you're looking for a quiet place to yourself, you'll find it here, on all but the busiest of weekends.

Campsites, facilities: There are four sites (three are walk-in sites). Picnic tables, fire pits, and a vault toilet are provided. There is no drinking water. Leashed pets permitted.

Reservations, fees: Reservations are not accepted. There is no fee. Open early May through mid-September.

Directions: From Vernal, drive north on Hwy. 191 for 21 miles and turn west (left) on the Red Cloud-Dry Fork Loop. After 3.2 miles, stay left on the Red Cloud Loop and continue 5.6 miles to Kaler Hollow on the right side of the road.

GPS Coordinates: N 40° 42.137' W 109° 36.919'

Contact: Vernal Ranger District, 435/789-1181.

71 IRON SPRINGS

Scenic rating: 7

on the Red Cloud Loop Scenic Byway in the eastern Uinta Mountains

Map 4.2, page 184

Iron Springs is a group campground for ATV riders and other off-road enthusiasts on the eastern slopes of the Uinta Mountains. A vast system of back roads and off-road trails weaves through this part of the high, plateau-like range. The campground can be accessed via the Red Cloud Loop Scenic Byway. This back-road byway is as popular in winter with snowmobilers as it is in the summer. The camp loop at Iron Springs leads to sites beneath a forest canopy of aspen and Engelmann spruce trees. These trees provide shade and shelter for the campground. Deer can be spotted in and around the campground near dusk. If you prefer free camping and can get by without the facilities, dispersed camping can be found across the road from Iron Springs.

Campsites, facilities: There are two group sites for up to 50 people. Picnic tables, fire rings, drinking water, and vault toilets are provided. Leashed pets permitted.

Reservations, fees: Reservations are required for the group sites at 877/444-6777 or online at www.recreation.gov and must be made a minimum of four days in advance. Sites are $20. Open mid-May through mid-September.

Directions: From Vernal, drive north on Hwy. 191 for 21 miles and turn west (left) on the Red Cloud-Dry Fork Loop. After 3.2 miles, stay left on the Red Cloud Loop, continue 1.3 miles and turn left into the Iron Springs Campground.

GPS Coordinates: N 40° 42.131' W 109° 33.400'

Contact: Vernal Ranger District, 435/789-1181.

72 PARADISE PARK

Scenic rating: 7

in the Uinta Mountains in the Ashley National Forest

Map 4.2, page 184

Paradise Park Campground is located on the edge of Paradise Reservoir in the eastern Uinta Mountains. The open meadows of the park are accessed via a long, bumpy dirt road. This high-mountain environment is popular with ATV riders and anglers. The Paradise Guard Station Cabin built in 1922 is located across the meadow from the campground. The cabin is available for rent and is especially popular with snowmobilers in winter. It sleeps four and has a wood stove for heat. The campground is set below the level of the earthen dam among scattered lodgepole pine and spruce trees. The

sites and loop are fenced in and offer easy access to the reservoir. Boating and fishing are possible on the reservoir, which is stocked with rainbow trout. Hiking is available on the nearby 8.5-mile Deadman Loop Trail.

Campsites, facilities: There are 15 sites for tents and RVs up to 25 feet in length and one cabin. The campground has picnic tables, fire pits, vault toilets, and garbage service. There is no drinking water. The cabin has running water (available seasonally), two bunk beds, table and chairs, fire grill, propane stove, vault toilet, and a refrigerator. Leashed pets are permitted in the campground but not in the cabin.

Reservations, fees: Reservations are accepted for the cabin only at 877/444-6777 or online at www.recreation.gov; they must be made a minimum of five days in advance and can be arranged up to 120 days in advance. Sites are $5, and the cabin is $25. Open June through September.

Directions: From the intersection of Rte. 121 and County Road 2728 in LaPoint, drive east on Rte. 121 for 0.6 mile. Turn north (left) and drive 6.7 miles and take the left fork. Continue 17.5 miles and turn right into the Paradise Park Campground.

GPS Coordinates: N 40° 39.903' W 109° 54.802'

Contact: Vernal Ranger District, 435/789-1181.

73 WHITEROCKS

Scenic rating: 8

in the Uinta Mountains in the Ashley National Forest

Map 4.2, page 184

Whiterocks Campground is located along the Whiterocks River in the southeastern Uinta Mountains. The campground layout winds through an inviting ponderosa pine, lodgepole, and aspen forest, with a gray-and-red boulder streambed on its west side. The access loop and parking slips are gravel with log barriers to keep vehicles on the driveways. Grass and sagebrush meadows surround the sites. There are views from the sites up to craggy white peaks. The sites have picnic tables on gravel pads and good flat places to pitch tents. A lodgepole fence around the campground keeps out the grazing livestock. There's fishing in the Whiterocks River, and spelunkers will be interested to know Whiterocks Cave is near the campground. The limestone cave is gated but can be visited with a permit from the forest service. The karst cave has about 1,000 feet of underground passages.

Campsites, facilities: There are 21 sites for tents and RVs up to 25 feet in length. Picnic tables, fire grills, drinking water, garbage service, and vault toilets are provided. Leashed pets permitted.

Reservations, fees: Reservations are not accepted. The fee is $8. Open mid-May through early September.

Directions: From the intersection of Hwy. 40 and Rte. 121 in Roosevelt, head north on Rte. 121 for 10 miles to Neola. Turn right, staying on Rte. 121, and continue five miles. Turn left and travel three miles to the town of Whiterocks. From Whiterocks, drive east on the Tridell Hwy. for two miles to the Whiterocks Loop Road. Turn north (left) and drive seven miles to a right fork for Forest Road 492. Turn right on Whiterocks Canyon Road and drive 6.4 miles to Whiterocks Campground on the left side of the road.

GPS Coordinates: N 40° 37.204' W 109° 56.531'

Contact: Vernal Ranger District, 435/789-1181.

74 RED FLEET STATE PARK

Scenic rating: 9

north of Vernal

Map 4.2, page 184

Red Fleet State Park sits above the beautiful waters of the Red Fleet Reservoir. The reservoir draws comparisons to Lake Powell with its layered sandstone geology and multi-fingered shape. Its name is inspired by the red-and-gray rock outcrops rising from the water like a fleet of ships. The sandstone here is from the Triassic period and contains many fossils, including such oddities as crocodile teeth and fossilized squid. As you might guess, this area was once a large inland sea. Red Fleet stands out as one of the prettiest state parks in Utah. The lake offers swimming, boating, and fishing. Sport-fishing species hooked on the lake include rainbow and brown trout, bluegill, and largemouth bass. The lake is visited by a variety of wildlife like rabbits, mule deer, and ground squirrels. Bird species seen here include mountain bluebirds, pinyon jays, owls, ospreys, and magpies. The campground is designed to capitalize on the wonderful views of the lake. The sites are divided into two unique areas: The RV-oriented area features back-in spots, barbeque grills, and picnic tables ringing a central grass lawn, while tent-friendly sites sit around the loop on a small knoll sporting sagebrush plants and other natural vegetation. The campground is immaculately maintained, with spotless barbeque grills and perfectly manicured grass. Perhaps its only negative aspect is the lack of tree cover for the sites.

Campsites, facilities: There are 38 sites for tents and RVs up to 30 feet in length. Sites 18–22 have full hook-ups. Sites 17 and 29 are wheelchair accessible. Covered picnic tables, barbeque grills, drinking water, modern restrooms, boat ramp, floating dock, garbage service, and a dump station are provided. Leashed pets permitted.

Reservations, fees: Reservations are accepted at 800/322-3770 or online at www.reserveamerica.com for the single and group sites. Single site reservations must be made a minimum of two days in advance and can be arranged up to 16 weeks in advance. Full hook-up sites are $25, tent sites are $13, extra vehicles are $8, and day use is $7. Open year-round.

Directions: From Vernal, drive north on Hwy.

191 for 11.5 miles. Turn right into Red Fleet State Park.

GPS Coordinates: N 40° 35.107' W 109° 26.607'

Contact: Red Fleet State Park, 435/789-4432, http://stateparks.utah.gov/stateparks/parks/red-fleet/

75 STEINAKER STATE PARK

Scenic rating: 7

north of Vernal

Map 4.2, page 184

Steinaker State Park hugs the shores of Steinaker Reservoir, a midsize reservoir north of Vernal. The lake offers fishing for rainbow and brown trout, green sunfish, bluegill, and largemouth bass. Wildlife at the park includes mule deer, jackrabbits, porcupines, elk, and coyotes. Boating, waterskiing, and swimming are popular on the lake, which can be accessed by a paved boat ramp with a floating dock. There are white sandy beaches for swimmers. The campground at Steinaker sits among sagebrush and junipers with a few larger cottonwood trees casting some shade on the sites. The campground has two tiers of sites, some raised up on a gently sloped hill, and others on lower, flatter ground. The lower sites offer better tent pitching opportunities on level tent pads. The sites are fairly tightly spaced and don't allow much privacy.

Campsites, facilities: There are 30 sites for tents and RVs up to 30 feet in length and one group area for 25–50 people. Sites 3–8 have full hook-ups. Sites 24 and 25 are wheelchair accessible and have raised tent pads. Amenities include covered picnic tables on cement pads, fire pits, barbeque grills, modern restrooms, drinking water, a dump station, a fish-cleaning station, and garbage service. Leashed pets permitted.

Reservations, fees: Reservations are accepted at 800/322-3770 or online at www.reserveamerica.com. Single site reservations must be made a minimum of two days in advance and can be arranged up to 16 weeks in advance, and group site reservations can be arranged up to 11 months in advance. There is a nonrefundable reservation fee of $8 for individual sites and $10.25 for group sites. Sites are $13, full hook-up sites are $25, the group site is $3 pp, and day use is $7. Open year-round.

Directions: From Vernal, drive north on Hwy. 191 for seven miles. Turn left and continue 1.7 miles to the Steinaker State Park.

GPS Coordinates: N 40° 31.082' W 109° 32.558'

Contact: Steinaker State Park, 435/789-4432, http://stateparks.utah.gov/stateparks/parks/steinaker/

76 DINOSAURLAND/ VERNAL KOA

Scenic rating: 3

in Vernal

Map 4.2, page 184

Vernal KOA is located north of Vernal on Highway 191, making it centrally located to explore Dinosaur National Monument and Steinaker and Red Fleet State Parks. The KOA is a spacious campground with a nice blend of tent camping, RV sites, and cabins. Aspen and cottonwood trees provide shade for the RV sites, which extend away from the office in a series of rows toward distant red-rock cliffs. The tent and cabins are set away from the RV section of the park, creating good separation for the different camping styles. The tent sites are on a green grass lawn with fire pits and are within plain view of each other. For an RV park, the tent area is very nice. The RV side of the park has a paved loop with pull-through sites for easy in-and-out. There is an extensive playground including miniature golf and a swimming pool for entertainment. In my opinion, this is the best RV park in the Vernal area.

Campsites, facilities: There are 52 full hook-up, pull-through RV (20, 30, 50 amps) sites, five back-in full hook-up sites, and eight partial hook-up sites for RVs up to 80 feet in length. There are also 15 tent sites, seven cabins, and two lodges. Amenities include picnic tables, fire pits, drinking water, a swimming pool (open seasonally), WiFi, cable TV, miniature golf, a playground, volleyball net, modern restrooms with showers, garbage service, and a dump station. Laundry and bicycle rentals are available. Leashed pets permitted.

Reservations, fees: Reservations are accepted at 800/562-7574 or online at https://koa.com/where/ut/44152/reserve/. Full hook-up sites are $35.99, partial hook-up sites are $29.95, tent sites are $25, and the cabins and lodges are $49.99–139.99. Open April 1 through October 31.

Directions: From the intersection of Hwy. 40 and Hwy 191 in Vernal, drive north on Highway 191 for one mile. Dinosaurland KOA is on the right side of the road.

GPS Coordinates: N 40° 28.193' W 109° 31.717'

Contact: Dinosaurland/Vernal KOA, 435/789-2148, www.koa.com/where/ut/44152/

77 FOSSIL VALLEY RV PARK

Scenic rating: 2

in Vernal

Map 4.2, page 184

Fossil Valley RV Park is in downtown Vernal on Hwy. 40. The campground is in an urban setting, on a major highway next to an auto repair shop. The RV park occupies a long, narrow yard with limited views up toward Dinosaur National Monument through the trees. Tightly spaced sites have grass lawns and are shaded by a mix of oak, aspen, box elder, and cottonwood trees. There are paved pull-through sites for RVs and trailers, and storage units are available for long-term residents.

Campsites, facilities: There are 18 sites (available for overnight stay) for RVs up to 60 feet in length. Picnic tables, drinking water, modern restrooms with showers, a dump station, and WiFi are provided. Laundry and cable TV are available. Leashed pets permitted.

Reservations, fees: Reservations are accepted at 435/789-6450. Full hook-up (30, 50 amps) sites are $27.50, partial hook-ups sites are $27, electricity-only sites are $26.50, and cable TV is $1.50. Open year-round.

Directions: From the intersection of Hwy. 191 and Hwy. 40 in Vernal, drive west 1.2 miles on Hwy. 40. Fossil Valley RV Park will be on the left side of the road.

GPS Coordinates: N 40° 27.110' W 109° 32.865'

Contact: Fossil Valley RV Park, 435/789-6450, www.fossilvalleyrvpark.com/

78 OUTLAW TRAIL RV PARK

Scenic rating: 3

south of Dinosaur National Monument

Map 4.2, page 184

Outlaw RV Park is conveniently located across Highway 40 from the Dinosaur National Monument Headquarters and Canyon Area Visitor Center. It's the closest RV Park to the monument. It's in a rural setting, although it's right on a major highway. For being so close to such beautiful country, Outlaw Trail RV Park isn't much to look at. A paved loop leads to a gravel yard and RV slips packed like sardines behind the office and laundry facilities. There are narrow grass strips between some of the parking slips and a basketball hoop and small playground for kids. Lots of permanent residents affect the character of the place, giving it more of a trailer park atmosphere than a RV campground. There are some limited views up to the Split Mountain formation in Dinosaur National Monument.

Campsites, facilities: There are 111 full hook-up (20-, 30-, and 50-amp) sites for RVs up to

60 feet in length and a limited tenting area. Picnic tables (at some of the sites), WiFi, playground, basketball hoop, drinking water, garbage service, and modern restrooms with showers are provided. Laundry is available. Leashed pets permitted.

Reservations, fees: Reservations are accepted at 435/781-6000. RV sites are $28.60 and tent sites are $14. Open April through November.

Directions: From the intersection of Hwy. 40 and Rte. 149 in Jensen, drive one block east on Hwy. 40. Outlaw Trail RV Park will be on the right side of the road.

GPS Coordinates: N 40° 22.159' W 109° 20.407'

Contact: Outlaw Trail RV Park, 435/781-6000.

79 SPLIT MOUNTAIN

Scenic rating: 9

in Dinosaur National Monument

Map 4.2, page 184

Split Mountain is a group area located on the scenic loop at Dinosaur National Monument. As the name implies, Split Mountain Campground sits across the river from a violently beautiful upheaval of red-and-yellow desert sandstone that has been divided by the calm yet powerful waters of the Green River. The river flanks the campground's east side, and an immaculate modern boat ramp (for multiday white-water rafting trips through the Split Mountain Gorge from Rainbow Park) is located just north of the campground. Nearby is the trailhead for the Desert Voices Nature Trail, a gently looping two-mile track through and around the area's intriguing rock formations. Midsize cottonwood trees shade the flat grass and sagebrush grounds. Long-eared jackrabbits can be seen hopping between well-spaced sites or in the picnic area.

Campsites, facilities: There are four group sites for up to 20 people per site, or 80 total.

Picnic tables, fire grills, drinking water (available seasonally), flush toilets (vault toilets only in the winter), garbage service, and aluminum recycling are provided. Firewood is available. Leashed pets permitted.

Reservations, fees: Reservations are required from Memorial Day to Labor Day and are accepted at 435/781-7759 or by mailing or faxing in the form at www.nps.gov/dino/planyourvisit/upload/splitmountainreserve.pdf. A $10 nonrefundable reservation fee is charged, and the group site fee is $25 per night. Camping during the off-season (mid-October through mid-April) is free and on a first-come, first-served basis. Open year-round.

Directions: From Vernal, drive east on Hwy. 40 for 13.4 miles to Jensen. Turn left on Rte. 149 and travel 8.8 miles. Turn left and continue one mile to the Split Mountain Campground.

GPS Coordinates: N 40° 26.658' W 109° 15.200'

Contact: Dinosaur National Monument, 435/781-7700, www.nps.gov/dino/planyourvisit/splitmountaincampground.htm

80 GREEN RIVER

Scenic rating: 8

in Dinosaur National Monument

Map 4.2, page 184   BEST

Green River Campground is located along the scenic auto tour of the Tilted Rocks in Dinosaur National Monument. Green River is the main campground in Dinosaur for individual camping. It sits on the banks of the muddy Green River after it flows out of the Split Mountain Canyon and before it enters a series of wide, meandering oxbows. While not as spectacular as Split Mountain, the scenery at Green River Campground is stupendous. The wildly crumpled and varied sandstone formations of the park, combined with the abundant life along the river's edge, make for an unforgettable setting. Unlike so many scenic destinations, the campgrounds at Dinosaur are located at the heart of the beauty, right beneath the towering rocks and beside the architect of it all, the Green River. This location at the center of the scenery makes Green River Campground one of the best public campgrounds for RVs in Utah. The paved loop leads to sites set under big cottonwood trees among sagebrush and Mormon Tea shrubs. The sites are close together and don't offer much privacy because of the campground's open layout and busy nature. There's fishing on the Green River, but be aware it's illegal to keep any of the threatened or endangered fish of the Upper Colorado River, including Colorado squawfish, humpback chub, bonytail chub, and razorback suckers.

Campsites, facilities: There are 88 sites for tents and RVs up to 32 feet in length. Picnic tables, fire grills, flush toilets, an amphitheater, drinking water, garbage service, and aluminum recycling are provided. Firewood is available. Leashed pets are permitted.

Reservations, fees: Reservations are not accepted. Sites are $12. Open mid-April through mid-October.

Directions: From Vernal, drive east on Hwy. 40 for 13.4 miles to Jensen. Turn left on Rte. 149 and travel 10.2 miles. Turn left and continue 0.5 mile to the Green River Campground.

GPS Coordinates: N 40° 25.342' W 109° 14.691'

Contact: Dinosaur National Monument, 435/781-7700, www.nps.gov/dino/planyour-visit/greenrivercampground.htm

81 RAINBOW PARK

Scenic rating: 9

in Dinosaur National Monument

Map 4.2, page 184 **BEST (**

Rainbow Park is a small campground at the put-in for Green River raft trips through Split Mountain Canyon. Rainbow Park can only be accessed by a dirt road but is well worth the journey, especially if you appreciate getting off the beaten path. On the way to Rainbow Park you'll pass McKee Spring Petroglyphs, one of the best, most accessible petroglyph panels anywhere in Utah. A collection of at least a dozen different panels lines the cliffs above the wash on both sides of the road. The panels can be reached via a short trail. This rock art is done in the classic Vernal style of the Fremont Indians and is around 1,000 years old. Rainbow Park sits on the outside of a huge sweeping bend on the Green River and is the boat launch for river rafting and a good fishing spot. Anglers should be aware that keeping endangered Upper Colorado River species is prohibited: Colorado squawfish, humpback chub, bonytail chub, and razorback suckers are all protected species. The sites sit above the river on a small bluff under broad-leaved deciduous trees. There are good, flat dirt tent pads and plenty of parking for RVs or boat trailers. Views from the site look out over the river and up to the beautiful red rock architecture of Rainbow Park. This is the quietest and least visited campground in the Utah section of Dinosaur National Monument.

Campsites, facilities: There are three sites. Picnic tables, fire grills, vault toilets, a boat ramp, garbage service, and aluminum recycling are provided. There is no drinking water. Leashed pets permitted.

Reservations, fees: Reservations are not accepted. There is no fee. Open year-round, but the access road is not maintained during the winter.

Directions: From Vernal, drive north on Hwy. 191 for 0.8 mile and turn right onto 3500 S (Brush Creek Road). After seven miles, turn left, drive 4.1 miles, and turn right onto the gravel road. Travel 12 miles, turn right, and continue one mile to the Rainbow Park Campground.

GPS Coordinates: N 40° 29.723' W 109° 10.456'

Contact: Dinosaur National Monument, 435/781-7700, www.nps.gov/dino/planyour-visit/rainbowparkcampground.htm

RED ROCKS AND EASTERN UTAH

© MIKE MATSON

BEST CAMPGROUNDS

Utah's eastern region is a red rock playground

for adventurers of all walks of life. This desert environment holds universal appeal to people from across the globe. It is a landscape of layers, where thousands of feet of sandstone bedrock have been exposed by the tectonic lifting and the erosive forces of wind, water, and time. At least eight distinct layers of sandstone have been exposed in the deep canyons carved by the Colorado and Green Rivers. This exposed rock landscape is on display in two distinctly beautiful national parks, Arches and Canyonlands.

Arches National Park was made famous by Edward Abbey's classic desert love letter *Desert Solitaire*, published in 1968. The novel recounts Abbey's ponderings from three seasons he spent working as a ranger in what was then Arches National Monument. The park's popularity has grown astronomically since then, but the red-rock landscape that makes it so special has stayed the same. The arches, bridges, fins, and pillars of the red rock wonderland are the result of the combined forces of extreme temperatures, water, ice, wind, and the gradual movement of an underground salt bed. The salt was deposited by an ancient ocean that covered the region some 300 million years ago. The inland sea evaporated, leaving behind a thick (thousands of feet in places) layer of salt, which was eventually covered with sedimentary rock. Over time, the rock exerted pressure on this salt layer, which in turn became unstable and began to flow. This dynamic layer shifted, buckled, and even liquefied in places, causing the overlying rocks to do the same. The rest of the story is the result of millions of years of physical weathering and erosion. Wind, water, ice, and gravity have slowly sculpted one of the most thrilling landscapes on the planet.

While Canyonlands isn't far from Arches, it offers a vastly different yet equally impressive landscape. Two of the Southwest's major rivers, the Green and the Colorado, come together in the bowls of Canyonlands in Cataract Canyon. Aside from the Grand Canyon, there is no more awesome vista in the American Southwest than the view down from Dead Horse Point State Park to the confluence of these two mud-choked waterways. Standing on the canyon rim, visitors can see 300 million years of geologic strata at one time. In total, 8,000 feet of rock are visible, from the top of the 12,000-foot La Sal Mountains to the river level at 4,000 feet. It's a mind-boggling scene – and one worth experiencing. Canyonlands offers three distinct regions: the Island in the Sky, the Maze, and the Needles. Each has its own charms, but all have one thing in common: the farther you explore into the backcountry, the more beauty they reveal.

These two national parks by no means encapsulate the slick-rock experience, as the canyons, buttes, mesas, and red rock geography spread out beyond their borders in every direction. The Bureau of Land Management (BLM) owns and manages much of the land adjacent to the national parks, where as many natural wonders are waiting to be enjoyed as in the parks themselves. There's more freedom to enjoy the landscape in different ways on BLM land, and you'll find rock climbers, hikers, mountain bikers, motorcyclists, and ATV drivers exploring it with gusto. There are easy hikes to beautifully weird arches, relaxing rafting trips on the silt-laden brown waters of the Colorado, or epic bike rides on Kokopelli's Trail. However you experience this region, it'll be more satisfying if you step out into the environment. Make the effort to get out and breathe in the bone-dry desert air, take off your shoes and wiggle your toes in the baking red sand, or dip a hand in the frigid and murky waters of the Colorado.

Most visitors drive the national park loops, look at the rock features, and call it a day. They're missing the essence of the landscape they came to see. Go find the subtlety of the desert – listen to the wind, feel the heat, and get to know it on its own terms.

There's a surprising diversity of campgrounds in the region, from alpine forest camps among quaking aspen in the La Sal Mountains to desert sites tucked into wild-mushroom-shaped rock forms at Goblin Valley State Park to full-service RV parks on the quiet banks of the Green River to some of the least visited wilderness in our country in the remote Maze district of Canyonlands National Park. Whatever your favorite way to camp, you'll find it here, so bring your backpack, bike, Jeep, skis, camera, boots, harness, or RV. Go out and discover the secrets of this corner of the desert. It'll satisfy your curiosity and keep you coming back for more. There's far too much to see in one trip, so realize you're not alone in wishing you could do more. But by all means, get started – you'll be happy you did!

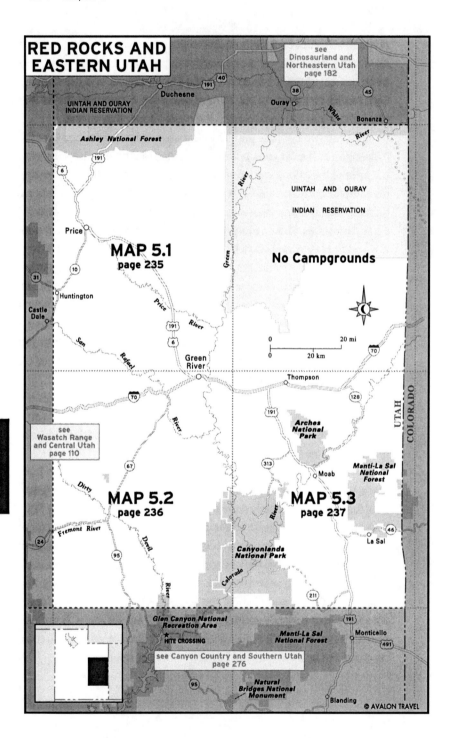

RED ROCKS AND EASTERN UTAH

see
Dinosaurland and
Northeastern Utah
page 182

Duchesne

Ouray

Bonanza

UINTAH AND OURAY
INDIAN RESERVATION

Ashley National Forest

UINTAH AND OURAY

INDIAN RESERVATION

No Campgrounds

Price

MAP 5.1
page 235

Huntington

Castle
Dale

0   20 mi

0   20 km

San Rafael River

Price River

Green
River

Thompson

see
Wasatch Range
and Central Utah
page 110

Arches
National
Park

Moab

Manti-La Sal
National
Forest

Dirty

MAP 5.2
page 236

MAP 5.3
page 237

Fremont River

Devil

La Sal

Canyonlands
National Park

Colorado River

UTAH

COLORADO

Glen Canyon National
Recreation Area

HITE CROSSING

Manti-La Sal
National Forest

Monticello

see Canyon Country and Southern Utah
page 276

Natural
Bridges National
Monument

Blanding

© AVALON TRAVEL

Map 5.1

Campgrounds 1-5
Pages 238-240

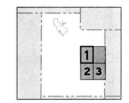

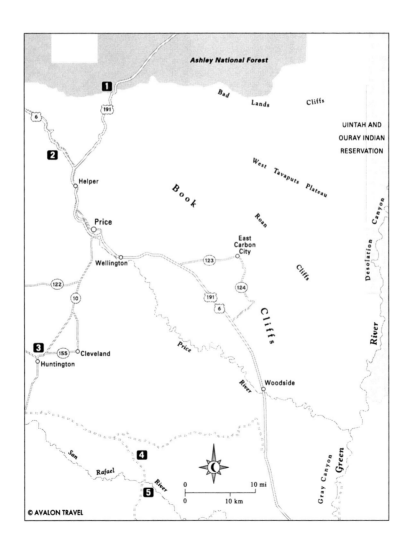

Map 5.2

Campgrounds 6-9
Pages 240-242

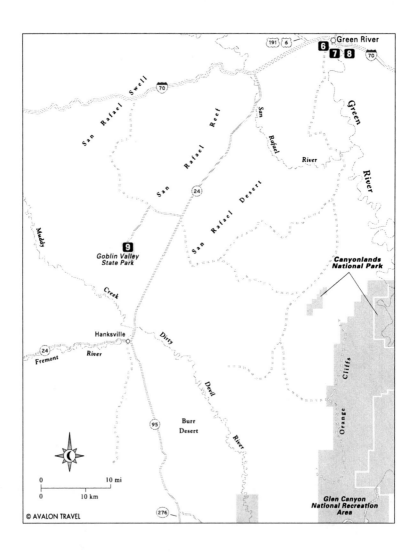

Map 5.3

Campgrounds 10-57
Pages 243-271

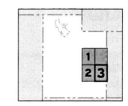

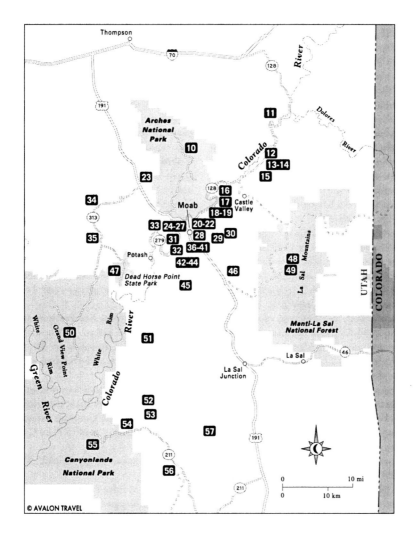

1 AVINTAQUIN

Scenic rating: 7

north of Price Canyon in Ashley National Forest

Map 5.1, page 235

Avintaquin Campground is located on the southern border of Ashley National Forest on Argyle Ridge. Argyle Ridge is a western arm of the West Tavaputs Plateau, a region the BLM is considering for oil and natural gas development. The campground is quiet despite being near Highway 191; it doesn't get a lot of use. The gravel loop has well-spaced sites in an aspen and Engelmann spruce forest. Many of the trees have been killed by bark beetles, but enough remain to provide plenty of shade and cover for the campsites. The forest setting is pleasant even in midsummer and provides a place to get away from it all. Tons of butterflies can be seen landing on the wildflowers between the sites, and deer may be spotted in the meadows near the campground entrance. Avintaquin is a forest retreat with simple yet adequate facilities.

Campsites, facilities: There are 17 individual sites for tents and RVs up to 30 feet in length. Site 10 is a group site for up to 50 people. Picnic tables, fire pits, vault toilets, and garbage service are provided. There is no drinking water. Leashed pets permitted.

Reservations, fees: Reservations are accepted at 877/444-6777 or online at www.recreation. gov and must be made a minimum of five days in advance. Individual sites are $5 and the group site is $25. Open late May through September.

Directions: From Price, drive 10 miles north on Hwy. 6 and turn northeast (right) onto Hwy. 191. Travel 15 miles on Hwy. 89 and turn left. Continue 1.1 miles and turn right into Avintaquin Campground.

GPS Coordinates: N 39° 53.020' W 110° 46.535'

Contact: Duchesne Ranger District, 435/738-2482.

2 PRICE CANYON

Scenic rating: 8

north of Price in the Price Canyon Recreation Area

Map 5.1, page 235

Price Canyon is located on Ford Ridge in the BLM's Price Canyon Recreation Area. The campground has good vistas across the Price Canyon to the distant Argyle Ridge and West Tavaputs Plateau. The camp loop sits among a mature ponderosa and pinyon pine forest. Scrub gambel oaks, sagebrush, and tall grass grow around the sites on the forest floor. The campground is relatively small and has well-spaced, walk-in sites branching off the gravel loop. The sites enjoy a good mix of shade and sun. Three group areas at Price Canyon are set among a particularly lovely grove of ponderosas. A nature trail heads out from the upper group area. There's rock climbing in the nearby Spring Canyon, and Price Canyon is the closest campground for climbers. In fact, it's one of the few campgrounds near Price.

Campsites, facilities: There are 18 sites and three group picnic areas. Picnic tables, fire grills, picnic area, and vault toilets are provided. There is no drinking water. Leashed pets permitted.

Reservations, fees: Reservations are accepted for the group picnic areas at 435/636-3600. Campsites are $8. Open mid-May through mid-October, weather permitting.

Directions: From Price, drive north on Hwy. 6 for 12 miles and turn left at the Price Canyon Recreation sign. Continue three miles up a steep, winding road to Price Canyon Campground.

GPS Coordinates: N 39° 45.612' W 110° 54.998'

Contact: BLM Price Field Office, 435/636-3600, www.blm.gov/ut/st/en/fo/price/recreation/pricerec.html.

❸ HUNTINGTON STATE PARK
🏊 🛶 🚐 ❄ 🏕 ♿ 🚗 ⛺

Scenic rating: 5

northeast of Huntington

Map 5.1, page 235

Camping here feels a bit like camping in a city park, with open grassy campsites and a paved parking loop next to the North Huntington Reservoir. The park is located in the Castle Valley at an elevation of almost 6,000 feet. At sunrise in early May, the distant red rock buttes, still holding the winter's snow, reflected in the calm waters of the lake. The lake is the impetus for the campground, providing summer fun in the form of boating, fishing, and swimming. Warm water temperatures in summer months and an excellent boat ramp make it a perfect spot for waterskiing. Sport-fishing species include largemouth bass, bluegill, green sunfish, channel catfish, and rainbow, brown, and tiger trout. In colder months, ice fishing is popular here as well. In addition to being a popular spot for water recreation, Huntington is a good place to break up a long drive, about midway between the mountains of northern Utah and southern desert destinations like Lake Powell and Moab.

Campsites, facilities: There are 22 campsites for tents or RVs up to 45 feet in length. Picnic tables, barbeque grills, modern restrooms with showers, a boat ramp, pull-through sites, a dump station, and drinking water are provided. Firewood is available. Leashed pets permitted.

Reservations, fees: Reservations are available for camping April 15–October 15 and can be arranged by phone at 800/322-3770 or online at www.reserveamerica.com. Single site reservations must be made a minimum of two days in advance and can be arranged up to 16 weeks in advance, with an $8 nonrefundable reservation fee. The fees are $16 for camping and $7 for day use. Open year-round.

Directions: From Huntington, drive northeast on Rte. 10 for two miles. Turn left into Huntington State Park.

GPS Coordinates: N 39° 20.716' W 110° 56.542'

Contact: Huntington State Park, 435/687-2491, http://stateparks.utah.gov/stateparks/parks/huntington/

❹ BUCKHORN WASH
🏕 ⛺

Scenic rating: 8

in San Rafael Swell

Map 5.1, page 235   **BEST (**

This minimally developed campground sits in an alcove of Navajo Sandstone in lovely Buckhorn Wash. Buckhorn Wash, like San Rafael Swell in general, is stunningly beautiful yet relatively undeveloped compared to many of Utah's parks. It offers an opportunity to see the distinctive architecture of the Navajo formation and find solitude at the same time. This area is popular with ATV enthusiasts and rock climbers. It's also just a half mile from the Buckhorn Wash Pictograph Panel. The campsites themselves don't offer anything other than rock fire rings and a natural setting to camp in. You will be able to find a flat sandy spot to pitch a tent or space to park a self-contained camper. This is one of the best free camping options in Utah. In addition to these sites, there are another handful of individual dispersed sites scattered along the road near the Buckhorn Wash Pictograph Panel. The road to the camping area is unpaved, and a four-wheel-drive vehicle is recommended.

Campsites, facilities: There are about a half dozen campsites off two spur roads in the campground. The left road is in better shape than the right, which is best navigated with a high-clearance vehicle. An open-air toilet and fire rings are provided. There are no picnic tables or drinking water. Leashed pets permitted.

Reservations, fees: Reservations are not accepted. There is no fee. Open year-round.

Directions: From Huntington, follow the BLM signs for the San Rafael Recreation Area.

Turn left on Center Street toward Lawrence. Turn left again after 2.8 miles, continue for 0.5 mile, and take the right fork to Buckhorn Draw. After 11.7 miles, you'll see a small campground with a toilet. The campground isn't labeled but is in a huge natural rock amphitheater on the east (left) side of the road. Look for the cave to the left.

GPS Coordinates: N 39° 08.023' W 110° 41.726'

Contact: BLM Price Field Office, 435/636-3600, www.blm.gov/ut/st/en/fo/price/recreation/NofI70.html.

⑤ SAN RAFAEL BRIDGE
🏕 🛖

Scenic rating: 6

on San Rafael River near Buckhorn Draw in San Rafael Swell

Map 5.1, page 235   BEST (

San Rafael River Campground is a BLM-run campground in the San Rafael Swell, one of the lesser-known parts of Utah's extensive canyon country. The campground sits on the floor of an open valley where Buckhorn Wash runs together with the San Rafael River. The valley is surrounded by an array of mesas and buttes skirted by aprons of eroding brown-and-red layers of soil and sandstone. The distinctive butte Bottleneck Peak stands guard over the campground. The campground is a short distance from the Buckhorn Wash Pictograph Panel, a substantial display of ancient rock paintings. These figures and images were painted over 2,000 years ago by the Barrier Canyon culture. Unfortunately, the campground doesn't do its surroundings justice. An unimpressive 12-site loop meanders through the grease wood shrubs and patches of bunchgrass. There is no shade in the campground, and the facilities are minimal. If you don't mind going without a picnic table, consider exploring the less developed camping a short distance up Buckhorn Wash; you may find it more appealing. The road to and from San

Rafael River Campground is unpaved, so a four-wheel-drive vehicle is recommended.

Campsites, facilities: There are 12 sites suitable for tents and small campers. RVs are not recommended because of the access road. Picnic tables, tent pads, and vault toilets are provided. There is no drinking water. Leashed pets permitted.

Reservations, fees: Reservations are not accepted. The fees are $6 per night. Open year-round.

Directions: From Price, take Rte. 10 south to Huntington. In Huntington, follow the BLM signs for the San Rafael Swell Recreation Area, taking a left on Center Street toward Lawrence. Take another left after 2.8 miles, follow the road for 0.5 mile, and take the right fork of the road to Buckhorn Draw. After an additional 11.7 miles, you'll see a small campground with a toilet. Continue past this camping area another 0.5 mile to the Buckhorn Wash Pictograph Panel. From the panel it's about four miles to the San Rafael River Campground.

GPS Coordinates: N 39° 04.778' W 110° 40.004'

Contact: BLM Price Field Office, 435/636-3600, www.blm.gov/ut/st/en/fo/price/recreation/NofI70.html.

⑥ GREEN RIVER STATE PARK
🚣 🏕 ♿ 🚐 🛖

Scenic rating: 4

in Green River

Map 5.2, page 236

Green River State Park features an inexpensive nine-hole public golf course at only $10 per round. While nothing like the gorgeous public links at Wasatch Mountain State Park, this open course is a fun opportunity for a casual round and an excellent chance for beginners to play without the pressure of a busy course. The park also features a well-maintained grassy campground with large cottonwood trees providing shade for many of the campsites. Occasionally, near dusk or dawn campers might spot a beaver or muskrat along the calm waters of the Green River. Also look for a variety of birds that intermittently visit the campground, including kingbirds, egrets, herons, hawks, owls, and warblers. The layout feels more like a public RV park than a campground and is definitely designed to accommodate larger vehicles. Tent campers will still find comfortable camping in the grass, but don't expect tent pads or a private wilderness experience. Green River is a good central location to stop for a night on the way to the wonders of Moab or southeastern Utah in general.

Campsites, facilities: There are 42 sites suitable for RVs up to 60 feet in length, and 40 of the sites are appropriate for tent camping. Picnic tables, barbeque grills, drinking water, modern restrooms with showers, garbage service, and a dump station are provided. Leashed pets permitted.

Reservations, fees: Reservations are accepted for camping March 15–October 15 at 800/322-3770 or online at www.reserveamerica.com. Single site reservations must be made a minimum of two days in advance and can be arranged up to 16 weeks in advance for an $8 nonrefundable reservation fee. Camping fees are $16 per night, and day use is $5. Open year-round.

Directions: Take Exit 160 off I-70 in Green River, turn left under the overpass, and take a right on Green River Boulevard (Business I-70). Continue 1.7 miles and turn right into Green River State Park.
GPS Coordinates: N 38° 59.379' W 110° 09.203'

Contact: Green River State Park, 435/564-3633, http://stateparks.utah.gov/stateparks/parks/green-river/.

⁊ GREEN RIVER KOA

🏊 🚣 🎣 🛖 🚴 🚐 ⛺

Scenic rating: 4

in Green River

Map 5.2, page 236

For where it's located, there's a surprising variety of things to do while camping at the Green River KOA. Across the street you'll find the John Wesley Powell Historic River Museum, where visitors can learn all about the fearless river explorer and his historic journey down the Green and Colorado Rivers. If you find yourself inspired by his early river trips and would like to float the river yourself, this calm stretch of the Green River is great place to canoe or kayak. Not interested in the river? Green River State Park's public golf course is within walking distance of the KOA campground. The grounds are well taken care of and offer visitors every option from tent camping to personal cabins. Views from the KOA look south across open plains and rolling desert. Long rows of gravel pull-through RV sites are shaded by broad-leaved deciduous trees. The sites are tightly spaced and offer little privacy, but there are well-watered lawn strips at each site. In the summer, the swimming pool provides a great way to cool down on hot afternoons.

Campsites, facilities: There are 77 sites with full hookups (20-, 30-, and 50-amp) for RVs up to 80 feet, a tenting area, and three cabins. A dog walk, playground, swimming pool (open seasonally), horseshoes, picnic tables, fire pits, drinking water, WiFi, garbage service, dump station, and modern restrooms with showers are provided. Cable TV, laundry, a convenience store, and firewood are available. Leashed pets are permitted (with breed restrictions) but are not allowed in the cabins.

Reservations, fees: Reservations are accepted at 800/562-5734 or online at https://koa.com/where/ut/44154/reserve/. Tent sites are $23.65, partial hookup sites are $29.70, full hookup sites with cable TV are $38.85, full hook-up sites without cable TV are $35.85, and cabins are $52.85 per night. Open year-round with limited service October 15–March 1.

Directions: Take Exit 160 off I-70 in Green River, turn left under the overpass, and take a right on Green River Boulevard (Business I-70). Continue 2.7 miles and turn right into Green River KOA.

GPS Coordinates: N 38° 59.543' W 110° 08.471'

Contact: Green River KOA, 435/564-8195, www.koa.com/where/ut/44154/.

⑧ SHADY ACRES RV PARK
🚐 🏠 🚴 ♿ 🚗 ⛰

Scenic rating: 3

in Green River

Map 5.2, page 236

Shady Acres RV Park borders the east side of the Green River State Park golf course and has a pleasant park feel to its grounds. It's near the gentle Green River and across the street from the John Wesley Powell Historic River Museum. Like the other Green River campgrounds, Shady Acres is a great base camp from which RV users can explore Canyonlands and Arches National Parks or the Moab area in general. It's also a good, central stop on I-70 to break up a long road trip. As the name implies, mature cottonwood trees provide shade and some respite from the relentless summer heat. There are pull-through RV sites in long neat rows. The sites have grassy strips in addition to tall trees. Views from the sites look out to the stratified red rock geology south of town.

Campsites, facilities: There are 97 RV sites with full hookups (30, 50 amps) for RVs up to 100 feet in length, 20 tent sites, and five cabins. Sites 75 and 76 are wheelchair accessible. A picnic area, modern restrooms with showers, drinking water, garbage service, playground, volleyball court, basketball court, WiFi, and cable TV are provided. A convenience store, car and RV wash, and laundry are available. Leashed pets permitted.

Reservations, fees: Reservations are accepted at 800/537-8674 or online at www.shadyacresrv.com. Tent sites are $19.99, truck or van sites with full hook-ups are $26.99, short pull-through sites with full hook-ups are $32.99, extra-long pull-through sites with full hook-ups are $34.99, and cabins are $42. Open year-round.

Directions: Take Exit 160 off I-70 in Green River, turn left under the overpass, and take a right on Green River Boulevard (Business I-70). Continue two miles and turn right into Shady Acres RV Park.

GPS Coordinates: N 38° 59.709' W 110° 09.323'

Contact: Shady Acres RV Park, 435/564-8290 or 800/537-8674, www.shadyacresrv.com.

⑨ GOBLIN VALLEY STATE PARK
🚵 🏠 ♿ 🚗 ⛰

Scenic rating: 7

southwest of Green River in San Rafael Swell

Map 5.2, page 236

Goblin Valley is a state park well worth a multi-day visit. Off the beaten path and often overlooked by the masses flocking to Utah's national parks, Goblin Valley is a geologic wonder all its own. A garden of wild-mushroom-shaped red rocks spreads across the valley floor. These deep, burnt red Goblins have been carved into unbelievable shapes by the erosive forces of water and wind. Spend a day hiking through this wonderland and another exploring Little Wild Horse Canyon, a nearby slot canyon. Little Wild Horse is a beautifully tight yet nontechnical slot canyon that is easy to get to, simple to navigate, and accessible to anyone who enjoys a good day hike. The Goblin Valley State Park Campground is new, well designed, and tucked right into some interesting rock fins and hoodoos. The sites sit on the red dirt desert floor and have covered picnic tables and built-up gravel tent pads. There's no vegetation of any kind in the campground, so the sites are all in open view and privacy is limited. There's an excellent group site set off from the rest of the loop. If you only visit one part of the San Rafael Swell, make it Goblin Valley!

Campsites, facilities: There are 25 sites for tents and RVs up to 59 feet in length and one group site for up to 35 people. Site 22 is wheelchair accessible. Amenities include tent pads, covered picnic tables, a dump station, modern restrooms with showers, drinking water, garbage service, barbeque grills and a metal windscreen. Firewood is available. Leashed pets permitted.

Reservations, fees: Reservations are accepted at 800/322-3770 or online at www.reserveamerica.com. Single site reservations must be made a minimum of two days in advance and can be arranged up to 16 weeks in advance, and group site reservations can be arranged up to 11 months in advance. There is a nonrefundable reservation fee of $8 for individual sites and $10.25 for group sites. Single sites are $16, the group site is $75, and the day-use fee is $7. Open year-round.

Directions: From Green River, drive west on I-70 for 11 miles to Exit 149. Drive south on Rte. 24 for 30 miles and turn right at the Temple Mountain/Goblin Valley Junction. Drive west for five miles and turn left (south), continuing six miles to Goblin Valley State Park. GPS coordinates: N 38° 33.705' W 110° 41.896'.

Contact: Goblin Valley State Park, 435/564-3633, http://stateparks.utah.gov/stateparks/parks/goblin-valley/.

⑩ DEVILS GARDEN
🏕 🚻 ♿ 🚐 ⛺

Scenic rating: 9

In Arches National Park

Map 5.3, page 237   BEST (

Arches National Park contains over 2,000 natural sandstone bridges and arches. The whole park has a teetering feel to it, like if the wind blew any harder, huge sculptures of soft red rock might crumble down all around. It doesn't, however, and it makes for some of the most fascinating geology in the world. Devils Garden is the only campground within the park and is conveniently located near some of the best, most popular hiking. Be sure to check out Delicate Arch; the relatively short hike is worth the effort to reach this great scene to photograph. You'll recognize it from Utah license plates and landscape calendars. Rock climbers will get a kick out of scaling Owl Rock, one of the shortest, least demanding desert towers in the area. Kids will love playing on and around the red rock landscape, making this campground one of the best in the state for families. Scrub juniper and pinyon pine trees grow out of the red dirt in the well-designed and spacious campground. The sites are well spaced and provide decent privacy for being in a relatively open desert environment. The sites are open with very little shade, so they can be extremely hot during the summer months. Being the only campground in a busy park, it can be hard to find a spot in any season, but there are slow times in the Garden too. Winter, early spring, and late fall all offer a very different experience in the Devils Garden Campground and in Arches National Park in general. Check with the rangers at the entrance station to see if there is space available before driving the 18 miles to the campground.

Campsites, facilities: There are 52 individual tent and RVs sites (up to 30 feet) for up to 10 people. Two group sites are available for up to 35 or 55 people, depending on the site. Site 7 is wheelchair accessible. Flush and pit toilets, picnic tables, fire grills, and potable water are provided. Bring your own wood or charcoal for fires and grills. Leashed pets permitted.

Reservations, fees: Up to 28 individual sites may be reserved for camping March 1–October 31, anywhere from 240 to four days in advance. The fee is $15 per night. There is a $9 fee for reservations. The 24 unreserved sites are first come, first served and can be booked starting at 7:30 A.M. at the park entrance station or visitors center. Group sites may be reserved between 360 and four days in advance and cost $3 pp, $33 minimum; no RVs are allowed in group sites. For reservations call 877/444-6777 or 518/885-3689 or visit www.recreation.gov. Open year-round.

Directions: From Moab, drive north on Hwy. 191 for five miles. Turn right into Arches National Park and continue 18 miles to Devils Garden Campground on the right side of the road.

GPS Coordinates: N 38° 36.501' W 109° 35.366'

Contact: Arches National Park Visitors Center, 435/719-2299, www.nps.gov/arch/planyour-visit/camping.htm.

11 DEWEY BRIDGE

🏃 🚲 🛥 🐎 🚐 ⛺

Scenic rating: 6

at the north end of the Colorado River Scenic Byway

Map 5.3, page 237   **BEST (**

Dewey Bridge Campground is located just south of the historic Dewey Bridge. The bridge itself was burned in April 2008 when a young boy was playing with matches downstream from the bridge. Built in 1915, the bridge was an important link between southeastern Utah and Grand Junction, Colorado. The campground is the farthest north in a string of 10 BLM campgrounds along the Colorado River on Route 128. The campground is also one of the access points for 140-mile Kokopelli's Trail, which extends from Loma, Colorado, to Moab, Utah. The trail is open to mountain bikes, horses, motorcycles, and ATVs and crosses a combination of improved dirt roads, old Jeep trails, single track, and exposed slick rock. The trail is usually ridden by mountain bikers in six days, traversing the Colorado Plateau and passing through mountains, canyons, and deserts, and is simply one of the best long-distance mountain bike rides in the world. The campground also has a boat ramp accessing the Colorado River, where white-water rafting trips put in. Aside from being a recreation hub, the campground itself is not particularly noteworthy. Recent removal of invasive tamarisk trees and the fire that burned the bridge have left the riverside sites looking blackened and barren. In true multi-use BLM style, cattle were grazing in site 5 while we visited. Sites 6 and 7 are shaded by a canopy of huge cottonwood trees. All in all, it's not a bad spot, but if you're driving in from the north you may want to continue south and explore some of the other BLM campgrounds along the scenic byway.

Campsites, facilities: There are seven sites for tents and small RVs. Vault toilets, fire grills, and picnic tables are provided. There is no drinking water. Leashed pets permitted.

Reservations, fees: Reservations are not accepted. The fee is $10 per site. Open year-round.

Directions: From Green River, drive east on I-70 for 44 miles and take Exit 204. Turn right and drive 2.6 miles southwest to Cisco. Turn right onto Rte. 128 and continue 11.6 miles to the Dewey Bridge Campground on the right side of the road.

GPS Coordinates: N 38° 48.676 W 109° 18.536

Contact: BLM Moab Field Office, 435/259-2100, www.blm.gov/ut/st/en/fo/moab/recreation/campgrounds/highway_128/Dewey_Bridge.html.

12 HITTLE BOTTOM

🏃 🛥 🐎 🚐 ⛺

Scenic rating: 8

northeast of Moab in the Richardson Amphitheater on the Colorado River Scenic Byway

Map 5.3, page 237

Featuring two wide boat ramps on the mud-brown Colorado River, Hittle Bottom is a popular put-in for Moab rafting day trips. The cottonwood-shaded picnic area is a great spot to get out of the midday heat, sit back, and enjoy the hustle and bustle as buses of sunscreen-covered rafters get briefed by their guides before launching off into the unknown. The campground is also the trailhead for the Amphitheater Loop Trail, a three-mile tour through the Richardson Amphitheater, the greater valley of red rock mesas and buttes, named after homesteader and early town leader Dr. Sylvester Richardson, who lived here with his wife in the 1880s. This small campground has a pleasant feel despite recent tamarisk removal.

The overall splendor of the valley, access to the river and hiking trail, and the small size of the campground make it one of the better BLM campgrounds along the upper stretch of the Colorado River Scenic Byway.

Campsites, facilities: There are 12 sites for tents and midsize RVs. Picnic tables, fire grills, a boat ramp, and vault toilets are provided. There is no drinking water. Leashed pets permitted.

Reservations, fees: Reservations are not accepted. The fee is $12 per site. Open year-round.

Directions: From Green River, drive east on I-70 for 44 miles and take Exit 204. Turn right and drive 2.6 miles southwest to Cisco. Turn right onto Rte. 128 and continue 18.2 miles to the Hittle Bottom Campground on the right side of the road.

GPS Coordinates: N 38° 45.603' W 109° 19.544

Contact: BLM Moab Field Office, 435/259-2100, www.blm.gov/ut/st/en/fo/moab/recreation/campgrounds/highway_128/Hittle_Bottom.html.

🔢 LOWER ONION CREEK
🏕 🚐 ⛺

Scenic rating: 7

northeast of Moab near Fisher Towers

Map 5.3, page 237

Onion Creek drains out of Fisher Valley by the wildly sculpted Fisher Towers before its confluence with the Colorado River. The Lower Onion Creek Campground is located along the creek in the Richardson Amphitheater. This broad valley is completely walled in by red sandstone mesas, buttes, and walls. The camp loop of unpaved red dirt and gravel leads to sites among tamarisk trees and sagebrush. Wild grasses grow around the red earth sites. The sites are open and exposed to the fierce desert sun but have incredible views up to the surrounding geology. The open nature of the campground leaves little room for privacy between sites. The

group site at Lower Onion Creek is set off by itself. There's mountain biking leaving from the campground on the Onion Creek Trail (seven miles one-way), open to hiking, biking, and horseback riding.

Campsites, facilities: There are four single sites and one group site for 15–50 people. Picnic tables, fire grills, and vault toilets are provided. There is no drinking water. Leashed pets permitted.

Reservations, fees: Reservations are accepted for the group site only at 435/259-2100. Single sites are $8, and the group site is $2.50 pp with a $10 reservation fee. Open year-round.

Directions: From Moab, drive north on Hwy. 191 for one mile and turn right onto Rte. 128. Continue for 22 miles and turn left into Lower Onion Creek Campground.

GPS Coordinates: N 38° 44.341' W 109° 19.557'

Contact: BLM Moab Field Office, 435/259-2100, www.blm.gov/ut/st/en/fo/moab/recreation/campgrounds/highway_128/lower_onion_creek.html

🔢 FISHER TOWERS
🥾 🐕 ⛺

Scenic rating: 8

northeast of Moab below Fisher Towers on the Colorado River Scenic Byway

Map 5.3, page 237

At the base of the mighty Fisher Towers, a tiny five-site BLM campground is perched above beautiful Richardson Amphitheater. The campground has a commanding view down the canyon to the Colorado River and the wild geography it is responsible for exposing. The towers themselves are massive red fins of rock protruding from the larger mesa to the north. They have a dubious reputation with rock climbers for their scary exposure and dirty, muddy rock. However, the rock is actually better quality than one might expect, and climbing there is a rite of passage for hardcore desert climbers. For everyone else, they are a

© MIKE MATSON

Fisher Towers and the San Juan Mountains along the Colorado River Scenic Byway

beautiful scenic attraction. A 2.2-mile trail starting at the campground wanders through stunning rock forms of gargoyles, pinnacles, fins, and towers. It eventually leads to a close-up view of the Titan, the largest of the towers. The campground is a small loop accessing five simple sites. The tent pads aren't particularly flat, and the whole campground seems to slope down-canyon. While the facilities are unimpressive, the views and proximity to the towers make this campground one of the most scenic in the Moab area. If you enjoy a bare-bones camping experience, you'll love it at Fisher Towers. Sunset is particularly beautiful at the campground, when the dark red towers glow with unique color and intensity, so don't forget your camera!

Campsites, facilities: There are five sites for tents or small self-contained campers or vans. Picnic tables, fire grills, vault toilets, and garbage service are provided. There is no drinking water. Leashed pets permitted.

Reservations, fees: Reservations are not accepted. The fee is $12 per site. Open year-round.

Directions: From Moab, drive north on Hwy. 191 for one mile and turn right onto Rte. 128. Continue for 22 miles and turn right at the sign for Fisher Towers. Travel 2.3 miles on an unpaved road to the Fisher Towers Campground.

GPS Coordinates: N 38°43.528 W 109°18.546'

Contact: BLM Moab Field Office, 435/259-2100, www.blm.gov/ut/st/en/fo/moab/recreation/campgrounds/highway_128/Fisher_Towers.html.

15 UPPER ONION CREEK

Scenic rating: 7

northeast of Moab near Fisher Towers

Map 5.3, page 237

Upper Onion Creek is located in the Richardson Amphitheater under red rock buttes, mesas, and towers. The impressive Fisher Towers and Castle Rock can be seen from the sites. Upper Onion Creek caters to horseback riders and horses. There are two group campsites with a corral that can accommodate up to eight horses. The water in Onion Creek is not recommended for horses because it has a high salt content. The campsites at Upper Onion Creek are accessed via an unpaved loop. The sites are open and exposed to the elements. There's very little vegetation around the sites aside from the occasional sagebrush.

Campsites, facilities: There are two group sites: Group site A is for 8–20 people and up to eight horses, and group site B is for 8–20 people. Picnic tables, fire grills, horse corral, and vault toilets are provided. There is no drinking water. Leashed pets permitted.

Reservations, fees: Reservations are accepted at 435/259-2100. Group sites are $2.50 pp plus a $10 reservation fee. Open year-round.

Directions: From Moab, drive north on Hwy. 191 for one mile and turn right onto Rte. 128. Continue for 21 miles, turn right onto Onion Creek Road, and continue 0.6 mile to the Upper Onion Creek Campground.

GPS Coordinates: N 38° 43.213' W 109° 20.300'

Contact: BLM Moab Field Office, 435/259-2100, www.blm.gov/ut/st/en/fo/moab/recreation/campgrounds/group_campgrounds/onion_creek_reservable.html

16 UPPER BIG BEND

Scenic rating: 4

northeast of Moab on the Colorado River Scenic Byway

Map 5.3, page 237

Upper Big Bend is the farthest north campground in what can be thought of as a complex of six similar BLM campgrounds hugging the bank of the Colorado River. Though the level of development, facilities, and feel of each campground are unique, all share similar views of the surrounding canyon and are closely bordered by the river on one side and the highway on the other. It is well worth your time to check out several of these campgrounds and choose the one that best fits your needs and preferences. For example, in comparison to other campgrounds nearby, Upper Big Bend feels dirty and neglected. Sites were dusty and hot, and there was garbage scattered around the fire grills during our visit. On the bright side, the campground is right across the street from the Big Bend Bouldering Area. This roadside rock-climbing area features at least 15 boulders with more than 75 "problems" or short routes up them. Even if you don't climb, look for the conspicuously chalked holds and imagine trying to pull yourself up on the tiny ledges and edges that make up these routes. You'll be amazed at what people can climb!

Campsites, facilities: There are eight tent sites. Picnic tables, fire rings, and open-air vault toilets are provided. There is no drinking water. Leashed pets permitted.

Reservations, fees: Reservations are not accepted. The fee is $8 per night. Open year-round.

Directions: From Moab, drive north on Hwy. 191 for one mile and turn right onto Rte. 128. Continue along the Colorado River for 8.1 miles to the Upper Big Bend Campground on the left side of the road.

GPS Coordinates: N 38° 38.957' W 109° 29.301'

Contact: BLM Moab Field Office, 435/259-2100, www.blm.gov/ut/st/en/fo/moab/recreation/campgrounds/highway_128/Upper_Big_Bend.html.

17 BIG BEND

Scenic rating: 7

northeast of Moab on the Colorado River Scenic Byway

Map 5.3, page 237

Big Bend is the largest and most developed of this cluster of BLM campgrounds along the Colorado River. Like the others, it sits in the heart of a beautiful desert setting and looks across the river to bold red rock cliffs and the southeastern edge of Arches National Park. Big Bend is a diverse campground that offers users a little bit of everything. There are lots of large open campsites with long parking spots for RVs. There are also smaller sites for tent camping, with tent pads tucked discreetly under oak and tamarisk trees. Some sites even access the river via short trails through the tamarisk. There are three group sites at Big Bend, all featuring covered pavilions: A and B are on the Colorado River and C is across the road in its own canyon. The loop road and parking areas are well-maintained gravel and are accessible to all types of vehicles. There are five overflow sites available across the road.

Campsites, facilities: There are 23 sites; most have adequate parking for large RVs and trailers. There are three group sites: Group site A is for 25–40 people, group site B is for 15–20 people, and group site C is for 15–30 people. All three can be reserved for groups up to 90 people. Site 5 and group sites A and B are wheelchair accessible. Picnic tables (group sites have covered pavilions), fire grills, vault toilets, garbage service, and aluminum recycling are provided. Leashed pets permitted.

Reservations, fees: Reservations are accepted for the group sites only at 435/259-2100. Individual sites are $12, and group sites are $3 pp plus the $10 reservation fee. Open year-round.

Directions: From Moab, drive one mile north on Hwy. 191 and turn right on Rte. 128. Continue along the Colorado River for 7.4 miles to the Big Bend Campground on the left side of the road.

GPS Coordinates: N 38°38.917' W 109° 28.795'

Contact: BLM Moab Field Office, 435/259-2100, www.blm.gov/ut/st/en/fo/moab/recreation/campgrounds/highway_128/Big_Bend.html.

18 OAK GROVE

Scenic rating: 8

northeast of Moab on the Colorado River Scenic Byway

Map 5.3, page 237

Not surprisingly, Oak Grove is a small, quiet tent campground tucked discreetly among a grove of gambel oak trees. For tent campers,

this campground is able to offer both sites with outstanding views of the scenery and others that are private and shaded. Sites 5–7 are particularly nice walk-in sites, shaded and protected by the broad-leaved trees. Sites 1–3 are open and perched above the Colorado River, looking down at its brown waters and up to the surrounding canyon walls. This campground is the most private, quiet, and appealing for tent campers among this group of BLM riverside campgrounds. While the campground is still close to the scenic byway, the protection provided by the oaks makes it feel more private than others along the road.

Campsites, facilities: There are seven tent camping sites for vehicles less than 22 feet. Picnic tables, fire grills, vault toilets, and garbage service are provided. There is no drinking water. Leashed pets permitted.

Reservations, fees: Reservations are not accepted. The fee is $12 per site. Open year-round.

Directions: From Moab, drive north on Hwy. 191 for one mile and turn right onto Rte. 128. Continue along the Colorado River for 6.9 miles to Oak Grove on the left side of the road.

GPS Coordinates: N 38° 38.591' W 109° 28.590'

Contact: BLM Moab Field Office, 435/259-2100, www.blm.gov/ut/st/en/fo/moab/recreation/campgrounds/highway_128/Oak-Grove.html.

19 HAL CANYON

Scenic rating: 7

northeast of Moab on the Colorado River Scenic Byway

Map 5.3, page 237

Hal Canyon is a nice compromise between Oak Grove and Big Bend Campgrounds. It provides a good balance of tent camping with RV sites. Gambel oak trees provide good separation between sites, and the campground has a small, quiet ambience without feeling cramped. There are good views up to the surrounding red rock canyon and of the dirt-choked Colorado River below. Again, compare it with surrounding facilities and choose the one that best suites your style.

Campsites, facilities: There are 11 sites for tents, several of which are suitable for midsize RVs. Picnic tables, fire grills, and vault toilets are provided. There is no drinking water. Garbage dumpsters are available 0.8 mile up the canyon at Big Bend Campground. Leashed pets permitted.

Reservations, fees: Reservations are not accepted. The fee is $12 per site. Open year-round.

Directions: From Moab, drive north on Hwy. 191 for one mile and turn right onto Rte. 128. Continue along the Colorado River for 6.6 miles to the Hal Canyon Campground on the left side of the road.

GPS Coordinates: N 38° 38.516' W 109° 28.603'

Contact: BLM Moab Field Office, 435/259-2100, www.blm.gov/ut/st/en/fo/moab/recreation/campgrounds/highway_128/hal_canyon.html.

20 DRINKS CANYON

Scenic rating: 5

northeast of Moab on the Colorado River Scenic Byway

Map 5.3, page 237

Drinks Canyon is the general name for three mini-campgrounds—Lower Drinks, Drinks, and Upper Drinks—that can effectively be considered one campground. Perhaps the best part of the Drinks Campgrounds is the tunnel view down the canyon toward Moab. At sunset, the filtered light creates the perception of looking down an endless canyon. Sites are surrounded by prickly pear cactus, big sagebrush, and gambel oak trees. The access loop drive is rather rocky for being

just off the highway, and a high-clearance, four-wheel-drive vehicle is recommended. This campground is a cheaper alternative to some of the more developed BLM sites in this area; in this case, the facilities seem to reflect the price.

Campsites, facilities: There are 17 sites suitable for tents. RVs are not recommended. Picnic tables, fire grills, and open-air vault toilets are provided. There is no drinking water. A garbage dumpster is available at the Big Bend Campground 1.2 miles up the canyon. Leashed pets permitted.

Reservations, fees: Reservations are not accepted. The fee ranges $5–8 per site depending on the specific location. Open year-round.

Directions: From Moab, drive north on Hwy. 191 for one mile and turn right onto Rte. 128. Continue along the Colorado River for 6.2 miles to the Drinks Canyon Campground on the left side of the road.

GPS Coordinates: N 38° 38.063' W 109° 29.048'

Contact: BLM Moab Field Office, 435/259-2100, www.blm.gov/ut/st/en/fo/moab/recreation/campgrounds/highway_128/Drinks.html.

21 GOOSE ISLAND

Scenic rating: 5

northeast of Moab on the Colorado River Scenic Byway

Map 5.3, page 237

This campground stares across the Colorado River at the huge Navajo Sandstone wall and rim that is the southern border to Arches National park. The steep, water-streaked face is impressive in its almost featureless purity. Nearby in Negro Bill Canyon, you'll find hiking to Morning Glory Arch and biking on the Porcupine Rim Trail. This is the most RV-friendly campground along the Colorado Scenic Byway. A large, flat, gravel loop driveway is right off the highway and provides easy access for RVs and other big rigs. Tent campers may prefer alternative sites if generator noise bothers them. The recent removal of tamarisk trees left a stark, barren feel to the sites, but this doesn't seem to affect the popularity of the campground.

Campsites, facilities: The 18 sites are all suitable for RVs and tents. There are two group sites: Group site A is for 15–25 people, and group site B is for 20–40 people. Picnic tables, fire grills, garbage service, and vault toilets are provided. Generators are permitted. There is no drinking water. Leashed pets permitted.

Reservations, fees: Reservations are accepted for the group sites only at 435/259-2100. Individual sites are $12, and the group sites are $2.50 pp plus a $10 reservation fee. Open year-round.

Directions: From Moab, drive north on Hwy. 191 for one mile and turn right onto Rte. 128. Continue along the Colorado River for 1.5 miles. Goose Island is on the left side of the road. GPS Coordinates: N 38° 36.580' W 109° 33.484'

Contact: BLM Moab Field Office, 435/259-2100, www.blm.gov/ut/st/en/fo/moab/recreation/campgrounds/highway_128/goose_island.htm.

22 NEGRO BILL CANYON
🚶 🚴 🏕 ⛰

Scenic rating: 5

northeast of Moab on the Colorado River Scenic Byway

Map 5.3, page 237

Negro Bill Canyon is named after a black prospector and rancher named William Gransraff who lived in the area in the 1870s. The canyon is the terminus of the famous Porcupine Rim mountain bike trail, which drops down from the Sand Flats Recreation Area to the east. The trail is a challenging but rewarding descent down sandstone ledges and single track from the canyon rim to the

Colorado River. The trail can be ridden one way by arranging a shuttle or as an all day loop ride. In addition, Negro Bill Canyon features a five-mile round-trip hike to Morning Glory Arch. The campground has recently been cleared of tamarisk trees and has all the appeal of a burned wasteland. Individual campsites are separated by charred black stumps and piles of ashes. There are no visual barriers between sites or privacy of any kind. On a positive note, this does leave open views up to the surrounding beauty of the canyon. Consider traveling a few miles upstream to any of the more attractive campgrounds while this campground recovers from what will eventually be a positive change.

Campsites, facilities: There are 17 tent sites. Picnic tables, fire grills, and open-air vault pit toilets are provided. There is no drinking water. A garbage receptacle is available at nearby Goose Island Campground. Leashed pets permitted.

Reservations, fees: Reservations are not accepted. The fee is $8 per site. Open year-round.

Directions: From Moab, drive approximately one mile north on Hwy. 191 and turn right on Rte. 128. Continue along the Colorado River four miles to Negro Bill Campground on the left side of the road. GPS Coordinates: N 38° 36.807' W 109° 31.874'

Contact: BLM Moab Field Office, 435/259-2100, www.blm.gov/ut/st/en/fo/moab/recreation/campgrounds/highway_128/Hal_Canyon.html.

23 ARCH VIEW CAMP PARK
🏊 🏕 🚐 ⛰

Scenic rating: 7

north of Moab on Highway 191

Map 5.3, page 237

Arch View Camp Park is located north of Moab near the junction leading to the Island in the Sky District of Canyonlands National

Park. It's also the closest RV park to Dead Horse Point State Park. The campground has scenic but distant views to the south of the La Sal Mountains and Arches National Park. Red sandstone cliffs rise above the campground to the west. Arch View is open and often breezy with small cottonwood trees that seem to provide little protection from the elements. The camp loop is gravel and leads to long rows of pull-through RV slips. The sites are close together and lack privacy. Tepees decorate the grounds around the office and an old, faded barn adds character to the resort. This full-service RV resort is the northernmost of its kind in the Moab area.

Campsites, facilities: There are 60 full hook-up (30, 50 amps) sites, 20 tent sites, and 14 cabins. Picnic tables, barbeque grills, pull-through sites, WiFi, volleyball court, swimming pool, modern restrooms with showers, garbage service, dump station, and tent pads are provided. A grocery store, gas station, and laundry are available. Leashed pets are permitted.

Reservations, fees: Reservations are accepted at 800/813-6622. Full hook-up sites are $28.95–35.95, tent sites are $18.95, and cabins are $39.95–97.95. Open March through mid-November.

Directions: From Moab, drive on Hwy. 191 for nine miles and turn right into the Arch View Camp Park.
GPS Coordinates: N 38° 40.618' W 109° 41.257'

Contact: Arch View Resort, 435/259-7854 or 800/813-6622, www.archviewresort.com/

24 RIVERSIDE OASIS RV PARK

🚐 🏕 ♿ 🚙 ⛰

Scenic rating: 5

north of Moab on Highway 191

Map 5.3, page 237

There couldn't be a better spot to have an RV park, equal distance from the center of Moab and the entrance to Arches National Park. This location is relatively close to just about everything you'd want to experience in Moab. Roads lead away from town in every direction like the legs of a spider, each accessing its own recreation opportunities and natural wonders. That's why staying here, just north of town, makes so much sense. The Riverside Oasis is a motel-campground hybrid of sorts, with everything from RV camping to white stucco, Southwest-style cabins. The campground does feel a bit like an oasis, with green grassy campsites shaded by straight lines of cottonwood trees and offering limited views of the surrounding red rock landscape. The tent sites enjoy large grass lawns with barbeque grills. This is one of the smaller, more intimate RV parks on this section of the road.

Campsites, facilities: There are 23 pull-through, full hookup (20-, 30-, and 50-amp) sites with cable TV, 17 large back-in sites with full hookups accommodating RVs up to 60 feet in length, 23 tent sites, six cabins, and a two-bedroom apartment on the premises (the apartment is not wheelchair accessible). Grass tent sites include a picnic table and barbecue grill; no wood fires are permitted. Amenities include WiFi, drinking water, garbage service, laundry, and showers. Pets are $5 extra and are not permitted in the tent areas, cabins, or apartment.

Reservations, fees: Reservations are accepted at 877/285-7757. Tent sites are $20 per night, RV sites with full hookups are $32–36 per night, group tent sites are $6 pp (20 person minimum), cabins are $40–45 per night, and the apartment is $100–125 per night. Open year-round.

Directions: From Center and Main Street in Moab, drive north on Hwy. 191 for 2.8 miles to Riverside Oasis on the left side of the road.

Contact: Riverside Oasis RV Park, 435/259-3424 or 877/285-7757, www.riversideoasis.com.

25 MOAB VALLEY RV RESORT

Scenic rating: 7

north of Moab on Highway 191

Map 5.3, page 237

The Moab Valley RV Resort is north of town near the turnoff for the Colorado River Scenic Byway, which accesses a slew of recreation opportunities including the bike trail at Negro Bill Canyon, the Porcupine Rim Trail, Colorado River rafting, and rock climbing at the Big Bend Bouldering Area. It's also close to the entrance to Arches National Park, which has only one campground option at Devils Garden. Consider Moab Valley a convenient, upscale alternative. The campground offers shady sites under broad-leaved trees. The sites have limited views east of town up to the red rocks and west over the Colorado River. The tent pads are level and made of whitewashed rock. Some of the tent sites are shaded by canopies. The tightly spaced RV sites have narrow grass strips with picnic tables.

Campsites, facilities: There are 69 RV sites with full hookups for RVs up to 60 feet in length, seven with partial hookups, 39 tent sites (some are covered), and 33 cabins. Amenities include restrooms with showers, drinking water, picnic tables, barbeques, a dump station, garbage service, a covered picnic area, gated entry, bike-washing station, seven-hole putting green, swimming pool, hot tub, laundry, WiFi, life-size checkers and chess games, horseshoes, tetherball, and playground. Tent sites include a barbecue grill and picnic table; no water or electricity is provided. Leashed pets are permitted in the RV sites only.

Reservations, fees: Reservations are accepted at 435/259-4469 starting in August for the following year. Tent sites are $20 per night, full hookup RV sites are $35–39 per night, and partial hookup sites for vans or trucks are $28 per night. Cabins are $42–75. Open March through November.

Directions: From Center and Main Street in Moab, drive 2.4 miles north on Hwy. 191 to Moab Valley RV Resort on the left side of the road.

GPS Coordinates: N 38° 36.057' W 109° 34.517'

Contact: Moab Valley RV Park, 435/259-4469, www.moabvalleyrv.com.

26 PORTAL RV RESORT

Scenic rating: 6

north of Moab on Highway 191

Map 5.3, page 237   BEST (

Portal RV Resort is one of the upscale RV parks that line the road on the north end of Moab. As with the other RV parks on this section of road, you couldn't pick a more central location to set up your base camp to explore the wonderland of Moab and the canyon country. The campground is adjacent to Matheson Wetlands Preserve, an 860-acre park owned by the Nature Conservancy, which has a one-mile boardwalk trail that leads to a wildlife-viewing blind. Muskrats, beavers, river otters, northern leopard frogs, mule deer, and over 200 species of birds can be seen in the wetlands. You won't find an RV park with better wildlife-viewing opportunities than this. The RV campground is currently expanding its facilities, adding more sites for big rigs. The trees are new, small, and don't provide much shade, but there are open views of the red cliffs to the north and west. The sites are mostly gravel and tightly spaced, extending in long rows west of the road. The new facilities, especially the pool, bathrooms, and other communal amenities are especially nice.

Campsites, facilities: There are 60 full hookup (20-, 30-, and 50-amp) sites for RVs up to 80 feet in length, 11 partial hookup sites, 10 tent sites, and four group tent sites. A dump station, enclosed dog run, picnic tables, drinking water, garbage service, barbeque grills, cable TV, and WiFi are provided. A general store, ice, laundry, and firewood are available. Leashed pets permitted.

Reservations, fees: Reservations are accepted at 435/259-6108 or online at www.portal-rvresort.com/reservations.html. Full hookup (50-amp), pull-through sites with cable TV are $45, back-in premium hookup (50-amp) sites with cable TV are $35, back-in regular hook-up sites are $31, partial hookup sites are $27.50, tent sites are $17.50, and group tent sites are $8 pp. Open year-round.

Directions: From Center and Main Street in Moab, drive north on Hwy. 191 for 1.7 miles to Portal RV Resort on the left side of the road.

GPS Coordinates: N 38° 35.661' W 109° 34.040'

Contact: Portal RV Resort, 435/259-6108, www.portalrvresort.com.

27 SLICKROCK RV PARK

Scenic rating: 5

north of Moab on Highway 191

Map 5.3, page 237

Slickrock RV is another conveniently located RV park between Moab and the entrance to Arches National Park. The resortlike park has all the amenities you desire, including a pool and game room. Tight rows cram over 100 sites of RVs onto this piece of property, so don't expect lots of privacy. Tent sites are backed up against a fence, which can feel either comforting or claustrophobic depending on your perspective. The tent pads are level, and some are covered with lean-to roofs. Many of the sites are shaded by large cottonwood and aspen trees. The yard is gravel with very little green besides the trees. All things considered, the location is the most attractive part of this campground.

Campsites, facilities: There are 95 full hookup RV sites, 21 sites with partial hook-ups, 11 car camping sites with no hookups, two group tent areas, 54 tent sites, and 14 cabins. Picnic tables, covered tent sites, fire rings, drinking water, garbage service, horseshoe pit, game room, playground, WiFi, cable TV, dog walk, and heated pool and hot tubs are provided. Laundry, convenience store, and showers are available. Leashed pets permitted.

Reservations, fees: Reservations are accepted at 800/448-8873, by email at info@slickrockcampground.com, or online at www.slickrockcampground.com. Full hookups (30 amps) with cable TV are $32; partial hookups are $27. No-hookup car camping and single tent sites are $20, double sites (up to four people) are $28, and group tent sites are $8 pp (10-person minimum). Cabins are $39. Open year-round.

Directions: From Center and Main Street in Moab, drive north on Hwy. 191 for 1.7 miles to Slickrock RV Park on the left side of the road.

GPS Coordinates: N 38° 35.661' W 109° 34.040'

Contact: Slickrock RV Park, 435/259-7660 or 800/448-8873, www.slickrockcampground.com.

28 UP THE CREEK

Scenic rating: 7

in Moab

Map 5.3, page 237

Up the Creek is a unique, privately owned tent campground in Moab. The walk-in, tent-only campground is located in a neighborhood setting along a quiet creek. While the sites are close together on the small lot, they're shaded by a canopy of cottonwood and other broad-leaved deciduous trees. There's a grass lawn to hang out on and beautiful flower gardens for decoration. The setting is truly peaceful. Up the Creek is a couple of blocks' walk from the shops and cafés on Main Street. It's also within riding distance of the Slickrock Bike Trail in the Sand Flats Recreation Area. If you're looking for a cool place to pitch your tent within walking distance of downtown Moab, this is your best option. Nice touches like carts to transport your camping gear from the car to your site show the owners really understand what makes a good tent campground. Travelers familiar with staying at hostels will enjoy this campground's similar feel. The small campground books up fast, so make reservations.

Campsites, facilities: There are 20 walk-in, tent-only sites. Amenities include picnic tables, drinking water, garbage service, and modern restrooms with showers. Pets are permitted for a $5 charge.

Reservations, fees: Reservations are recommended and are accepted at 435/260-1888 and require payment for the first night as a deposit. Sites are $20 for one person, $25 for two people, $30 for three people, $40 for four people, and a $5 charge for dogs. Open March through early November.

Directions: From Center and Main Street in Moab, drive south three blocks and turn left onto 300 S. Continue two blocks and turn right into Up the Creek Campground.
GPS Coordinates: N 38° 34.105' W 109° 32.834'

Contact: Up the Creek, 435/260-1888, www.moabupthecreek.com/

29 SAND FLATS RECREATION AREA

Scenic rating: 9

east of Moab

Map 5.3, page 237   BEST (

Combine expansive views toward the snow-covered La Sal Mountains with front-door access to the some of the most unusual and picturesque off-road terrain in the southwest and you'll have Sand Flats, one of the best campgrounds in the BLM system. Sand Flats is a lively crossroads of recreation and camping and helps make Moab the outdoor adventure epicenter it is. It is the trailhead for two legendary mountain bike trails, Slickrock and Porcupine Rim. Equally popular are the off-road Jeep trails that leave from Sand Flats and the many side roads around Moab.

Sand Flats is actually a complex of many small campground loops, each with a dozen or so campsites. The layout finds a nice balance between campground amenities and preserving the natural setting. Well-distributed sites work in and out of alcoves and fins of small, protruding red rock outcrops. The sites facing east enjoy gorgeous sunset views of the red rock landscape and snowcapped La Sal Mountains.

Campsites, facilities: Campgrounds are broken down into nine separate loops (A through H and Juniper) with a total of 124 campsites. There are two group sites: Radio Tower for up to 20 people and E-1 for up to 16 people. Picnic tables and fire grills are provided. Loops A through H have open-air vault pit toilets. There is no drinking water. Garbage disposal is available at the Slickrock trailhead parking lot. Leashed pets permitted.

Reservations, fees: Reservations are not accepted for individual sites. Group sites can be reserved by calling 435/259-2100. There is a $10 reservation fee for group sites with a minimum charge of $50 per night. The fee is $10 per individual site for up to five people (includes the day-use fee) and a $2 charge for any additional people or vehicles. There is a day-use fee for Sand Flats of $5 per vehicle or $2 when entering on a bicycle, good for three days. Pay camping fees at the entrance station. Open year-round.

Directions: From the intersection of Main and Center Street in Moab, drive east on Center Street to 400 East and turn right. Drive four blocks on 400 East and turn left onto Mill Creek Drive. Continue straight on Mill Creek Drive as it becomes Sand Flats Road. The entrance to the Sand Flats Recreation Area is 3.7 miles from downtown Moab.
GPS Coordinates: N 38° 34.567' N 109° 31.184

Contact: BLM Moab Field Office, 435/259-2100, www.blm.gov/ut/st/en/fo/moab/recreation/campgrounds/sand_flats_recreation.html.

30 JUNIPER

Scenic rating: 9

east of Moab in the Sand Flats Recreation Area

Map 5.3, page 237

Juniper Campground is part of the Sand Flats Recreation Area east of Moab. This beautiful plateau offers sweeping views up to the La Sal Mountains and fascinating red rock terrain. It accesses world-class backcountry adventures in the form of ATV and mountain bike trails like Porcupine Rim and Slickrock. This access is notable not only for its unique beauty, but because BLM ownership and Grand County management make it possible. Similar terrain can be seen in Arches and Canyonlands National Parks but not experienced on a mountain bike, motorcycle, or all-terrain vehicle because of the different rules and expectations of National Park designation. It's a unique spot and should be treated as such. Juniper Campground is more developed than Sand Flats Campground and may be more appealing to those who want a flat parking space, an enclosed toilet, and more structured setting. The campground looks brand new and is in a truly beautiful setting.

Campsites, facilities: There are 124 sites total in Sand Flats Recreation Area. Juniper is the final loop in the recreation area. Picnic tables, fire grills, and vault toilets are provided. There is no drinking water. Garbage disposal is available at the Slickrock trailhead parking lot. Leashed pets permitted.

Reservations, fees: Reservations are not accepted. The fee is $10 per individual site for up to five people (includes the day-use fee) and a $2 charge for any additional people or vehicles.

There is a day-use fee for Sand Flats of $5 per vehicle or $2 when entering on a bicycle, good for three days. Pay camping fees at the entrance station. Open year-round.

Directions: From the intersection of Main and Center Street in Moab, drive east on Center Street to 400 East and turn right. Drive four blocks on 400 East and turn left onto Mill Creek Drive. Continue straight on Mill Creek Drive as it becomes Sand Flats Road. The entrance to the Sand Flats Recreation Area is 3.7 miles from downtown Moab.

GPS Coordinates: N 38° 34.815' W 109° 25.719'

Contact: BLM Moab Field Office, 435/259-2100, www.blm.gov/ut/st/en/fo/moab/recreation/campgrounds/sand_flats_recreation.html.

31 JAYCEE PARK

Scenic rating: 5

northeast of Moab along the Colorado River on Potash Road

Map 5.3, page 237   **BEST (**

Jaycee Park is an intimate, walk-in campground with a communal layout. It's perfect for a large group of climbers who know each other or folks who don't mind mingling with other campers. Rock climbing is available at Wall Street climbing area just west of the campground on Highway 279. The sites are shaded by cottonwood trees and guarded by sandstone cliffs. They offer good, level tenting in the sandy soil. Like Williams Bottom, this campground is right off the road and lacks privacy. The tradeoff is convenience and proximity to great recreation. The Portal Overlook Trail starts in the parking lot, a four-mile round-trip trail that offers views down to the Moab Valley, the La Sal Mountains, the Colorado River, and the south portal. Mountain bikers also use this trail as a way down from the mesa top. Road biking is popular along the Colorado River on Potash Road. Also on Potash Road you'll find a large petroglyph panel marked by signs. This easily accessible panel puts Jaycee Park on the list as one of the best campgrounds for rock art.

Campsites, facilities: There are eight walk-in tent campsites. Picnic tables, metal fire grills, and open-air vault toilets are provided. There is no drinking water. Leashed pets permitted.

Reservations, fees: Reservations are not accepted. The fee is $10 per site. Open year-round.

Directions: From Moab drive northwest on Hwy. 191 for 1.5 miles and turn left onto Potash Road (Rte. 279). Continue 4.2 miles to Jaycee Park Campground on the right side of the road.

GPS Coordinates: N 38° 33.398' W 109° 35.438'

Contact: BLM Moab Field Office, 435/259-2100, www.blm.gov/ut/st/en/fo/moab/recreation/campgrounds/hgihway_279/j__c__park.html.

32 WILLIAMS BOTTOM

Scenic rating: 6

northeast of Moab along the Colorado River on Potash Road

Map 5.3, page 237   BEST (

This BLM Campground is a favorite of adventure-seekers because of its proximity to the Wall Street climbing areas, Poison Spider ATV and mountain bike trail, and Corona Arch hiking trail. In fact, there's a short but sweet crack climb right across from site 6. For those who enjoy the charms of relatively undeveloped camping, this is a low-key spot to stay for the night—or for a week. The sites are well spaced along a gravel driveway paralleling the highway and offer decent privacy. There are good, level tent-pitching options in the red sand beneath large cottonwood trees. Ubiquitous ants roam the sites, so be careful

to keep a tidy camp. With an unbroken wall of sandstone on one side and the highway on the other, things can feel a little cramped. You'll also probably notice the occasional truck barreling by in the night. However, if you're here to scale the rock, kayak the river, or bike and hike the local trails, there couldn't be a more convenient place to set up base camp. Don't miss the huge panel of petroglyphs near Wall Street.

Campsites, facilities: There are 18 sites for tents and small RVs. Picnic tables, fire grills, garbage service, and open-air vault toilets are provided. There are no established tent pads; just choose your spot in the red sand. There is no drinking water. Leashed pets permitted.

Reservations, fees: Reservations are not accepted. The fee is $8 per site. Open year-round.

Directions: From Moab, drive northwest on Hwy. 191 for 1.5 miles and turn left onto Potash Road (Rte. 279). Continue six miles to Williams Bottom Campground, located on the right side of the road.

GPS Coordinates: N 38° 32.311' W 109° 36.233'

Contact: BLM Moab Field Office, 435/259-2100, www.blm.gov/ut/st/en/fo/moab/recreation/campgrounds/hgihway_279/williams_bottom.html.

33 GOLD BAR

Scenic rating: 4

northeast of Moab along the Colorado River on Potash Road

Map 5.3, page 237

Gold Bar is the final of the three BLM campground as you drive southwest on curving Potash Road on the north bank of the Colorado River. The campground is near the trailhead of the short (1.5-mile) but rewarding Bowtie and Corona Arch Trail. Corona Arch is sometimes called Little Rainbow

Arch because of its similar character to the larger, well-known arch on Lake Powell. If you don't have time to visit Lake Powell, this trail is a much easier way to see a beautiful, similar arch. The campground is also only a few miles from the Poison Spider ATV and mountain bike trail, which climbs to the canyon rim and across the Behind the Rocks slickrock plateau. This trail is popular with Jeeps and off-road vehicles for its great vistas atop the plateau. It's also a good introduction to mountain biking in the Moab area. The campground is not the best of the BLM campgrounds located on the Potash Road. The seven individual sites are scattered around the perimeter of a parking lot of river rock and sand. Tamarisk trees line the river and provide limited shade for some of the sites. Like the other campgrounds on Potash, this campground is right off the highway. The group sites are much newer and more attractive than the individual spots, and they overlook the river.

Campsites, facilities: There are seven individual sites and four group sites for 15–30 or 30–90 people, depending on the site. All four group sites can be reserved as one site for up to 180 people. Picnic tables, fire grills, garbage service, and vault toilets are provided. There are paved, wheelchair-accessible pathways from the group sites to the vault toilets. There is no drinking water. Leashed pets permitted.

Reservations, fees: Reservations are accepted for the group sites only at 435/259-2100. Individual sites are $8. Group sites A, B, and C (covered pavilions) are $3 pp, and group site D is $2.50 pp (no covered pavilion), plus a $10 reservation fee. Open year-round.

Directions: From Moab, drive northwest on Hwy. 191 for 1.5 miles and turn left onto Potash Road (Rte. 279). Continue 9.8 miles to Gold Bar Campground on the left side of the road.

GPS Coordinates: N 38° 34.429' W 109° 37.986'

Contact: BLM Moab Field Office, 435/259-2100, www.blm.gov/ut/st/en/fo/moab/recreation/campgrounds/hgihway_279/gold_bar.html.

34 LONE MESA

Scenic rating: 7

north of the Island in the Sky District of Canyonlands National Park

Map 5.3, page 237

Lone Mesa Campground is a new group campground on BLM land north of the Island in the Sky District of Canyonlands National Park. There are five group sites designed for RV campers. The parking lot is huge and can accommodate basically any length RV or trailer. The campground is open and exposed to the elements, so bring plenty of shade. There are wide views out to red rock country around the campground. Lone Mesa offers a good alternative, especially for large groups, to the small, often full campgrounds inside the national park and in Dead Horse Point State Park.

Campsites, facilities: There are five group sites; A, B, and E are for 15–30 people, C is for 15–40, and D is for 10–20. Picnic tables, fire grills, garbage service, and vault toilets are provided. There is no drinking water. Leashed pets permitted.

Reservations, fees: Reservations are accepted at 435/259-2100. Group sites are $2.50 pp plus a $10 reservation fee. Open year-round.

Directions: From Moab, drive north on Hwy. 191 for nine miles and turn west (left) on Rte. 313 following signs to Canyonlands National Park. Continue eight miles on Rte. 313 and turn right into the Lone Mesa Group Area. GPS Coordinates: N 38° 63.365' W 109° 80.643'

Contact: BLM Moab Field Office, 435/259-2100, www.blm.gov/ut/st/en/fo/moab/recreation/campgrounds/group_campgrounds/lone_mesa.html

35 HORSETHIEF

Scenic rating: 7

just north of the entrance to Canyonlands
National Park on Route 313

Map 5.3, page 237

This new campground is an excellent alternative to the limited camping options in the northern part of Canyonlands National Park. The campground is a few miles from the Island in the Sky District of Canyonlands National Park and Dead Horse Point State Park. The large campground sits on a plateau-like landscape with expansive views to the southwest of the 11,000-foot peaks of the Henry Mountains. Well-spaced sites with flat gravel tent pads sit in a pygmy forest of pinyon pine and juniper trees. On the downside, these small trees and the scrubby sagebrush dotting the campground provide little shelter from the sun or wind. In this desert environment that regularly sees summer daytime temperatures above 100°F, this lack of shade is a real concern. Three gravel loops named after different horse breeds lead to sites with good privacy.

Campsites, facilities: There are 60 sites for tents and large RVs. Picnic tables, barbeque grills, garbage service, and vault toilets are provided. There is no drinking water. Leashed pets permitted.

Reservations, fees: Reservations are not accepted. The fee is $12 per site. Open year-round.

Directions: From Moab, drive north on Hwy. 191 for nine miles and turn left onto Rte. 313 following signs to Canyonlands National Park. Continue 12 miles on Rte. 313 and turn right onto a gravel road signed Horsethief Campground. Continue 0.5 mile to Horsethief Campground.

GPS Coordinates: N 38° 35.050' W 109° 48.854'

Contact: BLM Moab Field Office, 435/259-2100, www.blm.gov/ut/st/en/fo/moab/recreation/campgrounds/highway_313/horsethief.html.

36 CANYONLANDS CAMPGROUND

Scenic rating: 5

on Hwy. 191 north of Moab

Map 5.3, page 237

Part of what makes Moab such a popular tourist destination are the galleries, coffee shops, breweries, and bars that give it its unique character among small towns in Utah. If you're interested in staying within walking distance of town, the cluster of RV parks on the north side of town couldn't be more convenient. Canyonlands Campground is one of these full-service campgrounds. More like a mini-resort than a campground, Canyonlands has everything you could ever want for a comfortable stay and more. Long rows of shaded campsites stretch away from the highway to the west. The sites and loop are gravel. There are views from the sites down the Colorado River to the west and up to the entrance to Arches National Park.

Campsites, facilities: There are 66 full hookup sites, 24 partial hookup sites, 50 tent sites, and eight cabins. Picnic tables, fire rings, uncovered or covered tent sites, drinking water, WiFi, cable TV, pet walk, swimming pool, playground, garbage service, and a dump station are provided. Showers, a convenience store, and laundry are available. Leashed pets are permitted but not allowed in the cabins.

Reservations, fees: Reservations are accepted at 800/522-6848. Front tent sites are $23, back tent sites are $20, full hook-up (30- and 50-amp) sites on concrete pads with cable TV are $34, and water/electric sites on gravel pads with cable TV are $31. Group tent sites are $8 pp (10-person minimum), and cabins are $42–47. A three-night minimum is required Labor Day and Memorial Day. Open year-round.

Directions: From Center and Main Street in Moab, drive 0.6 mile south on Hwy. 191 to Canyonlands Campground on the left side of the road.

hiking in the Island in the Sky District, Canyonlands National Park

GPS Coordinates: N 38° 33.875' W 109° 32.987'

Contact: Canyonlands Campground, 435/259-6848 or 800/522-6848, www.canyonlandsrv.com.

37 MOAB RIM RV CAMPARK

Scenic rating: 7

south of Moab on Highway 191

Map 5.3, page 237

The Moab Rim Campark arguably has the best views of the all the Moab-area RV parks. Located south of town, the campground's sites look up at the La Sal Mountains and down the Spanish Valley. The minimally developed grounds retain a natural red rock feel. Scattered broad-leaved trees offer some shade, but many of the sites are out in the open. The tent sites are located on a level, green grass lawn. Being south of town and separate from the other larger RV parks, this campground feels unique, quiet, and private compared to its competition on the north side of Moab. The

pretty views and comfortable grass tenting areas make this a pleasant place to stay.

Campsites, facilities: There are 20 full hookup (30, 50 amps) sites, 10 partial hook-up sites, 20 tent sites, and seven cabins. Amenities include barbeque grills, picnic tables, fire pits, modern restrooms with showers, drinking water, garbage service, WiFi, and a bicycle-cleaning station. A dump station, cable TV, and convenience store are available. Leashed pets are permitted, but not in the cottage and in only some of cabins with a $5 cleaning fee.

Reservations, fees: Reservations are accepted at 888/559-6622. Full hookups with cable TV are $28, full hookups (30-amp) with water are $24, tent sites are $18, and group tent sites are $8 pp (eight person minimum). Cabins are $49–89 per night. Open year-round.

Directions: From Center and Main Street in Moab, drive 2.9 miles south on Hwy. 191 to Moab Rim RV Campark on the right side of the road.

GPS Coordinates: N 38° 32.601' W 109° 31.119'

Contact: Moab Rim RV Campark and

Cabins, 435/259-5002, www.moab-utah. com/moabrim/campark.html

38 SPANISH TRAIL RV PARK
🏠 🚐 ⛺

Scenic rating: 7

south of Moab on Highway 191

Map 5.3, page 237

Spanish Trail RV Park is located south of Moab on Highway 191 in Spanish Valley. Spanish Valley is bordered on the west by a long ridge of red sandstone and on the east by the La Sal Mountains. Both these scenic features can be seen from the sites at Spanish Trail RV Park. The campground is decorated with old wagon wheels and rose bushes. The gravel loop leads to long, pull-through RV sites that are shaded by deciduous trees and feature well-manicured, narrow grassy strips. The sites are close together and don't offer much privacy. The tent area has a grass lawn to pitch your shelter in. The campground is close to the highway, so expect road noise.

Campsites, facilities: There are 60 full hookup (30, 50 amps) sites for RVs up to 65 feet in length, seven partial hook-up sites, and three tent sites. Picnic tables, fire grills, a communal fire pit, a volleyball court, horseshoes, WiFi, cable TV, garbage service, modern restrooms with showers, and drinking water are provided. Laundry and a convenience store are available. Leashed pets permitted.

Reservations, fees: Reservations are accepted at 800/787-2751. Full hook-up sites are $34–36, partial hook-up sites are $28.95, and tent sites are $20. Open March 15 through November 15.

Directions: From Center and Main Street in Moab, drive south on Hwy. 191 for three miles. Spanish Trail RV Park will be on the right side of the road.

GPS Coordinates: N 38° 31.687' W 109° 30.261'

Contact: Spanish Trail RV Park, 800/787-2751, www.spanishtrailrvpark.com/

39 PACK CREEK RV PARK
🏠 🚴 ♿ 🚐 ⛺

Scenic rating: 4

east of Moab on Murphy Lane

Map 5.3, page 237

Pack Creek is tucked away in a rural setting on the outskirts of the east side of Moab. The campground is within biking distance of the Sand Flats Recreation Area, home to the Slickrock mountain bike trail. If you want to stay close to Sand Flats in an RV and would like the amenities of a full-service campground, Pack Creek is a convenient option. The property has limited views of the La Sal Mountains to the southwest. Pack Creek is family-owned and is proud to be 100 percent wind-powered. It draws its electricity from wind farms in Oregon and Wyoming through Utah Power's Blue Sky Program. The campground is behind a trailer park with lots of permanent residents. The trailer park feel spills over into the campground and RV park. The loop and parking slips are gravel.

Campsites, facilities: There are 20 full hookup (20, 30 amps) sites, seven partial hook-up sites (for RVs up to 55 feet in length), 15 tent sites, and a group tent site for up to 200 people. Picnic tables, barbeque grills, drinking water, WiFi, garbage service, a dump station, a playground, and restrooms with showers are provided. Laundry is available. Leashed pets permitted.

Reservations, fees: Reservations are accepted at 435/259-2982, by email at packcreekrv@ frontiernet.net, or online at www.packcreek-campground.com/reservations.asp. Full hookup sites are $25, partial hook-up sites are $20, tent sites are $17.50, and group sites are $5 pp. Showers are free to campers and $4 for noncampers. Open year-round.

Directions: From the intersection of Center and Main in Moab, drive east on Center Street for 0.2 mile and turn right on S 400 E. Continue 0.5 mile to Mill Creek Drive, turn left onto Murphy Lane, and drive 1.3 miles. Take another left, drive 0.9 mile, and turn right into the Pack Creek Campground.

GPS Coordinates: N 38° 32.975' W 109° 30.780'

Contact: Pack Creek Campground and RV Park, 435/259-2982, www.packcreekcampground.com.

40 MOAB KOA

Scenic rating: 7

south of Moab

Map 5.3, page 237

The Moab KOA Kampark is located south of Moab on Highway 191 as it heads out of town. This is one of the more scenic RV parks in Moab, with views of the La Sal Mountains and the red rock cliffs of the Spanish Valley. Being south of town, the KOA is near Ken's Lake and the start to the beautiful scenic loop drive through the La Sal Range. The campground is well taken care of and offers a host of amenities, including a swimming pool to cool off in on hot desert days. There are large, broad-leaved trees for shade between the sites. The sights are tightly spaced and don't offer much privacy. The KOA offers a separate tent camping area that actually resembles a regular campground.

Campsites, facilities: There are 48 full hook-up (20-, 30-, and 50-amp) sites, 25 partial hook-up sites, 38 tent sites, 23 cabins, and two lodges. Amenities include picnic tables, groceries, WiFi, propane, a swimming pool, miniature golf, horseshoes, bicycle rentals, a dump station, laundry, playgrounds, modern restrooms with showers, pull-through sites, garbage service, and drinking water. Leashed pets (with breed restrictions) are permitted, except in the two-room cabins and the lodges, and there's a $10 charge for pets in the cabins.

Reservations, fees: Reservations are accepted at 800/562-0372 or online at https://koa.com/where/UT/44105/reserve/. Full hook-up sites are $32.50, partial hook-up sites are $29.50, tent sites are $23.50, cabins are $48.50–61.50, and lodges are $149. Open March through October.

Directions: From Moab, drive south on Hwy. 191 for four miles (at Mile Marker 121). Turn left into the Moab KOA.

GPS Coordinates: N 38° 31.405' W 109° 31.405'

Contact: Moab KOA, 435/259-6682, www.moabkoa.com/

41 MOONFLOWER CANYON

Scenic rating: 8

southwest of Moab on Kane Creek Road

Map 5.3, page 237

Moonflower Canyon is a narrow, 50-yard-wide sandstone canyon with eight walk-in tent sites. A huge ancient cottonwood tree guards the entrance to the canyon. About half the sites are tucked around a gentle bend in the rock wall and are not visible from the road, providing some privacy. Be prepared, as there are no picnic tables at this site. There are good soft spots to pitch tents in the red sand desert floor. Adjacent to the campground is the Moonflower Canyon Petroglyph Panel. Here you'll find carvings of bighorn sheep, deer, and other mysterious characters. Perhaps more interesting is the log ladder system the ancients built into the rock chimney to the left of the carvings. This is probably the first rock-climbing route in the Moab area, established by the local Anasazi Indians in the 1200s. This route was more practical than fun, allowing access to the canyon rim.

Campsites, facilities: There are eight walk-in tent sites. Fire rings and an open-air vault toilet are provided. There is no drinking water. Leashed pets permitted.

Reservations, fees: Reservations are not accepted. The fee is $ 8 per site. Open year-round.

Directions: From the intersection of Center and Main Street in Moab, drive south on Main for 0.7 mile and turn right on Kane Creek Boulevard. Stay left at the junction with 500 W and continue for 2.4 miles on Kane Creek Road. Moonflower Canyon is on the left side of the road.

GPS Coordinates: N 38° 33.218' W 109° 35.097'

Contact: BLM Moab Field Office, 435/259-2100, www.blm.gov/ut/st/en/fo/moab/recreation/campgrounds/kane_creek_road/Moonflower_Camping_Area.html.

42 KING'S BOTTOM

Scenic rating: 3

southwest of Moab on Kane Creek Road

Map 5.3, page 237

The next five campgrounds line Kane Creek Road as it follows the Colorado River southwest out of Moab, climbs toward Hurrah Pass, and eventually pushes into the northeast corner of Canyonlands National Park. Kane Creek Road accesses off-road Jeep and mountain bike trails, rock climbing, camping, and, of course, endless red rock beauty. The first campground encountered on the way out of Moab is King's Bottom. The campground is 0.1 mile from the trailhead for the Moab Rim Trail. King's Bottom is another riverside BLM campground where tamarisk tree removal has temporarily had a devastating effect on the scenic quality and overall feel of the site. Rings of ash from burned timber and piles of charred tree trunks dot the small campground. This leaves the sites open and exposed to the elements, with little room for privacy. Hopefully these riparian areas can recover quickly and will benefit from the BLM program. In the meantime, it's worth looking for another campground, as there are many comparable options on Kane Spring Road and in the Moab area in general.

NOTE: This campsite is closed for reconstruction until spring 2009.

Campsites, facilities: There are seven tent sites. Picnic tables, fire rings, and open-air vault toilets are provided. There is no drinking water. Leashed pets permitted.

Reservations, fees: Reservations are not accepted. The fee is $8 per site. Open year-round.

Directions: From the intersection of Center and Main Street in Moab, drive south on Main for 0.7 mile and turn right on Kane Creek Boulevard. Stay left at the junction with 500 W and continue on Kane Creek Road for 2.2 miles. King's Bottom is on the right side of the road.

GPS Coordinates: N 38° 33.407' W 109° 34.961'

Contact: BLM Moab Field Office, 435/259-2100, www.blm.gov/ut/st/en/fo/moab/recreation/campgrounds/kane_creek_road/king_s_bottom_camping.html.

43 KANE SPRINGS

Scenic rating: 3

southwest of Moab on Kane Creek Road

Map 5.3, page 237

This privately owned campground has a huge piece of property in a prime location on Kane Creek Road. Kane Springs has views across the Colorado River to sheer, towering walls of red sandstone. The campground consists of two large flat fields along the Colorado River with hookups for RVs on one side and tent sites on the other. A few cottonwood trees in the tent camping area provide some shade. The fields and campsites are wide open and offer little separation or privacy between the sites. Unfortunately, the owners don't appear to have put much effort into the campground. Compared to other nearby campgrounds and RV Parks, Kane Springs doesn't offer much, especially for the price.

Campsites, facilities: There are nine sites with full hookups and 51 sites without hook-ups/tent sites. Picnic tables, restrooms with showers, drinking water, garbage service, and fire grills are provided. Leashed pets permitted.

Reservations, fees: Reservations are accepted for individual sites and are required for the group sites at 435/259-7821. The fees are $22 per site, $27.55 with hookups, $3 for a shower, $5 for an extra vehicle, and $5 extra charge for trailers. Open March 15 through October 31.

Directions: From the intersection of Center and Main Street in Moab, drive south on Main for 0.7 mile and turn right on Kane Creek Boulevard. Stay left at the junction with 500 W and continue on Kane Creek Road for 3.5 miles. Kane Springs Campground is on the right side of the road.

GPS Coordinates: N 38° 32.365' W 109° 35.652'

Contact: Kane Springs Campground, 435/259-7821, www.moab-utah.com/kanesprings/.

sites. Each site has a fire ring, but no other facilities. There is no drinking water. There is a vault toilet available at Hunter Canyon Campground about one mile farther up Kane Creek Road. Leashed pets permitted.

Reservations, fees: Reservations are not accepted. The fee is $8 per site. The pay station is one mile farther up Kane Creek Road at the Hunter Canyon Campground. Open year-round.

Directions: From the intersection of Center and Main Street in Moab, drive south on Main for 0.7 mile and turn right on Kane Creek Boulevard. Stay left at the junction with 500 W and continue on Kane Creek Road for six miles. Spring Site is on the right side of the road.

GPS Coordinates: N 38° 31.068' W 109° 35.726'

Contact: BLM Moab Field Office, 435/259-2100, www.blm.gov/ut/st/en/fo/moab/recreation/campgrounds/kane_creek_road/2.html.

44 SPRING SITE

Scenic rating: 7

southwest of Moab on Kane Creek Road

Map 5.3, page 237

These four campsites scattered along Kane Creek are as low-impact a campground as you'll find. Small tent sites have fire grills and little else, except a beautiful, cool setting near some of the clearest running water anywhere in the southwest. The sites are all shaded by old cottonwood trees, and the tight canyon walls give the area a protected, secluded feel. There are level, soft tent spots along the sandy banks above the creek and on the desert floor. Sites offer scenic views up to the surrounding canyon walls. This minimalist campground is popular with rock climbers who access the nearby Ice Cream Parlor crack-climbing area.

Campsites, facilities: There are four tent

45 HUNTERS CANYON

Scenic rating: 9

southwest of Moab on Kane Creek Road

Map 5.3, page 237

If you've ever wanted to camp in a slot canyon without backpacking to get there, this is the place to come. The canyon walls here don't get as narrow as some of Utah's best slots, but the canyon is steep and very narrow and unique for a walk-in campground. Many of the sites are for walk-in camping only and feel like a backcountry camping experience. Strolling into the nine campsites scattered along the dry wash, you can't help but crane your neck upward at the canyon walls that climb hundreds of feet above. Cottonwood trees provide a splash of green to the red landscape and shade from intense midday sun. Climbers, backpackers, or campers who are used to camping without facilities will feel most at home here. Bring everything you need and enjoy one of the best campgrounds in the Moab area. It's amazing that this secluded campground is only eight miles from the hustle and bustle of downtown Moab.

Campsites, facilities: There are nine tent sites. Fire rings and an open-air vault toilet are provided. There is no drinking water. Leashed pets permitted.

Reservations, fees: Reservations are not accepted. The fee is $8 per site. Open year-round.

Directions: From the intersection of Center and Main Street in Moab, drive south on Main for 0.7 mile and turn right on Kane Creek Boulevard. Stay left at the junction with 500 W and continue on Kane Creek Road for 7.1 miles. Hunter Canyon is on both sides of the road. GPS Coordinates: N 38° 30.592' W 109° 35.828'

Contact: BLM Moab Field Office, 435/259-2100, www.blm.gov/ut/st/en/fo/moab/recreation/campgrounds/kane_creek_road/2.html

46 KEN'S LAKE

Scenic rating: 8

in the Spanish Valley south of Moab

Map 5.3, page 237

Ken's Lake is a reservoir built in the late 1970s to provide drinking water for Moab residents and irrigation for agriculture. It is sometimes referred to as Mill Creek Reservoir. The lake is located at the base of the La Sal Mountains in the Spanish Valley south of Moab. The little reservoir is popular with anglers who cast for stocked rainbow trout and native brown trout, largemouth bass, and sunfish on its waters. Only nonmotorized boats are allowed on the reservoir. The open campground next to the lake enjoys awesome views of the La Sal Mountains and the red rock geology of the Spanish Valley. In the spring, Faux Falls courses down the red

rock in a torrent of white water just south of the reservoir and can be easily reached by a hiking trail or Jeep trail. The campground is also the trailhead for the 1.9-mile Lake Loop Trail and the 0.8-mile Rock Loop Trail. These trails are open to hikers and horses. The camp loop is gravel and leads to mostly open sites scattered with juniper trees on the red-dirt desert floor. The sites are relatively spread out, and the trees provide some privacy between sites. The parking slips have lots of room for RVs and trailers.

Campsites, facilities: There are 31 sites for tents and large RVs. Picnic tables, fire grills, vault toilets, and garbage service are provided. There is no drinking water. Leashed pets permitted.

Reservations, fees: Reservations are not accepted. The fee is $12. Open year-round.

Directions: From Moab, drive south on Hwy. 191 for seven miles to Old Airport Road. Turn left and continue 0.6 miles to a fork, then turn right onto Spanish Valley Drive. Stay left at the next intersection and after 0.5 mile turn left onto Ken's Lake access road. GPS Coordinates: N 38° 28.615' W 109° 25.352'

Contact: BLM Moab Field Office, 435/259-2100, www.blm.gov/ut/st/en/fo/moab/recreation/campgrounds/ken_s_lake.html

47 DEAD HORSE POINT STATE PARK

Scenic rating: 8

northeast of Canyonlands National Park

Map 5.3, page 237   BEST (

Dead Horse Point is an awe-inspiring place. The park is named after a narrow land bridge leading to a natural corral where, legend has it, cowboys used to round up wild mustangs, take the ones they wanted, and leave the rest to die. While you can't find any dead horses these days, you will find amazing vistas; the park overlooks the meandering

Colorado River and the multilayered canyon it has carved. More than 300 million years of geologic time is visible in the 2,000-foot drop between Dead Horse Point Overlook and the Colorado River. This overlook is as spectacular as any you'll encounter in Canyonlands National Park, making it one of the best spots for landscape photography in the Moab area. Although the Kayenta Campground is set back from the overlook, it still has a commanding view of the beautiful canyon country and rock walls below. The campground is in great shape with paved parking areas set between pinyon pine and juniper trees. The desert campground is mostly open, but wood picnic table dividers offer shade and privacy for the eating areas in the campsites. Drinking water is trucked in 32 miles from Moab, so please conserve water or bring your own.

Campsites, facilities: There are 21 campsites for tents and RVs up to 100 feet in length (all sites have 20-amp electricity hook-ups) and one group site for nine to 30 people. Site 9 is wheelchair accessible. Picnic tables (covered, with shelves, lights, and wind break),

barbeque grills (charcoal only, no wood fires are allowed), flush toilets, pull-through sites, drinking water, aluminum recycling, garbage service, and a dump station are provided. Leashed pets permitted.

Reservations, fees: Reservations are available and may be made a minimum of two days in advance and up to 16 weeks in advance at 800/322-3770 or online at www.reserveamerica.com. The group site may be reserved up to 11 months in advance. There is an nonrefundable reservation fee of $8 for individual sites and $10.25 for group sites. The camping fee is $20 per site, $10 for extra vehicles, and the day-use fee is $10. Open year-round.

Directions: From Moab, drive north on Hwy. 191 for nine miles and turn left onto Rte. 313, following signs to Canyonlands National Park. Continue for 15 miles on Rte. 313 and turn east (left) toward Dead Horse Point State Park.

GPS Coordinates: N 38° 29.122' W 109° 44.427'

Contact: Dead Horse Point State Park, 435/259-2614, http://stateparks.utah.gov/stateparks/parks/dead-horse/.

© MIKE MATSON

view from **Dead Horse Point State Park**

48 WARNER LAKE

🏃 🚲 🏊 🏕 🚐 ⛰

Scenic rating: 8

in the La Sal Mountains

Map 5.3, page 237

Warner Lake is a high mountain lake in the La Sal Range southeast of Moab. The La Sal Mountains are of volcanic origin and are the second-highest mountain range in Utah. Warner Lake offers fishing for brown, cutthroat, rainbow, and brook trout in a cool alpine environment at around 9,200 feet in elevation. The lake, open to nonmotorized boats only, is surrounded by a mix of long grassy meadows and lush forests. The campground sits in an aspen grove accented with an occasional Engelmann spruce or subalpine fir tree. The gravel loop accesses a combination of individual sites, group sites, and an old Forest Service Cabin. Views from the sites look up to Mann's Peak, which rises up to 12,272 feet. A network of trails starts near Warner Lake, leading to Miners Basin (two miles), Oowah Lake (two miles), Burro Pass (four miles), and Beaver Basin (five miles).

Campsites, facilities: There are 20 sites for tents and RVs up to 25 feet in length, one group area for up to 50 people, and one cabin for up to four people. Picnic tables, fire grills, and vault toilets are provided. There is no drinking water. Leashed pets permitted.

Reservations, fees: Reservations are required for the group site and cabin and are available for the individual sites at 877/444-6777 or online at www.recreation.gov; they must be made a minimum of five days in advance. Sites are $10; the group site and the cabin are $50. Open June through October, weather permitting.

Directions: From Moab, drive south on Hwy. 191 for seven miles to Old Airport Road. Turn left and continue 0.6 mile to a fork, then turn right onto Spanish Valley Drive. Stay left at the next intersection and drive 14 miles on La Sal Mountain Loop Road. Turn right at Forest Road 63 and continue eight miles to Warner Lake Campground.

GPS Coordinates: N 38° 31.080' W 109° 16.320'

Contact: Moab Ranger District, 435/259-7155.

49 OOWAH LAKE

🏃 🚲 🏊 🏕 ⛰

Scenic rating: 8

in the La Sal Mountains

Map 5.3, page 237

Oowah Lake offers excellent alpine trout fishing in the La Sal Mountains. The little lake is home to rainbow, cutthroat, brook, and brown trout. The campground is located at around 8,800 feet and offers an escape from the mid-summer heat of the southern Utah desert. The small campground has six tent-only campsites nestled into a dense Engelmann spruce and quaking aspen forest. The thick trees provide good privacy between the sites and plenty of shade. Oowah Lake is the trailhead for the Trans-Mountain Trail system and Burro Pass Trail. Burro Pass Trail is open to hikers and mountain bikers and climbs over 11,200 feet to Burro Pass. The views from the sometimes-rough trail look out over amazing vistas of the red rock country. A short trail also connects Oowah to the nearby Warner Lake.

Campsites, facilities: There are six tent sites. Picnic tables, fire grills, and vault toilets are provided. There is no drinking water. Leashed pets permitted.

Reservations, fees: Reservations are not accepted. Sites are $8. Open June through October, weather permitting.

Directions: From Moab, drive south on Hwy. 191 for seven miles to Old Airport Road. Turn left and continue 0.6 mile to a fork and turn right onto Spanish Valley Drive. Stay left at the next intersection and drive 12.5 miles on the La Sal Mountain Loop Road. Turn right on Forest Road 76 and continue 2.8 miles to the Oowah Lake Campground.

GPS Coordinates: N 38° 30.100' W 109° 16.180'

Contact: Moab Ranger District, 435/259-7155.

50 WILLOW FLAT

🥾 🚴 🏕 ♿ 🚐 ⛺

Scenic rating: 7

in the Island in the Sky District of Canyonlands National Park

Map 5.3, page 237   BEST (

Willow Flat is a small, conveniently located campground in the Island in the Sky district of Canyonlands National Park. The Island in the Sky is an expansive mesa overlooking stunning canyons carved by the Green River to the west and the Colorado River to the east. It is home to the White Rim Road, a multi-day mountain bike ride or four-wheel-drive adventure traversing the wild landscape. Willow Flat is the perfect place to camp if you plan on spending a couple of days in the Island in the Sky District. If you enjoy nature photography, consider spending a night at Willow Flat, waking up early, and taking sunrise photos of Mesa Arch, one of the iconic images of the American Southwest. The campground is also a short walk from the Green River Overlook, one of the best locations to watch or photograph a sunset in Canyonlands. Willow Flat is the only campground in the northern part of the park accessible by paved road. The tent sites have paved parking spots and are scattered among pinyon pine and juniper trees. Deer tracks are visible in the red dirt surrounding many of the sites. The sites are relatively spread out, though the open forest doesn't offer much privacy. Like all the national park campgrounds around Moab, Willow Flat is busy during high season in both the spring and fall. If you want to camp here, arrive early in the day. Expect the campground to fill up every night from mid-March through the end of June and again in September and October.

Campsites, facilities: There are 12 tent sites for tents and RVs up to 28 feet in length. Picnic tables, fire pits, and vault toilets are provided. There is no drinking water. Leashed pets permitted.

Reservations, fees: Reservations are not accepted. The fee is $10 per site. Open year-round.

Directions: From Moab, drive north on Hwy. 191 for nine miles and turn left on Rte. 313, following signs to Canyonlands National Park. Continue on Rte. 313 for 22 miles to the North entrance of Canyonlands National Park. From the park entrance, continue another seven miles and follow signs to the Willow Flat Campground. The campground is located on a short spur road accessing the Green River Overlook.

GPS Coordinates: N 38° 22.948' W 109° 53.282'.

Contact: Canyonlands National Park, 435/719-2313, www.nps.gov/cany/planyourvisit/camping.htm.

51 HATCH POINT

🚴 🏕 ⛺

Scenic rating: 8

in the Canyon Rims Recreation Area

Map 5.3, page 237

Hatch Point Campground is perched on a gently rising mesa above the deep rift carved by the Colorado River. Dead Horse Point State Park is visible to the north and much of Canyonlands National Park's Island in the Sky District can be seen to the west. An apron of slickrock spills down from the campground to an open grassland plateau below. The landscape seems to draw you out into it, pulling your eyes down the slope, wanting you to see what's beyond the distant canyon rim. (That can be seen, too, but not from the campground. The Needles overlook 13 miles south or the Anticline Overlook 10 miles to the north will satisfy that curiosity.) Hatch Point is the closest place to camp to visit either of these overlooks at sunrise or sunset for glowing photographs. The sites are scattered among pinyon pine, juniper, and thin-leaved yucca plants. The gravel parking spots and tent areas are not generally flat and tend to slope down-canyon. Hatch Point is a long drive from any paved road, but if you are interested in a primitive, remote, and beautiful campground, this is the spot. Look for pronghorn antelope as you approach the campground—we sighted a pair near the road on our drive to the campground.

Campsites, facilities: There are 10 sites for tents, small RVs, or campers. Picnic tables, fire rings, and open-air vault toilets are provided. Drinking water is available from mid-April through mid-October. Leashed pets permitted.

Reservations, fees: Reservations are not accepted. The fee is $12 per site. Open year-round.

Directions: From Moab, drive south on Hwy. 191 for 32 miles and turn west (right) at the entrance to Canyon Rims Recreation Area. Continue on this road 15 miles and turn north (right), following signs to campground and the Anticline Overlook. Continue seven miles on the gravel road to the Hatch Point Campground.

GPS Coordinates: N 38° 22.892' W 109° 37.005'

Contact: BLM Moab Field Office, 435/259-2100, www.blm.gov/ut/st/en/fo/moab/recreation/campgrounds/canyon_rims_recreation/2.html.

52 LOCKHART BASIN

Scenic rating: 7

in Lockhart Basin near Indian Creek east of Canyonlands National Park

Map 5.3, page 237

Undeveloped campsites line the road into Lockhart Basin. Although there are no facilities, many of these sites are as appealing as the Hamburger Rock sites. All the sites are exposed to the sun and wind, but if conditions are right, they offer a beautiful, free camping experience. An eclectic group of campers, including rock climbers visiting the popular Indian Creek climbing area, off-road vehicle enthusiasts, and

overflow campers from Canyonlands National Park, all share these sandy desert sites. The sites actually see heavy use because the rangers at the Canyonlands visitors center send people here when the park campground is full. Please camp where other people have camped in the past.

Campsites, facilities: Approximately 10–15 campsites line the road as it enters Lockhart Basin. There are no facilities other than scattered fire rings. Open-air vault toilets are available at both the Hamburger Rock Campground and farther down the road in Lockhart Basin. There is no drinking water. Leashed pets permitted.

Reservations, fees: Reservations are not accepted. There is no fee for camping. Open year-round.

Directions: From Moab, drive 35 miles south on Hwy. 191 and turn west (right) onto Rte. 211 toward Canyonlands National Park. Follow Rte. 211 for 30 miles and turn north (right) toward Lockhart Basin and Hurrah Pass. Look for the numerous undeveloped campsites on both sides of the road.

GPS Coordinates: N 38° 11.524' W 109° 40.222'

Contact: BLM Moab Field Office, 435/259-2100.

53 HAMBURGER ROCK

Scenic rating: 6

in Lockhart Basin near Indian Creek east of Canyonlands National Park

Map 5.3, page 237   **BEST(**

You'll understand why they call it Hamburger Rock as soon as you set eyes on the place. Beyond the quirky, Big Mac–shaped rock formation, there's not a lot of incentive to camp here. While the setting is undeniably pretty, with 360° views of red rock mesas, there's equally scenic camping available all along this unpaved BLM road for free. The sites surrounding Hamburger Rock offer little more than a picnic table and fire ring. Many of the spots don't even have a flat spot in the red dirt to pitch a tent. There's no shade to speak of in the campground, and privacy is limited because there are no visual barriers besides the rock itself. Despite a less-than-inspiring campground, this area is heavily used because of the limited camping options in Canyonlands National Park. When we visited, the sites at Hamburger Rock and along Lockhart Basin Road filled up quickly as the evening approached. If you plan on camping here, stake out a spot early in the day and don't assume sites will be available as the day progresses. Hamburger Rock's proximity to Canyonlands National Park, the Indian Creek rock climbing area, and the prolific Newspaper Rock petroglyph panel guarantee it will be busy except during the hottest and coldest parts of the year.

Campsites, facilities: There are eight sites. Picnic tables, fire grills, and an open-air vault toilet are provided. There is no drinking water. Leashed pets permitted.

Reservations, fees: Reservations are not accepted. The fee is $6 per site. Open year-round.

Directions: From Moab, drive 35 miles south on Hwy. 191 and turn west (right) onto Rte. 211 toward Canyonlands National Park. Follow Rte. 211 for 30 miles and turn north (right) toward Lockhart Basin and Hurrah Pass. Continue 1.1 miles over the bumpy road to Hamburger Rock Campground.

GPS Coordinates: N 38° 11.524' W 109° 40.222'

Contact: BLM Monticello Field Office, 435/587-1500.

54 NEEDLES OUTPOST
🚴 🛖 🚐 ⛰️

Scenic rating: 8

in the Needles District on the eastern border of Canyonlands National Park

Map 5.3, page 237

The privately owned and operated Needles Outpost literally hugs the eastern border of the Needles District of Canyonlands National Park. It's in a perfect location, because finding a site in the Squaw Flat Campground inside the park during high season can be near impossible. The Outpost is almost as convenient as Squaw Flat for exploring this section of the park. The campground sits beneath a low, broad red rock outcrop among juniper trees, big sagebrush, and bunchgrass, with views westward of the Needles formation. The quirky Needles Outpost even has an airstrip. Aero-camping anyone?

Campsites, facilities: There are 49 sites for tents and RVs for up to 30 feet in length. Picnic tables, drinking water, flush toilets, garbage service, and fire pits are provided. A general store, firewood, gasoline, restaurant, and showers are available. Leashed pets permitted.

Reservations, fees: Reservations are accepted at 435/979-4007 or by email at needlesoutpost@aol.com. Sites are $15 per night. Open March 15 through October 31.

Directions: From Moab, drive 35 miles south on Hwy. 191 and turn east (right) onto Rte. 211 toward Canyonlands National Park. Continue on Rte. 211 to the entrance to the national park. Just after entering the park, turn left and drive a short distance to the Needles Outpost Campground and store.

GPS Coordinates: N 38° 10.438' W 109° 44.510'

Contact: Needles Outpost, 435/979-4007, www.canyonlandsneedlesoutpost.com.

55 SQUAW FLAT
🚶 🛖 🚐 ⛰️

Scenic rating: 8

in the Needles District of Canyonlands National Park

Map 5.3, page 237   **BEST (**

Squaw Flat Campground is the only campground in the Needles District of Canyonlands National Park. The Needles formation is named for its red rock fins layered with

© MIKE MATSON

Squaw Flat Campground, Needles District, Canyonlands National Park

distinctive white bands. This region of the park sees far fewer visitors than the Island in Sky District farther north, despite offering an equally impressive landscape. The park service has focused its efforts on a single campground and has produced a quality facility. Two loops encircle a short, brown sandstone cliff. The sites are generally backed by rock in one direction with open views of grasslands and the distant Needles in the other. Gnarled ancient juniper trees give the campground a stately feel, and the constant voices of small birds chirping in their branches create a relaxing atmosphere. The campground is also the trailhead for several backcountry hikes including Big Spring Canyon, Squaw Canyon, and Chesler Park. These trails, combined with a collection of opportunities for backpacking into the wild Needles and Maze Districts of the park, make Squaw Flat one of the best campgrounds for hiking in Utah. Families should be sure to check out the campfire circle program at the

amphitheater. Squaw Flat Campground fills up often from late March through June and early September through mid-October.

Campsites, facilities: There are 26 campsites for tents or RVs up to 28 feet and three group sites for up to 11 to 50 people, depending on the site. Picnic tables, fire grills, tent pads, garbage service, aluminum recycling, drinking water, flush toilets, and dishwashing stations are provided. Leashed pets permitted.

Reservations, fees: Reservations are accepted for the group sites at www.nps.gov/cany/planyourvisit/upload/ReservationForm.pdf and can be arranged after the first Monday in January. Sites are $15, and the group sites are $3 pp. Open year-round.

Directions: From Moab, drive 35 miles south on Hwy. 191 and turn east (right) onto Rte. 211 toward Canyonlands National Park. Continue on Rte. 211 for 35 miles to the Squaw Flat Campground.

GPS Coordinates: N 38° 08.810' W 109° 47.828'

Contact: Canyonlands National Park, 435/797-2313, www.nps.gov/cany/planyourvisit/camping.htm.

56 INDIAN CREEK (CREEK PASTURE, SUPER BOWL, AND BRIDGER JACK MESA)

Scenic rating: 7

near Indian Creek east of the Needles District of Canyonlands National Park

Map 5.3, page 237

The Windgate Sandstone above Indian Creek east of Canyonlands National Park has become a destination for serious rock climbers from around the world. The sandstone cliffs feature perfectly parallel "splitter" cracks on otherwise featureless rock. These crack routes demand climbers stuff their hands and feet, sometimes painfully, into the cracks in order to haul themselves up the rocks. While crack climbing isn't exclusive to Indian Creek or even desert sandstone, the Windgate formation at Indian Creek offers crack systems so pure and sustained that it has become known the ultimate crack-climbing experience. Since Indian Creek was first "discovered" and climbed in 1976 by climbers like Billy Westbay, Jim Dunn, and Stewart Green, the area has exploded in popularity. As more and more climbers and other users visit this area, they have put pressure on the resources and campgrounds of this delicate desert environment. With limited developed camping options available, many climbers and campers have chosen to "poach" undeveloped sites along the road around Indian Creek. The land below the red rock walls of Indian Creek is a working ranch, called Dugout Ranch and operated by Heidi Redd. Heidi owns the land and grazing rights in a partnership with the Nature Conservancy. In an effort to accommodate climbers' needs, the BLM and the Nature Conservancy have developed three small dispersed camp loops for climbers (and other campers) to use near the walls of Indian Creek. Please respect Heidi's ranch and use these sites while visiting Indian Creek. Continued access to trails for classic climbs like Super Crack and Scarface depends upon it. The three areas are Creek Pasture, Super Bowl, and Bridger Jack Mesa. The unpaved loops offer relatively primitive sites with some picnic tables. At Creek Pasture you'll find a group area with a few picnic tables to supplement the otherwise natural setting. Super Bowl looks out over a broad, open plain to the towering wall of Windgate Sandstone. Bridger Jack Mesa is the most developed and popular of all three. Be sure to close the gate after you enter and keep your pets on a leash. In an effort to keep these camping areas free of charge, the BLM is trying a "pack it out" policy for human waste. Please use the waste disposal bags and leave a $2 donation to help cover the cost.

Campsites, facilities: There are 10 undeveloped sites at Creek Pasture and Super Bowl and 21 undeveloped sites at Bridger Jack Mesa.

Picnic tables and waste disposal bags are provided. Leashed pets permitted.

Reservations, fees: Reservations are not accepted. There is no fee. Open year-round.

Directions: Creek Pasture: From Moab, drive 35 miles south on Hwy. 191 and turn west (right) onto Rte. 211. Continue 28 miles, turn left, go past the gate, and continue 0.3 mile to the campground. GPS Coordinates: N 38° 09.948' W 109° 37.899'.

Super Bowl: From Moab, drive 35 miles south on Hwy. 191 and turn west (right) onto Rte. 211. Continue 27 miles, turn right, go past the gate, and continue 0.4 mile to the campground. GPS Coordinates: N 38° 08.762' W 109° 37.345'.

Bridger Jack Mesa: From Moab, drive 35 miles south on Hwy. 191 and turn west (right) onto Rte. 211. Continue 21 miles, turn left on Beef Basin Road, drive 0.8 mile, take a sharp right after the creek, and continue 0.9 mile to the campground. GPS Coordinates: N 38° 05.033' W 109° 35.391'

Contact: BLM Monticello Field Office, 435/587-1500.

57 WINDWHISTLE

Scenic rating: 7

in Canyon Rims Recreation Area

Map 5.3, page 237

The wind does whistle through this campground, but not any more so than other Moab-area campgrounds. The campground is actually named after a large slick rock dome west of the campground. Windwhistle is a medium-size BLM campground in the Canyon Rims Recreation Area. The south side of the campground is backed by the towering 200-foot red sandstone walls of Roan Bailey Mesa; however, expansive grassland stretches to the north, giving the whole place an open, airy feeling. The short 0.5-mile Windwhistle Nature Trail starts a bit awkwardly from the group camping area and takes about 20 minutes to tour a natural, red rock amphitheater. The informative trail brochure identifies about 20 native plant species and explains their historical uses and natural functions. You'll learn about everything from the prickly pear cactus to Mormon tea and glean a better understanding of the plant community you'll be camping in. The campsites are accessed via a gravel loop and sit in a pinyon pine and juniper forest. The short, squatty trees don't provide much shade or protection from the elements, but they do offer a little privacy for the sites. The paint is peeling off the wood picnic tables, leaving the facilities feeling a bit uncared for.

Campsites, facilities: There are 15 individual sites for tents and RVs up to 32 feet in length and one walk-in tent group site for up to 10–15 people. Picnic tables, fire rings, vault toilets, garbage service, and aluminum recycling are provided. Drinking water is available mid-April through mid-October. Leashed pets permitted.

Reservations, fees: Reservations are accepted for the group site only at 435/259-2100. Single sites are $12 and the group site is $2.50 pp with a $10 reservation fee. Open year-round.

Directions: From Moab, drive south on Hwy. 191 for 32 miles and turn west (right) at the entrance to the Canyon Rims Recreation Area. Follow the road six miles to the campground on the south (left) side of the road. GPS Coordinates: N 38° 10.558' W 109° 27.737'

Contact: BLM Moab Field Office, 435/259-2100, www.blm.gov/ut/st/en/fo/moab/recreation/campgrounds/canyon_rims_recreation/windwhistle_campground.html.

CANYON COUNTRY AND SOUTHERN UTAH

© MIKE MATSON

BEST CAMPGROUNDS

This chapter attempts the impossible: to describe

the potential camping experiences on a ribbon of starkly beautiful earth stretching from the green peaks of the Pine Mountain Wilderness in the west to the geographic oddity of the Four Corners in the east. In between these points rests a collection of national parks, monuments, recreation areas, state parks, and other public land worthy of a lifetime of exploration. What do all these parks celebrate, you might wonder? Rocks, is the simple answer. Take a closer look and you'll discover a massive, undulating rock landscape called the Colorado Plateau, 130,000 square miles in southern Utah, northern Arizona, northwestern New Mexico, and southwestern Colorado. The Colorado River and its tributaries carve into the sedimentary layers of the plateau in a complex of deeply cut canyons that must be seen to be believed. In one way or another, this combination of sandstone and erosion is responsible for sculpting the mind-blowing scenery of the iconic national parks of the southwest: the Grand Canyon, Zion Canyon, Bryce Canyon, Capitol Reef, Canyonlands, and Arches.

This region in Utah – Canyon Country, we'll call it – is the heart of the Colorado Plateau, which contains all or parts of four of these national parks. If you're visiting from outside Utah, this might be everything you have time to see, and you'll be amazed. Those who live here will probably want to return time and time again to explore all the nuances of the plateau.

Zion Canyon may be Utah's single most impressive natural wonder – and that's saying a lot. It was Utah's first national park and now draws two million visitors a year. But the hefty tourist traffic won't take away from the sense of awe you'll feel the first time you set eyes on the place. Sheer 2,000-foot walls of Navajo Sandstone rise up on both sides of the canyon in a neck-craning display of raw beauty. It seems impossible that the gentle, meandering Virgin River could have cut this deep into the earth. With great effort, the Civilian Conservation Corps built a number of world-class hikes in the park. Angel's Landing, a catwalk across a sandstone tightrope with adrenaline-producing drop-offs on either side, shouldn't be missed by those who enjoy a little exposure. And for those uninterested in a brush with vertigo, the less scary but equally impressive Observation Point trail gives an unforgettable view of the canyon from its eastern rim.

Where Zion is all about going into the canyon and experiencing it for yourself, Bryce Canyon is most impressive looking down from above.

Technically, Bryce Canyon is not actually a canyon, but a series of rock amphitheaters eroded from the richly colored limestone into wild formations described as everything from fins and spires to gargoyles or hoodoos. It's this combination of mind-bending natural architecture and a complex palette of iron oxide–induced coloring that makes the amphitheaters of this park so compelling. The hues of limestone in the Claron Formation range from glowing white to deep pink to bright orange. In the hours bracketing sunset and sunrise, when the sun is low on the horizon, the hoodoo rock formations seem to glow even more beautifully, the warm magic light drawing the best from this natural wonder. It's not surprising this is a favorite destination of nature photographers from around the planet.

Capitol Reef is Utah's least-celebrated national park. This is not because the park is deficient in scenery or lacking in majestic quality. Capitol Reef is simply harder to get to and less user-friendly than its more frequently visited neighbors. The neck of the park that extends into the Canyon Country Region we'll cover in this chapter is the perfect example of why this park is so lightly traveled. Waterpocket Fold is a remote geologic feature, stretching 100 miles north to south. The massive wrinkle in the earth is accessible from the north via the long, winding unpaved Norton Road or on the equally primitive Burr Trail from the west. The scale and geology of Waterpocket Fold is most easily understood from a bird's-eye view, where the massive formation can be taken in all at once. Waterpocket Fold is a classic example of a monocline, in which one side of the earth's crust has been bent and folded from a horizontal position to nearly vertical. Rock layers on the west side of this monocline were lifted nearly 7,000 feet above those on the eastern edge by the same forces that created the Rocky Mountains.

The southern tip of Canyonlands extends into the region discussed in this chapter, but a more thorough investigation into what the park has to offer is written in the *Red Rocks* chapter covering eastern Utah.

The national parks are really just the highlights of southern Utah. The region boasts a supporting cast of national monuments, recreation areas, state parks, and national forests that shouldn't be overlooked. Invariably, they are, leaving a silver lining of fewer crowds. So hit the road, take all the time you can, and discover the stupendous landscape of Canyon Country on the Colorado Plateau.

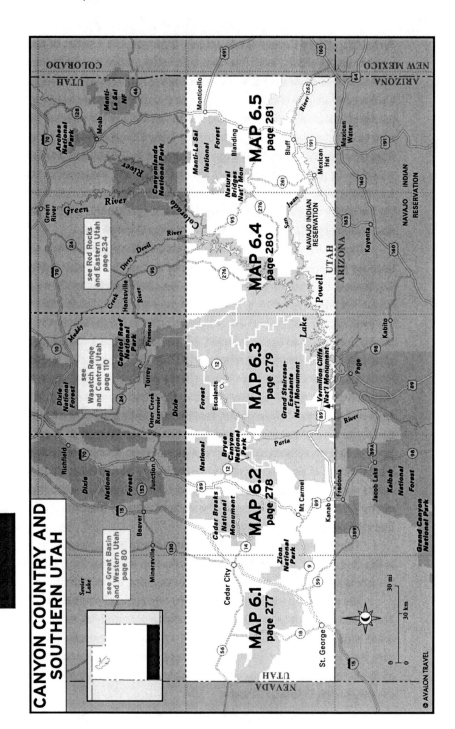

CANYON COUNTRY AND
SOUTHERN UTAH

see Great Basin
and Western Utah
page 80

MAP 6.1
page 277

MAP 6.2
page 278

MAP 6.3
page 279

MAP 6.4
page 280

MAP 6.5
page 281

see Red Rocks
and Eastern Utah
page 234

see
Wasatch Range
and Central Utah
page 110

© AVALON TRAVEL

Map 6.1

Campgrounds 1-23
Pages 282-294

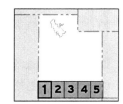

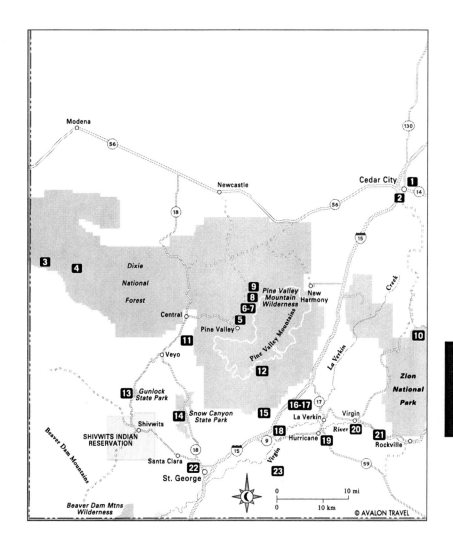

Map 6.2

Campgrounds 24-58
Pages 295-315

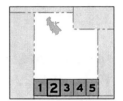

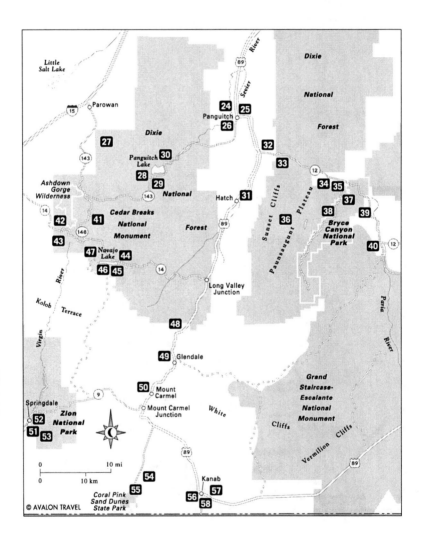

Map 6.3

Campgrounds 59-71

Pages 316-323

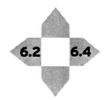

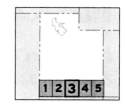

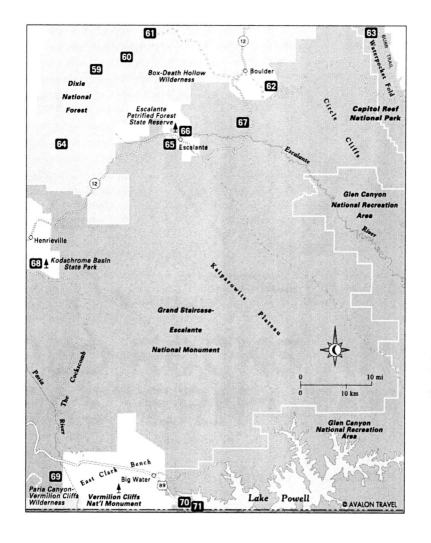

Map 6.4

Campgrounds 72-78
Pages 324-327

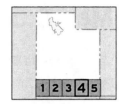

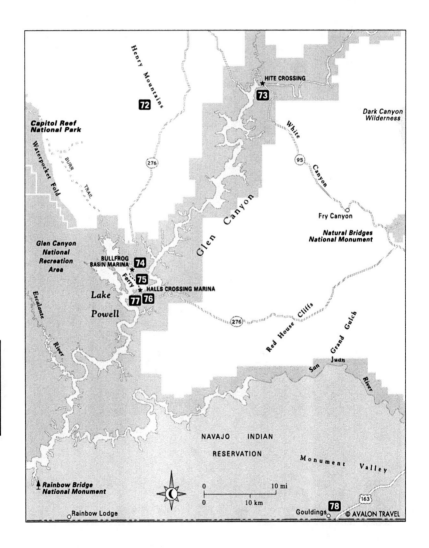

Map 6.5

Campgrounds 79-93
Pages 328-336

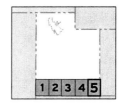

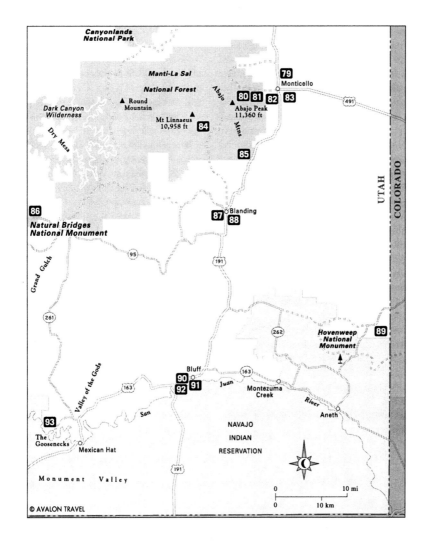

1 COUNTRY AIRE RV PARK

Scenic rating: 4

in Cedar City

Map 6.1, page 277

The Country Aire might be a bit polluted, as this RV park is right on the busy Main Street in Cedar City. It does offer better views than its competition, Cedar City KOA down the road. The mountains rise up to the northeast above the campground. The gravel loop has shaded, pull-through sites, and the facilities are well maintained and clean. Aside from the busy road and urban environment, this campground is actually a decent place to spend the night. Cedar City is surrounded by natural wonders, including the Cedar Breaks National Monument, Zion National Park, and the Dixie National Forest. The Country Aire puts you in the middle of all this.

Campsites, facilities: There are 53 full hook-up (20-, 30-, and 50-amp) sites. There are no tent sites. Amenities include WiFi, cable TV, picnic tables, swimming pool, pull-through sites, garbage service, laundry, drinking water, ice, and groceries. Leashed pets permitted.

Reservations, fees: Reservations are accepted at 435/586-2550. Full hook-up sites are $36. Open year-round.

Directions: From the intersection of Rte. 56 and Rte. 130, travel north on Rte. 130 for 1.9 miles to the Country Aire RV Park on the right side of the road.

GPS Coordinates: N 37° 42.470' W 113° 03.716'

Contact: Country Aire RV Park, 435/586-2550.

2 CEDAR CITY KOA

Scenic rating: 4

in Cedar City

Map 6.1, page 277

This KOA is off Main Street on the northern end of Cedar City. The large, well-kept campground has mature cottonwood trees that shade almost all sites. The sites are grass with gravel pull-through parking spaces. The campground is bordered by a residential neighborhood to the south and Main Street to the north. Overall, this is one of the nicer KOA facilities we've seen, but it comes up short in terms of location, scenery, and ambience. The whole facility appears very well maintained, and there are a nice variety of offerings from RV sites to a grass tent area to cabins. You'll also notice some permanent residents. In addition to being centrally located near a host of outdoor destinations, Cedar City is the proud home of the Utah Shakespearean Festival. The Festival's events usually run June through October. Open year-round and located less than an hour's drive from Brian Head Ski Resort, this KOA has potential to double as budget ski resort lodging. An all-you-can-eat pancake breakfast is available.

Campsites, facilities: There are 117 sites, 88 with full hook-ups (20-, 30-, and 50-amp) and 29 partial hook-up sites. A communal tent area and 14 cabins are also available. Picnic tables, drinking water, barbeque grills, pull-through sites, a dog run, cable TV, WiFi, dump station, swimming pool, playground, and horseshoes are provided. Laundry, groceries, and RV supplies are available. Leashed pets permitted.

Reservations, fees: Reservations are accepted at 800/562-9873 or online at https://koa.com/where/ut/44125/reserve/. RV sites are $39–55, tent sites are $27.50, and cabins are $50–70 per night. Open year-round.

Directions: From the intersection of Rte. 56 and Rte. 130, travel north on Rte. 130 for 1.1

miles to the campground. Cedar City KOA will be on the left side of the road.

GPS Coordinates: N 37° 41.827' W 113° 03.843'

Contact: Cedar City KOA, 435/586-9872, www.cedarcitycampgrounds.com/

3 PINE PARK

Scenic rating: 8

in the Dixie National Forest

Map 6.1, page 277

If you're looking for the middle of nowhere, Pine Park is just the spot. Located at the end of a long gravel road a few miles east of the Nevada border, this campground is as far off the beaten path as any in Utah. It sits at the bottom of a mystic valley, among shiny white rock outcrops and shaded by a canopy of stately ponderosa pines. The old pines grow around a quiet creek that runs through the small valley. The campground sees few visitors and is more of a mysterious scenic area than a developed campground. There are no developed sites, just nice spots to pitch a tent and enjoy the shade and solitude. The best sites are beside the creek right at the end of the road. Horseback riders, off-road motor bikers, ATV riders, and even mountain bikers may find some quality terrain and little-used trails in the area. If you enjoy exploring winding dirt roads that lead to, well, nowhere, you'll definitely love Pine Park. If not, it's probably not worth the effort.

Campsites, facilities: There are 11 primitive sites. Fire rings are the only facilities. Leashed pets permitted.

Reservations, fees: Reservations are not accepted. There is no fee. Open May through October.

Directions: From Enterprise, drive west on Main Street and continue 16 miles. Turn left on Forest Road 001. After one mile, take the left branch and drive 10 miles to the campground at the end of the road.

GPS Coordinates: N 37° 31.369' W 114° 01.433'

Contact: Pine Valley Ranger District, 435/652-3100.

4 HONEYCOMB ROCKS

Scenic rating: 8

in the Dixie National Forest

Map 6.1, page 277

The honeycomb rock formation is extremely featured, with textured pockets, alcoves, and small caves. Orange and mint green lichens cover the loose gray volcanic tuff. The campground is in a valley between the Upper and Lower Enterprise Reservoirs, formed behind earthen dams along Little Pine Creek on the western side of the Bull Valley Mountains. There's a boat ramp on the Upper Reservoir, which provides opportunities for boating and fishing. The quiet Forest Service campground loops around the rock feature, with sites tucked into the small caves and overhangs. It's a pleasant, protected spot because many of the sites are sheltered from the wind and sun by the rock itself. Gambel oak and pinyon pine trees help add to the shade and privacy. Keep your eyes peeled for jackrabbits hopping through the sagebrush flats around camp.

Campsites, facilities: There are 18 sites. Covered picnic tables on concrete pads, fire pits, vault toilets, garbage service, and water (be warned the water contains high levels of sodium). Leashed pets permitted.

Reservations, fees: Reservations are not accepted. The fee is $9 per site plus $5 for any additional vehicle. Open April through September.

Directions: From Enterprise, drive west on Main Street for 5.5 miles and turn left at the sign for Honeycomb Rocks. Continue 4.8 miles and turn right just past the reservoir. Drive 0.7 mile to the Honeycomb Rocks Campground.

GPS Coordinates: N 37° 31.088' W 113° 51.477'

Contact: Pine Valley Ranger District, 435/652-

3100, www.fs.fed.us/r4/dixie/recreation/camp-grounds/honeycombrocks.html

5 EQUESTRIAN

Scenic rating: 8

in Pine Valley Recreation Area of Dixie
National Forest

Map 6.1, page 277

The Pine Valley Wilderness is an oasis in the desert, an island of cool, forested mountains with striking, craggy cliffs reaching for the sky. Clear, cold snowmelt streams drop through mature ponderosa pine forests on their way to the desert floor below. The Pine Valley Recreation Area features five campgrounds dispersed within the forest canopy beneath the wilderness area. Equestrian is the first campground encountered upon entering the Pine Valley. As the name suggests, the campground is designed for horseback riders and their mounts. The site is perfectly positioned at the trailhead for the Browns Point, Whipple, and Forsyth Summit horse trails, which access some of the most impressive terrain in these beautiful mountains. The campground is open with dispersed gambel oak trees growing around sites. Grass and big sagebrush cover the ground surrounding the dirt camp spots. The sites are well spaced and offer some privacy despite the campground's open feel. There is adequate parking for RVs and trailers. The equestrian campground is reserved for horseback riders only. There are four other campgrounds in Pine Valley for campers without horses.

Campsites, facilities: There are 15 sites and four tent sites. All sites have hitching posts and some have corrals. Picnic tables on concrete pads, barbeque grills, flush and vault toilets, and drinking water are provided. Tent sites have fire pits and picnic tables (sites T1 and T2 don't have picnic tables). Firewood is available. Leashed pets permitted.

Reservations, fees: Reservations are accepted at 877/444-6777 or online at www.recreation.gov and must be made a minimum of four days in advance. In order to make a reservation, you must bring a horse. Single sites are $13, tent sites are $9, and extra vehicles are $6. Open May through September, weather permitting.

Directions: From St. George, drive 26 miles north on Rte. 18 and turn right onto the Pine Valley Highway. After 8.1 miles, turn left on Main Street in the historic town of Pine Valley. Continue 1.9 miles to Equestrian Campground, just beyond the entrance station to Pine Valley Recreation Area.

GPS Coordinates: N 37° 22.816' W 113° 28.992'

Contact: Pine Valley Ranger District, 435/652-3100, www.fs.fed.us/r4/dixie/recreation/camp-grounds/equestrian.html

6 PINES

Scenic rating: 8

in Pine Valley Recreation Area of Dixie
National Forest

Map 6.1, page 277

This campground is part of the Pine Valley Recreation Area. The Pines is the first in a series of four campgrounds sheltered by a lovely mature ponderosa pine forest. Stately trees cast shadows on the dirt and pine needle forest floor, accented with huge, gray, lichen-covered boulders. A clear stream tumbles gently over rocks and through quiet pools, where wary trout wait patiently for their next meal. It's hard to believe this cool mountain setting is just a short drive from St. George, which consistently posts the hottest temperatures in the state. Hiking and horseback riding are available on nearby trails into the Pine Valley Wilderness, and fishing is possible in the creeks running through the campgrounds and on the Pine Valley Reservoir. Small campers or vans will fit on the parking aprons, but no large trailers or RVs.

Campsites, facilities: There are 14 individual sites for tents and RVs up to 45 feet in length and one group area for up to 50 people. Sites 6 and 13 are wheelchair accessible. Picnic tables, barbeque grills, fire pits, vault toilets, drinking water, and garbage service are provided. The group site includes a large eating area with four picnic tables, barbeque grills, a cement volleyball court, and several tent areas. Firewood is available. Leashed pets permitted.

Reservations, fees: Reservations are required for the Pine Valley Group Site at 877/444-6777 or online at www.recreation.gov and must be made a minimum of four days in advance. Reservations are not accepted for the individual sites. Single sites are $12, double sites are $22, the group site is $42, and extra vehicles are $6. Open May through September.

Directions: From St. George, drive 26 miles north on Rte. 18 and turn right onto Pine Valley Highway. After 8.1 miles, turn left on Main Street in the historic town of Pine Valley. Continue 3.5 miles and turn right following the sign for Pines Campground.

GPS Coordinates: N 37° 22.540' W 113° 27.849'

Contact: Pine Valley Ranger District, 435/652-3100, www.fs.fed.us/r4/dixie/recreation/campgrounds/pines.html and for the group area www.fs.fed.us/r4/dixie/recreation/campgrounds/upperpines.html

⑦ BLUE SPRINGS
🏃 🛶 🏕 🚐 ⛰

Scenic rating: 8

in Pine Valley Recreation Area of Dixie National Forest

Map 6.1, page 277

Blue Springs is the next campground encountered as you drive into the Pine Valley Recreation Area. Like Pines, this campground is in an open, mature ponderosa pine forest. The left fork of the crystal-clear Santa Clara River flows through the campground. Many of the sites are adjacent to, or even surrounded by running water, adding to the area's cool, relaxing feel. This stream is snow-fed, however, and may dry up later in the summer. The campsites feature flat tent pads set between timeless boulders. The grounds are vigorously maintained by the camp host, and there's a fuel reduction program being implemented, meaning that many of the smaller trees have been selectively removed. There are inviting open meadows near the campground, where we noticed European white butterflies making the rounds. There's visible history in this campground, as well: In the early 1860s William Freleigh and Joseph Carpenter operated a keg factory on the site, offering Utah's Dixie region its first tubs, buckets, barrels, churns, bowls, and kegs made of native material. A descriptive sign marks the spot.

Campsites, facilities: There are 19 sites (numbered 39–58) for tents and RVs up to 45 feet in length. Picnic tables, barbeque grills, fire pits, vault toilets, drinking water, and garbage service are provided. Firewood is available. Leashed pets permitted.

Reservations, fees: Reservations are accepted at 877/444-6777 or online at www.recreation.gov and must be made a minimum of four days in advance. Single sites are $12, double sites are $22, and extra vehicles are $6. Open May through September.

Directions: From St. George, drive 26 miles north on Rte. 18 and turn right onto Pine Valley Highway. After 8.1 miles, turn left on Main Street in the historic town of Pine Valley. Continue to the Pine Valley Recreation Area entrance station. From the entrance station, drive 1.7 miles and turn right, go a short distance to a fork in the road, and turn right again into the Blue Springs Campground.

GPS Coordinates: N 37° 22.429' W 113° 27.653'

Contact: Pine Valley Ranger District, 435/652-3100, www.fs.fed.us/r4/dixie/recreation/campgrounds/bluesprings.html

8 SOUTH JUNIPER
🏃🏊🏕🚐⛺

Scenic rating: 8

in Pine Valley Recreation Area of Dixie
National Forest

Map 6.1, page 277

South Juniper is one of the smaller loops of these Pine Valley campgrounds. Like the others, it enjoys shade from pine trees. The running water provides a cool, peaceful atmosphere and supports lush green forest flora. A bridge crosses over the Left Fork of the Santa Clara River to the North Juniper loops from the campground. Birders can expect to spot three species of nuthatch, woodpeckers, western tanagers, mountain chickadees, and sharp-shinned hawks in the tall pine forest canopy above the campsites. Also look for mountain bluebirds in the open meadows. Dirt-floored campsites are scattered with long pine needles from the trees above. Being one of the last campgrounds on the road, this campground sees less overall traffic than Blue Springs and Pines, yet offers the same beautiful setting and equal access to the area's recreation.

Campsites, facilities: There are nine sites (numbered 29–38). Picnic tables, barbeque grills, fire pits, vault toilets, drinking water, and garbage service are provided. Firewood is available. Leashed pets permitted.

Reservations, fees: Reservations are not accepted. Single sites are $12, double sites are $22, triple sites are $36, and extra vehicles are $6. Open May through September, weather permitting.

Directions: From St. George, drive 26 miles north on Rte. 18 and turn right onto Pine Valley Highway. After 8.1 miles, turn left on Main Street in the historic town of Pine Valley. Continue straight to the Pine Valley Recreation Area entrance station. From the entrance

station, drive 1.7 miles and turn right and then left into the South Juniper Campground.
GPS Coordinates: N 37° 22.535' W 113° 27.626'
Contact: Pine Valley Ranger District, 435/652-3100, www.fs.fed.us/r4/dixie/recreation/campgrounds/juniperpark.html

9 NORTH JUNIPER
🏃🏊🏕🚐⛺

Scenic rating: 8

in Pine Valley Recreation Area of Dixie
National Forest

Map 6.1, page 277

This is the final campground in the Pine Valley Recreation Area. More of an extension to the South Juniper Campground than its own unit, this campground has the advantage of being small and at the end of the road. The handful of sites is set right on the Left Fork of the Santa Clara River. It is also the site of the historic White Elephant Sawmill, the first steam-operated sawmill in southern Utah, constructed in 1877. Pioneers John A. Gardner and Benjamin Burgess built and operated it. Come check out North and South Juniper before choosing your site in the Pine Valley. You may enjoy the smaller, less-developed feel at this end of the road. Big-rig drivers be aware, the tight camping loop at the end of the road may be difficult to turn a large vehicle around in.

Campsites, facilities: There are nine sites (numbered 20–28). Picnic tables, barbeque grills, fire pits, vault toilets, drinking water, and garbage service are provided. Firewood is available. Leashed pets permitted.

Reservations, fees: Reservations are not accepted. Single sites are $12, double sites are $22, triple sites are $36, and extra vehicles are $6. Open May through September, weather permitting.

Directions: From St. George, drive 26 miles north on Rte. 18 and turn right onto Pine Valley Highway. After 8.1 miles turn left on Main Street in the historic town of Pine

Valley. Continue straight to the Pine Valley Recreation Area entrance station. From the entrance station, it's 1.8 miles to the North Juniper Campground.

GPS Coordinates: N 37° 22.557 W 113° 27.442

Contact: Pine Valley Ranger District, 435/652-3100, www.fs.fed.us/r4/dixie/recreation/campgrounds/juniperpark.html

10 LAVA POINT

Scenic rating: 7

in the Kolob Terrace region of Zion National Park

Map 6.1, page 277	BEST

Free camping in a national park? Here's a rare gem. Located in the highlands of Kolob Terrace above Zion Canyon, this is a wonderful alternative experience to other campgrounds in the national park. Small, quiet, free, and cool, this campground is as different from the canyon floor as you'll find. Aspen and oak groves dot the pleasantly small loop. The park service is currently engaged in a fuel-reduction and aspen-restoration project around the campground. You'll notice some downed trees and burn piles, but they're far enough from the camping area to not have a negative impact on your experience. This is by far the most natural, wild campground you'll find anywhere in Zion, if not all of southern Utah's national parks. A short trail leads from the campground to the Lava Point Overlook, a great spot for views or sunset photography. Bring a long-reaching zoom lens and tripod for great shots of the distant canyon. From the overlook you'll get a top-down view of Zion Canyon. West Temple Mountain, the highest point in Zion, is visible, as are the tops of many of the canyon's dominant features. This campground is a great place to camp if you plan on hiking the famous Subway slot canyon from the bottom up. Make sure to pick up your permit ahead of time, because they can only be arranged at the main visitors center in Zion Canyon.

Campsites, facilities: There are six campsites for tents, small campers, and vans. Vehicles longer than 19 feet are not allowed on Lava Point Road. Picnic tables, fire grills, garbage service, and vault toilets are provided. There is no drinking water. Leashed pets permitted.

Reservations, fees: Reservations are not accepted. There is no fee. Open June through October, weather permitting.

Directions: Turn left off Rte. 9 on Kolob Terrace Road. Continue 20.4 miles and turn right. Drive 1.8 miles on a gravel road to Lava Point Campground.

GPS Coordinates: N 37° 23.024' W 113° 01.972'

Contact: Zion National Park, 435/772-3256, www.nps.gov/zion/planyourvisit/lava-point-campground.htm

sandstone waterfalls in the Subway slot canyon, Zion National Park

⓫ BAKER DAM

Scenic rating: 7

in Baker Dam Recreation Site

Map 6.1, page 277

This BLM-run campground is a popular spot to camp for families and Scout troops in spring and early summer before temperatures climb into the triple digits. The small Baker Reservoir is popular for fishing but is not open to motorized boats. The Wasatch Audubon Society describes Baker Reservoir and the riparian area around the Santa Clara River as a birding hotspot. Birders may spot green herons, common goldeneyes, common mergansers, and cinnamon teals on the water, and gray flycatchers and bushtits in the woodlands. An osprey pair nests above the lake as well. The campground offers wide-open vistas to orange-and-green-speckled hills, capped by craggy rock cliffs to the east. The camping loop is mostly open and exposed to the wind. Sagebrush, juniper trees, and the occasional yucca cactus grow in between small basalt boulders on the red desert floor. The sites feature established tent pads. Sites are relatively close together, and the place feels a bit exposed to the considerable elements, but overall the campground seems like a bargain for $6.

Campsites, facilities: There are 19 sites. Picnic tables, fire grills, vault toilets, and garbage service are provided. There is no drinking water. Leashed pets permitted.

Reservations, fees: Reservations are not accepted. Single sites are $6, double sites are $12, and extra vehicles are $6. Open year-round.

Directions: From St. George, drive 23 miles north on Rte. 18 and turn right at the sign for Baker Reservoir. Continue 0.6 mile to the Baker Dam Campground on the right side of the road.

GPS Coordinates: N 37° 22.665 W 113° 38.593'

Contact: St. George BLM Field Office, 435/688-3200, www.blm.gov/ut/st/en/fo/st__george/recreation/camping/baker_dam_campground.html

⓬ OAK GROVE

Scenic rating: 8

in Dixie National Forest

Map 6.1, page 277

This Forest Service campground sits in an oak grove near the base of the east side of the Pine Valley Mountains at the end of a long, winding, unpaved road. Leaving from the campground are several trails that access the Pine Valley Wilderness, including the one-mile Pine Trail and the three-mile Summit Trail, which crosses the range and connects to Whipple Valley. The quiet, forested campground is shaded by tall pine trees and has well-dispersed sites with plenty of privacy and space. Site eight has great views with a nearby gazebo. Expect to fight off huge horseflies in early summer, probably a result of the clear, cold creek coupled with horse trails. Views extend from the campground up to the surrounding craggy peaks and down to the western edge of the Colorado Plateau, Zion National Park, and beyond. This campground is definitely out of the way. If you're looking for solitude or to access the Pine Valley Wilderness, it's certainly a worthy destination, but otherwise, you may not find the unpaved road worth the effort.

Campsites, facilities: There are eight sites including two group sites. Picnic tables, drinking water, vault toilets, and a day-use picnic area are provided. Trailers are not recommended. Leashed pets permitted.

Reservations, fees: Reservations are not accepted. Sites are $5. Open May through early October, weather permitting.

Directions: From St. George, drive north on I-15 to Exit 23, turn left, and drive northwest. After 3.1 miles, take the right fork and continue six rough miles on Forest Road 032 to the Oak Grove Campground.

GPS Coordinates: N 37° 19.008' W 113° 27.187'

Contact: Pine Valley Ranger District, 435/688-3246, www.fs.fed.us/r4/dixie/recreation/campgrounds/oakgrove.html

13 GUNLOCK STATE PARK

Scenic rating: 7

south of the small town of Gunlock on Route 18

Map 6.1, page 277

South of the tiny town of Gunlock you'll find a state park, camping, and a pleasant respite from the desert heat on the shores of the Gunlock Reservoir. The lake was created by an earthen dam on the Santa Clara River in 1970 and named after William Hayes, a famous local sharpshooter nicknamed "Gunlock Bill." Recreational activities on the lake include boating, waterskiing, swimming, fishing, and birding. Boat-in camping is allowed in designated sites on the west side of the reservoir. Excellent birding is available in the BLM-managed riparian habitat below the dam. Those with a keen eye might spot green herons, common loons, western screech-owls, Bewick's wrens, yellow-breasted chats, blue grosbeaks, ladder-backed woodpeckers, hooded orioles, or great-tailed grackles. The reservoir is surrounded by an arid mountain landscape with white, red, and brown rocks dotted with dark green junipers. The campground is simple and small. Primitive campsites line the east edge of the lake, which is completely devoid of trees. Expect little shade or privacy—everything here is out in the open. Scattered around the sites are buckhorn cholla and Englemann prickly pear cacti. The cacti were blooming brilliant yellow and magenta during our visit in early June.

Campsites, facilities: There are four sites on the east side of the lake, and several boat-in campsites on the west side of the reservoir. Picnic tables, fire pits, garbage service, vault toilets, and a boat ramp are provided. There is no drinking water. Leashed pets permitted.

Reservations, fees: Reservations are not accepted. Sites are $10, and day use is $5. Open year-round.

Directions: From St. George, drive 19 miles north on Rte. 18 to the town of Veyo. Turn left toward the town of Gunlock. Drive 9.6 miles to Gunlock State Park.

GPS Coordinates: N 37° 15.295' W 113° 46.260'

Contact: Gunlock State Park, 435/680-0715, http://stateparks.utah.gov/stateparks/parks/gunlock/

14 SNOW CANYON STATE PARK

Scenic rating: 9

north of St. George

Map 6.1, page 277   BEST

Snow Canyon State Park preserves a red-and-salmon-colored desert rockscape accented with dark layers of desert varnish, lichen, and basalt. In the northern part of the park, lava flows from as recent as 10,000 years ago cap many of the red rock formations like chocolate frosting on a red-and-white layer cake. The desert floor is covered with a mosaic of flora, including narrow-leaved yucca, creosote, pinyon pine, rabbitbrush, scrub oak, and three-leaved sumac. The park is home to the endangered desert tortoise and many species of birds, including the lesser nighthawk, Costa's hummingbird, ash-throated flycatcher, rock and canyon wrens, northern mockingbird, and lesser goldfinch. The park features a paved trail for biking, many hiking trails, and good rock climbing on the red rock faces. Intensely varnished walls make for unique climbing on sharply in-cut holds on the Circus Wall, only a few hundred yards off the main road. In total, there are approximately 180 climbing routes in the park. The campground in Snow Canyon is located in the heart of the scenery. Tent sites and RV sites are in separate areas, making for a pleasant experience for both. The scenic walk-in tent sites have views south down-canyon, while paved, tightly spaced, full hook-up RV sites have covered eating areas that incorporate local lava rock into their design. Tent sites sport thoughtfully placed red sand tent pads under trees to maximize available shade. Solar-heated showers offer a much-needed opportunity to clean up on desert road trips.

Campsites, facilities: There are 14 full hook-up sites, 17 sites without hook-ups, and two group sites. Cottontail Group Area accommodates up to 35 people and Quail Group Area up to 50 people. Full hook-up sites have picnic tables and barbeque grills. The other sites have picnic tables and fire pits. Aluminum recycling, garbage service, drinking water, and modern restrooms with showers are provided. A dump station is available. Leashed pets permitted.

Reservations, fees: Reservations are accepted at 800/322-3770 or online at www.reserveamerica.com/. Single site reservations must be made a minimum of two days in advance and can be arranged up to 16 weeks in advance, and group site reservations can be arranged up to 11 months in advance. There is a nonrefundable reservation fee of $8 for individual sites and $10.25 for group sites. Full hook-up sites are $20, sites without hook-ups are $16, the group sites are $3 pp (with a $50 refundable cleaning deposit), and day use is $5. Open year-round.

Directions: From St. George, drive north on Rte. 18 for eight miles, turn left into the park, and continue 2.2 miles to the visitors center and campground.

GPS Coordinates: N 37° 12.168' W 113° 38.390'

Contact: Snow Canyon State Park, 435/628-2255, http://stateparks.utah.gov/stateparks/parks/snow-canyon/

15 RED CLIFFS

Scenic rating: 8

in the Red Cliffs Recreation Area

Map 6.1, page 277

The Red Cliffs is a pretty little BLM campground nestled into a scenic environment rich in history. The campground is within the 62,000-acre Red Cliffs Desert Reserve, which was designated to protect the threatened Mojave Desert Tortoise. Three trails leave from the site. The Red Cliffs Village Trail leads 1.5 miles to an Anasazi Indian ruin. A short path extends to

a point overlooking the Silver Reef Area, where silver was mined in the early 1900s. The third trail is a 0.5-mile interpretive trail identifying local plant species. The campground occupies both sides of small, slow-moving Quail Creek, which occasionally experiences powerful flash floods. Cottonwood trees line the stream bottom, and namesake Red Cliffs rise on either side. The campground is tucked into the canyon bottom, so it's well protected from the wind but, by the same token, hot during summer months. While large cottonwood trees shelter the group picnic area, some of the individual campsites enjoy only sporadic shade. The sites are spread out and private, though sounds carry and echo quite well in the canyon. Expect to hear your neighboring campers more than you see them. Keep an eye out for the large sagebrush lizards rustling in the bushes.

Campsites, facilities: There are 10 campsites, one of which is wheelchair accessible. Picnic tables, a picnic area, garbage service, drinking water, and vault toilets are provided. Leashed pets permitted.

Reservations, fees: Reservations are not accepted. The fees are $8 for camping and day use is $2. Open year-round.

Directions: From St. George, drive north on I-15 to Exit 22 and take a sharp right and drive 1.7 miles, turn right again, go under the freeway, and continue 1.5 miles to the campground.

GPS Coordinates: N 37° 13.371' W 113° 24.238'

Contact: St. George BLM Field Office, 435/688-3200, www.blm.gov/ut/st/en/fo/st__george/recreation/camping/red_cliffs_campground.html

16 ZION WEST RV PARK

Scenic rating: 5

in Leeds

Map 6.1, page 277

In the rural town of Leeds, west of Zion National Park and east of the Red Cliffs

Archeological Site, there are two RV parks sitting side by side. Worthy destinations like Snow Canyon State Park and the Pine Valley Recreation Area are also within striking distance of Leeds. Zion West RV is bordered to the south by farmland and has an open, spacious feel. The Red Cliffs can be seen across the fields to the southwest. RV sites run in long, neat rows and are shaded by broad-leaved trees. Paved driveway loops lead to gravel parking aprons. The log cabin office, TV clubhouse, and laundry facility complement the park's country feel. The laid-back, peaceful atmosphere of Zion West makes it my favorite of these two neighboring campgrounds.

Campsites, facilities: There are 36 full hook-up (30- and 50-amp) sites for RVs up to 60 feet in length. Amenities include modern restrooms with showers, pull-through sites, laundry, WiFi, drinking water, a dog walk area, and picnic tables. Leashed pets permitted.

Reservations, fees: Reservations are recommended from September through April and can be arranged at 435/879-2854. RV sites are $28.35, and tent sites are $18. Open year-round.

Directions: From St. George, drive north on I-15, take Exit 22, drive straight 0.3 mile, and turn right on Mulberry Lane. Drive three blocks to Zion West RV.

GPS Coordinates: N 37° 13.876' W 113° 21.829'

Contact: Zion West RV Park, 435/879-2854, www.zionwestrv.com/

🔢17 LEEDS RV PARK

Scenic rating: 4

in Leeds

Map 6.1, page 277

Leeds RV Park is one of two adjacent RV parks in the little hamlet of Leeds. Leeds is near a wide variety of southern Utah

recreation, from Zion National Park to the Pine Mountain Wilderness to local attractions like the historical Silver Reef mining area. Leeds RV offers an opportunity to stay smack in the middle of all these attractions. The park is located in a peaceful country setting bordering both farmland and neighborhoods. Most sites are shaded by trees, but some of the trees are young and small enough that they don't provide much relief. The driveway and parking spaces are gravel, and the RV park also has a motel attached. Check out the other RV park next door and choose the one that best suits your needs.

Campsites, facilities: There are 44 sites with full hook-ups (20-, 30-, and 50-amp) and 10 tent sites. Amenities include WiFi, cable TV, picnic tables, drinking water, modern restrooms with showers, laundry, picnic area, and horseshoe pit. Leashed pets permitted.

Reservations, fees: Reservations are accepted at 435/879-2450. RV sites are $23, and tent sites are $15. Open year-round.

Directions: From St. George, drive north on I-15, take Exit 22, drive straight 0.3 mile, and turn right on Mulberry Lane. Drive one block and turn left on Valley road. Pass Zion West RV and Leeds RV is the next property on the right side of the road.

GPS Coordinates: N 37° 13.976' W 113° 21.807'

Contact: Leeds RV Park and Motel, 435/879-2450 or 888/879-2450, www.leedsrvpark.com/

🔢18 QUAIL CREEK STATE PARK

Scenic rating: 8

northeast of St. George

Map 6.1, page 277

The campground is perched above the western shoreline of Quail Creek Reservoir, with a commanding overview of the lake, surrounding buttes, and in the distance the upper reaches of Zion National Park. Layered strata of gray, orange, and brown rock descend into the lake's clear blue waters. Boating is the recreation of choice here, and ski boats buzz continuous circles on the lake. Two spacious boat ramps provide easy entry and exit from the lake. Other aqua-centric recreational opportunities include fishing, scuba diving, sailing, windsurfing, and swimming. The sport-fishing species are largemouth bass, bluegill, black bullhead catfish, rainbow trout, and black crappie. Look for the large raptors, red-tailed hawks, and bald eagles occasionally spotted here. The campsites occupy small, terraced steps between lichen-painted boulders. The hillside is open and bare between relatively closely spaced sites, so expect to get to know your neighbors. Covered picnic tables offer a small swath of shade at the sites, otherwise completely exposed to the elements.

Campsites, facilities: There are 23 campsites. Sites 11 and 13 are wheelchair accessible. Covered picnic tables, barbeque grills, fire pits, drinking water, pull-through sites, garbage service, and flush toilets are provided. Leashed pets permitted.

Reservations, fees: Reservations are accepted at 800/322-3770 or online at www.reserveamerica.com; they must be made a minimum of two days in advance and can be arranged up to 16 weeks in advance. There is an $8 nonrefundable reservation fee for individual sites. Single sites are $13, extra vehicles are $7, and the day-use fee is $8. Open year-round.

Directions: From St. George, drive north on I-15 and take Exit 16. Drive east on Rte. 9 for 2.2 miles, turn left on Rte. 318, and continue two miles to the campground.

GPS Coordinates: N 37° 11.231' W 113° 23.708'

Contact: Quail Creek State Park, 435/879-2378, http://stateparks.utah.gov/stateparks/parks/quail-creek/

19 WILLOWIND RV PARK

Scenic rating: 5

in Hurricane

Map 6.1, page 277

Willowind RV is a few blocks off the main drag in Hurricane, the last major town west of the south entrance to Zion National Park. This huge, squeaky-clean RV park looks like it was just built. Paved driveways lead to neatly spaced rows of RVs next to long, narrow, grass lawn strips. Each site is shaded by large trees. There are ample pull-through spaces for RVs and trailers. Many of the sites were already occupied, some by long-term residents, but there was plenty of room for drop-in overnight guests. The campground is far enough off State Route 9 to be away from road noise, but with 165 sites, you might be more worried about other campers. Groups are welcome.

Campsites, facilities: There are 165 RV sites with full hook-ups (50 amps) and 10–12 tent sites. Amenities include picnic tables, modern restrooms with showers, drinking water, WiFi, cable TV, pull-through sites, garbage service, and a dump station. Laundry and phone hook-ups are available. Leashed pets permitted.

Reservations, fees: Reservations are accepted at 888/635-4154. RV sites are $30, Super RV sites are $40, and tent sites are $20. Open year-round.

Directions: From the intersection of Rte. 9 and 1150 W, head south for one block on 1150 W. Willowind RV will be on the left.

GPS Coordinates: N 37° 10.537' W 113° 18.564'

Contact: Willowind RV Park, 435/635-4154 or 888/635-4154, www.willowindrvpark.net/

20 ZION RIVER RESORT

Scenic rating: 5

in the town of Virgin on Route 9

Map 6.1, page 277

If you don't mind driving a little ways to your campground and appreciate a first-class RV resort with paved parking, green grass lawns, and nice facilities, then this is the spot. The Zion River Resort is located on State Route 9, near the turn-off for Kolob Terrace, in the northern corner of Zion National Park. It is a good place for a base camp if you'd like to see more of Zion than just the tourist madness of the main canyon. There is a plenty more to see out there with far fewer crowds, and this campground puts you closer to great trails and sights like the Subway, a deep, dark slot canyon carved out of the sandstone by North Creek, with tunnel-like subterranean feel. The RV resort is right on the Virgin River. A large rock-and-sand levy between the campground and the river holds back occasional flash floods. Unfortunately, it also blocks views and access to the Virgin River. There are distant views of red rock cliffs. Midsize trees provide some shade for sites. The paved pull-through parking aprons come with a small grass lawn. Overall, it's a nice, new facility, and the most expensive we've seen.

Campsites, facilities: There are 133 sites with full hook-ups (20-, 30-, and 50-amp), 11 tent sites, a group tent area, and three cabins. Picnic tables, fire grills, modern restrooms, garbage service, WiFi, a swimming pool, billiard table, playground, drinking water, and a dog run are provided. Laundry, a convenience store, and showers ($1) are available. Pets are permitted only in air-conditioned RVs, with a maximum of two dogs.

Reservations, fees: Reservations are accepted at 888/822-8594 or online at https://secure.areatravel.net/zrr/reservations2007.asp. Full hook-up, pull-through sites are $50–55, full hook-up, back-in sites are $45–50, tent sites are $36, the group tent site is $41, and cabins are $87–99. Open year-round.

Directions: From the town of Virgin, drive east on Rte. 9 toward Zion National Park; at mile marker 19 turn right into Zion River Resort. GPS Coordinates: N 37° 12.165' W 113° 10.657'

Contact: Zion River Resort, 435/635-8594 or 888/822-8594, www.zionriverresort.com/

21 MOSQUITO COVE

Scenic rating: 6

on Route 9 along the Virgin River outside Zion National Park

Map 6.1, page 277   BEST (

Mosquito Cove is a nice alternative to staying inside Zion National Park. The river-bottom site is undeveloped, free, and far less crowded than anything you'll find in Zion Canyon. There are no improvements at Mosquito Cove, it's simply an attractive place by the river with room for 20–40 campers. The scenery includes views up to distant red cliffs and the milky waters of the Virgin River itself. Big cottonwood trees provide shade and some privacy between sites. Self-contained campers or pickup trucks will feel most comfortable here; having a place to cook built into your vehicle, or even a portable picnic table is a big plus, otherwise you'll be dining in the sand with the ants. The ground is soft red sand, and so is the access "road." Regular passenger cars will have no problem accessing the camping area if things are dry, but getting stuck is certainly a possibility. Be aware this is a riverbed, so if a storm is threatening, a flash flood is a dangerous possibility. Please respect this free resource and limit your impact to an absolute minimum. Pack everything in and out. If the BLM feels this site is being abused, it will soon be closed or developed into a fee area. The camping is accessed via an unpaved road off the highway, which isn't ideal for RVs or larger vehicles; four-wheel drive is preferred but not strictly necessary.

Campsites, facilities: There's room for 20–40

sites. There are no facilities at this camping area. There is no drinking water. Leashed pets permitted.

Reservations, fees: Reservations are not accepted. Camping is free. Open year-round.

Directions: From the town of Virgin, drive east on Rte. 9 toward Zion National Park; the turn-off for the dispersed camping is on the right side of the road between mile marker 23 and 24. The turn-off is not well marked so watch closely.

GPS Coordinates: N 37° 10.258' W 113° 06.459'

Contact: St. George BLM Field Office, 435/688-3200.

22 MCARTHUR'S TEMPLE VIEW RV RESORT

🏊 🏕 ♿ 🚐 ⛺

Scenic rating: 2

in St. George

Map 6.1, page 277

This trailer park is in the city of St. George, across the street from the local high school. Don't come here looking for nature—you'll be disappointed by the passing traffic, concrete parking lots, and strip mall development. You will find a well-cared-for facility, with all the amenities you could ask for to entertain your kids and yourselves, or just a place to safely park your RV. You're also close to a movie theater, grocery store, and all the conveniences of a major town. A city park and baseball diamond are behind the RV park. Gravel RV parking strips look out onto the street. The majority of the RVs parked here are full-time residents, or at least haven't moved in a long, long time. I really wouldn't describe this as camping, but if for some reason you want to stay in town, this spot is a good option.

Campsites, facilities: There are 260 full hook-up (20-, 30-, and 50-amp) sites for RVs up to 45 feet in length and a tenting area. Many of the sites house permanent residents. Amenities include WiFi, cable TV, modern restrooms with showers, garbage service, pull-through sites, a swimming pool and hot tub, drinking water, billiards, horseshoes, a putting green, exercise rooms, and shuffleboard. Laundry and phone hook-ups are available. Leashed pets permitted.

Reservations, fees: Reservations are accepted at 800/776-6410 or online at https://secure. areatravel.net/templeviewrv/reservations3.asp. Full hookup sites are $38.95, and tent sites are $28.95. Open year-round.

Directions: From I-15, take exit 6 and turn left onto Bluff Street. Go approximately 0.3 miles to the stoplight and turn right onto Main Street. Continue up Main Street 0.4 mile. McArthur's Temple View RV will be on your right.

GPS Coordinates: N 37° 05.501' W 113° 34.953'

Contact: McArthur's Temple View RV Resort, 435/673-6400, www.templeviewrv.com

23 SAND HOLLOW STATE PARK

🏊 ⛵ 🏊 🏕 ♿ 🚐 ⛺

Scenic rating: 7

northeast of St. George

Map 6.1, page 277

Welcome to the land of expensive toys: tricked-out waterskiing boats, monster ATVs, and plush, bus-sized RVs. Everything is bigger and better here, including the reservoir and campground. The campground facilitates recreational opportunities, mostly of the off-road variety, either on the red dunes of Sand Mountain or in the blue waters of the Sand Hollow Reservoir. The camping area is both exposed and breezy, sitting high in the sandy desert. There are no substantial trees, just baking red earth and the hearty, drought-resistant flora that will grow in it, namely sage, rabbit brush, and prickly pear cactus. The sites are spread out between two huge, newly constructed loops (Sand Hollow is Utah's newest state park) and have plenty of room for everyone and their stuff. Thankfully, covered picnic tables offer shade from the omnipresent sun. If you're interested in camping right on the lake, primitive beach camping is available on the reservoir's eastern shore. Views look west to the distant lava-topped chasm of Snow Canyon. Sand Hollow is open year-round and experiences pleasantly mild winter temperatures, so consider an off-season visit as well.

Campsites, facilities: There are 50 full hook-up (15 amps) sites for tents and RVs up to 40 feet in length. Sites 8, 14, and 45 are wheelchair accessible. Amenities include covered picnic tables on concrete pads, barbeque grills, pull-through sites, full hook-ups, drinking water, garbage service, a dump station, and modern restrooms with showers. Leashed pets permitted.

Reservations, fees: Reservations are accepted at 800/322-3770 or online at www.reserveamerica.com; they must be made a minimum of two days in advance and can be arranged up to 16 weeks in advance. There is an $8 non-refundable reservation fee for individual sites. Primitive sites on the beach are $13, full hook-ups at the main campground are $25, and the day-use fee is $10. Open year-round.

Directions: From St. George, drive north on I-15 and take Exit 16. Drive east on Rte. 9.

After 4.4 miles, turn right on Sand Hollow Road, continue 3.9 miles, and turn left into Sand Hollow State Park.

GPS Coordinates: N 37° 07.215' W 113° 23.196'

Contact: Sand Hollow State Park, 435/680-0715, http://stateparks.utah.gov/stateparks/parks/sand-hollow/

24 PARADISE RV PARK AND CAMPGROUND

Scenic rating: 4

north of Panguitch

Map 6.2, page 278

Paradise RV Park is a sprawling gravel RV park a short distance north of Panguitch on Highway 89. There are distant views of Red Canyon and the Sevier Plateau to the east and the Tushar Mountains to the west. Panguitch is close to Red Canyon Recreation Area and equidistant to Cedar Breaks National Monument and Bryce Canyon National Park. The campground is surrounded by farmland. The store and RV park are a throwback to earlier

© MIKE MATSON

Cedar Breaks National Monument

times, with a Western feel and a relaxed, casual attitude. The amenities are minimal, with hook-ups being the only constant at every site; there are a handful of picnic tables scattered about the yard. Young trees have been planted that eventually should provide shade for many of the sites, but in the meantime, they're more comical than functional. The campground is easily recognizable by the elk statues outside the small convenience store and rock shop. If you're looking for an RV park that's outside of town, this is the most rural option in the Panguitch area.

Campsites, facilities: There are 60 RV sites, unlimited places to pitch a tent, and five cabins. Modern restrooms with showers, playground, drinking water, a few picnic tables, fire grills at the cabins, and garbage service are provided. Laundry, a small convenience store, and gift shop are available. Leashed pets permitted with a fee.

Reservations, fees: Reservations are accepted at 800/648-2268. RV sites with 50-amp hook-ups are $21, RV sites with 30-amp hook-ups are $18, partial hook-ups are $15, and tent sites are $10. There's also a $2 fee for dogs. Open May through October.

Directions: From Panguitch, drive north on Hwy. 89 for 1.5 miles. Paradise RV Park will be on the west (left) side of the road.

GPS Coordinates: N 37° 51.665' W 112° 26.312'

Contact: Paradise RV Park and Campground, 800/648-2268.

25 HITCH-N-POST

Scenic rating: 3

in Panguitch

Map 6.2, page 278

The Hitch-N-Post RV Park is a small gravel park right off Highway 89 in the small country town of Panguitch. Panguitch is close to Red Canyon Recreation Area and an equal distance from the hoodoo wonderlands of Cedar Breaks

National Monument and Bryce Canyon National Park. You'll have no problem spotting the campground, with its elevated water tank sign and Western motif. Small trees offer a little shade for a few of the sites, but for the most part the campground is open and unprotected. Tent sites are grass, and the campground has a group fire ring. Being right on the highway, road noise is unavoidable. After driving countless dirt roads in Southern Utah, we were happy to take advantage of the Hitch-N-Post's $0.75 car wash.

Campsites, facilities: There are 40 full hook-up (20-, 30-, and 50-amp) RV sites and six tent sites. Picnic tables, barbeque grills, modern restrooms with showers, WiFi, drinking water, and a dump station are provided. A car wash, laundry, and gift shop are available. Leashed pets permitted.

Reservations, fees: Reservations are accepted at 435/676-2436 or online at www.hitchn-postrv.com/852/936.html. RV sites are $25 and tent sites are $15. Open year-round.

Directions: From the intersection of Hwy. 89 and Rte. 143, drive four blocks north on Hwy. 89 and turn right into the campground.

GPS Coordinates: N 37° 49.792' W 112° 26.133'

Contact: Hitch-N-Post Campground, 435/676-2436, www.hitchnpostrv.com/

26 PANGUITCH KOA

Scenic rating: 5

in Panguitch

Map 6.2, page 278

The Panguitch KOA is by far the nicest of the three RV parks in Panguitch. The quiet setting on State Route 143 feels much more secluded than the RV parks right off Highway 89. Cottonwood trees provide some shade for many of the sites, which have limited views up to the Sevier Plateau and Red Canyon to the east. There are plenty of long, pull-through sites for big rigs. Located on Route 143, the KOA is one step closer to the recreation opportunities of Panguitch Lake and Cedar Breaks

National Monument. A grass volleyball court, horseshoe pits, and a swimming pool give the place a city-park feel and distinguish it from the other Panguitch RV campgrounds. The grass lawn and trees are more appealing than the gravel pit atmosphere you'll find at the competitors' sites.

Campsites, facilities: There are 25 full hook-up (20-, 30-, and 50-amp) sites, 18 partial hook-up sites, and 10 tent sites. Picnic tables, barbeque grills, a swimming pool, grass volleyball court, horseshoes, modern restrooms with showers, drinking water, garbage service, a covered picnic area, and WiFi are provided. Firewood and bicycle rentals are available. Leashed pets permitted.

Reservations, fees: Reservations are accepted at 800/562-1625 or online at https://koa.com/where/ut/44107/reserve/. Full hook-up sites are $35.49, partial hook-up sites are $28.49, and tent sites are $20.49. Cabins are $48.49 per night, and there is a $5 fee for pets. Open April 15 through October 15.

Directions: From the intersection of Hwy. 89 and Rte. 143, drive south on Rte. 143 for five blocks and turn left into the Panguitch KOA.

GPS Coordinates: N 37° 48.881' W 112° 26.096'

Contact: Panguitch KOA, 435/676-2225, www.koa.com/where/ut/44107/

27 YANKEE MEADOWS

Scenic rating: 7

near Yankee Meadows Reservoir in Dixie National Forest

Map 6.2, page 278

Yankee Meadows Campground features flat, open sites in an attractive forest of spruce and aspen trees. The red gravel loop accesses flat parking areas and simple, functional sites. Randomly spaced refrigerator-sized basalt boulders and short grass share space in the red dirt campsites. Single and double sites accommodate a variety of group sizes. The campground is one mile from Yankee Meadows Reservoir, where boating and fishing are the most popular recreational pursuits. Fishing for brook and rainbow trout is best during spring and fall at the lake. The reservoir is surrounded by evergreen forest, and views extend up the gently rising Markagunt Plateau. This part of the Dixie National Forest is particularly popular with ATV riders, and many trails are accessible near the campground.

Campsites, facilities: There are 29 sites. Picnic tables, fire grills, fire pits, vault toilets, garbage service, pull-through sites, and drinking water are provided. Leashed pets permitted.

Reservations, fees: Reservations are not accepted. Single sites are $10, and double sites are $18. Open late May through early September, weather permitting.

Directions: From Parowan, drive south on Rte. 143 for three miles and turn left onto the first road on your left. Continue six miles to the Yankee Meadows Campground.

GPS Coordinates: N 37° 45.119' W 112° 46.284'

Contact: Cedar City Ranger District, 435/865-3200, www.fs.fed.us/r4/dixie/recreation/campgrounds/yankee.html

28 PANGUITCH LAKE NORTH

Scenic rating: 8

on the Markagunt Plateau in Dixie National Forest

Map 6.2, page 278

This excellent Forest Service campground overlooks Panguitch Lake from a wooded hillside. The lake provides boating and fishing opportunities, but it can't be accessed from the campground directly. Panguitch Lake's cool waters are an ideal environment for rainbow, brook, cutthroat, and brown trout, and the fishing has improved in recent years as a result of the removal of Utah chub. Historically, the fishing must have been noteworthy as well, as Panguitch is a Paiute name meaning "big fish." Hikers, bikers, horseback riders, and ATV users all enjoy many trails in the area. In winter, (campground closed) ice fishing and snowmobiling are popular. In the campground, a mosaic of ponderosa pines varying in age and diameter provide the perfect balance of shade and views. The sites are adequately spaced, especially considering the size of the campground and popularity of the area. Near the impressive group area, a small amphitheater with wood benches and a rock-framed stage overlooks the lake. The constant buzz of insects, occasionally broken by the higher-pitched buzz of hummingbirds, is more comforting than a nuisance. Pine needles and small, red-brown basalt rocks decorate the dusty forest floor and campsites. The loop and parking aprons are paved. The large group picnic area features horseshoe pits, a central fire ring circled by benches, and plenty of long picnic tables for large parties. Pleasant temperatures—even when the rest of the state is blistering in a heat wave—combined with a beautiful forest and access to a mountain lake make this one of the best Forest Service facilities in this part of the state.

Campsites, facilities: There are 49 sites for tents and RVs up to 35 feet in length, two group sites for up to 35 people, and a group picnic area. Picnic tables, fire grills, modern restrooms, drinking water, horseshoes, a volleyball court, and garbage service are provided. Firewood is available. Leashed pets permitted.

Reservations, fees: Reservations are accepted at 877/444-6777 or online at www.recreation.gov and must be made at least four days in advance. Single sites are $12, double sites are $20, and extra vehicles and day use are $6. The Evergreen and Blue Springs Group Sites are $40, and the picnic area is $45. Open early June through early September, weather permitting.

Directions: From Panguitch, drive south on Rte. 143 for 16 miles. Panguitch Lake North campground will be on the north (right) side of the road.

GPS Coordinates: N 37° 42.092' W 112° 39.370'

Contact: Cedar City Ranger District, 435/865-

3200, www.fs.fed.us/r4/dixie/recreation/campgrounds/panguitchnorth.html

29 PANGUITCH LAKE SOUTH

Scenic rating: 6

on the Markagunt Plateau in Dixie National Forest

Map 6.2, page 278

The Panguitch Lake South Campground is surprisingly different from the North Campground across the highway. The loop and parking areas are unpaved, which makes the place dustier. This campground also doesn't share the lake views with its neighbor, and the overall feel just doesn't compare. An aspen and ponderosa pine forest protects the sites and offers shade and a peaceful environment. The campground is cut out of a steep hill, and most of the tent sites seem to slightly retain the slope. The South Campground is much smaller than North, and cheaper, too. So, if every dollar counts or if you can't stand the noise of RV generators, this side of the highway is a better option. Both facilities offer the same access to a plethora of recreational opportunities on and around Panguitch Lake. Because they're within a few hundred yards of each other, it's certainly worth taking a spin around both layouts and picking the one that best suites you.

Campsites, facilities: There are 19 individual sites. Trailers are not recommended. Picnic tables, fire grills, modern restrooms, and drinking water are provided. Firewood is available. Leashed pets permitted.

Reservations, fees: Reservations are not accepted. Sites are $10; extra vehicles and day use are $5. Open early June through early September, weather permitting.

Directions: From Panguitch, drive south on Rte. 143 for 16 miles. Panguitch Lake South campground will be on the south (left) side of the road.

GPS Coordinates: N 37° 42.032' W 112° 39.317'

Contact: Cedar City Ranger District, 435/865-3200, www.fs.fed.us/r4/dixie/recreation/campgrounds/panguitchsouth.html

30 WHITE BRIDGE
🏊 🐕 🎣 ⛺

Scenic rating: 7

in Dixie National Forest

Map 6.2, page 278

Just off the Patchwork Parkway Scenic Byway (Route 143), a small bridge with painted white rails crosses Panguitch Creek and enters a midsize Forest Service campground. The campground sits below sagebrush-covered hills among cottonwood, pinyon pine, and juniper trees. This is the first campground encountered on the way toward the Markagunt Plateau, a broad alpine plateau capped by Brian Head Ski Resort and the wildly eroded Cedar Breaks National Monument. Fishing for rainbow trout is popular along Panguitch Creek and farther up the scenic byway on Panguitch Lake. The paved loop accesses shaded sites along the river and open sites with covered picnic tables. At 7,900 feet, this campground is lower, with warmer temperatures, and is more exposed than the other Forest Service sites farther up the road, making it best for visits early or late in the season.

Campsites, facilities: There are 28 sites for tents and RVs up to 24 feet in length. Picnic tables, fire grills, garbage service, drinking water, flush and vault toilets, and a dump station are provided. Leashed pets permitted.

Reservations, fees: Reservations are accepted at 877/444-6777 or online at www.recreation.gov and must be made at least four days in advance. The fee is $12 per site; extra vehicles and day use are $6. Open early June through early September.

Directions: From Panguitch, drive south on Rte. 143 for 12 miles. White Bridge Campground will be on the north (right) side of the road.

GPS Coordinates: N 37° 44.737' W 112° 35.276'

Contact: Cedar City Ranger District, 435/865-

3200, www.fs.fed.us/r4/dixie/recreation/campgrounds/whitebridge.html

31 RIVERSIDE RESORT AND RV PARK
🏊 🐕 ♿ 🎣 ⛺

Scenic rating: 5

north of the town of Hatch

Map 6.2, page 278

The Riverside Resort and RV Park is a wide-open campground in a flat field by the Sevier River. The campground is part of a facility that includes a motel, restaurant, gift shop, and general store in addition to camping accommodations. Above all else this campground feels open and spacious, with no shortage of room. In fact, there's a five-acre meadow available to play or just hang out in. The facilities are adequate, but not particularly appealing. Expect a casual but rustic camping experience. The RV parking areas are dirt and surrounded by a mix of grass, weeds, and native vegetation. Tent sites are tucked among tamarisk trees by the river. Tent sites with or without shade are available. All sites have views of red cliffs above the campground. While there are campgrounds closer to all southwestern Utah's mega-destinations, this RV park puts you right in the middle of Zion, Cedar Breaks, and Bryce Canyon. It isn't a bad location to set up a base camp.

Campsites, facilities: There are 47 full hookup (30, 50 amps) sites and 15 back-in sites with partial hook-ups. Amenities include picnic tables, barbeque or fire grills, cable TV, modern restrooms with showers, drinking water, a restaurant, store and gift shop, swing set, and basketball court. Firewood and WiFi are available for a fee. Leashed pets permitted.

Reservations, fees: Reservations are accepted at 800/824-5651 or online at http://convoyant.com/resnexus/reserve/book.aspx?ID=151&ResID=21009. Full hook-up sites are $28–33, and partial hook-up river sites are $28. Open year-round.

Directions: From Hatch, drive north on Hwy.

89 for one mile, entering the campground on the right.
GPS Coordinates: N 37° 39.659' W 112° 25.631'
Contact: Riverside Resort and RV Park, 435/735-4223 or 800/824-5651, www.riversideresort-utah.com/rv_park.shtml

32 RED CANYON RV PARK

Scenic rating: 4

southeast of Panguitch on Route 12 near the junction with Highway 89

Map 6.2, page 278

If the Red Canyon Forest Service campground is full, Red Canyon RV Park is a nearby alternative. The site isn't much to look at but is certainly close to Red Canyon Recreation Area and Bryce Canyon National Park. At Red Canyon you'll find Bryce-like rock hoodoo formations and a great variety of trails to enjoy them on. There's everything from a short 20-minute loop through the rocks to an eight-mile paved bike route to all-day horseback-riding opportunities. The RV park itself is simply an open piece of land with gravel, pull-through sites and a couple of large strips of grass for tent campers. The weeds seem to be winning the battle with the grass, and there's little to no shade for any sites, so take a look at the place before you decide to stay. On the bright side, the camp host is very friendly and forthcoming.

Campsites, facilities: There are 25 sites with full hook-ups (30, 50 amps) for RVs up to 40 feet in length, one site with partial hook-ups, six without hook-ups, eight rustic cabins, two modern cabins, and 20 tent sites. Modern restrooms with showers, picnic tables for tent sites and covered picnic tables for RV sites, pull-through sites, barbeque grills, garbage service, and cable TV are provided. Leashed pets permitted.

Reservations, fees: Reservations are accepted at 435/676-2690 (April–October) and 435/673-2689 (November–March). RV

sites are $27, tent sites are $11, and cabins are $30–45. Open mid-March through mid-October, weather permitting.
Directions: From Panguitch, drive south seven miles on Hwy. 89 and turn east (left) on Rte. 12. Continue 0.7 miles to the Red Canyon RV Park on the left side of the road.
GPS Coordinates: N 37° 44.927' W 112° 21.640'
Contact: Red Canyon RV Park, 435/676-2690, www.redcanyon.net/rc_rvpark/

33 RED CANYON

Scenic rating: 9

in Dixie National Forest

Map 6.2, page 278   BEST (

With the sunset reflecting off the burning red Bryce-like hoodoos and a gentle breeze kissing the bows of the beautiful ponderosa pines, the cool evening air feels almost too good to be true. Could we really be on the Colorado Plateau in late June? At a higher elevation than most of southern Utah, this campground is a true pleasure. Loop B's elevated sites have views across the canyon at the hoodoos forming a natural red amphitheater. Loop A is lower and closer to the road, but the sites are still tranquil on the pine needle–covered forest floor. Many sites feature level tent pads. The campground is conveniently located only a half hour from the wonders of Bryce Canyon National Park, but it has its own worthy rock forms to explore. Consider it a perfect place to camp away from the crowded mega campgrounds in Bryce or a destination in itself. A paved bike trail heads up Route 9 for eight miles toward Bryce Canyon, and there are several short, scenic trails through the Forest Service–run Red Canyon. Try walking the one-mile Pink Ledges Trail just after sunrise to take advantage of the soft, early morning light on the colorful rock. If an evening stroll is your preferred activity, the Buckhorn Trail leaves right from site 23 and ascends 0.9 mile to a scenic vantage point above the canyon. With abundant hiking trails, beautiful scenery, and a new, well-cared-for campground, Red Canyon is one of the best Forest Service campgrounds in Utah.

Campsites, facilities: There are 37 sites for tents and RVs up to 45 feet in length. Picnic tables on cement pads, barbeque grills, fire pits, garbage service, pull-through sites, flush and vault toilets, a group picnic area, and drinking water are provided. Showers and a dump station are available. Leashed pets permitted.

Reservations, fees: Reservations are not accepted. Single sites are $12, double sites are $24, and additional vehicles are $6. Open mid-May through early October, weather permitting.

Directions: From Panguitch, drive south seven miles on Hwy. 89 and turn east (left) on Rte. 12. Continue 3.8 miles to the Red Canyon Campground on the right side of the road. GPS Coordinates: N 37° 44.586' W 112° 18.636'

Contact: Powell Ranger District, 435/679-9300, www.fs.fed.us/r4/dixie/recreation/campgrounds/redcanyon.html

34 BRYCE CANYON PINES RV PARK AND CAMPGROUND

Scenic rating: 7

on Route 12 near Bryce Canyon National Park

Map 6.2, page 278

This campground is a convenient place to stay to explore the wild hoodoos and majestic rock scenery of Bryce Canyon National Park, with all the amenities of a full-service RV park. It's a short drive from the entrance to the park. This is one of the most natural RV parks in Utah and offers a viable alternative if the park campgrounds are full. While there isn't much in the way scenic views, the open, pine forest setting is quite nice. Development is minimal,

and it's a nice blend of hotel-like facilities combined with an authentic camping experience. Long dirt parking areas have enough space for RVs, but the sites are appropriate for tents as well.

Campsites, facilities: There are 26 full hookup (20, 30 amps) sites and 15 no hook-up/tent sites. Picnic tables, rock fire rings, portable toilets, some fire rings, WiFi, pull-through sites, modern restrooms with showers (at main building), and drinking water are provided. A swimming pool, recreation room, gas station, laundry, and a small convenience store are available. Leashed pets permitted.

Reservations, fees: Reservations are accepted at 800/892-7923 or online. RV sites are $25, tent sites are $17, and group tent sites are $4 pp. Open April 1 through October 31.

Directions: From Panguitch, drive seven miles south on Hwy. 89 and turn east (left) on Rte. 12, continuing 10.6 miles to the Bryce Canyon Pines RV Park and Campground on the right side of the road. GPS Coordinates: N 37° 42.668' W 112° 13.028'

Contact: Bryce Canyon Pines RV Park and Campground, 435/834-5441, www.brycecanyonmotel.com/campground/

35 RUBY'S INN RV PARK AND CAMPGROUND

Scenic rating: 5

near Bryce Canyon National Park

Map 6.2, page 278

Ruby's Inn is a large complex of lodging, shops, gas, and campgrounds near the entrance to Bryce Canyon National Park. This is the closest private campground and lodging to Bryce and therefore a good alternative to staying in the park. The campground sprawls out behind the lodges into an open pine forest. Some sites are in the open, and others are tucked into the canopy of trees. The facility seems well kept and offers lots of amenities you won't find in the park. A wide range of services include a post office, mountain bike rentals, scenic flights, horseback trail rides, and a free park shuttle. The trade-off is that the surrounding environment isn't nearly as scenic as the pine-forested campgrounds in Bryce. The sites here are very tightly spaced, so expect to get to know your neighbor. Open tent-camping spots are located around the RV sites in a forest area.

Campsites, facilities: There are 147 full hook-up sites, 21 partial hook-up sites, three group camping areas, nine tepees, and five cabins. Picnic tables, modern restrooms with showers, drinking water, WiFi, swimming pool, hot tub, dish-washing station, garbage service, and dump station are provided. Laundry is available. Leashed pets permitted.

Reservations, fees: Reservations are accepted at 866/866-6616 or online at https://secure. areatravel.net/rubysinn/reservations_camp. asp for RV sites, cabins, and tepees. Tent sites are on a first-come, first-served basis. Full hook-up sites are $31, tent sites are $20, and partial hook-up sites and tepees are $28. Open year-round.

Directions: From Panguitch, drive south on Hwy. 89 for seven miles, then turn east (left) on Rte. 12. Continue 14 miles east on Rte. 12 and turn south on Rte. 63. The campground is beyond the main lodge and general store on the right-hand side.

GPS Coordinates: N 37° 40.086' W 112° 09.513'

Contact: Ruby's Inn RV Park, 800/468-8660, www.brycecanyoncampgrounds.com./bryce-canyon-campground.html

36 KING CREEK

Scenic rating: 7

in the Dixie National Forest

Map 6.2, page 278

King Creek Campground has a pine forest setting with access to a beautiful reservoir. The Tropic Reservoir is on the East Fork of the Sevier River near Bryce Canyon National Park. The campground enjoys shade from the large trees but still maintains an open, spacious feel. Sites have pine needles on the forest floor and cement pads for eating areas. The campground has recently been improved with paved trails to some of the sites to increase access for people with disabilities. Views in the campground are limited to the surrounding forest. Recreational activities are possible on Tropic Reservoir. The lake is accessed by a boat ramp, and fishing is popular. ATV riders will enjoy the Fremont, East Fork, and Paunsaugunt ATV Trails.

Campsites, facilities: There are 38 sites, a group area for up to 150 people, plus 10 sites of dispersed camping along the East Fork of the Sevier River. The dispersed sites are primitive sites with rock fire rings and little else. Be sure to bring everything you need if you plan on camping in these sites. Picnic tables on cement pads, barbeque grills, modern restrooms and vault toilets, and drinking water are provided at the King Creek Campground. Firewood is for sale. A dump station is available. Leashed pets permitted.

Reservations, fees: Reservations are required for the group site at 877/444-6777 or online at www.recreation.gov and must be made at least four days in advance. The group site is $40 for up to 50 people, $80 for 51–100 people, and $120 for 101–150 people. Individual sites are $10, and extra vehicles are $5. Open mid-May through early September, weather permitting.

Directions: From Panguitch, drive south on Hwy. 89 for seven miles and turn east (left) on Rte. 12. Travel 11.5 miles east on Rte. 12 and turn right onto East Fork Road, signed for King Creek. Continue seven miles, turn right, and drive 0.5 mile to the King Creek Campground.

GPS Coordinates: N 37° 36.522' W 112° 15.494'

Contact: Powell Ranger District, 435/679-9300, www.fs.fed.us/r4/dixie/recreation/ campgrounds/kingcreek.html, for the group site www.fs.fed.us/r4/dixie/recreation/

campgrounds/kingcreekgroup.html, and for dispersed camping, www.fs.fed.us/r4/dixie/recreation/campgrounds/East_Fork.pdf

37 NORTH

Scenic rating: 8

in Bryce Canyon National Park

Map 6.2, page 278　　　**BEST**

Bryce Canyon National Park is an outdoor photographer's dream. The park displays brightly colored, wildly formed hoodoo rock formations accessed by a well-designed road to various viewpoints and overlooks. Without fail, at sunrise and sunset you'll find a collection of tripod-toting photographers waiting patiently at the canyon rim to capture the best light of the day. Join them—or just take pictures in your mind—but make sure you're around to experience the light show at the magic hour when the rock shows its true colors. The best way to be at the canyon rim at the right time is to camp in the park. Bryce Canyon National Park has two campgrounds of similar size in very close proximity to each other near the entrance to the park. The first campground reached after the entrance station is the North Campground. North is set on gently undulating ground in an open ponderosa pine forest. The security and shelter this forest provides can feel like a welcome treat after the exposure of the surrounding open desert. The campground is within spitting distance of the park visitors center and the ultra-scenic canyon rim. The paved, multi-loop layout is well designed with good separation between sites and maintains a natural feel despite its heavy use. Separate loops designated for RVs and tents allow different camping styles to happily coexist in different necks of these woods. The dirt-floored sites are bit dusty because of heavy use, but that's to be expected in a busy national park. Be sure to step out of the tent or trailer at night and check out the dazzling display of stars. Clean air and a lack of light pollution make for some

of the best stargazing anywhere; to celebrate, the Bryce Canyon Astronomy Festival is held the last weekend in June.

Campsites, facilities: There are 107 sites. Loops A and B are for RV campers, where vehicles must be over 20 feet in length and generators are allowed 8 A.M.–8 P.M. Loops C and D are for tent campers; maximum vehicle length is 20 feet. A dump station is available south of the campground for a fee. Picnic tables, flush toilets, drinking water, a campfire circle, recycling containers, barbeque grills, garbage service, and fire grills are provided. Leashed pets permitted.

Reservations, fees: Reservations are accepted for 32 of the sites from early May through September and can be made from two to 240 days in advance. Sites are $15. At least one of the loops is open year-round, weather permitting.

Directions: From Panguitch, drive south on Hwy. 89 for seven miles and turn east (left) on Rte. 12. Continue 14 miles east on Rte. 12 and turn south (right) on Rte. 63. Travel south on Rte. 63 for 4.5 miles to the park entrance and visitors center. The campground is on the left, 0.1 mile from the visitors center.

GPS Coordinates: N 37° 38.222' W 112° 10.152'

Contact: Bryce Canyon National Park, 435/834-5322, www.nps.gov/brca/planyourvisit/northcampground.htm

38 SUNSET

Scenic rating: 8

in Bryce Canyon National Park

Map 6.2, page 278　　　**BEST**

Bryce Canyon draws visitors from all over the world. Its colorful geology has been so widely publicized it has almost become a cliché. Even so, looking out over the canyon for the first time is an indescribable and powerful experience and shouldn't be missed. The most complete way to experience the park is to camp in one of the two park service campgrounds. Sunset Campground is just past North Campground, about 1.2 miles from the park entrance and directly across from the Sunset Overlook. Like North, the campground is spread out under the shelter of a ponderosa pine forest, and it, too, has separate loops for RVers who'd like to use their generators and tent campers who'd rather listen to the sounds of nature. The campground is much flatter than North. A short trail leads from the campground to Sunset Point on the amphitheater rim. At the rim is the trailhead for a collection of great day-hike trails snaking through the hoodoo landscape inside the amphitheater. Sunset's easy access to these trails makes it one of my favorite campgrounds for hiking in Utah.

Campsites, facilities: There are 101 sites and one group site for 7–30 people. Sites 223, 224, 309, and the group site are wheelchair accessible. Loop A is for RV campers, where vehicles must be over 20 feet in length and generators are allowed 8 A.M.–8 P.M. Loops B and C are for tent campers, with a maximum vehicle length of 20 feet. Picnic tables, barbeque grills, fire grills, drinking water, flush toilets, a campfire circle ring, and garbage service are provided. A dump station is available at North Campground for a fee. Leashed pets permitted.

Reservations, fees: Reservations are only accepted for the group site at 877/444-6777 or online at www.recreation.gov. Reservations are accepted for the group site from May through September and can be made from two to 240 days in advance. The group site is $40 for seven people (minimum) plus $3 pp up to a maximum of 30 people. Single sites are $15. Open May through October, weather permitting.

Directions: From Panguitch, drive south on Hwy. 89 for seven miles, then turn east (left) on Rte. 12. Continue 14 miles east on Rte. 12 and turn south on Rte. 63. Travel south on Rte. 63 for 4.5 miles to the park entrance and visitors center. The campground is on the right, 1.2 miles from the visitors center.
GPS Coordinates: N 37° 37.374' W 112° 10.371'

Contact: Bryce Canyon National Park, 435/834-5322, www.nps.gov/brca/planyourvisit/sunsetcampground.htm and for the group site, www.nps.gov/brca/planyourvisit/sunsetgroupsite.htm

39 BRYCE PIONEER VILLAGE RV PARK AND CAMPGROUND

Scenic rating: 4

in the town of Tropic

Map 6.2, page 278

The Bryce Pioneer Village RV Park and Campground looks like it was an afterthought for this motel. The RV and tent spaces take up unused parking lot space and help pat down the weeds growing out of the gravel. There is no shade for the any of the sites. There are picnic tables at the sites and some redeeming distant views of the pink cliffs of the Aquarius Plateau to the east. Tropic is about 11 miles from the entrance to Bryce Canyon National Park. Plan to stay here only if you don't care at all about the aesthetic character of a campground. Consider using one of the other many options in the Bryce area.

Campsites, facilities: There are 10 RV sites with full hook-ups (20, 30 amps) and six tent sites. Picnic tables, a dish-washing station, drinking water, and modern restrooms with showers are provided. Leashed pets permitted.

Reservations, fees: Reservations are not accepted. Full hook-up sites are $18, and tent sites are $12. Open March 1 through October 31.

Directions: From Cannonville, travel north on Rte. 12 for five miles to the town of Tropic. Bryce Poineer Village RV Park is on the left side of the road.
GPS Coordinates: N 37° 37.318' W 112° 04.957'

Contact: Bryce Pioneer Village RV Park and Campground, 435/679-8536, www.bpvillage.com/

40 BRYCE VALLEY KOA

Scenic rating: 4

in Cannonville

Map 6.2, page 278

This KOA campground is located in the tiny town of Cannonville, conveniently positioned between the destinations of Bryce Canyon National Park and Kodachrome Basin State Park. Both parks are favorites of outdoor photographers because of their amazing multihued rocks, which burn saturated red at sunrise and sunset. This KOA is the closest campground outside of Kodachrome Basin State Park, which was nearly full when we visited. The campground is not as pretty as the parks it's near, but it does have more to offer than its run-of-the-mill RV park first impression. This KOA is a lesson in not judging a book by its cover, or more appropriately, not judging a campground from the road. After a little more exploration, we discovered the back side of the campground, with a hidden tent loop totally separate and far more scenic than the roadside RV slips. The back loop sports the best views of the surrounding hills and cliffs. A Western-style lodgepole pine fence hems in the property, but the sites have a very open, sometimes windy feel. Birds were chirping in the trees, which provided sporadic shade for some sites.

Campsites, facilities: There are 49 full hookup (20-, 30-, and 50-amp) sites, 18 tent sites, and seven cabins. Picnic tables, fire grills, pull-through sites, kitchen areas, a playground, pet walk, basketball court, swimming pool, modern restrooms with showers, garbage service, and drinking water are provided. Amenities include a small general store, WiFi, a dump station, laundry, RV supplies, and ice. Leashed pets permitted (with breed restrictions).

Reservations, fees: Reservations are accepted at 888/562-4710 or online at https://koa.com/where/ut/44151/reserve/. RV sites are $28–38, tent sites are $22–28, and cabins are $40–60. Open March 15 through November 15.

Directions: Upon entering the town of Cannonville on Rte. 12, the Bryce Valley KOA is located at the intersection of Rte. 12 and Red Rock Road.

GPS Coordinates: N 37° 34.183' W 112° 03.372'

Contact: Bryce Valley KOA, 435/679-8988 or 888/562-4710, www.brycecanyonkoa.com

41 POINT SUPREME

Scenic rating: 7

on the Markagunt Plateau in Cedar Breaks National Monument

Map 6.2, page 278   **BEST**

Cedar Breaks National Monument is one of the wonderful places in Utah that remains under the radar because the state boasts so much amazing scenery. If Cedar Breaks were anywhere else, it would undoubtedly be a national park, but because the rock formations in Bryce Canyon are so similar, Cedar Breaks remains one of Utah's best-kept secrets. Like Bryce, the park sits well above the surrounding desert, topping out above 10,000 feet on the Markagunt Plateau, and is a welcomed break from the summer heat. The Point Supreme Campground loop occupies a ridge overlooking open meadows painted with wildflowers in midsummer. Visitors can expect to see the speckles of red Indian paintbrush, white columbine, yellow cinquefoil, purple shooting stars, and pink wild roses, both in the meadows and on the canyon rim. In fact, the summer flower display is so spectacular here that a Cedar Breaks National Monument Wildflower Festival is held annually in early July. Campsites overlook the lovely meadows or are tucked into clumps of Engelmann spruce trees, many of which are dead or dying from a spruce bark beetle epidemic. A quaint little amphitheater is well positioned in a field of flowers. Gravel parking areas and tent pads ranging from off kilter to nonexistent don't quite live up to the expectations of a park service campground, but overall it's still a good facility in an amazing setting. The lack of crowds and easy access to a beautiful park more than make up for the minor shortcomings in facilities.

Campsites, facilities: There are 28 individual sites. Site 27 is wheelchair accessible. Picnic tables, fire grills, pull-through sites, a picnic area, flush toilets, drinking water, and an amphitheater are provided. Leashed pets permitted.

Reservations, fees: Reservations are not accepted. The fee is $14 per site. Open June through September, weather permitting.

Directions: From Cedar City, drive 18 miles east on Rte. 14 and turn north (left) on Rte. 148. Continue for six miles; the turnoff for the campground will be on the right.

GPS Coordinates: N 37° 36.667' W 112° 49.889'

Contact: Cedar Breaks National Monument, 435/586-9451, www.nps.gov/cebr/planyourvisit/camping-fees.htm

42 CEDAR CANYON

Scenic rating: 7

in Dixie National Forest

Map 6.2, page 278

Cedar Canyon Campground is built into a lovely spruce forest on Route 14 near the Ashton Gorge Wilderness Area just west of Cedar Breaks National Monument. It's tucked discreetly away, in a location you might not even notice if you weren't looking for it. It has a different feel than the other campground in the Cedar Breaks area and is especially appealing if you prefer the protection provided by thick stands of alpine spruce. Look and listen for hummingbirds engaging in aerial combat—and hope their high-pitched maneuvers drown out the cars cruising past on the adjacent highway. Despite its proximity to the road, which isn't very busy at night, this campground

is actually a nice little forested loop. The small, quiet Coal Creek runs through the campground. Dense stands of spruce and aspens surround the widely spaced campsites and offer shade and shelter on sunny summer days. Just up the road there are some nice pink hoodoo formations, but the campground itself doesn't offer a lot to do. It does put you within a short drive of Cedar Breaks National Monument, Brian Head Ski Resort, and the general beauty of the Markagunt Plateau.

Campsites, facilities: There are 18 sites for tents and RVs up to 24 feet in length and one group site for up to 35 people. Picnic tables, fire grills, vault toilets, drinking water, and garbage service are provided. Firewood is available. Leashed pets permitted.

Reservations, fees: Reservations are accepted at 877/444-6777 or online at www.recreation. gov and must be made at least four days in advance. Individual sites are $12, and the group site is $40. Open early June through early September, weather permitting.

Directions: From Cedar City, drive 13 miles east on Rte. 14. Cedar Canyon Campground is on the north (left) side of the road.

GPS Coordinates: N 37° 35.502' W 112° 54.271'

Contact: Cedar City Ranger District, 435/865-3200, www.fs.fed.us/r4/dixie/recreation/campgrounds/cedarcanyon.html

43 DEER HAVEN

Scenic rating: 7

in Dixie National Forest

Map 6.2, page 278

Deer Haven is a group-oriented campground located at nearly 9,000 feet, near the Ashdown Gorge Wilderness Area. Open grassy meadows accented with the splash of red Indian Paintbrush wildflowers are complemented by mature stands of aspen. These groves of white-barked trees are ideal habitat for mountain bluebirds, as well as providing shade and comfort for campers in a cool alpine environment. The campground feels relatively undeveloped, with gravel drives and parking spaces combined with a mix of walk-in tent areas and single campsites. It also features an amphitheater with a large group fire circle. While the campground is designed for group use, there is a loop of individual sites as well. The 32.5-mile Virgin River Rim Trail crosses the access road at the entrance to the campground. This mountain-bike trail meanders through the Dixie National Forest high country and offers great views of the Kolob Plateau, Zion National Park, and the Pine Valley Mountains; it can be ridden in 7–10 hours point to point by strong riders with a shuttle. Deer Haven is also near the Cedar Break National Monument with nearby roads offering views of its scenic geology and distant vistas toward Zion National Park.

Campsites, facilities: There are 10 individual walk-in sites and 10 units in a large group area able to accommodate RVs up to 24 feet in length. Picnic tables, fire rings, flush and vault toilets, drinking water, an amphitheater, and a large parking area are provided. Leashed pets permitted.

Reservations, fees: Reservations are required for the group site at 877/444-6777 or online at www.recreation.gov and must be made at least four days in advance. Reservations are not accepted for the individual sites. Individual sites are $10, the group site is $55 for 50 people plus $1 pp for up to 200 people, and extra vehicles and day use are $5. Open early June through early September.

Directions: From Cedar City, drive 16 miles east on Rte. 14, turn right on Webster Flat Road, and continue 2.1 miles to the campground.

GPS Coordinates: N 37° 34.409' W 112° 54.540'

Contact: Cedar City Ranger District, 435/865-3200, www.fs.fed.us/r4/dixie/recreation/campgrounds/deerhaven.shtml

44 DUCK CREEK

Scenic rating: 7

in Dixie National Forest

Map 6.2, page 278

Duck Creek Campground is the largest campground in this part of the Dixie National Forest. Located near the turnoff to Navajo Lake on Route 14, the Forest Service campground is a centrally located spot. The campground acts as a base from which to explore the scenic high country of Point Supreme, the spectacular Cedar Breaks overlooks, and the subtle, recreation-rich Navajo Lake area. In the immediate vicinity of the campground, Duck Creek and Duck Creek Pond both offer good fishing. Right across the road, Duck Creek Visitors Center offers information about the plethora of recreation in the area. Five campground loops weave beneath the canopy of ponderosa pine, aspen, and spruce. Sites are nestled in among the trees, protected from the sun, and well spaced for a large, busy campground. The campground has an amphitheater and special ATV parking to accommodate one of its biggest user groups. The facilities are first rate and include a pay phone and volleyball court. The campground's only drawbacks stem from its size and popularity—expect it to be busy and well loved.

Campsites, facilities: There are 94 sites for tents and RVs up to 35 feet in length and four group sites. Duck Creek and Ponderosa Group Areas can accommodate up to 150 people and Roundup and Wagon Train Group Areas up to 50 people. There are 27 sites that are wheelchair accessible. Picnic tables, fire grills, flush and vault toilets, drinking water, garbage service, a volleyball court (bring your own net/ball), an amphitheater, and a dump station are provided. Firewood is available. Leashed pets permitted.

Reservations, fees: Reservations are accepted at 877/444-6777 or online at www.recreation.gov and must be made at least four days in advance.

Single sites are $12, double sites are $20, triple sites are $30, and the day-use fee is $6. Ponderosa and Duck Creek Group Areas are $55 for the first 50 people plus $1 pp for up to 150 people. The Wagon Train and Roundup Group Areas are $55 (up to 50 people). Open early June through early September, weather permitting.

Directions: From Cedar City, drive 28 miles east on Rte. 14. Duck Creek Campground will be on the north side (left) of the road.

GPS Coordinates: N 37° 31.127' W 112° 41.930'

Contact: Cedar City Ranger District, 435/865-3200, www.fs.fed.us/r4/dixie/recreation/campgrounds/duckcreek.html

45 SPRUCES

Scenic rating: 7

in Dixie National Forest

Map 6.2, page 278

Spruces is the first of three campgrounds along Navajo Lake. Navajo Lake is one of Southern Utah's few natural lakes and is fed by numerous springs and lava tubes. The lake is approximately three miles long and sits at 9,042 feet on the Markagunt Plateau. Its waters empty into both Duck Creek and Cascade Falls. Hills blanketed in alpine spruce trees rim the north shore of the lake, while three developed Forest Service campgrounds and the Navajo Lake Lodge occupy the southern shore. Rainbow and brook trout are stocked annually and provide good fishing. Boating is popular here; a boat-launch facility and boat rentals are available at the Navajo Lake Lodge. The spruce bark beetles have taken their toll on the local forests, and Spruces Campground has been cleared of the dead trees, leaving the campground with a very open feel and views of the lake. Sites are built into the hillside on small, terraced benches as the slope rises away from the lake. Some sites have level gravel tent pads built into the landscape. Lava boulders, grass, and scattered aspen and spruce trees break up the

otherwise open, exposed sites. Parking spots and the campground loop are paved.

Campsites, facilities: There are 25 sites for tents and RVs up to 24 feet in length and six walk-in tent sites. Picnic tables, fire grills, flush toilets, drinking water, and garbage service are provided. Firewood is available. Leashed pets permitted.

Reservations, fees: Reservations are not accepted. Single sites are $12, double sites are $20, and extra vehicles and day use are $6. Open early June through early September, weather permitting.

Directions: From Cedar City, drive 25 miles east on Rte. 14, turn right on Navajo Lake Road, and continue 2.4 miles to the Spruces Campground.

GPS Coordinates: N 37° 31.124' W 112° 46.464'

Contact: Cedar City Ranger District, 435/865-3200, www.fs.fed.us/r4/dixie/recreation/campgrounds/spruces.html

46 NAVAJO LAKE

Scenic rating: 8

in Dixie National Forest

Map 6.2, page 278

Navajo Lake is the second Forest Service Campground encountered along the southern shore of its namesake lake. The Navajo Lake Campground is similar and close to the Spruces Campground but has a few noticeable differences. More trees seem to have survived the spruce bark beetle epidemic, and the campground enjoys more shade as a result. Bluebell wildflowers grow between sites, which attract butterflies like European whites and painted ladies. Lava rocks are scattered about the sites, and grass grows where the trees have been removed. The trees give the campground a more balanced feel than Spruces. The campground sits right on the lake shore and has a boat ramp with lake access and parking for anglers. The lakeside loop is more open and sits along the shore, while a second loop on the south side of the road works up the hill away from the lake. The upper loop features seven walk-in sites (sites 18–24) set off to themselves for tent campers.

Campsites, facilities: There are 16 single sites, four double sites for tents and RVs up to 24 feet in length, and seven walk-in tent sites. Picnic tables, fire grills, drinking water, and flush toilets are provided. Leashed pets permitted.

Reservations, fees: Reservations are not accepted. Single sites are $12, double sites are $20, tent sites are $10, and extra vehicles and day use are $6.

Directions: From Cedar City, drive 25 miles east on Rte. 14, turn right on Navajo Lake Road, and continue for 3.2 miles to the Navajo Lake Campground.

GPS Coordinates: N 37° 31.273' W 112° 47.361'

Contact: Cedar City Ranger District, 435/865-3200, www.fs.fed.us/r4/dixie/recreation/campgrounds/navajolake.html

47 TE-AH

Scenic rating: 7

in Dixie National Forest

Map 6.2, page 278   **BEST (**

Te-ah Campground is the last Forest Service Campground encountered on Navajo Lake. Te-ah has a different feel than both Spruces and Navajo Lake Campgrounds, which hug the lake shore and overlook its waters. Te-ah sits above the wetlands at the west tip of Navajo Lake. It doesn't provide access to the lake; in fact, one of the loops doesn't even have views of the lake. Te-ah has two distinct loops, both paved. The lower loop is open with some views of the lake, and sites are grassy with clumps of aspen trees. The small trees do not provide much shade. The upper loop has a forested feel, cut out of groves of aspen and spruce. These trees provide privacy and adequate separation between the well-spaced sites. Wild turkey and deer are often spotted in the campground. In addition to boating and

fishing opportunities on Navajo Lake, Te-ah provides close proximity to mountain biking on the Virgin River Rim Trail. With a group site specifically set up for mountain bikers, Te-ah makes the list as one of the best campgrounds for biking. It also is the trailhead for the short half-mile Pinks Trail, which leads to the pink cliffs from the upper campground loop.

Campsites, facilities: There are 41 sites and one group site (Site 33) for up to 30 people, set up for mountain bike tour groups. Sites 17, 18, and 23 are wheelchair accessible. Picnic tables, fire grills, flush and vault toilets, garbage service, drinking water, and pull-through sites are provided. The group site includes a bike rack and a bike-washing station. Firewood is available. Leashed pets permitted.

Reservations, fees: Reservations are accepted at 877/444-6777 or online at www.recreation.gov and must be made at least four days in advance. Single sites are $12, the group site is $30, and extra vehicles and day use are $6. Open late May through early September, weather permitting.

Directions: From Cedar City, drive 25 miles east on Rte. 14, turn right on Navajo Lake Road, and continue for 4.3 miles to the Te-ah campground.

GPS Coordinates: N 37° 31.985' W 112° 49.115'

Contact: Cedar City Ranger District, 435/865-3200, www.fs.fed.us/r4/dixie/recreation/campgrounds/teah.html

48 ZION-BRYCE KOA

Scenic rating: 6

five miles north of Glendale on Hwy. 89

Map 6.2, page 278

The Zion-Bryce KOA is one of the more scenic KOAs in Utah. Views from the campground look across a narrow valley at basalt columns and up to pink rock hoodoos in the other direction. Antique plows and farming equipment greet visitors at the office and entry to the facility.

It occupies a convenient central location from which to explore a variety of southwestern Utah's hotspots. The closest major destinations are the east entrance to Zion, Cedar Breaks National Monument, Bryce Canyon, and the Canyons of the Escalante. The campground itself is set on a gently sloping hillside as it works back down toward Highway 89. The grounds are grassy, with a gravel driveway and parking spaces. There is very little separation between sites; tent sites in particular are tightly packed along a wood fence. Despite being in a rural setting, the campground is still close to the major highway.

Campsites, facilities: There are 22 full hook-up (20-, 30-, and 50-amp) sites and 50 partial hook-up sites for RVs up to 75 feet in length. Tent sites are designated A through Q, and there are three cabins. Picnic tables, fire pits, grassy tent sites, pull-through sites, a swimming pool, a playground, drinking water, WiFi, garbage service, and modern restrooms with showers are provided. Firewood, a convenience store, ice, and bicycle rentals are available. Leashed pets permitted.

Reservations, fees: Reservations are accepted at 800/562-8635. RV sites are $25–32, tent sites are $22, and cabins are $38–$42. Open May 1 through September 30.

Directions: From Glendale, drive north on Hwy. 89 for five miles and turn left into the campground.

GPS Coordinates: N 37° 23.116' W 112° 34.564'

Contact: Zion-Bryce KOA, 800/562-8635, www.koa.com/where/ut/44131/

49 BAUER'S CANYON RANCH RV PARK

Scenic rating: 6

in Glendale

Map 6.2, page 278

This RV park is part of a working ranch with unique character in the little country town of Glendale. The campground is bordered by an orchard and enjoys scenic views of the hills around town. The grounds are set back a block from the highway in a quiet, relaxing setting. Tent campers will appreciate the separate area designated to pitch their shelters along a narrow, grassy strip under apple trees. RV sites have gravel parking aprons with grass lawns. The country-Western theme of the RV park is genuinely exuded by the owner. Ask about Dutch oven cooking and chuckwagon cookouts that can be arranged for your group. Fishing is possible in a stream that runs through the ranch and is stocked with rainbow trout by Utah Fish and Game. In my opinion, this is by far the nicest RV park along this stretch of Highway 89.

Campsites, facilities: There are 21 full hook-up (20-, 30-, and 50-amp) sites and 10 walk-in tent sites. Picnic tables, a dump station, modern restrooms with showers, pull-through sites, garbage service, and drinking water are provided. Laundry is available. Leashed pets permitted.

Reservations, fees: Reservations are accepted at 888/648-2564 or online at www.bauersrv.com/reservation.htm. Tent sites are $10, and full hook-ups are $24. Open March 1 to November 1.

Directions: From the town of Mount Carmel Junction, drive nine miles north on Hwy. 89 to the town of Glendale. Bauer's Canyon Ranch RV Park is on the left side of the road.

GPS Coordinates: N 37° 19.096' W 112° 35.945'

Contact: Bauer's Canyon Ranch RV Park, 435/648-2564, www.bauersrv.com

50 MT. CARMEL CAMPGROUND AND TRAILER PARK

Scenic rating: 5

in Mount Carmel

Map 6.2, page 278

Intimately close to Highway 89, this trailer park might only be a few miles from the east side of Zion National Park, but in terms of ambience and splendor, it might as well be another planet! Of course, with full hook-ups for $15, how can you really complain? The small gravel yard is shaded by tall trees, which provide some degree of privacy from the road. The RV park, on the banks of Muddy Creek, is beside a small motel. Its atmosphere is very laid back and casual, and you won't feel any pressure to keep up with the Joneses here! The campground is owned and operated by a friendly woman who came over from her house down the street to answer all our questions.

Campsites, facilities: There are 10 pull-through RV sites, six tent sites, and one cabin. Picnic tables, modern restrooms with showers, drinking water, and garbage service are provided. Leashed pets permitted.

Reservations, fees: Reservations are accepted at 435/648-2323. Full hook-up sites are $15 and tent sites are $10. Open early April through November, weather permitting.

Directions: From the town of Mount Carmel Junction (the intersection of Rte. 9 and Hwy. 89), drive two miles north on Hwy. 89. Mt. Carmel Campground will be on the left as you enter Mount Carmel.

GPS Coordinates: N 37° 14.505' W 112° 40.274'

Contact: Mt. Carmel Campground and Trailer Park, 435/648-2323, www.visiteastzion.info/mcrvpark.html

51 SOUTH

Scenic rating: 8

in Zion National Park

Map 6.2, page 278

Zion National Park features two huge, conveniently located campgrounds at the entrance to the Zion Canyon: South and Watchman. Zion Canyon is a stunningly beautiful place, a massive canyon carved by the Virgin River as it drops off the western edge of the Colorado Plateau. The erosive power of eons of flash floods paired with the slow but steady uplift of an immense chunk of the earth's crust has created an inspiring scene unparalleled anywhere in the world. Cliffs of 2,000 feet, ranging in color from milky white to crimson red to chocolate brown, wall in the canyon on either side. Recreation opportunities in the canyon are endless and can be accessed from the campground by free park service shuttles that leave every 6–8 minutes. Some of the best hikes include Angel's Landing, Observation Point, The Narrows, Riverside Walk, Hidden Canyon, and the Emerald Pools. Rock climbing is popular on Zion's steep, often featureless sandstone walls, and big wall climbers consider it second only to Yosemite for its long sustained routes. Canyoneers love Zion for its deep, dark, technically challenging slot canyons, many of which require swimming through frigid pools of water, scrambling over and around chalkstones, and rappelling off fixed anchors. South Campground is better suited to tent campers than Watchman, with smaller sites with tent pads. The campground is shaded by large cottonwood trees and has soaring views to the cliffs above. The beauty of the place can't be denied, but South Campground is huge and sprawling and can feel more like a small town than a camp. If you visit in the busy season (mid-March through October), you'll be sharing the place with hundreds of others. The sites are packed together and are close to the road. Don't expect much privacy or a wilderness experience.

Campsites, facilities: There are 127 campsites; three are wheelchair accessible. Picnic tables, fire grills, modern restrooms, drinking water, garbage service, and a dump station are provided. Generators are allowed 8–10 A.M. and 6–8 P.M. Leashed pets permitted.

Reservations, fees: Reservations are not accepted. Sites are $16. Open March through September.

Directions: From Springdale, drive east on Rte. 9 to the south entrance of Zion National Park; South Campground is 0.5 mile from this entrance on the right. Those traveling to Zion from the east should be advised vehicles over 7'10" in width or 11'4" in height must have an escort to pass through a narrow tunnel on Rte. 9.

GPS Coordinates: N 37° 12.237' W 112° 59.032'

Contact: Zion National Park, 435/772-3256, www.nps.gov/zion/planyourvisit/south-campground.htm

52 WATCHMAN

Scenic rating: 8

in Zion National Park

Map 6.2, page 278   **BEST (**

Watchman Campground is adjacent to South, and the second campground encountered upon entering Zion Canyon. Both campgrounds are a short walk from the park visitors center and the shuttle bus stop. The shuttle accesses copious recreation opportunities, from family-friendly walks to multi-day rock climbs. Permits and information are available at the visitors center, and equipment can be rented from several full-service outfitters in Springdale. Watchman Campground caters more to RVs and big rigs and has sites with electric hook-ups, but it offers some nice tent sites as well. This huge collection of RV sites in such a dramatic setting make Watchman one the best public campgrounds for RVs in Utah. The campground is actually quite lush and green for being in the desert canyon, due to its close proximity to the Virgin River and the small irrigation canals you'll see running between sites. The sites themselves have red gravel parking spots and are tightly packed into the campground. The campground has a modern amphitheater with a huge list of ranger-led programs to engage kids and families. Check at the visitors center to see what's on tap when you arrive. Like South Campground, the whole complex remains busy throughout the high season. Arrive early in the day or make reservations ahead of time to be safe.

Campsites, facilities: There are 95 sites with electrical hook-ups (30 amps) and 69 tent-only sites, seven of these for groups. Two sites are wheelchair accessible. Picnic tables, fire grills, drinking water, recycling, garbage service, an amphitheater, dump station, and flush toilets are provided. Generators are not permitted. Leashed pets permitted.

Reservations, fees: Reservations are accepted for the months of March through October. They can be made up to six months in advance at 877/444-6777 or online at www.recreation.gov. During the rest of the year, sites are first-come, first-served. Sites with electric hook-ups are $18, riverside electric hook-up sites are $20, and tent-only sites are $16. Group sites are $3 pp (minimum of nine people and maximum of 50 people). Open year-round.

Directions: From Springdale, drive east on Rte. 9 to the south entrance of Zion National Park; Watchman Campground is 0.7 mile from this entrance on the right. Those traveling to Zion from the east should be advised that vehicles over 7'10" in width or 11'4" in height must have an escort to pass through a narrow tunnel on Rte. 9.

GPS Coordinates: N 37° 11.871' W 112° 59.260'

Contact: Zion National Park, 435/772-3256, www.nps.gov/zion/planyourvisit/watchman-campground.htm

53 ZION CANYON CAMPGROUND AND RV RESORT

Scenic rating: 7

in Springdale outside the south entrance to Zion National Park

Map 6.2, page 278

You won't find an RV park that's any closer to the south entrance of Zion National Park. This motel and RV park is a short stroll from the park's gates and is surrounded by the towering cliffs that attract visitors from around the world. Views in every direction are quite spectacular. And the park shuttle bus stops right at the front door. There are dozens of shops, cafés, restaurants, galleries, and a beautiful new public library within walking distance as well. Trees shade many of the sites at this campground on the west bank of the Virgin River. The grounds look a little run-down and aren't very appealing, but considering how much there is to do around the campground, it isn't a bad option.

Campsites, facilities: There are 85 full hookup (20-, 30-, and 50-amp) sites, 20 partial hook-up sites, and 100 no hook-up/tent sites. A swimming pool (open seasonally), playground, river access, dump station, cable TV, fire pits, barbeque grills, pull-through sites, modern restrooms with showers, and picnic tables are provided. A convenience store and laundry are available. Pets are allowed only in air-conditioned motor homes.

Reservations, fees: Reservations are accepted at 435/772-3237 or online at www.zioncamp. com/reservation_form.php. RV sites are $30, tent sites are $25, and group tent sites are $8 pp. Open year-round.

Directions: Enter Springdale on Rte. 9 and continue to 0.5 mile before the entrance to Zion. Zion Canyon RV and Campground will be on the right.

GPS Coordinates: N 37° 11.631' W 112° 59.580'

Contact: Zion Canyon Campground and RV Park, 435/772-3237, www.zioncamp.com

54 PONDEROSA GROVE
🏇 🏕 🚐 ⛰

Scenic rating: 7

west of Kanab and north of Coral Pink Sand Dunes State Park

Map 6.2, page 278

Ponderosa Grove is a small, quality BLM campground on the way to Coral Pink Sand Dunes State Park. The campground sits on the edge of the BLM's 14,830-acre Mosquito Mountain Wilderness Study Area. Hiking, wildlife-

viewing, and nature photography are popular in Mosquito Mountain area. The Ponderosa Grove loop circles under widely spaced ponderosa pines bordered on the west by a small grass meadow. Sagebrush and bunch grass grow between sites in a high desert environment. The facilities are well taken care of, and the small campground has a different feel than the heavily used sites at Coral Pink Sand Dunes State Park. There is a group site with fire grills and five picnic tables available. Temperatures can be hot here and the tiny black flies and no-see-ums vicious, but it's a lovely setting near a great state park and a large BLM natural area. If conditions are windy and the state park feels like a sandstorm, this campground offers a good alternative.

Campsites, facilities: There are nine sites for tents and RVs up to 24 feet in length and two group sites. Picnic tables, fire grills, fire pits, garbage service, and vault toilets are provided. There is no drinking water. Leashed pets permitted.

Reservations, fees: Reservations are not accepted. Single sites are $5, and the group site is $5 plus $1 pp. Open year-round.

Directions: From Kanab, drive north 7.2 miles on Hwy. 89 and turn west (left) on Hancock Road. Continue 7.4 miles to Ponderosa Grove. The campground will be on the northwest (right) side of the road.

GPS Coordinates: N 37° 05.346' W 112° 40.332'

Contact: Kanab Field Office, 435/644-4600, www.blm.gov/ut/st/en/fo/kanab/recreation/camping.html

55 CORAL PINK SAND DUNES STATE PARK
🏇 🏕 ♿ 🚐 ⛰

Scenic rating: 8

east of Kanab

Map 6.2, page 278   BEST (

Coral Pink Sand Dunes State Park protects a unique and substantial collection of pink sand dunes straddling the Utah/Arizona border. The park attracts heavy use from ORV and dune-buggy riders who play endlessly on the ever-shifting sands. It's also a favorite spot for outdoor photographers who try to capture the deep red and pink tones and abstract shapes and patterns of the sand forms at sunrise and sunset. Kids will love exploring the constantly shifting sand, making this one of the best parks in the state for camping with the whole family. The park is home to a variety of desert mammals including kit foxes, coyotes, mule deer, and jackrabbits. It's also the only place in the world you'll find the Coral Pink Sand Dunes tiger beetle. The campground sits west of the main sand dunes in a pinyon pine and juniper forest with sagebrush and rabbit brush cozying up to the sites. Sites have flat, sandy spots for tent camping and pull-through parking for RVs. Views look east to red-and-pink cliffs rising above the dunes and west at sunset over distant peaks. This campground is another one of the shining stars in Utah's state park system. Sites are both well spaced and designed, and they access a small, yet wonderful natural area. Temperatures in summer are hot but tolerable, and the open area cools off quickly at night, unlike some campgrounds in the southwest corner of the state.

Campsites, facilities: There are 22 individual sites and one group site for up to 40 people. Picnic tables, fire grills, modern restrooms with showers, drinking water, garbage service, a dump station, and a picnic area with a barbeque grill are provided. Firewood and ice are available. Leashed pets permitted.

Reservations, fees: Reservations are accepted at 800/322-3770 or online at www.reserveamerica.com. Single sites are $16, the group sites is $75, and day use is $6. Open year-round.

Directions: From Kanab, drive north 7.2 miles on Hwy. 89 and turn west (left) on Hancock Road. Continue 9.3 miles on Hancock Road, turn left, and drive 3.3 miles to the entrance to Coral Pink Sand Dunes State Park.

GPS Coordinates: N 37° 02.204' W 112° 43.866'

Contact: Coral Pink Sand Dunes State Park, 435/648-2800, http://stateparks.utah.gov/stateparks/parks/coral-pink/.

56 KANAB RV CORRAL

Scenic rating: 5

in Kanab

Map 6.2, page 278

The Kanab RV Corral is by far the most upscale of the Kanab RV parks. It's located a few blocks off busy Highway 89, making it the quietest in town. The nice facilities and peaceful location help make it the most popular as well. A paved drive and gravel parking make for easy access for RVs of any size. Sites are shaded by trees, and picnic tables sit on red rock strips. The sandstone and lava rock decorations blend together in a Xeriscape-style landscape. The campground has views up the red rock cliffs above town.

Campsites, facilities: There are 40 full hookup (20-, 30-, 50-amp) sites. Tents are not allowed. A swimming pool, WiFi, modern restrooms with showers, drinking water, a croquet field, horseshoes, a dog run, garbage service, and gazebos are provided. Laundry and ice are available. Leashed pets permitted.

Reservations, fees: Reservations are accepted. Full hook-up sites are $28. Open year-round.

Directions: From the intersection of Hwy. 89 and Alternate Hwy. 89, drive south on Alternate Hwy. 89 for one block; Kanab RV Corral will be on the east (left) side of the road.

GPS Coordinates: N 37° 02.403' W 112° 31.561'

Contact: Kanab RV Corral, 435/644-5330, www.kanabrvcorral.com/

57 CRAZY HORSE CAMPARK

Scenic rating: 4

in Kanab

Map 6.2, page 278

The Crazy Horse Campark occupies a rural lot on the east side of Kanab on Highway 89. Kanab is the gateway town to some of Utah's most sought-after rock formations, including the

Buckskin Gulch slot canyon in the Vermilion Cliffs National Monument

Wave, wildly popular with photographers, and Buckskin Gulch, the longest slot canyon in the world. Throngs of vacationers pass through the little town on their way to surrounding scenic hotspots like Lake Powell, the Grand Canyon, Vermillion Cliffs, and Grand Staircase-Escalante. The park is right on busy Highway 89, which makes it easy to find, but it can be noisy at night. It does have views up to red rock hills north of town. The campground looks a little downtrodden, but that doesn't seem to affect its popularity. A gravel loop accesses sites well shaded by big cottonwood trees.

Campsites, facilities: There are 44 full hookup (20-, 30-, and 50-amp) sites, 30 partial hook-up sites, six tent sites, and one group tent site that can accommodate up to nine tents. Picnic tables, drinking water, barbeque grills, fire rings, pull-through sites, a dump station, garbage service, game parlor, horseshoes, a playground, and a swimming pool (open seasonally) are provided. Leashed pets permitted.

Reservations, fees: Reservations are accepted at 435/644-2782. The fee for full hook-ups is $23, water and electric is $20, and tent sites are $16. Open year-round.

Directions: From the intersection of Hwy. 89 and Alternate Hwy. 89, drive east 0.5 mile on Hwy. 89; Crazy Horse is on the north (left) side of the road.

GPS Coordinates: N 37° 02.586' W 112° 31.014'

Contact: Crazy Horse Campark, 435/644-2782.

58 HITCH-N-POST RV PARK

Scenic rating: 3

in Kanab

Map 6.2, page 278

The Hitch-N-Post is a centrally located RV park, a spot to tie up the horse (or RV) and stumble to a local watering hole. The whole town of Kanab is within walking distance, so feel free to tie one on. Beware of the bikini ban, though, a little-known local law that banned not only bikinis but Speedos and cut-off shorts at the new public pool. The local ordinance enjoyed a short life in the spring of 2008. Even if you disagree with conservative local policies,

Kanab is good place to stock up or spend the night before heading out for a more liberating adventure in the surrounding natural playgrounds. As you might imagine, being right in town, the Hitch-N-Post RV Park is small and has tightly spaced RV slips alongside some permanent trailers. An abundance of trees provide important shade, and old Western trinkets, antique bottles, and deer antlers lining the roof of the office give the place unique character.

Campsites, facilities: There are 14 full hook-up (20-, 30-, and 50-amp) sites, three partial hook-up sites, five tent sites, and three cabins. Picnic tables, drinking water, WiFi, garbage service, pull-through sites, and modern restrooms with showers are provided. Leashed pets permitted.

Reservations, fees: Reservations are accepted at 800/458-3516. The fees for full hook-ups are $22 (30 amps) and $24 (50 amps), tent sites are $16, and cabins are $24–28. Open year-round.

Directions: From the intersection of Hwy. 89 and Alternate Hwy. 89, drive east one block to the Hitch-N-Post on the south (right) side of the road.

GPS Coordinates: N 37° 02.586' W 112° 31.014'

Contact: Hitch-N-Post RV Park, 435/644-2142, www.hitchnpostrvpark.com/

59 BARKER RECREATION AREA (BARKER RESERVOIR)

Scenic rating: 8

on the Aquarius Plateau in Dixie National Forest

Map 6.3, page 279

Barker Reservoir is on Boulder Mountain, on the Aquarius Plateau where temperatures are at least 15 to 20°F cooler than the surrounding desert. The plateau has over 1,000 small alpine lakes, most of which are only accessible by trail. This area is considered by fly fishermen to rival the Uinta Mountains as one of the best in the state. Barker Reservoir offers boating and fishing, and a nearby trailhead accesses seven small backcountry lakes where anglers cast for rainbow and brook trout. This campground is cut out of an endless aspen grove with white-barked trees extending outward in every direction. It should be noted the campground isn't actually on the lake, nor can you see the lake from the sites. The 13 sites are well spread out along a large loop. Some of the sites don't really have tent pads, and the whole loop has a very open feel. These highlands are bear country, so use the provided bear vault garbage containers and keep the animals wild. The access road (Forest Road 149) offers scenic views of the Aquarius Plateau and the distant Grand Staircase-Escalante National Monument.

Campsites, facilities: There are 13 individual sites and three group sites. Old Lady Young group site can accommodate up to 100 people, while Porter Equestrian and Gates group sites can hold up to 35 people. Picnic tables, fire rings, drinking water, bear vault garbage containers, and vault toilets are provided. Leashed pets permitted.

Reservations, fees: Reservations are accepted at 877/444-6777 or online at www.recreation. gov and must be made at least seven days in advance. Single sites are $8, the Old Lady Young group area is $40 (up to 50 people, add $0.50 pp over 50 people), Gates and Porter group areas are $35, and extra vehicles are $4. Open mid-May through early September.

Directions: From Escalante, take Rte. 12 west 3.7 miles to the Barker Reservoir sign. Turn right after the sign onto a gravel road and go 0.1 mile to a second Barker Reservoir sign. Immediately after the sign turn right onto Forest Road 149 and continue 12 miles to a Y intersection. Take the left fork, staying on Forest Road 149, and continue 3.4 miles to the campground.

GPS Coordinates: N 37° 55.249' W 111° 48.980'

Contact: Escalante Ranger District, 435/826-5400, www.fs.fed.us/r4/dixie/recreation/campgrounds/barker.html

60 POSY LAKE

Scenic rating: 8

on the Aquarius Plateau in Dixie National Forest

Map 6.3, page 279

Posy Lake is an alpine lake surrounded by an evergreen and aspen forest. The lake sits at 8,600 feet in elevation on the southern flank of Boulder Mountain, part of the Aquarius Plateau in central Southern Utah. The campground's lofty elevation and forest setting make it a cool respite from the desert summer heat. Wildlife is abundant in and around the campground. Deer and elk can be spotted resting and grazing in the forest, and a beaver lodge is conspicuously located on the southeast shore of the lake. Wild turkey and other waterfowl frequent the area as well, and we noticed a brightly colored yellow-and-black swallowtail butterfly puddling in the sand near the boat ramp. You'll see lava boulders strewn around the campsites and enjoy the shade provided by the forest canopy. The sites are well spaced, and the hilly setting makes them feel even more spread out than they are. The group site is particularly nice and overlooks the lake from the top of a small hill. The lake has a small boat ramp, floating docks, and a fish-cleaning station to accommodate trout fishermen. The Posy Lake Campground is accessed via Posy Lake Road, also known as Hell's Backbone Road. It crosses a spectacular, narrow bridge built by the Civilian Conservation Corps during the Great Depression, which offers breathtaking views into Box-Death Hollow and surrounding canyons. Nearby trailheads access the storied Box-Death Hollow, and many recreation opportunities await to the south in the Grand Staircase-Escalante National Monument.

Campsites, facilities: There are 26 sites and one group site for up to 35 people. Trailers over 24 feet in length are not recommended. Picnic tables, fire grills, a fish-cleaning station, drinking water, a small boat ramp, two docks, bear vault garbage containers, and vault toilets are provided. Leashed pets permitted.

Reservations, fees: Reservations are required for the group site at 877/444-6777 or online at www.recreation.gov and must be made at least seven days in advance. The fee is $8 for individual sites, the group site is $35, and additional vehicles are $4. Open May through September.

Directions: From Escalante, drive 9.4 miles on Forest Road 149 and turn right on Forest Road 152 and continue 10.7 miles to the Posy Lake Campground.

GPS Coordinates: N 37° 56.160' W 111° 41.644'

Contact: Escalante Ranger District, 435/826-5400, www.fs.fed.us/r4/dixie/recreation/campgrounds/posylake.html

61 BLUE SPRUCE

Scenic rating: 7

on the Aquarius Plateau in Dixie National Forest

Map 6.3, page 279   BEST (

Blue Spruce Campground is a quiet, shaded campground set in the high forest of the Aquarius Plateau in central Southern Utah. Located at around 7,800 feet, Blue Spruce is a good spot to escape the summer heat and enjoy the cool, clear Pine Creek. Watch for elk and deer that also come here to capitalize on the combination of cooler temperatures and abundant shade in the meadows and forest around the campground. The primitive campsites are simple yet functional and fit right in to the quiet environment. Driving into the campground you'll cross the impressive Hell's Backbone Bridge, built by the Civilian Conservation Corps and spanning deep-cut canyons carved by Box-Death Hollow and Sand Creek. Along the road (Forest Road 153) is the trailhead to explore Box-Death Hollow. The hike accesses wild backcountry in the form of tight, deep canyons sliced into

Navajo Sandstone by Pine and Death Hollow Creeks before they join the Escalante River. With the Forest Service–managed Aquarius Plateau to the north and BLM-run Grand Staircase-Escalante National Monument to the south, this campground is in the middle of a huge tract of protected wilderness. For those looking to escape everything, this spot won't disappoint.

Campsites, facilities: There are seven sites. Picnic tables, fire grills, a vault toilet, bear vault garbage containers, and drinking water are provided. Leashed pets permitted.

Reservations, fees: Reservations are not accepted. The fee is $7, and it's $4 for additional vehicles. Open late May through early September.

Directions: From Escalante, drive north 18 miles on the Hells Backbone Road (Forest Road 153), turn left on Forest Road 145, and continue to the Blue Spruce Campground.

GPS Coordinates: N 37° 58.456' W 111° 39.128'

Contact: Escalante Ranger District, 435/826-5400, www.fs.fed.us/r4/dixie/recreation/campgrounds/bluespruce.html

62 DEER CREEK

Scenic rating: 7

on Burr Trail in Grand Staircase-Escalante National Monument

Map 6.3, page 279

Deer Creek Campground is the only developed campground along Burr Trail, the long, winding road accessing the immense Canyons of the Escalante region in the Grand Staircase-Escalante National Monument. On its way to Waterpocket Fold, Burr Trail winds through huge, solidified, yellow sand dunes with stately ponderosa pines clinging to the cracks and crevasses of the ancient rock forms. It also accesses some incredible slot canyon hikes, including multi-day backpacking and long, rewarding day hikes. Deer Creek crosses

the road and is one of the only year-round streams in the area. The campground itself is managed by the BLM and developed in its signature minimalist style. The site is down in the creek bottom, and when we visited there was not a breath of air moving. In an act of mercy, huge cottonwood trees line the creek and shade the campground. Red sand sites are small, primitive, and appropriate for tent camping only. The parking areas are small and the loop is not trailer- or RV-friendly. Look for red sagebrush lizards scampering across the rock and sunning themselves in the sites. The campground was empty when we were there and probably rarely fills to capacity, though our visit was midweek. If all the sites are full, there are lots of opportunities for dispersed undeveloped camping farther down Burr Trail.

Campsites, facilities: There are seven sites. Picnic tables, fire pits, barbeque grills, and a pit toilet are provided. There is no drinking water. Leashed pets permitted.

Reservations, fees: Reservations are not accepted. The fee is $4. Open year-round.

Directions: From Boulder, drive 6.4 miles on Burr Trail and turn left into Deer Creek Campground.

GPS Coordinates: N 37° 51.315' W 111° 21.333'

Contact: Grand Staircase-Escalante National Monument, 435/826-5499.

63 CEDAR MESA

Scenic rating: 8

in Waterpocket Fold in Capitol Reef National Park

Map 6.3, page 279   BEST (

Cedar Mesa Campground is located in the remote and beautiful Waterpocket Fold in Capitol Reef National Park. Reaching the campground is an adventure in itself, driving down the long and bumpy Notom-Bullfrog Road. The National Park Service recommends contacting the visitors center for current road and weather conditions before driving out to the campground, as the road can become impassible during heavy rain. The relatively primitive sites are set in an open juniper and pinyon pine forest under the awesome geology of Waterpocket Fold. These short trees provide a little shade for the sites, but the campground can get extremely hot during summer. Prickly pear cacti grow out of the brown soil around the sites. The trees provide some separation between the sites, and the campground in general is about as private a camping experience as you'll find inside a national park. The 3.5-mile Red Canyon Loop Trail starts at the campground and leads into a wide box canyon. This is a rare free, developed campground inside a national park.

Campsites, facilities: There are five sites. Picnic tables, fire grills, and a vault toilet are provided. There is no drinking water. Leashed pets permitted.

Reservations, fees: Reservations are not accepted. There is no fee. Open year-round.

Directions: From Capitol Reef's visitors center, drive east on Rte. 24 for nine miles. Turn south (right) onto Notom-Bullfrog Road and continue 22.5 miles. Turn right into Cedar Mesa Campground.

GPS Coordinates: N 38° 00.260' W 111° 05.030'

Contact: Capitol Reef National Park, 435/425-3791, ext. 111, www.nps.gov/care/planyourvisit/primitivecampsites.htm

64 PINE LAKE

Scenic rating: 6

in the Dixie National Forest

Map 6.3, page 279

Pine Lake is a shallow, island-dotted reservoir fed by a small stream and set in an open valley hemmed in by pink, red, and white cliffs. The campground is a short walk from the lake and occupies a meadow with scattered pine, fir, and juniper trees. According to the camp host, the campground is popular in summer with families and especially with Boy and Girl Scout troops. The lake is great for trout fishing; species include Bonneville, cutthroat, rainbow, and brook trout. Look closely for a glimpse of the abundant wildlife in the campground and around the lake. The hosts have spotted deer, wild turkeys, muskrats, antelopes, elk, black bears, and skunks. Nearby you'll find access to the Great Western and Henderson Canyon ATV trails. With abundant trees for shade, this high-elevation site (8,300 feet) is a great spot to escape the summer heat. The gravel loop leads to spread-out sites between clumps of trees. Expect crowds in July and August and relative calm during the rest of the summer.

Campsites, facilities: There are 33 sites for tents and RVs up to 45 feet in length and four group sites. The Clay Creek group area can accommodate up to 35 people, the Wild Iris and Yellow Pine group areas up to 50 people, and John's Valley up to 100 people. Picnic tables, fire grills, drinking water (available only during the summer months), and vault toilets are provided. Leashed pets permitted.

Reservations, fees: Reservations are accepted (required for group sites) at 877/444-6777 or online at www.recreation.gov and must be made at least seven days in advance. Individual sites are $9, group sites are $40 for up to 50 people and $80 for 51–100 people, and extra vehicles are $5. Open year-round.

Directions: From Panguitch, head south for seven miles on Hwy. 89 and turn east on Rte. 12. Continue 14 miles and turn north onto the John's Valley Road (Forest Road 22). Travel 10.6 miles and turn right onto Clay Creek Road (Forest Road 132) and drive seven miles to the campground.

GPS Coordinates: N 37° 44.631' W 111° 57.046'

Contact: Escalante Ranger District, 435/826-5400, www.fs.fed.us/r4/dixie/recreation/campgrounds/pinelake.html

65 BROKEN BOW RV CAMP

Scenic rating: 3

in Escalante

Map 6.3, page 279

Broken Bow RV Camp greets travelers as they enter the town of Escalante on Route 12 from the west. Escalante is one of the gateways to the Grand Staircase-Escalante National Monument, home of wild sandstone formations, deep-cut canyons, and endless desert wilderness. The monument is an adventurous explorer's dream, with few paved roads and even fewer travel restrictions. It isn't, however, an RV-friendly place; in addition to a shortage in paved roads, the park sorely lacks developed campgrounds. So RV users are left to seek other accommodations. Broken Bow in Escalante is one option. The RV park doesn't offer much in the way of curb appeal, with its block-long gravel lot and trailer park appearance. Sites are shaded by cottonwood trees, but the designated tent area is disappointing, just a spot to sleep among the dirt and weeds. On the bright side, Broken Bow is under new ownership, which seems interested in making improvements and is seeking suggestions on developing the tent camping area. Hopefully as time passes the facilities will be upgraded.

Campsites, facilities: There are 28 pull-through RV sites with full hook-ups (20-, 30-, and 50-amp), two rustic cabins, and a small area for tents. Picnic tables, fire grills, modern restrooms with showers, drinking water, garbage service, WiFi, and a dump station are provided. Laundry is available. Leashed pets permitted (with breed restrictions).

Reservations, fees: Reservations are accepted at 888/241-8785. Full hook-up sites are $26 (50-amp) and $24 (30-amp), partial hook-ups are $21, sites without hook-ups are $18, and tent sites are $13. Cabins are $35–45 per night. Open year-round.

Directions: From the west side of Escalante, drive a half block east on Rte. 12. Broken Bow RV Camp is on the right side of the road.

GPS Coordinates: N 37° 46.224' W 111° 36.583'

Contact: Broken Bow RV Camp, 888/241-8785, www.brokenbowrvpark.com/

66 ESCALANTE PETRIFIED FOREST STATE PARK

Scenic rating: 7

one mile west of the town of Escalante

Map 6.3, page 279

Desert hills surround the campground and small Wide Hollow Reservoir, where canoeing, fishing, swimming, and bird-watching are popular summer activities. Sport-fishing species include rainbow trout, largemouth bass, and bluegill. A one-mile hiking trail leads out of the east end of the campground and climbs up a short mesa to the petrified forest. The petrified forest features some beautifully colored and remarkably intact petrified wood, with some pieces as wide as five feet across. Panoramic views from atop the mesa are an added benefit to the hike. The small, cozy camp loop encircles modern restrooms and lies on the east bank of the reservoir. There are large cottonwood trees by the shore of the lake, but they don't shade all the sites. The campground was almost full when we visited, and there isn't much space between sites. A group of tent campers were occupying the grass area next to the restrooms, giving the whole place a cramped feel. Overall, though, it isn't a bad spot to camp, and the collection of petrified wood is an interesting destination.

Campsites, facilities: There are 22 campsites, one group site for up to 30 people, and eight additional overflow walk-in sites. The maximum RV length is 50 feet. Covered picnic tables, tent pads, barbeque grills, fire grills, a covered picnic area, and modern restrooms with showers are provided. Firewood is available. Canoe rentals are available for $5 per hour. Leashed pets permitted.

Reservations, fees: Reservations are accepted at 800/322-3770 or online at www.reserveamerica.com. Single site reservations must be made a minimum of two days in advance and can be arranged up to 16 weeks in advance, and group site reservations can be arranged up to 11 months in advance. There is a nonrefundable reservation fee of $8 for individual sites and $10.25 for group sites. The fee is $16 for individual sites, $25 for full hookup sites, and $50 for the group area. Open year-round.

Directions: From Escalante, travel west on Rte. 12 for one mile, turn right onto North Reservoir Road, and follow this road a short distance to the campground.

GPS Coordinates: N 37° 47.215' W 111° 37.863'

Contact: Escalante Petrified Forest State Park, 435/826-4466 http://stateparks.utah.gov/stateparks/parks/escalante/

67 CALF CREEK
🏃‍♂️ 🛶 🏕 ⛰

Scenic rating: 8

east of Escalante in Grand
Staircase-Escalante National Monument

Map 6.3, page 279 **BEST (**

Lower Calf Creek Falls is an impressive 126-foot waterfall that cascades over green-algae-painted Navajo sandstone in the Grand Staircase-Escalante National Monument. The falls can be reached from the campground via a 5.5-mile round-trip trail, which passes a Fremont pictograph panel and ancient granary ruin en route. The campground is located in the base of a deep canyon and is reached by the wildly exposed and aesthetic All American Road Scenic Route (Route 12). The campground occupies both sides of Calf Creek and is shaded by a grove of oak trees. The creek can be accessed from many of the sites via a trail with steps leading right into

the flowing water. Fishing for brown trout is possible along Calf Creek. The sites vary tremendously at this campground, with some shaded by trees, others tucked into the red rock itself, and a few out in the open. So be sure to take a look around before settling on one. Also check out the cool footbridge leading across the creek.

Campsites, facilities: There are 14 sites. Vehicles over 25 feet are not recommended. Picnic tables, flush toilets (in the day-use area), vault toilets (in the campground), drinking water, and fire grills are provided. Leashed pets permitted.

Reservations, fees: Reservations are not accepted. The fee is $7 per site and $2 for day use. Open year-round.

Directions: From Escalante, drive 14.4 miles on Rte. 12 and turn left onto the campground access road.

GPS Coordinates: N 37° 42.642' W 111° 24.888'

Contact: Grand Staircase BLM Field Office, 435/826-5499.

68 KODACHROME BASIN STATE PARK
🏃‍♂️ 🏕 🚐 ⛰

Scenic rating: 10

east of Cannonville

Map 6.3, page 279 **BEST (**

As the park ranger told us at the entrance station, "This is not a drive-through park—you at least have to get out and walk the nature trail." He couldn't be more right. The real magic of Kodachrome Basin State Park didn't reveal itself until we took a sunset hike that led us up to the bluffs above the campground to enjoy a light show of the low-angled sun on the diverse rockscape. This park features many of the wild formations you'll encounter on the Colorado Plateau within a compact canyon. The west wall of the canyon drops low enough to extend the "magic hour" photographers love, letting the colors grow richer with each passing minute.

If you have any interest in nature photography, you'll be happy to spend a night here. The night sky is incredible, too, because the park is far away from any source of light pollution. In the wee hours of the night you'll see the Big Dipper hanging over the northern rim of the canyon. Kodachrome Basin is a great place to bring the whole family. The short, scenic trails are perfect for hikers of all ages, and fascinating geology creates a natural playground for kids. The campground loop is small and sociable, with sites not far from each other. Pinyon pines and juniper provide a little bit of privacy, but you'll hear and see your neighbors plenty. The facilities are nice and well taken care of, and overall it's a great place to camp. Word is out and the campground is busy for its size, so make reservations or arrive early to avoid being disappointed.

Campsites, facilities: There are 27 individual sites for tents and large RVs and two group sites for up to 35 people. Site 18 is wheelchair accessible. Picnic tables on cement pads, barbeque grills, fire pits, pull-through sites, modern restrooms with showers, and a dump station are provided. Firewood is for sale from the Boy Scouts. Leashed pets permitted.

Reservations, fees: Reservations are accepted at 800/322-3770 or online at www.reserveamerica.com. Single site reservations must be made a minimum of two days in advance and can be arranged up to 16 weeks in advance, and group site reservations can be arranged up to 11 months in advance. There is a nonrefundable reservation fee of $8 for individual sites and $10.25 for group sites. Single sites are $16, group sites are $50 (plus $3 pp above 16 people with a maximum of 35 people) and the day-use fee is $7. Open year-round.

Directions: From Cannonville, drive south nine miles to Kodachrome Basin State Park. GPS Coordinates: N 37° 31.179 W 111° 59.226'

Contact: Kodachrome Basin State Park, 435/679-8562, http://stateparks.utah.gov/stateparks/parks/kodachrome/

camping at the White House

69 WHITE HOUSE
🏃 🏕 ⛰

Scenic rating: 7

on the Utah/Arizona border just north of the Paria Canyon-Vermilion Cliffs Wilderness

Map 6.3, page 279   **BEST (**

White House Campground is a relatively primitive BLM campground used almost exclusively by hikers planning to take one of Utah's two most coveted hikes, Buckskin Gulch and the Wave. Buckskin Gulch is the longest continuous narrow slot canyon in the world and one of Utah's best backpacking trips. The Wave, found within an area known as Coyote Buttes, is particularly popular with outdoor photographers who come to record their artistic take of the colorfully flowing rock form. Europeans tourists, especially Germans, have had a special fascination with the Wave since German filmmaker Gogol Lobmayr made a nonverbal nature film featuring the aesthetic spot. Both hikes require a permit, which can be obtained in advance online, or in a lottery at the ranger station the day before the hike. It's well worth your time to secure the permit in advance, as there's no guarantee it'll be available the day of your hike. The White House Campground isn't a bad spot; it's just designed more for function than beauty. Picnic tables have been strategically placed under the largest juniper trees to maximize afternoon shade. If you visit anytime in the summer months, you'll understand why. The place is hot. Really hot. Beside the juniper trees there's lots of pink sand and some cool rock formations. A dry wash runs through the campground, and long-eared jackrabbits come out once things start to cool off in the evenings.

Campsites, facilities: There are five walk-in tent sites. Picnic tables, vault toilets, and fire pits are provided. There is no drinking water. Water is available at the Paria Ranger Station. Leashed pets permitted.

Reservations, fees: Reservations are not accepted. The fee is $5 per site. Open year-round.

Directions: From Kanab, drive east on Hwy. 89 for 43 miles, then turn right following signs for the Paria Ranger Station. At the ranger station, stay left and continue two miles to the White House Campground.

GPS Coordinates: N 37° 04.799' W 111° 53.411'

Contact: Kanab Field Office, 435/644-4600, www.blm.gov/ut/st/en/fo/kanab/recreation/camping.html

70 LONE ROCK

🏊 ⛵ 🚤 🎣 🚐 ⛺

Scenic rating: 8

near the outlet of Lake Powell at Glen Canyon Dam

Map 6.3, page 279

Lone Rock Campground is your primitive camping option on the farthest western arm of Lake Powell. The beach site looks across at a huge lone rock jutting out of the reservoir's

waters. During summer, RVs, tents, umbrellas, beach towels, and pale-skinned tourists line the shore of the lake. The free-for-all beach scene and laissez-faire management style stand in stark contrast to the intensively developed RV-park-style campground at nearby Wahweap Marina. Dispersed, undeveloped waterfront camping is somewhat unusual in a national park service–managed campground, and people blissfully take full advantage. Swimming, boating, sunbathing, beer drinking, and general beach lounging are the most popular activities at Lone Rock. ATV and dune-buggy drivers congregate here to enjoy a system of sandy off-road trails. The beach camping is completely devoid of trees and exposed to the sun, so come prepared with your own shade, as well as tables, chairs, and other supplies.

Campsites, facilities: There are no designated campsites. A modern restroom with an outdoor cold-water shower, vault toilets, a dump station, garbage service, and drinking water (available seasonally) are provided. Open fires are permitted but must be contained to within a four-foot area. Leashed pets permitted.

Reservations, fees: Reservations are not accepted. The fee is $10. Open year-round.

Directions: From Kanab, drive east on Hwy. 89 for 64 miles, turn left on Rte. 277, and continue down to the Lone Rock dispersed camping area.

GPS Coordinates: N 37° 00.984' W 111° 32.719'

Contact: Glen Canyon National Recreation Area, 928/608-6200, www.nps.gov/glca/planyourvisit/campgrounds.htm

71 WAHWEAP

🏊 ⛵ 🚤 🎣 ♿ 🚐 ⛺

Scenic rating: 7

near Glen Canyon Dam on Lake Powell, on the Utah-Arizona border

Map 6.3, page 279

Wahweap Marina is the main access point for the southwest end of Lake Powell. Lake Powell, a colossal reservoir on the Colorado River created by the controversial Glen Canyon Dam, is a man-made wonder and recreation favorite of boaters from all over the southwest. You're just as likely to spot license plates from California, Arizona, New Mexico, and Nevada at Wahweap as those from Utah. The marina campground is operated by the Glen Canyon National Recreation Area concessionaire and has the feel and amenities of an upscale private RV park. The campground is uphill from the shore of Lake Powell but has views down to the water and the surrounding red rock scenery. Long, paved driveways lead to row upon row of RV sites, with huge, concrete parking spaces for their accompanying boats and other toys. The designated tent sites have gravel tent pads. In general, the sites have a few small trees and bushes but are relatively exposed to the wind and sun, which is what you'd expect in this barren landscape. The campground seems to go on forever, looking and feeling a bit like a small civilization, so don't come with expectations of privacy or solitude. You'll have to find that in the remote side canyons of the lake.

Campsites, facilities: There are 139 full hook-up (30, 50 amps) sites, 112 tent sites, and one group tenting area with six sites (for 9–30 people). Site 23 is wheelchair accessible. Modern restrooms, picnic tables, fire grills, barbeque grills, pull-through sites, boat ramp, dump station, WiFi, swimming pool, drinking water, and garbage service are provided. A small store, showers, and laundry are available. Leashed pets permitted.

Reservations, fees: Reservations are accepted at 888/896-3829 or online at www.lakepowell.com/rv-campgrounds.cfm#WW. Full hookup sites are $43, and tent sites are $19. Open year-round.

Directions: From Page, Arizona, at the intersection of Hwy. 89 and Rte. 98, drive four miles north on Hwy. 89, turn right onto Wahweap Marina Road, and continue six miles to the Wahweap RV Park and Campground.
GPS Coordinates: N 36° 59.928' W 111° 29.867'

Contact: Wahweap RV Park and Campground, 928/645-2433, www.lakepowell.com/rv-campgrounds.cfm#WW

72 STARR SPRINGS

Scenic rating: 7

south of Henry Mountains off Route 276

Map 6.4, page 280

The Starr Springs BLM site is near the base of 10,723-foot Mount Hillers in the Henry Mountains, nestled into a grove of gambel oak trees. The campground is near the buildings of Starr Ranch. In the 1880s, Al Starr chose this site as the base for his mining and horse operations. A stonemason built a well-crafted house and cellar, the remains of which are still visible. The entire operation was deserted before completion due to a drought. The campground is a noted birding destination. Birders might spot a wide variety of feathered friends including common nighthawks, western scrub jays, pinyon jays, gray flycatchers, Western wood-pewees, olive-sided flycatchers, blue-gray gnatcatchers, cedar waxwings, and black-throated gray warblers. The small campground loop is most appropriate for tents, small vans, and pickup trucks. RVs and larger vehicles not only won't fit in the parking areas, but they will have trouble negotiating the tight loop. Gambel oaks offer shade for most of the small, secluded sites. Starr Springs is a stopover option on the way to and from Bullfrog Marina on Lake Powell.

Campsites, facilities: There are 12 sites. Picnic tables, fire pits, drinking water, barbeque grills, and vault toilets are provided. Leashed pets permitted.

Reservations, fees: Reservations are not accepted. The fee is $4 per site. Open April through November.

Directions: From Hanksville, drive 26 miles south on Rte. 95. Turn right at the junction with Rte. 276 and continue 17 miles to the turnoff for Starr Ranch. Follow the gravel road for five miles to the campground.

GPS Coordinates: N 37° 50.939' W 110° 39.798'

Contact: Henry Mountains Field Station, 435/542-3461.

73 HITE

Scenic rating: 7

at the northeastern tip of Lake Powell

Map 6.4, page 280

Hite sits at the northeastern tip of Lake Powell where the churning, muddy waters of the Colorado River flow out of Cataract Canyon and into the lake. Red sandstone walls rise all around you in enormous scale, giving the whole place such an immense feel it seems ridiculous there's even a boat ramp here. But Hite is the take-out point for Cataract Canyon, the end of an amazing multi-day river odyssey, and one of the launching points for boating adventures on Lake Powell, so it all makes sense from a functional standpoint. The 600-foot boat ramp is almost comical in the fact that it doesn't actually reach the lake's receded waters. The water level of Lake Powell fluctuates greatly depending on recent precipitation trends in the region and has left the boat ramp high and dry. You'll notice the telltale bathtub ring from the lake's historic high point. Hite Campground will be a disappointment if you're expecting a National Park Service–quality facility. Perhaps appropriately for the surroundings, the camping facilities are very primitive. The red dirt campground loop doesn't even look like it's been graded and accesses an open parking area for RVs and possible places to pitch a tent. A few wooden picnic tables are scattered around, but they have piles of heavy rocks stacked on top, as if to keep them from blowing away in the wind. There are modern restrooms a short walk away, but if there are any other creature comforts you'd like, plan on bringing them with you.

Campsites, facilities: There are no designated campsites. Picnic tables, fire rings, flush toilets, a fish-cleaning station, drinking water, a dump station, and garbage service are provided. Leashed pets permitted.

Reservations, fees: Reservations are not accepted. The fee is $6 pp ($12 maximum per vehicle). Open year-round.

Directions: From Hanksville, drive 50 miles south on Rte. 95 and turn right onto the campground access road.

GPS Coordinates: N 37° 52.420' W 110° 23.546'

Contact: Glen Canyon National Recreation Area, 928/608-6200, www.nps.gov/glca/planyourvisit/campgrounds.htm

74 BULLFROG

Scenic rating: 8

on the northern shore of Bullfrog Bay on Lake Powell in Glen Canyon National Recreation Area

Map 6.4, page 280

Bullfrog Campground is located above Bullfrog Bay and Marina on Lake Powell. Bullfrog Bay is approximately midway up the 186-mile-long Lake Powell, making it a good central spot to camp or launch a boat. Bullfrog Marina is one of the major launching points for houseboat vacations on Lake Powell. It's also a main access point for powerboats and even sea kayaks looking to explore and play on the central waters of the Lake. Some of the major destinations in this central part of the lake include the Defiance House Ruin (in Forgotten Canyon), Knowles Canyon, and the Tapestry Wall. At Bullfrog Marina there's a six-lane paved boat ramp, small grocery store, post office, gas station, and boat slips. The large campground loop and parking slips are paved. Sites are sporadically shaded by broad-leaved trees and look down to Bullfrog Bay on Lake Powell. Grass grows around many of the sites and helps add a little bit of life to the desert setting.

Campsites, facilities: There are 78 sites for tents and RVs up to 35 feet in length. Picnic tables, fire grills, drinking water, a dump station, garbage service, and flush toilets are provided. Leashed pets permitted.

Reservations, fees: Reservations are not accepted. Sites are $20. Open March through October.

Directions: From the Bullfrog ferry dock, drive one mile north on Hwy. 276. Bullfrog Campground will be on the left side of the road.

GPS Coordinates: N 37° 31.201' W 110° 43.158'

Contact: Glen Canyon National Recreation Area, 435/684-3000, www.nps.gov/glca/planyourvisit/campgrounds.htm

75 RV PARK AT BULLFROG MARINA

Scenic rating: 8

on the northern shore of Bullfrog Bay on Lake Powell in Glen Canyon National Recreation Area

Map 6.4, page 280

Bullfrog Marina is one of the main access points on Lake Powell for boaters coming from the north. The marina is located on Bullfrog Bay about midway up the lake. Bullfrog Marina is a huge facility with all the amenities you might need for your visit to the lake, including a small grocery store, gas station, gift shop, post office, boat slips, a six-lane boat launching ramp, and an RV park. The Bullfrog Marina RV Park is not affiliated with Bullfrog Campground, which is run by a private concessionaire. Check in at the front desk at Defiance House. The campground offers sites shaded by deciduous trees and views down the hill to Bullfrog Bay and to the incredible geology of Lake Powell. The sites are close together and don't offer much privacy, especially in the busy season.

Campsites, facilities: There are 24 full hookup (30 amps) sites for RVs up to 50 feet in length. Tents are not permitted. Picnic tables, barbeque grills, drinking water, pull-through sites, garbage service, and modern restrooms with showers are provided. Leashed pets permitted.

Reservations, fees: Reservations are accepted at 888/896-3829. Sites are $38.54. Open year-round.

Directions: From the Bullfrog ferry dock, drive one mile north on Hwy. 276. The Bullfrog's Painted Hills RV Park will be on the right side of the road.

GPS Coordinates: N 37° 30.976' W 110° 43.682'

Contact: Bullfrog Marina and Resort, 435/684-3000, www.lakepowell.com/rv-campgrounds.cfm#PH

76 HALL'S CROSSING

Scenic rating: 8

on the southeast shore of Bullfrog Bay on Lake Powell in Glen Canyon National Recreation Area

Map 6.4, page 280

Hall's Crossing is located on the southeast shore of Bullfrog Bay on Lake Powell. Bullfrog Bay is at approximately the midpoint of 186-mile Lake Powell. Hall's Crossing is the end point for the *John Atlantic Burr Ferry* that shuttles cars across Lake Powell from Bullfrog to Hall's Crossing. The crossing saves drivers about 150 miles of driving around the northern end of the lake. Hall's Crossing Campground offers sites with expansive views of the lake's waters and the wild red rock landscape. The sites are open and exposed to the desert sun, which can be oppressive, so bring your own shade. Temperatures in this part of the Colorado Plateau regularly exceed 100°F in the summer, so head to the lake for relief. Lake Powell is a boating paradise: Powerboats, sea kayaks, and houseboats all have their place on its seemingly endless surface. Swimming, fishing, hiking, canyoneering, and exploring opportunities are everywhere at Lake Powell. Set up camp and head for the water.

Campsites, facilities: There are 63 single sites and two group sites. Picnic tables, fire grills, drinking water, a dump station, garbage service, cold showers, and flush toilets are provided. Leashed pets permitted.

Reservations, fees: Reservations are not accepted. Sites are $18. Open April through October.

Directions: From the Hall's Crossing ferry dock, drive two miles south on Hwy. 276. Hall's Crossing Campground will be on the right side of the road.

GPS Coordinates: N 37° 26.404' W 110° 42.207'

Contact: Glen Canyon National Recreation Area, 435/684-7000, www.nps.gov/glca/planyourvisit/campgrounds.htm

77 HALL'S CROSSING RV RESORT AND MARINA

Scenic rating: 8

on the southeast shore of Bullfrog Bay on Lake Powell in Glen Canyon National Recreation Area

Map 6.4, page 280

Hall's Crossing is at the southern end of the *John Atlantic Burr Ferry* route; the ferry transports cars, trucks, and RVs across Bullfrog Bay on Lake Powell, eliminating about 150 miles of driving for travelers on Route 276, much like the historic *Lee's Ferry* once did across the Colorado River. Hall's Crossing is much more than just a point of transit. It offers a marina, one of Lake Powell's busiest recreation centers. The lake is one of the Southwest's best and most special boating destinations. The Hall's Crossing side of the lake sees far less traffic than the Bullfrog side, and therefore offers an opportunity for a quieter, more peaceful Lake Powell experience. Compared to the busy

facilities at Wahweap and Bullfrog Marinas, Hall's Crossing seems almost deserted. On the other hand, compared to the majority of Lake Powell's little-used surface, it can feel like a small city. The RV park at Hall's Crossing is a small paved loop offering pull-through sites for RVs.

Campsites, facilities: There are 33 full hookup (30 amps) sites for RVs up to 60 feet in length. Tents are not permitted. Picnic tables, barbeque grills, a dump station, pull-through sites, garbage service, drinking water, and modern restrooms with showers are provided. Motorboat rentals, groceries, ice, and laundry are available. Leashed pets permitted.

Reservations, fees: Reservations are accepted at 888/896-3829. Sites are $38.25. Open year-round.

Directions: From the Hall's Crossing ferry dock, drive two miles south on Hwy. 276. Hall's Crossing RV Resort and Marina will be on the left side of the road.

GPS Coordinates: N 37° 28.406' W 110° 42.708'

Contact: Hall's Crossing RV Resort and Marina, 435/684-7000, www.lakepowell.com/rv-campgrounds.cfm#VC

78 GOULDING'S MONUMENT VALLEY RV PARK

Scenic rating: 8

in the town of Monument Valley

Map 6.4, page 280   **BEST**

Goulding's Monument Valley Campground is connected to Goulding's Lodge. The campground offers a full-service RV park with views of Monument Valley, a Navajo Tribal Park encompassing an incredible collection of sandstone pinnacles, mesas, and buttes. The valley has been used as the dramatic backdrop for many Hollywood Western movies, so many visitors' first reaction is, "Haven't I been here before?" Goulding's is the closest campground in Utah to Monument Valley. Deep red sandstone cliffs rise above the campground, and in the distance the mesas and buttes of Monument Valley beckon. The sites are open and don't offer much shade. The open layout capitalizes on the surrounding scenery but can leave campers exposed to the elements in the middle of hot summer days. The tent sites offer level tent-pitching options on the red dirt desert floor. Goulding's Lodge offers guided tours of Monument Valley and the wonders of the surrounding desert. Goulding's proximity to this awe-inspiring landscape makes it one of the best campgrounds in Utah for nature photography.

Campsites, facilities: There are 66 full hookup (30, 50 amps) sites, 67 tent sites, and three cabins. Picnic tables, barbeque grills, WiFi, cable TV, a swimming pool, modern restrooms with showers, garbage service, and drinking water are provided. Laundry, guided tours, and a grocery store are available. Leashed pets permitted.

Reservations, fees: Reservations are accepted at 435/727-3231 or online at https://s28.rezrobot.com/member/Dates.asp?Robot_ID=5184. Full hook-up sites are $38, tent sites are $24, and cabins are $69. Open year-round (limited service November through mid-March).

Directions: From the intersection of Hwy. 163 and Monument Valley Road, drive west on Monument Valley Road for two miles. Goulding's Monument Valley RV Park will be on the right side of the road.

GPS Coordinates: N 37° 00.393' W 110° 12.116'

Contact: Goulding's Monument Valley, 435/727-3231, www.gouldings.com/english/campground.htm

79 MOUNTAIN VIEW RV PARK
🏕️ 🚐 ⛺

Scenic rating: 4

in Monticello

Map 6.5, page 281

Mountain View RV Park occupies a lot on the east side of Highway 191 in the sleepy, scenic town of Monticello. Monticello sits at the base of the obscure yet beautiful Abajo, a.k.a. Blue, Mountains. Like all the RV park options in Monticello, Mountain View RV Park is right on Highway 191. Views from the park extend east up to the Abajos and open out west to rangeland. The gravel yard has nicely manicured grass tent sites and pull-through RV spots. The fields and horse pasture of a farm to the south of the RV park give it a distinct rural feel. Cottonwood trees provide shade for many of the sites. The yard is small and quarters close, so don't expect much privacy.

Campsites, facilities: There are 29 full hookup (30, 50 amps) RV sites and five tent sites with small picnic tables. Modern restrooms, cable TV, pull-through sites, drinking water, and garbage service are provided. Showers and laundry are available. Leashed pets permitted.

Reservations, fees: Reservations are accepted at 435/587-2974. The fee is $22. Open May through October.

Directions: From the junction of Hwy. 191 and Hwy. 491, drive 0.5 mile north on Hwy. 191.

GPS Coordinates: N 37° 52.882' W 109° 20.490'

Contact: Mountain View RV Park, 435/587-2974.

80 BUCKBOARD
🏕️ ⛺

Scenic rating: 8

on the slopes of the Abajo Mountains in Manti-La Sal National Forest

Map 6.5, page 281

Buckboard Campground has a very alpine feel, in a mountain setting high above the surrounding desert. The grounds are lush and green, with grass and gambel oak encroaching on dirt tent pads. Clear mountain streams flow by the campground, and countless deer graze the nearby meadows near sunset. There's no cooler place to run from the desert heat in this part of the state. The campground and facilities have an older, almost forgotten feel to them, like the Forest Service feels there are better places to spend its dwindling budget. That's too bad, because it's a lovely setting and a unique atmosphere for this part of Utah. Bring your own drinking water. While there are water spigots at the campground, signs warn that the water isn't potable.

Campsites, facilities: There are 11 individual sites and two group tent areas for up to 25 tents and 100 people. Picnic tables, fire grills, garbage service, and vault toilets are provided. There is no potable water. Leashed pets permitted.

Reservations, fees: Reservations are accepted at 877/444-6777 or online at www.recreation. gov and must be made at least five days in advance. Sites are $10, and group sites are $30–40. Open June through October.

Directions: From Hwy. 191 in Monticello, turn west on 200 South and follow it as it turns into Abajo Drive. Drive seven miles west on Forest Road 105 to Buckboard Campground on the left side of the road.

GPS Coordinates: N 37° 52.855' W 109° 26.927'

Contact: Monticello Ranger District, 435/587-2041.

81 DALTON SPRINGS
🏕️ 🏔️

Scenic rating: 8

on the slopes of the Abajo Mountains in Manti-La Sal National Forest

Map 6.5, page 281

Tired of crowded Moab? Need to escape the scorching midday heat and crowded trails? Head south on Highway 191 and check out the beautiful Abajo Mountains. The range, like both the La Sal and Henry Mountains, is made of igneous rock, a relatively hard volcanic rock that cooled slowly underground and is therefore more resistant to erosion than the sandstone of the Colorado Plateau. Topping out at 11,362 feet, the Abajos are in a totally different climate than the surrounding canyonlands and can be quite refreshing during warmer months. Aspen and gambel oak trees shade Dalton Springs campground, with clear running water cascading nearby. The campground feels lush and green, like an island in the sky. While views from the campground are limited by the forest, experiencing the dichotomy of desert canyons below and alpine tundra above is well worth the drive. The campground is older and not well loved, so don't expect sparkling facilities. Bring your own water; for some reason, no campgrounds in this area have potable water.

Campsites, facilities: There are 17 sites for tents and small RVs. Picnic tables, fire grills, pull-through sites, and vault toilets are provided. There is no drinking water. Leashed pets permitted.

Reservations, fees: Reservations are not accepted. The fee is $10 per site. Open June through September.

Directions: From Hwy. 191 in Monticello, turn west on 200 South and follow it as it turns into Abajo Drive. Drive five miles west on Forest Road 105 to the Dalton Springs Campground on the left side of the road.

GPS Coordinates: N 37° 52.446 W 109° 25.889'

Contact: Monticello Ranger District, 435/587-2041.

82 WESTERNER RV PARK
🏕️ ♿ 🚐 🏔️

Scenic rating: 4

in Monticello

Map 6.5, page 281

Touring all the obscure golf courses in southern Utah? Or more likely heading north from visiting Monument Valley or Mexican Hat and need a place to spend the night? Westerner RV Park is the first option at the southern end of the small town of Monticello. It's got a well-shaded yard with grassy sites under a canopy of maple trees and is within walking distance of Hideout Golf Club. The public Hideout Golf Club is named after the many visitors who historically found refuge in the canyons and hideouts in the nearby mountains. The spot was a favorite for Native Americans, cowboys, and fugitives alike. The RV park seems to be the most popular in Monticello, despite its location right on the major highway. Like most RV parks, the sites are tightly spaced and privacy is minimal.

Campsites, facilities: There are 28 full hook-up (20-, 30-, and 50-amp) RV sites, a few of which double as tent sites. Picnic tables, modern restrooms with showers, cable TV, garbage service, and a dump station are provided. Laundry is available. Leashed pets permitted.

Reservations, fees: Reservations are accepted at 435/587-2762. The fee is $22 for full hook-ups and $18 for no hook-ups and tent sites. Open April through November.

Directions: From the junction of Hwy. 191 and Hwy. 491, drive south on Hwy. 191 for five blocks and turn right into Westerner RV Park at Golf Course Lane.

GPS Coordinates: N 37° 51.915' W 109° 20.589'

Contact: Westerner RV Park, 435/587-2762.

83 BAR TN RV PARK

Scenic rating: 4

in Monticello

Map 6.5, page 281

Bar TN RV Park is a convenient stopover on long Southwest road trips, or it could be a base camp to explore more intimately the Abajo Mountains or the southern entrance to Canyonlands National Park. Local Monticello attractions include a public golf course at Hideaway Golf Club and the Bull Hollow Raceway. The Bar TN is owned and operated by the multitalented Mr. and Mrs. Barton, both of whom have Masters degrees in education in addition to running the RV park and Verdure Livestock. The RV park has a gravel loop and trees to provide shade. An old, Western-style office greets travelers as they enter the campground. Sites are close together and the property is right off the Highway 191, so expect noticeable road noise at night.

Campsites, facilities: There are 16 RV sites with full hook-ups (20-, 30-, and 50-amp), a few tent sites, and two cabins. Amenities include picnic tables, cable TV, drinking water, modern restrooms with showers, dump station, garbage service, and a covered picnic table. Leashed pets permitted.

Reservations, fees: Reservations are accepted. Full hook-up sites are $25, tent sites are $15 and cabins are $33. Open March through November.

Directions: From the junction of Hwy. 191 and Hwy. 491, drive three blocks south on Hwy. 191.

GPS Coordinates: N 37° 52.067' W 109° 20.600'

Contact: Bar TN RV Park, 435/587-1005, www.bar-tn.com/rv-park.html

84 NIZHONI

Scenic rating: 7

in the Manti-La Sal National Forest

Map 6.5, page 281

This Forest Service campground is located on the lower flanks of the Abajo Mountains. Views from the campground look up to the 10,938-foot Mount Linnaeus. A hiking trail leaving the campground leads to a 700-year-old Anasazi cliff dwelling and granary ruin site. The campground loop weaves through gambel oak and ponderosa pine trees, and sites are surrounded by desert sage. The setting is a combination of forest and open meadows with flowing long grass. The parking aprons are gravel, with grass growing in many of the sites. Cool temperatures combined with ample shade make this campground a good place to escape hot days in the surrounding desert. On the way to Nizhoni, you'll notice the Dry Wash Reservoir, where local Scout troops practice their water skills.

Campsites, facilities: There are 21 sites and two group sites able to accommodate up to 100 people. Picnic tables, fire rings, vault toilets, and drinking water are provided. Leashed pets permitted.

Reservations, fees: Reservations are accepted at 877/444-6777 or online at www.recreation. gov and must be made at least five days in advance. Sites are $10; extra vehicles cost $5. The group areas are $30–40, and camping is allowed in the group sites for $15 if they are not reserved. Open mid-May through late October.

Directions: From Blanding, drive north on Hwy. 191 for two miles, turn left onto County Road 2191, and travel 0.7 mile to the stop sign. Turn right onto Mountain Road and continue 10 miles to the campground.

GPS Coordinates: N 37° 46.941' W 109° 32.380'

Contact: Monticello Ranger District, 435/587-2041.

85 DEVILS CANYON
Scenic rating: 7

in Manti-La Sal National Forest

Map 6.5, page 281

Devils Canyon has an alpine feel to the air even though it's on the benches below the Abajo Mountains. The mountains are visible to the north, and views to the south stretch out across the vast desert. Rabbits and deer frequent the campground in the evenings before sunset. Pinyon pine and juniper trees grow in and around the sites, and lower desert sage covers the brown soil. Paved, level parking aprons provide access to clean, well-developed sites. Picnic tables sit on concrete pads, keeping things tidy and reducing the impact on the desert soil. The campground has two separate loops: The lower loop

is open and closer to the highway, while the upper one is tucked into a pine forest. While sites in the upper loop enjoy more privacy from dense vegetation, the lower loop sites offer better views and an open, free feeling. At night the campground is quiet and peaceful.

Campsites, facilities: There are 42 sites for tents and RVs up to 45 feet in length. Site 2 is wheelchair accessible. Picnic tables on cement pads, fire rings, vault toilets, and drinking water are provided. Leashed pets permitted.

Reservations, fees: Reservations are accepted at 877/444-6777 or online at www.recreation. gov and must be made at least five days in advance. The fee is $10 per site. Open April through October.

Directions: From Monticello, drive 13 miles south on Hwy. 191, turn right onto the campground access road, and continue 0.5 mile to the campground.

GPS Coordinates: N 37° 44.195' W 109° 24.686'

Contact: Monticello Ranger District, 435/587-2041.

86 NATURAL BRIDGES
Scenic rating: 7

in Natural Bridges National Monument

Map 6.5, page 281   BEST (

Natural Bridges National Monument preserves a unique geologic wonder called White Canyon. The canyon is home to a collection of spectacular natural bridges formed by the undercutting, erosive properties of long-gone streams. The largest bridge in White Canyon is called Sipapu, meaning "place of emergence" in the Hopi Indian language. This is the world's second-largest natural bridge. White Canyon is of historic interest, protecting ancient Puebloan ruins. A scenic drive leads to White Canyon and all the natural bridges. This nine-mile loop is open year-round. Natural Bridges is a long drive from just about everywhere, and as a result the campground can be very busy. When we arrived in waning evening light, we were very disappointed to find the campground full. We felt even worse for the touring cyclist pulling in after us, who was at the tail end of a hundred-mile day in the rain. The campground is a tight loop of closely spaced sites in the red desert sand. A juniper and pinyon pine forest provides some shade and privacy for campers. Sand tent pads keep shelters out of the dirt and protect cryptobiotic soils from too much trampling. The campground caters to tents and small RVs and won't accommodate vehicles longer than 26 feet. If you do arrive to a full campground, there is undeveloped overflow camping on BLM land near the monument at the intersection of Highway 95 and Highway 261. There are no facilities at the overflow site.

Campsites, facilities: There are 13 sites. Maximum vehicle length is 26 feet. Picnic tables, fire grills, and vault toilets are provided. Drinking water is available at the visitors center. Extra vehicles must be parked at the visitors center. Leashed pets permitted.

Reservations, fees: Reservations are not accepted. The fee is $10. Open year-round.

Directions: From Blanding, drive south four miles on Hwy. 191 and turn left at the junction with Hwy. 95. Drive 38 miles west on Hwy. 95 and turn north (right) on Hwy. 275, following signs to the monument. Natural Bridges Campground is at the end of Hwy. 275.

GPS Coordinates: N 37° 36.556' W 109° 59.020'

Contact: Natural Bridges National Monument, 435/692-1234, www.nps.gov/nabr/planyourvisit/things2do.htm

87 BLUE MOUNTAIN TRADING POST RV PARK

🏕️ 🚙 ⛺

Scenic rating: 6

in Blanding

Map 6.5, page 281

Blanding is a good central location for exploring the extreme southeast corner of Utah. It is almost equal distance to Canyonlands National Park, Goosenecks State Park, Natural Bridges National Monument, and Hovenweep National Monument. History buffs and those who enjoy learning about native cultures will like the Edge of Cedars State Park museum in town. While there aren't a lot of public campgrounds in the area, there are two RV parks in Blanding, and this is definitely the better of the two. It has nice views over farmland to distant red rock features and a well-kept, clean feel. Sites are neatly arranged and tightly spaced in a gravel lot. There's a small store featuring Indian arts and crafts. On the downside, it's right on Highway 191 and there isn't a lot of shade.

Campsites, facilities: There are 23 sites with full hook-ups (30, 50 amps) for RVs up to 70 feet in length, and tenting is possible in these sites. Amenities include laundry, picnic tables, barbeque grills, modern restrooms with showers, pull-through sites, drinking water, and WiFi. Leashed pets permitted.

Reservations, fees: Reservations are accepted. The fee is $26. Open March 15 through October 31.

Directions: From the intersection of Hwy. 191 and Center Street in Blanding, drive 2.3 miles south on Hwy. 191 and turn right into the campground.

GPS Coordinates: N 37° 35.880' W 109° 28.744'

Contact: Blue Mountain Trading Post RV Park, 435/678-7840, www.bluemountainrvpark.com/

88 BLANDING GOFER KAMPARK

🏕️ 🚵 🚐 ⛺

Scenic rating: 3

in Blanding

Map 6.5, page 281

Gofer Kampark is in the small town of Blanding right off Highway 191. Blanding is a frequent stopover spot for travelers making their way north from southeastern Utah attractions like Goosenecks State Park, Monument Valley, and Natural Bridges National Monument. The quiet town is also the home of Edge of Cedars State Park, a museum protecting and displaying a pre-Columbian Pueblo Indian ruin and pottery. There's no camping at the state park, but there are two RV parks in town. Blanding Gofer Kampark is one of the options. The RV park has gravel pull-through parking for RVs, and trees provide shade for the sites. The campground is across from the public baseball diamond and is tucked apologetically behind a gas station. The urban yard has a run-down, overlooked feel. Take a look at the Blue Mountain Trading Post as another option.

Campsites, facilities: There are 50 full hook-up (20-, 30-, and 50-amp) sites and 16 tent sites. Amenities include WiFi, a dump station, laundry, a small playground, drinking water, pull-through sites, and modern restrooms with showers. Leashed pets permitted.

Reservations, fees: Reservations are not accepted. Full hook-up sites are $20, and tent sites are $14. Open year-round.

Directions: From the intersection of Hwy. 191 and Center Street in Blanding, drive 1.3 miles north on Hwy. 191 to the campground. GPS Coordinates: N 37° 36.772' W 109° 28.726'

Contact: Blanding Gofer Kampark, 435/678-2770, kampark@yahoo.com.

Hovenweep National Monument

© MIKE MATSON

89 HOVENWEEP

Scenic rating: 8

In the Hovenweep National Monument

Map 6.5, page 281   BEST (

Hovenweep National Monument is one of the best-kept secrets of the Four Corners Region. Hovenweep is a Ute/Paiute word meaning "deserted valley." What's so impressive about this particular deserted valley is the structures left by ancient inhabitants. Towers, multi-room pueblos, and small cliff dwellings leave a record of a culture that thrived in this canyon until as little as 700 years ago. While the monument is a substantial drive from almost anywhere, it offers a more intimate view of ancient ruins than you'll find in the more heavily visited Mesa Verde National Park. Hikes of varying length access six different groups of ruins. The Hovenweep Campground is a short distance from the main Little Ruin Canyon and enjoys views to the east of the Sleeping Ute Mountains across the border in Colorado. Juniper and pinyon pine trees grow between well-designed and -maintained sites. Parking aprons are gravel. Like the park in general, the campground appears to get little use because it's so far out of the way. A small amphitheater overlooks a shallow ravine. The eight-mile round-trip Holly Ruins Trail leaves directly from the campground. The trail leads to a complex of ruins that straddles the Colorado border.

Campsites, facilities: There are 31 sites for

tents and RVs up to 36 feet in length. Semi-covered picnic tables, flush toilets, drinking water, a dish-washing area, aluminum and plastic recycling, garbage service, and fire grills are provided. Leashed pets permitted.

Reservations, fees: Reservations are not accepted. The fee is $10 per site. Open year-round.

Directions: From Blanding, drive south 15 miles on Hwy. 191 and turn east (left) on Rte. 262. Follow Rte. 262 nine miles. Continue straight toward Hatch Trading Post. Follow the paved road as it bends south, following signs to Hovenweep National Monument. Nine miles after Hatch Trading Post, turn north (left) again and continue to the park entrance.

GPS Coordinates: N 37° 22.999' W 109° 04.254'

Contact: Hovenweep National Monument, 970/562-4282, www.nps.gov/hove/planyour-visit/things2do.htm

90 COTTONWOOD RV PARK

Scenic rating: 3

in Bluff

Map 6.5, page 281

Cottonwood RV is tucked away a couple of blocks off Highway 191 as it bends through the tiny town of Bluff. Bluff is near a collection of southern Utah's best-kept secrets. Treasures like Hovenweep National Monument, Monument Valley Tribal Park, Goosenecks State Park, and Natural Bridges National Monument are all within one hour's drive of Bluff. While camping is possible in some of these parks, this farthest southeast corner of the state is by no means overflowing with camp-grounds. If you're interested in a full-service RV park, the town of Bluff may be the best option for a base camp. Cottonwood RV Park is definitely a low-key place to spend the night. The spacious campground is decorated with pioneer-era farming relics. Rusty old wagon

wheels are even built into the stucco office architecture. Open campsites have views of the surrounding red rock landscape, but there is little shade or protection from the relentless southern Utah sun. The RV area is gravel, and tent sites are grassy. Cottonwood does have the advantage over its competitors of being far enough off the main road to be quiet and peaceful. In fact, when we visited the camp-ground it felt eerily empty, though I am not sure if that was an effect of the large layout or a reflection of the facility's overall popularity. Be forewarned that the help wasn't around when we visited and was rude on the phone.

Campsites, facilities: There are 23 full hook-up (20-, 30-, and 50-amp) sites, two electric-ity-only sites, and eight tent sites. Cabins are available. Amenities include WiFi, modern restrooms with showers, drinking water, a playground, basketball court, and garbage service. Leashed pets permitted.

Reservations, fees: Reservations are accepted. Full hook-up sites are $23–24, tent sites are $16, and cabins are $65. Open March 15 through November 15, weather permitting.

Directions: From Blanding, drive 26 miles south on Hwy. 191 to the town of Bluff. Turn left on 400 W, continue one block, and turn left again on Larkspur. Continue straight into Cottonwood RV. The office is on 300 W and Main Street.

GPS Coordinates: N 37° 16.812' W 109° 33.866'

Contact: Cottonwood RV Park, 435/672-2287, www.cottonwoodrvpark.us/

91 CADILLAC RANCH

Scenic rating: 4

in Bluff

Map 6.5, page 281

Cadillac Ranch is a newly finished RV park in the desert town of Bluff. Bluff is known for its long and varied history, starting with the ancient cliff-dwelling and basket-weaving cultures that inhabited the area until about A.D. 1300. Their ruins and rock art petroglyphs can be seen at nearby sites like Sand Island Campground and Hovenweep National Monument. The tradition of native art lives on, and Bluff remains a hot spot for arts and crafts. The distinguishing feature at Cadillac Ranch is a small pond that creates a unique landscape for an RV park. Fishing and paddleboating are both possible on the pond. An ostrich farm borders the park as well, adding to its quirky feel. Tent sites have grass lawns and are shaded by trees. RV parking spaces are gravel, and each has a single rock and young tree. Limited views look north to the 300-foot sandstone bluffs after which the town was named.

Campsites, facilities: There are 15 sites with full hook-ups (30, 50 amps), two with partial hook-ups, and 10 tent sites. Picnic tables, barbeque grills, WiFi, fire rings, modern restrooms with showers, pull-through sites, garbage service, and a basketball court are provided. Paddleboat rentals are available. Leashed pets permitted.

Reservations, fees: Reservations are recommended and can be arranged at 800/538-6195. Open year-round.

Directions: In the town of Bluff on Hwy. 191, Cadillac Ranch is on the southeast side of the highway at 640 E Main.

GPS Coordinates: N 37° 16.961' W 109° 33.080'

Contact: Cadillac Ranch RV Park, 800/538-6195, www.bluffutah.org/cadillacranch/

92 SAND ISLAND

Scenic rating: 7

four miles south of Bluff

Map 6.5, page 281   BEST

Sand Island is a BLM campground along the San Juan River. It's the launching point for San Juan River rafting trips through the amazing Goosenecks of the San Juan. The river can be floated on Class I–III rapids for up to 84 miles over six days, terminating at the southeastern arm of Lake Powell. In addition to the Goosenecks Canyon, this float accesses backcountry petroglyph sites and Anasazi ruins. Sand Island Campground is also the site of a huge Anasazi petroglyph panel. The rock art runs for at least 200 feet along a dark section of desert varnished rock and is notable for its flute player figures in the San Juan basket-weaver style. Lots of modern additions to the panel take away somewhat from its character, but it's still a very impressive site. The campground features a short hike along the Sand Island Nature Trail, where you might spot a few of the many birds that utilize the riparian habitat. Look for scrub jays, canyon wrens, and many others during spring migration. This campground is also a convenient place to spend the night if you plan on visiting Goosenecks State Park or the Valley of the Gods, neither of which have any camping to speak of. The campground is well designed with two separate loops, one by the boat ramp and the other close to the petroglyphs. Flat gravel parking spots access tidy, secluded spots. Some sites are by the river; when we visited, several riverside sites were swamped by the swollen, muddy San Juan, so consider the weather report before setting up camp.

Campsites, facilities: There are 17 campsites in two loops. In Loop A, vehicles over 22 feet are not permitted. Picnic tables, fire grills, drinking water, vault toilets, and garbage service are provided. Leashed pets permitted.

Reservations, fees: Reservations are not accepted. The fee is $10 per site. Open year-round.

Directions: From Bluff, drive west on Hwy. 191 for four miles; the entrance to the campground will be on the left.

GPS Coordinates: N 37° 15.723' W 109° 36.974'

Contact: Monticello Field Office, 435/587-1504, www.blm.gov/ut/st/en/fo/monticello/recreation/camping.html

© MIKE MATSON

Goosenecks of the San Juan, Goosenecks State Park

93 GOOSENECKS STATE PARK

Scenic rating: 9

near the town of Mexican Hat

Map 6.5, page 281

Goosenecks State Park is the ultimate "drive-through" scenic location. The park is simple, yet breathtakingly beautiful. The overlook gazes down on the meandering waters of the San Juan River and the massive Gooseneck Canyon it has carved. The gorge cuts down through more than a thousand feet of the Pennsylvanian Hermosa Formation. The river twists and winds through the deep canyon, flowing over five miles while only getting one mile closer to its ultimate end, its confluence with the Colorado River and Lake Powell. Look for kayakers and rafters, floating lazily through the meandering turns. If you stick around long enough, they'll come by for another pass. Views extend beyond the canyon rim to Arizona's Monument Valley and the Valley of the Gods, both worthy destinations in their own right. The campground at Goosenecks State Park is very primitive. Two large parking areas offer a place to park an RV or pitch a tent. The overlook is open and exposed to the sun and wind, both of which can pose a considerable challenge. Come prepared and don't expect much from the facilities.

Campsites, facilities: There are no designated sites. There are two large open parking areas where camping is permitted. There are a handful of picnic tables and fire rings scattered around, a vault toilet, and a small covered picnic area. There is no drinking water. Leashed pets permitted.

Reservations, fees: Reservations are not accepted. There is no fee. Open year-round.

Directions: From Bluff, drive 21 miles southwest on Hwy. 163 and turn north (right) onto Rte. 261. Continue 0.8 mile, turn left onto Rte. 316, and travel 3.3 miles to Goosenecks State Park.

GPS Coordinates: N 37° 10.470' W 109° 55.654'

Contact: Goosenecks State Park, 435/678-2238, http://stateparks.utah.gov/stateparks/parks/goosenecks/

RESOURCES

RESERVATIONS

National Recreation Reservation Service (NRRS)

The NRRS is the reservation system for public campgrounds in Utah. Many of the Forest Service campgrounds and some of the National Park campgrounds can be reserved through the NRRS.
877/444-6777
TDD: 877/833-6777
www.recreation.gov/

Utah State Parks Reservations

Reserve America is the online reservation service used by the Utah State Parks. It also maintains a call center if you prefer to make your reservation by phone.
800/322-3770
www.reserveamerica.com/

NATIONAL PARKS AND FEDERAL RECREATIONAL LANDS PASS

The National Parks Service now sells the **America the Beautiful** pass, an annual recreation pass granting access to most federally owned lands. The pass costs $80 ($10 for seniors and free to disabled citizens) and admits the bearer plus up to three additional adults in the same vehicle to federal recreation areas for one year. The Interagency Pass Program gives pass holders access to National Park Service, U.S. Department of Agriculture, Forest Service, Fish and Wildlife Service, Bureau of Land Management, and Bureau of Reclamation lands and parks.
www.nps.gov/fees_passes.htm

U.S. FOREST SERVICE

The United States Department of Agriculture Forest Service administers land in seven different national forests in Utah. In addition, the forest service manages the Flaming Gorge National Recreation Area. Each national forest is broken down further into ranger districts. Questions about campgrounds should be addressed to the ranger district in which they are located.

For detailed maps of Forest Service lands, contact the Forest Service or purchase maps online.

Main Offices
WASHINGTON OFFICE
1400 Independence Ave., SW
Washington, D.C. 20250-0003
800/832-1355
www.fs.fed.us/maps/

INTERMOUNTAIN REGION
324 25th Street
Ogden, UT 84401
801/625-5306
www.fs.fed.us/r4/

Ashley National Forest
SUPERVISOR'S OFFICE
355 North Vernal Ave.
Vernal, UT 84078
435/789-1181
fax 435/781-5142
www.fs.fed.us/r4/ashley/

DUCHESNE/ROOSEVELT
RANGER DISTRICT
Duchesne Office
85 West Main
P.O. Box 981
Duchesne, UT 84021
435/738-2482
fax 435/781-5215

Roosevelt Office
650 West Hwy. 40
P.O. Box 127
Roosevelt, UT 84066
435/722-5018
fax 435/781-5237

FLAMING GORGE NATIONAL
RECREATION AREA
Flaming Gorge Ranger District
25 West Hwy. 43
P.O. Box 279
Manila, UT 84046
435/784-3445
fax 435/781-5295
www.fs.fed.us/r4/ashley/recreation/flaming_
  gorge/index.shtml

VERNAL RANGER DISTRICT
355 North Vernal Avenue
Vernal, UT 84078
435/789-1181
fax 435/781-5142

Uinta-Wasatch-Cache National Forest
SALT LAKE CITY
ADMINISTRATIVE OFFICE
8236 Federal Building
125 South State Street
Salt Lake City, UT 84138
801/236-3400
www.fs.fed.us/r4/uwc/

EVANSTON DISTRICT AND
VISITOR CENTER
1565 Hwy. 150, Suite A
P.O. Box 1880
Evanston, WY 82930
307/789-3194

HEBER RANGER DISTRICT
2460 South Highway 40
P.O. Box 190
Heber City, UT 84032
435/654-0470

KAMAS DISTRICT AND VISITOR CENTER
50 East Center Street
P.O. Box 68
Kamas, UT 84036
435/783-4338

LOGAN RANGER DISTRICT AND
VISITOR CENTER
1500 East Hwy. 89
Logan, UT 84321
435/755-3620

MOUNTAIN VIEW DISTRICT AND
VISITOR CENTER
321 Hwy. 414
P.O. Box 129
Mountain View, WY 82939
307/782-6555

OGDEN RANGER DISTRICT
Union Station Visitor Center
2501 Wall Avenue
Ogden, UT 84401
801/625-5306

SALT LAKE RANGER DISTRICT AND
VISITOR CENTER
3285 East 3300 South
Salt Lake City, UT 84109
801/466-6411

SPANISH FORK RANGER DISTRICT
44 West 400 North
Spanish Fork, UT 84660
801/798-3571

PLEASANT GROVE RANGER DISTRICT
390 North 100 East
Pleasant Grove, UT 84062
801/785-3563

PROVO ADMINISTRATIVE OFFICE
88 West 100 North
Provo, UT 84601
801/342-5100
www.fs.fed.us/r4/uwc/

SPANISH FORK RANGER DISTRICT,
NEPHI OFFICE
635 North Main
Nephi, UT 84648
435/623-2735

Dixie National Forest
ADMINISTRATIVE OFFICE
1789 North Wedgewood Lane
Cedar City, UT 84721-7769
435/865-3700
www.fs.fed.us/r4/dixie/index.shtml

ESCALANTE RANGER DISTRICT
P.O. Box 246
Escalante, UT 84726-0246
435/826-5400

CEDAR CITY RANGER DISTRICT
1789 North Wedgewood Lane
Cedar City, UT 84721-7769
435/865-3200

PINE VALLEY RANGER DISTRICT
196 East Tabernacle, Suite 40
St. George, UT 84770
435/688-3246

POWELL RANGER DISTRICT
P.O. Box 80
Panguitch, UT 84759-0080
435/676-9300

Manti-La Sal National Forest
599 West Price River Dr.
Price, UT 84501
435/637-2817
www.fs.fed.us/r4/mantilasal/

FERRON-PRICE RANGER DISTRICT
115 West Canyon Road
Ferron, UT 84523
435/384-2372

MOAB RANGER DISTRICT
62 East 100 North
Moab, UT 84532
435/259-7155

MONTICELLO RANGER DISTRICT
P.O. Box 820
Monticello, UT 84535
435/587-2041

SANPETE RANGER DISTRICT
540 North Main
Ephraim, UT 84627
435/283-4151

Fishlake National Forest
Administrative Office
115 East 900 North
Richfield, UT 84701
435/896-9233
www.fs.fed.us/r4/fishlake/

BEAVER RANGER DISTRICT
575 South Main St.
P.O. Box E
Beaver, UT 84713
435/438-2436

FILLMORE RANGER DISTRICT
390 South Main Street
Fillmore, UT 84631
435/743-5721

FREMONT RIVER RANGER DISTRICT
138 South Main Street
P.O. Box 129
Loa, UT 84747
435/836-2800

RICHFIELD RANGER DISTRICT
115 East 900 North
Richfield, Utah 84701
435/896-9233

Sawtooth National Forest
2647 Kimberly Rd. East
Twin Falls, ID 83301
208/737-3200
www.fs.fed.us/r4/sawtooth/

MINIDOKA RANGER DISTRICT
3650 South Overland Ave.
Burley, ID 83318-3242
208/678-0430

BUREAU OF LAND MANAGEMENT (BLM)

The BLM manages 12 million acres of public land in Utah including the Grand Staircase-Escalante National Monument.

Main Offices

BLM UTAH STATE OFFICE
440 West 200 South, Suite 500
Salt Lake City, Utah 84145-0155
801/539-4001
TDD: 801/539-4133
fax 801/539-4013
www.blm.gov/ut/st/en.html

PUBLIC LANDS INTERPRETIVE ASSOCIATION
6501 Fourth Street NW, Suite I
Albuquerque, NM 87107
505/345-9498 or 877/851-8946
www.publiclands.org/home.php

Field Offices

CEDAR CITY BLM FIELD OFFICE
176 East D.L. Sargent Drive
Cedar City, UT 84721
435/586-2401
fax 435/865-3058
www.blm.gov/ut/st/en/fo/cedar_city.html

GRAND STAIRCASE-ESCALANTE NATIONAL MONUMENT
Kanab Headquarters
190 East Center
Kanab, Utah 84741
435/644-4300
fax 435/644-4350
www.blm.gov/ut/st/en/fo/grand_staircase-escalante.html

FILLMORE BLM FIELD OFFICE
35 East 500 North
Fillmore, Utah 84631
435/743-3100
fax 435/743-3135
www.blm.gov/ut/st/en/fo/fillmore.html

KANAB BLM FIELD OFFICE
318 North 100 East
Kanab, UT 84741
435/644-4600
fax 435/644-4620
www.blm.gov/ut/st/en/fo/kanab.html

MOAB BLM FIELD OFFICE
82 East Dogwood
Moab, Utah 84532
435/259-2100
fax 435/259-2106
www.blm.gov/ut/st/en/fo/moab.html

MONTICELLO BLM FIELD OFFICE
435 North Main Street
P.O. Box 7
Monticello, Utah 84535
435/587-1500
fax 435/587-1518
www.blm.gov/ut/st/en/fo/monticello.html

PRICE BLM FIELD OFFICE
125 South 600 West
Price, UT 84501
435/636-3600
fax 435/636-3657
www.blm.gov/ut/st/en/fo/price.html

RICHFIELD BLM FIELD OFFICE
150 East 900 North
Richfield, UT 84701
435/896-1500
fax 435/896-1550

SALT LAKE BLM FIELD OFFICE
2370 South 2300 West
Salt Lake City, UT 84119
801/977-4300
fax 801/977-4397
www.blm.gov/ut/st/en/fo/salt_lake.html

ST. GEORGE BLM FIELD OFFICE
345 East Riverside Drive
St. George, UT 84790
435/688-3200
fax 435/688-3252
www.blm.gov/ut/st/en/fo/st__george.html

VERNAL BLM FIELD OFFICE
170 South 500 East
Vernal, UT 84078
435/781-4400
fax 435/781-4410
www.blm.gov/ut/st/en/fo/vernal.html

NATIONAL PARK SERVICE

There are five national parks in Utah. In addition, the National Park Service manages six national monuments and the Glen Canyon National Recreation Area.

National Parks

ARCHES NATIONAL PARK
P.O. Box 907
Moab, UT 84532-0907
435/719-2299
fax 435/719-2305
www.nps.gov/arch/

BRYCE CANYON NATIONAL PARK
P.O. Box 640201
Bryce Canyon, UT 84764-0201
435/834-5322
www.nps.gov/brca/

CANYONLANDS NATIONAL PARK
2282 SW Resource Blvd.
Moab, UT 84532
435/719-2313
fax 435/719-2300
www.nps.gov/cany/

CAPITOL REEF NATIONAL PARK
HC 70 Box 15
Torrey, UT 84775
435/425-3791, ext. 111
fax 435/425-3026
www.nps.gov/care

ZION NATIONAL PARK
P.O. Box 1099
Springdale, UT 84767-1099
435/772-3256

fax 435/772-3426
www.nps.gov/zion/

National Monuments

CEDAR BREAKS NATIONAL MONUMENT
2390 West Hwy. 56, Suite 11
Cedar City, UT 84720
435/586-9451
fax 435/586-3813
www.nps.gov/cebr/

DINOSAUR NATIONAL MONUMENT
4545 E. Hwy. 40
Dinosaur, CO 81610-9724
435/781-7700
fax 970/374-3003
www.nps.gov/dino/

HOVENWEEP NATIONAL MONUMENT
McElmo Route
Cortez, CO 81321
970/562-4282
fax 970/562-4283
www.nps.gov/hove/

NATURAL BRIDGES NATIONAL MONUMENT
HC 60 Box 1
Lake Powell, UT 84533-0001
435/692-1234
fax 435/692-1111
www.nps.gov/nabr/

RAINBOW BRIDGE NATIONAL MONUMENT
P.O. Box 1507
Page, AZ 86040
928/608-6200
fax 928/608-6259
www.nps.gov/rabr/

TIMPANOGOS CAVE NATIONAL MONUMENT
R.R. 3 Box 200
American Fork, Utah 84003
801/756-5238 (summer only) or
801/756-5239

fax 801/756-5661
www.nps.gov/tica/

National Recreation Areas
GLEN CANYON NATIONAL
RECREATION AREA
P.O. Box 1507
Page, Arizona 86040
928/608-6200
fax 928/608-6259
www.nps.gov/glca/

STATE PARKS
There are more than 40 state parks in Utah.

Administrative Offices
UTAH STATE PARKS AND RECREATION
1594 West North Temple, Suite 116
P.O. Box 146001
Salt Lake City, Utah 84114
801/538-7220 or 877/887-2757
http://stateparks.utah.gov/

UTAH STATE DEPARTMENT OF
NATURAL RESOURCES
P.O. Box 145610
1594 W. North Temple
Salt Lake City, UT 84114-5610
801/538-7200
www.nr.utah.gov/

OTHER RESOURCES
UTAH DEPARTMENT OF TRANSPORTATION
511 (within Utah)
866/511-UTAH (866/511-8824)
www.dot.state.ut.us

UTAH DIVISION OF WILDLIFE RESOURCES
1594 W. North Temple
Salt Lake City, Utah 84116
801/538-4700
fax 801/538-4745
http://wildlife.utah.gov/index.php

Index

Acknowledgments

I'd like to thank the scores of National Park Service, National Forest, Bureau of Land Management, State Park, and private campground employees and campground hosts who assisted in the writing of this book. I'd also like to express my appreciation to the editorial team at Avalon—especially Tiffany Watson, Sabrina Young, Brice Ticen, and Tabitha Lahr—for guiding me through the process of writing this book. Finally, I'd like to thank my wife, Sonja, for her tireless work on this project, and her unending enthusiasm, love, and support.

www.moon.com

DESTINATIONS | ACTIVITIES | BLOGS | MAPS | BOOKS

MOON.COM is all new, and ready to help plan your next trip! Filled with fresh trip ideas and strategies, author interviews, informative blogs, a detailed map library, and descriptions of all the Moon guidebooks, Moon.com is all you need to get out and explore the world—or even places in your own backyard. As always, when you travel with Moon, expect an experience that is uncommon and truly unique.

 O U T D O O R S

"Well written, thoroughly researched, and packed full of useful information and advice, these guides really do get you into the outdoors."

−GORP.COM

ALSO AVAILABLE AS FOGHORN OUTDOORS ACTIVITY GUIDES:

250 Great Hikes in
  California's National Parks
California Golf
California Waterfalls
California Wildlife
Camper's Companion
Easy Biking in Northern
  California
Easy Hiking in Northern
  California

Easy Hiking in Southern
  California
Georgia & Alabama Camping
Maine Hiking
Massachusetts Hiking
New England Biking
New England Cabins
  & Cottages
New England Camping
New England Hiking

New Hampshire Hiking
Southern California
  Cabins & Cottages
Tom Stienstra's Bay Area
  Recreation
Utah Camping
Vermont Hiking
Washington Boating
  & Water Sports

MOON UTAH CAMPING

Avalon Travel
a member of the Perseus Books Group
1700 Fourth Street
Berkeley, CA 94710, USA
www.moon.com

Editor: Tiffany Watson
Series Manager: Sabrina Young
Copy Editor: Valerie Sellers Blanton
Graphics Coordinator: Tabitha Lahr
Production Coordinator: Tabitha Lahr,
    Christine DeLorenzo
Cover Designer: Tabitha Lahr
Illustrations: Bob Race
Map Editor: Brice Ticen
Cartographer: Kat Bennett

ISBN: 978-1-59880-195-8
ISSN: 1-59880-195-3

Printing History
1st Edition – April 2001
2nd Edition – May 2009
5 4 3 2 1

Some photos and illustrations are used by permission and are the property of the original copyright owners.

Front cover photo: camping at Arches National Park © Michael DeYoung / Corbis
Title page photo: Delicate Arch, Arches National Park © Mike Matson
Table of contents photos: Sandstone waterfalls, Subway, Zion National Park; mountain goat, Big Cottonwood Canyon; wildflowers on Mount Timpanogos © Mike Matson
Back cover photo: © Al Valeiro / Getty Images

Printed in the United States by RR Donnelley

Keeping Current

We are committed to making this book the most accurate and enjoyable camping guide to the state. You can rest assured that every campground in this book has been carefully reviewed in an effort to keep this book as up-to-date as possible. However, by the time you read this book, some of the fees listed herein may have changed and campgrounds may have closed unexpectedly.

If you have a favorite gem you'd like to see included in the next edition, or see anything that needs updating, clarification, or correction, please drop us a line. Send your comments via email to feedback@moon.com, or use the address above.

CPSIA information can be obtained at www.ICGtesting.com
Printed in the USA
LVOW10s0909230714

395654LV00005B/16/P